SOCIOLOGY

Diversity, Conflict, and Change

Kenneth J. Neubeck
University of Connecticut

Davita Silfen Glasberg
University of Connecticut

Boston   Burr Ridge, IL   Dubuque, IA   Madison, WI   New York   San Francisco   St. Louis
Bangkok   Bogotá   Caracas   Kuala Lumpur   Lisbon   London   Madrid   Mexico City
Milan   Montreal   New Delhi   Santiago   Seoul   Singapore   Sydney   Taipei   Toronto

To Gig, Michael, Kara, and Christopher Neubeck
To Gillian and Morgan Silfen Glasberg

 Higher Education

SOCIOLOGY: DIVERSITY, CONFLICT, AND CHANGE

Published by McGraw-Hill, a business unit of The McGraw-Hill Companies, Inc., 1221 Avenue of the Americas, New York, NY 10020. Copyright © 2005, by The McGraw-Hill Companies, Inc. All rights reserved. No part of this publication may be reproduced or distributed in any form or by any means, or stored in a database or retrieval system, without the prior written consent of The McGraw-Hill Companies, Inc., including, but not limited to, in any network or other electronic storage or transmission, or broadcast for distance learning.

Some ancillaries, including electronic and print components, may not be available to customers outside the United States.

This book is printed on acid-free paper.

3 4 5 6 7 8 9 0 DOC/DOC 0 9 8 7

ISBN 0-07-250476-5

Library of Congress Control Number: 2004102606 (soft cover)

Publisher: *Phillip A. Butcher*
Sponsoring editor: *Sherith H. Pankratz*
Developmental editor: *Katherine Blake*
Senior marketing manager: *Daniel M. Loch*
Producer, media technology: *Jessica Bodie*
Project manager: *Diane M. Folliard*
Senior production supervisor: *Carol A. Bielski*
Senior designer: *Gino Cieslik*
Lead media project manager: *Marc Mattson*
Photo research coordinator: *Alexandra Ambrose*
Art editor: *Emma C. Ghiselli*
Photo researcher: *Emily Tietz*
Cover/ Interior design: *Maureen McCutcheon*
Typeface: *10.5/12 Times Roman*
Compositor: *Thompson Type*
Printer: *R.R. Donnelley and Sons Inc.*

www.mhhe.com

Kenneth J. Neubeck is a professor emeritus of Sociology at the University of Connecticut, where he served as director of the university's undergraduate minor in human rights. He is coauthor (with Noel A. Cazenave) of *Welfare Racism: Playing the Race Card Against America's Poor* (Routledge, 2001). This monograph, an analysis of the impact of racism on U.S. welfare policy, won five distinguished scholarship awards in 2002, including awards from three sections of the American Sociological Association. He is also the author of the book *Corporate Response to Urban Crisis,* along with many articles on racism, poverty, and welfare reform. In addition, Professor Neubeck is coauthor of two textbooks published by McGraw-Hill: *Sociology: A Critical Approach* (1996), written with Davita Silfen Glasberg, as well as *Social Problems: A Critical Approach* (1997), written with Mary Alice Neubeck. The fifth edition of the latter text is under development, with Professor Glasberg as a newly added coauthor. Professor Neubeck is the recipient of the American Association of University Professors Career Excellence Award in Teaching/Mentoring. He has long been an activist on civil rights and anti-poverty issues, and most recently has been working with advocacy groups on such issues as racial equity in welfare reform and on the living-wage campaign.

Davita Silfen Glasberg is a professor in the Sociology Department and the director of graduate studies at the University of Connecticut. In January, 2004, she became the director of the university's undergraduate minor in human rights. She received her Ph.D. in sociology from the State University of New York at Stony Brook in 1983. She has authored or coauthored three books and more than two dozen journal articles on issues concerning finance capital, the state in finance capitalism, and political economy, the most recent of which was *Corporate Welfare and the Welfare State: Bank Deregulation and the Savings and Loan Bailout* (with Dan Skidmore), published by Aldine de Gruyter (1997). She is currently working on a book about power, oppression, and the state, as well as a study of predatory lending and the Community Reinvestment Act. Her special interests are political sociology, political economy, and systems of inequality.

Contents in Brief

Contents

9   Deviance, Crime, and Social Control   254

10   Social Change and Social Movements   292

15 Families   468

16 Religion   504

PART 3   THINKING ABOUT THE FUTURE

17 Emerging Issues   536

SOCIOLOGY: DIVERSITY, CONFLICT, AND CHANGE is an outgrowth of our long-standing commitment to helping students develop a sociological imagination that will frame the way they look at the world around them. By using our own sociological imaginations, we have achieved an enhanced understanding of the powerful influence of the intersections of race, class, and gender inequalities—as well as inequalities of able-bodiedness, age, and sexual orientation—in shaping the lives of individuals in significant ways. The great expansion of sociological literature addressing this issue over the last decade indicates that we are not alone in this regard. Moreover, judging by the excitement of colleagues about our completion of this book, it seems that there are many instructors who would very much like to transfer this insight into their classrooms.

This text is designed to stimulate students' sociological imaginations by using core sociological concepts to explore basic issues that may challenge their taken-for-granted world.

In order to stimulate students' sociological imaginations, we begin each chapter with a set of basic questions, broad in scope, relating to the topics to be discussed in the chapter, and we introduce the core sociological concepts as we answer those questions. In this way, students learn that sociological concepts are not just glossary terms to be memorized for exams but, more importantly, useful tools for real-world analysis. Our hope is that their sociological imaginations will serve students well long after they have left our classrooms by empowering them to form their own questions about the world they confront every day, to search for answers to these questions, and not be satisfied with easy or superficial answers.

Organization and Conceptualization

We begin *Sociology: Diversity, Conflict, and Change* with an introductory chapter in which we discuss the importance of the sociological imagination and the core sociological concepts upon which this imagination relies. We follow this with a chapter covering the diversity of methods sociologists use to gather the information needed to address their research questions and generate knowledge essential to the exercise of the sociological imagination. Here, we also explore the political and ethical concerns to which sociologists must remain sensitive when conducting research.

In the first part of the text, students are introduced to core sociological concepts that most sociologists consider to be at the heart of the discipline. We stress the significance of these concepts for analyzing the organization and operation of society, covering topics ranging from the most "macro" (the importance of a society's position in the world-system) to the most "micro" (the impact of socialization on individuals). We also explore how systems of inequality intersect so as to affect individuals' lives. We end this section with an examination of social change and social movements as core concepts to help students understand that systems *can* be changed—that people can effectively challenge and alter society. Without exposure to that conceptualization prior to being introduced to the various societal institutions, students are likely to view institutions as inexorable and unchangeable. We want students to understand their power to effect change.

The second part of the text focuses on six institutional spheres that are central to the cumulative experiences of members of society. Here, students are exposed to bodies of research literature pertaining to social structures with which they have come into contact but about which most students have thought very little. In this part of the text we show students how the sociological imagination can be put to work to shed new light on how the institutions they often take for granted affect them—for better or for worse.

We close the text with a final chapter on emerging issues—recent problems or trends that people are beginning to confront—which challenge the sociological imagination. The chapter is organized around the issue of intensifying globalization and its significance for cultural, political, and social constructions of aging, environmental racism, war and terrorism, and the digital divide. Indeed, while we were in the midst of writing this book, the terrorist attacks of September 11, 2001, dramatically altered the lives of many people. We had to return to several chapters to revisit and rethink issues because social reality now existed in a world that would never be quite the same again. In closing with emerging issues, we wish to encourage students to utilize their sociological insights to understand and respond in an empowered way to changing societal conditions they will encounter in the future.

Key Features

Integration of Race, Class, and Gender Issues

Our interest in issues pertaining to race, class, and gender led us to integrate materials on these and related topics into virtually every chapter. Consistent with this approach, Chapter 7 ("Systems of Inequality") moves beyond the conventional chapter-length treatment of class-based social stratification found in most texts. In Chapter 7 we not only discuss class inequality, but we also give equal attention to systems of racial and gender inequality, as well as systems of inequality based on age, state of able-bodiedness, and sexual orientation.

Chapter 8 ("Intersections of Race, Class, and Gender")

This unique chapter flows logically from our treatment of various systems of inequality. In this chapter these systems are viewed as a matrix within which most individuals are simultaneously members of socially dominant and socially subordinate groups. Topics treated in this chapter (such as the ways in which our system of gender inequality affects women who are privileged by virtue of their class and race) increase students' awareness of the diversity of people's experiences with inequality, a diversity that traditional treatments of stratification tend to ignore.

Coherence of Chapters

Each chapter in this text is organized around a central set of questions that helps to frame the discussion and enhance the chapter's coherence. Concepts are introduced as vehicles or sociological tools with which to address these questions. Thus, we avoid presenting students with a text that reads like a dictionary of terms. Instead, students see how sociological concepts and perspectives can be usefully mobilized to expand their understanding of social life, the world around them, and their own position and experiences in that world.

Social Forces/People's Lives

Each chapter contains a boxed reading in which an individual speaks of life experiences that reflect—to use C. Wright Mills's terms—"public issues" rather than "personal troubles." These readings, which we have chosen to call "Social Forces/People's Lives," help to ground sometimes abstract concepts and ideas in terms that are easy for students to grasp. For example, in Chapter 3 a young man in Mauritania struggles with life as a slave in the new global economy. In Chapter 12 a journalist chronicles the daily difficulties of living as a minimum-wage worker in a labor market where such work is increasingly dominant. In Chapter 14 families restructure themselves to fill the parenting void left by those who have been deployed to fight the war in Iraq.

Chapter Summaries

At the end of each chapter the major points are summarized in the form of an enumerated list.

"Thinking Critically" Discussion Questions

At the end of each chapter, there is a series of provocative questions that are intended to promote discussion, debate, and exercise of the sociological imagination. The questions, under the heading "Thinking Critically," encourage students to consider the implications of facts outlined in the chapter and often call upon them to relate these facts to their own lives.

Key Terms and Glossary

Key terms are highlighted in boldface type in the chapter narrative. These terms are listed (with page references) at the end of each chapter and defined in a glossary at the end of the text.

Graphics

Tables and figures provide data that are useful and relevant to the text discussion. Figures are carefully captioned to assist student understanding.

Ancillary Materials

Sociology: Diversity, Conflict, and Change is augmented by a number of supplementary learning and teaching aids.

For the Student

Online Learning Center Website (OLC)

The Online Learning Center website that accompanies this text, www.mhhe.com/neubeck, offers a variety of resources for the student. In addition to various study tools, students will find chapter objectives, chapter outlines and overviews, interactive chapter quizzes, annotated lists of weblinks, suggested readings, Internet exercises, census updates, and flashcards of key terms.

PowerWeb

Available as an option, PowerWeb allows students to supplement their learning experience using Internet-based course materials. It includes current articles, curriculum-based materials, weekly updates with assessment, informative and timely world news, refereed weblinks, research tools, student study tools, interactive exercises, and more.

Reel Society Interactive Movie CD-ROM 1.5

Available as a separate package option, this professionally produced movie on CD-ROM demonstrates the sociological imagination using actors in campus life scenarios. Viewers take on the role of one of the characters and influence key plot turns by making choices for them. Through it all, a wide variety of issues and perspectives are addressed relating major sociological concepts and theories to students' lives. Go to www.mhhe.com/reelsoc, for further details.

For the Instructor

The Instructor's Manual, Test Bank, Computerized Test Bank, and PowerPoints are available to instructors on the **Instructor's Resource CD (IRCD):**

Instructor's Manual

The Instructor's Manual provides chapter summaries, learning objectives, lecture ideas and discussion questions, suggestions for assignments and exercises, suggested additional readings, suggested films/videos, and an annotated list of weblinks. The Instructor's Manual can also be downloaded from the Instructor's side of the Online Learning Center website.

Test Bank

The Test Bank offers approximately 75 multiple-choice, 15 true-false, and 5 essay questions for each chapter in the text. The Test Bank can be downloaded as a Word file from the IRCD. It is also available on the IRCD as a **Computerized Test Bank.**

PowerPoint Slides

A collection of tables and figures from the text, augmented by additional graphics, allows instructors to add visual content to their lectures. The PowerPoints are also available on the Instructor's Online Learning Center.

Instructor's Online Learning Center (OLC)

The password-protected Instructor's side of the OLC contains a variety of resources, activities, and classroom tips. The Instructor's Manual, PowerPoint slides, and more can be accessed electronically on this site.

The Classroom Performance System (CPS)

This revolutionary wireless response system gives you immediate feedback from every student in the class. CPS units include easy-to-use software for creating and delivering questions and assessments to your class. Each student simply responds with his or her individual wireless response pad, providing instant results. Suggested CPS questions specific to Neubeck and Glasberg's *Sociology: Diversity, Conflict, and Change*, are available on the Instructor's Online Learning Center. CPS is the perfect tool for engaging students while gathering important assessment data. Go to www.mhhe.com/einstruction for further details.

PageOut: The Course Website Development Center

Online content for *Sociology: Diversity, Conflict, and Change* is supported by WebCT, eCollege.com, Blackboard, and other course management systems. Additionally, McGraw-Hill's PageOut service is available to help instructors get their course up and running online in a matter of hours, at no cost. (No programming knowledge is required.) When you use PageOut, your students have instant, 24-hour access to your course syllabus, lecture notes, assignments, and other original material. Students can even check their grades on-line. Material from the Online Learning Center (OLC) can be pulled into your website. PageOut also provides a discussion board where you and your students can exchange questions and post announcements. To find out more about PageOut, ask your McGraw-Hill representative for details, or go to http://www.mhhe.com/catalogs/solutions/pageout.html.

Acknowledgements

Many people have contributed to the successful completion of *Sociology: Diversity, Conflict, and Change*. Our appreciation goes to the very able and professional staff at McGraw-Hill, with special thanks to Katherine Blake, Sherith Pankratz, Diane Folliard, Phil Butcher, and David and EmilyTietz. We also benefited from counseling regarding text users' interests provided by McGraw-Hill sales representative Janie Pittendreigh.

We are greatly indebted to our wonderful graduate students who have provided research assistance: Beth Frankel-Merenstein, Courtney Merrill, Rachel Sullivan,

Andrew Fullerton, and Medora Barnes. We would have been lost without the very capable administrative assistance of Arlene Goodwin and Jeanne Monty.

We would also like to thank our respective families for their love and support, patience and good humor: Gig, Michael, Kara, and Christopher Neubeck, and Gillian and Morgan Silfen Glasberg. It is to them that we dedicate this book.

The following academic reviewers commissioned by McGraw-Hill also deserve our thanks for their helpful comments and suggestions:

Jan AbuShakrah, Portland Community College

Pat Allen, Los Angeles Valley College

Tracy Burkett, College of Charleston

Kelly Dagan, Illinois College

Julia Fox, Marshall University

Laurie Gordy, University of South Carolina at Spartanburg

Dawn Hinton, Saginaw Valley State University

Jay Hughes, Georgia Southern University

Christine Linsley, St. John Fisher College

Nelda Pearson, Radford University

Kathy Rowell, Sinclair Community College

Karen Schaumann, Eastern Michigan University

Randy Stoecker, University of Toledo

Darlene A. Townsend, Spokane Community College

J.R. Woodward, Montana State University

Pidi Zhang, Georgia Southern University

Last, but not least, we would like to thank each other. We have learned a great deal from each other throughout this process, and we have had tremendous fun along the way. What more could one ask for? It's been a real slice!

Kenneth J. Neubeck
Davita Silfen Glasberg

SOCIOLOGY

Diversity, Conflict, and Change

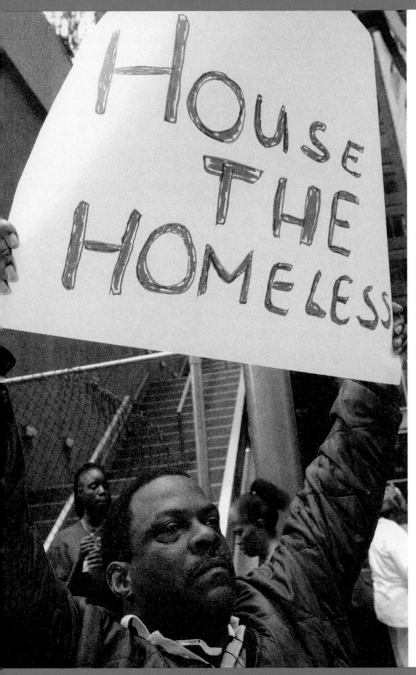

Chapter One

The Sociological Imagination

A glance at newspaper headlines or television nightly news reveals political turmoil and civil strife, military violence, serious economic breakdowns, famines, and natural disasters in societies around the world. In comparison to many other societies, the United States seems relatively calm and tranquil, even as it has had to contend with recent terrorist acts and their aftermath. Beneath this relative tranquility, however, millions of people in the United States face problems that leave them yearning for relief and anxious for change in their circumstances.

Many, for example, have difficulty finding or keeping decent-paying jobs. Others find themselves living in tension-filled and abusive partner or family situations. Still others face prejudicial attitudes and discriminatory treatment. Individuals sometimes view such experiences as their own personal burdens to bear and fail to appreciate just how widely their problems may be shared. The discipline of sociology can contribute to our understanding of the sources of such commonly experienced problems and help offer solutions.

Sociology is the scientific study of society, of the ways in which society is organized and operates, and of the factors contributing to both societal stability and social change. Sociologists are interested in analyzing how people create, maintain, and go about altering the society in which they live. They are also interested in analyzing the effects that various features of society have on its members. Sociology provides research-based knowledge about the organization and operation of society that can often help individuals to put their personal problems in perspective and perhaps deal with them more effectively. It does this by encouraging people to view the sources of their problems in a larger context.

We titled this textbook *Sociology: Diversity, Conflict, and Change.* The term "diversity" in the subtitle is very important, for in chapters that follow we will underscore the fact that people's lives are very much influenced not only by who they are, but by *what* they are. In U.S. society, individuals' opportunities and **life chances** (the ability to experience life and all its beneficial offerings) are unequally distributed. They vary by whether people are affluent or poor, male or female, white or of color. People's lives are also affected by virtue of their being either young or old, able-bodied or experiencing a disability, heterosexual or homosexual.

As you will see in subsequent chapters, sociological research has generated a great deal of knowledge about class, gender, and racial inequalities, as well as many other factors that shape people's experiences in society. Such knowledge not only contributes to a better

continued

understanding of the sources of harmful societal conditions that can and should be changed; sociological knowledge may also point to ways to go about making the changes. Sociologists' research findings and advice thus have often proven useful to politicians, planners, policymakers, journalists, intellectuals, and social workers and reformers concerned with contemporary social problems.

Sociology differs in significant ways from other social sciences. The discipline of psychology, for example, focuses primarily on the internal mental functioning of individuals and its effects on their behavior. In contrast, sociologists are principally concerned with the impact of social groups and societal conditions on people's thinking and behavior. Sociologists seek to understand how and why people are influenced by their group memberships, their everyday social interactions with others, and the broader social, economic, and political conditions under which they function.

Psychologists and sociologists do at times overlap in the interests of their academic disciplines and share insights. For example, some sociologists and psychologists share common interests in the specialized area of social psychology, which includes such research arenas as attitude formation and change, the behavior of people in small groups, and the socialization process through which people learn to participate in social life. But in general it is correct to say that sociologists are more prone than psychologists to be interested in the "big picture," which means looking at how the organization and operation of society affect its members, as well as how its members' thinking and behavior affect society.

Sociologists also trade ideas with their social science colleagues in economics and political science. Sociologists, however, view economic and political systems as only two of many types of social institutions central to the functioning of society. Finally, there is a good deal of common ground between sociology and anthropology in their concepts and research concerns. Although there are many exceptions, anthropologists have historically emphasized the study of non-Western, preliterate societies, particularly their cultural characteristics, while sociologists have tended to emphasize analysis of the organization and operation of industrialized societies, particularly those in the West.

Earlier we defined sociology as the scientific study of society, of the ways in which society is organized and operates, and of the factors contributing to both societal stability and social change. This chapter addresses the following questions:

- What is the "sociological imagination" and how does sociology contribute to it?
- What major theoretical perspectives have historically shaped sociology?
- What are some of the highly useful concepts that have come out of these perspectives?

As we address these questions, we hope readers of this book will begin to share our own sense of excitement and enthusiasm about the discipline of sociology.

Personal Troubles and Public Issues: Dana's Story

Before moving to a discussion of the sociological imagination, we begin with a story about Dana, a sincere and pleasant young woman of 19. Dana grew up in a racially and ethnically diverse middle-class neighborhood with her parents and two younger brothers. She was a relatively good student in high school, although she was the first to admit she coasted whenever she could. To provide the family with basic necessities, Dana's parents were both employed. They gave up vacations in order to put a small amount of money aside each month to help pay for their children's college costs. Dana and her brothers found part-time jobs to pay for their personal expenses. They enjoyed few luxuries. Dana's family was proud last year when she went off to a public college that had a good reputation. She was one of the first children of color in the neighborhood to go to this college. It was just affordable with Dana's summer earnings and a modest loan from the financial aid office. She was on track. But now her world is falling apart.

Dana's father was laid off over six months ago when his employer, a large manufacturing firm where he had worked his way up to a middle-management position, downsized its number of employees to reduce labor costs. To his dismay, the best job he was able to find was that of evening shift supervisor at a telemarketing firm. As a typical service-sector job, it paid far less and had fewer benefits than his manufacturing firm position, and thus it represented downward mobility. Dana's father wondered how much being in his early fifties had to do with his limited job prospects or if his physical disability, the result of a car accident, counted against him. He took it for granted that his dark skin could be a liability.

Dana's mother had been employed ever since her youngest child was old enough to care for himself after school. But her salary as a data-input worker in an insurance company was not sufficient to offset the family's drop in income from her husband's job change. When Dana inquired about more financial aid, the college aid office told her that the federal government had tightened the eligibility rules in response to a stagnant economy and reduced tax revenues. The school couldn't give her anything more. Even with the part-time jobs she was holding down, Dana could not afford to stay at college.

When Dana arrived home, she found her family in turmoil. Stress seemed to be ripping apart her parents' marriage. Mutual hostility and periodic outbursts of physical abuse marred their relationship. Dana's father had always been strict but fair with his children. Now he behaved unpredictably and at times drank to excess. Her brothers sought refuge with their friends, trying to avoid their father. They were also beginning to get into trouble at school; her mother was receiving a stream of calls and notes from school authorities. Dana spent a lot of time in her room, anxiety-stricken and chronically depressed by the overwhelming facts of her difficult situation. Away from her friends, and too frightened to approach her parents, Dana suffered alone.

If Dana and her family were part of a small handful of people in our society facing crises associated with employment difficulties and family discord, we might simply suggest that they all get counseling and wish them well. It would be logical to conclude they were just suffering from what sociologist C. Wright Mills called **personal troubles**—matters involving a person's character and his or her relations with others. Personal troubles typically can be resolved in local environments by those directly involved (Mills, 1959). But a substantial body of social science research suggests that the kinds of crises and challenges confronting Dana and her family are extremely widespread (Newman, 1999; Sklar, Mykyta, and Wefald, 2002).

White-collar employees—including those in supervisory and middle-management positions—increasingly find themselves subject to job insecurity and unemployment due to corporate downsizing and layoffs. Here, the jobless stand in line hoping to be chosen for another position.

Mills, a renowned scholar whose writings were often very critical of the workings of U.S. society, made a distinction between personal troubles and public issues. **Public issues** "have to do with matters that transcend local environments of the individual" (Mills, 1959: 8). When millions of men and women in our society are unable to achieve economic success and job security, as is so often the case today, this is a public issue. The individuals involved cannot all correct their plight simply by an act of personal will. Rather, it is necessary to look at what is wrong with the economy as an institution in order to determine what steps can be taken to improve employment opportunities and incomes. This may require the active intervention of other major social institutions, such as the state.

Dana's father, caught up in a situation that he may consider his personal trouble, reflects a larger public issue. "Deindustrialization" of the U.S. economy, the decline of secure, well-paying jobs in the goods-producing manufacturing sector, and their replacement with often lower paying jobs that involve providing services—is now a fact of life in the United States (Newman, 1999). Dana's father is but one of many blue-color and white-collar workers who have found their work lives and economic situations transformed and disrupted by the deindustrialization process.

The plight of Dana's family reflects other public issues that go beyond personal troubles and resist individual-level solutions. Despite antidiscrimination laws, millions of adults face discrimination in the labor market on the basis of their skin color or age. Approximately 40 million Americans have disabilities and many confront hiring prejudices on the part of employers. Women across U.S. society continue to face pressures to bear the bulk of child care and domestic responsibilities in their households. This situation, combined with sex discrimination in the work force, makes it difficult for women to perform successfully as sole providers of the family income (Albelda and Tilly, 1997). Unemployment and other job-related problems may have a damaging impact on personal and family life, fostering tensions and even contributing to family violence (Neubeck and Neubeck, 1997).

Studying sociology can help us become sensitive not only to the difference between personal troubles and public issues but also to the connections that often exist between the two. People like Dana's father frequently view job loss, downward mobility, and economic stress as their own personal trouble and accept the full burden of responsibility for it. They blame themselves, and may be blamed by others, for their plight. The solution to personal troubles rests with the individuals involved. But when many people experience these same troubles, and the causes lie with forces and decisions that are largely beyond their control, it is more appropriate to treat such personal troubles as a public issue. In that case both the causes and solutions lie with how the society is organized and run.

The Sociological Imagination in Action

C. Wright Mills coined the term **sociological imagination** to refer to a way of thinking that enables individuals to understand how they are affected by broad features of the society in which they live. In *The Sociological Imagination* (1959), Mills noted that many people tend to get so caught up in their own "personal orbits" of everyday life that they often ignore what is happening in the larger society. Family, school, work, and personal relationships absorb much of people's attention, time, and energies. Yet their personal orbits are very much open to influence by broad societal trends and key events.

As discussed in the "Social Forces/People's Lives" reading, the sociological imagination strives to understand (1) how society is presently structured or organized, (2) how and why it seems to be changing, and (3) how people's personal "biographies" or individual life experiences fit within and are affected by the society's structure and the flow of social change. Mills believed the sociological imagination gives power to anyone possessing it. It allows individuals to identify problematic circumstances they share with others, circumstances over which they may seek to capture some control. Let's look briefly at Dana's father's situation. How might exercising the sociological imagination be useful to him and members of his family?

Many people like Dana's father are losing their jobs because of shifts in the capitalist world economic system. The dominant economic position occupied by the United States since World War II has been undergoing challenge by Japan, members of the European Union, and a host of other capitalist nations that are successfully competing to provide manufactured goods for the world market. To deal with the competition and meet their profit goals, corporations in the United States have been taking steps to reduce production costs and increase efficiency. Often this means downsizing or trimming the ranks of management and other supervisory and white-collar staff, substituting automated machinery for blue-collar workers, and moving some production activities to low-wage plants elsewhere in the United States or abroad. The pursuit of profit maximization has led some corporate executives to engage in "corporate deviance," in this case unethical and illegal financial practices which at times (as in the case of Enron) have led to criminal charges, corporate bankruptcies, and extensive employee job loss.

Many of the manufacturing jobs that have disappeared in the United States due to deindustrialization have been replaced by jobs in the service sector (e.g., finance, communications, real estate, retail sales, health care, food services). But high-level service jobs often require skills that former manufacturing workers do not possess, and the skill level requirements and pay levels of many of the new service-sector jobs are often less than those for the blue-collar and white-collar jobs that are disappearing. Some argue that the pace at which U.S. manufacturing-sector jobs have been lost has increased since the mid-1990s when the U.S. government established new economic relations with Mexico and Canada (under the North American Free Trade Agreement, or NAFTA). Both the world and domestic economies are undergoing a major reordering, reflecting decisions being made by top-level corporate and political elites. Members of the U.S. labor force are experiencing effects of these decisions, over which they exercise no say.

Using a sociological imagination, Dana's father's might view his predicament more constructively. He could see how deindustrialization, downsizing, and economic difficulties are troubling millions of workers in the United States, and that he is by no means alone or to blame for his plight. He might see value in joining collectively with others to actively press for needed political and economic solutions on the local, state, and national levels. Finally, were Dana and other family members to view problems families like theirs are having with employment and income as a public issue, they would see the importance of giving Dana's father needed support and encouragement. Each family member could do more to help the others cope, and they might opt to join with people caught up in a similar predicament in mobilizing politically to demand solutions.

Our goal in writing this book is to help readers develop a sociological imagination. The sociological imagination can help individuals understand the importance of acting with others to affect history and thereby influence the series of life experiences that constitute individual biographies. The sociological imagination can help people who are struggling under harmful societal conditions to avoid placing blame on themselves or innocent others for situations that they did not create. The sociological imagination can redirect attention toward more productive and appropriate analyses and strategies for social change from which many can benefit (Johnson, 1997).

To help readers develop this imagination, we draw on a number of core concepts used by sociologists. **Core concepts** are fundamental ideas that are helpful in analyzing features of U.S. society as well as those of other societies. They provide a language to use in formulating research questions that lead us to take a deeper look at society's workings. Armed with facts from such research, people are in a better position to determine what, if anything, they might hope to change.

The core concepts used by contemporary sociologists in the United States derive from or reflect the influence of major intellectual traditions that have historically shaped the discipline. In the next section we will address these intellectual traditions and some of the core concepts that flow out of them.

Sociology: Intellectual Traditions and Core Concepts

Sociology's European Roots

The actual origins of sociology lie in antiquity. For hundreds of years, social thinkers and philosophers in the East and West have expressed views on the workings of the organized social life of their own and other societies. Contemporary sociological thinking in the United States, however, has been most directly influenced by intellectual developments arising in the late eighteenth and nineteenth centuries, particularly in France and Germany. This was a time when rapid and radical social changes were occurring in European societies (Ritzer and Goodman, 2004). Social movements, like the one that led to the French Revolution in 1789, challenged and undermined hierarchical social relationships between the rich, aristocratic classes and the poor, common people. These relationships had long been taken for granted by elites and common people alike as part of the natural order of things. In addition, advances in science opened up alternative ways of thinking about the natural and physical worlds, prompted by exciting new ideas and discoveries. The increasing stature of science threatened the traditional monopoly over truth and knowledge claimed by church authorities.

Research and technological innovations fostered new means of producing goods as well as advances in transportation and communication. These provided the basis for the Industrial Revolution, which dramatically changed many people's lives. The expansion of trade with the colonies and with non-European nations, along with changes in domestic production, meant that fewer European workers were needed in traditional agricultural pursuits and more were needed to labor in newly built factories. Increasing numbers of families were forced to leave rural farms, estates, and villages and seek out a livelihood in these factories, which were often located in growing urban centers. In these centers an emerging class of business owners and merchants was busy accumulating political and economic power and aggressively using this power to further its interests in profits and wealth accumulation.

The late eighteenth and nineteenth centuries were disruptive and unsettling, as more and more people across Europe experienced the loss and transformation of their traditional ways of life. It was also an era in which many people—including the intellectuals of the day—worried about high rates of crime, widespread squalor, street rioting, and threats of rebellion by impoverished workers and unemployed people in the burgeoning cities. This, then, is the social, economic, and political context within which early European sociological thinkers developed their ideas.

European scholars approached the study of society out of deep concern over the harmful social conditions they observed (Zeitlin, 2000). Impressed by breakthroughs in the physical and natural sciences made possible by the systematic use of scientific methods, these scholars believed it was possible to study society scientifically as well. The knowledge generated, early sociologists believed, could be employed to help solve social problems. Sociologists were not to study society simply to accumulate information about it, but were to generate knowledge that could be used to guide social progress.

Almost from the very beginning, however, sociologists found it difficult to agree on how to approach the study of society and its problems (Zeitlin, 2000). What concepts should be used to analyze the workings of society? What were the societal problems that needed to be solved? Disagreements among scholars over such issues gave rise to two European intellectual traditions whose impact on sociological thinking lingers even to this day. We will refer to these two traditions as the "functionalist perspective" and the "conflict perspective."

Social Forces/People's Lives

The Sociological Imagination

C. WRIGHT MILLS

In his classic work *The Sociological Imagination,* C. Wright Mills exhorts us to develop a "quality of mind" that will enable us to view our lives and the lives of others within their larger historical and social context. While Mills's language refers only to "men," thus seeming to exclude women, it is clear that he intended his words to be a call to all humanity.

NOWADAYS men often feel that their private lives are a series of traps. They sense that within their everyday worlds, they cannot overcome their troubles, and in this feeling, they are often quite correct: What ordinary men are directly aware of and what they try to do are bounded by the private orbits in which they live; their visions and their powers are limited to the close-up scenes of job, family, neighborhood; in other milieux, they move vicariously and remain spectators. And the more aware they become, however vaguely, of ambitions and of threats which transcend their immediate locales, the more trapped they seem to feel.

Underlying this sense of being trapped are seemingly impersonal changes in the very structure of continent-wide societies. The facts of contemporary history are also facts about the success and the failure of individual men and women. When a society is industrialized, a peasant becomes a worker; a feudal lord is liquidated or becomes a businessman. When classes rise or fall, a man is employed or unemployed; when the rate of investment goes up or down, a man takes new heart or goes broke. When wars happen, an insurance salesman becomes a rocket launcher; a store clerk, a radar man; a wife lives alone; a child grows up without a father. Neither the life of an individual, nor the history

of a society can be understood without understanding both.

Yet men do not usually define the troubles they endure in terms of historical change and institutional contradiction. The well-being they enjoy, they do not usually impute to the big ups and downs of the societies in which they live. Seldom aware of the intricate connection between the patterns of their own lives and the course of world history, ordinary men do not usually know what this connection means for the kinds of men they are becoming and for the kinds of history-making in which they might take part. They do not possess the quality of mind essential to grasp the interplay of man and society, of biography and history, of self and world. they cannot cope with their personal troubles in such ways as to control the structural transformations that usually lie behind them

Surely it is no wonder. In what period have so many men been so totally exposed at so fast a pace to such earthquakes of change? That Americans have not known such catastrophic changes as have the men and women of other societies is due to historical facts that are now quickly becoming "merely history." The history that now affects every man is world history. Within this scene and this period, in the course of a single generation, one sixth

The Functionalist Perspective

The **functionalist perspective** is often associated with French thinker Auguste Comte (1798–1857), who helped to popularize the term "sociology," and even more so with his fellow countryman Émile Durkheim (1858–1917). This perspective posits that human society is a naturally stable, harmonious social system. The stability of the social system is maintained by a culture that includes values, rules, and of mankind is transformed from all that is feudal and backward into all that is modern, advanced, and fearful. Political colonies are freed; new and less visible forms of imperialism installed. Revolutions occur; men feel the intimate grip of new kinds of authority. Totalitarian societies rise, and are smashed to bits—or succeed fabulously. After two centuries of ascendancy, capitalism is shown up as only one way to make society into an industrial apparatus. After two centuries of hope, even formal democracy is restricted to a quite small portion of mankind. Everywhere in the underdeveloped world, ancient ways of life are broken up and vague expectations become urgent demands. Everywhere in the overdeveloped world, the means of authority and of violence become total in scope and bureaucratic in form. Humanity itself now lies before us, the supernation at either pole concentrating its most co-ordinated and massive efforts upon the preparation of World War Three.

The very shaping of history now outpaces the ability of men to orient themselves in accordance with cherished values. And which values? Even when they do not panic, men often sense that older ways of feeling and thinking have collapsed and that newer beginnings are ambiguous to the point of moral stasis. Is it any wonder that ordinary men feel they cannot cope with the larger worlds with which they are so suddenly confronted? That they cannot understand the meaning of their epoch for their own lives? That—in defense of selfhood—they become morally insensible, trying to remain altogether private men? Is it any wonder that they come to be possessed by a sense of the trap?

What they need, and what they feel they need, is a quality of mind that will help them to use information and to develop reason in order to achieve lucid summations of what is going on in the world and of what may be happening within themselves. It is this quality, I am going to contend, that journalists and scholars, artists and publics, scientists and editors are coming to expect of what may be called the sociological imagination.

The sociological imagination enables its possessor to understand the larger historical scene in terms of its meaning for the inner life and the external career of a variety of individuals. It enables him to take into account how individuals, in the welter of their daily experience, often become falsely conscious of their social positions. Within that welter, the framework of modern society is sought, and within that framework the psychologies of a variety of men and women are formulated. By such means the personal uneasiness of individuals is focused upon explicit troubles and the indifference of publics is transformed into involvement with public issues.

> "The sociological imagination enables us to grasp history and biography and the relations between the two within society."

The first fruit of this imagination—and the first lesson of the social science that embodies it—is the idea that the individual can understand his own experience and gauge his own fate only by locating himself within his period, that he can know his own chances in life by becoming aware of those of all individuals in his circumstances. In many ways it is a terrible lesson; in many ways a magnificent one. We do not know the limits of man's capacities for supreme effort or willing degradation, for agony or glee, for pleasurable brutality or the sweetness of reason. But in our time we have come to know that the limits of "human nature" are frighteningly broad. We have come to know that every individual lives, from one generation to the next, in some society; that he lives out a biography, and that he lives it out within some historical sequence. By the fact of his living he contributes, however minutely, to the shaping of this society and to the course of its history, even as he is made by society and by its historical push and shove.

The sociological imagination enables us to grasp history and biography and the relations between the two within society. That is its task and its promise.

Source: C. Wright Mills, *The Sociological Imagination*, New York: Oxford University Press, 1959, pp. 3–5.

practices that are widely shared. People become participants in a society by learning its culture. This occurs through a process known as socialization.

The socialization process includes learning how to fill existing social positions and to perform necessary social roles in major social institutions, such as the family, the economy, religion, and the political system. Each of these institutions is said to be interdependent and interrelated with other institutions, and to serve critical functions

Peasants and workers rose up against the wealthy and privileged classes during the French Revolution of 1789, inspired by the belief that the extreme social, political, and economic inequalities existing in France were neither natural nor inevitable and needed to be changed.

for society as a whole. The various features of society—from social institutions to systems of inequality—are said to be there for a reason and should be changed using great caution, if at all.

From the functionalist perspective, the appropriate relationship of the individual to society is one of accommodation and adaptation. Individuals are constantly being born, participating in social life, and then dying. Yet society and its institutions go on regardless of the changes in societal membership. The ongoing operation and continuity of society require that everyone cooperate with the socialization process, carried out by social institutions such as the family, religion, and education. Through the process of socialization, individuals are groomed for their appropriate places in society's division of labor. Along with a commonly shared culture, the cooperation among people called for by the division of labor itself is important to societal stability. In the big scheme of things, the needs of society are far more important than the needs of those individuals who participate in it.

The functionalist perspective assumes that human nature contains a tendency toward irrational behavior that must be kept in check by proper socialization. When individuals are not adequately socialized, their behavior is likely to depart from shared values, rules, and practices. Deviant behavior can be highly disruptive to stability and harmony within the social system. Important positions and social roles may not be adequately performed, and this can interfere with societal functioning.

Thus from the functionalist perspective it is important for society to develop means to exercise social control over deviant behavior and to discourage society's members from engaging in it. Minor expressions of deviant behavior can usually be dealt with informally by those who find them offensive (e.g., teachers, neighbors, family members, friends); formal agencies of social control (e.g., police, courts, prisons) exist to handle the most serious cases of deviance.

Punishment of society's deviants is said to serve as a reminder and reaffirmation of the cultural values and rules that its members share. Most individuals are either responsive to the socialization process or coerced to conform by the ever-present weight of cultural values, rules, and negative sanctions for deviant behavior. Individuals' conformity with society's demands contributes to order, without which, from the functionalist perspective, there can be no social progress (see Figure 1.1).

🌐 Émile Durkheim: Influential Functionalist Thinker

Émile Durkheim, a nineteenth-century French thinker whose sociological writings are still widely read and cited, has been perhaps the most influential proponent of the functionalist perspective. Durkheim's writings range across a wide variety of topics (Ritzer and Goodman, 2004). He addressed the importance of culture and the functions played by commonly shared moral values, beliefs, ceremonies, and rituals in encouraging societal harmony and stability. In more contemporary societies, where population diversity may outweigh commonalities among people, Durkheim saw stabilizing functions also played by the complex division of labor, arguing that it renders people and their activities highly interdependent. Durkheim saw social order similarly being helped along by the appearance and consequent condemnation of deviant behavior such as criminal acts. Condemnation of deviance functioned to remind members of diverse societies that they shared certain fundamental values.

Durkheim also stressed the important function of **social facts.** These are social and cultural features of a society, existing independently of the individuals who make it up, which influence people's behavior. The size and makeup of the general population, dominant ideas and ways of thinking, the division of labor, groups to which people can belong—all are examples of social facts. Durkheim believed that analyses using social facts would lead to highly valuable sociological explanations of human behavior, reducing reliance on frequently problematic biological or psychological explanations. He showed, for example, that the members of different religious denominations have different rates of suicide, suggesting that the groups in which one holds membership (a social fact) can help explain even highly personal acts. In other words, suicide rates can be explained sociologically and without recourse to biological or psychological explanations.

Finally, Durkheim also brought a functionalist perspective to bear in his thinking about inequality in society (Kerbo, 2003). In Durkheim's view, if contemporary society and its division of labor were to function properly, and social progress was to occur, individuals with the appropriate talents had to be encouraged and permitted to move into those positions to which they were best suited. The rewards (money, power, prestige) attached to different positions were often highly unequal. However, this was less important to Durkheim than the undermining of social order that could occur if people grew disruptive because they could not move into positions where they could exercise their talents. In his stress on the importance of meeting society's needs for order, Durkheim failed to see inequality as a matter for concern.

Functionalist thinkers like Comte and Durkheim articulated ideas that very much expressed the views and supported the interests of the privileged classes in European society. But, although in retrospect functionalist thinkers may have acted as apologists for the status quo in their theorizing about how society works, they also embraced and emphasized core concepts that still serve as important tools for analyses of the organization and operation of society. Aspects of this intellectual tradition are reflected later in this book when, for example, we discuss the functions of different social institutions, culture, views on socialization, and explanations for class inequality and deviant behavior.

If the functionalist perspective emphasizes the importance of order as a prerequisite for social progress, a second intellectual tradition emphasizes the role of conflict in bringing about change. Proponents of the "conflict perspective" argue that struggles between groups with different degrees of wealth, prestige, and power are to be expected and are necessary if social progress is to occur (see Figure 1.1).

Measure	Functionalist Perspective	Conflict Perspective
Notable features of society	Common culture, stability, harmony	Societal diversity, power differences, systematic inequalities
View of human nature	Irrational, in need of control	Rational or "good"
Individuals' relation to society	Individuals should adapt to societ's needs	Society should be organized to meet its members' needs
Sources of deviant behavior	Failure of people to be adequately socialized	Alienation of people from harmful features of society
View of deviance	Disruptive, dangerous	Inevitable
Basis for social progress	Order in society	Conflict leading to transformation of society
Means to social progress	Conformity to social roles and the demands of social institutions	Social movements for fundamental societal change
Influential European thinkers	Comte, Durkheim	Rousseau, Marx, Weber

FIGURE 1.1 **Functionalist and Conflict Perspectives** The functionalist and conflict perspectives are two European intellectual traditions that continue to have an impact on sociological thinking. Each views society in quite a different way.

The Conflict Perspective

Like the functionalist perspective, the **conflict perspective** represents an intellectual tradition within sociology whose roots go back to late-eighteenth- and nineteenth-century Europe and the changes under way at that time. Thinkers within this second tradition emphasize social splits and divisions that often characterize human society. Whereas proponents of the functionalist perspective tend to emphasize what societal members have in common (e.g., common cultural values), conflict perspective proponents stress heterogeneity and diversity within society. In the rapidly industrializing capitalist societies of the late eighteenth and nineteenth centuries, wealth and income, prestige, and power were very visibly unequally distributed.

Unlike functionalist thinkers like Comte and Durkheim, social thinkers adopting a conflict perspective tended to side with the common people regarding the widespread injustices being inflicted by the privileged and powerful and in seeing a need for radical social change. Their views were dismissed and condemned by members of Europe's privileged classes. Jean Jacques Rousseau (1712–1778) found class inequality in pre-Revolutionary France to be unnatural and in violation of human nature. It had to be fought. Karl Marx (1818–1883) concluded that industrial **capitalism**—an economic system in which the means of production were owned by relatively few—would produce class inequalities so severe as to call forth worker-led social movements leading to the system's downfall. Both were disturbed by the unequal distribution of life chances and opportunities among society's members that systematic political and economic inequalities promote and maintain.

The conflict perspective accepts the notion that human society is naturally harmonious and stable, but it sees the creation of systems of inequality (such as class inequality under capitalism) as producing outcomes that are contrary to social order. Social movements can be expected to arise as people refuse to submit to unjust and harmful conditions within systems of inequality from which they see no escape. Conflict is to be expected, as groups or classes holding little power or privilege struggle to improve their lot while the advantaged strive to protect what they have. A society with haves and have-nots is inherently unstable. From this perspective, social progress often requires social conflict.

Proponents of the conflict perspective tend to adopt a more positive view of human nature than proponents of functionalism. Human beings are seen as being fundamentally rational or "good." The conflict perspective holds that individuals are capable of acting effectively on behalf of their own best interests. Karl Marx, for example, was generally respectful of workers' ability to make the right choices when it came to bringing about needed social change, encouraging them to do so in political pamphlets like *The Communist Manifesto.*

Persons who question the societal status quo, who refuse to adapt to the demands of authority and the rules of the existing order, are viewed from the functionalist perspective as poorly socialized deviants. From the conflict perspective, however, such persons instead may be seen as expressing their alienation from an oppressive and exploitative social system that fails to meet their needs. Order cannot depend on socializing deviants into the existing social system, for the system is harming them. Such a situation regularly arises whenever a social system is organized and operated to systematically benefit only a few.

Hence, unlike the functionalist perspective, the conflict perspective places priority on the well-being of society's members. Their physical and psychological needs are of primary concern, and proponents of the conflict perspective argue that society and its institutions should be organized in ways that meet these needs. The failure of the social system to meet many of its members' needs makes their lives intolerable, and this situation gives rise to social movements to bring about change. Social progress occurs out of the conflict such movements produce, and conflict thus is as necessary as it is inevitable.

Karl Marx: Proponent of Radical Change

To nineteenth-century German thinker Karl Marx, perhaps the most important feature of any society was the nature of its economic system. In his view, the economy significantly affects a society's culture and value system, its class structure and class relations, and the functioning of the state.

Marx was particularly critical of the European industrial capitalist economy of his day. It was an economy based on the private ownership of the means of production (e.g., factories, mines, transportation systems) by a relatively small number of affluent individuals who comprised a **bourgeoisie** or capitalist class. The overwhelming majority of society's members—who constituted a **proletariat** or working class—could survive only by selling their labor power to the capitalists. The latter took advantage of the workers' desperation, profiting mightily by paying workers very low wages and requiring that they labor under the worst of conditions. Workers who did not like the situation could leave or were fired. The state sided with the capitalists by passing laws that prohibited workers from organizing and unionizing and provided police to forcibly suppress protests and protect capitalists' property.

Marx believed that a society organized around capitalism was highly unstable, conflict-prone, and contained the seeds of its own destruction. Conflict between the bourgeoisie and the proletariat was inevitable, given the contradictions in their self-interests. Yet, he noted, workers often blamed their suffering on fate, higher powers, or their own poor decisions. Workers possessed what Marx called **false consciousness,** in that they did not understand that capitalism itself created their poverty and misery. Marx believed this false consciousness would eventually give way to **class consciousness,** wherein workers would understand that capitalism itself was the problem and that their poverty and poor working conditions could be ended only with **socialism,** or worker ownership of and control over the society's means of production.

As a proponent of the conflict perspective, Marx believed that social progress required conflict. He assumed that economic exploitation of the proletariat by the bourgeoisie would eventually spark widespread worker rebellion and radical change that would benefit the majority of society's members. Marx's analyses have been highly influential and have provided inspiration and a rationale for participation in social movements for exploited and impoverished people in many nations. Marx's writings have also been important to sociologists interested in developing a conflict perspective on the present-day dynamics of capitalism, the class structure, and capitalism's impact on society's members.

Max Weber: Student of Social Stratification and Bureaucracy

While Karl Marx is often considered the central figure in the development of the conflict perspective, it is just as important to mention contributions that his fellow German sociologist Max Weber (1864–1920) made to this intellectual tradition. Weber was nowhere near as critical of capitalism as was Marx. Moreover, Weber placed more emphasis than did Marx on the importance of analyzing features of a society other than its economic system, such as its political and cultural characteristics. Weber is best understood as developing many of his ideas in reaction to Marx, providing his own approaches to some of the issues with which Marx was concerned (Zeitlin, 2000).

Like Marx, Weber was interested in inequality. But he did not limit his analyses to capitalism and to classes defined in terms of those who either owned or did not own society's means of production. His interest in inequality encompassed differences in individuals' political power and prestige. Weber noted that power and prestige did not always derive from property ownership. In some instances important social positions, such as religious or military positions, carried power and prestige but not wealth. Moreover, power and prestige were at times rooted in an individual's charisma, personality characteristics to which others responded by granting that person respect or authority. Weber thus emphasized the importance of analyzing **social stratification** in society, or the bases on which different positions and the people in them are ranked or "stratified" from high to low in terms of wealth and income, prestige, or power.

Weber viewed the unequal distribution of power and conflict as central features of society. But, unlike Marx, Weber associated these phenomena with trends that went beyond capitalism. Weber observed that traditional ways of organizing social life in Western societies, which relied heavily on past practices and the authority of elders, were rapidly being displaced by more scientific and rational approaches. This shift was reflected in the growing use of bureaucratic forms of organization to carry out business activities and governmental affairs. A **bureaucracy** is an organization in which people perform specialized roles under a system of explicit rules and within a hierarchy of authority.

Weber viewed bureaucracy as a highly efficient tool for getting various societal tasks accomplished. He was, however, very concerned over the implications of society becoming more and more bureaucratized and run by bureaucratic elites, those in top organizational positions. Just as capitalism was a problem to Marx, bureaucracy was a problem to Weber. Weber was pessimistic that the trend toward bureaucratic domination could be overcome, suggesting instead that the hierarchical social relations characterizing bureaucratic organization (in business, government, religious institutions) would give rise to constant conflicts and struggles between bureaucratic elites and the rank and file over elites' exercise of power and authority.

Reflecting Back on Dana's Story

Social thinkers like Rousseau, Marx, and Weber helped launch an intellectual tradition that encouraged contemporary sociologists to utilize core concepts such as capitalism, bureaucracy, class, power, and social movements in their efforts to understand the workings of society. Core concepts important to the conflict perspective will play a prominent role in the chapters that follow. Indeed, we already drew on such concepts in discussing how a sociological imagination might help one see Dana's family problems as connected to public issues.

For example, Dana's father's loss of his manufacturing-sector position stemmed from his firm's putting profit maximization before the jobs of workers, a decision being made by many firms within the U.S. economic system of *capitalism.* Needing more financial aid, Dana found that she would now have to drop out of college as a result of the limits on aid established by the federal government *bureaucracy.* Her father's downward mobility, coupled with her mother's limited earning ability, had made the *class* position of Dana's family less secure. Helpless to solve their problems simply on their own as individuals, members of Dana's family might be able to gain *power* by joining with others in *social movement* activities to demand change.

Consideration of the functionalist and conflict perspectives raises some interesting questions. Can people successfully avoid adaptation to the demands being made on them by the social system in which they are embedded? Can people ignore, resist, or even alter the system? To what degree can Dana's family, and people facing similar problems, realistically hope to alter the trajectory of their biographies? In thinking about such questions, it is helpful to consider a third intellectual tradition that

Replacing blue-collar workers with robots in the manufacturing process may increase a company's productivity and help maximize its profits; however, the workers who are displaced by robots must bear the hardships of unemployment while facing a shortage of decent-paying jobs.

has helped to shape contemporary sociology in the United States.

Symbolic Interactionism: People Constructing Social Reality

The functionalist and conflict perspectives approach society and its key features from very different standpoints, and each also has a different conception of the relationship of the individual to society. The functionalist perspective views people's lives as by necessity being "determined" by society and its institutions, to which people had best adapt. The conflict perspective likewise views society as placing constraints on people, but in ways that foster alienation, not adaptation, and that may prompt people into movements for social change (Figure 1.1).

Among contemporary sociologists there is disagreement over the degree to which people are pushed to behave in certain ways by prevailing features of society, whether it be the demands of shared cultural values (the functionalist perspective) or social conditions that do harm (the conflict perspective). Are human beings really little more than robots who march in response to abstract "laws of society" or other social forces? Or are people active agents? Do people's minds count? To what degree and in what ways do people exercise their own "free will" to act autonomously within and upon society?

The term **human agency** is often used to refer to the ability of humans to react to and change the social conditions surrounding them. It stands in contrast to the term **social determinism,** which is used to stress the importance of society's features as determinants of what happens to individuals. How much emphasis sociologists should place on the role of human agency in understanding the operation and course of society is a key issue within contemporary sociology. This question is addressed by a third sociological perspective, one that focuses on people's thinking and behavior on the level of their everyday social interactions.

Symbolic interactionism is an intellectual tradition that evolved in the United States out of the scholarship of such sociologists as George Herbert Mead (1863–1931) and W. I. Thomas (1863–1947). Proponents of symbolic interactionism have often been highly critical of functionalist and conflict perspectives, arguing that they overemphasize the significance of external social forces, such as cultural values or systems of inequality, in determining individuals' behaviors. Indeed, symbolic interactionism arose in the United States partly in response to the failure of the functionalist perspective to treat individuals as mindful social actors.

Symbolic interactionists acknowledge that individuals are influenced by the social environments in which they find themselves. However, they stress that individuals are also active, autonomous agents who, unlike robots, initiate thought and behavior. Proponents point to the important fact that human beings are capable of self-reflection and self-criticism, as well as efforts at self-development and change. People also can think imaginatively, and they actively interpret and bestow meaning on situations and events. All these activities are possible due to humans' use of language and other symbols in combination with social interaction.

Symbolic interactionism focuses on such topics as the ways in which shared meanings among individuals develop or change through social interaction. It addresses the role that social interaction plays in the individual's development of a sense of "self." And, of particular importance to scholars of social movements and social change, symbolic interactionism explores how people, interacting through the medium of language and other symbols, construct understandings of external reality on which they then may act.

From a symbolic interactionist perspective, the reality that is objectively "out there" is not nearly as important as the reality that subjectively exists in people's minds. Symbolic interactionism will, for example, inform aspects of our discussion of the importance of language in constructing social reality, our treatment of how individuals develop social identities, including gender identity, and our discussion of the processes by which people come to be labeled by others and to see themselves as deviants.

Different Perspectives, Different Voices: The Benefits

We have presented the functionalist, conflict, and symbolic interactionist perspectives as distinct intellectual traditions. In the United States, sociologists have tended to lean toward one or the other of these traditions in their attempts to understand the workings of society. Others have moved back and forth between traditions over the course of their careers. Today sociologists commonly borrow core concepts from different intellectual traditions, finding some concepts more useful than others in their analyses. Our own interest in "personal troubles" and "public issues" has led us to draw heavily on concepts central to the conflict perspective in writing this book. However, we also freely rely on many concepts that are central to alternative ways of viewing society and its participants, such as the functionalist and symbolic interactionist perspectives.

In recent decades the influence of voices that were often muted or largely ignored by mainstream sociology has grown much more prominent. In part, this has occurred as the sociological community in the United States—long dominated by white, male academics—has become much more diverse and inclusive. Today, for example, this community is coming to appreciate the intellectual power and unique contributions of important sociologists of color such as W. E. B. Dubois (1868–1963) and Oliver Cromwell Cox (1901–1974), pioneers in analyzing racial inequalities. The sociological community is likewise very much aware of the pathbreaking contributions to understanding gender inequalities by women in sociology, particularly since the 1960s (Lengermann and Niebrugge, 2000; Rogers, 2001). In recent years, the voices of scholars of color and feminist sociologists have encouraged new ways of thinking about how the intersections of race and ethnicity, class, and gender simultaneously affect people.

Much of the diversity and scholarly creativity within sociology has come from the discovery of new questions and new ways to use the discipline's core concepts as steppingstones to knowledge about society, whatever the intellectual traditions with which they are historically associated. In chapters that follow, we define and flesh out sociology's core concepts and show how contemporary sociologists have used them in their scholarly work. Such concepts are central to the exercise of the sociological imagination.

Reflecting the contributions of different perspectives and different voices, sociology seeks to provide a systematic, evidence-based understanding of the world humans have constructed. At its best, sociology does more than simply identify obstacles to change. It points to contradictions within society that are potential change levers, suggests public issues around which people can organize, and stimulates continual assessments of the status quo. In short, sociology is meant to be done, studied, and used for the betterment of humanity.

CHAPTER SUMMARY

1. Sociology is the scientific study of society, of the ways in which society is organized and operates, and of the factors contributing to both societal stability and social change.

2. Sociology is useful in that it can help people distinguish between their own "personal troubles," or problems that individuals might hope to solve, and "public issues," socially harmful societal conditions whose solution requires collective political action.

3. To understand the difference between personal troubles and public issues, a way of thinking called the "sociological imagination" is helpful. That imagination is fueled by knowledge about how society is presently structured, how and why it seems to be changing, and how features of society affect people's biographies.

4. A sociological imagination allows people to play an active role in influencing the directions their biographies are likely to take. Human beings need not simply be passive objects to whom life happens. Working alongside like-minded others, people have the capacity to exercise influence and capture some control over their series of life experiences.

5. Contemporary sociology is influenced by important intellectual traditions that we have termed the functionalist, conflict, and symbolic interactionist perspectives. While quite different in their ways of perceiving society and its members, each has contributed to the core concepts that sociologists use in asking research questions and generating new knowledge about the workings of society.

6. The functionalist perspective stresses the importance of order and stability within society as a prerequisite for social progress. It examines functions served by different features of society and the contributions they make to the organization and operation of society as a whole. Core concepts associated with the functionalist perspective include culture, socialization, deviant behavior, and social control.

7. The conflict perspective emphasizes features of society that can be harmful to people's life chances. This perspective suggests that social progress may require conflict in order to end harmful conditions. Core concepts associated with the conflict perspective include capitalism, class, systems of inequality, power, bureaucracy, and social movements.

8. The symbolic interactionist perspective focuses on people as active and autonomous agents. Symbolic interactionists explore how individuals come to view and define themselves as well as the ways in which people use language and other symbols to interpret and bestow meaning on situations and events. Core concepts associated with this perspective include the self, social identity, and the construction of social reality.

THINKING CRITICALLY

1. A marriage that ends in divorce is usually dismissed as the couple's own personal trouble and a matter of their individual failings. Yet the divorce rate is very high; some 50 percent of all marriages end in divorce. How might our understanding of the causes of divorce be enriched were we to view it as a public issue?

2. In the early 2000s, many students graduating from college had a difficult time finding jobs. Some experienced unemployment. Others could find only part-time or temporary positions or were forced to take low-paying full-time jobs that often did not require a college education. Who or what is to blame for this situation? How does the way one answers that question suggest different solutions?

3. Do you believe that members of society can change harmful social conditions under which they or others are living? To what degree and in what ways do people have "free will" to make such changes? If there are obstacles, who or what are they? What might be needed for these obstacles to be overcome? Give examples.

4. C. Wright Mills believed that the sociological imagination would be empowering to anyone possessing it. A counterargument might hold that the accumulation of knowledge about how the surrounding social world affects us could prove to be overwhelming, even paralyzing. Where do you stand in this argument?

KEY TERMS

bourgeoisie, *(16)*
bureaucracy, *(17)*
capitalism, *(15)*
class consciousness, *(16)*
conflict perspective, *(14)*
core concepts, *(8)*
false consciousness, *(16)*

functionalist perspective, *(10)*
human agency, *(18)*
life chances, *(3)*
personal troubles, *(5)*
proletariat, *(16)*
public issues, *(6)*
social determinism, *(18)*

social facts, *(13)*
social stratification, *(17)*
socialism, *(16)*
sociological imagination, *(7)*
sociology, *(3)*
symbolic interactionism, *(18)*

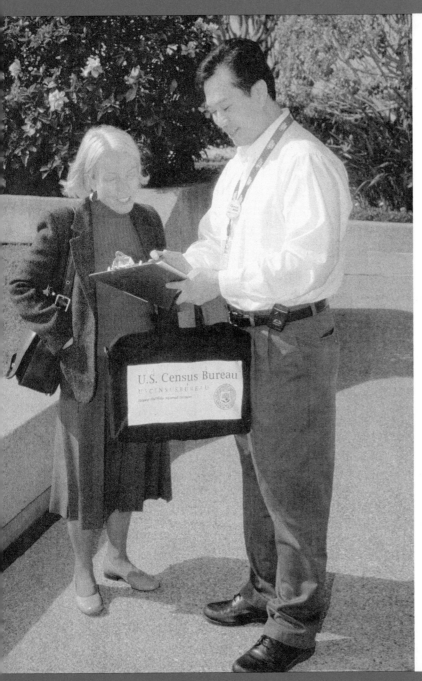

Chapter Two

Research Methods

To exercise the sociological imagination, as discussed in Chapter 1, the ability to distinguish between opinion and fact when it comes to discussing the workings of society is important. Many people base their knowledge of the social world upon "facts" handed down from others in the past or on traditional thinking, without questioning whether the facts still hold true (or ever did). Other people make hasty generalizations about social groups or various features of society largely based on their personal experiences. While one's personal experiences may themselves be valid, this does not mean that they are necessarily typical, that they are correctly understood or interpreted, or that they can be broadly generalized.

Sociologists make special efforts not to fall into the trap of confusing opinion with fact. They tend to be cautious or even skeptical about ideas concerning the workings of society, even ideas that many people take for granted as being true. Sociologists seek to base their observations about society on facts that have been scientifically established through objective investigation and systematic data gathering. When sociologists report their research findings, they describe the methods and data that produced them. If they receive funding for their research projects, they reveal its sources. This information helps other researchers assess the probable validity of the research findings being reported.

Sociologists use a variety of research methods to conduct their investigations. These methods are important tools, for they are the means by which sociologists seek to generate new knowledge. No one research method is intrinsically "better" than another, just as a hammer is no "better" a tool than a screwdriver or pliers. As a unique tool, each research method has its appropriate uses, as well as its relative advantages and disadvantages. The toolbox of different research methods is invaluable to furthering understanding of how society is organized and operates and of the factors contributing to social stability and change. To say that the effective use of research methods makes the sociological imagination possible is no exaggeration.

Whatever the research methods sociologists choose to use, opportunities for unethical behavior may arise in the course of carrying out investigations. In addition, sociological research could in some instances conceivably be conducted for purposes that contribute to social injustice. Like other professionals, sociologists have a responsibility to pursue their activities ethically and to avoid bringing harm to others.

This chapter focuses attention on several questions:

- What are the main research methods that sociologists use in their investigations?
- What are the relative advantages and disadvantages of the different methods?
- What kinds of ethical issues may at times arise for sociological researchers?
- What is the importance of the political context in which research is conducted?

continued

The Research Process

Use of Hypotheses and Open-Ended Research Questions

Social scientists are trained to use a variety of different **research methods**—procedures designed to establish facts about the social world. These methods include experimental research, field research, historical research, and survey research (Babbie, 2000; Schutt, 2001). Usually such research methods are used to gather information relevant to hypotheses. A **hypothesis** is a carefully formulated statement that may be either verified or discarded on the basis of the examination of relevant data. At times, the hypotheses being tested have important implications for social policy.

For example, a sociologist may formulate a hypothesis that states "Mother-headed families receiving welfare, whose heads enter the labor force under federal and state welfare reform requirements, are likely to rise out of poverty." The sociologist would then gather data on the work behavior and poverty circumstances of such mothers to see whether the hypothesis receives support. In testing a hypothesis, researchers look for systematic relationships between the variables contained in their statements. **Variables** are attitudes, behaviors, or conditions that can vary.

There are two main types of variable, "independent" and "dependent." An **independent variable** is one that affects another variable. A change in the independent variable causes the other variable to change. A **dependent variable** is the one in which change is caused. In short, when an independent variable changes, a change in the dependent value should follow. Sociologists use statistical techniques to manipulate (change) independent variables in order to see whether and to what extent dependent variables then undergo change. In the example above, the sociologist is interested in whether welfare-reliant mothers' entry into the labor force (the independent variable) results in their families rising out of poverty (the dependent variable).

Sometimes researchers feel that they do not know enough about a given social phenomenon to develop and test specific hypotheses about it. In such instances researchers may pursue **open-ended research questions.** They are "open-ended" in the sense that no particular answers are necessarily assumed. Rather, questions are posed in ways that may generate new and at times detailed information. Open-ended questions can be very exploratory, leaving the sociologist a good deal of flexibility in deciding what he or she will consider relevant and useful data sources.

For example, a sociologist may ask "Why is there a high rate of hunger within the U.S. population?" Sources of data bearing on this question might include people patronizing soup kitchens and food banks; caseworkers in social service agencies and homeless shelters; staff of public health clinics, hospitals, and schools; leaders of antihunger groups, and government officials. In the "Social Forces/People's Lives" reading, Loretta Schwartz-Nobel's observations about the extent of hunger in the United States underscore the importance of formulating adequate answers to this question if hunger is to be eliminated.

Steps in the Research Process

The sociological research process proceeds through a series of steps (see Figure 2.1). After becoming interested in a particular social phenomenon, and having reviewed existing scholarly literature to learn more about it, the researcher determines the hypothesis to be tested or the research question to be pursued. Next, the researcher chooses a research method. The method selected depends, in part, on the hypothesis or research question. Some methods will be more appropriate than others to answer the questions posed by the researcher's investigation. He or she then gathers data relevant to the hypothesis or research question (or draws on data already gathered by others). The researcher analyzes these data, records the findings, and reaches conclusions.

Finally, sociological researchers disseminate information about their inquiries. This often involves preparation of a report that describes the purpose of the research, the method(s) used, an explanation of how the data produced were analyzed, the findings, and the conclusions reached. Often, the report will include recommendations for further research. If the research was commissioned by a sponsor (e.g., a government agency, foundation, or private firm), the sociologist will give the report to the sponsor. Sociologists also disseminate information about their research in professional journals and books, in the mass media, and through public presentations.

To illustrate the principal methods used in sociological research, we will examine some well-known and classic studies that examine the relationship between schooling and class inequality, a topic to be taken up in more detail in Chapter 13. As we will see, different questions about this relationship, explored with various research methods, have led to valuable insights. The studies to be discussed have been widely cited by sociological researchers and have contributed to debates that continue to this day over how to eliminate the unequal educational opportunities confronting students from low-income backgrounds. The studies chosen employ experimental research, field research, survey research, and historical research. Finally, to round out our discussion of research methods we will discuss analyses of data that have previously been collected by others.

Types of Research Methods

Experimental Research

Most of us are familiar with experimental research from school science courses. In the physical sciences, **experimental research** is conducted to find out how a particular organism or object is affected by different types of treatment selected by the researcher. Although by no means the research method used most frequently by sociologists, some do find it useful notwithstanding the practical and ethical considerations experimentation with human beings imposes. Like other scientists, some sociologists even conduct studies in laboratories where they are able to maximize control over experimental procedures and conditions. The basic principles guiding the experimental research method are much the same in both laboratory and natural (nonlaboratory) settings.

Establishing Experimental and Control Groups

Researchers begin by establishing at least two groups to be studied. The first, called the **experimental group,** is the one to which the researcher will give special treatment

Social Forces/People's Lives

People Going Hungry

LORETTA SCHWARTZ-NOBEL

When children in a U.S. city are seen foraging for discarded food in a Dumpster, their hunger may seem like an exceptional situation that perhaps should be addressed by their parents or guardians. Yet hunger affects tens of millions of people in the United States. The sociological imagination can help us see hunger as a public issue that perhaps requires new social policies in order to be effectively addressed.

THERE is a road near my house called Haverford Road. I have driven on it often but I never really knew where it led. One day last summer when the expressway was closed, I checked my map and decided to follow the road as an alternate route to the center of Philadelphia. After about fifteen minutes, my familiar-looking neighborhood began to change into a distinctly poorer one. Ten minutes later, it looked as if I had entered a third world country. Some of the stores had rusted iron bars across their windows, others had been closed down altogether and their doors were nailed shut. Many of the houses still appeared lived in but most had boarded-up windows. There was graffiti, broken glass and trash everywhere.

I stopped at a red light and instinctively turned to lock my doors, then I saw two young girls and a boy standing next to a large dark green trash Dumpster at the side of the road.

I watched the older girl, who was about six and rail thin, climb onto the boy's shoulders. She leaned forward and grabbed a white paper bag. Ignoring the flies that circled the bin, she jumped off the boy's shoulders, opened the bag and tore a leg from the carcass of a partly eaten chicken. She solemnly handed the leg to the littler girl, then, without speaking, the older girl and the boy began devouring the rest.

The younger girl, who was only about two, stepped off the curb and toddled toward me wearing a dirty yellow dress and carrying the chicken leg. There was a cross around her neck and desperation in her large, almond-shaped brown eyes. She pressed her sticky fingers against my car door then opened her mouth and smiled. As I smiled back, I looked at her more closely and saw something black moving across her tongue. Then I looked down at her hand and saw that there were ants, dozens of ants, on the chicken leg.

The driver behind me beeped his horn. The boy looked up and saw me. He shouted something I couldn't understand, then frantically grabbed the little girl.

"Wait," I called, forgetting the neighborhood, forgetting the car behind me, forgetting everything. But all

in order to determine its effect. The second group, the **control group,** differs only in that it is not subjected to the same special treatment. The control group serves as a baseline of comparison to the experimental group. If the experiment is well designed, differences in thinking and behavior between the two groups should reflect the differences in their treatment. The cause of the differences, if any, is assumed to stem from researcher-designed conditions. Experimental research is typically used to test very specific hypotheses. Unusual experimental outcomes may lead to new ideas to explore, and thus to further hypothesizing and experimentation.

All researchers, regardless of the methods that they use, try to design their research in ways that avoid bias. **Bias** refers to unwanted influences that can produce three children had already flown out of sight and disappeared like fireflies into a dark, narrow alley, leaving only the iridescent magic of their life spark indelibly etched in my mind. They ran because they thought that they had done something wrong. They ran because they believed that they were the criminals instead of the victims. They ran because they did not know that there is a Haverford Road and children as desperately hungry as they are in every city, town and village in America.

Like many of us, they did not know that there is a hidden epidemic in this country. Sometimes it strikes children suddenly and without warning. At other times it starts before their birth and lasts an entire lifetime. Often, it is passed from one generation to the next, damaging not only the spirits of its young victims but their immune systems, physical strength and intelligence as well. Now and then there is a remission and occasionally there is a long-term cure, but it can also be fatal or permanently damaging, especially for the very young.

A young child's brain grows so rapidly that, by the age of two it has achieved 80 percent of its full development. If adequate nutrients are not available during this critical period, the brain's weight and size may be irreversibly compromised. The result may be a child who is mildly to moderately retarded for the rest of his or her life.

As the Harvard Physicians Task Force pointed out, in the end it all comes down to food. In its mildest form, and for short periods, all children have known hunger. But for most of them that uncomfortable craving is a symptom, not a disease. Hunger that continues because there is no food to eat becomes malnutrition, a torturous physiological experience that affects all of the body's most important functions and makes children desperate enough to eat anything they can find . . . .

The hidden epidemic in America is hunger. Now, in the new millennium, once again it is running rampant through urban, rural and suburban communities. It is affecting blacks, whites, Asians, Christians, Jews, and nonbelievers alike.

The physical suffering and the losses it causes to the bodies, spirits and brains of children are as debilitating and potentially fatal as the most serious diseases. But hunger is not caused by a virus or a bacteria. This silent American epidemic is caused by people, by acts of man, not acts of God or nature . . . .

The cure is easily within our reach. We have the money and we have the food. We need only the courage to see, the compassion to respond and the leadership to change our course.

If any other rapidly spreading epidemic was weakening the health, minds and spirits of 36.2 million Americans and keeping 12.1 million children under the age of twelve from growing up healthy or growing up at all, there would be headlines in every major newspaper about it every day. But hunger is America's silent and hidden disease. More than 36 million Americans are suffering from an epidemic that still remains largely unacknowledged at the highest political levels. Our leaders often speak of poverty, but "hunger" is a word that is almost never publicly mentioned. Even in President Bush's inaugural address in 2001, the word "hunger" was never spoken.

Perhaps that is because, as [presidential candidate] George McGovern pointed out back in 1972, "To admit the existence of hunger in America is to confess that we have failed in meeting the most sensitive and painful of human needs. To admit the existence of widespread hunger is to cast doubt on the efficacy of our whole system."

SOURCE: Loretta Schwartz-Nobel, *Growing Up Empty: The Hunger Epidemic in America* (New York: HarperCollins, 2002), pp. 1–5.

research results which are invalid or without foundation. In the case of the experimental method, avoidance of bias begins with the way in which subjects are assigned to the experimental and control groups. Typically, researchers will select a sample of subjects. A **sample** consists of a set of subjects that is representative of the total population of subjects. The sample is chosen at **random,** meaning that every individual in the total population has an equal chance of being selected. Then, those selected for the sample are assigned to the experimental and control groups at random. In this way possible sources of bias in assignment will be extremely small.

Avoiding bias also requires the researchers to take care that only members of the experimental group receive the special treatment whose effect is being investigated.

1. Observing, hearing about, or reading about a social phenomenon of interest.

2. Reviewing existing scholarly literature to learn more about the phenomenon.

3. Framing hypotheses or research questions that, if addressed, will generate valuable new knowledge and understandings.

4. Selecting an appropriate research method (or methods).

5. Gathering data that will address the hypotheses or research questions.

6. Analyzing the data gathered, reaching conclusions based on the findings.

7. Disseminating information about the research project, its findings and its conclusions through reports, articles, books, or public

FIGURE 2.1 **The Research Process in Brief** Sociologists typically follow a series of steps in conducting their research, proceeding very systematically as they choose an appropriate research method, engage in data-gathering and analysis, and disseminate their research results.

Moreover, researchers must be prepared to assess the effects of unexpected factors that may influence what occurs in the experimental or control group. Such cautions are necessary if other social scientists, repeating the same experiment, are to come up with the same findings.

Laboratories provide researchers with maximum control over an experiment because they impose artificial conditions on the two groups. But people do not live in laboratories, and the conditions to which they are normally subjected are not as neatly timed and delineated as those of laboratory experiments. Laboratory research may thus produce findings that may be reproducible by other laboratory researchers but that do not necessarily apply to people's thinking and behavior in the "real" world. Hence it is desirable to conduct experimental research in natural settings when possible.

Obviously, many natural settings are not easily replicated or cannot even be imitated in a laboratory. A public school is such a setting. Yet, oddly enough, schools actually resemble research laboratories in some ways. For example, school staff members provide students with an "experimental treatment" in the form of teaching, and they expect this treatment to have a certain outcome in the form of learning. In the example of experimental research we describe next, researchers manipulated the treatment of students by teaching staff.

Research Example: Teacher Expectations and Student Performance

Students from poor and working-class backgrounds, on average, have long been observed to get lower scores on intelligence quotient (IQ) tests and other standardized tests of achievement than do students from the more affluent middle and upper classes. Researchers Robert Rosenthal and Lenore Jacobson wondered whether the lower achievement could at least in part be due to low expectations on the part of teachers toward children of the less affluent. The researchers thus set out to test the following hypothesis: "Within a given classroom those children from whom the teacher expected greater intellectual growth would show such greater growth" (Rosenthal and Jacobson, 1968a: 61).

The researchers conducted their experiment in a West Coast elementary school whose students came for the most part from low-income families. Rosenthal and Jacobson began by giving the children in all six school grades a test. The teachers were deceived into thinking that the test results would predict which students would bloom intellectually over the school year. The researchers then gave the teachers a list consisting of 20 percent of the school's students who should be expected to do well. The researchers had compiled this list by randomly selecting students, such that the "difference between the special children and the ordinary children . . . was only in the mind of the teacher" (Rosenthal and Jacobson, 1968a: 175). The so-called special children comprised the experimental group, and the other 80 percent of the school's children comprised the control group. Members of the experimental group would, presumably, be subject to different treatment by their teachers under the expectation that they would intellectually spurt ahead.

At the end of the school year, each student was given the same test again, and the gains made by the experimental and control groups were compared. The experimental-group students not only experienced intellectual growth (at least as measured by the test) but were perceived by their teachers as displaying more positive learning and other behavioral characteristics than control-group students.

Some controversy surrounds this classic study because of mixed results in subsequent efforts by other researchers to replicate it. Still, Rosenthal and Jacobson's innovative experiment made a major contribution in suggesting that the nature of teachers' interactions can play an important role in the intellectual growth of children from less affluent backgrounds. School experiences that discourage intellectual growth can contribute to poorer children's social and economic marginalization as adults and help to perpetuate class inequalities.

Advantages and Disadvantages of Experimental Research

To summarize, then, experimental research methods are modeled after methods used in the physical sciences. When experimental and control groups are carefully chosen and all safeguards against bias and invalid results are put in place, experiments can provide important insights into people's thinking and behavior. Experiments have several advantages: They can demonstrate causal links between experimental treatments and predicted outcomes; they provide researchers with a high degree of control over independent and dependent variables in order to exclude sources of error; and they can be used to study changes in people's thinking and behavior over time.

Disadvantages include the sometimes artificial character of experimental settings; the possibility that people aware of their involvement in an experiment may adjust their behavior with this knowledge in mind; and practical limits to the size of samples for many experiments. The latter may limit the generalizability of findings.

Relatively few sociologists use laboratory-based experimental methods, and these are mostly scholars whose research lies within the specialized area of social psychology. Other sociologists look for ways to employ the principles of experimental research in nonlaboratory settings. For example, it has become commonplace for sociologists to participate in the evaluation of experimental government "pilot programs" to help policymakers determine if they should be implemented on a wider scale. This type of experimentation has taken place in such areas as education, health care delivery, job training, and welfare reform.

Field Research

When researchers leave their offices and go out among people to observe or speak with them firsthand, they are conducting **field research.** Direct observation can be useful either when little is known about a group or particular type of social setting or when enough is known to warrant hypotheses about the group. In the first case, the social scientist may enter the research site with few preconceptions and observe the entire situation just long enough to draw some conclusions about group members' thinking and behavior. When the social scientist already knows enough to have formulated a testable hypothesis before entering the field, direct observation will be much more limited in its focus; only observations pertaining to the hypothesis will be of interest to the researcher.

🌐 Making Field Observations

The purpose of the study, the types of data needed, and the situation at hand determine the method the researcher uses. **Passive observation** entails simply watching, listening, and recording events for later analysis and interpretation. In **participant observation,** the researcher plays an active role, even to the point of becoming an actual participant in the activities of those being observed. Participant observation may prove especially helpful if the social scientist is attempting to better understand matters from the position and viewpoint of others.

Whichever observation technique is used, researchers must decide how to handle the issue of revealing their identity and purpose (Goode, 1996). Should the observations be done covertly or overtly? Should subjects know they are being studied? Would the known presence or participation of the researcher in a group's activities influence behavior and events in ways contrary to the researcher's objectives? There is also the issue of privacy. What rights to privacy do those being studied have? Are there times when people deserve the opportunity to give their informed consent to be research subjects? Thinking back, you will no doubt see ways in which such questions could be readily discussed in regard to the experimental research of Rosenthal and Jacobson.

Field research tends to take place in one particular site, within a given time period, and with a specific sample of people. How do we know whether the findings

Children have their first contact with schooling at very young ages. Sociologists have investigated the key role that elementary school teachers' expectations can play in their students' lives through positive encouragement of each individual learner.

based on observations of one group at one site will be applicable or generalizable to other people and other settings? One may be more confident in the findings if other researchers come up with similar findings elsewhere. Unfortunately, sometimes a research situation is so unusual that the research may not be repeated easily. Because those reading field researchers' findings have not been observers, they must place a great deal of trust in the researchers' honesty, observational skills, and interpretive judgments. Finally, field research—while often rewarding—is also highly labor-intensive. Investigators may have to devote a great deal of time, often over long periods, to gathering observations. This was certainly the case in the well-known study we have chosen to illustrate the use of this research method.

🌎 Research Example: Manufacturing Classroom Failure

Aware of Rosenthal and Jacobson's experimental research, sociologist Ray C. Rist conducted a highly acclaimed study that further explored ways in which schools may actually nurture class inequalities (Rist, 1973). In contrast to Rosenthal and Jacobson's experimental method, Rist chose to pursue his investigation through direct observation of teacher–student interaction in the classroom. He conducted field research in an urban elementary school in the Midwest, observing a group of children from the time they entered kindergarten until they entered the second grade.

Rist began by looking at pre-enrollment information about each child, all of which was available to the kindergarten teacher. For example, the school social worker reported on which children about to enroll in kindergarten came from families receiving welfare. Rist noted that none of the pre-enrollment information directly related to the children's academic capabilities or potential. Yet, armed with this information and firsthand observation of the appearance and demeanor of each child, by the eighth day of kindergarten the teacher in the classroom where Rist was observing had established permanent seating assignments.

Seated at Table 1, closest to the teacher, were the better dressed children in the classroom. None came from families reliant on welfare. Table 1 children seemed most at ease in the school setting, interacted confidently with the teacher and their peers, and tended to speak standard American English. At Tables 2 and 3 were less well-attired children. They were more likely to be from families receiving public assistance, appeared restrained in their interactions, and were likely to speak in street dialect, if they spoke at all.

The teacher told Rist that the students she placed at Table 1 were her "fast learners," while those at the other two tables "had no idea of what was going on in the classroom" (Rist, 1970: 422). Thereafter, she focused most of her time, attention, teaching, and affection on Table 1 children and effectively wrote off the children at Tables 2 and 3 as unteachable. As he watched the process of differential treatment of the children unfold, Rist concluded that those the teacher had earmarked for school success were the children who were most similar—in their background, appearance, and behavior—to offspring of the educated middle class, the same class of which the teacher was a member.

Children who are not taught usually do not test well either. Hence, Rist was not surprised that formal tests of IQ and reading skill that were later used to sort the students into "ability groups" in the first and second grades produced groupings that closely replicated the kindergarten teacher's initial table placements. Tables 2 and 3 students lagged academically behind their more fortunate peers from the first grade on. Rist asked a rhetorical question: "Given the treatment of low-income children from the beginning of their kindergarten experience, for what class strata are they being prepared other than that of the lower class?" (Rist, 1970: 448–449). Using a different research method than did Rosenthal and Jacobson, Rist shed light on some actual classroom practices that provide differential and more negative treatment to low-income children.

Advantages and Disadvantages of Field Research

Field research has a number of advantages. These include the ability of researchers to observe behavior as it occurs, to be flexible in determining what to consider as data, and to obtain information about people in natural settings. Field research also sometimes allows sociologists to study groups engaged in "deviant behavior" who would be unlikely to cooperate with other research methods, such as questionnaire surveys.

Disadvantages lie in the difficulties the researcher may face in gaining entry to and cooperation from a group, the possibility that personal limitations or prejudices may affect the researcher's observations, practical difficulties in recording and analyzing what can be substantial amounts of data, time commitments involved in doing the research, and problems in establishing the reliability of observations when two or more researchers must alternate in field research of long duration.

Sociologists have used field research to gather data in a wide range of settings, including poverty-stricken neighborhoods, college dormitories, tattoo studios, race track stables, factory assembly lines, communities in suburbia, nude beaches, private schools, hospital emergency rooms, working-class bars, the headquarters of religious cults, and homes of the wealthy. Field research has vastly increased our knowledge of the social forces and conditions affecting human behavior and has challenged many stereotypes and false assumptions about different populations.

Survey Research

Perhaps you have been asked to fill out a written questionnaire or answer a series of questions over the telephone or in person. Or maybe you have participated in a course evaluation in college. If so, you have participated in a survey. A **survey** is a set of questions administered to a sample of people.

Survey Procedures

When social scientists use surveys to investigate a topic, they must follow strict procedures. The most important is choosing the sample. Surveying every single person in the population under study is usually impractical for researchers. Care, then, must be taken to use proper techniques to choose a sample that is representative of the population about whom the researcher is seeking to generalize. To avoid bias, the researcher selects randomly from this population. For example, researchers wishing to study views on people of color moving into a close-knit white suburban neighborhood may decide to seek interviews at every third home on each block.

The wording used for survey questions must be as neutral as possible. Frequently, researchers will pretest their questions and rephrase any that seem biased or confusing to subjects. Both sample selection and survey-question development are carried out in accordance with rules designed to minimize sources of bias and error that might cast doubt on the research results.

Surveys may be undertaken simply to gain descriptive information or to gather data relevant to previously formulated hypotheses. In the example we present here, the researcher was interested in gathering descriptive information on students' experiences with their course curricula.

Research Example: Gatekeeping in High Schools

In her classic study *Keeping Track: How Schools Structure Inequality* (1985), Jeannie Oakes explored the connection between high school education and class inequality. Most high schools in the United States have formal or informal school-wide policies of **tracking** (Lucas, 1999). In many instances, tracking involves dividing course offerings into academic (college-bound) and one or more vocational (employment-bound) curricular programs, or "tracks." The different tracks are supposed to prepare students for what teachers, counselors, and school administrators believe they should be doing after graduation. Some schools may subdivide various academic subjects into separate classes designed for different ability levels. Students are assigned, often after standardized achievement tests and teacher recommendations, to a given classroom ability level.

Sociological field research on people who must rely on soup kitchens has provided new insights into the extent and causes of food insecurity and hunger in the United States. Such research has helped policy makers base their decisions on facts rather than on stereotypes about those in need of food assistance.

Oakes examined the tracking experiences of students surveyed in 25 high schools located in 13 different communities. Each school was carefully selected to represent the population of students in U.S. secondary schools. Her findings pointed to distinct patterns of placement in tracks. Students from low-income backgrounds and students of color were found to be disproportionately present in the non-college-bound tracks. Once students were placed, they were exposed to very different course content. Those in college preparatory classes were presented with knowledge similar to that which they would later encounter in college and university courses. In the non-college-bound classes, students were exposed to extremely basic materials often requiring little more than rote learning.

Oakes's research results led her to criticize tracking policies. Students from economically disadvantaged backgrounds, particularly students of color, were likely to be channeled away from courses, knowledge, and high school credentials that could facilitate future upward mobility. Oakes concluded that high schools act as **gatekeepers:** they function to open up different doors of opportunity for different populations (Page, 1991). It is noteworthy that high school dropout rates are highest for students in non-college-bound tracks, suggesting that track placement by itself can lower students' educational aspirations and commitment to schooling.

◐ Advantages and Disadvantages of Surveys

Surveys are advantageous when one wishes to learn about the thinking and behavior of large populations. Since the ability to sample means that everyone in the population does not need to participate in the survey, costs can be kept down. People who are widely dispersed geographically can easily be reached by mail (standard or electronic) or phone if necessary. Respondents to phone or mail surveys often accept assurances of anonymity, which may make it easier to gain information about sensitive topics. Sampling and data analysis may often be done quickly and efficiently with the aid of computer technology.

Survey research also has disadvantages. A survey usually provides information about people's behavior and thinking only at a given point in time. Arranging and conducting surveys using face-to-face interviews can be time-consuming and require special interpersonal skills. The quality and dependability of survey results hinge on the representativeness of the sample chosen to be surveyed, the care with which questions are constructed, and the degree to which respondents are cooperative and truthful. But even with these disadvantages, surveys have become an important source of data for sociologists and other social scientists, as well as for decision makers in business and government. We may have escaped being part of someone's experiment or field research, but few of us have escaped being surveyed.

Historical Research

We have seen how research using experimental, field, and survey methods has in each case made a different kind of contribution to our understanding of the relationship between schooling and class inequality. Our next example of a research method shows that social scientists may also look at the historical record in order to understand the workings of society.

⊕ Uses and Sources of Historical Data

Much of the research in the social sciences deals with contemporary phenomena. But many researchers are concerned with establishing facts about the past. This approach is known as **historical research.** Sociologists using this method may want to gain more understanding of people's behavior in contemporary society by comparing it with that of an earlier era. Or they may want to determine origins of present-day practices. The motivation for historical research may be to understand patterns of continuity as well as change in society over time. Frequently, two or more of these motivations operate at the same time. Historical research may help test a strictly defined hypothesis, but it may also be used to answer questions that are open-ended. Usually, the questions pursued go beyond "Who?" "What?" "When?" and "Where?" Social scientists go one step further and want to know *why* history looks like it does.

Historical research involves using available data to recreate the past. Data may be found in **primary sources,** such as original records and diaries, official documents, and eyewitness accounts. In recent years a great deal of attention has been given to the use of oral history as a primary source: People are interviewed and asked to recount perceptions and make observations about earlier life experiences. This source of data may be particularly useful when written sources are inadequate or lacking. Data may also be found in **secondary sources,** such as historical data described in the publications of scholars.

⊕ Research Example: The Origins of School Tracking Practices

The desire to better understand the present-day relationship between schooling and class inequality informs the well-known study *Schooling in Capitalist America* by Samuel Bowles and Herbert Gintis (1976). These researchers wanted to determine why tracking systems were originally established in order to more fully understand their contemporary significance. Bowles and Gintis, using secondary sources for the most part, traced the origins of these policies back to the beginnings of mass public education in the United States well over 100 years ago.

The world of work back then, as is even more the case today, was a hierarchy of varying occupational levels. Each level required different degrees of skill and allowed for different amounts of autonomy, responsibility, and privilege. Bowles and Gintis found that public schooling was, from the very beginning, designed to guide individuals toward these different levels. To carry out this process, the economic and political elites who organized mass public education deemed it necessary to sort children into various curricular tracks. Tracking systems were rationalized as the most efficient way to make sure each child received a school experience appropriate to his or her potential. However, biases in track assignments destined many poor and working-class children for the lower rungs of the occupational ladder, while children of the more privileged middle and upper classes usually received quite a different education and hence had quite different occupational trajectories.

Bowles and Gintis asked if the objectives of those economic and political elites who maintained control over mass public education in the nineteenth century are still being played out today. In their view this is indeed the case: Schooling is organized to serve the labor needs of hierarchical workplaces. However, schooling does not seem to be performing this function satisfactorily in the eyes of many of today's employers. Indeed, much of the recent corporate interest in improving the quality and effectiveness of U.S. public schools stems from employers' desire to increase worker productivity at different levels of the occupational structure.

In short, historical research can help shed light on a variety of social phenomena. This research method has been used to better understand the evolution of relations between developed and underdeveloped nations, the factors producing revolutions and other movements for social change, the effects of technology on the workplace, the origins of the modern welfare state, the changing nature of the health care system and the medical profession, and approaches to the definition and handling of crime, mental illness, and other forms of "deviant behavior."

🌐 Advantages and Disadvantages of Historical Research

Perhaps the key disadvantage of historical research is the possibility of inaccuracy and bias in the sources. Primary sources such as eyewitness accounts may exaggerate or fabricate reality, contain errors of fact, or be intentionally self-serving. Documents are often not intended for research purposes, and their content may be built around a depiction of reality that departs from actual events. Secondary sources are written from a scholar's point of view. The selection of source material and the meaning the scholar derives from his or her selection must be assessed critically. Anyone conducting historical research thus must be satisfied with the closest approximation of reality possible, based on review of all available information. Social scientists are obligated to be meticulous in documenting the sources of their historical data, for others must be able to judge the credibility of their research.

The principal advantage of historical research is its helpfulness in understanding not only the past but also the present: Knowledge of history provides a unique context within which we can better assess present-day issues. Indeed, Jeannie Oakes's pathbreaking work on the significance and implications of tracking as a gatekeeping process was clearly assisted by the historical research on the origins of tracking published several years earlier by Bowles and Gintis.

While we face many public issues today that are new and unprecedented, most of the issues we grapple with are not. Contemporary phenomena such as school failure, unemployment, poverty, substance abuse, different forms of criminal behavior, discrimination, and family-related problems—to mention just a few—may be rendered less mystifying and more open to change when viewed within a historical

Sociologists have used historical research to analyze the organization and operation of such key societal institutions as education. They have found that, since its beginnings in the nineteenth century, mass public education in the United States has sought to teach respect for authority and the state. Requiring that students salute the flag is one way to transmit such values.

context. Moreover, we may find out that certain strategies being proposed for addressing these phenomena have never worked and thus be more open to thinking about new approaches.

Analyses of Existing Data

Secondary Data Analysis

Not all research requires that social scientists go out and gather their own data. Sociological researchers often rely on data that have already been gathered by others, data that often had originally been collected for totally different purposes. When such data are analyzed by sociologists engaging in their own research, they are performing **secondary data analysis.**

An enormous volume of data is readily available for secondary data analysis. Most of these data are in the form of statistics, often generated by government agencies. For example, federal census data on the characteristics of the U.S. population are available for the nation as a whole as well as by region, state, city or town, and on down to the neighborhood level. The federal government also generates statistics on such topics as education, health care, employment, and immigration. Both government agencies and many business groups collect data to track government spending, assess the effects of government programs, and determine the need for new legislation. Nonprofit organizations and advocacy groups frequently develop data concerning social problems and policy issues with which they are concerned. Much of this information, particularly that generated by government, is in the "public domain." This simply means that anyone interested can access and use it.

⬤ Advantages and Disadvantages of Using Existing Data

Being able to analyze data already gathered by others is invaluable in saving sociological researchers a great deal of time and money. In some instances, sociologists are even able to serve in roles that influence the kinds of data being gathered, particularly by government agencies. On the other hand, not all secondary data are in the public domain, especially data collected by corporations and business groups. Data that are generally available are not always as up-to-date as a researcher may wish, and researchers needing data extending over a period of years may find gaps or inconsistencies in what has been collected. Finally, data originally intended to be used for quite different purposes do not always provide the best fit with the kinds of research questions that sociologists are seeking to answer. Nonetheless, secondary data analysis is an important research method on which many sociological researchers rely.

Research Ethics and Politics

The different types of research methods illustrated above generate facts that can help us exercise the sociological imagination. Yet the conduct of sociological research and the reporting of findings do not take place in a vacuum. Under certain circumstances, unless care is taken, research may cause harm to people. Researchers have an obligation before they even begin an investigation to consider the ethical and political implications of what they are about to do (Babbie, 2000). Failure to do so not only may be harmful to others but is likely to increase the difficulty future researchers face in obtaining the cooperation and legitimacy they need to pursue their own inquiries. This is not to say that researchers must avoid controversy. Newly discovered facts are often controversial, if only because they may be differently interpreted depending on one's personal or group values. Rather, social scientists must be reflective and ready to take responsibility for the impact of their research undertakings.

The Ethics of Research

Perhaps the most well-known case of research generating widespread debate over ethics is Laud Humphreys's work published under the title *Tearoom Trade* (1975). Humphreys was interested in male-to-male sexual behavior. He decided to investigate the sexual behavior and social backgrounds of men who visited public restrooms of a midwestern city park for mutually consenting, but anonymous and highly impersonal, sexual encounters. Humphreys's research findings exploded the popular stereotype that such men lead very deviant lifestyles in general. Most of the men were married, had families, and were respected members of their communities. They came from all walks of life, occupations, and professions. Few were exclusively homosexual in their sexual orientation. Yet, when Humphreys reported his findings, the facts were forced to compete with a torrent of debate about the ethics of his research procedures. Let us briefly describe what he did that raised debate.

Humphreys gathered his data using the field research technique of participant observation. His research took place in a park located in a major midwestern city. To observe the sexual behaviors of the men in question, he offered to play the role of lookout at the park's public restrooms, warning of the arrival of possible intruders (including the police). Besides systematically keeping track of the patterns of sexual behavior he observed, Humphreys also managed to take down the automobile license numbers of the men. Using friendly contacts in the local police department, but telling them only that he was performing some kind of "market research," Humphreys located the home addresses of his subjects. Using a disguise to avoid being recognized as the restroom lookout, Humphreys interviewed the men as part of a survey he said he was conducting on the health of males in the community. In this way he was able to gather a wide variety of information on their lifestyles and backgrounds.

One of the ethical issues Humphreys's procedures raised was that of individuals' rights to privacy. Some researchers argued that the subjects' privacy rights were invaded by Humphreys, both in his participant observation and through the interviews. Others argued that Humphreys had rights as a scientist to pursue and to disseminate new knowledge. Another issue was that of deceit; he had pretended to be a lookout at the restrooms, a market researcher at the police station, and a survey interviewer at the subjects' residences. Some researchers argued that deceit was often the only way to gain access to groups who are likely to reject being studied. Others argued that this type of activity spawned distrust among citizens and violated fundamental values about what kinds of behavior were just and fair.

But Humphreys's critics went beyond the issues of privacy invasion and deceit. They pointed out that he risked doing harm to the subjects by seeking out their identities and places of residence. If, despite safeguards that Humphreys had established, their identities had somehow leaked out, the lives of these men could have been ruined. As it was, once the research findings and sociologists' debate over his methods entered the public arena and were picked up by the mass media, some of the men—clearly panicked—privately sought reassurance from Humphreys that their anonymity was not in jeopardy. Perhaps others, who chose not to contact him, lived in a state of fear. Psychologically, one could argue, harm was done.

The debate among sociologists over the ethics of Humphreys's research methods was useful because it helped make members of the discipline more aware of their responsibilities to their research subjects. The American Sociological Association, a scholarly organization to which most professional sociologists belong, has a Code of Ethics. This code requires that people being studied give the researcher their informed consent. Such consent may be waived under certain conditions, according to the code:

> Despite the paramount importance of consent, sociologists may seek waivers of this standard when (1) the research involves no more than minimal risk for research participants, and (2) the research could not practicably be carried out were informed consent to be required. (American Sociological Association, 1997: Section 12.01)

The Code of Ethics addresses the principle of keeping information provided by research subjects confidential. For example, the code states:

Sociologists have an obligation to ensure that confidential information is protected. They do so to ensure the integrity of research and the open communication with research participants and to protect sensitive information obtained in research. . . . Confidential information provided by research participants . . . is treated as such by sociologists even if there is no legal protection or privilege to do. Sociologists have an obligation to...not allow information gained in confidence from being used in ways that would unfairly compromise research participants. (American Sociological Association,1997: Sections 11, 11.01)

Adherence to the code's principles of confidentiality may, in unusual circumstances, place a sociologist in conflict with legal authorities. Rik Scarce, who has done research on animal rights and environmental activists, was jailed for almost six months in 1993. Scarce had refused to answer a federal grand jury's questions about research interviews he conducted with members of a group called the Animal Liberation Front (ALF). In 1991 ALF members allegedly broke into a research laboratory at Washington State University, released mink, coyotes, and mice that were being used for experiments, and did $150,000 worth of damage. Police were unable to locate the suspects. Scarce, jailed under a charge of civil contempt, took the position that he would not breach any guarantees of confidentiality he might have made to the subjects of his research. As he put it:

I am concerned that activists in the environmental movement may refuse to speak to me if I testify . . . Other social scientists might find themselves less able to gain the trust of sources . . . [Social scientists] also would be less willing to go out and do research which in some instances does require of us that we grant promises of confidentiality. (Monaghan, 1993)

Researchers put themselves at great risk if they break the law themselves in order to be able to gain access to and maintain rapport with a group they are studying. Sociologist Patricia Adler, who studied upper-level drug smugglers and dealers, acknowledges witnessing criminal behavior, including drug transactions that occurred in her own home. In addition, she admits to possessing and consuming marijuana and cocaine along with her research subjects. Adler states that it would have been impossible for a non–drug user to gain admittance and acceptance into the drug underworld that she studied. In the course of her research, Adler risked the serious dangers of arrest in a drug "bust" and police seizure of her research materials as "evidence" of her own and others' criminal behavior (Adler, 1985).

The Politics of Research

In addition to the ethical issues in the conduct of their research, the fact that all research is conducted within a larger political context can raise further issues for researchers (Neuman, 2003). Whereas ethical concerns usually involve sociological research methods and the handling of data, political issues can arise from the purposes or substance of the research and the uses to which findings may be put. A well-known case in point involved "Project Camelot," a research project that became the object of international condemnation.

In the early 1960s the U.S. Department of the Army asked researchers at American University to engage in a research project that would enable it to "predict and influence politically significant aspects of social change in the developing world" (Horowitz, 1967: 47). At that time, Latin American nations—in which a number of U.S. corporations had important investments—were the army's principal focus. In many such nations, impoverished people were rebelling against strong, often brutal dictatorships. The army wanted research conducted that would help it predict where rebellions were most likely to occur so it could help these Latin American governments head them off. It was, in short, a research project aimed at helping the powerful remain powerful. Those social scientists who agreed to participate in Project Camelot accepted, whether consciously or not, that political bias.

Project Camelot was to cost millions of dollars over a three-year period and was to draw on social science expertise across the United States and in Latin America as well. Yet, less than a year after Project Camelot began, the army dropped the whole idea. The U.S. government was highly embarrassed when news of the research leaked to the mass media. Governments and scholars around the world strongly condemned the United States for this planned intrusion into other nations' internal affairs and the political uses it was making of social scientists.

The widespread controversy surrounding Project Camelot alerted sociologists to the importance of understanding the interests of their sponsors, the implications of the research questions they were being asked to pursue, and the sponsors' intended uses of the research findings. The controversy made many sociologists sensitive to the potentially harmful political uses to which their skills and knowledge can be put. In our view sociologists have an obligation—much like that of medical researchers—to pursue knowledge that will aid in reducing human suffering and enhancing human potential. By that criterion, research like Project Camelot should simply not take place.

CHAPTER SUMMARY

1. Sociologists study society in order to generate knowledge helpful in exercising the sociological imagination.

2. In studying society, sociologists seek to base their conclusions on facts that have been scientifically established through objective investigation and systematic data gathering.

3. The research methods used by sociologists are usually intended to gather data relevant to a hypothesis, a statement that may be verified or discarded on the basis of the data collected. Sociologists also may ask open-ended research questions when not enough is known about a social phenomenon to state a hypothesis.

4. In pursuing their research questions, sociologists may engage in experimental research, field research, surveys, or historical research in order to establish facts about the social world. Sociologists also often engage in secondary data analysis.

5. Experimental research involves studying the effects of treating members of an experimental group and a control group differently under carefully controlled conditions.

6. Field research entails direct personal contact with those whose attitudes or behaviors are being studied, using such techniques as passive or participant observation.

7. Surveys involve the gathering of data from individuals through questionnaires or interviews, making possible the study of large populations.

8. Historical research involves the study of both continuity and changes in various aspects of society over time, utilizing primary or secondary data sources.

9. Secondary data analysis entails analyzing already-existing data gathered by others, often for quite different purposes.

10. In carrying out their research, sociologists have a special obligation to conduct themselves in ways that avoid bringing harm to people. This means being fully aware of the ethical and political implications of their research, including the unintended uses to which their research findings could be put.

THINKING CRITICALLY

1. Assuming that you had the education, training, skills, and resources, which aspect of society would you most like to study and why? What, specifically, would you want to find out? How would you go about doing so? What research methods do you think you would use? What kinds of problems do you think you would run into in doing your research?

2. To gain access to groups that are likely to resist being the objects of sociological research, sociologists sometimes conceal their professional identities and intentions. What issues does this raise in your mind, and where do you stand on them? Are there situations where people's rights to privacy must come before the sociologist's right to freedom of scientific inquiry? What would be an example?

3. In this chapter we discussed research which suggests that U.S. public education operates in ways that deny equal educational opportunities to children from less affluent backgrounds. We also mentioned research which suggests that men who have sex with other men come from all walks of life and that many are married men with families. Sociological research findings like these may make some people uncomfortable. In your view, is this good or bad?

4. Discuss the differences between fact and opinion. What opinions concerning poor people and recipients of welfare are contrary to actual facts? Where do you think these opinions come from? Do they easily change when those who hold them are presented with factual information? Why or why not? What are the risks of basing policies regarding the poor on opinions and not facts?

KEY TERMS

bias, *(26)*
control group, *(26)*
dependent variable, *(24)*
experimental group, *(25)*
experimental research, *(25)*
field research, *(30)*
gatekeepers, *(34)*
historical research, *(35)*

hypothesis, *(24)*
independent variable, *(24)*
open-ended research question, *(24)*
participant observation, *(30)*
passive observation, *(30)*
primary sources, *(35)*
random, *(28)*

research methods, *(24)*
sample, *(27)*
secondary data analysis, *(37)*
secondary sources, *(35)*
survey, *(33)*
tracking, *(33)*
variables, *(24)*

Macro Social Structures

Most people interact regularly with a relatively small handful of other individuals. Yet each person's daily existence is likely to be affected by many other unseen, unknown people throughout the world. Ask yourself the following questions:

- How are the world and the societies in which people live organized to link individuals in meaningful ways?
- How might your life be affected by people halfway around the world and from all walks of life, and how might you affect them?
- Is the way societies are organized unchangeable, or do people have an ability to resist and affect the patterns of social organization?

To begin to explore these questions, look at the labels inside the clothes you are wearing. Where were the garments made? If you drive a car or own a stereo, where was it manufactured? And have you or has someone you know been sent as a member of the U.S. military to another country to participate in an armed conflict (perhaps in Iraq in 2003, Afghanistan in 2001, or Kuwait in 1991), to deliver medical and food supplies to an embattled nation (maybe in Somalia in the 1990s), or to join a peacekeeping mission (say, in Bosnia or Kosovo in the 1990s), or simply to be part of an ongoing presence (in Europe or Asia)?

Your answers to these questions should illustrate to you that no one is isolated from the rest of the world. On the contrary, everyone is part of a world-system, linked to other countries through the economic and political relationships forged between countries. Moreover, each individual is linked to society through participation in its central institutions, including the family, education, religion, economy, and the state. The shaping of individuals' lives can be understood in terms of how each person is positioned within these three levels of social structure: the world-system, society, and its institutions. These are the three levels of what sociologists refer to as macro-level social structures, and they are the focus of this chapter. People can affect these macro structures through collective actions, thereby introducing flexibility and change into such structures. This notion is explored in more depth at the end of the chapter and throughout the book.

Social Structure

Social systems are the ongoing ways that groups of people organize themselves and relate to one another in order to survive. Individuals are born into and die out of social systems, or they immigrate into or migrate out of social systems. But the social structures remain in place even as individuals enter and leave. What are these social structures, and how do they affect individuals as members of these social systems? Sociologists refer to **social structure** as the means of organizing recurring patterns of relationships within a social system. **Macro-level social structures** are large-scale mechanisms that organize and distribute individuals in an entire society, as opposed to small-scale, or interpersonal, structures (on the midlevel or micro level; see Chapter 4). Social structures can be arranged along a continuum, from the most macro to the most micro (see Figure 3.1). The more macro structures contain the elements of the more micro structures below them.

Note that the focus here is not on individuals and their personalities; rather, what is important is how the positions that individuals occupy in society are organized and related. Social structure is analogous to an apartment building in which tenants may come and go but the building itself remains intact. Some members of the social system die or leave, new ones are born or migrate into it, but the social structures remain to organize the positions that these individuals fill. For example, national and international labor markets are large-scale structures that organize tasks of production and distribution of goods and services in our society and around the world. They also operate as a sorting mechanism, distributing individuals into jobs to carry out these tasks. Individual workers and managers may retire, quit, or die, and others may be hired to replace them. But the way the jobs are organized to produce and distribute goods and services remains unaltered by the changes in individuals performing the work: Managers decide what to produce, how much to produce, how to produce it, and how much to pay workers to get the job done. Workers, in turn, follow the orders dictated from management and are paid a negotiated wage in exchange for their labor. That structure of work does not change even though personnel may come and go. So it is with social structures: Individuals come and go, but the way society is organized largely remains stable.

The patterns produced by the organization and distribution of individuals in society are beyond any single individual's day-to-day control, but they remain powerful and significant forces in contouring people's existence. They shape people's experiences, possible alternatives for action, their worldview, and their feelings about themselves. What,

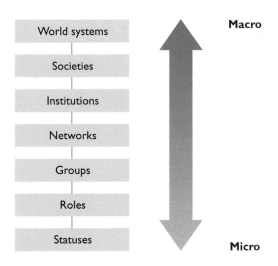

FIGURE 3.1 **Social Structures** Social structures fall on a continuum from those on the most micro-level to those on the most macro-level. The more macro-structures contain the elements of the more micro-structures below them on the continuum; thus, world-systems are the most complete form of social structure because they contain all of the social structures nested below them.

then, are these macro-level social structures, and how do they contour individuals' lives?

Let us begin by considering how individuals may be affected by events and relationships in other countries.

- How is it possible for issues and problems to affect individuals across oceans and continents?
- How do people influence what happens in their nation and around the world?
- In what ways are all people members of an organized world-system?
- How is this relevant to individual experience?

The World-System

All nations are connected to each other in a **world-system.** This is the most complete macro-level structure, encompassing all other levels of social structure. A world-system is an international social system of "cultural, normative, economic, political, and military relations"; these are organized around the exchange of goods and services (Chase-Dunn, 1998: 348). In a world-system, nations may trade goods and services, share common goals in international treaties, allow foreign productive facilities and military bases to locate within their borders, share a common history or heritage, or exchange labor. Such relationships are not necessarily between equal partners, and they need not produce equal or mutually beneficial outcomes. Indeed, they often do not (Peet, 1999).

Let's consider the role different countries play in producing the world's goods and services. There is a **global division of labor** in which the work required to produce these goods and services is broken into separate tasks, each performed largely by different groups of countries or groups within countries. Some countries may be classified as **core nations,** in which production is based on technology that relies more on machinery than on human labor and in which human labor is relatively skilled and highly paid. Such countries tend to be wealthy, yet most of the people who live in them are not. Examples of core nations include the United States, Great Britain, Japan, Canada, and Germany.

In **peripheral nations,** production is based on technology that relies more on cheap human labor than on expensive machinery. Such countries are typically quite poor; however, not everyone who lives in the periphery is poor. Elites in peripheral nations tend to be wealthy compared with the poverty of the masses. Examples of peripheral nations include Bangladesh, Vietnam, Sri Lanka, Nicaragua, Zaire, and Lesotho.

Finally, still other countries may be classified as **semiperipheral nations.** These are countries in which production is based on a mixture of intermediate levels of machinery and human labor and in which human labor is semiskilled and paid intermediate levels of wages. Such countries are neither as poor as peripheral countries nor as wealthy as core countries. And as with core and peripheral nations, wealth and poverty coexist within their populations. Examples of semiperipheral nations include India, Mexico, Egypt, Kuwait, and South Africa (Chase-Dunn, 1997; Wallerstein, 1974) (see Figure 3.2 for a map of the global distribution of these classifications).

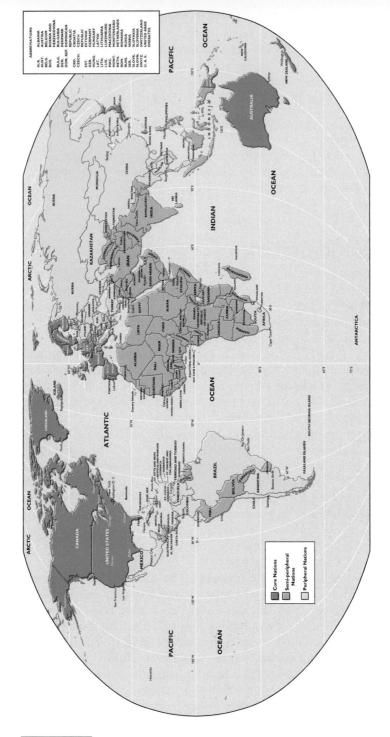

FIGURE 3.2 **The World-System of Global Inequality** The various roles nations play in the global division of labor to produce and distribute the world's goods and services create economic inequality between nations. Notice that the core nations are concentrated in North America and Western Europe (with the exceptions of Japan and Australia), with peripheral nations concentrated in Central America, Southeast Asia, and Africa, and semiperipheral nations concentrated in Eastern Europe, Asia, and South America.

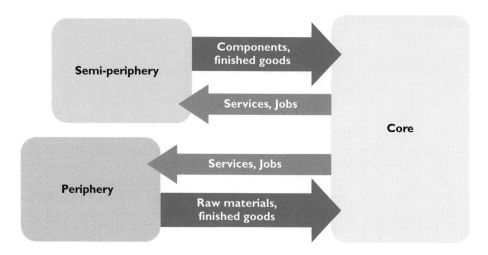

FIGURE 3.3 Global Division of Labor   In the global division of labor, core nations export jobs and services (particularly financial and management services) to the periphery and semiperiphery. Meanwhile, the periphery sends raw materials and finished goods to the core, and the semiperiphery sends finished goods and components to be assembled into finished goods to the core. These are not equal exchanges, however. The advantage remains with the core nations.

Each type of country plays a different role in producing and consuming the world's goods and services. In the global division of labor, peripheral and semi-peripheral countries provide the raw materials needed for production and manufacture more and more consumer goods, which the core nations consume. Meanwhile, the economies of core nations increasingly revolve around service-sector operations, such as finance, management, sales, and information processing (see Figure 3.3). We return to an analysis of the dynamics of producing this division of labor in Chapter 10, but our question for now is: How do these global patterns and relationships affect individuals' lives?

Global Patterns and Their Consequences for Individuals' Life Chances

Where people live in the world system affects their individual **life chances**, or their quality of life and their very likelihood of survival. The physical space on Earth is shared by 6.2 billion people, a population that is currently growing at a rate of 1.5 percent each year. But that space is not shared equally; nearly four-fifths of Earth's population live in peripheral nations, where extreme poverty and hunger run rampant. Population growth rates are higher in these nations than in the core nations. In peripheral nations the **death rates** (the number of deaths in a given year per 1,000 people in the population) are lower than **birth rates** (the number of births in a given year per 1,000 people in the population) (www.census.gov International Database Table 008). These rates are greatly affected by age distributions in the world population, with 87 percent of those under age 25 (prime childbearing years) living in peripheral countries. Contrast this to more affluent core countries where the number of people aged 65 and older is growing faster than those under 25 (www.census.gov International Database Table 094).

Some observers argue that poverty and hunger in peripheral nations are caused by the strong population growth rates in such nations. This analysis implies that poverty and hunger are personal problems that can be solved by individuals choosing to have fewer children. However, a conflict perspective (see Chapter 1) would ◄ pp. 14–15 emphasize the extremely widespread poverty and hunger in peripheral nations. This observation suggests that hunger and poverty are public issues rather than personal problems and that their cause may lie in how the structure of the world system affects the distribution of power and resources between and within nations (Lappe and Collins, 1986). For example, the wealthiest fifth of the world's population consumes 86 percent of all global resources, compared to the poorest fifth, who consume 1.3 percent (U.N. Human Development Programme, 1998). How does the structure of the world system contribute to this pattern of global inequality?

The position of peripheral countries in the world-system's division of labor affects population dynamics and the life chances of everyone living in these nations, from birth on. Both the land and the resources are controlled by a small privileged class, an elite group interested primarily in generating private profits by trading with large corporations in the core. Much of the land is thus used to produce cash crops (those grown for profitable sale rather than immediate consumption or barter by the grower) and luxury commodities (such as sugar, coffee, and cocoa), rather than the food needed for survival by most of the people in the peripheral country itself. As a result, chronic malnutrition or undernutrition and poor health severely limit the life chances of the vast majority of people living in these countries.

Additionally, the cultivation of a limited number of cash crops for many years requires the use of chemical fertilizers to replenish lost minerals and pesticides to protect the crops. After years of exposure to these chemicals, many workers suffer from debilitating and life-threatening diseases. Moreover, when countries emphasize cash crops grown for profit, they must increasingly rely on technology to make production more efficient and raise profits. This displaces human labor and provokes widespread unemployment. Unemployment, malnutrition, and lack of control of fertile land combine to undermine the life chances of working people in the periphery. In particular, women and children suffer most.

Statistics show a stark gap between life chances in wealthy core nations and those in poor peripheral ones. As Table 3.1 indicates, adults can expect to live decades longer and infants have a far greater chance of survival in the core nations. In many core countries the number of children who die in the first year of life per 1,000 live births per year (i.e., the **infant mortality rate**) is 7 or fewer. In contrast, in some peripheral countries in Africa and Asia, anywhere from 70 to more than 100 infants per 1,000 live births die before their first birthday. Moreover, it is relatively rare for children in the core to die before age 5 (1 per 1,000 people in the total population). Those who do die are usually victims of accidents. In contrast, *half of all deaths in peripheral countries are children under 5 years old,* and the typical cause of their deaths is not accidents but disease (World Bank, 2000; *Economist Book of Vital World Statistics,* 1990). In peripheral nations malnutrition severely increases

TABLE 3.1 Global Contrasts: Wealth and Survival, 1999

Nation	GNP per Capita (U.S. $)	Infant Mortality	Life Expectancy (per 1000 live births)	
			Males	Females
Japan	$32,230	4	78	84
United States	30,600	7	74	80
Germany	25,350	5	74	81
Sweden	25,040	4	77	82
France	23,480	5	75	83
Pakistan	470	91	60	62
Haiti	460	71	47	51
Bangladesh	370	73	60	60
Yemen	350	82	58	62
Nigeria	310	76	52	52
Ethiopia	100	107	44	46

Source: World Development Indicators database, World Bank, 2000 (www.worldbank.org/data) and Central Intelligence Agency, *The World Fact Book, 2000* (www.odci.gov/cia/publications/factbook).

children's susceptibility to diseases. For example, when water supplies are contaminated, intestinal irritations like diarrhea become deadly, so that diarrhea is one of the major causes of death among these children. The poor distribution of food and unequal control over arable land often impose a death sentence on children in peripheral countries.

In many peripheral and semiperipheral countries multinational corporations based in core nations conduct manufacturing for export. But the people they employ do not derive many benefits. For example, in electronics factories in the Philippines, young women who work 8 to 12 hours per day peering into microscopes strain their eye muscles and endanger their eyesight. Workers in garment industries (who are primarily women) commonly work in sweatshops where severe overcrowding and inordinately long days with few if any breaks threaten their well-being (Soyer, 1999). And slave labor remains a common and rapidly increasing feature of production in the global economy, as the "Social Forces/People's Lives" reading describes (Bales, 1999). Wages are extremely low, even by local standards of living, endangering workers' general health because their low wages are hardly enough to subsist on, much less support families. While the average hourly wage for factory workers in the United States in 1998 was $18.56, it was $5.03 in Korea, $5.24 in Taiwan, and $1.83 in Mexico (U.S. CIA: World Factbook, 1999). In Vietnam, the athletic footwear manufacturers Nike and Adidas pay average monthly wages of $30 per worker (Egan, 1998). In some of these nations' factories, exposure to toxic chemicals and fumes causes lung and respiratory diseases, miscarriages, cancer, and other life-threatening diseases (Ortiz, 1999). Some corporations respond to workers' complaints of less-than-living wages and unsafe work conditions by automating, replacing people with technology. This only increases unemployment, poverty, and hunger among workers in the periphery and semiperiphery.

Since these workers do not own or control the corporations they work for, and since they are typically not unionized, changing production arrangements to improve their life chances becomes extremely difficult. Recent developments, however, suggest that such resistance is not impossible. For example, fair trade coffee networks have developed, linking small producers in Latin America with consumers in the Northern Hemisphere "around the values of solidarity and fairness" and rejecting the corporate values of capital accumulation at the expense of human rights (Renard, 1999). Environmental nongovernmental organizations (NGOs) like Greenpeace, the Sierra Club, and Friends of the Earth have also had some success in pressuring individual transnational corporations in peripheral countries to assume greater corporate responsibility toward the environment in their production processes (Fabig and Boele, 1999).

In a global system, core countries aren't immune from hardship either. When peripheral countries' economies are in crisis, these nations may sharply increase their exports to core countries like the United States and flood core markets with cheaper goods. These cheaper goods then compete with more expensive products, undermining sales of domestic goods. Declines in sales of domestic products may produce widespread layoffs and unemployment in affected U.S. industries, such as textiles, garments, computers, and electronics. In addition, poverty in peripheral countries produces a cheap labor pool that can be exploited by multinational corporations based in the core. When U.S. corporations move their plants to the periphery to take advantage of the cheap labor, workers in the United States lose jobs. Mass migration of unemployed and impoverished workers into the United States also affects U.S. workers' wages and job opportunities. Corporations can pay migrants substantially lower wages, thereby creating competitive pressures between workers. That competition enables employers to pay U.S. workers lower wages as well. All of this works to the benefit of corporations. The social structure of global relationships thus affects people in both peripheral and core countries.

The Role of Raw Materials in the World-System

Dependency on imported raw materials affects the U.S. economy, its military relations, and its population. For example, heavy dependence on foreign sources of oil leaves the United States vulnerable to political and economic upheavals over which it has little control. In 1973, when the Organization of Petroleum Exporting Countries (OPEC) restricted its production and export of oil, the United States suffered a serious recession. Industries that relied on oil and petroleum products for production had to pay four times as much for these raw materials. Production became much more costly, raising the price of consumer goods. The resulting decline in consumption, together with the increased costs of production, caused thousands of U.S. workers to lose their jobs and left everyone suffering from dramatic inflation in prices. High inflation rates reduced the amount of goods and services that wages were able to purchase, thereby lowering their standard of living. In the year 2000, when oil producers restricted production in an effort to enhance prices, the cost of home heating fuel and gasoline soared in the core nations, leaving many poor families, as well as elders on low-level fixed incomes, to choose between food and fuel. Many in the middle class felt the economic pinch as well.

Reliance on imported oil also affects international political relations. When Iraq's invasion of Kuwait in 1991 threatened U.S. access to Mideast oil, President George H.W. Bush mobilized the most massive military force since the Vietnam war. As a result, thousands of people found their employment and education disrupted and their lives at risk when their reserve units were sent to the Persian Gulf area. In many families, income dropped sharply while wage earners were away at war. And, of course, some Americans lost their lives, many others suffered injuries, and still others endured the emotional turmoil of being captured as a prisoner of war. It is unlikely that U.S. decision-making leaders would have cared so deeply about Iraq's invasion of Kuwait had oil not been involved. Note, for example, that the United States did not mobilize military forces when the Soviet Union invaded Afghanistan in the 1980s, when the Taliban in Afghanistan began its campaign against the rights of women in that country in the 1990s, or when the Bosnian Serbs slaughtered Muslims in their "ethnic cleansing" campaign in that same decade. Note, too, that while gross human rights violations in the Balkans did not persuade the United States to exercise its military strength, the geographic significance of Yugoslavia did. Its position on the global map allows access to oil-rich areas in the Black Sea and Caspian Sea, thus making it important to the United States in its quest for global resources (Chossudovsky, 1997). It is not difficult, then, to understand the willingness of the United States and its core allies to send troops to the former Yugoslavia in 1999 (Chomsky, 1999; Gervasi, 1996).

Moreover, while the effect of such military ventures on the indigenous populations in the periphery is clear, people in the core nations are not immune. The 1991 U.S. attack on Iraq caused outbreaks of political conflict in the United States. Many people questioned whether U.S. troops should be sent to war to protect access to Mideast oil. But those who protested against the war often found themselves labeled unpatriotic by powerful political elites and by members of the public who supported the war. Similar charges were lodged against people who protested the buildup toward war against Iraq in 2003, which was politically framed more as a war against terrorism than a war to secure oil resources for the United States. Thus economic and trade relations between countries can seriously affect the social and political relations within them. This is in part why so many people felt compelled to protest the World Trade Organization (WTO) in Seattle in 1999 and 2000. The WTO is an international bureaucracy, dominated by countries in the core, whose mission is to reduce economic conflicts or differences in order to smooth the way to the international production and trade of goods and services. Essentially, the WTO is supposed to mediate the global economy of primarily

Trade arrangements between nations are not always mutually beneficial, and often create serious social and political consequences within the individual countries. That is why large groups of protestors such as this one demonstrate against the World Trade Organization when it meets to promote international trade agreements.

The Rise of the New Slavery

KEVIN BALES

The global division of labor has stimulated a rise in slavery throughout the world, a practice many believe was a thing of the past. While slavery in fact continues to thrive in the twenty-first century, it has taken on a new character that distinguishes it from the old slavery of the nineteenth century. In the old slavery, the slave belonged to the owner as a possession. Owners had to take care of their slaves in order to protect their investment. In the new slavery, slaves are not owned as possessions; rather, because of their extreme poverty and lack of power, they are controlled by exploiters as captive labor. Exploiters may subject slaves to extensive abuse until they die, or they may dispose of them when they are no longer useful. In this reading, Bilal, a slave in the African country of Mauritania, describes the inhumanity of his daily existence and his inability to escape from his situation.

FOR thousands of years people have been enslaved ... Slavery [has] never disappeared; instead, it [has taken] a different form. The basic fact of one person totally controlling another remains the same, but slavery has changed in some crucial ways.

Two factors are critical in the shift from the old slavery to the explosive spread of the new. The first is the dramatic increase in world population following World War II .... The greatest growth has been in those countries where slavery is most prevalent today. Across Southeast Asia, the Indian subcontinent, Africa, and the Arab countries, populations have more than tripled and countries are flooded with children. Over half the population in some of these countries is under the age of fifteen. In countries that were already poor, the sheer weight of numbers overwhelms the resources at hand. Without work and with increasing fear as re-

sources diminish, people become desperate and life becomes cheap. Especially in those areas where slavery had persisted or was part of the historical culture, the population explosion radically increased the supply of potential slaves and drove down their price.

The second crucial factor is that at the same time that the population was exploding, these countries were undergoing rapid social and economic change. In many developing countries modernization brought immense wealth to the elite and continued or increased the impoverishment of the poor majority.... Traditional ways of life and subsistence have been sacrificed to the cash crop and quick profit.... The forced shift from subsistence to cash-crop agriculture, the loss of common land, and government policies that suppress farm income in favor of cheap food for the cities have all helped bankrupt millions of peasants and drive them from their

private corporate producers by moving countries toward common policies about labor laws, environmental regulations, economic restrictions such as trade tariffs, immigration laws and restrictions, and so on.

Some people consider the WTO to be the international agent reinforcing and maintaining the peripheral status of poorer nations (Brecher, Costello, and Smith, 2000). They point to the effects of the North American Free Trade Agreement land—sometimes into slavery. . . . Because the political elites in the developing world focus on economic growth, which is not just in their collective self-interest but required by global financial institutions, little attention is paid to sustainable livelihoods for the majority. So while the rich of the developing world have grown richer, the poor have fewer and fewer options. Amid the disruption of rapid social change, one of those options is slavery. . . . Bilal . . . was one of many slaves who work in the [Mauritanian] capital distributing water. . . . Bilal rises before dawn. He has slept somewhere around his master's house in the sprawl of Nouakchott, perhaps on the back porch or under a cardboard shelter in the walled yard. His breakfast is some rice or leftovers served by the slave women who got up earlier to begin cooking for the household. By dawn he is on the street driving his donkey and cart to a public well where he laboriously fills his two sixty-liter barrels by hand. The well is just a hole in the ground with some bricks arranged around its edge. There is no tap or standpipe or pump, no pulley or crank—just a large metal can attached to a rope. Working quickly, pulling up bucket after bucket, Bilal pours the water through a makeshift funnel into his barrels. Once they are filled, another slave steps in to begin filling his barrels, and Bilal starts his round.

The slaves hauling water fan out across the city, stopping at most houses. With a bit of rubber hose they siphon water into bottles, buckets, barrels, and water tanks. Sometimes they are called to building sites to provide the water for making concrete or mortar, sometimes to garden plots. Bilal will haul at least one load of water back to his master's house, and perhaps another load or two will go to his master's relatives. The local currency is the ouguiya (200 ouguiya = $1), and Bilal collects about one ouguiya per liter from those who pay for his water. When his barrels are exhausted, he returns to one of the public wells to refill them, sometimes having a moment of rest and conversation as he waits in line with other slaves hauling water. His day is a constant round of filling his barrels and hauling the water from house to

house. Bilal's master expects him to sell at least 800 liters a day in addition to the water he hauls for his master's family, making it necessary for Bilal to go to the well between seven and ten times. The rest of the time he is in constant motion, working through the hottest part of the day without rest, keeping up the pace until sundown. At sundown he must return to his master's house, to hand over the money he has collected and to do other work (usually cleaning or hauling) until he can sleep around midnight. The next day is the same; every day is the same, seven days a week. If he returns to his master without the expected amount of money, he is berated or beaten and his food is cut back. If he has a break from the work it will come in the rainy season, a short and chancy thing in Mauritania, when his master will send him back to the country to help with the planting.

Bilal is about twenty years old, and he was brought to the city by his master three years ago. . . .

"What I really want," he said, "is a salary—a fixed amount of money for the work I do." He knows now that other people sometimes work for salaries, that they have jobs and at night go to their own homes. "But when I asked my master about a salary, he told me it was better this way, that he gives me food, maybe a little pocket money, and that I should stay in his household—what can I do?" There is a very little Bilal can do; he is trapped. He has no money and no other way of making money. He knows how to sell water, but the donkey, cart, and barrels belong to his master. Away from his master he has nowhere to live and no way to pay for a rented room. "If I complain, my master will send me back to the countryside where he has even more control over me," he told me. In addition, Bilal and the others know what can happen to escaped slaves. They have heard the stories of slaves hunted down and killed by their masters, and they know that the courts rarely take any action against the killers.

SOURCE: Kevin Bales, *Disposable People: New Slavery in the Global Economy* (Berkeley: University of California Press, 1999), pp. 12, 13, 101–103.

(NAFTA) of 1994, in which trade and investment barriers between Canada, the United States, and Mexico were relaxed to encourage trade. Supporters of NAFTA argued that the policy would equalize wages in the three countries, increasing Mexican wages to U.S. levels and thus discouraging illegal immigration and encouraging consumerism to benefit the economies of all. After just five years, NAFTA had served to depress wages by 29 percent in Mexico, thrusting 60 percent of the

Mexican labor force below the poverty line (Wallach and Sforza, 1999). Furthermore, the push for mediating the differences in environmental laws between the countries has meant relaxation of the tougher laws in Canada and the United States, resulting in an increase in toxic waste dumping and an increase in public health problems. One 12-year border study found a connection between the boom in border-area production in the *maquiladoras* (foreign-owned assembly plants where low-paid workers assemble imported parts in the production of goods for export) in Mexico and severe birth defects in both Mexico and the United States (Wallach and Sforza, 1999). Critics saw NAFTA as a smaller scale WTO, which they argued would produce the same intensification of inequality on a global scale, and thus they launch protest demonstrations against the WTO every time it meets. These protests are frequently met with the full force of military and police power to subdue the demonstrators and protect the meetings and their attendees, and thus the economic agenda of the core nations represented at WTO meetings.

In addition to protecting U.S. trade interests, the military often facilitates international production. A strong U.S. military presence in or around countries in which multinational corporations have a stake helps secure the political environment. This military presence often requires treaties and leases to forge political interrelationships between countries. Such arrangements involve an unspoken understanding that issues like human rights violations may be overlooked in the interest of preserving the agreements. For example, for many years the United States did little to acknowledge the beating, torture, and killing of dissenters in the Philippines, in part because the Philippine dictatorship had been avowedly anticommunist, a position consistent with U.S. economic and political interests. International relations in the world-system, then, affect the structure and experiences of whole nations and the people in them.

To sum up, where individuals are located in the global division of labor strongly influences their lives. Factory workers all over the world live less well than corporate executives, but factory workers in Mexico, the Philippines, and Vietnam are far more poverty-stricken than their counterparts in the United States.

Also important is where people are located within the society that links them to the world-system. Just as there is differentiation between nations, there is differentiation within them. What is the relationship between the individual and the larger society of which he or she is a member?

Societies

The world-system is a network of many nations and societies. A **society** is an organization of people who share a common territory, govern themselves, and cooperate to secure the survival of the group. Not all societies are nations; there may be several societies within a single nation. For example, in the United States many surviving populations of Native Americans constitute societies within the national boundaries of the country. Similarly, before its breakup, Yugoslavia contained within its boundaries several societies, including Serbs, Muslims, and Croatians; Spain contains a society of Basques; and Iraq, Iran, and Turkey share the society of Kurds. In Israel, societies of Jews and Palestinians live a tense and frequently violent coexistence. Sometimes the presence of many societies in a single nation can produce diversity, richness of history, and gradual change. Other times, the presence of many societies within a single nation can become a source of serious conflict and sometimes war. In Iraq, Iran, and Turkey, for example, Kurds are persecuted and Shiites and Sunni Muslims clash for dominance and control. In Yugoslavia in 1991, Serbs, Muslims, and Croatians resumed old conflicts in a struggle for control of land, a struggle that continues even now. And in Israel, despite ongoing efforts to forge a treaty for coexistence, tensions between Jews and Palestinians often erupt in violence.

Nations are political entities with clearly defined geographic boundaries usually recognized by neighboring nations. Nations are generally characterized by the viewpoint and interests of their dominant societies. Thus, although nations may contain several societies, not all these societies are necessarily equal in power or benefit equally from social, political, and economic arrangements. For example, the Kurds in Iraq were oppressed by a more powerful prevailing society under Saddam Hussein. And although blacks in South Africa are now in the political majority, for many years they were exploited and oppressed economically, socially, and politically by the dominant white society in that country. In the United States, Native Americans do not share the political or economic power of the nation's white-dominated society. Indeed, the dominant legal system may render aspects of Native American culture illegitimate. For example, federal laws prohibit Native Americans from using in their traditional rituals substances that the federal government defines as illicit drugs despite the fact that such substances may have been an integral aspect of their societies' rituals for centuries.

Two Views of Social Structure

Some sociologists adopt a **functionalist perspective,** in which they view societies as adaptive social structures that help human beings adjust to their physical, political,
pp. 10–12 economic, and social environment (Parsons, 1951) (see Chapter 1). When changes or challenges occur in that environment, the structure of a given society becomes the mechanism for organizing responses, adjustments, or preemptive strategies. For example, our use of fossil fuels has contributed to the greenhouse effect, a phenomenon that occurs when carbon dioxide released and trapped in the atmosphere by the burning of fossil fuels raises Earth's temperature. Functionalists would argue that U.S. society has made structural adaptations so that it can continue to survive. U.S. political structures have enacted and enforced clean-air and recycling laws, and its economic structure has made fossil fuels more expensive to discourage unnecessary use. Thus society functions to adapt to the greenhouse effect. In this sense, society's structure is functional or beneficial in meeting its members' needs.

In contrast, other sociologists offer a **conflict perspective** on social structure
pp. 14–15 (Chapter 1). They challenge the assumption in the functionalist analysis that all of society's members benefit from the way society is structured and from the ways it adapts to challenges. Moreover, they argue that policies are often driven by power struggles. These critics point out that some groups enjoy advantages and privileges that allow them to impose their views on others and to influence the adaptive strategies society may adopt. In this analysis, the way society is organized significantly affects not only how (and if) people might alter their lifestyle in response

Global inequalities in the world-system commonly encourage policies and practices that benefit wealthy and powerful elites but that may be harmful to workers and the poor as well as to the environment. In the rainforests of Central and South America, millions of acres of forest are cleared annually for timber or to make room for factories or grazing land.

to environmental challenges but also who benefits and who is hurt by the strategies chosen (Foster, 1999; Lowe, 1994).

What forces might influence decisions concerning energy policy? In the United States, the power of large-scale corporations, particularly energy and utility corporations, greatly influences that policy. The nation's energy policy today emphasizes an increasing reliance on nonrenewable, potentially hazardous sources of energy such as nuclear power plants. After the United States had gone to war to protect its access to cheap foreign oil in 1991, President George H.W. Bush put forth a national energy policy that reflected a corporate agenda. The proposal called for a renewed investment in nuclear power generation as an alternative to reliance on oil and other fossil fuels; it made no provision for the development of less hazardous renewable sources of energy (such as solar, wind, or geothermal energy) or for conservation measures. Such a policy largely benefits the energy corporations, and their wealthy stockholders, that own the nuclear power plants, at the expense of the rest of society. Similarly, current policies relaxing environmental restrictions against cutting mature trees in national forests in the United States favor the logging industry's interests, and proposals to allow oil drilling in Alaskan national forests favor energy corporations' interests, at the expense of the environment.

In many underdeveloped countries, global inequalities in the world-system encourage policies that favor the wealthy elites, reinforce oppression of workers, and may intensify environmental challenges. Large landowners in countries like Brazil cut down millions of acres of rain forest a year to export wood or to create more land for cattle grazing in order to export beef to industrialized nations. Since trees are the natural consumers of the carbon dioxide released by burning fossil fuels, massive deforestation in peripheral countries contributes to the greenhouse effect (Durning, 1994). Thus the structural position of countries in the world-system affects policies that in turn can affect Earth's environment. Indeed, protestors against the World Trade Organization in Seattle in 2000 raised precisely these issues.

Notably, even political and economic power cannot protect corporate executives from the personal effects of global warming. At some point, it would seem, health issues should outweigh the profit motive in steering energy policy. For example, certain rare medicinal plants used to treat life-threatening illnesses may be found only in the rain forests now undergoing destruction. Thus far, however, health issues have not been connected to energy policy changes. People tend to address the greenhouse effect in terms of personal lifestyle issues (such as whether to buy large, fuel-inefficient cars like sports utility vehicles, whether to carpool to save gas usage, and whether to invest in solar energy for one's own home). Framed this way, the hazards are analyzed as personal problems of lifestyle rather than as public issues of energy policy driven by profit motives.

Societies respond to the need to adapt to their environment in many ways, *always influenced by their social structures.* Thus a given problem has no single, universal response. For example, some societies may respond to the threat of the greenhouse effect by outlawing the burning of fossil fuels altogether. Others may attempt to reduce the use of fossil fuels for some purposes but not for all. Still others may ignore the threat, seeing it as minimal in the near future.

The strategies societies develop to respond to environmental challenges affect not only their own survival but that of the entire world-system. For example, if societies choose to rely on nuclear power as an alternative to burning fossil fuels, they run the risk of nuclear accidents that may poison the air, land, and water of other societies in the world-system. In 1986, the accident at the Chernobyl nuclear power plant in the Soviet Union contaminated a large area of land and water in that nation and the radiation drifted into several neighboring countries. On the other hand, societies that insist on burning fossil fuels may be contributing to the growing threat of the greenhouse effect, and that will affect everyone.

How, then, do societies resolve the problem of survival, and how are individuals linked in the process of social survival? How do factors such as one's class, gender, and race or ethnicity affect each person's relationship to the larger society? How does society control and distribute access to important resources? These questions point to social structures called institutions.

Institutions

To survive, every society must successfully address the same fundamental social needs. Sociologists using the functionalist perspective call these needs **functional imperatives** (Parsons, 1951). Talcott Parsons identified six basic functional imperatives:

1. All societies must *organize the activities of their members* to obtain the basic goods and services necessary for survival (such as food, clothing, shelter, fuel, potable water), without irreparably upsetting a balance with the environment. Societies can obtain food by relying on what they find growing around them, or they can cultivate products that may or may not deplete the fertility of the soil. Alternatively, societies can trade with other societies for food, or they can invade another country or society to seize its food, perhaps at a cost to their national security.

2. Societies must *protect their members* from both external and internal threats. External threats include invasion by other societies and destructive natural disasters like hurricanes, tornadoes, and earthquakes. Internal threats include crimes like robbery, murder, rape, and embezzlement as well as health epidemics like AIDS, SARS, measles, polio, and the flu.

3. All societies must *replace members* lost by death or emigration. One strategy may be to encourage increased reproduction, as many Orthodox Jewish leaders have done to replace members lost in the Holocaust. Alternatively, societies may provide incentives to draw immigrants from other societies, as the United States did in the 1800s to mid-1900s to attract the large labor force needed for industrial expansion. Another way to replenish labor is to seize people from other societies, as slave traders did during the 1700s to 1800s. While slaves certainly did not officially count as full citizens of U.S. society, they did count as greatly needed labor. As such, they filled a particular position in the social structure of plantation life, and slavery represented one strategy for replenishing diminished labor power in society.

4. Whenever societies gain new members, they must *transmit knowledge* of the rights, obligations, responsibilities, and expectations of appropriate behavior to the newcomers (whether they are native-born children or adult migrants). New members must also be taught the skills they will need to participate as productive members of the society.

5. All societies must *motivate both new and continuing members* to fulfill their responsibilities and conform to expected behaviors. This may be accomplished by a variety of approaches, among them providing meaning and purpose to activities and behaviors or using force and punishment.

6. Finally, societies must *develop mechanisms for resolving conflicts.* Otherwise, conflicts may disrupt a society's ability to satisfy other needs and may even destroy that society altogether.

The social structures that all known societies possess to fulfill these fundamental social needs are called **institutions.** These structures develop the standardized methods that societies use to cope with problems of survival. Most members of society accept these conventional coping mechanisms as legitimate, but some members may debate about their value. The dominant groups in society are generally able to prevail over the interests and viewpoints of the nonelite or subordinate groups in society. For example, dominants in the United States strongly insist on defining the institution of the family as a heterosexual married couple and their offspring, a viewpoint reinforced by a wide range of laws. However, organized challenges by gay couples have pressed for such changes as the extension of health benefits for life partners and the right of gays to adopt children. In 2000, the Vermont legislature passed a bill recognizing gay civil unions as legitimate. Several other states now have similar policies. Thus resistance and organized challenges to the powerful groups' view may affect the content and operation of institutions.

Despite debates about or changes in their form, institutions as social structures survive over time. Because they strongly influence our lives, they often become the focus of attempts at change. How can the problems experienced by individuals be viewed within the context of societal institutions? To answer this question, it is important to first establish what it is that institutions do.

Five basic institutions can be found in all known societies: the *family, religion, economy, education,* and *the state.* Each institution is intended to address one or more of the functional imperatives determining society's survival. Sociologists who adopt a functionalist perspective call such goals the **manifest functions** of the institution. However, in carrying out these functions, institutions also produce unintended and often unrecognized outcomes or consequences, or **latent functions** (Merton, 1968). In addition, when institutions carry out their manifest functions, they also sometimes inadvertently produce consequences that reduce the adaptability and flexibility of societies and hence may threaten the very survival of the society the institutions are presumably there to secure. It is important to note that not all latent functions are necessarily negative; some positive outcomes may occur as well that were not intended or even noticed. For example, the greenhouse effect's threat to the environment is an unintended consequence of the operation of powerful interests in economic institutions. This unintended threat to the environment produced by economic institutions fulfilling their manifest functions has also produced the unintended outcome of greater awareness of how people live and growing creativity in balancing lifestyles with the health of the ecosystem.

Functionalists argue that, in general, the purpose of institutions is to provide for the collective or common good by attending to the survival needs of society. However, a conflict perspective points out that institutions often serve some portions of the societal population better than they serve others. Institutions may even provoke or exacerbate systemic inequalities between groups within society. For example, when the United States went to war against Iraq in early 1991, the state was fulfilling its function of protecting U.S. society from external threats. Indeed, President George H.W. Bush argued that it was necessary to go to war to "protect our way of life," because Iraq's invasion of Kuwait threatened U.S. access to Mideast oil. However, an examination of who actually went to the gulf among the U.S. troops indicates that the "way of life" of certain groups was exposed to disproportionate risk.

The troops (particularly the ground troops) were overwhelmingly from the working class. Of the chief executive officers of the nation's top 20 corporations and members of the president's Cabinet, none had children involved in the war (Lacayo, 1990; Siegel, 1991). Moreover, people of color were disproportionately represented among the troops in the gulf. The percentage of African Americans and Latinos or Latinas in the ground troops was much larger than their proportion in the U.S. population. Of the troops who went to the gulf, 30 percent were African American; more than half of the women on active duty in the army were of color. And on one Native American reservation, 70 members of a total population of 3,600 went to the gulf (Women's International League for Peace and Freedom, 1991). This pattern repeated itself as the United States went to war against Iraq in 2003: fully one-third of the active-duty troops were people of color (Thomas, 2003). Why are persons of color and working-class whites so predominant in the U.S. troops mobilized to serve in war?

When the United States discontinued the military draft system in 1973, the country began to rely on an all-volunteer army. With unemployment and poverty among African Americans and Latinos/Latinas running double and triple the rate among white Americans, many people of color turned to the military as one of the few sources of employment and social mobility available. Others joined the military reserves as a way to afford college tuition. An army survey concerning recruits' reasons for joining the military found that 39 percent needed the money for college, and 26 percent needed job skills and training or income from service (DeParle, 1990). Although such motivations are not quite as strong for women as for men (Segal et al., 1998), many of the women in the military still cite similar reasons for volunteering: "for college money, technical training, a way out of a pink-collar ghetto filled with dead ends" (Quindlen, 1991). In many ways, poverty had led the

Poverty and racial inequality in the United States have resulted in an all-volunteer military in which the rank-and-file personnel are largely poor and working-class, and people of color. Thus, those who are at greatest risk during war, such as these soldiers in Iraq in 2003, are the least likely to benefit from the way of life they are protecting.

chronically disadvantaged to become the ones who jeopardized their lives in order to preserve "our" way of life. Note that there is a hierarchy within the military as well, with people of color found more commonly in the nonelite branch of the army than in the more elite branches of the navy, marines and air force. For example, African Americans constitute over 40 percent of the personnel in the army but only 18 percent in the navy and 16 percent in the marines and the air force (U.S. Department of Defense, 1999). This suggests that one latent function of the war mobilization was to reinforce racial inequality, whereas the manifest function was to protect U.S. society from external threats to its survival.

Sociologists using a conflict perspective often point out that when institutions reinforce inequalities, they are unintentionally introducing elements that may actually *erode* a society's ability to operate. For example, inequality limits the possibility that all of society's members will have an equal opportunity to develop their creative talents and skills. Inequality also may provoke hostility and distrust of society's ability to be fair or to reward hard work and accomplishment regardless of gender, race and ethnicity, class, age, religion, sexual orientation, or a host of other characteristics. Such distrust and hostility may weaken loyalty to the society among those who feel they have been unfairly denied rewards, and they may resist fulfilling responsibilities, obligations, and expected behaviors (Tumin, 1966). Hence inequality as a consequence of institutions' operations may actually threaten the institutions' ability to ensure a society's survival. At the very least, inequality may lead certain members of society to disregard socially prescribed responsibilities and obligations.

Whereas a functionalist perspective emphasizes the needs institutions are there to meet, a conflict perspective asks who benefits and who is hurt by the way institutions operate to meet these fundamental societal needs. Who benefits and who is hurt by the unintended consequences or latent functions of our institutions? Keep these questions in mind as you read about institutions on the following pages, where the functionalist and the conflict approaches are compared in an analysis of key institutions.

The Family

Functionalist sociologists view the **family** as the institution whose manifest function is to contribute new members to society. Families also teach the new members what is expected of them, and they try to motivate members to fulfill those expectations. The family may help contain and resolve conflicts within it, including disputes over inheritance. Finally, it ideally resolves the issue of the support of members of society whose capacity to produce may be limited (such as the young, the very elderly, and the infirm). However, while the family attends to these important manifest functions, it may also produce several unintended consequences.

A conflict perspective, in contrast, would note that families may reinforce racial and ethnic, gender, and class inequalities in the way they transmit expectations regarding appropriate behaviors and goals. Girls and boys may be assigned chores that reinforce traditional gender distinctions: Girls may be expected to baby-sit and wash dishes; boys may be expected to take out the garbage or help with household or car repairs (Antill et al., 1996). Children of the working class may be taught behaviors and skills that are consistent with jobs requiring little or no autonomy and creativity, while children of the middle class may be instilled with expectations of autonomy, creativity, initiative, and responsibility (Holstrom, Karp, and Gray, 2002). Gender, however, can affect families' class influences on children's socialization: Women in relatively prestigious positions often place significantly more value on autonomy than men in similar positions (Xiao, 2000), perhaps because of these women's heightened awareness of the importance of their hard-won empowerment.

Similarly, families may reinforce prejudice and discrimination on the basis of race or ethnicity, religion, and sexual orientation. Parents, guardians, older relatives, and siblings are important sources of such values, stereotypes, and preconceptions of superiority and inferiority of different groups (Dennis, 1981). As families fulfill their functions, they may unknowingly perpetuate inequalities, hostilities, and unnecessarily low aspirations and goals. Over time these prejudices can undermine society's ability to develop human resources and form a consensus, both of which may strengthen a society's ability to survive.

Families can also perpetuate economic inequalities by consolidating their wealth through marriages between wealthy families or through inheritance. Kanfer (1993), for example, offers a detailed historical analysis showing how three generations of the Oppenheimer family achieved highly concentrated wealth in South Africa through their monopolistic hold over the DeBeers diamond mines, and ultimately over the world's diamond market. By the early 1990s, the Oppenheimer family controlled 90 percent of the global supply of diamonds.

Instead of facilitating conflict resolution, families may actually produce the unintended consequence of increased conflict and violence. For example, some families in southern states were instrumental in instigating lynchings to avenge perceived injustices or insults against family members (Cutler, 1969). Their actions tended to inflame the existing conflicts rather than resolve them.

In addition, in a context of diminishing resources and increasing external pressures, family conflict in the form of domestic violence and child abuse may increase. Domestic violence in the United States does not occur in the vacuum of family structures. Society itself provides the context for using violence to resolve conflict. This can be seen in both popular culture and political relations. For example, television and film graphically show the use of violence as a method of resolving differences. Furthermore, the United States has a long history of participation in international wars to resolve global conflicts. Film footage on the U.S. labor movement (1900s–1980s), the civil rights movement (1950s–1970s), the antiwar movement (1960s–1970s), and protests against the World Trade Organization (2000) chronicles the use of force and violence by military and police organizations to quell challenges to government policies. And private videos have documented police violence directed against people of color, as in the 1991 beating of Rodney King in Los Angeles. So prevalent is the use of violence in society that it is not surprising if it comes to be accepted as a legitimate form of conflict resolution at home.

On the other hand, some families may transmit expectations of behaviors that challenge the predominant ones. Some parents, for example, argue against violence and in favor of nonviolent ways of resolving conflicts. And some children are repelled by the state-sponsored violence and war they see in news clips and by the violence they see in their own or friends' families. Their sense of justice may be energized when they see people being clubbed or beaten, for example, or even killed. Indeed, nightly news footage of the horrors of the Vietnam war did more to raise a public outcry against the war than any debate ever could. In such instances, individual reactions to the social setting can affect the latent functions of the institution.

When families teach their children to challenge or question institutional arrangements and their limitations, they may open the door to changing social institutions, such as the family itself. The tension between alternative and dominant expectations and behaviors in families does not necessarily indicate a breakdown of the institution. It may become a front edge of change in the structure of the family as an institution. Different conceptions of family and different needs will give rise to a variety of forms of that institution: childless couples, gay and lesbian couples (perhaps with children), "blended" families of partners and their children from previous relationships, and so on. These variations can potentially challenge inequalities of race, class, and gender. For example, new divisions of labor may necessarily arise that do not conform to traditional gender-based divisions. Whoever is available for child care must do the baby-sitting; whoever is available may have to cook dinner if the family is to eat; and so on. Then, too, the gender construction of the household may not be conducive to a traditional division of labor—if there are no women, or if there may be only women, for instance. These issues will be explored in greater detail in Chapter 15.

Religion

Functionalist sociologists emphasize that the institution of **religion** manifestly motivates members to comply with their responsibilities and obligations by assigning meaning and purpose to such activities. It attempts to reinforce the family's transmission of appropriate behaviors and goals to new as well as continuing members of society, and it parallels the family's role as a mechanism of conflict resolution. And religious institutions reinforce the family's legitimacy by sanctifying and protecting the family as an important institution.

However, a conflict perspective suggests that religious institutions often reinforce gender inequalities by promoting notions of appropriate and inappropriate gender behaviors and reproductive roles within the family. This typically means that sexual intercourse (and therefore parenthood) is forbidden until a couple has been formally married. The father is considered the breadwinner and authority figure ("head of the family"); the mother is the caregiver, housekeeper, and child rearer and is subordinate to the father. Such interpretations of appropriate family roles imply that departures from this model are in many ways sacrilegious. Indeed, one young single mother in Nigeria became the focus of an international outcry in 2002 because she was sentenced to death by stoning for bearing a child out of wedlock. Two years later she was cleared on a technicality by a panel of Muslim judges. Religious institutions thus often sanctify a particular family form, such as the nuclear heterosexual family, and denigrate or punish others (especially homosexual family forms and heterosexual cohabitation without marriage). This reduces society's ability to adapt to changes.

Religious institutions may also underscore gender inequalities within their own power structure. For example, the Roman Catholic church does not recognize the legitimacy of women as priests. The Orthodox branch of Judaism similarly neither recognizes the legitimacy of women as rabbis nor allows women to be included in minions reading the Torah or leading services. Orthodox men and women cannot sit together in synagogues to pray; men who pray each morning include a passage in which they thank God they were not born a woman. Some interpretations of Islamic religion do not recognize women as equal to men; men are dominant and superior to women. In some fundamentalist Islamic countries women must cover themselves completely when outside the home by wearing the traditional chador. Islamic women in Saudi Arabia are not permitted to drive. Whenever they wish to go anywhere, they must have a male as both a chauffeur and an escort. Women in Afghanistan were forced by the Taliban to leave their jobs, and they were forbidden to attend school.

Religious institutions often strictly define family and marriage roles, and those who depart from these roles as sacrilegious. In March 2002, a court in Nigeria following strict Islamic Shariah law sentenced this young single woman, Amina Lawal, to death by stoning because she bore a child out of wedlock. Lawal was acquitted in September 2003 after human rights groups around the world took up her cause and Nigeria faced international isolation.

Finally, religious institutions may unintentionally reinforce existing inequalities and social problems by emphasizing belief in an afterlife, when sufferers will be rewarded. This attitude may impede attempts to improve present-day social conditions and increase society's survivability.

But despite their general tendency toward conservatism, some religious institutions challenge existing inequalities (Smith, 1996). Both Conservative Judaism and Reform Judaism recognize women as equal to men; they allow men and women to sit together in temple, encourage women to participate in prayer services, and permit women to function as rabbis. Some more liberal Muslims note that nothing in the Koran specifically indicates that women are less valuable than men, or that women must necessarily live circumscribed roles. Some Christian and Jewish religious groups have begun to accept homosexuals as legitimate church members as well as leaders. Black churches in the United States were instrumental in challenging racial inequalities as part of the civil rights movement (McAdam, 1999; Morris, 1984). And many religious groups have actively opposed inequality and have participated in antipoverty activities for decades. Indeed, faith communities have become vocal partners with labor organizations in the United States in their push for a living wage and in their protests against welfare "reform" in the 1990s. And in Latin America, many churches preach Liberation Theology, emphasizing protest against poverty and oppression.

Another unintended consequence of religion as an institution can be an increase in conflicts rather than the decrease of hostilities and the development of peaceful consensus. Some religions have for centuries nurtured hostilities toward one another as competitors for souls. Wars such as the Crusades have been waged in the name of God, church, and religion. People who have not conformed to the prevailing religious dogmas have been killed, as in the Salem witch trials in colonial America, the Spanish Inquisition of the thirteenth century, and in Islamic Iran and Afghanistan. Indeed, Iran's religious political leaders issued an international death warrant against novelist Salman Rushdie in 1989 when they decided that his book *The Satanic Verses* was a blasphemous attack against Islam and God. The role of religion in social conflict will be examined in Chapter 16.

The Economy

In the United States, the institution of the **economy** includes corporations, organized markets, the banking community, international trade associations, labor unions, and consumer organizations. In noncapitalist societies, the economy might include the state-controlled production collectives, worker cooperatives, bartering and trading systems, and so on. For functionalists, the purpose of economic institutions is primarily to produce and distribute goods and services throughout society. They also discipline and motivate members of society to perform their role in the production, distribution, and consumption of goods and services. In a capitalist economy, workers (including managers) are motivated to do their jobs through the rewards of salaries, wages, and bonuses or the punishments of unemployment and poverty.

A conflict perspective, in contrast, would emphasize that the economy is often imperfect in achieving its manifest purposes and in reality produces unintended consequences depending on how people design that institution. For example, the economy in some socialist countries (such as the former Soviet Union), where the profit motive is not the principal guide to economic activity, may not produce the consumer goods people need to survive; instead, the economy may focus on state-defined needs, such as military production. A capitalist economy does not always produce the goods and services that people need to survive, either, but in this case the situation occurs because the economy focuses on profits. Grain and cheese may be warehoused and milk dumped into the ocean (despite great hunger here and abroad) because marketing too much of these products can reduce their profitability. Drugs needed to treat rare diseases, or products designed to help physically challenged individuals participate more fully in society's mainstream, may be difficult to find or very expensive because the market is considered too small to be profitable.

Yet corporations may produce many goods and services that are profitable but not needed. In spite of mounting evidence of the dangers to both smokers and nonsmokers alike, cigarettes will continue to be manufactured because of their profitability. Manufacturers are targeting younger consumers through advertisements and sponsorship of sports events and concerts. These marketing strategies are apparently working: while the percentage of smokers in all age groups has declined in the last 20 years, the decline has been slowest among 12 to 17 year olds, and more than a third of all teenagers are "active smokers by the time they leave high school" (National Institute on Drug Abuse, 1999:1). Young consumers are replacing the losses among older, more educated, and health-conscious consumers. Thus the economy as an institution provides incentives to produce harmful or useless goods and disincentives to produce important, needed goods. People often pressure the state to step in to control harmful consequences, demanding more ordinances regulating smoking in public places such as elevators, airplanes, restaurants, stores, and offices.

The economy can also reinforce class, racial and ethnic, and gender inequalities. When workers' wages are kept low to increase corporate profitability, the workers are less able to purchase the goods they produce. Low wages thus reduce the consumption of goods and services produced, thereby periodically provoking recessions and unemployment and aggravating class inequalities.

Seniority systems within both corporations and labor unions institutionalize racial and gender inequalities. This is because a "neutral" principle of "last hired, first fired" ensures that women and people of color —historically more likely than white males to be the last hired—will continue to be the most vulnerable to recessions and corporate downsizing.

Inadequate access to jobs, coupled with racial discrimination in the labor market, perpetuates class and racial inequalities by assigning different economic roles to different races and classes. In the face of dwindling opportunities, the poor, both whites and persons of color, are more likely to volunteer for military service as a job. Thus the people who are least likely to benefit from the existing economic structure become the ones most likely to endanger their lives to protect it and the superior advantages it provides others.

In the United States the economy is supposedly based on a system of free enterprise and open competition, suggesting equal opportunity for all members of society. However, the economy actually protects the advantages of the already-privileged. Large corporations that dominate most industries prevent small businesses from entering an industry and competing successfully. For example, small mom-and-pop clothing stores, grocery stores, and restaurants find it difficult to compete with the price advantages of large national department stores like Wal-Mart and fast-food chains like McDonald's. Many go bankrupt as the national chains continue to grow and expand. And relatively small auto producers like the American Motors Corporation have found it impossible to remain competitive with General Motors, Ford, and Chrysler (indeed, Chrysler eventually bought American Motors; by 1998 Chrysler itself was bought by Daimler-Benz, making it an even larger firm in an industry with fewer and fewer separate, competitive auto producers).

When the economy fails to equitably and adequately produce and distribute the basic goods and services needed for survival, those members of society who are denied them may turn to other, sometimes illegal ways to survive. For example, when the Soviet Union existed, a thriving underground economy of black-market trading developed there to give consumers access to commodities (commonly at very high prices) that were unavailable to them through state-run stores. In the United States, some women consider prostitution an opportunity for employment in an economy that offers few jobs (although, to be sure, not all prostitutes make a lucrative living in a safe environment; many are exploited by pimps and work under very dangerous conditions). Drug trafficking provides a lucrative (although extremely risky) source of income. Thus, although not all crimes are the result of economic need, and not everyone with desperate economic needs commits crimes, one unintended consequence of the way the economy is organized may be increased crime.

More advantaged members of society may also receive unintended incentives for criminal behavior. Executives are more likely than assembly-line workers to embezzle corporate funds because the structure of the corporation places them in a position to do so. In the United States, for example, lack of regulatory oversight of the savings and loan institutions in the 1980s facilitated executive abuse, embezzlement, and fraud, costing taxpayers billions of dollars (Calavita and Pontell, 1991). In the same decade, illegal insider trading of stocks became a common practice among stockbrokers (Zey, 1993). One consequence of our economy may be that people place a greater emphasis on the value of money and personal gain than on the value of integrity and societal or collective gain.

The priority of profit making in the U.S. economy also provides incentives for corporate crimes. For example, Pacific Gas & Electric Company (PG&E) profited by discharging massive amounts of chromium 6, a cancer-causing chemical that is potentially highly toxic to anyone exposed to it, and allowing it to seep into the groundwater of Barstow, California (a case made famous by the film *Erin Brockovich)*. Although PG&E knew about the extreme toxicity of the chemical as early as 1965, it continued its practice but did not notify the community or the local fire department as required by law. Instead, the company watched as the entire community drank, bathed, swam, and cooked with the contaminated water, and it supplied contaminated water to the all-volunteer fire department (Ascenzi, 2000). By 1996, after severe clusters of cancer, birth defects, and miscarriages began surfacing in the small town and Erin Brockovich doggedly pursued the case against the PG&E's

resistance, the firm was forced to pay a settlement of $333 million to residents of Barstow. PG&E had maintained its profitability at the cost of human lives and at the expense of the taxpayers, who ultimately will have to pay to clean up such sites.

These latent consequences of the economy combine to weaken its ability to ensure adequate production and distribution of basic goods and services to all. Increasingly, then, other institutions, such as the state, the family, and religion, must redirect societal priorities to discourage the profit motive from overwhelming society's basic needs. Some of these issues will be taken up in greater detail in Chapters 11 and 12.

Education

When functionalist sociologists study the institution of **education,** they see a system whose manifest function is to transmit the skills that all young members of society need to become productive members of the economy as adults. Thus the purpose of schools is to teach basic skills such as reading, writing, and math. In the United States, free public education is available to all children up to the age of 18. The Supreme Court's 1954 decision *(Brown v. Topeka Board of Education)* that separate educational institutions based on race are inherently unequal underscored the government's commitment to equal education for all.

A conflict perspective reveals, however, that in the United States, schools in fact *reproduce* inequality as an unintended consequence through a variety of mechanisms. For example, most school systems fund their budgets through local property tax revenues. This method of funding creates unequal school budgets, since school systems located in wealthy areas with high property values have access to greater tax revenues than do those in poor locales with low property values. For example, in 1998–1999 the city of Bridgeport, Connecticut, spent $7,814 per student on a student population that was 88 percent children of color; in contrast, the nearby affluent community of Westport spent $11,638 per pupil on a student population that was 95 percent white. Greater per-student expenditures appear to have contributed to a more advantageous environment for success in Westport: 86 percent of Westport students go on to attend a four-year college, compared with 47 percent in Bridgeport. Compare the proportions of students in these school districts who pursue higher education to those who

The unequal funding of schools based on property tax revenues can have a pronounced effect on students' learning opportunities and future success. Here, students at an affluent private school enjoy the use of individual laptop computers, a luxury unlikely to be found in public schools in economically disadvantaged communities. In an age when computer literacy and access to technology is increasingly important, such inequality in educational resources is likely to reproduce economic and racial inequalities.

enter the military instead. In Westport, only 3 percent of the high school graduates went into the military, but 17 percent of Bridgeport's graduates did so (Connecticut Department of Education, 1999). Why do per-student expenditures affect such high school outcomes as college attendance versus military service? Students in wealthy school systems tend to study an enriched curriculum in well-appointed facilities with low student-to-teacher ratios; students who attend school in poor systems commonly study a spare curriculum in deficient facilities (including lack of adequate books) with high student-to-teacher ratios. The method of providing local school budgets thus recreates past patterns of class and racial inequalities.

Another latent function of education is mate selection. This is because our educational institutions are structured to place large numbers of similar-aged people in the same school or classroom. While this may be the most cost-efficient manner of imparting basic knowledge, it has the unintended consequence of serving as a marriage and mate-selection mechanism at the high school and college levels. By matching privileged students with one another and economically disadvantaged students with one another, schools and colleges seriously reduce the possibility that an upwardly mobile, college-educated individual will mate with someone less advantaged or less educated, whose chances of mobility are limited. Thus the educational institution reproduces economic inequalities and unequal access to mobility.

Schools also perform the latent function of mitigating pressures on the economy during recessions by delaying the entry of young adults into a tight labor market. Indeed, many college graduates in the early 1990s, faced with the worst job market for college graduates in more than a decade, opted for graduate school as a haven from unemployment (McFadden, 1991). Schools therefore reinforce the legitimacy of the economy by reducing the pressures that could be created on a restricted labor market if all high school and college graduates demanded jobs simultaneously.

On the other hand, educational institutions can also be powerful mechanisms for social change. When skills taught by schools include independent, critical, and creative thinking, they produce the potential for challenges to society to alter inequalities and discrimination (Ayers, Hunt, and Quinn, 1998; Finn, 1999). It was to prevent such challenges that the antebellum South prohibited teaching African American slaves to read. More recently, critical thinking in colleges and universities and the consequent challenges to institutions promoted pressures to pass and implement civil rights laws and to question U.S. involvement in Vietnam.

The State

The **state** is the structure of the political system that includes all governmental branches and agencies, which together exercise power and authority over a particular nation. This is different from the notion of **government**, the people who govern within that structure who determine overall policy direction and make laws. Government, then is but one of several elements of the state. While people in governing bodies make laws, these laws are enacted or implemented by other administrative agencies; the military and police enforce the laws; and the judiciary interprets the laws, resolves the disputes in their application, and applies sanctions for transgressions. The state, then, is composed of the people in governing bodies together with people in administrative and enforcement agencies. In the United States, for instance, the government is Congress and the president, state legislators and governors, municipal and town councils and mayors, and other policy-making bodies (such as Boards of Education). The administrators of the laws and policies passed by these decision makers include bureaucracies such as the Department of Labor, the Environmental Protection Agency, and the Department of Health and Human Services. The military and police forces (including the various branches of the armed services) help enforce the policies passed by Congress and signed into law by the president, both within the United States and abroad. The judiciary, including the Supreme Court, criminal courts, civil courts, and courts of appeal, interpret the laws and policies Congress passes and may impose sanctions against those who do not comply. Together, these various agencies and branches, both elected and nonelected, are the state in the United States.

Functionalist sociologists conventionally view the state as an institution designed to protect society's members from internal and external threats. To meet this obligation, the state frequently becomes the only institution that can legitimately use force and violence, doing so through its police force and militia (Weber, 1947). Except in police states, there are controls on state power as well. When the state exceeds legitimate use of its power, even its agents can be brought to trial, as in the case of police officers who brutally beat up suspects.

The state also establishes penal and civil codes to formally define standards of acceptable and unacceptable behaviors, responsibilities, and obligations, and it specifies sanctions for violations of these standards. These codes help transmit prevailing standards and expectations and motivate society's members to comply with them. Ideally, the laws also serve to resolve conflicts through clearly defined legal processes, to be conducted in courts before impartial judges and a jury of one's peers.

Finally, the state is designed to aid the economy by developing social welfare programs that distribute goods and services to individuals the economy cannot support. By enhancing the ability of the poor to consume goods and services, such programs indirectly support the private producers and the economy.

On the other hand, a conflict perspective on the state reveals activities that may reproduce race and class inequalities. When the state is controlled by interests that are already advantaged (e.g., white, wealthy, corporate interests), its legitimate use of force and violence may be directed against challengers to the system. As noted earlier, this has historically been the case in the U.S. labor and civil rights movements.

At other times, the state may become the agent of change. In the United States the state is not a single entity controlled by an absolutely powerful elite. Instead, the state is composed of several levels of government in a hierarchy that allows the federal government, within limits, to act to force local governments to change. For example, the federal government used individual states' National Guards to enforce court-ordered school desegregation in southern states in the 1950s.

The state may reinforce advantages of corporations over labor and advantages of the affluent over the poor through its tax structure. A study by Citizens for Tax Justice reported that in 1996, as a group, the wealthiest members of U.S. society paid 81 percent less in taxes than the total paid by the poorest members as a group. This occurred because of hidden entitlements and tax breaks for the affluent and an emphasis on regressive sales and excise taxes, as opposed to progressive ability-to-pay income taxes (Citizens for Tax Justice, 1996). Sales taxes are regressive in that everyone, regardless of income, must pay the same tax on purchases. This means that the poor pay a higher proportion of their income than do the wealthy on food, clothing, transportation, fuel, and so on.

Moreover, the tax structure provides the affluent with tax breaks that are not accessible to the poor, thereby reducing the affluents' share of the total tax burden. For example, mortgage interest is tax-deductible. Since far more people in the middle and upper classes than in the poor and working classes are likely to own their homes, such a deduction mainly benefits the wealthier taxpayers. Indeed, although only 20 percent of U.S. taxpayers earned more than $50,000 per year in 2000, they were the recipients of more than 75 percent of mortgage deductions. And while an income of $50,000 per year is not considered wealthy by current standards, four-fifths of U.S. workers earn less than that amount (www.irs.gov/taxstats)—thus mortgage tax breaks are inaccessible to the vast majority of the population. A mortgage tax deduction, then, not only reduces the tax burden of the relatively privileged few; it also becomes a form of welfare for them.

This same tax policy, manifestly designed to encourage home purchases, may have the indirect latent consequence of stimulating job creation in the construction and supply industries (lumber, concrete, brick, plumbing, electrical supplies, durable goods, shipping and moving, etc.). The state as an institution thus may serve the latent function of reproducing inequality while simultaneously stimulating upward mobility through the creation of jobs in high-paying industries.

The state may reinforce other inequalities as well. The Medicaid program, for example, is manifestly designed to extend health care to the poor, thereby reducing economic inequalities and promoting a healthy work force. However, since the program focuses largely on acute care needs, it neglects the needs of the chronically ill and people with physical and mental disabilities, thus underscoring and aggravating such persons' problems.

Furthermore, the state may reinforce dominant ideologies in its development and implementation of laws. For example, while civil rights legislation legally ensures equal rights regardless of race, sex, ethnicity, religion, or physical ability, in fact people of color, women, individuals with disabilities, and religious minorities may find their protections limited by the various ways the laws are interpreted. Moreover, some minority interests remain unprotected, even in the written policy. Homosexual equal rights, frequently under attack, are often defined as outside the realm of the state. Thus one consequence of the structure and process of the American state is continued domination by privileged wealthy, white, largely male, and often corporate interests.

The state does not always provide equal protection under the laws. People of color frequently charge that they are harassed or unfairly treated by police, courts, prisons, and laws that remain insensitive to issues of discrimination (Free, 1996; Mauer, 1999; Russell, 1998a). Studies in several cities have noted that prosecuting lawyers often challenge African Americans during jury-selection processes and effectively keep them off juries that are likely to hear cases involving African American defendants (Kennedy, 1997; *Harvard Law Review,* 1988). This raises the questions of whether these defendants are being tried by a jury of their peers and whether the judicial system is neutral. Moreover, people of color are frequently the target of police brutality and excessive use of force on the streets, as evidenced by the Stolen Lives Project (1999), which has documented more than 2,000 such cases nationally, and are also the victims of denigration and excessive force and violence at the hands of their guards in prisons (Johnson, 1990; McQuiston, 1990).

Unequal protection is also manifested as a class issue. Since the 1980s, the U.S. government has initiated policies that more heavily favor the wealthy. The ability of the affluent to drastically reduce their share of the federal tax burden (and thus indirectly of the state tax burden) through deductions, writeoffs, and loopholes has effectively meant that they have decreased their financial support of public services at all levels. Faced with reduced funding, the local levels of the state are finding it difficult to maintain adequate police forces, and the protection provided to the public is often insufficient. At the same time, however, the affluent do not suffer. Instead, they purchase their own protection by hiring private security guards. Thus the state's decision to shift the responsibility of protection to the local level, coupled with its policy of tax structures that overwhelmingly favor the wealthy, means that the state provides unequal protection to society's members on the basis of class (Cole, 1999).

Similarly, gender is an issue in the state's unequal approach to crime. Women who have been raped still complain of being psychologically raped a second time by insensitive police, lawyers, judges, and other members of the judicial system who inquire about their previous relationships and their manner of dress when these women attempt to bring their attackers to justice. Debates continue over whether a victim's past relationships are admissible evidence during a rape trial. And many communities still treat spouse or partner abuse as a private matter of domestic dispute to be dealt with by the parties involved, rather than as a violation of the law. Fortunately, communities are increasingly treating such abuse as a crime of assault and battery, thereby opening the possibility for greater state protection of women. However, protection of women is still imperfect; once an attacker has served the specified term, the state does not typically follow up with restrictions for the attacker.

There is some evidence to suggest that a pattern defines who receives less-than-perfect protection. Those groups in society who have relatively little power, particularly women, people of color, homosexuals, and the poor, have found themselves to be the victims of state neglect, at best, and of violence at the hands of agents of the state, at worst. The state appears to provide the best protection to those who already benefit most from the way the state is organized and who have the power to ensure that this organization continues. In particular, the affluent in the United States, who are largely white, have historically had the power to protect the state from serious challenges and in turn have benefited from its protection of their safety, their affluence, and their position.

Institutions as Dynamic Structures

Institutions are not inexorable and unchangeable. The form and content of institutions such as the family and the state may vary from one society to another or from one time period to another within a single society. There may also be several simultaneous alternative forms of a given institution within a single society. But the institution itself in some form or another remains identifiable as an institution everywhere. For example, many contrasting structural forms may be classified as family: nuclear families (two parents of opposite sex who are married and their offspring), extended families (nuclear families plus other related individuals, such as grandparents, aunts, uncles, cousins), single-parent families, childless couples, gay and lesbian couples, live-in couples (two people of opposite sex who are not married), blended stepfamilies, and so on. All are families, grouping individuals into a common living arrangement to obtain the necessary goods and services for survival. They all transmit to their members the knowledge and skills needed to function in society. And they sometimes replenish the population.

Institutions, then, are not set in concrete. They are dynamic structures that respond to changes and challenges. But what remain, regardless of alterations in form, are structures of organized social life that are designed to satisfy fundamental social needs and that often produce unintended consequences.

The basic institutions do not operate in isolation either. They interact and affect one another. For example, the institutions of the economy and the state affect the family and education. When the state determines that education systems must be funded by property tax revenues, it affects schools' curricula and facilities and thus how effective these will be. In this way, decisions made by the state reinforce the schools' consequence of perpetuating class (and often racial) inequality. When the economy is in a recession, it affects the family by altering the employment status of family members. This may in turn affect gender roles as well as reinforce class inequalities, since low-wage production and service workers are typically the first and hardest hit in a recession. When the state awards child custody primarily to the mother (except in extreme cases) during a divorce, but does not enforce child-support payment responsibilities, it is reinforcing gender inequalities (Weitzman and Maclean, 1992). So great are the inequalities in earnings between males and females and the gendered division of paid and unpaid labor (i.e., housework) that in the first year after a divorce the mother's income typically declines substantially while the father's *improves* (Morgan, 1991). More recent research indicates that men's incomes are most likely to increase after divorce if they were the sole or primary breadwinner; men whose partners contributed substantially to the total household income actually lost income after divorce (McManus and DiPrete, 2001). This suggests that one latent consequence of traditional roles in marriage is the reproduction of gendered inequalities after divorce, since the state does not typically evaluate women's unpaid labor as equal to the monetary income paid to men who work outside the home. Moreover, the state's approach to child-custody arrangements also has the latent consequence of supporting some family forms and undermining others. Single parenthood becomes an economic liability, whereas the nuclear family becomes an asset. These issues will be elaborated in Chapter 15.

Social Movements: Challenge and Change

Although institutions may produce inequalities, people are not powerless to affect how they fulfill their functions. **Social movements,** for example, are organizational structures within which individuals working together may alter how institutions, whole societies, and even world-systems operate. In Poland in the 1980s, workers organized in the outlawed union Solidarity were able collectively to strike, ultimately shifting the Polish communist government by 1989 to one that permitted free elections of noncommunist leaders. Prior to this, elections were not part of the country's political structure, and participation in government was limited to Communist Party members.

The feminist movement in the United States (which has been, in fact, several movements, depending on the kinds of changes sought) has had some success in obtaining legislation and Supreme Court decisions designed to promote social and political rights, greater control over reproduction, and greater protection from sexual harassment. There is still a gulf between legislation and implementation, and legislation still does not guarantee equal economic rights, but the feminist movement has succeeded in weakening many traditional gender barriers to participation in U.S. society.

Black South Africans, organized in the outlawed African National Congress (ANC), collectively defied the white minority government, holding mass funerals and demonstrations and enlisting world support for their struggle. Together, they succeeded in forcing the white government to dismantle the discriminatory institution of apartheid in 1994. Under that system, blacks were not allowed to vote; were segregated in public as well as private facilities, housing, education, and transportation; were forced to relocate into tribal "homelands" designated by the government; and were denied the right to freedoms of assembly, speech, and movement. Such restrictive institutional practices would have been daunting for an individual to alter, but the collective pressure applied by the ANC and its international allies facilitated a change in South African social and political structures that many had thought impossible. Today the ANC holds the reins of government in South Africa after the first election in which South Africans of all racial and ethnic groups were allowed to vote.

The civil rights movement in the United States linked individuals and groups (such as churches, civic groups, student groups, and local and national black organizations) in a coalition to pressure and change institutions that reinforced racial inequality. Their efforts led to the Supreme Court ruling that separate educational institutions on the basis of race are inherently unequal. This fundamentally altered the structure of schools' populations, if not the manner in which schools are funded. Pressure from the movement also ultimately elicited civil rights legislation mandating voting rights and equal opportunity and affirmative action programs.

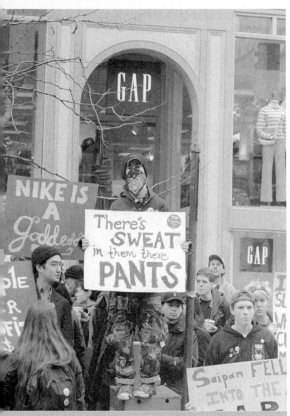

Social movements are important social structures for stimulating social change, especially for those who are not ordinarily among the powerful. Students in the United States and around the world have organized a movement to demand an end to the use of sweatshops to produce merchandise sold in their schools and in stores such as the Gap.

These laws made it illegal to deny access to political, educational, or occupational opportunities on the basis of race. And while the civil rights movement's efforts have certainly not eradicated racism or eliminated the inequalities that white-dominated institutions may reproduce, they have altered in some ways how such institutions operate.

The disability rights movement has been somewhat less visible, but it has been fairly successful in redressing grievances and inequalities generated against people with disabilities by social institutions. Part of its success may be traced to the public perception that, unlike more stigmatized groups (such as gays and the poor), the disabled are a "worthy" minority. Moreover, disabilities affect all races, classes, and genders, making it likely that every individual knows someone who is disabled. Thus the disability rights movement may face a less hostile public than other groups. Whatever the reason for its success, however, the movement has been able to produce important institutional changes. In many cases legislation has given the disabled greater access to public transportation. The movement's efforts have also resulted in making buildings more accessible, with ramps to accommodate wheelchairs, elevators with floor indicators in Braille, and bathrooms with wider stalls, low handles, and raised seat levels. Many cities also construct sidewalks that slope at street corners so wheelchairs can negotiate the streets. And in some cities "walk–don't walk" lights emit loud signals so that visually impaired pedestrians can know when it is safe to cross the street. Efforts of the disability rights movement helped gain passage of the Americans with Disabilities Act in 1990, legislation that facilitates broader inclusion of people with disabilities into the mainstream of society.

And the burgeoning United Students Against Sweatshops movement in the United States is quickly building a potential ability to affect trade and production processes in the world-system. It is pressuring well-endowed universities to refuse to enter into licensing contracts with manufacturers who produce goods with exploited child labor and workers who are paid less than living wages in underdeveloped countries. For example, in 2000 the University of Michigan, among several major universities, refused to renew its licensing agreement with Nike because that firm would not agree to the general principles and guidelines against the use of sweatshops (Featherstone, 2000).

This discussion of social movements suggests that changing institutions may be a very long, slow process but that change is not impossible. It also suggests how individuals may affect macro structures. Individuals acting alone are not likely to be successful; but when people join together in a common effort, they can, in fact, collectively act as agents to alter these structures. We will explore this more fully in Chapter 10.

Moreover, the discussion of social movements raises the question of how individuals are linked to macro levels of structure. Just as there are macro-level structures, there are micro-level and midlevel structures that distribute and organize individuals locally, defining positions and behaviors of individuals and linking them to the macro structures. These more local structures are examined in the next chapter.

CHAPTER SUMMARY

1. Social systems link individuals to one another as organized mechanisms for survival. When these linkages are organized and recurring, they form social structures, some of which are quite large and complex.

2. Everyone is situated within a world-system; the society in which an individual lives is only one part. Changes in the relationships among the world-system's components—for example, the invasion or domination of one nation by another—can have ramifications that reach right down into the lives of individuals in societies around the world. Individuals' personal lives are not explicable without reference to where their own society stands within this world-system. The powerful core position of the U.S. economy in the world-system has begun to erode in recent years as, for example, other nations successfully compete against the United States in international markets. This has affected everything in the United States, from the ability of individuals to find decent-paying jobs to the quality and cost of public services upon which people depend.

3. Just as all persons are linked to the world-system through their societal membership, so are they linked to their own society through participation in its institutions. In one way or another, everyone has some kind of relationship to the central institutions of family, religion, the economy, education, and the state. The functioning of these institutions influences individuals' biographies directly, often affecting them differently depending on their race or ethnicity, class, and/or gender. These factors come to be organizing principles around which institutions frequently operate. For example, in times of economic stagnation, the persons who experience the highest rates of unemployment tend to be those working in the lowest paying jobs and are thus most likely to be individuals of color and females. In comparative terms, then, those who are white, affluent, and male are less likely to lose their jobs, and if they do, they are likely to find work sooner.

4. As relationships among components of the world-system change, the operations of entire societies may be affected, and within societies the functioning of central institutions may exact costs from some people and not others. Less frequently, concerted collective actions undertaken by individuals may alter

institutional and societal operations; even the world-system itself may consequently undergo change.

5. While it is true that each person is part of a much larger set of structures through participation in institutions, society, and the world-system, people are not entirely powerless to affect how these macro structures operate or are organized. Change occurs at all levels of this set of structures, whether out of consensus on the need for change or out of conflict over the status quo. Each individual can be involved with others in making change; people need not be only acted upon by society.

THINKING CRITICALLY

1. Global trade and production relationships form macro structures that influence our daily existence. Consider the man in the "Social Forces/People's Lives" reading: How does the global division of labor affect him? Discuss how these relationships affect your own life.

2. Select an important and current problem facing nations all over the world (such as population growth, nuclear danger, AIDS, food shortage, homelessness). Analyze how different social structures in at least two different nations may contribute to how these nations approach the problem.

3. Examine your own family (or your religious organization or the educational system you attend) and identify the manifest and latent functions it performs. Describe how the institutions may produce the latent functions you identify.

4. At the start of the chapter you were asked where your clothing was made and where your car or stereo was manufactured. What social structures contributed to bringing these items into your possession? What are the manifest and latent functions of these structures in the manufacture of consumer goods?

4. You may know someone (perhaps yourself) who has been stationed with a military unit somewhere in the world. Identify the location of the military assignment, and discuss the social structures that may have contributed to the assignment. Discuss the manifest and latent functions of the assignment. How did the social structures affect the daily life of the individual stationed abroad? How did they affect his or her family?

KEY TERMS

birth rates, *(49)*
conflict perspective, *(57)*
core nations, *(47)*
death rates, *(49)*
economy, *(66)*

education, *(69)*
family, *(62)*
functional imperatives, *(59)*
functionalist
   perspective, *(57)*

global division of labor,
   (47)
government, *(70)*
infant mortality rate, *(50)*
institutions, *(60)*

latent functions, *(60)*
life chances, *(49)*
macro-level social structures, *(46)*
manifest functions, *(60)*
nations, *(57)*

peripheral nations, *(47)*
religion, *(64)*
semiperipheral nations, *(47)*
social movements, *(75)*
social structure, *(46)*

social systems, *(46)*
society, *(56)*
state, *(70)*
world-system, *(47)*

Chapter Four

Social Structure: Micro Level and Midlevel

One of the most fascinating features of society—although often taken for granted—is the degree to which people's daily lives are patterned and organized. For the most part, individuals' daily interactions with others are not random. Rather, they reflect the variety of social positions that each individual occupies, as well as the interpersonal relationships and group memberships that these positions require or make possible. In this chapter, we explore questions such as the following:

- What are social statuses and roles, and how are people's lives tied to and shaped by them?
- What are the distinguishing characteristics of social groups, and why are group and organizational memberships important for individuals?
- How do bureaucratic and democratic forms of organization differ in their features and in their impact on people?
- What functions do social networks play in people's lives and how do individuals' access to social networks vary along the lines of class, race, and gender?

Like Chapter 3, this chapter introduces sociological concepts useful for thinking about how society is organized and the types of demands that people face by virtue of being participants in society. Knowledge about the ways in which society is organized can help in the development of a sociological imagination by increasing understanding of both sources of social order and sources of social conflict and change.

Most human beings spend very little time alone or in isolation from others. From birth, people are engaged in ongoing social relationships. At first relationships are with members of the family, neighbors, and playmates. Later, additional social relationships develop with other people in school, in clubs, on sports teams, at places of worship, and at work. Any setting in which people regularly interact—from a street in a low-income

continued

neighborhood to a corporate boardroom—provides opportunities to enter into and maintain social relationships.

As we saw in Chapter 3, the term **social structure** refers to the organization of recurrent and patterned social relationships. Chapter 3 focused on macro-level forms of social structure, including world-systems, societies, and institutions. Macro-level social structures entail large-scale mechanisms that organize social relationships within and between entire societies. In this chapter we examine micro-level and midlevel forms of social structure. p. 46

Micro-level social structure refers to social relationships based on interaction between small numbers of individuals, for example, between family members or between occupants of a dormitory floor. Such relationships often take place within the context of "primary groups," which are discussed in a later section. Social structure at this level is small-scale, or micro, in the sense that the interpersonal social relationships involved, while important, involve relatively few people.

In contrast, we use the term **midlevel social structure** to refer to larger webs of social relationships. "Secondary groups" and social networks, also to be discussed later, are examples of midlevel social structure. At this midlevel, participants are involved in varied forms and degrees of interaction with others. Consider a restaurant as a midlevel form of social structure. Restaurant wait staff interact with a changing cast of customers at their tables, while maintaining ongoing relationships with the floor manager, the bartender, cooks, and table-clearing staff. Midlevel social structure differs from micro level in the greater number, formality, and complexity of the social relationships in which individuals are enmeshed.

As we will see, at both micro and midlevel the nature, frequency, and content of the interaction that takes place between individuals are often guided by role expectations. Different role expectations accompany the various social statuses or positions that individuals occupy. In the examples above, there are certain widely held role expectations as to how people who hold positions as family members, dorm floor residents, wait staff, or cooks will behave. But because people are typically participants in many micro and midlevel social structures at the same time, they frequently find themselves caught up in role expectations that are contradictory or conflicting and at times impossible to meet. We will consider this topic as well.

Finally, this chapter addresses ways in which particular midlevel forms of social structure in which people are involved impact on and help to shape their lives. For example, secondary groups in which people participate may be democratically organized or fashioned along the lines of a bureaucracy. We examine how these two ways of organizing activities call for very different types of social relationships among group participants and may have very different effects on their behavior and thinking. Similarly, most people are involved in social networks, another form of midlevel social structure. The nature of the social networks in which people participate—in effect, the ties people develop within and outside their own social circles—can have important life consequences, as we will see.

Overall, then, this chapter seeks to encourage sociological thinking in response to the following question: What is the importance of participation in social structures at the micro level and midlevel for the biographies and lived experiences of individuals?

Status

People participate in a variety of micro- and midlevel social structures. People's social positions in these structures are referred to by sociologists as their **status.** The term "status" is often used interchangeably with the term "prestige." But here we are using "status" to refer to the social position a person occupies regardless of the prestige of that position. For example, a young person may occupy the status of daughter and granddaughter, as well as sister, at home; student, girlfriend, and basketball player at school; and sales clerk at work. People typically occupy multiple statuses or social positions, some of which change over time. A person is likely to be a daughter and sister far longer than a point guard or girlfriend. One's biography can be mapped by tracing the many statuses an individual has occupied.

Achieved and Ascribed Status

The ability to assume some statuses depends on whether individuals possess the right combination of resources, talent, motivation, and—most important of all—opportunity. An **achieved status** is a social position that is largely contingent on the structure of opportunities open to an individual. One thus achieves the status of wife, truck driver, business executive, or amateur skydiver. In contrast, **ascribed status** refers to a social position over which one has no control. In some cases ascribed

status is linked to characteristics determined at birth. Sex, race, class, and nation of origin are particularly powerful forms of ascribed status present at birth. And, throughout life, sexual orientation, the presence or absence of disability, and age provide additional sources of ascribed status.

It is important to note that ascribed status can easily function as an impediment to upward mobility in society. One cannot readily change one's ascribed race or sex, and discrimination against women and people of color continues to be a serious problem experienced by millions of people in U.S. society. Many individuals achieve mobility upward within the class structure, yet most members of U.S. society remain at or near the class position of the parents to whom they were born. This is particularly the case for those who suffer discrimination in the world of work (Kerbo, 2003).

An achieved status is a social position that a person comes to occupy on the basis of resources, talent, motivation, and especially opportunity. When actress Halle Berry won the 2002 Oscar for Best Actress for her role in Monster's Ball, *she became the first black woman to win this award in the 74-year history of the Academy Awards.*

Master Status

The meaning people attach to a given status may change over time and place. Thus, being female or male, a person of color or white, gay or heterosexual, experiencing a disability or being able-bodied may mean different things in different contexts. Not all status positions are equally important or salient, either to the individual occupying them or to other members of society. But at times one status occupied by an individual tends to override all others, dictating how a person is likely to be treated. For such cases, sociologists use the term **master status.** A female college professor or attorney may find that her sex is more salient than her professional credentials in determining how she is treated by many others, even colleagues.

One's master status may enhance or limit opportunities. One of the clearest examples of this involves people experiencing disabilities. Disabilities may interfere with many life activities, such as being able to hold down employment, attend school, or care for members of a household. There are some 35 million to 43 million people with disabilities in the United States (estimates vary by source and definition of disability), only a small proportion born with the disabilities with which they are challenged. Many adults with disabilities have not completed high school, and the overwhelming majority are not engaged in paid employment, even though most want to work. Poverty among those experiencing disability is much higher than it is among those who are able-bodied. Discrimination, based on the stereotype that to have a disability is to be "defective" and less than human, is widespread (Russell 1998; Shapiro, 1993).

In 1989 a committee of the U.S. Senate conducted hearings on the proposed Americans with Disabilities Act, a significant civil rights bill that became federal law in 1990. The hearings documented the miserable treatment that people with disabilities faced, treatment contributing to their isolation and segregation from those privileged to be able-bodied (U.S. Congress: Senate, 1989). The hearings also uncovered discrimination against caregivers, as well as persons thought to have a disability even if this was no longer, or had never been, the case.

The Senate committee heard testimony from a young woman with cerebral palsy who was denied admission to a movie theater by its owner. It also learned about a zookeeper who would not admit children with Down syndrome because he feared they would upset the chimpanzees; a child with a disability whose teacher claimed he should be excluded from school because his appearance "produced a nauseating effect on his classmates"; a woman who was fired because she was caring for her son, who was suffering from the effects of AIDS; people with arthritis, cancer survivors, and others who were fired or denied jobs not because they could not do them but because of discrimination; and people with disabilities who were denied access to public transportation and accommodations, medical treatment, and housing. The Americans with Disabilities Act of 1990 is intended to provide people with disabilities the same civil rights protections available to people of color and women, persons also often accorded a devalued master status.

Master status has a great deal to do with the distribution of power and the ability of dominant groups in society to decide what is "normal." In a society in which political power is concentrated in the hands of the able-bodied majority, to be otherwise is to be vulnerable to stigmatization and stereotyping, common prerequisites for discriminatory treatment. This is true even though people with disabilities are members of a "minority group" that any person can involuntarily join at any point in life. Likewise, in a society in which political power largely rests in the hands of persons who are heterosexual, gay males and lesbians, along with persons who are bisexual or transgender, are vulnerable to mistreatment. The imposition of unwanted master statuses is possible as long as men have more power than women, whites more power than people of color, the young more power than the elderly, and the affluent more power than the poor. The nearby "Social Forces/People's Lives" reading, in which Vanessa Hua speaks of being made uncomfortable by others because she and her partner are a mixed-race couple, underscores how negative master status treatment can affect people's everyday lives.

Roles

We previously said that people typically occupy multiple social positions or statuses. The behaviors expected of people in these positions are referred to as **social roles.** Social roles are not necessarily rigid proscriptions, although they are often linked to prevailing social norms. Some roles are more flexible than others, permitting the role player more room for innovation and experimentation. For example, the social role of college instructor probably allows more flexibility in ways to go about fulfilling the role than that of airline pilots. Failure to fulfill some roles properly can result in more severe sanctions than others. A bank clerk who is short money from his or her cash drawer may be summarily fired; a doctor whose work is suffering due to addiction to prescription narcotics is likely to be referred by a panel of peers for counseling.

Role Strain

When persons respond to role expectations that others attach to the positions they occupy, they may experience **role strain.** Role strain refers to the distress experienced by an individual when a particular role contains contradictory demands. Consider the role of mother, when this position is occupied by an impoverished woman. Out of economic desperation, mothers at times must look to the state to help meet their need for family income support. Yet a mother receiving welfare is often faced with role strain. She needs a minimum income to support her children. If she enters the welfare rolls, she is liable to be publicly stigmatized and condemned for so-called welfare dependence. Under current "welfare reform" policies she will be pressured by welfare officials to leave the rolls—voluntarily or involuntarily—as soon as possible and be a "self-sufficient" provider for her children. On the other hand, if she leaves her children in order to be employed and to try to provide for her children in that way, she may be criticized as a "bad mother" by those who feel that the daily care of children—not working outside the home—should be a mother's first and foremost priority (Edin and Lein, 1997).

To make the role strain faced by such mothers even worse, competent, affordable day care, after-school care, and overnight care are in woefully short supply in the United States. Consequently, most working mothers rely on family, friends, and neighbors to care for their children. But not all mothers have social networks adequate to the task. Mothers who are forced by welfare officials to take on day, evening, or night shift employment may at times have little choice but to leave their children home alone (as "latchkey kids") or in less-than-reliable child care situations. These mothers not only may put their children at risk; they also put themselves

Social Forces/People's Lives

Color Colors Everything

VANESSA HUA

In the United States, skin color may determine one's master status, overriding other characteristics that an individual possesses. Mixed-race couples regularly experience the meaning others automatically attach to skin color, at times in negative ways. Vanessa Hua, a young Asian American woman in a mixed-race relationship, comments on how Asian females with white male partners are frequently viewed.

WE were strolling one night toward a French bistro in San Francisco.

"Chink lover," spat out a man who passed by us.

I didn't hear what he said, but my boyfriend, Marc— now my fiancé—told me. I flushed and turned around, enraged. By then, the man had crossed the street and was on the next block. Still, I yelled after him, screaming that he was the one alone and a loser.

I could have laughed it off, made jokes about how exhausted he must be, insulting the legions of mixed-race couples living in the Bay Area. He was just a drunk in gym shorts.

Instead, I was embarrassed. Although he was rude, I felt as if I had committed the transgression. His insult wasn't even aimed at me but at Marc, who was tainted by his association with an Asian woman.

The remark left us uneasy. Marc said it was unfair that I was angry at him for not defending me. The drunk wasn't worth the effort. I worried that he didn't understand what it meant to be a minority. But if we stayed upset, we would have let the name-caller succeed—so we made up.

But why did our relationship enflame the man on the street? What did a white man with an Asian woman symbolize?

at risk of getting into trouble with government child protection agencies. In many instances mothers struggling to rise to the employment demands of welfare policy have been accused of neglect and have had their children taken away by the state (Roberts, 2001). Which way should an impoverished woman go about meeting the role expectations of "mother" when faced with such contradictory expectations and demands?

Role Conflict

Along with role strain, **role conflict** can exact costs from people. Role conflict occurs when the demands on a person from two or more of the roles he or she must fulfill are at odds. Consider, for example, the case of a college student talented enough to be awarded a scholarship to play basketball. Playing college-level ball is a dream for many young people—including low-income youths who see few other routes to upward mobility and financial success. With rare exceptions, play at this level is a prerequisite to selection by a professional team. Even though the statistical proba-

A few months later, on a trip to Thailand, we made a game of spotting what we dubbed "odd couples"; tall, gangly foreigners with tiny Thai women. They held hands, dined together at open-air cafes and snuggled on the beach.

In private, I wavered from anger—"that's exploitation"—to moral relativism—"she's doing what she needs to survive, and he's finding comfort the only way he can."

In public, I spoke loudly in English and wore my Tevas and other backpacking garb in an attempt to appear American and not as someone's paid consort.

It didn't work. Even Thais mistook me for one of them, pitching me deals in their language as we walked by restaurants or the airport.

I didn't want to be lumped together with the prostitutes and the girlfriends who came with a fee.

Maybe that's what bothered me so much about the jerk on the street—his implication that all Asian women were somehow lower than white men. That only women with desperate financial need and lonely men would cross the color line.

When my fiance asked for my father's blessing before he proposed, Dad warned that my career was important to me. Marc replied that my ambition was part of what he loved about me.

The two of us met in Spanish class and practiced what we learned in Peru, Panama, Mexico and in the Mission District.

Last fall, on a trip to the North Carolina's Outer Banks, a friend predicted that Marc and I would last. I drove and he navigated so well together—proof, she said, that we were meant to be.

In the Bay Area, every few months, the debate over Asian women/white men flares up on the online site Craigslist. The arguments always tread the same ground: Asian women steal white men from white women, wimpy whites seek subservient Asians, Asians try to social-climb out of their race.

The common explanation: "I know this is true because it happened to me."

What irks me is their belief that personal experience makes someone an authority. Behind their arguments is the assumption that all interracial relationships are the same, and by corollary, so are the people in them.

There is a long history of white male domination in Asia, with its women among the spoils of war. I don't deny that patterns emerge from cumulative experience. But I don't want to be grouped with other people who look like me, just as other individuals do not want to be confused with me.

SOURCE: Vanessa Hua, "Prejudice Still Haunts Mixed-Race Couples," *San Francisco Chronicle*, April 4, 2003, p. D20.

bility that a college player will make it into the pros is extremely small, many young persons nonetheless harbor this fantasy.

Yet the role of student and the role of athlete do not necessarily coexist easily. Some of the young people recruited to play college basketball lack skills as students. More frequently, the demands made on athletes by their school's coaching staff conflict with those being made by professors. College athletes may find themselves caught in an impossible dilemma: They can cut back on time devoted to developing as an athlete and draw the wrath of coaches, or cut back on time invested in being a student and risk losing the grades necessary to maintain athletic eligibility.

Colleges vary greatly in how they react to the student athlete's role conflict. Some schools work hard to support the student role, an important consideration given how few players will actually turn pro. College players will need a track record of academic success to compete for jobs when their athletic careers are over, which is right after college for just about all. Other schools exploit the athlete role, using whatever tricks are necessary to maintain student athletes' eligibility to play and losing interest in players when their eligibility is lost or runs out. In such

Being both a full-time student and a varsity athlete can easily produce role conflict. Football players often find it frustrating and difficult to figure out how to fulfill the competing demands and expectations attached to these two separate roles.

settings, the graduation rate for athletes is very low and nongraduates are faced with very limited employment opportunities when they leave school.

Role Sets

In thinking about role conflict, noting that individuals occupy **role sets** is also useful. Any given role exists in relationship to a set of many other roles, and the individual is therefore simultaneously subject to various expectations and demands from people fulfilling all these other roles. For example, a person fulfilling the social role of student may have to simultaneously satisfy the expectations of individuals with such roles as teacher, academic adviser, roommate, fellow student, friend who is not a student, partner, parent, or employer. A student must find ways to deal with the situation whenever it becomes impossible to adequately fulfill the expectations of all those who are part of his or her role set.

The kinds of role strains and role conflict that people face, and the ways in which strains and conflicts are handled, constitute yet another element of people's individual biographies. Efforts to solve role strain and conflict may become the front end of change, as when people break out of roles or defy others' role expectations.

The complex interactions between many individuals performing complementary social roles in role sets leads us to take up the topic of "groups." Sociologically speaking, what is a group and why is group membership significant to individuals?

Groups and the Individual

Just about everyone in U.S. society has at some time attended a concert or sporting event. People arrive along with hundreds of others, find a seat, hope to enjoy themselves, and participate by clapping and cheering. Such an audience is not, in sociological terms, a "group." Rather, it is a **social aggregate,** a collection of individuals with no real interpersonal ties or patterned social relationships.

Classrooms of college students, especially if they are small in size, often evolve from social aggregates to something much closer to what sociologists mean by the term group. The first day of class most people don't know one another and may have little basis for interaction. As time goes on, students begin to recognize one another in and out of class, share gripes and lecture notes, study together for exams, form ties, and develop social relationships. As the professor comes down the hall to enter class, she is likely to hear a lively chorus of conversations that is quite different from the relative silence that may have greeted her entry on the first day.

In a sociological sense, a **group** occurs only when there is regular interaction among an aggregate or collection of individuals. The interaction provides a basis for a sense of group membership and can facilitate the emergence of leadership and status differences within a group. Through interaction people enter into orderly and predictable relationships with one another. Social order is assisted by the formation and acceptance of rules of group behavior, or **norms.** For example, a group norm may be "Never snitch on a friend" or "Men don't work at the office without a coat and tie." If new members join the group, they must learn and adhere to its norms. Failure to adopt these norms will make it difficult for a new member to form or retain the social ties and relationships integral to group participation.

Human beings are social animals. They rely on group memberships for everything from friendship to economic survival. Because of this, the groups in which people are involved form an important part of their personal biographies. Individual members can shape the character of their group, but the group's character also helps shape the thinking and behavior of its individual members. For example, inspirational or charismatic leaders (Weber, 1947) may give specific direction to a religious group, but participation in collective rituals and ceremonies helps members arouse one another's sense of group belonging and the desire to remain involved. Given the influence of groups, sociologists feel it is important to examine the types of groups in which people typically find themselves.

Primary Groups

Sociologists generally distinguish between two different types of groups, primary and secondary. The term **primary group** was introduced many years ago by sociologist Charles Horton Cooley (1929). Primary groups tend to be made up of a relatively small number of people who interact frequently face-to-face. Group members share important connections that bring them together, such as common kinship ties, school attendance, residential location, or employment at a workplace. Their frequent interaction gives rise to a sense of group identity and to the emergence of norms, which both guide members' behavior and contribute to group solidarity. The prototypical example of a primary group is the family. Primary groups can be a source of friendship, companionship, and support, yet they may also give rise to serious conflict. Because relationships within primary groups are often both binding and intense, these groups play a central role in people's everyday lives.

A classic study by sociologist Herbert Gans (1982) revealed the importance of primary groups to people's biographies. Gans was interested in looking at the everyday lives of white working-class families. He chose a run-down, low-income neighborhood in Boston's West End, considered a slum by city officials and planners (the West End neighborhood would later be torn down and its residents dispersed as part of "urban renewal"). Gans found that the lives of working-class people in the neighborhood revolved around what he termed a "peer group society." In Gans's words,

> The primary group is a peer group society because most of the West Enders' relationships are with peers, that is, among people of the same sex, age, and life-cycle status. (Gans, 1982: 37)

Members of primary groups typically have a good deal of face-to-face interaction and develop strong ties with one another over time. Here, a small group of close friends relaxes at a beach outing.

Males and females each had their own primary group peer affiliations, and these in turn were roughly divided by different ages and generations. Adult peer groups were primarily based on family and kinship. Members shared common interests and ethnic backgrounds (most were Italian Americans) and came together regularly. The adult peer group not only provided companionship and a sense of belonging; it was also a source of news and entertainment. It was a setting in which individuals could express their unique personalities and feel they were making a well-received contribution.

The opportunities for personal expression provided by the peer group society were in marked contrast to what the adult men, for example, experienced in their low-wage factory and service jobs. For them, the peer group was a place to escape to from the "outside world" of poorly paid, insecure employment. Given the nature of the jobs they could find, the men viewed work in highly utilitarian terms: It was necessary but not enjoyable, and it provided them with means to participate in the peer group society. For example, it enabled men to play the role of hosts at group get-togethers and to lay claim to the prestige associated with being successful providers and breadwinners.

According to Gans, for adult women the peer group society performed other functions. The women spent most of their free time and communicated most often with relatives and friends of the same sex; Gans felt that their emotional involvement with the peer group surpassed that with their husbands. He believed this was the case because of their families' very marginal and insecure economic position and the heavy stresses of working-class life. Faced with the ever-present possibility of losing a husband through illness or workplace accident, or through separation or divorce, the women looked to their same-sex peer group members for support that would be available at all times.

The peer group society Gans described also played a negative role. In some ways it encompassed and trapped its members, channeling their thinking and behavior along certain lines. For example, one norm of the peer group was that members focus on being liked and noticed within the group (*person orientation*). This orientation came at the expense of focusing on particular objectives such as pursuing a career or improving one's material circumstances (*object orientation*). Being object-oriented violated group norms because it involved detaching oneself from group life to focus time and attention outward in directions that did not support the peer group society. Object-oriented individuals were made to feel like traitors pursuing selfish aims. So, if a person wished to enjoy the benefits of the peer group society, he or she often had to suppress aspirations for involvement and success in the "outside world" that conflicted with the norm of person orientation.

The peer group, therefore, was alternately a comfort and a source of oppressive confinement. Given its benefits, along with the fact that it was linked heavily to family and kinship, the peer group society—as a primary group—could not be rejected by its members lightly.

The example provided by the working-class peer group society may lead to thinking about one's own primary group memberships. As a primary group, the peer group society revolved around intimate, face-to-face relationships. Each individual developed strong bonds with the others and could depend on the group for support. In return, each member was expected to adhere to the norms of the group. Expressing ideas not shared by others in the group could result in criticism and even rejection by the group's members. How do the features of primary groups of which you have been a member—at home, in high school or college, or at work—compare with those of the peer group society? What benefits or rewards have you gained from being a member of such primary groups? What disadvantages or costs have been associated with your involvement? The answers to such questions can help you assess the importance of primary groups in shaping your own life experiences and thus the ongoing composition of your biography.

Secondary Groups

Secondary groups are very different social phenomena from primary groups, although certainly they are as much a part of people's daily lives. In contrast to primary groups, secondary groups are usually larger, more formally structured, and formed for a purpose, such as accomplishing a certain task (providing fire protection) or achieving a particular goal (making a profit manufacturing and selling cars). Examples of secondary groups include schools, colleges, government agencies, military services, corporations, unions, and voluntary associations. (The latter are secondary groups in which members' involvement is a really a matter of choice, participation usually takes only a small portion of members' time, and commitment to the group and its purpose may be highly variable. The Girl Scouts and the National Rifle Association are examples.) Secondary groups vary in composition from relatively few members to thousands of members. The degree and intensity of interaction and personal involvement are ordinarily less than that found in a primary group.

Note, however, that primary groups frequently form as people become acquainted through participation in secondary groups, as is the case when a group of people become close friends at school or in the workplace. Indeed, the large size and impersonal nature of many secondary groups often prompts participants to form primary group relationships with others for the personal rewards and benefits these relationships can provide. Moreover, as we will see later in our discussion of informal organization within bureaucracies, the formation of primary groups can affect the functioning of secondary groups.

In contrast to a primary group, secondary group members may come and go; their emotional ties to the group are ordinarily not strong enough to make leaving a serious problem. A secondary group typically continues to accomplish its tasks or pursue its goals even as its membership changes. Individuals become members for a limited purpose and may use their membership in the secondary group to accomplish a personal objective. Even if people are not members of particular secondary groups that exist around them, they usually have some contact with such organizations and feel the impact of these groups' presence.

While employees of a large firm, members of the military, or students at a public university tend to be a heterogeneous collection of people, members of some secondary groups often have more in common than simply the fact of their group affiliation. In the example we describe below, that of a voluntary association, the members happen to have a great deal in common: class position, sex, and race.

In comparison to the amount of knowledge that sociologists have generated about the thinking and behavior of "ordinary people," such as those in the peer group society studied by Herbert Gans, much less is known about the everyday lives of U.S. society's elites. Affluence and power enable elites to have a great deal of privacy, and such persons have little incentive to admit researchers into their personal domains. Nevertheless, the research of sociologist G. William Domhoff (2002) has provided some data on elites (see also Kerbo, 2003). According to Domhoff, social and economic elites constitute an upper class in the United States whose members regularly interact and often intermarry. Their great wealth, high annual incomes, and privileged lifestyles distinguish them from members of other classes. Domhoff estimates that the upper class makes up no more than 0.5 percent of the U.S. population. It is also overwhelmingly white. Upper-class activities often include membership in private clubs (e.g., country clubs, hunt clubs, men's clubs, and women's clubs).

Exclusive private clubs that cater to the upper class are examples of secondary groups. It is extremely difficult for sociologists (or nonmembers generally) to gain access to them. However, Domhoff carried out extensive research on such clubs, and we draw on his work here. The example we use is the Bohemian Club of San Francisco, founded in 1872. For more than 100 years the club has provided a summer camp outside the city, one primarily attended by wealthy men, top corporate elites, and important political figures and government officials (Domhoff, 2002). Located on a 2,700-acre forest site called Bohemian Grove, the camp attracts as many as 2,500 men to its annual two-week summer session each July. The membership and guest lists have included most of those who have been president of the United States in past and recent decades, top military officials, as well as numerous chief executives and directors of the nation's largest corporate firms. Besides political and economic elites, some well-known celebrities and university intellectuals are usually in attendance.

Bohemian Grove provides a setting in which some of U.S. society's most powerful and influential men can come together privately once a year to engage in informal and off-the-record talk about business and politics, establish or reaffirm social relationships, engage in recreation, and be entertained. Participants reside and attend one another's dinners and parties in over 120 campsites or lodges with names like Cave Man, Owl's Nest, and Hill Billies. Over the course of the two weeks they swim, canoe, hike, play cards and dominoes, attend talks, and involve themselves in events that have become fraternitylike traditions at Bohemian Grove. Camp attendees act out lighthearted roles in amateur talent shows, participate in camper rituals, and dress up for large-scale, annual ceremonial spectacles with names like

"Cremation of Care." The latter, a camp opening ceremony, "involves the burning of an effigy named Dull Care, who symbolizes the burdens and responsibilities that these busy Bohemians now wish to shed temporarily. More than 250 Bohemians take part in the ceremony as priests, elders, boatmen, and woodland voices" (Domhoff, 2002: 52).

In Domhoff's view, such clubs contribute to the national cohesiveness of the upper class and tie its members together across geographic and institutional boundaries. In the case of Bohemian Grove, cohesiveness is facilitated by participants' retreat from their everyday activities, where they are sometimes at odds in their political and business dealings. In the camp, they relax in a setting that functions to promote a sense of collective upper-class brotherhood that clearly resembles a fraternity. Membership in the Bohemian Club is highly restrictive and both the club and the camp are off-limits to the public. This exclusivity adds to participants' feelings of being part of a very special in-group, as members of the upper class and their guests bond with one another through club activities.

The Bohemian Club is a voluntary organization and an example of a secondary group, in this case one that caters largely to white male members of the upper class (on private clubs catering to women of the upper class, see Kendall, 2002). The workings of different secondary groups influence people's biographies in a variety of ways. Apart from the makeup of their membership, the organizational forms that secondary groups take is of importance to sociologists. In the next section we discuss how experiences that people have participating in secondary groups can be affected by the group's bureaucratic or democratic structure.

Group Structure: Bureaucratic versus Democratic Organization

Secondary groups can be structured in different ways. In this section we focus on two particular organizational forms in which people may at times participate: bureaucratic and democratic organizations. People's lives are shaped in important respects by the structure of the organizations in which they are involved. Thus it matters whether a society is characterized more heavily by bureaucratic or by democratic organizations. Most societies contain a range of types of organizations, but some societies tend to be more bureaucratic or more democratic than others in their organizational makeup.

Bureaucratic Organization

The term **bureaucracy** is used generically by people complaining about an experience with a large, impersonal organization, often a business or a government office. People frequently refer to organizational "red tape" that interferes with getting things done or of inflexible "bureaucrats" who say things like "I just work here; I don't make the rules." Sociologists, however, use the term bureaucracy to refer to the way in which certain secondary groups are organized. Such groups may or may not be responsive to people's needs, but that is not their defining feature.

Features of Bureaucracy

As was mentioned in Chapter 1, the rise of bureaucratic forms of or- pp. 16–17 ganization was central to the thinking of German sociologist Max Weber, one of the European social thinkers of the late nineteenth and twentieth centuries whose ideas contributed to the development of contemporary sociology. Weber saw the spread of bureaucracy as a dominant or master trend in the Western world. In his writings, he identified five features of the ideal-type, or model, bureaucratic organization that continue to prove useful to sociologists as they analyze features of present-day society (Weber in Gerth and Mills, 1968):

1. The organization contains a clear-cut division of labor: Every member is responsible for particular tasks.
2. Authority is organized in a hierarchy: Everyone (except of course the individual at the top) reports to someone whose directives are considered legitimate and to be obeyed.
3. The activities of all members of the organization are governed by a set of formally established, written rules and regulations.
4. Members are to carry out their organizational responsibilities impartially and without the exercise of favoritism or bias toward others.
5. Recognition, rewards, and status in the organization are based upon meritorious performance.

Bureaucracy and Control in the Workplace

To some extent, most work settings are organized in accordance with the foregoing features. One might ask why this is the case. What functions does bureaucracy perform? In his widely acclaimed historical analysis addressing this question, Richard Edwards (1979) examined the evolution of work organizations in the United States. In his view, whereas significant changes in ways of organizing work have occurred over the last couple of centuries, the central issue facing employers has remained the same: how to get as much work as possible out of workers for the least amount of money. In Edwards's view, resolving this problem has required that employers deal with the issue of how workers are to be controlled.

Before the Industrial Revolution, work organizations were relatively small operations in which the "boss" ran the enterprise. Whether the owner or hired supervisors oversaw the work, power over workers was exercised personally and directly. Edwards termed this type of structure *simple control,* a form of organization that still persists today in small firms. In the late nineteenth and early twentieth centuries, as firm owners relied more on technologically advanced machinery and the assembly line became common, power over workers came to be exercised by the impersonal demands of technology. The machinery and other apparatus in the workplace limited the activities of each worker and dictated the pace of work. On an assembly line, for example, working too slowly quickly becomes apparent and laggards can then be disciplined. Edwards called this form of structure *technical control.* Technical control of workers still exists in many of today's factories, although automation and robotization have greatly reduced the proportion of the U.S. labor force employed in assembly-line settings.

During the twentieth century, as work organizations increased in size and the white-collar office sector grew, *bureaucratic control* became dominant in the workplace. Bureaucratic control operates by surrounding people with rules. Employers require that their workers conform to standardized job descriptions, and they evaluate employee job performance on checklists and rating forms. Of course, it is possible to create new job descriptions, alter old ones, and make judgments about job performance, but the power to do so is in the hands of those who occupy the top positions in the organizational hierarchy. The individuals who have the ability to make and change the organization's rules tend to be far removed from the average worker. This is particularly the case in large organizations. Under bureaucratic control, the power over workers wielded by top organization officials is masked. For it is the rules—not distant bosses—that workers experience as coercive and controlling. For many workers, one consequence of bureaucratic control is dissatisfaction and alienation (Ehrenreich, 2001; Fraser, 2001; Garson, 1994).

Even persons occupying managerial positions in bureaucratic work organizations are confined and controlled by the nature of the activities and relationships bureaucracy promotes. Sociologist Robert Jackall (1988) demonstrated this in his research on corporate managers. While corporate managers hold positions of substantial responsibility and receive generous financial remuneration, bureaucracy has important effects on their everyday lives. Here, Jackall sums up the impact of bureaucracy:

> Bureaucratic work shapes people's consciousness in decisive ways. . . . [It] regularizes people's experiences of time and indeed routinizes their lives by engaging them on a daily basis in rational, socially approved purposive action; it brings them into daily proximity with and subordination to authority, creating in the process upward-looking stances that have decisive social and psychological consequences . . . and it creates subtle measures of prestige and an elaborate status hierarchy that, in addition to fostering an intense competition for status, also makes the rules, procedures, social contexts, and protocols of an organization paramount psychological and behavioral guides. (Jackall, 1988: 5–6)

Jackall's interviews with corporate managers revealed that they were under pressure to conform to an organizational code of morality that often differed from their own. As one former corporate vice president put it, "What is right in the corporation is not what is right in a man's home or in his church. What is right in the corporation is what the guy above you wants from you. That's what morality is in the corporation" (Jackall, 1988: 6). Jackall's research suggests that conformity to an organization's code of morality (its workplace norms) is a key prerequisite for personal success in the world of corporate managers. Research on other categories of white-collar personnel in bureaucratic work organizations, such as persons in sales positions (Oakes, 1990), has revealed similar demands for conformity. On occasion, the corporate code of morality may be loose enough to allow shocking acts of large-scale corporate corruption and malfeasance, as illustrated by the revelations of illegal financial activities involving top officials at Enron and other large corporations in the early 2000s.

Bureaucracy and the Declining Power of Workers

In the past century a large percentage of the U.S. labor force has come to be employed by large, bureaucratic organizations—in both the public and the private sectors. For example, 15.5 percent of the labor force—more than 20 million people—work for agencies of government at all levels. Over 2 million work for the federal government alone (U.S. Bureau of Labor Statistics, 2001). Figure 4.1 illustrates the vast range of federal offices. Moreover, it has been estimated that 20 percent of our industrial labor force is employed by a mere 16 of the very largest U.S. corporations (Neubeck and Neubeck, 1997).

Relatively few employees have very much collective power within their own workplace. The organized labor movement, which traditionally worked to increase the power of workers vis-à-vis employers, has weakened in recent decades. Unions have been adversely affected by the elimination of many unionized industrial jobs and by a climate of employer hostility toward their concerns and activities. Unionized workers on average have higher pay and benefits, better working conditions, and more on-the-job protections of their rights than do nonunion workers. Today, however, unions represent less than 14 percent of the U.S. labor force, down from a peak of 35 percent in the mid-1950s (Rubin, 1996; Zweig, 2000). Moreover, the unionization rate is much higher among government workers today (37.5 percent) than among workers in the private sector (9.0 percent) where the vast majority of people are employed (U.S. Bureau of Labor Statistics, 2001).

The typical large, bureaucratic work organization discourages collective activity by workers through its complex reward structure: the substantial numbers of job titles, occupational levels, pay scales, and symbols of prestige that differentiate workers from one another. One feature of bureaucratic control, then, is the way in which it differentiates and divides people, making it very difficult for workers across an organization to be aware of the things they all have in common. White-collar and blue-collar workers, or professional and nonprofessional staff, often fail to realize that they share many of the same workplace problems, such as declining job security and difficulty getting the resources they need to do their work well.

The Bureaucratized Society

Bureaucracy is so common in U.S. society that many people can hardly imagine another way to organize human activity. Large bureaucratic organizations have come to pervade people's everyday lives (Jaffee, 2002). Their subtle influence extends outside the immediate workplace through the promotion of "corporate culture." The latter has encouraged the "McDonaldization" of our eating practices around corporate-designed foods and fast-food eating places, values emphasizing material consumption, and the routinization and rationalization of human activities in a wide range of other settings (Ritzer, 2000, 2002).

Sociologist Gary Fine's provocative study of Little League baseball (1987), for example, suggests that even this popular youth sport has fallen to bureaucratization. Little League's bureaucratic organization no doubt helped to facilitate and has been reinforced by the expansion in size and league activities since Fine completed his study (see www.littleleague.org). Little League, Inc., an organization with mil-

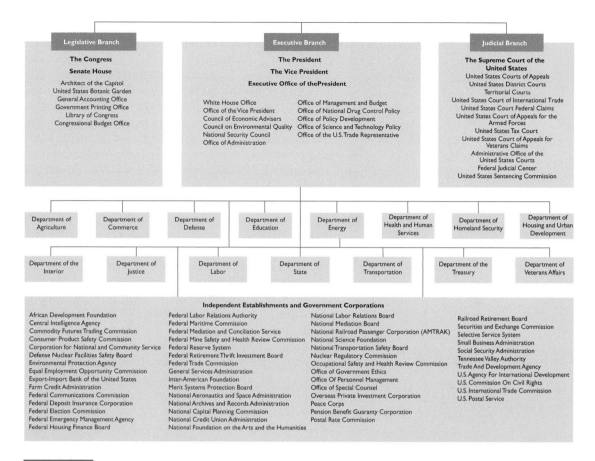

FIGURE 4.1 **Branches, Departments, and Agencies of the Federal Bureaucracy** In the United States, many of the functions of federal, state, and local governments are carried out through bureaucratic organizations. The federal bureaucracy is not only very large, but also highly complex. (Source: Office of Federal Registrar, *United States Government Manual, 2002/2003.* Washington, D.C.: U.S. Government Printing Office, 2002, p. 21.)

lions of dollars in assets, operates under a charter awarded by the federal government. Under this charter, Little League is considered to be a quasi-governmental agency whose revenues are exempt from taxes. The charter calls for Little League to file an annual report on its finances and philosophy with the U.S. House of Representatives. Little League is also required to "shape its mission to the needs of the United States government (particularly in dealing with foreign leagues)" (Fine, 1987: 6). Presumably, this means accepting the responsibility of "promoting America" as part of its involvement in international competitions (Fine, 1987: 261).

As of 2001, there were 7,330 local Little Leagues with almost 2.4 million baseball players, along with an additional 362,000 softball players (www.littleleague.org). Fine characterizes local leagues as "branches of a large bureaucratic organization" (1987: 7). Each league has a board of directors to oversee its operations, coaches to

Bureaucratization of organizations can even extend to children's play activities. The Little League, in which many children participate as baseball and softball players, is organized along bureaucratic lines.

supervise the children and teach them how to play, umpires to interpret and enforce the official rules, and players who are expected to occupy their assigned positions and perform well. The entire operation of the game—from the length of the basepaths to the number of innings to be played—is governed by decisions made by Little League, Inc. With its division of labor, hierarchy of authority, rules and regulations, and recognition based on merit, Little League baseball is an expression of the master trend toward bureaucratization. In the realm of sports, this master trend is especially evident at the professional level—particularly baseball, basketball, hockey, and football—which are essentially activities run by corporations in which players are employees. Many of those who play such professional sports (as well as those who umpire games) have unionized and on occasion even gone out on strike to assert their collective interests as workers.

Writing in the early twentieth century, German social thinker Robert Michels (1962) argued that bureaucratization of human activities was inevitable. He thought that the inevitability of bureaucracy was virtually a social law (much like a law of physics). In Michels's view, organization life is subject to an **iron law of oligarchy:** All organizations, even those that purport to be organized in accordance with democratic ideals, tend to be ruled by a few. According to Michels, persons who come to occupy an elite organizational status—whether by appointment or election—come to enjoy the special benefits and privileges associated with it. They find they have access to knowledge, resources, prestige, and powers that rank-and-file organizational members lack. Consequently, such elites are likely to manipulate and control others in ways calculated to allow them to retain their positions. Even democratically elected elites are said to act in such ways, doing whatever it takes to gain reelection. In Michels's view, organizational elites seek to protect their own interests over and above the interests of other organizational members and those of the organization as a whole. But, as the next section outlines, there is reason to doubt bureaucracy's inevitability and the existence of such an "iron law."

Democratic Organization

If bureaucracy involves control *of* people, **democracy** involves control *by* people. In organizations structured in accordance with bureaucratic principles, most members have little or no power to shape the policies that affect them; in those structured along democratic lines, group members are empowered to participate in shaping these policies precisely because they will be affected. Democratizing decision-making processes in already existing organizations may be considered a radical idea in a society whose organizational life tends to be highly bureaucratized. When people demand a say in decisions that affect their lives, they are demanding power. In the United States, just as in virtually every other nation in the world, such demands can be occasions for sharp conflict when made in an organization where power has traditionally been monopolized by a few top members who are "in charge."

Democratic Workplace Cooperatives

Despite Robert Michels's view that people are subject to an iron law of oligarchy that makes bureaucracy inevitable, work organizations do exist in the United States and in many other societies that incorporate principles of democratic organization. They are intriguing not only because they are relatively uncommon, but because they contradict the notion that the only way to successfully organize work is to institute a bureaucratic system or some other form of top-down control of workers (Melman, 2001).

Sociologists Joyce Rothschild and J. Allen Whitt studied democratically controlled workplace cooperatives in the United States. Such cooperatives have a history going back to the late eighteenth century. Rothschild and Whitt suggest that since the late 1960s there has been a new wave of creation of such organizations as "alternative newspapers, arts and handicraft shops, food co-ops, publishing houses, restaurants, health clinics, legal collectives, natural foods bakeries, auto repair cooperatives, and retail stores" (1986: 11; see also GEO, 2001). Such cooperatives are organized at the local, grassroots level, are small in size (often 10 to 20 members), and frequently arise from members' commitment to progressive social change. Their nonbureaucratic organization typically reflects political values that view personal empowerment and involvement in the democratic process as fundamental goals.

Cooperatives are usually organized as a **direct democracy,** in which all members participate in decision making on issues of concern. Their size makes this possible. Direct democracy contrasts sharply to the system of political governance in the United States, which is often called a **representative democracy.** Ideally, the tens of millions of U.S. voters elect others (the president, representatives, senators) to make decisions for them that serve their interests. Those elected are said to be put in office to represent the "will of the people." But this representative democracy chronically falls short of the ideal, and many of "the people" often feel that their interests are going unmet. In contrast, organizations set up to allow direct democracy, in theory at least, provide opportunities for all group members to express their needs and work with others in getting these needs met.

Features of the Democratic Workplace

Just as the ideal-type, or model, bureaucracy described by Max Weber has certain key features, the workplace cooperatives studied by Rothschild and Whitt had a set of common characteristics as well:

1. Power is shared within the membership as a whole, and decision making involves discussion, negotiation, and consensus.

2. Rules are minimal; members are assumed to be capable of using discretion and common sense in conducting their activities.

3. There is a sense of community. People do not limit their interactions to the work tasks at hand but feel free to develop close relationships with one another.

4. The division of labor is minimal. Members share their knowledge and take turns rotating jobs when possible.

5. Material rewards are secondary to those otherwise derived from involvement in the group. Just as there is no hierarchy of authority, rewards are shared equally or nearly so.

From this list one might think that cooperatives are utopian forms of organization. But Rothschild and Whitt's research indicates that their members must be ready to confront challenges. For example, democratic decision making can be time-consuming. Differences among group members can at times be very intense and disturbing. Personality characteristics that may mesh well in bureaucratically controlled areas of life, such as a need for authority figures or an inability to make decisions in the face of ambiguity, may create problems when they unexpectedly emerge in a democratic setting. Majority rule under democratic decision making is not a protection against poor decisions. And cooperatives may face external challenges—legal, economic, political, and cultural. Some fail because of internal and/or external challenges or conflicts that cannot be overcome. But many do not fail, and they may often provide enormously rich experiences for their members.

Democratically-run work organizations at times find ways to cooperate with and help to sustain one another. For example, in the San Francisco Bay Area, over 55 work cooperatives ranging from clinics to cafés participate in the Network of Bay Area Worker Collectives (GEO, 2001). In some instances, cooperatives' activities cross national borders. A U.S.-based cooperative, Equal Exchange, functions as part of an international cooperative network. This organization purchases coffee from small democratic work cooperatives in Latin America and Africa and sells it through retail establishments—including other cooperatives—in the United States (see www.equalexchange.com).

Some of the most noteworthy examples of workplace cooperatives are outside the United States. In Japan, older workers who have been laid off and are unable to find work using their experience and skills have formed cooperatives, as have retired workers. Income is shared among the workers, and they are able to have health insurance and other benefits important to elders (Evanoff, 2001).

Although most cooperatives are small in terms of the number of workers involved, some are quite large. In such instances, combinations of direct and representative democracy may be necessary to maintain workers' participation in democratic decision making. In the Basque region of Spain, workers own and control large-scale manufacturing cooperatives in the industrial city of Mondragón; they produce stoves, refrigerators, steel, and other goods for an international market (Cheney, 2002). In the state of Kerala, in southern India, an industrial cooperative operates with over 30,000 workers who produce packaged food and tobacco products (Isaac, Franke, and Raghavan, 1998).

These examples suggest that work organizations and other secondary groups do not have to be structured in accordance with bureaucratic principles in order to operate effectively. The issue of how organizations are to be structured is really an issue of the distribution of power—who will have it, and how it will be exercised.

How Bureaucratic and Democratic Organizations Affect People's Lives

Those whose lives are heavily encompassed by highly bureaucratized organizations will behave and feel very differently than those who conduct their lives primarily in democratically organized settings. Bureaucratic organizations expect people to accommodate to their will, to become objects to whom things happen. Highly bureaucratized structures are likely to discourage spontaneity, innovative ideas, or creative group efforts that may call the status quo into question. The more a society is pervaded by bureaucracy, the more its organizational structures exert pressure on and control over the thinking and behavior of its members.

Within democratic organizations people can more easily become subjects who make events happen. Democratic forms of organization can empower participants, providing them with degrees of freedom to decide how to conduct their own affairs. Persons who feel alienated and disgruntled when denied a say in what is going on around them may find that democratic structures open up new opportunities for the expression of their personalities and the achievement of personal goals. This is not to say that in democratic organizations "anything goes" and there are no restraints on members. Participants in democratic structures usually arrive at, if they do not start out with, rules of operation and social norms as to the range of behavior and thinking they are willing to tolerate. These rules and norms, however, may periodically be discussed, criticized, and changed by rank-and-file organization members, something that is unlikely to occur in bureaucratic work organizations that are run from the top down.

Today, people's lives often involve a mixture of daily experiences with bureaucratic and democratic organizations. A person may work in an office, follow the office rules, fulfill the narrow set of duties outlined in a job description, and jump whenever the boss calls. But outside of work that same person may attend an evening meeting of the local parent–teacher organization, functioning as a democratically elected officer; participate with peers in a lunch-hour gathering of a free-wheeling book discussion group that was spontaneously organized; accept an invitation to hear (and decide whether to work on behalf of) a political party candidate; and spend a weekend hunting with fellow members of the collectively owned and operated Fish, Fur and Feather Club. While people's biographies are affected by participation in bureaucratic organizations, democratic structures shape their biographies in important ways as well.

In societies whose overall mode of governance is dictatorial or authoritarian, political elites may use military and civilian bureaucracies to monitor and control many aspects of people's lives. In such societies, people at times rebel and seek to create democratic organizational structures. Most nations in Latin America, a region long characterized by oppressive military dictatorships, have made a transition to greater democratic rule in recent years in response to popular social movements and political upheavals. Nations in eastern Europe and the former Soviet Union were shaken apart by social movements that were at least in part a reaction to the concentrated bureaucratic power of their respective states. The democracy movement in the People's Republic of China, brutally crushed in 1989 by tanks in Beijing's Tiananmen Square, will very likely reappear. Resisting bureaucratic control is one way in which many people have sought to gain more say over the directions in which their own biographies will go.

Informal Organization

Max Weber's classic model focused on bureaucracy's formal characteristics (its hierarchy of authority, rules and regulations, etc.). Yet anyone who has worked in a bureaucratic setting knows that informal relationships spring up among groups of employees. Often these relationships have little or nothing to do with the bureaucratically prescribed division of labor or people's official job descriptions. Sociologists use the term **informal organization** to refer to social structures that emerge spontaneously as people interact and develop interpersonal ties within bureaucratic settings. Informal organization is evidence for the existence of primary groups within a bureaucratically organized workplace.

Some Functions of Informal Organization

The importance of informal organization was first noted in pathbreaking organizational research conducted way back in the 1930s (Roethlisberger and Dickson, 1939). Researchers at Western Electric Company's Hawthorne Works in Chicago, where electrical components were assembled, were interested in helping the firm's management increase levels of production. The researchers assumed that one way to do this was to alter working conditions. They selected a group of workers and observed their reactions to changes in conditions, such as the amount of light in the workroom and the timing of rest breaks. But no matter what the researchers changed, they found no consistent relationship between workplace conditions and worker productivity.

The researchers continued their experiment. Finally they realized that the workers themselves created mutually accepted norms that guided their rates of production. According to management, these norms resulted in less than the optimal amount being produced. The researchers tried to understand this restriction of output. It turned out that the workers were holding back their productivity out of fear. They believed that if management knew they could produce more, it would increase their production quotas without increasing their pay or would decide fewer workers were needed and lay some off. This research was taking place during the Depression of the 1930s, a time of extremely widespread unemployment and scarcity of jobs.

Within their group, the workers denounced and ridiculed those who broke ranks and produced above the norm, calling them "rate-busters" and "speed kings." At the same time, a worker who lagged too far below the norm was criticized as a "chiseler," who could possibly draw unwanted attention from management. Since most workers were concerned with earning and maintaining the respect and regard of their peers, few chose to deviate from the pressures to conform. The researchers concluded that informal relationships are important in influencing productivity levels and that the output of any individual worker should be considered a function of the informal organization in which that person participates.

Sociologists have conducted numerous studies in a variety of work settings and found informal organization to be operating and demanding conformity to its norms (Jaffee, 2002). At times, informal relationships actually facilitate work accomplishment, particularly when bureaucratic rules get in the way of handling problems or when established channels stifle communications that are important to organizational functioning. Workers may informally pass along knowledge to one another that enables work to be done more safely and efficiently than official bureaucratic procedures would allow. In some settings informal organization results in activities that distract workers from the mind-numbing nature of their labor and thus actually contributes to their productivity.

While many work organizations are bureaucratically organized, workers often spontaneously develop their own patterns of informal organization and primary group relationships. These manufacturing company workers share a laugh during a break in the workplace routine.

Managers and workers obviously occupy very different positions in bureaucratic work organizations. As such, they often have very different perspectives on the work to be done and on the respective roles each should play in the process. Based on in-depth interviews, sociologist Randy Hodson found that workers are often motivated in the workplace by their own agendas rather than those of management. While informal organization may facilitate organizational operations, workers may also choose not to comply with managerial directives. Their behaviors can include resistance to being managed, as well as autonomous, often creative efforts to control and structure the work they must do (Hodson, 2001).

Workers' Resistance to Management

Worker resistance to being managed can take the form of disrupting and sabotaging bureaucratic routine (Hodson, 1991, 1995; Sprouse, 1992). Let us look at two dramatic examples drawn from the auto industry in the latter part of the twentieth century. In the first example, workers actively resisted management's efforts to plan their role in production. In the second example, workers rebelled in similar ways against a new supervisor's efforts to "shape things up" and enforce previously neglected bureaucratic rules. Auto company managements have sought to overcome the types of disruptive worker behavior contained in these examples and increase control over workers by replacing more and more of them with automated and computerized production machinery, including mechanical robots, and increasing bureaucratization of the production process. Nonetheless, these studies demonstrate that resistance to bureaucracy is possible through informal organization in the workplace.

When Bill Watson (1971) took a temporary summer job in a Detroit auto factory, he was overwhelmed by the frenetic human activity demanded by the constantly moving assembly line. Workers resembled robots, tied to their specialized function and place along the line. The assembly line ran inexorably at a pace that always seemed just slightly too fast. It seemed to dominate all human social interaction, or what little was possible given the incredible noise. Yet Watson quickly became aware, on the basis of participant observation in this work setting, that not all was what it seemed on the surface.

Watson found that the workers were engaged in daily and often overt struggles with management over everything from working conditions to the quality of the autos being produced. The struggles were made possible and carried out through an informal organization consisting of networks of "fictive kin": chains of friends and acquaintances across the auto plant who kept up channels of communication, did favors for one another, and looked for ways to cooperate in subverting management. The fictive-kin network extended outside the plant, through the taverns and bars surrounding it, and into local working-class neighborhoods where many of the auto workers resided.

Workers used the fictive-kin network to establish their own rest break system. Workers in different parts of the plant would find ways to sabotage and break down the assembly line at a specified hour on a given day, allowing everyone time to talk, read, or move about the plant to visit friends. When workers were asked to assemble engines out of parts known to be defective, the fictive-kin network rolled into action. Assembly workers either broke parts or misassembled the engines, and workers responsible for inspection cooperated by rejecting the engines and pulling them off the line.

The fictive-kin network made possible a great deal of organized theft. Workers would distract security guards at plant gates while peers smuggled out tools and auto parts. Similar organized distraction allowed workers to smuggle items into the plant. Chaise lounges were brought in, hoisted through ceiling traps in the bathrooms, and placed on the roof. Workers who could manage to "disappear," protected by false excuses given to supervisors by peers, were often able to escape the racket, heat, and oil-filled air by hiding on the roof for brief periods.

The summer heat in the plant was debilitating. Workers in one area responded by holding sporadic fire hose fights; participants were protected by a network of lookouts who warned them whenever supervisors were coming. For a while those involved wore their wives' shower caps to work, a symbol which management could not fathom but which brought glee to coworkers across the plant.

One of management's bureaucratic rules stipulated that workers had to cease work 10 minutes before their shift was over in order to wash their hands. Workers felt that this was a waste of time, since they could wash their hands in less than 10 minutes. Using the fictive-kin network, they agreed to wash for only a few minutes, line up at the exit door, howl the sound of the shift whistle, and proceed to charge out early. For a time the supervisors were unable to mobilize enough counterforce to stop them.

Efforts to enforce conformity to bureaucratic rules among workers who have devised their own ways of accomplishing mind-numbing work may likewise foster rebellion. Ben Hamper, a riveter on a General Motors assembly line, describes workers' feisty reaction to a new supervisor's efforts in this regard:

Enter the new boss, a self-proclaimed "troubleshooter." He had been enlisted to groom the rivet line into a more docile outpost . . . With a tight grip on the whip, the new bossman started riding the crew. No music. No Rivet Hockey. No horseplay. No drinking. No card playing. No working up the line. No leaving the department. No doubling up. No this, no that. No questions asked. No way. After three nights of this imported bullyism, the boys had had their fill. Frames began sliding down the line minus parts. Rivets became crosseyed. Guns mysteriously broke down. The repairmen began shipping the majority of the defects, unable to keep up with the repair load. Sabotage was rather drastic; however it was an effective way of getting the point across. We simply had no other recourse. Sometimes these power-gods had to be reminded that it was we, the workers, who kept the place runnin'. . . This new guy was nobody's dummy. He could see it all slippin' away, his goon tactics workin' against him. He pulled us all aside and suggested that we return to our old methods. (Hamper, 1992: 206)

Do these workers appear irrational? And whatever happened to the old-fashioned work ethic?

Consider the context in which they are made to labor: Assembly-line systems of production are designed by management to leave workers with very little or no say over what they will produce, how it will be produced, the pace of production, and the quality of the end product. Job dissatisfaction and alienation among assembly-line workers tends to be high. Yet, while assembly lines minimize workplace freedom, U.S. society simultaneously values democracy and individual rights. The behavior of the autoworkers described by Watson and Hamper might be said to represent one expression of the fundamental contradiction between bureaucratic control and democratic values, in this case through the medium of informal organization.

Organizational memberships help to shape people's biographies, but so do the social networks in which people participate. These networks often involve relationships and ties that link the primary and secondary groups with which people are affiliated to other such groups.

Social Networks

Some 40 years ago, social psychologist Stanley Milgram published an article in which he asked the question, "Starting with any two people in the world, what is the probability that they will know one another?" Taking the U.S. population as a case in point, his answer was that there was a chance of 1 in 200,000. Milgram presented a model showing it was highly probable statistically that any two people in the United States could be linked up through a range of 2 to10 intermediary acquaintances (Milgram, 1967). Milgram's article stimulated research into his claims and may have prompted some sociologists to take a greater interest in the subject of **social networks.** Networks can be described as the complex patterns of social relationships and ties to others in which individuals are caught up.

Strong and Weak Network Ties

Sociologist Mark Granovetter (1973) was among the first to stress the importance of distinguishing between "strong" and "weak" ties. Some ties are interpersonally

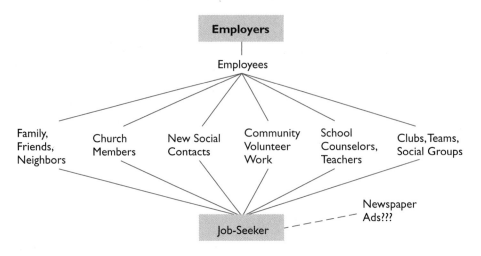

FIGURE 4.2 **The Social Network to Employment** In searching for jobs, individuals who must rely on help-wanted ads in newspapers are likely to be at a disadvantage when compared to those who are able to make their employment needs known and learn of job openings through social networks in which they are involved.

strong, as in the case of primary groups. Strong ties develop, for example, among family members and friends. Other ties are weak, as with casual acquaintances and people to whom we might have indirect ties through relatives or friends. Ties that are weak are often typical of our relationships with many others who are in the secondary groups of which we are members. Weak ties may also link us to people in primary and secondary groups other than those to which we belong. They can connect us to people who move in more distant social circles. With computerized communication linkages available through the Internet, we can even develop weak ties with people living on other continents.

The importance of social networks, and strong versus weak ties, has been underscored in research into how people find jobs. Newspaper job listings turn out to be far less important in successfully locating employment than the networks in which people are enmeshed (Montgomery, 1992). Figure 4.2 illustrates the relative importance of personal ties in obtaining employment.

Networks function, in effect, as a form of **social capital**—a crucial social resource that all people possess to a greater or lesser degree. Success in finding jobs has been found to depend not only on having access to social networks and on their size, but on the relative proportion of weak and strong ties which one's networks contain. In general, if people have to rely most heavily or entirely on strong ties (family, friends), they run out of job-locating assistance very quickly. Those with extensive weak ties (acquaintances, indirect links to friends of friends or to members of other groups) are much more advantaged in this regard. Weak ties, then, have been found to be indispensable in exposing people to a wider range of job information and opportunities (Montgomery, 1992).

Networks and Social Advantage

People differ in the degree to which they possess social capital—in this case access to networks and to weak or strong interpersonal ties. But they differ as well as to the relative advantages they possess in terms of what they can achieve through activating such ties and networks. Indeed, variation in social network possession, use, and pay-off occurs rather systematically along the lines of race and ethnicity, class, and gender. The affluent, men, and whites have more extensive, richer, and varied networks than do the less affluent or poor, women, and people of color. The latter populations also have fewer weak ties and tend to rely more on strong ties for help with job searches, job advancement, and attainment of higher earnings and bonuses (Ling, 2000).

Using women as an example, researchers have found that those who must take on the primary responsibility for child rearing (especially of very young children) have smaller social networks and fewer ties than men or women without such responsibilities (Munch et al., 1997). Women engaged in care giving are drawn more heavily into relationships with family and friends, while their male partners are sustaining and developing their ties outside these circles. Likewise, sex segregation in the labor force means that women who work outside the home tend to develop ties on the job with those in lower paying occupations like their own, while men are more likely to develop ties with other men who hold similarly higher paying positions. Differential access to social networks and the nature of the ties in these networks contribute to the difficulty that women face in competing for jobs on an equal basis with men in the labor force (Ling, 2000).

In short, the networks available to those who are already privileged help them to sustain that privilege. As sociologist Nan Ling put it:

> Resource-rich networks are characterized by relative richness not only in quantity but in kind—resource heterogeneity . . . Members of such networks enjoy access to information from and influence in diverse socioeconomic strata and positions. In contrast, members in resource-poor networks share a relatively restricted variety of information and influence. (Ling, 2000: 787)

Insofar as the social networks in which people of color, nonaffluent people, and women participate are resource-poor, this lack of social capital poses invisible but very concrete barriers to achievement, upward mobility, and social equality.

The statuses and roles, groups, organizations, and social networks into which people's lives are woven are in actuality somewhat fragile, requiring individual and collective acquiescence and collusion in order to persist. People can and do choose to challenge or change social structures within and through which they relate to one another, thus contributing to the dynamic quality of what would otherwise be extremely stagnant social arrangements.

CHAPTER SUMMARY

1. Social structure, the organization of recurrent and patterned social relationships, provides the framework within and through which human beings relate to one another. Micro-level social structure involves social relationships based on

interaction between small numbers of individuals. Midlevel social structure refers to larger webs of social relationships.

2. Individuals occupy many different social positions and are involved in a variety of micro- and midlevel social structures. The social positions or statuses that people occupy, and the roles they are expected to perform, organize and define their participation in groups, organizations, and social networks. Statuses and roles may restrict individuals' activities as well as provide opportunities for people to explore their talents and capabilities.

3. A status is a social position occupied by an individual. An achieved status is entered into based on an individual's opportunities and decisions. In contrast, an ascribed status is beyond an individual's real control and is often determined at birth. A master status is so socially important to some that it overrides other statuses in terms of how that person may be treated. Some master statuses are unwanted by those who occupy them, but are imposed by dominant groups in positions of power.

4. Statuses are accompanied by roles, or sets of expectations as to how those occupying a particular social position are to behave. Individuals may find that a role they are expected to play has contradictory demands, leading them to experience role strain. People may also experience role conflicts, as when different roles or sets of roles carry competing expectations. Such strains and conflicts can prove stressful to the individuals involved.

5. Unlike social aggregates or collections of individuals with no real interpersonal ties, social groups are based on recurrent interaction and established social relationships. Individuals participate in many social groups during the course of their lives and are often participants in a variety of groups simultaneously. All groups have rules or norms of behavior to which members are expected to conform.

6. Groups may be either primary or secondary. Primary groups are smaller in size and may entail more frequent and informal face-to-face interaction with other group members than secondary groups. The secondary groups in which people participate are likely to be organized around one of two basic principles: bureaucracy or democracy. To the degree that organizations are bureaucratic, individuals are likely to feel that they are objects to whom things happen. In contrast, members of democratic organizations feel more like actors empowered to shape the social scene.

7. Most workplaces in U.S. society are organized in accordance with the features of bureaucracy, one of which is a formal hierarchy of authority. Bureaucracy calls for top-down control of workplace activities and its spread has contributed to the declining power of workers. Bureaucracy in the workplace is not inevitable. Democratic workplace cooperatives exist, proving that workplaces need not be subject to oligarchy or rule by a few. Nonetheless, many arenas of social life in U.S. society reflect the strong influence of bureaucratization.

8. Members of bureaucratic organizations frequently form or enter into primary group relationships within the organizational setting. Referred to as expressions of informal organization, such relationships within bureaucratic workplaces may serve to offset bureaucracy's oppressive tendencies and even empower workers to actively resist top-down control.

9. People's access to and participation in social networks is a crucial social resource or form of social capital. Network ties may be weak or strong. Those who have the most numerous, diverse, and rich network connections are typically people who are privileged by virtue of class, race or ethnicity, or gender. The social networks in which people are involved help determine their life chances, including opportunities for employment and upward mobility.

THINKING CRITICALLY

1. Sociologists believe that the thinking and behavior of youths are strongly influenced both by their families and by the peer groups to which they belong. Use examples to characterize the influence these two primary groups have on a teenager. Does their relative influence change over time? How so?

2. Consider the features of the ideal-type, or model, bureaucracy that German sociologist Max Weber identified. Apply these features to an organization for which you have worked. How does the organization resemble the ideal type, and how does it differ?

3. We have said that bureaucracy is extremely common in U.S. society. What arguments could be made for and against organizing many more of our secondary groups, such as schools and workplaces, along democratic principles? What do you see as the obstacles to doing so?

4. Think about the various social roles you occupy and the behavioral expectations associated with these roles. In what situations do you experience role strain or role conflict? How successful are you, usually, in resolving it? Why?

5. The "Social Forces/People's Lives" reading describes a young mixed-race couple who sometimes face problems when others treat their skin color as a master status. Do people single out a particular ascribed status of yours (e.g., race, ethnicity, gender, sexual orientation) and consider it more definitive of "who and what you are" than any of your other personal characteristics? When do you notice this occurring? How does this affect you?

KEY TERMS

achieved status, *(83)*
ascribed status, *(83)*
bureaucracy, *(93)*
democracy, *(98)*
direct democracy, *(99)*
group, *(89)*
informal organization, *(102)*
iron law of oligarchy, *(98)*
master status, *(84)*

micro-level social structure, *(82)*
midlevel social structure, *(82)*
norms, *(89)*
primary group, *(89)*
representative democracy, *(99)*
role conflict, *(86)*

role set, *(88)*
role strain, *(85)*
secondary group, *(91)*
social aggregate, *(88)*
social capital, *(106)*
social networks, *(105)*
social role, *(85)*
social structure, *(82)*
status, *(83)*

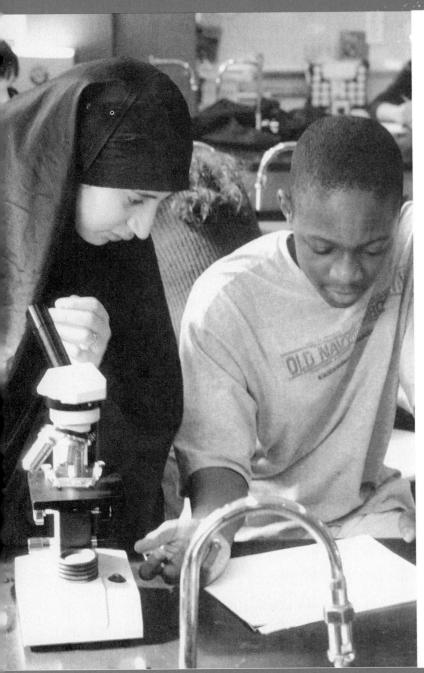

Chapter Five

Culture

In Western societies people marry one spouse at a time, whereas in many African and Asian societies marriage to several spouses simultaneously is not unusual. Western families commonly contain two or more children; but in China, state-enforced policies have limited families to one child. Women in Western societies take their freedom of movement for granted; women in Saudi Arabia are not even permitted to drive; and women in Taliban-controlled Afghanistan were not permitted to hold jobs, attend school, or leave home unescorted by a male family member. Dogs and cats are pets in Western societies, not meals; cows may be food but are not regarded as sacred objects, as they are among Hindus in India. These varied social practices are part of what is called culture. Where do these patterns of social practices come from, and why are they different in different societies?

When sociologists conventionally use the term **culture,** they are generally referring to a shared way of life among the members of a society. Culture is an agreement among a society's members about appropriate behavior, values, beliefs, history and heritage, rituals that should be respected and observed, and so on. The members of a society share a way of life described by a set of blueprints that show "what must be done, ought to be done, should be done, may be done, and must not be done" (Williams, 1965: 23). These blueprints are learned understandings of acceptable and expected patterns of behaviors. But who decides what these patterns are?

Karl Marx and Friedrich Engels noted that "the ideas of the ruling class are in every epoch the ruling ideas" (1970: 64). In their view, those who control the production of material wealth in a society also control the production of knowledge, as well as systems of ideas (or **ideology**) and insight, and in this way control the production of an entire way of life. Thus, a society is highly likely to create a culture that justifies reinforces, and reproduces the privileges, advantages, and power of its ruling class.

Antonio Gramsci (1971), writing around 1927, expanded this insight with his notion of **cultural hegemony:** The ideas and values of the dominant class are diffused throughout society's institutions and imposed on society's less powerful members. Since the members of the dominant class enjoy privileged access to its institutions, as well as to the media, they are in a position to promote the values that support and legitimize their privileged or dominant position. That position also enables them to tolerate only those dissenting viewpoints that do not fundamentally challenge the existing order and to squelch any views that do. The dominant members of society are thus able to define the boundaries of debate and discussion, thereby encouraging the incorporation of their ideologies into the thinking of subordinate members. Culture, then, can be a powerful influence on people's behaviors by restricting their actions and thoughts within "safe" ranges that do not seriously undermine the existing order.

continued

The provocative observations of Marx, Engels, and Gramsci challenge the common assumption that cultures are little more than a blend of the shared contributions of many different groups. Their analysis, therefore, raises several questions:

- Is it true that those who control wealth and production also control the culture?
- If so, how is diversity possible? What do all or most members of society have in common?
- Is the individual powerless to alter the dominant culture, or do individual and collective efforts make a difference?
- How successful are different groups in gaining widespread acceptance for their ideas?
- To what degree and in what ways can individuals and minorities resist the ideas of dominant groups within society?

Conventionally, sociologists treat culture as a relatively static entity handed down from one generation to another with little or no significant resistance and only superficial modifications. But another way to view culture is as a contested terrain characterized by an ongoing dynamic process of resistance and change: People may challenge both prevailing definitions of acceptable and appropriate behaviors and existing social arrangements.

- Who has the power to determine the elements of culture?
- How do the dominant groups in society convey their cultural perspectives and how do others convey challenges to those perspectives?

In this chapter we explore these questions by examining the components of culture, including norms, values, sanctions, language, subcultures, and countercultures.

Norms

When you come into a classroom, you generally know how to behave. You must sit down, open a notebook, and have a pen or pencil ready to take notes. You know that you should not play a boom box or chat on a cell phone during class, you should raise your hand to speak, and you should not swear at the teacher or stand up and shout at friends across the room during a lecture. And you're aware that you should wear clothing to class. How do you know all this without receiving a written list of rules from each individual teacher?

Norms are standards that define the obligatory and expected behaviors of people in various situations. They reflect a society's beliefs about correct and incorrect behaviors. Once these behaviors become second nature, members of society do not have to consciously analyze every situation and decide what their appropriate actions ought to be. Norms also can inhibit the type of thinking that might result in challenges to the dominant members of society. For example, the norms defining appropriate classroom behavior reduce the chances that a student will challenge the teacher's authority in class. Similarly, norms served for generations to inhibit the idea that women and African Americans in the United States could challenge their disadvantaged position in society (we discuss how this situation changed later in the chapter).

On the other hand, norms also help society control inappropriate or harmful behaviors. For example, until very recently, sexual harassment of women was widely perceived as normative, something women had to learn to live with and endure. Norms are now beginning to define such behavior as inappropriate and unacceptable. Similarly, driving under the influence of alcohol and drugs is now normatively defined as unacceptable, as are other harmful behaviors such as assault, rape, murder, and drug trafficking. And smoking in public places is increasingly frowned upon, if not defined as illegal in some settings.

Normative indoctrination, or the teaching of norms to individuals, is so successful that people often are taken by surprise when they encounter behaviors that do not conform to prevailing norms. That is, when people's unconscious expectations for behavior are suddenly violated, they experience **culture shock.** For example, on one episode of the popular television show *Survivor,* contestants ate live beetle larvae and roasted rats. The revulsion viewers expressed illustrated the collective culture shock at having to confront eating norms that contradict those that are commonly unexamined and taken for granted. People often remain equally unaware of the norms about physical beauty until they see someone whose face is disfigured. Such a person is considered "ugly," less than valuable, and frequently isolated (Hawkesworth, 2001; Hughes, 1999). In some cases, people may audibly gasp, look away with revulsion, or even scream when confronted with severe facial disfigurement. In other cases, individuals with facial disfigurements are likely to be stared at, pitied, scorned, discriminated against, or made the object of derision.

Culture shock can also be seen in the way some people react to homosexuality. People are largely unconscious of the social assumption that heterosexuality is the only legitimate basis of sexual relationships. Yet when confronted with members of the same sex kissing or openly expressing physical attraction, people may react with shock, revulsion, anger, derision, ridicule, discrimination, or violence. For example, more than half of the public television stations in the United States refused to air the PBS program *Tongues Untied,* about African American homosexuals. In its listing of the broadcast, *TV Guide* warned that the subject matter was not suitable for all audiences. *TV Guide* does not always post such warnings for sexually explicit programs involving heterosexuals. Indeed, fairly explicit heterosexual interactions occur daily on network afternoon dramas, but the program listings appear without warnings.

Culture shock may be a reflection of **ethnocentrism,** in which one's own culture is held to be the standard against which all other cultures are evaluated. Here, the individual not only notices the differences between cultures but ranks them as superior and inferior, with his or her own culture as the superior one. For example, many people in the United States are unable to appreciate the fact that for Hindus in India cows are sacred; no matter how hungry people might be, they may not eat cows there. To many Americans, such a status accorded to the cow even in the face of extreme hunger may indicate an inferior culture. Evaluating India as having an inferior culture on this basis is an expression of ethnocentrism.

There are three types of norms, based on their level of importance to the dominant members of society: folkways, mores, and laws. The negative **sanctions,** or punishments, meted out to violators of norms vary in severity depending on the type of norm being transgressed.

Folkways

Folkways, the least formal or important norms, involve everyday conventional routines. They belong to the category of behaviors that *should* and *should not* occur, as specified by society or a social group. Folkways may include such things as how many meals members eat per day, when meals are eaten, and what should be eaten at each one. They also include rituals of deference and public deportment, such as where to stand and whom to look at during conversations or public outings. For example, in the United States, one is expected to maintain an invisible bubble of personal space even when involved in conversations with others. Violation of personal space is tolerated only in unavoidable circumstances such as crowded trains and elevators; even then, one is expected to avoid eye contact as a means of respecting a minimum of personal space. In contrast, people in Latin America consider it rude to hoard personal space; they will attempt to get physically close to their fellow conversants. Imagine the social dance likely to develop as a person from the United States and someone from Brazil attempt to have a conversation, with the U.S. person backing away and the Brazilian advancing closer, both attempting to conform to their own folkways.

Sanctions imposed on violators of folkways are often relatively mild expressions of reprimand, such as stares, frowns, laughter, throat clearing, or tongue clucking. In the hypothetical conversation described above, the person from the United States may frown or stare at the Brazilian or may even laugh nervously, and the Brazilian is likely to do the same. Both are undergoing the culture shock of having a conversational partner violate the expected social behaviors defining roles and physical positions, and each may interpret the violation differently. Each may alternatively interpret the other's behavior as rude, curious, eccentric, deranged, aggressive, or hostile.

Mores

Mores are more formal and important norms than folkways. They generally include behaviors defined as those that absolutely must or must not occur. Members of society view these norms as absolutes because violation of them is believed to threaten the group's ability to function or its very existence. Given the increased level of importance accorded to mores, violations of mores typically meet with more severe sanctions than do violations of folkways. Transgressors face the imposition of shame, ostracism, and sometimes exile. Mores may include rules governing marriage-partner selection. For example, many societies require that mates be selected from the same ethnic, racial, religious, economic, political, or social group. Marriages between people from different groups are seen to threaten a group's existence by diluting its practices and its heritage or by dispersing the group's accumulated material wealth. Intermarriages may be subject to a range of sanctions, including excommunication from a church, abdication of royalty, beating of the "intruding" partner, and refusal to acknowledge the marriage as legitimate. Among certain groups of Orthodox Jews, the family of an individual who has married a non-Jewish partner will sit shiva, a mourning ritual. From that moment on the family will act as if the transgressor had died; many will not even permit the name of the transgressor to be mentioned, and all evidence of the person's existence, past and present, will be destroyed.

Most societies maintain mores defining heterosexuality as the only legitimate sexual orientation. Sexual relationships between individuals of the same sex are at best unacknowledged and at worst punished. In the United States, for example, gay males and lesbians are often ridiculed, chastised, denied housing and employment, subjected to violence, ignored by family members, and erroneously blamed for social problems such as AIDS or child pornography. Gay partnerships have not been legally recognized as valid marriages, even though the partners may be mutually devoted for many years. While this is changing, few employers allow homosexuals to extend health insurance coverage to their partners, as married heterosexuals are allowed to do.

Laws

Laws constitute the most formal and important norms. Laws are the folkways and mores deemed so vital to dominant interests that they become translated into written, legal formalizations that even nonmembers of the society (such as visitors) are required to obey. For example, in many communities in the United States no one may purchase alcohol before noon on Sundays; in some communities, alcohol sales are completely forbidden on Sundays, despite the fact that many people do not regard Sunday as the Sabbath. In most states, no one under the age of 21 is permitted to purchase alcoholic beverages, and that includes international visitors who may be allowed to purchase and consume alcohol at a younger age in their own country.

People do not often consciously recognize norms until they are confronted with a situation that does not conform to their unspoken expectations. Norms defining heterosexuality as the prerequisite for a socially acceptable sexual relationship are sharply challenged in the culture shock of the obvious love and affection these two men feel for each other and which they publicly display as heterosexual couples commonly do.

When laws are not firmly based on norms shared by the majority, they are difficult to enforce. The constitutional amendment prohibiting the sale of alcohol was repealed in 1933 because so many people regularly violated it. The amendment was championed primarily by the Protestant middle class, with the support of labor and socialist organizations, in an attempt to impose its norms and values on the rest of society. More recently, although many states maintained laws forbidding private, consensual practices defined in the statutes as sodomy, these laws were routinely ignored by homosexuals and heterosexuals alike. These laws were difficult to enforce, both because of the private nature of the act and because the laws were so commonly violated. The Supreme Court in 2003 finally found such laws unconstitutional. Today there remain schisms in the social cohesion underlying laws such as those forbidding the possession and use of marijuana, an example of laws that continue to be challenged and may change in the future.

Laws concern issues that are so important to dominant interests that sanctions against violations are formalized in the written legal codes and are likely to be quite severe. But one latent consequence of these sanctions is the reproduction of class and racial inequality (Reiman, 2000). For example, monetary fines typically penalize the poor more than the wealthy. The poor are also at a disadvantage in raising bail in order to remain out of jail while awaiting trail. In addition, people of color pay considerably more, sometimes twice the bail, than whites to secure their freedom before trial.

Regardless of whether one believes that sanctions are fair or uniformly applied, the fact that they occur regularly suggests that norms are not necessarily shared and embraced by all members of society. Where, then, do norms come from?

Values

Folkways, mores, and laws are shaped by the value system defined by the dominant members of society. **Values** are assumptions and judgments made about the goods, goals, or states of existence that are deemed important, desirable, and worth striving (or dying) for. For example, in the United States respect for private property is a fundamentally important value, as are individual rights to privacy and freedom of expression. Values shape the normative system by defining the criteria for judging which behaviors will and will not be tolerated. However, values do not necessarily *determine* people's behaviors. Norms define the dominant perception of the ideal behaviors in specific situations; they are not necessarily a reflection of real or actual behaviors. Thus, although an important value in the United States is the right of individuals to privacy, it is still fairly common for children to have their personal belongings examined by their teachers and school administrators, for workers to have their private lives investigated by employers, and for individuals' credit histories to be sold to any buyer (Manning, 2000).

Because of the gap between ideal norms and actual behavior, societies generally feel the need to impose negative sanctions (or punishments of violations of norms). For example, jails and courts are overcrowded with hundreds of thousands of violators of society's most important norms—laws (especially drug laws). And parents routinely talk about the need to find effective punishments for children who do not comply with family rules: Is a removal of privileges ("grounding") enough? Is a spanking too much? Many people violate norms, and such widespread violation indicates that norms are not necessarily shared by all. Similarly, not everyone accepts the prevailing value system advocated by dominant groups. Both the norms and values of dominant groups meet with resistance and challenge.

Furthermore, the prevailing value system may contain contradictory values that give rise to debate, challenge, and varying interpretations. For example, one ostensible value in the United States is the right to life. As such, laws strictly prohibit the taking of human life. Killing another person is considered the most heinous of offenses. Yet the prohibition against taking a life is suspended during war and under circumstances defined as "self-defense," and some states reserve the right to take a human life in capital punishment. And some people view abortion as a violation of the right to life. Ironically, to protest the operations of abortion clinics, some abortion opponents have used violence (and, in several cases, murder of physicians performing abortions in Florida, New York, and Massachusetts, such as the 1998 sniper killing of Dr. Barnett Slepian in his Amherst, New York, home). Contradictory values may serve to help shape a normative system by generating debate and conflict. The process of developing various perspectives through debate, and of resolving the conflict, may help identify the priorities of values and the norms to which those values point us.

The Relationship between Values and Norms

Conventional wisdom holds that norms and values in the culture are the glue that binds society together as a positive, coherent unit, enabling its members to function smoothly and peaceably. However, sometimes the value system gives rise to norms that actually serve to oppress some people. We shall examine the value system inherent in a patriarchy to show this relationship between values and norms.

A **patriarchy** values male dominance as a natural, inalienable right, thereby enforcing the inferiority and subordination of women. Normative behaviors derived from this value include institutional discrimination against women in education and in the labor force, resulting in restricted opportunities, lower wages for work, and relative economic, social, and political deprivation (Cubbins, 2001).

Patriarchal values also encourage the treatment of women as property. This is evident in Christian marriage rituals in which the bride is "given away" by a male (usually her father or uncle) to the male she is about to marry. Similarly, in some Jewish marriage rituals the bride's father walks her halfway down the aisle; then he turns her over to the groom, who walks her the remaining way to the rabbi performing the ceremony. At the conclusion of many wedding ceremonies the presider announces "I now pronounce you man and wife," suggesting that the woman now belongs to the man. Many couples today prefer "husband and wife," which represents their relationship as partners rather than as a man and his possession.

While marriage rituals seem relatively innocuous, the fact that they frequently go unquestioned suggests the power of patriarchy to define values. More extreme cases of patriarchal definitions of female inferiority involve violence against women (Dobash et al., 2000, Kurz, 2001). Even though U.S. culture assumes that women's male partners are to be their protectors, it is also a culture that links masculinity with anger and violence (Kindlon, Thompson, and Barker, 2000). It is not surprising, then, to find these norms coalesce so that women are more likely to become homicide victims in the United States than in 25 other core countries, and account for 70 percent of all female murder victims in these countries (Hemenway et al., 2002). Furthermore, while men in the United States are more likely to be murdered away from home and by a stranger, women are more likely to suffer violence at the hands of their intimate male partners at home (Hemenway et al., 2002). Indeed, one study found that in 86 percent of the cases of female homicide the perpetrator was either the victims' current or former partner (Morton et al., 1998).

In extreme cases the intersection of patriarchy as power and privilege and cultural conceptualizations of women as objects and possessions can often become institutionalized into a "rape culture" in which rape and other forms of violence against women are accepted as a common feature of society (Cuklanz, 2000; Feltey, 2001). For example, in the 1990s and into 2000, Serbs in Bosnia, Croatia, and Kosovo used systematic rape of women as a standard strategy of war to punish and terrorize populations viewed as inferior. Evidence suggests, however, that such a rape culture can be resisted and challenged: The Silent Witness Initiative in the United States notes that homicide rates of women often decline in locales with a greater presence and availability of women's shelters and rape crisis centers and in states that had legislation addressing domestic violence (www.silentwitness.net/old_site/html/results.html).

Patriarchy also implies that women are objects for the sexual pleasure of males. This means women must make themselves attractive partners for sexual pleasure (as well as for reproduction). For many women, being attractive means being thin, and this value leads them to engage in various health-threatening behaviors, such as smoking, and eating disorders, particularly anorexia (voluntary starvation) and bulimia (binge purging). At least 90 percent of the diagnosed cases of these life-threatening disorders are females (www.nationalalcoholscreeningday.org/eat/eat-athlete.htm). Both anorexia and bulimia have tended to be treated as personal troubles, that is, as psychological and medical problems of individuals. Recently, however, more and more researchers have suggested that patriarchal values combined with corporations eager to cash in on the cult of thinness have promoted eating disorders based on the notion that "one can never be too rich or too thin" (Brand, 2000; Hesse-Biber, 1996; Poulton, 1997). Similarly, the tobacco industry aggressively promoted smoking to women as a weight-control tool, despite mounting evidence of its dangers, especially to women (Stauber and Rampton, 1995).

Thus, far from simply organizing society into a positive, unified structure that is beneficial to all members, norms and values may create an oppressive culture for some members. Such oppression may have dire consequences for those who are victimized by the culture. But the normative system is not all-powerful; there is often resistance to the oppression that some members of society feel. (We also discuss resistance to the dominant culture in this chapter's sections on subcultures and countercultures.) The question we now ask is: How do societies transmit the prevailing normative system, and how do people challenge that system?

Culture and Language

Culture contains prevailing knowledge, or "facts" as a particular society construes them; beliefs and assumptions about the way the world works or ought to work; values defining what is important; customs and rituals; and symbols. Together, these elements are a society's **nonmaterial culture,** the body of abstractions defining the way its members think and live. A society's **material culture** consists of the physical artifacts that define the society: a flag, style of dress, means of transportation and housing, and so on.

The key to the abstractions of nonmaterial culture is **language.** Language consists of patterns of written symbols, audible sounds, and gestures that convey meanings. These meanings are usually shared by the members of a society, so when some members use them, others understand the gist of what is being communicated. Through the exchange of language members of society have access to experience and history beyond their own immediate time and place. It is not necessary to have lived in concentration camps in 1940s Germany to know about the Holocaust and its horrors, or in Hiroshima in 1945 to appreciate the devastating effects of nuclear weapons. Nor is it necessary to put one's hands in a fire to learn that it burns. This is because language can categorize objects and events that share perceived or assumed common elements.

Language has three main cultural functions: It can describe the world; it can create or construct individuals' vision of social reality; and it can be a vehicle to challenge and change social reality. Let's examine each of these functions.

Language: Describing the World

Language may simply describe the world around us. For example, people may categorize as wars all conflicts that attempt to resolve differences by means of weapons and bloodshed. Thus, even though people today were born after the American Revolution, the Civil War, and World War I, these are widely agreed to all be wars. An analysis of why these wars occurred or who was right and who was wrong is not necessary to understand that these were all wars, because they share the common elements of weapons, death, and conflicting interests. And this understanding may be extended to the present day, defining as wars such events as armed disputes between urban gangs, the invasion of Kuwait by Iraq, the extended conflicts in the Balkans and the Middle East, and the 2003 use of U.S. military forces against Iraq.

Language: Constructing Reality

Beyond just reflecting reality, language can also *construct,* or define, reality (Berger and Luckmann, 1966; Sinke, 1999). This is because the structure of language contains hidden assumptions about the world around us. For example, the English language contains many implicit assumptions about gender abilities, worth and value, and appropriate behaviors and roles (Sorrels, 1983). When people use words like "fireman," and "congressman," they are conjuring a mental image of a male, thereby constructing a reality which assumes that only men fight fires and serve in Congress. Such assumptions are similarly reinforced when people use gendered pronouns, such as "the doctor . . . he" and "the nurse . . . she" or "the teacher . . . she" and "the principal . . . he." Even the use of the generic "man" to refer to all of humanity constructs perceptions of a male as the embodiment of humanness. This may have the consequence of rendering females invisible and inconsequential. In contrast, words like "firefighter" and "congressperson" draw attention to the notion that females as well as males hold these positions.

In fact, anthropologists Edward Sapir (1949) and Benjamin Whorf (1956) suggested that people's understanding of the world around them can be limited by their language: they know the world only by the very words they learn and use, a view

Social Forces/People's Lives

American Dreamer

BHARATI MUKHERJEE

The United States has always been a multicultural amalgamation of people from many diverse nations, ethnicities, and religions. This raises several questions: Who is "American"? What does it mean to be an "American"? What is "American culture"? Must one relinquish membership in and identity with a previous culture in order to become a member of a new one? Consider the struggles of the woman in this reading as she navigates between two worlds.

THE United States exists as a sovereign nation, "America," in contrast, exists as a myth of democracy and equal opportunity to live by, or as an ideal goal to reach.

I am a naturalized U.S. citizen, which means that, unlike native-born citizens, I had to prove to the U.S. government that I merited citizenship. What I didn't have to disclose was that I desired "America," which to me is the stage for the drama of self-transformation.

I was born in Calcutta and first came to the United States—to Iowa City, to be precise—on a summer evening in 1961. I flew into a small airport surrounded by cornfields and pastures, ready to carry out the two commands my father had written out for me the night before I left Calcutta: Spend two years studying creative writing at the Iowa Writers' Workshop, then come back home and marry the bridegroom he selected for me from our caste and class.

In traditional Hindu families like ours, men provided and women were provided for. My father was a patriarch and I a pliant daughter. The neighborhood I'd grown up in was homogeneously Hindu, Bengali-speaking, and middle-class. I didn't expect myself to ever disobey or

disappoint my father by setting my own goals and taking care of my future.

When I landed in Iowa 35 years ago, I found myself in a society in which almost everyone was Christian, white, and moderately well-off. In the women's dormitory I lived in my first year, apart from six international graduate students (all of us were from Asia and considered "exotic"), the only non-Christian was Jewish, and the only nonwhite an African-American from Georgia. I didn't anticipate then, that over the next 35 years, the Iowa population would become so diverse that it would have 6,931 children from non-English-speaking homes registered as students in its schools, nor that Iowans would be in the grip of a cultural crisis in which resentment against immigrants, particularly refugees from Vietnam, Sudan, and Bosnia, as well as unskilled Spanish-speaking workers, would become politicized enough to cause the Immigration and Naturalization Service to open an "enforcement" office in Cedar Rapids in October for the tracking and deporting of undocumented aliens.

In Calcutta in the '50s, I heard no talk of "identity crisis"—communal or individual. The concept itself—of a

referred to as the **Sapir-Whorf hypothesis.** Thus, if an individual's language has only one word to describe economic deprivation, the wide range and degrees of the experience of insufficient money may become difficult to appreciate: Is the cash flow problem temporary or chronic, conscious and deliberate (as in a vow of poverty) or beyond one's control, crushingly fundamental so as to deprive one of the necessities of life or simply a limitation to one's ability to obtain luxuries? This power of language to restrict people's perceptions can be seen in the difficulty of translating person not knowing who he or she is—was unimaginable in our hierarchical, classification-obsessed society. One's identity was fixed, derived from religion, caste, patrimony, and mother tongue. A Hindu Indian's last name announced his or her forefathers' caste and place of origin. A Mukherjee could *only* be a Brahmin from Bengal. Hindu tradition forbade intercaste, interlanguage, interethnic marriages. Bengali tradition even discouraged emigration: To remove oneself from Bengal was to dilute true culture.

Until the age of 8, I lived in a house crowded with 40 or 50 relatives. My identity was viscerally connected with ancestral soil and genealogy. I was who I was because I was Dr. Sudhir Lal Mukherjee's daughter, because I was a Hindu Brahmin, because I was Bengali-speaking, and because my *desh*—the Bengali word for homeland—was an East Bengal village called Faridpur. The University of Iowa classroom was my first experience of coeducation. And after not too long, I fell in love with a fellow student named Clark Blaise, an American of Canadian origin, and impulsively married him during a lunch break in a lawyer's office above a coffee shop.

That act cut me off forever from the rules and ways of upper-middle-class life in Bengal, and hurled me into a New World life of scary improvisations and heady explorations. Until my lunchbreak wedding, I had seen myself as an Indian foreign student who intended to return to India to live. The five-minute ceremony in the lawyer's office suddenly changed me into a transient with conflicting loyalties to two very different cultures....

I negotiated the no-man's land between the country of my past and the contintent of my present. Shaped by memory, textured with nostalgia for a class and culture I had abandoned, this novel quite naturally became an expression of the expatriate consciousness.

It took me a decade of painful introspection to put nostalgia in perspective and to make the transition from expatriate to immigrant....

I am a naturalized U.S. citizen and I take my American citizenship very seriously. I am not an economic refugee, nor am I a seeker of political asylum. I am a voluntary immigrant. I became a citizen by choice, not by simple accident of birth.

Yet these days, questions such as who is an American and what is American culture are being posed with belligerence, and being answered with violence. Scapegoating of immigrants has once again become the politicians' easy remedy for all that ails the nation. Hate speeches fill auditoriums for demagogues willing to profit from stirring up racial animosity ...

The United States, like every sovereign nation, has a right to formulate its immigration policies. But in this decade of continual, large-scale diasporas, it is imperative that we come to some agreement about who "we" are, and what our goals are for the nation, now that our community includes people of many races, ethnicities, languages, and religions....

The multicultural mosaic implies a contiguity of fixed, self-sufficient, utterly distinct cultures. Multiculturalism, as it has been practiced in the United States in the past 10 years, implies the existence of a central culture, ringed by peripheral cultures. The fallout of official multiculturalism is the establishment of one culture as the norm and the rest as aberrations. At the same time, the multiculturalist emphasis on race- and ethnicity-based group identity leads to a lack of respect for individual differences within each group, and to vilification of those individuals who place the good of the nation above the interests of their particular racial or ethnic communities....

What excites me is that as a nation we have not only the chance to retain those values we treasure from our original cultures but also the chance to acknowledge that the outer forms of those values are likely to change ...

SOURCE: *Mother Jones* magazine, Jan. Feb., 1997

ideas from one language to another, because not all words or phrases have exact counterparts in all languages. Many a frustrated speaker can often be heard to say, after a failed attempt to communicate between two languages, "It loses something in the translation!"

The power of language to construct social reality is captured in the **Thomas theorem,** or the **definition of the situation** (Thomas, 1928): If people define a situation as real, the consequences of that definition will be quite real whether that definition is accurate or not. For example, if society accepts a definition of women as inferior to men, the consequences may be behavior that reinforces the definition as correct. Members of society, including school administrators, prospective employers, and those holding political power, may believe that women are incapable of tasks requiring intellect, independent initiative, authority, responsibility, and physical strength and stamina. The all-too-real consequences set in motion by this definition of the situation may be women's economic, social, and political disadvantage and deprivation. We discuss sexism in greater detail in Chapter 7. Because the very language suggests that men are superior to women, men are considered more qualified for leadership positions, jobs requiring skill and responsibility (which are frequently higher paying jobs), and decision making in politics and the home.

The idea that women are inferior in the culture is also expressed in the terminology many men traditionally apply to women—descriptive words such as "girls," "dolls," "broads," "babes," and so forth. When one executive says to another, "I'll have my girl call your girl," the statement renders both their secretaries inferior. Through one small sentence, each secretary becomes a child, her boss's possession, and his servant. Thus the Thomas theorem describes how language and ideas reinforce each other in the social construction of reality.

Language use similarly reinforces stereotypes defining racially linked perceptions. The use in the English language of "black" as a metaphor for "evil" and "white" as a descriptor of "good" and "pure" contributes to cultural images linking racially defined categories of people with such characteristics. For example, villains in film are commonly dressed in black and described as having a "black heart," while the heroes wear white and are described as "pure of heart." African Americans and other dark-skinned people become culturally defined as somehow inherently aggressive, violent, criminal, untrustworthy, and mean-spirited, while light-skinned people become culturally defined as inherently honest, fair, well-mannered, law-abiding, and well-intentioned.

Similarly, the words used to describe physical and mental impairment also construct individuals' perceptions of various human conditions and the people who have them. The term "handicapped person" implies that an individual who has a physical or mental disability is a "limited person" (Stroman, 1982: 47). The use of such wording defines the person in terms of her or his physical or mental disability and precludes the understanding that the disability is merely one aspect of an entire human being. This social construction affects how people without disabilities respond to those who have an impairment. People with disabilities are frequently seen as unattractive, unintelligent, immature, incapable of competently performing jobs requiring responsibility, unable to adequately parent children, and incapable of living independently. Replacing the term "handicapped person" with the phrase "person with a disability" reorients the social construction to one in which a specific impairment is seen as only a part of a person. Stroman (1982) suggests that "handicap" be reserved to describe the limitations that culture imposes on the disabled through stereotyping and labels. In doing so, Stroman acknowledges the power of language to socially construct reality, and he suggests using that power to *resist* the prevailing social constructions. By using noticeably different words, it is possible to call attention to the inadequacy of the words more commonly used and raise society's consciousness about the realities these words create. Thus language can also be used to challenge or change culture.

Language: Vehicle for Change

The important role of language in the social construction of reality indicates that individuals who control language have the power to control culture. Those who determine the "appropriate" words for denoting various experiences and objects can strongly influence the way everyone else views the world around them, as well as their own place and the places of others in that world. Language is the means by which culture is passed on (including social constructions of advantage and disadvantage) from generation to generation and to new members of society. But language also allows people who are less powerful to introduce change into culture. As noted above, people can alter established social constructions by deliberately using common words in new ways or by generating new concepts that heighten society's awareness of the power of existing words (Hall and Bucholtz, 1995).

This is also what "politically correct" speech often does. Consider, for example, the effect of changes in the words used to refer to people of color in the United States. Through much of the 20th century African American men were commonly called "boy," a derisive pejorative term that dismissed their value as adult human beings. This socially constructed cultural consciousness helped shape the real consequence of denial of the rights and privileges normally accorded to eligible (i.e., white) adult men: voting rights, meaningful jobs (beyond slavery), education, and decent housing. By the 1960s, activists rejected the term "boy" (and its later pejoratives "colored" and "nigger") and instead worked to reframe the social construction of race in the use of "black" as a self-identifier infusing greater dignity and empowerment in a racially charged culture. More recently, many people have noted that "black" still focuses on skin color as a biological marker. Instead, they use the term "African American" to highlight the cultural history of kidnaping and enslavement that is distinct from all other, more voluntary immigrant groups. Notice that the change in words draws attention to different cultural issues and ideas, which in turn shape individuals' consciousness. The controversy over "politically correct" speech, then, may be a reflection of the power of language: Such use of language is a forceful expression of challenge and resistance to cultural assumptions favoring dominant groups (whites in this example).

▎Corporate Culture

The discussion of language indicates the ongoing struggle between dominant and subordinate members of society to socially construct reality or to challenge and change these. But what shapes the definition of what is important in society? That is, where do norms and values come from? At the beginning of the chapter, we introduced the idea that powerful groups in society are in a position to define society's norms and values. In the United States, values derive in part from the production and consumption of goods and services for profit. Cultural ideologies create relationships and structures that promote and enhance the production of private profit. Sociologists refer to this fundamental aspect of U.S. culture as the **corporate culture.** Corporate culture includes values based on the cult of **competitive individualism** (Cummings and del Taebel, 1978; Lipset, 1990), in which members of society are taught to believe that individuals are completely responsible for their own personal economic conditions. As such, economic success (wealth) or failure (poverty) is held to be the result of individual effort and competitive capabilities. Individuals who are wealthy are presumed to have earned their privileged economic position; if they did not deserve it, they would not have it. Similarly, many people believe that poor people deserve their poverty because of sloth, laziness, lack of motivation or initiative, or lack of competitive capabilities. If not for these personal failures, the poor would not be poor.

The notion that some people are poverty-stricken because of a lack of motivation to work hard, earn a living, or gain an education is called the **culture of poverty** (Billings and Blee, 2000; Lewis, 1959). This viewpoint assumes that the poor share a value system, or normative culture, that differs from mainstream norms and values because of the effect of poverty on their lives. According to this argument, the circumstance of being poor shapes people's adaptive strategies so that they to come to value instant gratification, shun formal education, disrespect law and order, and adopt cynical attitudes about the value of hard work and effort (Banfield, 1974). And they are likely to pass these values along to their children, dooming several generations to be poor. The analysis implies that poverty permanently deprives the poor of any competing cultural input beyond their immediate environment, an implication often interpreted to suggest that the poor consciously embrace the value system of the culture of poverty and thus hinder their own ability to break out of the cycle of poverty. This was the ideological underpinning of welfare reforms of the 1990s in the United States. Since work was assumed to be the antidote to poverty, the poor would be coerced out of poverty by being cut off from welfare benefits and forced to adopt the presumably absent work ethic to work outside the home. Not only do such policies ignore the work ethic possessed by most poor people; the culture of poverty thesis does not consider the larger structural constraints that are important factors in producing poverty. For example, can valuing hard work and education ensure upward mobility for individuals if there are not enough jobs paying living wages for all the people who want and need them? Many adults who are poor work full-time, year-round.

The success of transmitting mainstream values can be seen in public opinion polls regarding economic success issues. In a 2002 survey by Pew Research Center, 61 percent of the respondents believed that individual failures were major factors for poverty. Yet 61 percent of these respondents recognized that most people who are poor work but can't earn enough money to avoid poverty, suggesting that poverty is beyond the control of individuals (http://roperweb.ropercenter.uconn.edu). Apparently, even when a majority of people recognize the role that the economy and society play in generating poverty, most still believe that the poor are themselves to blame because of deficient personal characteristics. This contradiction indicates that the twin ideologies of culture of poverty and competitive individualism are powerful, pervasive, and tenacious, even in the face of contradictory information.

These ideologies, transmitted through schools and the workplace, support an acceptance of corporate culture and inhibit any independent thinking that might challenge these notions. For example, is it appropriate or accurate to consider economic achievement in terms of a competition that has winners and losers? Does each generation of contestants begin the competition on a level playing field regardless of their parents' or previous generations' economic positions? Might such a competition, in fact, be rigged at the outset, with some beginning with greater advantages to support success and others carrying heavy institutional hindrances throughout? Is individual effort the most important factor in determining economic success? Are there institutional arrangements and practices in the economy and the state that might shape opportunity structures, making individual effort less important?

U.S. corporate culture is disseminated to other cultures when firms go abroad in search of profits in new markets and when the relatively better-off in many countries seek to enjoy the lifestyle that seems to be accessible to so many in the United States. That is why McDonald's golden arches can be found in Russia, Mexico, Japan, India, and many European countries. Coca-Cola and Pepsi ads can be seen all around the world in dozens of languages, as can the logos of many, if not most, of the Fortune 500 corporations.

Most of these firms not only sell products in an international marketplace; they also maintain manufacturing plants abroad, particularly in underdeveloped nations where labor can be exploited cheaply. Such inroads make possible a sharing of foods, music, and material goods, but they also spread corporate culture, in which generating profits takes precedence over other cultural norms and ideologies (Held et al., 1999). Sociologist George Ritzer refers to this exportation of U.S. corporate culture around the world and the consequent homogenization of global culture as the **"McDonaldization" of society** (2000b). This term does not mean simply that one corporation—McDonald's—is taking over the world. Rather, it suggests a more widespread issue of **cultural leveling,** in which the diverse and distinctive differences between cultures become blurred as they increasingly come to resemble each other because of the common, dominating presence of corporate culture.

Many countries encourage the presence of U.S. corporations as part of a conscious economic development strategy, but such strategies can also have an enormous cultural impact (Held et al., 1999). For example, corporate producers can disrupt agrarian cultures as land use and labor activities shift from farming to manufacturing. Sunrises and sunsets, growing seasons, and weather patterns no longer mark the daily clock and annual calendar. Instead, the day and year are organized around the assembly line, production shifts, and workweeks, all dictated by the

Multinational corporations often export their culture to other nations. Starbuck's coffee shops can be found in many different countries, although their menus may be written in various languages and alphabets. Cultivating recognition of corporate cultural images and demand for the product can be quite lucrative in nations with large populations or pockets of great affluence.

market for material goods. Rituals and norms associated with agriculture become less meaningful in the face of corporate culture. Less visible, but no less important, is the impact on family and community structures and cultural heritages. Rural farming and fishing communities can no longer compete with the economy of scale posed by large corporate agribusinesses and fisheries, so the community members leave in search of employment in overcrowded cities.

Notably, despite the powerful influence of corporate culture, it is not absolute or immune to change. As more individuals articulate criticisms and organize into action-oriented groups, the likelihood increases that there will be challenges to the spread of corporate culture and its negative effects.

Agents of Cultural Transmission

How is it possible for members of a large society to learn the subtle and not-so-subtle values, norms, and rituals of the dominant culture? Which members have the power to transmit and impose their cultural assumptions on others? What mechanisms and processes enhance this transmission? Do these processes produce an all-powerful, dominant culture, or is there some degree of resistance, challenge, and diversity?

Several agents combine to facilitate transmission of the dominant group's culture, most notably, schools, the media, the workplace, and the toy, game, and recreation industries. Other agents that may variably reinforce this process include the family, religion, and peers. We deal with the processes and agents of cultural transmission, or socialization, in great detail in the next chapter and in Chapter 13. Here, we focus broadly on the special role that schools and the media play in reinforcing the dominant culture.

Mass Media

The mass media are major transmitters of culture. Television broadcasts entertainment that reflects stereotypes of acceptable and unacceptable behaviors and values across a wide range of dimensions, including race or ethnicity, class, gender, age, physical and mental ability, and sexual orientation. The format of the programs often invites viewers to laugh at, despise, or belittle cultures other than the dominant one in the United States. For example, *The Simpsons* has a running joke that depicts Pakistani immigrants as ignorant convenience-store owners and confused taxicab drivers. While broadcasters may be showing some sensitivity to how they present diversity, they have a very long way to go. By 2000, the National Association for the Advancement of Colored People and Latino/Latina groups began to publicly criticize the television and film industries for their inadequate representation of people of color in front of the cameras as well as behind them. Consequently, too few faces of color turn up in popular culture, and thus pejorative stereotypes are unlikely to be challenged.

News programmers reflect the interests of society's major power groups—corporations and the wealthy, for example, in capitalist nations like the United States—in the stories they select as important, the subjects they choose for interviews, and the way they treat the stories they present. This is not surprising: The media are themselves controlled by major corporate entities and the primary sponsors of programming are corporate advertisers (McChesney, 1999; McChesney, www.fair.org/extra/9711/gmg.html). Notably, in a survey of journalists 40 percent admitted that they deliberately refrained from reporting on important stories or "softened the tone" of reports "to avoid harming the financial interests of their own news organization or embarrassing an advertiser" (Pew Research Center for the People and the Press, 2000).

Television commercials encourage a materialistic consumer mentality, regardless of the necessity, safety, or effectiveness of products. Consider, for example, the controversies over the advertisements for highly sugared cereals and junk food that children watch along with their Saturday morning cartoons. (The cartoons themselves are often little more than half-hour commercials for toys, movies, and other merchandise related to the main characters of the shows, as witnessed in the marketing phenomenon of Pokemon.)

Researchers have long noted the power of commercials and the media to entice consumers to feel the need for products that may be unnecessary, ineffective, frivolous, beyond people's means, or even harmful. The modern world is dominated, both in print and electronic media, by corporate logos, advertising jingles and catchphrases, and visual images that create a reality that contradicts and often undermines the everyday reality of the individual (McAllister, 1996; Parenti, 1993).

In his examination of U.S. culture, *Culture against Man,* Jules Henry describes advertising as "an expression of an irrational economy that has depended for survival on a fantastically high standard of living incorporated into the American mind as a moral imperative" (1963: 45). That is, people are encouraged to believe that it is their duty to maintain a very high level of consumption in order to support the economy. Limited personal budgets are not an obstacle: Credit cards help even those with relatively meager incomes to consume beyond their means in order to make their contribution to this civic cause (Manning, 2000). Age apparently is no obstacle, either: The advertising industry now uses child psychologists to make advertising more effective by stimulating consumerism and demand among children (Solomon, www.fair.org/media_beat991007/html). Advertising creates a consumer culture in that it defines individuals' needs and then entices people to fulfill them by purchasing goods and services, an activity that is the lifeblood of capitalism. Indeed, referring to consumerism as a moral imperative is not so far-fetched; experts proclaim that the U.S. economy was slow to rebound from the recession of the early 1990s because consumers were not spending enough to fuel the recovery.

In *Who Rules America?* (2002), G. William Domhoff examines what he calls the ideology process, the use of commercials, direct mailing, television-programming productions, and full-page newspaper ads to contour public opinion and the normative system. Domhoff identifies as a major force the Advertising Council, an organization dominated by corporate interests. It sponsors conferences "where academics, journalists, and other cultural experts can brainstorm with corporate leaders about problems of ideology and public opinion," thereby helping to solidify the dominant ideology (Domhoff, 2002: 109).

The Advertising Council transmits an ideology favoring dominant interests to the rest of the population in its campaigns of advertising in the public interest. These commercial spots tend to promote the sanctity of free enterprise; to encourage voluntarism in groups like the Red Cross and United Fund (as opposed to pressing for corporate responsibility or state-funded social welfare programs), ignoring the fact that voluntarism and charity are often too haphazard and unpredictable methods to deal with serious need; to present pollution and conservation as problems of individual behavior rather than public issues of corporate misconduct, abuse, and responsibility; and to stress the importance of religion in American life. These are issues and viewpoints that the "corporate-dominated boards and advisory committees [of the Advertising Council] believe to be in the public interest" (Domhoff, 2002:108). Since the Advertising Council uses more than 80 percent of the public service airtime that television networks are required by law to provide, its ads, even if unsuccessful, still deprive viewers of exposure to opposing points of view.

On the other hand, when television producers are less dependent on corporate advertisers, they are freer to promote and reinforce values and norms that challenge corporate culture. For example, much of the funding for public television comes from membership dues and federal support. Therefore, it is easier for children's programs like *Mr. Rogers, Sesame Street, Zoom,* and *Barney and Friends* to promote values of sharing, acceptance of others, and racial and gender equality.

The media, as corporate entities, also tend to choose stories and present them in such a way as to manipulate public opinion about foreign policies that support corporate interests. This filtering process serves to stifle or at least marginalize dissent and to mobilize acceptance and support of corporate interests (Chomsky, 1997; Parenti, 1993). For example, the media may define victims of violence who challenge U.S. corporate dominance as "unworthy" of coverage and victims who are supportive of that dominance as "worthy" (Elias, 1986; Herman and Chomsky, 1988). Thus the U.S. media loudly protested the injustice of the murder of a Polish priest ("worthy" victim) by the police in then-communist Poland but gave scant coverage to the murders of the archbishop of El Salvador and numerous clergy ("unworthy" victims) protesting treatment of the poor by landowners in El Salvador, killed by paramilitary troops who had been trained by Green Berets at Fort Bragg, North Carolina. The amount and kind of coverage accorded stories, then, influence perceptions of what U.S. interests are and, in turn, help "manufacture" citizens' consent to foreign policies consistent with corporate interests.

Schools

In addition to the media, schools are cultural-transmission agents. While there is a growing and powerful movement toward a multicultural perspective in curricula, teachers and boards of education often aid the transmission of dominant culture. They determine the subject matter and perspectives to be taught and then select the appropriate textbooks for that curriculum. In the United States, this policy has often meant that both the curricula and the textbooks—for political and social history, literature, and science—emphasize the dominant white, male, Western perspective, ignoring or downplaying the contributions, and, at times, the very existence, of females, members of the working class, people of color, or non-Western peoples (Loewen, 1995).

The movement in the United States to broaden and enrich curricula by making them more inclusive encourages teachers and textbook writers to adopt a perspective of **cultural relativity.** This perspective considers other cultures and their points of view as worthy of respect and understanding. It treats others' cultural practices as valid within their own context. More recently, however, there has been a shift to a perspective of **multiculturalism.** Whereas cultural relativity focuses on the perspective of another culture, multiculturalism acknowledges the heterogeneity within societies, examines the contributions and the intersection of many different groups at crucial moments in history, and explores the factors that differentially affect the experiences of each group. For example, cultural relativism might ask people to view slavery as supporting the economy of the South and the profit "needs" of plantation owners. In contrast, a multicultural perspective invites individuals to explore the roles that each group played in the larger political economy and to examine the power differences between slaves and slaveholders. For example, multiculturalism has brought about a shift in the New York State public school curriculum. The new approach no longer treats Christopher Columbus and the Spanish explorers as benign heroes and native populations as violent and uncivilized. Students are now exposed to primary and secondary sources describing the brutal and exploitative treatment of native populations by the explorers.

Schools in most, if not all, societies, regardless of their political or economic structure, reinforce the dominant culture of their society in addition to providing basic knowledge and skills. In their book *Schooling in Capitalist America* (1976), Bowles and Gintis describe how schools in U.S. society have historically sought to foster common ideological values and perspectives under the guise of mass public education. More often than not, they argue, what is taught are the *ideals* of democracy rather than the realities. Some schools today do encourage critical thinking and discussion about the difference between political ideals and reality. However, many of them still teach that the United States is a government of the people, by the people, and for the people, thereby ignoring existing power structures.

Schools can also transmit culture more subtly. In the very way they are structured, schools urge students to acquiesce to bureaucratic rules, regulations, and authorities. This encourages the students to accept authority outside of school as normal and legitimate. While the degree of authority children should have in schools is debatable, as is the viability of running all institutions on strict democratic principles, schools themselves clearly violate the virtues of democracy they extol in their curricula. They frequently override students' right to privacy by searching their lockers for contraband, instituting random drug testing, and restricting students' freedom of expression in student publications (http://archive.aclu.org/issues/student/hmes.html). Student activism, however, sometimes succeeds in challenging such contradictions of democracy. In schools where they have learned the lessons of the Bill of Rights, students protest intrusions on their rights, and sometimes they win in the courts. Thus they see the conflicts that are inherent in democratic societies and act to confront them.

Schools and the media often combine as cultural transmitters. Whittle Communications, for example, in 1989 introduced Channel One television, a news service, into public school systems in every state (except Nevada, Alaska, and Hawaii) and the District of Columbia (DeVaney, 1994; U.S. Congress: Senate, 1991). The schools received free media equipment from Whittle Communications in exchange for allowing 12 minutes of news each day plus 2 minutes of commercials to be aired in the classroom. Critics vehemently objected to using students as a captive audience for a barrage of messages promoting consumption (Apple, 1992; Greenberg and Brand, 1993). Many state boards of education—including those in New York, California, and North Carolina (Johnson, 1989; Mater, 1989; Walsh, 1990), became convinced that Channel One was inappropriate and banned the broadcast from their public schools. Many other school systems, however, drawn by the attraction of free media equipment and a new medium for instruction, have invited the powerful cultural transmitter into their classrooms. By 2003, Channel One, now owned by K-III Communications, was being broadcast to over 8 million students in12,000 middle and high schools around the country (www.fair.org).

Channel One is hardly the first mechanism corporations have used to transmit corporate culture to schoolchildren. More than 3,000 large corporations regularly produce and distribute videos, films, posters, comic books, and coloring books to children in public schools (*Business Week,* 1980; Manning, 1999). Teachers faced with severely tight budgets are more than happy to have the free materials. These materials, however, often carry a hidden agenda, defending the legitimacy of various industries, extolling the virtues of their products, and narrowing the critical vision of students. Consider the math exercise book for third graders that uses Tootsie Rolls or M&M candies to teach counting; a business course for elementary and middle school students that demonstrates the value of work by exploring "how McDonald's restaurants are run" (Manning, 1999:11); a scoreboard at a football stadium or basketball gym supported by corporate sponsors whose logos and advertisements dominate the vision of all who wish to see the score; or computers donated by corporate sponsors that ensure no student will log on without having to see a barrage of corporate ads; or a school bus whose sides are covered with corporate ads, as are the walls in the halls and cafeteria of the school, bombarding students with corporate culture throughout their day.

Corporate culture has made similar inroads into higher education, as corporations increasingly become major providers of research funding, endowments, and faculty chairs, underwriters of campus athletics and social events, financiers of campus buildings and laboratories, and so on. That crucial economic role increasingly positions corporations to wield tremendous power to affect curriculum and knowledge production decisions that are more traditionally covered by the norms of academic freedom of individual professors and scholars (Aronowitz, 1998, 2000; Croissant, 2001). For example, a major corporation may use its role as provider of research grants to influence the kind of scholarship researchers pursue or the development of courses that are consistent with its needs (often to the detriment of more critical courses which do not), as well as exerting editorial control over the production and publication of scholarship (Press

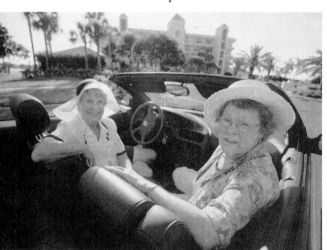

Subcultures can develop around such factors as religion, race, ethnicity, age, economic circumstances, or sexual orientation. Here, two women relax as members of one of the age subcultures that have emerged in middle-class and affluent retirement communities around the country, particularly in the warmer climates of Florida and Arizona.

and Washburn, 2000). Thus the central role economic institutions play in society enables them to influence other institutions like education and to shape them to promote and disseminate cultural norms and values that are consistent with business interests. Corporate culture, then, becomes the product of that power.

Subcultures

We have so far discussed culture as a single, powerful national phenomenon that everyone experiences. However, there is cultural variation *within* society. Although there may very well be a prevailing dominant culture, people are not necessarily bound to it or forced to conform like powerless robots. Rather, they can experience a great deal of diversity within society and its dominant culture. A wide variety of groups exist whose members participate in the larger society and its institutions but who share values, norms, heritages, and rituals that differ from those of the dominant culture. Sociologists call these groups **subcultures.** Members of subcultures do not necessarily reject the dominant culture, but they embrace their own subculture as valid and important.

Subcultures can be based on a variety of factors, including religion, race, ethnicity, age, economic circumstances, and sexual orientation. Gay male and lesbian subcultures have flourished in large urban areas and in smaller towns (often university towns) where there are meeting places and organizations to support their social and political activities. A loose national network provides information about supportive, thriving gay and lesbian communities. Thus, while gay males and lesbians are active participants in the dominant culture—in jobs, educational and religious institutions, and politics at all levels—they often also participate in a subculture containing shared norms and values that support the legitimacy of their sexual orientation.

Age subcultures also thrive in the United States. Communities of middle-class and wealthy retirees, particularly in the warmer climates of Florida and Arizona, continue to multiply. Residents' lifestyles are arranged around leisure activities and health care issues and information. Restaurants in such communities typically provide health-conscious menus and less costly early evening meals ("early bird specials"). Support groups abound for widowed people, for those with critically ill partners, and for those who are critically ill themselves. So do clubs and organizations that offer opportunities to meet other retirees, information regarding retirement benefits and entitlements, and chances to get involved in political issues affecting senior citizens. Some planned retirement communities and condominiums maintain social activities and classes and develop "blue books" establishing norms to govern residents' behaviors, including restrictions on the minimum age of residents and on the maximum length of visits by younger people (especially if they bring young children with them).

Economic circumstances can also impose a subcultural existence on people. El-liot Liebow's study, *Tally's Corner* (1967), and that of Elijah Anderson, *A Place on the Corner* (1978), used research methods of participant observation to examine how poverty and unemployment structured the lives of the men in two different city neighborhoods. The loss of self-esteem caused by inadequate job opportunities created the subculture of the street corner, a gathering place for men whose lives were characterized by shaky and failed marriages, sometimes by illegal activities, and often by shallow and fluid relationships (because of evictions from homes, prison terms, migrations in search of jobs, and so on). The men did not willingly embrace a culture of poverty. Rather, they were thrust into the street-corner subculture by poverty and by limited or nonexistent opportunities that marginalized them from mainstream society and made them appear unmotivated to settle down.

The economic circumstances of the men in Mitchell Duneier's participant observation study, *Slim's Table* (1992), were clearly better than those of the men in Liebow's and Anderson's studies: These working-class African American men in Chicago had jobs. Every day at about the same time "the regulars" stopped into the Valois Cafeteria to break up the monotony of the workday with cheap, home-cooked food and, more important, to hang out together with the other regulars, sharing stories, offering mutual support, and providing meaning about life's challenges. Like the men on Tally's Corner and Anderson's streetcorner, the subculture that the men at Valois created by hanging out together was carved out of the intersecting experiences of their work, class, race, gender, and families. They may have had a greater sense of choice because of their more comfortable economic status than the men in the other two studies, but their subculture clearly was just as structured by economic and social circumstances.

In addition to economic and social factors, subcultures are often also structured by norms and **rituals** (regularly practiced formal ceremonies, usually marking important personal or social events). Many ethnic and religious groups observe rituals and holidays and share folkways of foods, dances, music, and other everyday habits that are part of their ethnic heritage. For example, Jews who participate fully in American political and social life often still observe Passover and Hanukkah (Festival of Lights), as well as other Jewish holidays. Orthodox Jews observe their Sabbath even as they participate in the secular world: They leave work early on Friday to get home before sundown, and they avoid the use of electricity until sundown on Saturday. Many Jewish children are bar mitzvahed (boys) and bat mitzvahed (girls) at age 13 as a rite of passage to adulthood. Participants at such events typically dance the hora, a spirited dance of joy and celebration. Each Jewish holiday and ritual is marked by a remembrance of history and custom, a reaffirmation of heritage and roots, and a recommitment to maintaining that connection. At the same time, Jews live and fully participate in the larger, non-Jewish society and culture.

It is not always easy for subcultures to maintain such clear and solid connections to their heritage. Jews in the former Soviet Union had to practice their religion in secrecy or not at all. There is a long history of persecution and attempted genocide of Jews, from Jewish enslavement under the Pharaoh to banishment and oppression during the Spanish Inquisition to extermination during the Holocaust. And in the United States today, Jews continue to be the object of serious anti-Semitism. The results of a 1998 survey by the Anti-Defamation League indicate that 12 percent of the people in the United States harbor negative attitudes toward and stereotypes about Jews. The survey found that the number of people who maintain such stereotypes dropped from 20 percent in 1992. And where in 1992 one-third of the respondents

Members of subcultures maintain their own rituals and customs even as they participate in the dominant cultures of their societies. Here, several generations of African Americans gather to share in the candle-lighting ritual of Kwanzaa, a holiday celebrating African-American heritage and values.

believed that Jews have too much power, by 1998 only 13 percent still harbored that attitude. While these figures indicate clear progress in a reduction of some anti-Semitic attitudes, the survey also found that in 1998 56 percent of the respondents continued to believe that Jews stick together more than any other groups in the United States, an increase over the 50 percent who held this belief in 1992 (Anti-Defamation League, 1999). It is clearly a difficult challenge for the subculture of Jews in the United States to maintain its heritage in such an improving but still hostile atmosphere.

Many ethnic groups have similar histories of oppression; two examples are Native Americans and African Americans. African Americans' ancestors were kidnapped from their tribes in Africa and sold as slaves in colonial America. Torn from their cultures, and unable to communicate with slaves from other tribes who spoke different languages, many lost their cultural connections. Only through concerted, conscious efforts by many African Americans have some threads of African culture been retrieved and nurtured by embracing folkways that emphasize the subcultures' validity. Many African Americans, for example, celebrate Kwanzaa, a festival developed by Maulana Karenga and first observed in 1966. It reinforces and honors African heritage according to the principles of unity, self-determination, collective work and responsibility, cooperative economics, purpose, creativity, and faith. During this holiday, celebrants may wear traditional African dress; decorate their homes in the African colors of red, black, and green; arrange a table centerpiece containing the symbols of the harvest and of children; and share a feast with traditional African music and dancing in tribute to their ancestors. Some African Americans have changed their Anglo-American names to Muslim or African ones; prominent examples are writer and civil rights activist Kwame Toure (formerly Stokely Carmichael), boxing legend Muhammad Ali (born Cassius Clay), and basketball great Kareem Abdul-Jabbar (born Lew Alcindor). African crafts (such as batik), music, and dance are increasingly introduced in concert halls, community centers, and schools in African American neighborhoods as vivid reminders of the importance of the African American culture. And an increasing number of students have begun attending graduation ceremonies with a thin, multicolored shawl draped over the traditional cap and gown indicating African unity and pride.

Native Americans have also had to work militantly to preserve their heritage, all but obliterated by the genocidal westward expansion of the dominant white population in the United States (LaDuke, 1999). The remaining members of the various Native American nations are recapturing the rituals, spiritual practices, folk medicine, language, dance, norms, dress, and material aspects of their culture (such as pottery, jewelry making, textiles, and architecture).

The ability of ethnic and religious subcultures to piece together and preserve their often-threatened or lost cultural heritages is a testament to their strength and resilience. Indeed, many such subcultures are now so well preserved and maintained that their members often bring parts of their subcultures with them as they participate in the larger society. Such sharing by a wide variety of subcultures diversifies and enriches the larger society. In this way, even dominant cultures can change over time as they adapt to the new cultural elements. Sociologists refer to the gradual sharing and incorporation of a diversity of cultures into the dominant culture as **cultural diffusion.**

Many aspects of this diffusion can be seen in the mainstream culture of the United States. For example, rock music popular in youth subculture is now often used in product commercials. And fashions frequently borrow and incorporate styles from other cultures. In their 1993 line of men's clothing, designers in New York City featured the "Hassidic look": simple black suits, plain brimmed hats, and long, white, fringed scarves, which constitute the conventional dress of many Orthodox Jewish men. Indian saris and bindhis were popularized in the United States by pop culture figures like Madonna and Gwen Stefani in the late 1990s. Foods of many ethnic subcultures have become standard American fare: pizza from Italy, frankfurters from Germany, tacos from Mexico, sushi from Japan, falafel from the Middle East, and so on. American music and dance incorporates salsa from Latin America; reggae and ska from the Caribbean; jazz, rap, hip-hop, and blues from African American culture; and zydeco from black Creoles. The noted pop and rock star Paul Simon deliberately uses the music forms and instruments of black South African groups and Latin American and Caribbean cultures in his mainstream music. And many schools in the United States have changed their Christmas parties to "winter holiday celebrations," in which children often learn Hanukkah, winter solstice, and Kwanzaa songs in addition to the more traditional Christmas carols. Note, however, that the cultural forms absorbed from subcultures are relatively innocuous. The norms that still prevail tend to be those established by the dominant groups in society. To thrive, then, a subculture must maintain its identity apart from and in addition to the mainstream culture.

Sometimes dominant groups adopt aspects of subcultures as a safety valve mechanism. Doing so reduces the probability of open hostility and challenge to the dominant culture. For example, Arizona initially refused to recognize Dr. Martin Luther King Jr.'s birthday as a state holiday. That decision evoked protest marches and boycotts, all of which stopped when the state finally reversed its position and adopted the holiday in 1992. A similar struggle erupted in 2000 in Wallingford, Connecticut. Including King's birthday in the dominant culture of Arizona and Connecticut calmed race relations and reduced the probability that hostile challenges to the state would escalate.

Changes in cultures are not necessarily swift or immediate, however. There is often a lapse between the time a new subculture, technology, or idea is introduced and the time it is accepted and incorporated into the existing dominant culture. Sociologists refer to this time gap as **cultural lag.** For example, the civil rights movement has succeeded in getting legislation passed that legally protects people of color from discrimination. However, the notion that they are equal to whites is still not fully accepted by all. This is not to say that racism in the United States is impossible to eradicate; but the concept of cultural lag points to how the more innocuous aspects of African American culture can become incorporated into the dominant culture while African Americans themselves still struggle against racism in the mainstream.

Countercultures

Dominant corporate and wealthy interests shape U.S. culture, particularly its norms and values. In spite of this pervasive influence, the persistence of subcultures suggests that the power of such interests is not absolute. Even more telling is the persistence of **countercultures.** A counterculture is a specific type of subculture whose members embrace values, norms, rituals, and lifestyles that directly challenge the dominant culture. Whereas members of other subcultures participate in both the dominant culture and their particular subculture, members of countercultures reject the mainstream and challenge its pressures to conform.

The best-known, relatively recent example of a counterculture is the "hippie" movement of the late 1960s and early 1970s. Members of this loose counterculture denounced the legitimacy of the corporate culture and rejected its values of a button-down nine-to-five work ethic and competitive individualism, its emphasis on private property and the amassing of material goods ("conspicuous consumption"), its norms of state violence and aggression as means of resolving conflicts and threats (both domestically and internationally), and its reliance on modern technologies that threaten the environment. Moreover, the counterculture rejected mainstream norms of exclusivity in sexual relationships and the right of the state to legislate individual behaviors such as drug use. In essence, the counterculture challenged what it referred to as "the Establishment." Many in the movement were young people who joined urban collectives and rural communes to jointly produce or buy their own food, communally raise their children, eschew the "rat race" of traditional jobs, foster cooperation instead of competition, and drastically reduce or eliminate their reliance on technology. Many communes also endorsed illicit drug use and non-normative sexual practices. Ironically, many communes reverted to sexist divisions of labor, relegating household chores and child care largely to women. Many also developed mainstream patriarchal power structures, with men dominating the decision-making process. While not all communes replicated mainstream sexism, its presence in some countercultural settings suggests the powerful influence mainstream norms and values can have.

Gangs can also be seen as countercultures. They tend to emerge from poverty and disenfranchisement from the mainstream's economic, social, and political opportunity structures. In the United States, where the Census Bureau indicates that 23.4 percent of African American families and 22.7 percent of Latino/Latina families live below the poverty line, it is not surprising to find that 46 percent of gang members are Latino/Latina and 34 percent are African American (U.S. Dept. of Justice, 1999; U.S. Census Bureau, 1999). There are also several very active Asian American gangs in New York, Los Angeles, and other major cities (Huff, 1996; Vigil, 1997).

Gangs come in a variety of forms, including social gangs, neighborhood street gangs, and organized-crime gangs. Our discussion here focuses on the neighborhood street gangs. Many of these have spread from specific urban neighborhoods to other neighborhoods, entire cities, or more suburban areas. These gangs often use illegal weapons and violence to commit crimes and control neighborhoods.

Gangs are typically organizations of alienated youths whose experiences remind them that the mainstream culture disdains and disrespects them. Gang members are frequently poorly educated and many live in substandard housing. They are chronically unemployed because urban education systems often do not provide adequate skills training and because there are fewer and fewer jobs for those without such training. Youth gangs can be seen as a countercultural response to blocked opportunities (Long and Ricard, 1996; Sheldon, Tracy, and Brown, 1997). But gangs are not necessarily typical only among poor, urban minorities: increasingly gangs are emerging in more affluent white suburbs where youth alienation and stagnated opportunities combine with the romanticized portrayal of gangs in movies and videos as icons of rebellion and empowerment to appeal to and attract a wider audience (Monti, 1994; Wooden, 1995). Gangs reject many of the values and norms of the mainstream and form their own often violent and predatory countercultures. For example, dominant cultural norms stipulate that only the state can use force and violence to resolve disputes and that individuals must settle conflicts through negotiations or legal processes. Gangs challenge this notion by brazenly investing powers of violence with individual members. Gang violence also repudiates mainstream norms that call for deference to institutional authorities, such as those in schools and in the criminal justice system; it becomes a means of eliciting a semblance of respect, based on fear, from other gang members as well as the larger community. Gangs often respond to

Gangs often function as countercultures for disenfranchised youths. Members of this gang reject the dominant cultural definition of femininity as docility and adopt their own cultural code of toughness, including norms governing how to dress and adorn one's body, a system of gestures and body language, and violent initiation ceremonies.

the unavailability of jobs in the mainstream economy by participating in drug trafficking, which can be lucrative although highly dangerous. Larceny and robbery may also be part of gang activity (Anderson, 1999; Hagedorn, 1998).

Gangs reject mainstream culture in more symbolic ways as well. For example, their members' dress (such as the widespread use of bandannas as "colors" identifying gang affiliation), hairstyles, tattoos, and language defy the dominant folkways. Gangs also represent an alternative to mainstream definitions of family as one's unit of procreation and parentage. The gang itself becomes an extended family providing protection as well as approval and support for delinquent and violent acts not accepted by the larger society (Clark, 1991; Kaplan, Johnson, and Bailey, 1987), or it acts as a surrogate family when even the opportunity for developing the traditional form virtually disappears (Moore and Hagedorn, 1996).

In a unique participant observation study of several female gangs in New York City, Campbell (1991) showed how such gangs reject the dominant culture's restrictive gender roles and establish their independence through the use of violence. While she disagreed with the notion that female gangs represent a counterculture, her descriptions of three of them suggest otherwise. For example, her findings indicate that female gangs will not accept members who are not able to "take care of themselves." Prospective members must demonstrate that they are willing and able to engage in a fight. In some instances, once the gangs have established this ability, members are initiated into the gang in a violent ritual called "jumping in." In this initiation they must endure (and perhaps defend themselves against) severe beatings by other gang members for a period of 10 seconds.

Members in the gangs also form strong ties with other members; they do not allow men to come between the "sisters." Members frequently demand extreme loyalty to the gang, over and above boyfriends and even family. Female gangs thus repudiate the mainstream gender prescriptions of females as docile and dependent and as antagonistic rivals.

In some ways, gangs provide an interesting demonstration of how a counterculture can, in fact, embrace dominant cultural values while establishing very different and challenging norms. For example, gangs often accept the mainstream value of economic success and all the material comforts such success affords. But, faced with blocked opportunities, the gangs resort to their own norms for acquiring wealth, such as drug trafficking, robbery, larceny, and extortion of "protection" money from local small businesses (Clark, 1991). Some gangs have spread beyond the local "turf" battles and have organized "franchises" in many cities. These intercity franchises facilitate the movement of stolen goods and drugs. The national network this creates frustrates law enforcement agencies, which have tried in vain to control such gang activities. Gangs' countercultures thus become a parody of mainstream values, even as the gangs adopt normative behaviors that defy the legitimacy of the dominant culture.

CHAPTER SUMMARY

1. Culture is a social construction created by members of society. But not all members' viewpoints concerning values and norms are equally powerful in influencing the contours of mainstream culture. Since culture is transmitted from one generation to another, those members who have enjoyed prior privilege, advantage, and power are in a stronger position than others to impose their values and norms on everyone else. Similarly, since culture is diffused from one society to another, those societies with greater power and advantage are better able to influence the cultures of others.

2. Mainstream culture shapes individuals' biographies by defining what is acceptable and unacceptable and what is normal and abnormal in regard to behavior and life circumstances. These culturally defined restrictions narrow people's vision of legitimate alternatives. In addition, punishments for violations of these norms may reduce the likelihood that people will challenge existing rules and guidelines and may sometimes prevent them from even considering alternatives. Individuals who depart from the dominant culture may be marginalized and condemned by members of mainstream society.

3. Language, as the key to cultural transmission, is a powerful vehicle for constructing reality. Individuals who control what constitutes legitimate language usage can significantly influence the definitions of appropriate and inappropriate behaviors, viewpoints, and values. They can also shape what people consider to be real and viable and what never even occurs to them as possible.

4. Although the ideas, values, and norms of dominant groups tend to define the dominant culture, cultural diversity and resistance can still exist. The persistence of subcultures, for example, testifies to the fact that diverse values and normative systems can thrive even as the members of the subcultures participate in the mainstream culture. And the presence of countercultures illustrates the power of human effort to challenge and reject mainstream, dominant norms and values and to push at their boundaries. Moreover, in addition to functioning as the key to the social construction of reality by society's dominant members, language may also be used by the less powerful to sharpen people's consciousness about that social construction and to introduce new ways of seeing the world and ultimately helping to change the dominant culture.

5. Culture, then, is not simply a body of ideas and practices handed down unchanged from one generation to the next. It is a process of power struggles and contested constructions of social reality involving various members of society. These struggles are part of an ongoing historical process in which groups possessing variable resources and abilities strive to articulate and preserve the legitimacy of their social worlds. We examine this process of organized struggle over the social construction of reality and cultural content in Chapter 10.

THINKING CRITICALLY

1. In the "Social Forces/People's Lives" reading, the author describes her internal struggle to balance her ethnic identity with her status as an American citizen. Consider your own ethnic heritage. Do you have conflicts similar to those the author describes? What does being an "American" mean? Must you give up your ethnic identity in order to be fully "American"?

2. Many variables may contribute to the development of a subculture. Consider the variety of statuses you have. Which of these might shape a subcultural existence for you? Why? Describe the elements of your subculture that depart from mainstream culture. Do these differences draw sanctions from the larger normative system? Why?

3. Think about situations you have encountered in which the norms differed significantly from those with which you are familiar. How did you react? Why? What norms did these differences define for you?

4. Consider the textbooks, ideas, and materials to which you were exposed in elementary school and high school. Make a list of the images, ideas, norms, and values focused on in your schools. How closely did they conform to mainstream culture, and how much did they challenge it? Were you invited to debate the ideas presented in the classrooms and in the texts? How? How were uninvited challenges received?

5. Much debate has centered around the notion of "politically correct" language. What is politically correct language? What values does such language invoke?

Why might there be considerable resistance to the use of politically correct language? What role does such language play in society?

KEY TERMS

competitive individualism, *(124)*
corporate culture, *(124)*
counterculture, *(135)*
cultural diffusion, *(134)*
cultural hegemony, *(111)*
cultural lag, *(135)*
cultural leveling, *(125)*
cultural relativity, *(128)*
culture, *(111)*
culture of poverty, *(124)*
culture shock, *(113)*
ethnocentrism, *(113)*

folkways, *(114)*
ideology, *(111)*
language, *(119)*
laws, *(115)*
material culture, *(118)*
McDonaldization of Society, *(125)*
mores, *(114)*
multiculturalism, *(129)*
nonmaterial culture, *(118)*
normative indoctrination, *(113)*
norms, *(112)*

patriarchy, *(117)*
rituals, *(132)*
sanctions, *(113)*
Sapir-Whorf hypothesis, *(120)*
subculture, *(131)*
Thomas theorem (definition of the situation), *(121)*
values, *(116)*

Chapter Six

Socialization

When you entered your first college class, you probably knew that you had to take a seat in the classroom rather than sit at the desk in front of the room, take out a notebook and a pen to take notes, raise your hand to speak rather than simply call out, and come to class dressed in clothing like jeans and a shirt rather than a bathing suit or pajamas. You also are likely to hold certain attitudes about what you expect of others in your environment: You expect that if you're the first to arrive in the lecture hall you may select any seat you wish; the next person to enter the room may also select any seat, but not the one right next to yours, and not the one you selected. You may also have some ideas about what your classmates should look like and about who you would consider a good candidate for a date. And you are likely to have some ideas about what you might like to do when you graduate and what your realistic options are. How do you know all of this, and where did these ideas come from?

Sociologists have long recognized that social attitudes and behaviors such as these are learned because of the great variability in cultural patterns throughout the world. As members of a society, individuals learn and adopt social attitudes. Such attitudes are not genetically programmed; people learn them. Are your attitudes similar to or different from those of your friends, your family, or your teachers?

Answer the following questions as honestly as you can: If one person of a two- earner couple has to quit work and remain at home because of a family situation, how should the couple decide which person will quit? Do you believe the United States is full of opportunity for anyone willing to work hard? Would you hesitate to marry someone who has a physical disability? Would you be willing to go to war if the president asked you to, even if you didn't understand the reasons for the United States to be involved? What if you didn't agree with the reasons? Suppose you wanted to lease your home to tenants and you receive two similar offers, one from a female-headed family and one from a two-parent family. Which one would you rent your house to, and why? Should the school board of your child's elementary school be permitted to hire a kindergarten teacher who happens to be gay? Suppose you are on the admissions board of a prestigious medical school, and you have one opening left. Two applicants come before you with similar grades and board exam scores. One is the daughter of an unemployed coal miner, and the other is the son of a member of the U.S. Congress. Which applicant will you admit? Would you buy a home in a neighborhood in which most people were not of your race? Should legal marriage be possible for gay men or lesbians? Should capital punishment be abolished? Should retirement be mandatory for everyone at age 65?

Your responses reflect your attitudes on a number of social issues. People are not born with such attitudes; these are learned. This raises several questions about their origins:

continued

- **How does this learning occur?**
- **Who does the teaching?**
- **To what degree is the individual a passive recipient in this process?**
- **Can an individual transform the persons doing the teaching?**
- **What sorts of social roles and identities do people learn?**
- **What are the possible limitations to the process?**

This chapter examines how sociologists study the learning process sociologists call socialization.

Socialization as a Learning Process

Human beings are social animals by nature, and are among the most dependent of animals at birth: When humans are born, the muscles and the nervous, skeletal, and digestive systems are not fully developed, and individuals cannot care for themselves. People rely on other humans to nurture and protect them. But the need for other human beings does not end when individuals learn to walk and feed themselves. Along the way, individuals become members of society. The ongoing process of learning the ways of one's culture is called **socialization.** During this lifelong process, individuals acquire and modify their social identities. People learn, accept, reject, and modify the norms, values, assumptions, and expectations of the societies in which they live. Finally, members of society develop the political lenses through which they view and analyze their surroundings.

Social scientists often debate the relationship between what people inherit and what they learn. Sociologists call this the **nature-versus-nurture debate.** Some sociologists argue that many social behaviors appear to be inherited genetically (e.g., intelligence and the capacity to learn, aggression or passivity, and sexual orientation) (Kagan, Resnick, and Snidman, 1988). The study of the biological basis of social behavior is known as **sociobiology.** Other sociologists view social characteristics as primarily socially constructed, influenced by such environmental factors as power in relationships and learning. If social traits were biologically determined, they say, such immense variation within families and societies and between cultures in social behaviors and attitudes would be unlikely (Wilson, 2000).

Yet studies of twins separated at birth and raised apart suggest that some social traits may develop independently of individuals' social environment. Twins raised apart often exhibit surprisingly similar traits, such as shyness, in spite of very different upbringings and surroundings (Bouchard and McGue, 1990). How can the contradictions of evidence in the nature-versus-nurture debate be reconciled? Many sociologists take a middle ground. They argue that although the *potential* for expressing some social traits may indeed be inherited, striking evidence shows that social characteristics are unlikely to develop without social interaction between individuals as well as between individuals and a variety of social agents.

For example, children deprived of social contacts do not thrive physically and tend to be socially and emotionally immature. This is often the case with institutionalized children (Cermak and Groza, 1998). In fact, even when infants in institutions are given the best basic care in terms of food, clothing, hygiene, and shelter, their social development is slow at best without regular play and human interaction (Cummins and Dunt, 1988). Consider Anna, a child whose unmarried mother, fearful of her grandfather's fury, kept the child in an attic where she was fed but otherwise largely ignored. When Anna was found, she was a six-year-old child who could not even sit up, much less walk, and she could not talk; she was unable to express any emotion, other than to bite the social workers who worked with her (Davis, 1940). In another case, Genie's father locked her away before she was two years old in an isolated room with no human contact beyond the brief visits by family to bring her food. She remained locked away for 11 years, until her mother, herself abused by Genie's father, escaped and took Genie with her. Like Anna, Genie could not speak or stand up straight, and she could walk only in the clumsy fashion of a toddler; she was not toilet-trained, and her emotional expression was confined largely to animal-like noises. Doctors described her as primitive and barely human (Curtiss, 1977). Adults who are deprived similarly to Anna and Genie, such as prisoners in solitary confinement for long periods of time, tend to regress to infantile behaviors (e.g., assuming a fetal position and thumb-sucking). These cases suggest that the provision of the basic physical needs for survival such as food and water is not sufficient to ensure social development or even physical development of the human being in the absence of human contact.

Notably, evidence suggests that children who were deprived of social interaction early in their lives improve in language, social skills, and muscle control when stimulated by increased human contact (Scarr, 1982). In the case of Anna described above, social workers intensively provided interaction and care, and within four years she was able to talk and attempt conversations and could perform basic functions of daily life, such as brushing her teeth and washing her hands, keeping her clothing clean, walking, and even running. Her emotional range increased regularly (Davis, 1948). Genie showed similar progress once under the intensive care of social workers and physicians. Although both children's eventual development was well behind that of most children of their ages, their astonishing progress highlights the essential importance of human interaction for developing and reinforcing social characteristics. However, they do not tell us exactly *how* individuals learn to adopt certain attitudes and behaviors. In short, how do individuals become members of society? What is the *process* of socialization? Who participates in this process, and what role do they play?

Symbolic Interactionist Perspective

Several theorists maintain that individuals develop social identities through **symbolic interaction,** an interpersonal process using language and other symbols, and sanctions. It is through that interaction process that individuals come to learn the values and norms of their society: they learn how to behave, what to think, and what to expect of others. Let's look, for example, at what this might entail for some sociologists.

Charles Horton Cooley: The Looking-Glass Self

The sociologist Charles Horton Cooley (1902) argued that people acquire a sense of who they are by evaluating themselves through the eyes of others, imagining how these others might react to a particular behavior. He calls this identity the **looking-glass self.** People see themselves as they believe others see them, perhaps altering behaviors they believe others disapprove of. Cooley argued that these others need not be present during this process; people's assumptions and ideas of how they are likely to react are sufficient. For example, when you wish to speak in class, you know you should raise your hand and wait to be called on, and then avoid using slang and profane words. You do not need a specific teacher in front of you to tell you this every semester and for every class; you become aware over the years as a student that this is what is expected of you, and you are likely to act accordingly.

Cooley's analysis of the looking-glass self did not distinguish among the various others whose perceptions individuals anticipate. Are the opinions of all others equally important to people when they see themselves through others' eyes? Some sociologists, like George Herbert Mead, did not think so.

George Herbert Mead: Significant and Generalized Others

Sociologist George Herbert Mead (1934) believed that the child's primary group relationships (e.g., family, peers) were crucial, as "significant others," to the development of the self. Harry Stack Sullivan (1953) later argued that the most important primary group member is the mother, who becomes the child's significant other. Since an infant is so dependent on its mother for nurturance and survival, he argued, the mother becomes uniquely important to the child; her judgment and approval are critical in developing the child's sense of self and identity. Later, researchers found that fathers are also significant (Lamb, 1997). In fact, anyone who functions as a child's primary caregiver may be viewed as the significant other. Such persons could be grandparents and other family members, foster or adoptive parents, or day care workers (Pooley et al., 2000).

As the child matures, the process of acquiring social identity and self-awareness extends to play. For example, children try on a variety of roles through dress-up and playacting. As they mature further, children develop a generalized understanding of how people around them expect them to behave and of what their place is among those people through role-playing. They no longer need the actual presence of known individuals in order to understand their own roles and identities. They now evaluate their behavior through a **generalized other.** Here, play and pretend are highlighted as critical elements in social development (Barnett, 1977).

Mead's analysis speaks of the process of shaping a sense of self as if it occurs only in children. In fact, many different **significant others,** people who are vitally important to individuals in their daily existence, may appear throughout the life cycle. Anyone who is centrally important to individuals at a particular point in their lives—on-the-job mentors, for example, or coaches, advisers, or partners—may take on the role of significant other. Indeed, many couples in the United States refer to each other as "my significant other." Some researchers argue that a significant other does not have to be someone with whom the individual is intimate or even another person at all. For example, television may act as significant other for some people (Newton and Buck, 1985). For others, some notion of a spiritual higher being is sufficient.

Mead's analysis of how individuals acquire social identities suggests that the process of self-development is reflexive, involving the individual as an active agent rather than as a passive recipient. That is, developing a self-identity involves an interaction "between identification by others and self-identification, between objectively assigned and subjectively appropriated identity" (Berger and Luckmann, 1966:132). Thus socialization subjects may resist or reject others' definitions of "appropriate" behaviors. However, the focus in Mead's analysis remains the socialization subject. This focus implies that the socialization process moves in one direction only: The agent socializes the subject.

Children often play at adult roles during games of dress-up. Here, a child plays doctor to a "sick" teddy bear patient, mimicking the adult world of work.

Symbolic Interaction as a Dynamic Process

More recent analyses using a symbolic interaction perspective suggest that the interaction process is a dynamic one: *Both* parties get socialized rather than just one; adults get socialized as well as children. For example, although parents and other primary caregivers may indeed teach the child about appropriate behaviors, the child may also socialize the caregivers, altering their behaviors, values, or attitudes (Peterson and Rollins, 1987). When labor and management engage in negotiations, management is certainly attempting to indoctrinate the workers about appropriate attitudes and behaviors, but the workers are also teaching management about appropriate interaction and bargaining styles, acceptable demand levels, and so forth. Both parties are in fact altering their behavior patterns. Even when one party is clearly more powerful than the other, that power is not absolute. There is usually some room for each side to modify its position in response to the socialization it has undergone.

Conflict Perspective

Sociologists using a **conflict perspective** argue that socialization processes are, in fact, typified by struggles. Conflict theorists examine the internal as well as external struggles experienced in the process of socialization. They also tend to view socialization as ongoing throughout the life cycle. As individuals encounter new situations and challenges in their lives, they are always shaping and reshaping their social identities. As they move from school to the work world or from single life to marriage, for example, people learn new sets of expectations, some of which may challenge previous social constructions of themselves. Even though some statuses (e.g., race and sex,) do not change, people's sense of what they mean may change over time. Other statuses may actually change (e.g., age, family status, working status, sexual orientation, and physical and mental capacities and capabilities), prompting a personal reconceptualization of self and a reevaluation of expectations. Conflict theorists argue that as people confront and resolve these changes and challenges, they form and redefine their social identity.

Conflict in Social Psychological Explanations

Learning a social identity and how to interact in society is not a smooth or easy process. Many observers have noted how rife with conflict such learning can be. For example, the noted psychologist Sigmund Freud (1946/1930) described a conflict involving a primitive, almost feral self that he called the **id** in unsocialized infants, a driving, self-centered force that compels individuals to focus on their own personal pleasure. While the need to satisfy personal demands for pleasure is biologically natural, he argued, it is quite at odds with the requirements of the larger society. Social norms largely do not accept public displays of sexual gratification or defecation on public streets, even if these are widely acknowledged as satisfying actions. People learn to control the urge for instant gratification, primarily by parents setting limits and punishing children's failure to remain within those limits identifying appropriate times and places for satisfaction of personal pleasures. That learning process helps establish the development of the **ego,** which Freud defined as the rational self that controls the urges of the id. Freud argued that the individual also develops a **super-ego,** or conscience, as a result of this learning process. Even in the absence of a punishing other to help remind the ego to control the id, the superego functions as that restraining force. Here, the superego is the internalized parental voice, reinforcing the limiting rules of social behavior. The individual's personality and social behavior thus are the site of constant conflict between the id, the ego, and the superego.

Where Freud's analysis emphasized how children become socialized into social beings, psychologist Erik Erikson (1963) argued that individuals develop their identities and attitudes about the world throughout the entire life cycle as they resolve various developmental conflicts and crises. Although he specified the life stages during which each crisis typically occurs, he argued that individuals may always return to earlier crises and rework them or complete unresolved ones. How people resolve these crises shapes their social identities (see Figure 6.1).

The basic conflict during infancy concerns reliance on others to provide food, shelter, protection, and comfort. Infants resolve this problem by developing either *basic trust* or *basic mistrust* that the world around them can be counted on to provide consistently for their needs. Toddlers encountering challenges of personal control (e.g., during toilet training) resolve their crisis with either a *sense of autonomy,* if control is mastered, or a *sense of shame and doubt,* if control proves difficult to achieve. Preschool children, whose main challenge is to learn to perform basic tasks independently, develop either a *sense of initiative* born of successful attempts at

Old Age	Integrity versus Despair
Maturity	Generativity versus Stagnation
Young Adulthood	Intimacy versus Isolation
Adolescence	Identity versus Role Confusion
School Age	Industry versus Inferiority
Preschool	Initiative versus Guilt
Early Childhood	Autonomy versus Shame, Doubt
Infancy	Trust versus Mistrust

FIGURE 6.1 **Erickson's Stages of Psychosocial Development** Erik Erikson underscored the role of culture in personality development throughout the life cycle. Consider your own personality development: Which developmental stages are you currently struggling with? (Source: Adapted from Erik Erikson, *Childhood and Society,* 2nd ed. New York: W.W. Norton & Company Inc., 1950.)

mastery or a *sense of guilt* from repeated failures. Older children confront increasingly challenging academic and physical skills. If they learn that mastery of these skills involves the often frustrating process of trying, failing, and trying again, they are more likely to develop a *sense of industry* and a willingness to work through failures. If they learn that not mastering a task immediately is a personal failing and a character flaw, they are more likely to develop a *sense of inferiority.* Adolescents face the challenge of establishing a clear definition of self. Success in defining "who I am" resolves the crisis with a *sense of identity;* failure to resolve the identity crisis may result in *role confusion.*

Beyond adolescence, Erikson saw three more crises. Young adults face the tension of establishing close personal relationships, many of which may not last for very long. Such crises resolve either in a *sense of intimacy* and a willingness to make oneself vulnerable to another or in a *sense of isolation* and a refusal or reluctance to risk getting close to others. Adults must resolve the crisis of maintaining a *sense of generativity,* involving productiveness and growth, or they may develop a *sense of stagnation,* of being in a rut or not being challenged or excited about their work or lifestyle. Elderly adults, particularly at retirement, resolve the crisis of identity shift either with a *sense of integrity,* feeling they have performed well and lived a good life, or a *sense of despair,* feeling they have wasted their lives or lost sight of their goals.

Conflict in Structural Explanations

Freud's and Erikson's analyses certainly emphasized conflicts in socialization of individuals as social members of society, but they focused on individuals' psychological processes. In contrast, W. E. B. Du Bois (1989/1903) examined the conflicts resulting from the intersection between identity processes and larger social structures and relationships. He argued that African Americans commonly formed dual, sometimes "warring" identities separated by what he referred to as a *veil*. As strategy for survival in a racist world, the veil allows African American individuals to see themselves as black persons with an individual consciousness while also seeing themselves through white eyes. This does not mean the individual forgets that he or she is African American; but power inequalities based on race require African American people to be conscious of how whites are likely to see them and expect them to behave and to conform to racist expectations, such as deferment to whites, as a matter of survival. This is because whites control so much that can affect African Americans' life chances, including jobs, housing, education, health care, and legal justice. The veil functions to preserve and protect the African American identity for expression in safe and supportive circumstances and to send that identity underground in more threatening situations. This dual identity, Du Bois argued, produces "this peculiar sensation, this double-consciousness, this sense of always looking at one's self through the eyes of another" (1989/1903:5). A similar analysis of this double consciousness can also be seen among Asian Americans (Min, 1996; Spickard, 1997).

Whereas Cooley spoke of the looking-glass self affecting all individuals in their identity formation, Du Bois referred to the conflict that specifically affects the identity of persons of color in a white-dominated society. In Du Bois's analysis, the perceptions of the (white) "other" are likely to devalue the worth of the individual's identity because of racist stereotypes and assumptions rather than the actual behavior of the individual, and thus have the power to make those assumptions matter. The concept of the veil, then, highlights both the internal conflicts individuals struggle with in the development of a general social identity and the external conflicts between persons of color and the white-dominated world in which they must live in particular.

Further complicating the conflict surrounding the development of identity is the rise in multiracial identities. Increasingly, sociologists are recognizing that previous social constructions of racial identity as matters of black versus white (which later broadened to include categories of Latino, Asian American and Pacific Island, and Native American) are no longer valid. Individuals' identities are often defined more by overlaps of a wide range of ethnic and racial backgrounds and heritages as a result of immigration and intermarriage (Root, 1996). This means that identity formation is frequently marked by conflicts in the negotiations between sharply different cultures and loyalties (Hall and duGay, 1996). Du Bois's veil is likely to produce not just a double consciousness, but a more complicated multiple consciousness. The logistics of maintaining several such identities is surely characterized by heightened tension and conflicts as individuals seek to develop positive multiracial identities in a white-dominated society. At least one study, on the other hand, found that many individuals feel that multiracial identity actually liberates them rather than isolating and marginalizing them, because their membership in several racial and ethnic groups broadens their social consciousness and makes them wiser and more socially astute. In such cases, race is no longer a matter of imposed social constructions; rather, race is chosen by individuals (Korgen, 1998).

Resocialization processes often involve a degradation ceremony, during which an individual's previous identity is broken down in order to shape a new identity. At prison boot camp, each new recruit is given a uniform bearing a prison number. This becomes their new identity, replacing their name, and they are frequently subjected to verbal assaults on their dignity, individuality, and previous identity.

Socialization, Conflict, and Social Structure

Erikson's and Du Bois's analyses introduce conflict rather than consensus as the central characteristic of the socialization process. However, Erikson's model is based on the assumption that specific roles and tasks belong to particular life stages, and it defines success and failure narrowly. And because of Erikson's psychoanalytical perspective, his analysis assumes psychosocial development to be more a personal problem of individual struggles and conflicts than the result of structural restrictions. For example, if an adolescent girl is told she cannot participate in football because she is not strong enough, the feeling of inferiority she might develop would be seen as the result of a personal failure to resolve a developmental crisis. Yet it seems more likely that her feeling of inferiority would be the result of systematic discrimination and differential treatment in the social structure, a point emphasized by Du Bois. Sometimes both personal and social elements are at work. Consider an elderly woman who feels a sense of despair. She may have failed to resolve some personal crises, but she also may feel the burden of a social structure that limits her opportunities, perhaps sharply reduces her income, restricts her access to outlets for usefulness, narrowly defines her roles, and accords "senior citizens" little respect.

Looking at the role of both internal and institutional conflicts suggests that the process of identity development does not necessarily produce a uniform outcome for all. Some people may, in fact, resist and reject the dominant group's definition of appropriate and inappropriate behaviors. What happens in such cases? In some instances, sanctions may be imposed to punish or correct the "inappropriate" behavior.

For example, homosexuals, whose very existence violates the prevailing mores of heterosexuality, often suffer the intense sanctions of being ostracized or harassed, denied employment or fired. Children who display "gender-inappropriate" behaviors may be called names, ostracized by their peers, and "redirected" by guidance counselors who try to steer them to more "appropriate" behaviors and aspirations. Those who violate the mores against intimate interracial relationships may experience similar sanctions.

When informal sanctions are insufficient to alter an individual's resistance, dominant groups may sometimes attempt to reeducate, or resocialize, the transgressor. **Resocialization** is a process in which the individual's previous self is dismantled and replaced with a new, more acceptable social identity (Fein, 1990; Ichilov, 2002). Sometimes individuals undergoing resocialization may be relocated to entirely new and unfamiliar locations called **total institutions,** in which they are completely isolated from the rest of society as well as from their ordinary surroundings and social networks for an extended period of time. In such environments the individual's life is carefully controlled and the process of resocialization more easily accomplished (Goffman, 1961).

New military recruits experience this situation in boot camp, where they undergo a fairly intense process of resocialization designed to break down civilian values of individuality, freedom of expression, and freedom of choice and replace them with new values. The recruits learn to accept orders unquestioningly, to subordinate individuality to country or troop, and to respect rank, the flag, and the uniform. They learn to accept narrowly defined conceptions of appropriate dress and hairstyles and to suspend personal opinions concerning a broad variety of issues, both personal and global. In some cases, the process may involve a **degradation ceremony,** in which socialization agents assail and devalue the subject's existing identity in an effort to break it down and build an entirely new one (Garfinkel, 1956). For example, drill instructors in military boot camp may publicly call resistant or struggling recruits pejorative names or challenge the manhood of male recruits by referring to them with women's names and attributing feminine characteristics to them. Officers may penalize the recruits by assigning them to publicly demeaning chores, such as cleaning bathrooms with a toothbrush, or denying them privileges such as leave time. Goffman (1961) found that similar processes occur among prisoners and patients at state mental hospitals.

Resocialization may also occur in more subtle ways. Changes in life circumstances can bring about transformations of one's social identity. For example, no total-institution setting is required for the changes that accompany the shifts from student to worker, from childless person to parent, from worker to retiree, and so on.

At the same time that individuals develop a social identity, they also undergo a constant process of political socialization. In this process they may internalize a political identity of who they are and how they should behave in the political and economic institutions of society. Moreover, individuals may learn to accept the dominant social structure and its inequalities as just, fair, and legitimate. Socialization, then, can be a means of political control, in which the dominant group may influence and shape individuals' perceptions of acceptable or appropriate political attitudes and behaviors (e.g., voting is an acceptable way to express dissatisfaction, but rioting is not), limit their conception of valid options for action, and legitimize its rule and ideology.

Agents of Socialization

How do people come to be socially and politically socialized? Who or what are the agents of socialization? **Socialization agents** can be classified as primary groups such as family members and peers; secondary groups such as schools, religious and work organizations; mass media and language usage; toys, games, and recreational activities; and institutions such as the state. As we pointed out in Chapter 3, institutions operate to address the functional imperatives of societal survival as their manifest function. One of these is to teach the knowledge and skills necessary to be contributing members of society and to motivate members to perform their roles. Those institutions that perform this function are clearly agents of socialization. But socialization can also occur as a latent function of institutions as they address the other basic imperatives as well.

pp. 59–60

Family

Just as family reinforces "appropriate" social and gender roles, some observers also believe that birth order acts as a passive socialization agent (Steelman and Powell, 1985). One's birth-order position in the family may greatly affect siblings' interactions as well as parent–child interactions. These interactions become part of one's socialization experiences.

For example, firstborn children (if they are not twins) tend to be more strictly disciplined, to receive more attention, to remain in school longer, and to be higher achievers than later-born siblings. With second-born children, parents are more relaxed and tend to be less authoritative; such children may therefore have more relaxed relationships with others and be more playful than firstborns. Second-borns may also be more diplomatic negotiators than firstborns, because they are smaller than older siblings and must therefore rely more on reason and rationality than on brute strength. It is important to note, however, that these social characteristics are based on a middle-class model of the family. Birth-order characteristics may be complicated by such factors as the age and spacing of siblings and parents' differential expectations based on gender, class, ethnicity, and family structure (Kilbride, Johnson, and Streissguth, 1977).

Peer Groups

Peer groups constitute an alternative **reference group** to family members. A reference group is a group to whom individuals look for approval, guidance, and role models. Peer groups may be an important factor influencing study habits, work aspirations, and lifestyle goals (Allen, McManus, and Russell, 1999). Children and adolescents often develop a greater sense of autonomy from adults by forming coalitions with peers (McLellan and Pugh, 1999). In extreme cases, gangs and other countercultural groups may develop to challenge authority. Adults who work together often form informal groups of peers that may counteract rules of managers or corporate culture (see Chapter 4). pp. 102–105

People who are subject to systematic prejudice or disapproval may look to peer groups to help resist being stigmatized and reinforce the validity of their autonomy. For example, the many formal and informal gay and lesbian peer groups found in high schools, colleges, and urban areas serve this dual purpose. Students of color on predominantly white campuses frequently look to peer groups to affirm their validity in the dominant group's culture. And women often form peer groups as a way to countervail patriarchal treatment and share information that challenges the prevailing attitudes toward women's appropriate roles, rights, and abilities.

Schools

Schools reproduce the dominant culture of society by socializing students about what is valued and appropriate in the culture and what is not (Rodden, 2001; Spyrou, 2000). For example, curricula and texts that stress white, male, privileged European contributions to U.S. society and ignore the legitimacy of contributions of people of color, women, and the working class reproduce a limited set of cultural values (Deegan, 1998; Parker, 2001). In-school celebration of Christian holidays (such as Christmas) but not of other ethnic or religious groups' holidays (such as Hanukkah, Kwanzaa, or winter solstice) makes Christianity seem more valuable and legitimate than other credos. Similarly, if schools honor the birthdays of Washington and Lincoln but not Dr. Martin Luther King, they teach children that King's contributions to U.S. society are less important. The celebration of the dominant groups' culture and the failure to acknowledge the importance of others may socialize whites and Christians to an identity of superiority and privilege while socializing people of color and non-Christians to an identity of marginality and inferiority.

The dramatic rise of day care as a common experience of many preschoolers increases the role of such "schooling" facilities as socialization agents. Day care teachers have the potential, as surrogate parents for at least part of the day, to teach very young children core values. While taking turns, sharing, resolving conflicts without violence, and developing good manners are among the common themes many day care centers foster, attitudes related to gender, race, and class position may also be transmitted by teachers.

Religious Organizations

Religious organizations socialize us to adopt particular attitudes and behaviors that may or may not be consistent with the dominant culture. For example, an ideology that stresses sacrifice and asceticism, obedience to a higher authority, acceptance of one's lot in life as part of a plan of that higher authority, heterosexual love and marriage, tradition, and hard work is consistent with the values of the dominant culture in the United States. These principles contribute to a social identity based on conformity, which makes it less likely that oppressed or exploited groups subject to this ideology will challenge the authority and privilege of the dominant groups.

Schools frequently function as agents of socialization, teaching students core cultural values. The rise of day care as a common daily experience of an increasing number of preschoolers places day care workers in the same capacity as socialization agents.

On the other hand, some religious teachings stress nonacceptance of poverty, challenge of higher authorities if they are oppressive or punitive, civil disobedience, and the legitimacy of nontraditional lifestyles. This religious position has occurred as a social movement in Latin American Catholic churches, where it is referred to as **Liberation Theology.** This theology may pose a countervailing influence to dominant socialization forces. Indeed, in parts of Mexico as well as Central and South America, the poor are encouraged by local clergy to believe that challenging landowners and political authorities who see fit to oppress and starve them, deprive them of dignity and civil and human rights, and otherwise abuse them is entirely appropriate.

In the United States, African American churches played a pivotal role in the civil rights movement from the 1950s to 1970s. Unitarian and mainline Protestant denominational churches have come to recognize the legitimacy of women as clergy, and many Conservative and Reformed Jewish synagogues have come to accept female rabbis. The Episcopal Church now accepts priests who are homosexual and has generally played an active role in the gay, lesbian, bisexual, and transgender movement. Religious organizations throughout the world were often visible and vocal opponents to the Vietnam war, giving legitimacy to such opposition. More recently, churches in the United States have provided asylum for Central American refugees escaping oppression by their governments. Not only have these churches provided refugees with food, clothing, and shelter, but they have also protected them from deportation by U.S. immigration authorities. The participation of religious institutions in the antiwar and asylum movements lends institutional support to people who challenge their governments, both here and abroad. Religious doctrine, then, can contribute to a social identity that includes the entitlement to protest and challenge oppression. It can also contribute to a social identity based on a notion of social justice and altruism.

The Workplace

The workplace acts as both a formal and an informal socialization agent, reinforcing capitalist social relations of production. For example, on-the-job training is a formal mechanism of workplace socialization, in which one is taught rules, regulations, expectations of behavior, and recognition of authority figures and status symbols. Individuals who train closely with a mentor tend to become dependent on the mentor, and therefore more susceptible to influence (Shire, 1999).

Training in groups can produce a team spirit that reinforces dominant workplace values. For example, military training in boot camp emphasizes the importance of duty to country, a strong sense of "us" against "them," and the necessity of a buddy system for survival against a common enemy. Corporate softball and bowling teams reinforce many similar principles and create a sense of family and loyalty among the workers for that firm.

Group training can, however, also produce camaraderie among trainees *against* corporate and military authority figures and become a source of resistance to the workplace organization. For example, during the Vietnam war, instances of organized violent retaliation by recruits against abusive or overzealous officers occurred frequently. Assembly-line workers may develop group loyalty to one another in the face of exploitative or overly harsh management, devising ways to set more comfortable rates of productivity and, in extreme cases, sabotaging output. Computer hacking is now emerging as a new form of corporate sabotage, sometimes involving the dissemination of sensitive information about executives and managers who workers view as dictatorial or arbitrary. While these examples describe conflicts between workers and management, group training can sometimes also produce intragroup forces to conform. The classic Hawthorne studies discussed in Chapter 4 revealed ◀ pp. 102–103 how an informal group of workers punished those whose productivity exceeded the group's informally set rate. The group also covered for colleagues whose productivity fell short for various reasons (Roethlisberger and Dickson, 1939).

Some have noted gender biases in on-the-job training and interaction patterns, such as mentor relationships. Employers place men in advantageous interaction systems more frequently than they do women; the men thus become part of a network tapped for promotion opportunities. Such gender differentiation in training and work opportunities serves to reproduce stereotypical gender differences.

The Media

Media are very powerful, pervasive agents of socialization. Television can play a positive role in the development of language and reading readiness skills, as well as the assimilation of basic arithmetic facts. Programs like *Sesame Street,* in particular, have been highly successful in this area. In addition, *Sesame Street, Barney,* and

Mr. Rogers' Neighborhood promote prosocial values like cooperation, helping others, sharing, and self-control.

On the other hand, much debate centers on the effects of media violence on antisocial behaviors (Barker and Petley, 1997; Dudley, 1999). Some studies have found that early and frequent television viewing is associated with increased aggression in children and teenagers (Barry, 1993; Cannon, 1993). Many observers agree that the increasing level of violence in both television programs and films teaches viewers of all ages that brute force and violence are acceptable and appropriate avenues for redressing grievances and solving problems (Grossman and DeGaetano, 1999). Some evidence suggests that programming containing violence particularly targeted against women tends to heighten women's feelings of vulnerability and lack of power (Reid and Finchilescu, 1995). Such perspectives can alter women's freedom of movement as they seek to protect themselves from perceived threats to which they may be subjected because they are female.

The power of media may also come from what they do *not* show. By limiting the kinds of people individuals see, especially in positive roles, largely to white, middle-class, heterosexual, able-bodied people, the media contribute to **symbolic annihilation** (Tuchman, Daniels, and Benet, 1978), or "the absence of experience of a group of people in the media" (Lont, 2001:119). The dearth of people of color, gays and lesbians, people with disabilities, or the poor, and of their voices talking about their experiences as valid, suggests that these people do not exist or are unimportant. This can happen in other settings besides media, but it is especially important in media, since this is such a significant source of information for many people.

As influential as media can be, however, their power in shaping individuals' identities has limits. For example, while adolescents may not necessarily be able to choose to avoid exposure to the socialization information provided by their parents, schools, and religious organizations, they do have much greater power to select the media messages and information they consume. As a result, they may be more able to "self-socialize" with challenging or contradictory information, values, norms, and so on, thereby minimizing the power of other socialization agents (Arnett, 1995).

Toys, Games, and Recreation

In addition to the usual components of media (such as films, television, newspapers, and magazines), toys, games, and recreational activities serve as socialization agents (Fromberg and Bergen, 1998). Individuals learn much about cultural values from the rules and concepts of various board games. For example, Monopoly rewards greed and cutthroat competition: the winner is the player who bankrupts all the other players. The game of Risk, with its goal of world domination, rewards aggression. Other games also reinforce prevailing social values. Trivial Pursuit rewards the ability to spit back odd bits and pieces of memorized information rather than the ability to present a coherent, critical analysis of a problem.

While most board games and sports tend to emphasize the concepts of competition and winning and losing, some do stress cooperation. For example, Bertel Ollman's game Class Struggle sought to deliberately counter Monopoly by rewarding cooperation and an organized struggle against capitalism (interestingly, no major toy company would market the game). Group games of jump rope, particularly Double Dutch, succeed only when everyone cooperates to keep the game going by ensuring that the rope turns with a constant rhythm and accommodates the jumper. And while team sports emphasize competition between teams, they also reinforce the notion of cooperation for the common good among the team members.

Children remain fairly creative in how they approach games, however, and that creativity may pose limits to the power toys and games have in forcing them to acquire their intended values and norms. Children often alter the rules provided by the makers of manufactured games, sometimes changing them midgame, and sometimes creating entirely new games using the basic pieces out of the box. Further, the interaction process of play provides opportunities for children to actively explore and question the rules, the apparent use of toys (such as doctor kits, kitchen sets, and black dolls by white children), and their meanings (Best, 1998).

The State

Finally, the state itself is an important socialization agent in its efforts to eliminate "deviance." Laws formally codify the norms of dominant groups, so that noncompliance is likely to be sanctioned with the loss of rights and freedoms, resources, and rewards. For example, welfare reform laws, passed by the affluent and predicated on the false assumption that poverty is caused by individual laziness and lack of a work ethic, ultimately require recipients of welfare to accept work that is available regardless of pay, hours, or lack of benefits. Should a mother whose family receives welfare object (often because there are preschool children or ill family members needing care at home, for example), the state reserves the right to deny her and her children welfare. Similarly, the state normatively defines legitimate political action as voting. Those who violate that norm by participating in protests and demonstrations are often subject to intense state sanctions by police: pepper spray, tear gas, rubber bullets, arrests, clubbings, beatings, and sometimes death. Witness, for example, the treatment of civil rights demonstrators during the 1960s who were attacked by police using powerful firehoses. Antiwar demonstrators at Jackson State and Kent State universities in 1970 were shot at and killed by the National Guard. More recently, demonstrators against the World Trade Organization in Seattle in 1999, and against the corporate-dominated Republican and Democratic national conventions in 2000, received the full force of the state's power in an effort to punish and disperse protestors and discourage future demonstrations.

Sometimes gender norms prohibit the social control agents from resorting to force and violence. For example, the Million Mom March against guns and violence on Washington, D.C., in 2000 elicited no use of tear gas or pepper spray and no arrests. Motherhood norms hinder the state from viewing women with babies as threatening and from using the level of violence against them more commonly used against primarily male demonstrators.

Taken together, these socialization agents tend to encourage the adoption of dominant values and norms. But beyond a general assimilation of cultural norms and values, what specific roles do these agents socialize us to internalize? There is evidence that they work to reinforce and reproduce roles relating to class, gender, and race, as well as roles and attitudes concerning political values and norms.

Class Socialization

Families, workplaces, and schools play an important part in class socialization, reproducing and perpetuating class positions and roles. Consider the different socialization processes undergone by professional, technical, and managerial workers, on the one hand, and blue-collar, clerical, and service workers, on the other. The latter operate in a work environment that requires little autonomy or creative initiative. They are rewarded for accepting orders and following directions. Professional, managerial, and technical workers are more likely to get rewards for exercising autonomy, independence, creativity, and initiative in decision making and problem solving (Kohn, 1977). These differential work experiences and reward structures reproduce class differences: They affect how these workers view themselves as well as how their children perceive them as role models (Grant and Sleeter, 1988).

Family

Class differences may persist because parents strive to prepare their children for the work world they are likely to join when they become adults (Majoribanks, 1987). This preparation for future roles is what sociologists call **anticipatory socialization** (Mortimer and Simmons, 1978). Research shows, for example, that the higher parents' socioeconomic status, the more likely they are to emphasize independence in socializing their children, a reflection in part of the presumed qualities needed for the occupations of managers and professionals such children are anticipated to fill. In comparison, parents with lower socioeconomic status are more likely to emphasize obedience in socializing their children, a quality characteristic of rank and file or nonmanagerial jobs requiring workers to follow the orders of managers and supervisors (Flanagan, 1999). Research also suggests that this pattern is often affected by gender. One study found that middle-class African American women's parents held higher expectations for them than the parents of working-class African American women held for their daughters (Hill, 1997). These different levels of expectations are likely to affect how parents prepare their daughters for their future roles, be they in the work force or in the home.

Affluent private schools act as class socialization agents, inculcating their students with the values and assumed privileges associated with wealth and power. Here, students at a private prep school chat in their well-endowed library. They are likely to view such complete and state-of-the-art resources as unquestioned entitlements rather than as luxuries that one must struggle to attain.

Some researchers have noted, however, that class-based differences are declining as middle-class and working-class child-rearing practices become more similar (Alwin, 1984; Amato and Fowler, 2002). Why is this convergence taking place now? It may well be that shrinking working-class opportunities in manufacturing and increasing middle-class opportunities in lower paying service-sector jobs may be making the work experiences of both more similar. Both contend with work that is likely to offer low pay, few benefits, and little job stability. In addition, increasing reliance by firms on contingency or temporary workers for skilled and managerial work makes the work world of the middle and upper-middle classes more like that of the part-time and seasonal workers in the service sector. As such, parents' perceptions of the probable work world their children will face may very well be increasingly similar, and this in turn may affect how they socialize their children.

Schools

Schools also participate in socializing children for their future roles in the labor market. Teachers and guidance counselors make assumptions concerning appropriate future education or work roles for students and therefore appropriate curriculum tracks. Affluent students sent to private prep schools are prepared to assume power positions, while students in public schools are more likely to be prepared for following such leaders (Brint, 1998). The class membership, race, and gender of a student may influence school staff more than his or her actual skills and talents (Grant and Sleeter, 1988). Teachers and counselors also tend to emphasize varying degrees of obedience, the necessity to follow rules and take direction, and independent thinking (Franklin, 1986). School officials tend to reward behaviors that they see as consistent with perceptions of future roles; inconsistent behaviors are punished. Taken together, these forces operate to perpetuate differential class positions.

Differential treatment of students on the basis of class becomes a **self-fulfilling prophecy,** a phenomenon in which people achieve to the level expected of them rather than the level of which they may actually be capable. Thus when teachers assume that poor and working-class children are not capable of achieving high academic performances expected of middle-class and affluent children, lower-class and working-class children are likely to exhibit poor performance and feelings of inferiority (Rhem, 1999; Rosenthal and Jacobson, 1992). Indeed, even when such children succeed later in life as educators and researchers holding advanced degrees, they frequently express feelings of the **imposter syndrome,** of somehow having fooled those around them into thinking that they are deserving of recognition, respect, and acceptance (Morris and Grimes, 1996; Ryan and Sackrey, 1984).

Gender Socialization

Many socialization agents are important forces in the shaping of gender identities. They therefore contribute significantly to reproducing stereotypical gender roles.

Family

Families may reproduce gender roles by overtly assigning different household chores along traditional gender lines: girls baby-sit, cook, and wash dishes; boys take out garbage and do yardwork (Burns and Homel, 1989). Different parental expectations for academic performance may also reinforce gender differences. Parents often send their children messages about male and female abilities and appropriate future work roles (Howard and Hollander, 1997). Similar gendered information frequently crosses cultural divides around the world (Harkness and Super, 1996). Noted one observer, "Girls are raised to 'keep the home fires burning.' Boys are raised to do battle" (Abbott, 1998:1).

The division of household chores between parents also sends a powerful message to children about gendered domestic work roles (Cunningham, 2001). Studies indicate that women do the majority of domestic labor, thereby defining it as women's responsibility (Demo and Acock, 1993). Even when women work full time outside the home, they still perform most of the household chores, a situation some observers have referred to as the **second shift** (Hochschild with Machung, 1997; Stohs, 2000). Such role models teach children that the appropriate behavior for women includes cooking, cleaning, and caring for children, regardless of the time spent working outside the home. Similarly, they imply that a man's appropriate role is that of paid worker who is not expected to assume household or child care responsibilities.

Schools

Schools also reinforce gendered social roles. For example, researchers have documented the differential treatment accorded males and females in the classroom that reinforces a sense of inferiority and lack of initiative among female students (Sadker and Sadker, 1994; Spade, 2001). Boys are far more likely than girls to be given specific information that guides improvement of their performance (Boggiano and Barrett, 1991). Boys also receive greater encouragement to reach for higher standards for themselves. Girls are thus denied an important part of the education process that encourages students to strive for excellence. Instead, the vague praise girls may receive often implies that whatever they accomplish, however flawed, is "good enough," that it is not necessary for them to try for better achievement.

Researchers have found that school tracking often is based on gender (Kubitschek and Hallinan, 1996). Girls tend to be tracked away from math and science and toward the humanities, social sciences, and secretarial studies. They are often encouraged to enter nurturing or helping professions, such as teaching (especially at the preschool and elementary school levels), nursing, social work, and clerical work. Boys tend to be tracked toward math and science, sports, and physically demanding vocations. They are pushed toward more autonomous professions, such as medicine, science and technology, law, business, engineering, and finance or toward physical vocations in fields like auto mechanics and electromechanical technology (Peltz, 1990).

Textbooks used in schools explicitly and implicitly reinforce gender roles through both their content and their form. For example, literature texts are often dominated by the works of white men, with a few notable exceptions (such as Emily Dickinson). History texts give scant attention to the serious contributions of women in American and world history. Even in college-level sociology texts, discussions of women tend to be restricted to a single chapter on gender or sprinkled in chapters on topics such as the family and socialization, which have traditionally included women (Ferree and Hall, 1996).

One study of photographs that accompany sociology texts found that only one-third of the pictures contained women of any race. Race and sex were treated as mutually exclusive categories: White women were depicted as women, while women of color were depicted for their race. Moreover, the study found that, overall, white male images dominated the textbook photographs, most particularly in the chapters on politics and economics (Ferree and Hall, 1996). The message here, in sociology textbooks of all places, is that white males are the important actors in the most crucial institutions, whereas women play a role primarily in the family.

Funding for high school and college athletics, including equipment, travel, and scholarships, tends to reward females less than males (with the notable exception of cheerleading). This inequality is reinforced by the lack of opportunities for women's professional sports. Even in cases where women's sports do receive some institutional support, it lags significantly behind that of men's sports. The lack of positive rewards or adequate funding to support women's sports discourages females from pursuing such activities. This reinforces notions that women are genetically predisposed to dislike sports, are not strong, and have little physical endurance.

Work

Work roles in the paid labor market are also sharply divided along gender lines, which sends a strong message to people about appropriate and inappropriate work aspirations for boys and girls. Most occupations in industrialized societies are characterized as predominantly male or predominantly female. In the United States in 1998, almost 60 percent of the women in the paid labor force could be found in fewer than 50 job categories (out of a total of 219 defined by the Census Bureau) that were predominantly female, which means that at least 80 percent of the employees doing those jobs were women (www.census.gov/statabs, Table 675). Such an arrangement identifies specific work activities based on one's sex and can contribute to the gendered development of aspirations and training for future work roles. Indeed, when individuals pursue "gender-inappropriate" jobs they frequently report pressures from family, peers, teachers, and employers to reconsider. This often happens to men who choose to work as day care providers, kindergarten teachers, and nurses, an experience illustrated in popular culture. Take, for example, the man in the movie *Meet the Parents* who suffered the disrespect and severe disapproval of his future father-in-law when he announced that he was a nurse. Similarly, when Ross and Rachel hired a man as a nanny for their new baby on the television show *Friends,* an entire episode of jokes revolved around questions concerning his masculinity. Eventually they fired him, the ultimate sanction for being the "wrong" sex for the job and for "poor socialization."

This stereotyping may be changing somewhat. More men are beginning to take female-dominated jobs because of shrinking job opportunities in their previously male-dominated jobs. As more men do so, the gender-typing of jobs may be likely to play a reduced role in gender socialization.

Media

The media also contribute to stereotypes of gender roles. In some media, for example, stark images depict men as aggressive and dominating actors and women as docile, submissive objects (Dines, 1992a). Television and films tend to offer very limited roles for women, and those they do often perpetuate female stereotypes and caricatures. Actresses frequently lament the scarcity of roles for strong leading women; they tend to be cast in secondary roles as insecure, punishing, spoiled, prudish, or childish females (Hanania, 1999; Lont, 2001). And although many situation comedies depict men in buffoonish stereotypes, a wide and diverse array of images of men counter these. In comparison, the images of women tend to be more restricted to sharp and demeaning caricatures; in the absence of countervailing images of women, the stereotypes become more significant. Moreover, stereotypical buffoonish men tend to be depicted primarily as working-class men, suggesting that there is something about their class, not their gender, that causes them to behave so poorly (Butsch, 1995). Many critics have noted a repeated theme in films of the early 1990s: Women are sold to men by other men. This was the case in *Honeymoon in Vegas, Mad Dog and Glory,* and *Indecent Proposal.* Television reinforces this view of women as objects: The portrayal of women in videos seen on MTV, where sex and violence are often casually fused, offers teenagers a sadomasochistic perspective of women as victims and emphasizes women's physical appearance as sex objects (Gow, 1996; Maio, 1990).

The gender bias in media is not surprising, given the industry's power structure. One study of Fortune 1000 media and telecom corporations found that while 44 percent of network and national cable news anchors were women, they remained severely underrepresented in the boardroom: Only 10 percent of executive and 12 percent of corporate board members were women (Annenberg Public Policy Center, 2001, cited in Pozner, 2001). Regardless of who reads the news to viewers, those who make the decisions about what to broadcast, whether it is news or entertainment programming, determine what images people see. And when the decision makers are predominantly men, it is likely that male interests, perspectives, and experiences will dominate the programming.

Why does the pattern of gendered media images matter? Research shows that children as young as toddlers imitate behaviors they see on television and that this copying intensifies through adolescence (Comstock and Paik, 1991). Therefore, media images of gender can be powerful socializers. In children's television, very few roles are given to females. Even on the award-winning *Sesame Street* most of the muppet characters are male; it was not until 1994 that a female muppet (named Zoe) was introduced to join Miss Piggy as a main character on the show.

Notably, there are encouraging signs of change. Children's shows like *Kim Possible* are beginning to showcase strong, intelligent female characters. In adult programming, the popular television series *Murphy Brown, Roseanne,* and *Grace Under Fire* in the 1980s and *Felicity,* and *The Profiler* in the 1990s all featured independent, powerful central female characters. By 2003, these few shows were gone from prime time, but others have continued the trend: *Alias* and *Buffy the Vampire Slayer* depict strong females as the main characters. Witness as well Amy Brenneman's role as a judge and Tyne Daly's role as her intelligent, independent mother on *Judging Amy,* several formidable women who are lawyers and district attorneys on *The Practice* and the three *Law and Order* series, and the women on *CSI* and *CSI: Miami* who are top-notch forensic scientists.

That such roles are increasing is a real sign of progress, but there is much work to be done. That such characters stand out reaffirms the persistence of gender stereotypes in television. And there are signs of retreating to the earlier, more traditional stereotypes of limited female roles. This can be seen, for example, in the spoiled, whiny "airhead" types on *Friends* and *Just Shoot Me,* the ineffective women on *Will and Grace,* and the full-time homemakers on *Everybody Loves Raymond.* Moreover, a study of prime-time television in 2000–2001 done by Children Now, a child policy and advocacy organization, found a continuation of gendered images. Men dominated prime time, totaling 65 percent of the characters portrayed in that time slot. The marital and parental statuses of females were twice as likely to be identified as those of males. And while women are seen crossing over into traditionally male jobs, no such crossover of men to traditionally female jobs occurred at all (www.childrennow.org, "Fall Colors 2000–01").

Gender roles are generally depicted as appropriate when they are heterosexual. The media, particularly television, still are more likely to treat gay males and lesbians as oddities in overdrawn caricatures, when they portray them at all. Indeed, a very sensitive portrayal on *thirtysomething* in the late 1980s of two homosexual men sitting in bed discussing the horror of losing friends to AIDS was never rerun because of intense objections to the scene by ABC's standards and practices censors. More recently, the show *Will and Grace* is often credited with bringing homosexuality into the mainstream of television culture, yet some critics point out that it continues to rely on stereotypes of male homosexuals as feminine and infantile in their behavior (Battles and Hilton-Morrow, 2002).

However, encouraging signs suggest that television is becoming more comfortable with more positive, accepting images of gays. Since the coming out of Ellen DeGeneres's lesbian character on *Ellen* in April 1997, television has portrayed gays who are comfortable in their identity and productive members of society. Examples include *Will and Grace* (in spite of its stereotypes of gays), an affirmative depiction of a gay wedding on *Felicity,* an intimate kiss between two women on *Ally McBeal,* and a feature-length positive treatment of lesbian relationships on HBO's *If These Walls Could Talk, II,* in which a woman struggles for dignity, inclusion, and recognition as a grieving widow by the family of her deceased long-term lesbian partner.

There are also encouraging signs of the ability of media to challenge dominant values and norms. For example, one study found that subjects tended to have a more sympathetic, positive attitude toward homosexuals after viewing the documentary *The Times of Harvey Milk,* about a gay legislator murdered in California in 1978 (Riggle, Ellis, and Crawford, 1996). The film had premiered in 1984 and was aired on PBS in 1985, a time when affirmative portrayals of gays and lesbians were still uncommon.

Toys, Games, and Recreational Activities

Toys and games teach children a great deal about "appropriate" and "inappropriate" gender roles (Johnson, Christie, and Yawkey, 1999). Even the packaging plays a part. For example, boxes showing girls playing with dolls and tea sets and boys playing with erector sets, or doctor kits showing a boy as the doctor and a girl as either patient or nurse, send children a message of who is "supposed" to play with these toys or who is "supposed" to assume a particular role when they play. Indeed, girls are encouraged to view the distorted body form of the Barbie doll as the ideal, while boys learn to idolize the aggression of such "action figures" as G.I. Joe, Transformers, and He-Man.

Games are subtle, but powerful, gender socialization agents. For example, Chutes and Ladders is a very popular game among preschoolers and very young elementary school children. The game explicitly defines "good" behaviors (rewarded with advancement to the finish) and "bad" behaviors (punished with slides back toward the start). Notably, the behaviors identified in the pictures on the game board are gender-specific. Good behaviors depict girls planting flowers, baking a cake, nursing an injured dog, and sweeping the floor while boys mow the lawn, rescue a distressed cat in a tree, and find Mom's purse. Bad behaviors show girls eating too many chocolates (girls must be careful not to jeopardize their figures) and breaking dishes by attempting to carry too many (girls are not strong enough to carry more than a few), and they depict boys reading comic books instead of the history textbook, breaking a window with a baseball, and pulling a cat's tail. Games such as Sweet Valley High and the Barbie Game teach adolescent and preadolescent girls to fit the stereotype of catty, backbiting females as they compete for boyfriends and prom dates.

Video games tend to reinforce conventional gendering as well (Cassell and Jenkins, 1998). One study found that females were absent in more than 40 percent of the games containing characters, rendering females unimportant or invisible. In almost one third of the remaining games containing characters females were depicted as sex objects, and they were targeted for violence in more than one-fifth of the games (Dietz, 1998). To discover, then, that video games are frequently considered boys' toys (Game Boy), or to find that video arcades are largely populated by boys, is no surprise. The research suggests that the messages contained in these games, coupled with the themes of violence against women in the media, may be socializing them to accept as normal the treatment of women as objects and as targets of aggression (Gilmore and Crissman, 1997). The perception of video games as a male preserve may also encourage the more general notion that the world of computers itself belongs more to males than females.

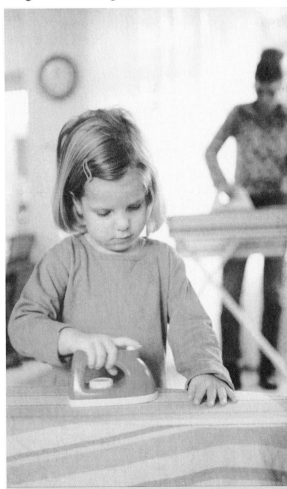

Gendered toys and games encourage children to adopt traditional gendered behaviors and aspirations. Here, a preschool girl perfectly mimics her mother's household chore with her toy iron and ironing board.

On the other hand, although female athletics receive less funding than male athletics, sports have in fact become an increasingly important source of activity for girls, largely as the result of protests against sex discrimination in school athletics. The state has been pressured to adopt legislation mandating equal access to and funding for educational activities for both boys and girls. This has resulted in a dramatic increase in funding and participation opportunities for girls in athletics (although still not equal to the funding and participation opportunities for boys). By 2000, national participation and interest in women's basketball had grown, as had interest in women's soccer and ice hockey, in both schools and the Olympics as well as professional sports. Of considerable concern, however, is the backlash to affirmative action. While the Supreme Court in 2003 reaffirmed the principle of affirmative action, legal disputes, including those challenging Title IX, the provision of the Educational Amendments of 1972 that has been crucial in the increase of funding for girls' and women's athletics, continue to work their way through the courts. If successful, these cases may roll back the progress made by women in sports. This is likely to be an area of struggle and contention for some time.

Language and Gender Socialization

Language use plays an important role in gender socialization (O'Barr, 2001). For example, the use of the generic pronoun "he" and the term "man" to refer to any member of the human species invokes an image of a male, thereby excluding women from individuals' consciousness as important members of humanity (Frank and Anshen, 1983; Miller and Swift, 1991). The media only reinforce this perception when they pointedly refer to a "woman lawyer," "woman senator," or "woman autoworker." Such terms as "fireman" (instead of "firefighter"), "workman's compensation" (in place of "workers' compensation"), and "manpower" (as opposed to "labor power") also underscore the power of language and media to devalue women and elevate men as the important members of society. The *New York Times,* widely regarded as the newspaper of record, resisted eliminating sexist language in its reporting for decades. Only recently have the editors agreed to use "Ms." instead of "Miss" or "Mrs." to describe women in its articles. Why is this change important? Formal titles like "Miss" or "Mrs." clearly identify women by their relationships to men, whether these are relevant to the story or not. The term "Ms.," like the term "Mr.," makes marital status irrelevant to the story and focuses reporting on women in their own right.

Women are more likely than men to be pejoratively described by their sexuality. One study found 220 English words used to negatively describe sexually active women but only 22 describing sexually active men (Stanley, 1977). This language discrepancy reinforces the sexual double standard applied to men and women in their socialization, where "nice" girls are chaste and virginal until marriage but "real" boys are sexually experienced by the time they "settle down" with a partner. More recent research suggests that the use of degrading terms by males to describe women's genitals suggests a continuation of pejorative and derogatory language directed at women (Murnen, 2000).

Effectiveness of Gender Socialization

How successful are all these agents of gender socialization in reinforcing gender stereotypes of appropriate and inappropriate behavior? Gilligan, Lyons, and Hanmer (1990) studied socialization and development of adolescent girls in a girls' school in the United States, and they found striking evidence that these agents are indeed formidable. According to the researchers, girls tend to go through a "moment of resistance" around age 11, in which they experience a clear confidence in their abilities, insights, integrity, and potential roles in the world around them. However, as they get older, girls begin to understand and heed the restrictive messages that socialization agents in their culture send to them—they begin to believe that women are invisible and unimportant in their culture. By age 15 or 16, the girls in the study were less outspoken, less sure of their abilities and intelligence, and more docile than the preadolescents. The resistance was gone, or had at least gone "underground"; the girls were more likely to preface their statements and observations with comments such as "This may be silly," and they repeatedly said "I don't know." The researchers' findings suggest that socialization agents are quite powerful in shaping girls' social identities to conform to gender stereotypes (Gallas, 1998).

The difficulty of generalizing the findings of Gilligan, Lyons, and Hanmer stems from the fact that their study was based on an elite, gender-segregated school. Are their findings gender-specific? Or might they be age-specific to both boys and girls? A 1992 survey found that although both boys and girls do indeed suffer a decline in self-esteem as adolescents, the decline is more pronounced for girls (American Association of University Women, 1992). Another study found that while girls begin kindergarten well ahead of boys in all areas except science, they finish high school *behind* boys in almost all areas because systematic gender bias in the classroom boosts boys' and undermines girls' confidence (Sadker and Sadker, 1994).

The effectiveness of gender socialization of both boys and girls is also evident in their respective recreational activities, peer interactions, and language use. Sex segregation in peer and play groups begins very early among preschoolers (Schofield, 1981), and it continues in school friendships as children select same-sex tablemates in the lunchroom and in the playground at recess. These groups begin to reinforce gender roles for both boys and girls. Later, schools, families, and communities support team sports as common, validating experiences for boys, a reflection of the persistent stereotype that competitive and aggressive behavior is masculine, not feminine (Messner, 2001). This view is reinforced by disproportionate media coverage of men's professional sports and use of male star athletes in advertisements. One result of all this support is that large areas of playground space are controlled by boys playing baseball, football, basketball, street hockey, and so on. Girls often play games such as jump rope and hopscotch, which involve turn taking and cooperation and require relatively little playground space (Thorne, 1989, 1993). While there have been important advances in organized competitive sports for girls in many schools throughout the United States, owing largely to federal legislation mandating equal opportunity for both boys and girls to participate in school sports, these still lag behind school and media support for boys' athletics.

Boys, then, dominate the "gendered turf" of the playground, where they learn that competition, aggression, and sometimes violence are "normal" aspects of being male. Such lessons extend beyond team sports, as boys' interactions frequently involve contests, challenges and dares, insults, and dictated commands (Fine, 1986; Goodwin, 1980). Girls, in contrast, learn to express disagreement more indirectly, through secrets and shifting alliances (Maltz and Borker, 1983). Instead of using commands and orders, girls learn to use inclusive suggestions, such as "let's" do something (Goodwin, 1980). The gendered messages are obvious: Boys are leaders who dictate orders to others, control greater resources, and confront conflicts and challenges; girls are subordinate to boys in that they control fewer resources, follow rather than lead, and avoid or ignore conflicts. Indeed, research has found that girls tend to more positively respond to female peers who use an inclusive, communal style of interaction, in contrast to boys, who tend to respond more positively to male peers who adopt a more individually goal-oriented style (Hibbard and Buhrmester, 1998).

Thus family, schools, work, media, toys and games, the state, and language use operate together in the process of gender socialization, reproducing and reinforcing stereotypes of appropriate and inappropriate gender roles and behaviors. Moreover, the domination in all these agents of heterosexual images and assumptions strongly discourages consideration of homosexuality as a viable and acceptable alternative and together effectively promote a sense of **compulsory heterosexuality,** the adoption of a heterosexual public persona as a prerequisite for acceptance in mainstream society (Nielson, Walden, and Kunkel, 2000; Renold, 2000). For such reasons, young people who know they are, or believe they might be, gay or lesbian are made to feel very negative about themselves.

On the other hand, gender socialization appears to be imperfect. Many women and men transcend its powerful messages and successfully challenge them. For example, in the workplace and in educational institutions, an increasing number of women are breaking barriers considered impenetrable by previous generations. Look at the proportion of female students in your classroom. Perhaps the professor standing before you is a woman. Look, too, at the increases in women in school and professional and Olympic sports, including basketball, soccer, and ice hockey. And notice the increasing number of women executives in corporations and politicians in Congress and governor's mansions all over the United States. Consider, as well, the Houston Oilers football player who in 1993 refused to play in a football game because his wife was giving birth to their first child. He risked a heavy monetary fine and suspension from the team, but after a major public outcry supporting his denial of traditional gender roles and condemning his punitive coach, the team's management rescinded the sanction. More recently, when the highly successful attorney Cherie Blair gave birth to their fourth child in 2000, her husband, Prime Minister Tony Blair of Great Britain, took a brief parental leave of absence. Such cases depart from the norm, but the fact that they happen at all suggests that gender socialization, while powerful, is far from absolute in shaping gender identity.

Racial Socialization

Just as the various agents play a critical role in class and gender socialization, they are vital transmitters of racial socialization. Racial socialization reinforces racist stereotypes and race-based roles that legitimize racial inequality. The agents that are particularly influential here are family, schools, media, and toys.

Family

The family is an important source of values and norms of interaction for children, and it is within families that stereotypes about groups may take on added significance (O'Connor, Brooks-Gunn, and Graber, 2000). Children may go through race-based rites of passage that emphasize white superiority and black inferiority. For example, Sarah Putton Boyle experienced a "racialized" rite of passage as a white child in the South in the 1950s when she rebuffed an African American child's invitation to play. Here is her poignant description of the event:

> Crushing back my desire both for his company and for fun, I answered stiffly, "No, I can't." Then I added with proper Southern-lady courtesy, "How are you?" My mother had watched the exchange . . . [and] she said, "Mother saw and heard everything. That was a good girl." (Boyle, 1962: 22).

When families reward "appropriate" behavior regarding rules and boundaries of interracial interaction, they send a clear message to white children and children of color about the children's "proper" places in society.

On the other hand, some families' socialization processes may encourage resistance to prevailing racial attitudes. For example, African American parents must often teach their children ways to interact with a white-dominated law enforcement system in order to safeguard themselves when they have not violated any laws. Thus, although most families of all races want to impart to their children a sense of the children's places in the social structure and an understanding of social norms, African American families must do so in the context of racism. Unfortunately, that context may not allow their children to develop a positive self-image or pride of group membership. The challenge for people of color, then, is to stand between their children and a hostile environment to reinterpret the significance of the prejudicial attitudes and discrimination likely to confront them (Hill, 1999; Thornton, 1998). Yet not all African American families actively pursue this socialization route.

What factors, then, influence whether and how a family will offer racial socialization information? Age of the child may be one factor. A study of African American families suggests that in general racial socialization most frequently emphasizes an appreciation for culture rather than a preparation for bias or a promotion of mistrust. However, parents are more likely to shift toward a focus on preparing their children for bias and discrimination or to more overtly promote wariness of others as their children grow older (Hughes and Chen, 1997). Research also shows that the sex of the child may affect the process: African American adolescent males appear more likely than females to receive cautionary messages about the racist roadblocks they will commonly confront; African American adolescent females are more likely to receive socialization information stressing racial pride (Bowman and Howard, 1985; Stevenson, 1995). Fathers rather than mothers, especially fathers in the Northeast as opposed to those in the South, were more likely to offer survival strategies for existing in a racially hostile environment; widows and never-married women were less likely to offer such information (Thornton et al., 1990). Apparently, gender helps determine who will deliver the messages that challenge negative stereotypes and racist barriers to achievement as well as who is likely to receive them. Militance and challenge are more characteristic of behaviors considered appropriate for males.

This is not to say that women never receive and send racial socialization messages that encourage resistance to prejudice and discrimination. Just consider such women as civil rights activist Rosa Parks, who challenged racism in the early 1960s by refusing to give up her seat on a bus to a white passenger; attorneys Anita Hill, who testified about sexual harassment by Clarence Thomas in the Senate hearings for confirmation of his Supreme Court nomination in the 1980s, and Lani Guinier, a highly active and vocal federal civil rights advocate; and award-winning writers Maya Angelou, Alice Walker, and Toni Morrison. Research does suggest, however, that men are far more likely to be socialized in this way. That such challenges occur at all underscores the role family can play as a proactive socialization agent contradicting racial messages stressed by other agents.

Schools

Schools reinforce racial inequality and racial socialization through a variety of mechanisms. One of these is funding. Because school budgets depend on property tax revenues and state matching funds, much better funding is available for schools in middle-class districts than for schools in poor and working-class districts (Walters, 2001). Housing discrimination patterns, coupled with widening economic gaps between whites and people of color, suggest that these funding practices are likely to contribute to widening racial inequality as well. Differential funding often occurs *within* districts, where school boards may allocate money unequally from school to school. One study in New York found that teachers' pay in predominantly white suburban Scarsdale averaged $81,410 annually, compared with teachers' annual salaries of $47,345 in heavily Latino/Latina and African American New York City, a pay gap of more than 58 percent (Stern, 1998). Funding and allocation decisions can produce differential educational experiences on the basis of race and class (Swan, 1995).

Texts and curricula also often contain a racial and ethnic bias. As noted earlier, textbooks tend to exclude racial minorities from analyses of U.S. history. In one early study, only 8 out of 45 social science textbooks mentioned Latinos or Latinas, and only 2 talked of Chicanos/Chicanas (Kane, 1970). Another early study found a similar sparsity of references to Native Americans in texts (Bowker, 1972). When people of color were mentioned, they tended to be depicted in pejorative terms (Shaw-Taylor and Benokraitis, 1995; Wills, 1994). Although textbook publishers have grown more sensitive to this issue, progress is still needed. Photographs of people of color are most likely to appear in textbook chapters on race-related issues rather than being integrated throughout the book. Some disciplines' textbooks still tend to ignore race-related issues altogether. For example, studies found that introductory economics and American government textbooks tend to "race code" contemporary poverty as an African American problem but exclude African Americans in more sympathetic portrayals of Depression-era poverty (Clawson, 2002; Clawson and Kegler, 2000). Anthropology and criminal justice textbooks tend to ignore problems of racism in their presentations (Farrell and Koch, 1995; Shanklin, 2000). Yet another study noted that introductory sociology textbooks fail to present race-related information outside of specific chapters (such as those on race and ethnicity, family, and stratification) (Ferree and Hall, 1996).

Schools reinforce racial inequality through interactions between students and teachers. One study found that while African American female students are more likely than white female students to seek contact with and help from their teachers, the African American students are more likely to be ignored or turned away (American Association of University Women, 1992). When teachers do respond to students of color with positive feedback, the praise offered is likely to be more qualified ("that report wasn't bad"; "your project was pretty good, but it could have been neater") than that offered to white students (American Association of University Women, 1992; Freiberg, 1991). Evidence also suggests that teachers' expectations of students' performances are influenced by race and class (Dei et al., 1997). For example, teachers often have higher prior expectations of white and middle-class students' abilities than of economically poor students and those of color (Allen-Meares, 1990).

Such prior expectations get frozen early on in the process of tracking, with the result that students of color are often placed in slower or non-college-bound programs of study. Such students find it difficult to earn college preparatory credits, and they enjoy fewer opportunities for educational and occupational advancement. Evidence suggests that an early placement in a slower track on the basis of race tends to become permanent and impedes academic advancement, regardless of early abilities (Jencks and Phillips, 1998; Oakes, 1995).

Language also plays a part in tracking decisions. Schools tend to devalue languages other than standard English, a position that reinforces white superiority. For example, many educators have decried African Americans' use of nonstandard English, or Ebonics, saying it lacks the rules and syntactical organization of standard English. However, studies have shown that Ebonics, while certainly different, is just as regulated by rules as standard English (Baratz and Baratz, 1970). Unfortunately, teachers have more power than students to make their interpretations of language use matter. As a result, African American students who use nonstandard English get labeled as less intelligent than white students or as slow and requiring a less advanced track of study (Woodford et al., 1997). It is important to note that standard English is the language of high-paying occupations in the United States, so preparing students of color to compete for these jobs must include teaching them standard English. The point here is that, while doing so, rather than conveying that different languages and linguistic styles are appropriate for specific circumstances, teachers may simply denigrate students' common usage.

On the other hand, dialects such as Ebonics can in fact be an important vehicle for resistance and identity formation. Ebonics has been found to provide a framework for the development of greater group cohesion and identity and to provide a vocabulary of resistance to dominant group conceptions of African American inferiority and an empowering celebration of self for those who are often excluded from the mainstream (Green and Smart, 1997; Smitherman and Cunningham, 1997).

Schools may reinforce racial socialization through their very structure, in the lack of role models within their personnel. In 1999, only 7.3 percent of elementary and secondary public school teachers were African American, 4.3 percent were Latino/Latina, and 1.8 percent were Asian/Pacific Islander (www.census.gov/statabs, Table 268). By the time students enter college (if they do, in fact, go to college), the proportion of faculty of color dips to 4.9 percent African American, 2.6 percent Latino, 5.5 percent Asian/Pacific Islander, and less than 0.05 percent Native American (U.S. Dept. of Education, 1997 available at www.nces.ed.gov/quicktables). This does not necessarily mean that schools intentionally restrict the number of minority faculty, but the decline in role models among teachers does send a visual message to all students that people of color are not as intelligent or capable of holding positions of authority as whites.

Media

In addition to schools, the media are powerful transmitters of racial socialization (Williams, B., 1999). For example, many African American and Latino/Latina actors complain that they are typically cast as drug dealers or users, pimps, prostitutes, rapists, murderers, or muggers but are rarely given positive leading roles (Dennis and Pease, 1996; Entman and Rojecki, 2000; Rodriguez, 1997). The NAACP and Latino/Latina and Asian American critics in the entertainment industry have forcefully condemned this persistent pattern (Jackson, 2000; Lichter and Amundson, 1997).

A similar bias occurs in radio broadcasting. For example, one study of national radio stations found that in seven major U.S. urban markets the voices that dominated the airwaves were overwhelmingly white: 88 percent of the daytime hosts and news anchors were non-Latino/Latina white (Rendall and Creeley, 2002). Although the situation has improved somewhat with the addition of Juan Williams and Tavis Smiley, positive roles are still more remarkable than typical.

Television, too, shows this bias. Indeed, a study of prime time television in 2000–2001 done by Children Now found that people of color remained marginal, and that the greatest racial diversity occurred not in central, continuing roles but in nonrecurring characters. Whites were more likely than people of color to be portrayed in professional occupations; African Americans were more likely to be portrayed in law enforcement–related positions. And only people of color played the roles of domestic workers, nurse/physicians' assistants, and unskilled laborers, with most of these concentrated among Latinos/Latinas (www.childrennow.org, "Fall Colors 2000–01").

Moreover, television has not remained consistently vigilant about increasing the affirmative presence of actors of color in a diversity of roles. Both television and films continue to rely heavily on racial and ethnic stereotypes. And where there has been an increase in the number of television shows dominated by African Amercian characters, these have been largely restricted to Warner Brothers (WB) and Universal Paramount Network (UPN), not the major networks. Notable exceptions that do not rely on negative stereotypes include the 1980s *Cosby Show*'s positive portrayal of a successful African American family, which was important for the perceptions of both white and African American viewers of families of color as respectable, well-educated, and stable (Havens, 2000; Rhym, 1998). More recently, *Bernie Mac* and *My Wife and Kids* depict middle-class couples struggling successfully with issues confronting many African American and middle-class families. *Boston Public*'s African American principal is strong, intelligent, and professional. But the more standard fare on television perpetuates racial stereotypes, reinforcing negative racial images and making people of color objects of derision. For example, *The George Lopez Show* relies on stereotypes of Mexican Americans.

Television and print news media are often swift to seize on racist stereotypes in their reporting. For example, when Susan Smith claimed an African American carjacker kidnapped and killed her two young sons in South Carolina in 1994, both the police and the press readily and uncritically accepted her story. Later it became clear that she herself had sent her sons, strapped in their carseats, to their death when she deliberately submerged her car in a lake. The repeated emphasis in the press on the racial overtones of the case served to reinforce racist stereotypes of the violence of African American males and the danger they pose for whites.

Toys, Games, and Recreational Activities

The toys children play with may also reinforce racist stereotypes. In 1949 Crayola, the leading manufacturer of crayons, introduced a peach-colored crayon that it labeled "flesh," implying that normal skin color is peach, not black, brown, yellow, or red. Flesh remained on the market for over a decade, but was discontinued in 1962 when Crayola bowed to pressures from the civil rights movement. Crayola was less sensitive to the implications of labeling another color "Indian Red." This color label remained on the market until 1999, when it was changed to "chestnut" (http://kids.inforplease.lycos.com).

Dolls are also persuasive toys. In a classic study (Clark and Clark, 1947), when children were confronted with two dolls, one white and one black, one-third of the African American children selected the white doll as the one resembling themselves. Both white and African American children in the study tended to identify the white doll as good and the black doll as bad. Research suggests that the preponderance of white dolls available in toy stores continues to affect racial socialization and perceptions of beauty and goodness. For example, 65 percent of the African American preschoolers in one study selected a white Cabbage Patch doll over a black version of the doll (Powell-Hopson and Hopson, 1988). Another study done in the West Indies produced similar results, which the author attributed to the continued cultural impact of white colonialism (Gopaul-McNicol, 1995). On the other hand, toys and books do have the power to alter racist stereotypes. In one study, two-thirds of both white and African American preschoolers chose the black doll after exposure to a half hour of stories containing positive images of the black doll (Gopaul-McNicol, 1988).

The use of racist stereotypes as team mascots and logos, both in school and in professional sports, reinforces the image of some groups as less-than-human or civilized. In particular, Native American references are often used as team names (Redskins, Braves, Indians, etc.) in part because of the cultural image of these

Social Forces/People's Lives

White Christmas in the Dollhouse

LONNAE O'NEAL PARKER

Toys and games are meant to entertain children and the young-at-heart. But along the way, they transmit to those who play with them a great deal of cultural information about race, class, gender, political identities, and normative expectations. The woman in this reading describes her own struggles with this insight as she attempts to grant her daughter's wish for a doll.

WE reached a quiet milestone in my house this Christmas. We bought my youngest daughter her first **white** doll. In truth, my husband bought it. I'm not sure I would have been able to actually lay down the cash, but my husband did so if not with my blessing, at least without my vehement opposition.

We have two **girls,** an 8-year-old and a 4-year-old (plus a 7-month-old son), and we had never bought a **white** doll for either. For years, I had been clear on this point. I had **white** dolls growing up. Cherubs with cornflower blue eyes and gossamer yellow hair. Beautiful little things. And along with the Breck **girl** and the Superfriends and Miss Clairol and Farrah Fawcett and Amy Carter and every image attached to every thing of worth and value and popularity in the culture, they helped teach me that I was not. My hair was all wrong. It was dark brown, not blond. And it wouldn't lie straight. You could break the comb trying to fix it in the morning. And it needed hair grease.

My **white** doll was a stand-in for my fantasies of something prettier. Something better than little brown **girls** with unstraight brown hair.

When my first daughter was born, I first vowed not to buy dolls. But I caved under pressure when she was about 2. Then I vowed I would not pay money for playthings that would teach her to covet something she would never have. I think we would have been okay with that approach if Sydney could have remained sheltered in the house forever.

My black neighbors gave my child her first **white** doll. It was a naked hand-me-down baby, and Sydney was enchanted. She christened it "**White** Baby," and it quickly replaced "Brown Baby" and "Kenya" and an African princess Barbie with a gold-flecked head wrap in Sydney's affections.

For about a week, **White** Baby ruled. Then she mysteriously disappeared. Stayed gone for several months until Sydney found her tucked away at the bottom of the front closet. This began a pattern. **White** Baby would go on the lam for long stretches before turning up strangely contorted to fit behind the potatoes in the pantry, or in the basement or the back of the garage. I even enlisted the help of relatives to hide it away.

Because **White** Baby caused me existential angst.

groups as aggressive, violent, savage, and fear-inspiring. The team names are typically combined with demeaning logos, as the savage image of the Brave and the unflattering caricature of the Cleveland Indian. Other groups (and certainly white European Americans as the dominant group) escape such treatment, at least in part because of power differentials: Whites own and control teams and the designation of names, logos, and mascots. African Americans and Latinos/Latinas have historically been more politically successful than Native Americans in resisting and challenging these depictions. This is beginning to change: Native Americans are becoming

I could not throw away the doll just because it was **white**—what would that say about me?—but I would not allow my daughter to adore something that might cause her to hate herself. So I did what we do. I hid it away so I didn't have to deal. Turns out, it was Sydney who reminded me that the world had changed. That all my issues did not need to be her own.

One day she asked me if it was okay to have **white** friends. And when I said of course, she asked, "Then why can't I play with **white** dolls?"

Very clearly, the answer was that she could. Play. With one **white** doll.

Sydney was later joined by her sister, Savannah. **White** Baby was supplanted by other dolls, mostly Barbies. And while I never bought **white** dolls, I always let the **girls** keep the two or so they got each year as gifts. **White** dolls over that cutoff simply rested in peace in the back of my pajama drawer.

This approach mostly worked, although there have been a few incidents. My brother-in-law, who lives in North Carolina, took my nephew and my **girls** to the toy store last year. He told them they could each get a toy of their choice. Sydney wanted a doll, but they didn't have any brown ones. "My mama doesn't let me buy **white** dolls," she said loudly, in the middle of Kay-Bee Toys.

It was a moment that we are supposed to be past in American culture. It is unfashionable now to have a baldly racial moment. Despite the occasional Trent Lott and his monsters from the id, lots of people act as if we can go from the civil rights movement to perfect reconciliation in one or two strides. It is simply too untidy to contemplate anything different. So I apologized to my brother-in-law for my daughter's remark. But then I pointed out, it wasn't like any of the little **white girls** in the stores were lining up with black baby dolls either.

This Christmas Eve, I was stuck at work and my husband was doing the last-minute shopping. He had already been to about five stores and he had one brown

Bratz doll, Sasha, for Sydney. But maintaining the balance of power in my house meant Savannah had to have a Bratz doll, too. And the only one left was Slumber Party Chloe. And she wasn't just **white,** she looked like Miss Helsinki.

So I braced myself. But I didn't tell my husband not to buy it. After all, Halle Berry won an Academy Award and Queen Latifah models for Revlon. On Channel 9, anchor J.C. Hayward interviews D.C. Del. Eleanor Holmes Norton, and in my house we read "Happy to be Nappy." Surely we were ready for this momentous step.

Christmas morning, the doll went over fine. Although I was slightly traumatized, or perhaps it was transfixed, by Chloe's butt-length spun-gold hair, Savannah made no comment—she just grinned. It turns out my mother-in-law bought a blond "My Beautiful Mermaid" for Sydney (this after the store ran out of black dolls and a blond Rapunzel Barbie was just too over the top), so each of them had a **white** doll of her own.

The day after Christmas, Sydney showed me her new doll's hair. she had rolled it up the night before and it was bouncing and behaving and swaying just fine. "That's beautiful, honey," I told her, and made a note to self:

> With all the strides we have made, with all the images of black beauty and power and success around her, with all the love I can heap on her, I will not, I will not, I will not be afraid of little blond dolls.

Then I smiled to myself. Because if I sense there's a problem, there's always room for one more in the bottom of my pajama drawer.

SOURCE: Lonnae O'Neal Parker, "White Christmas in the Dollhouse," *The Washington Post,* December 27, 2002, p. C1.

more vocal in their protests and their demands that use of these images end. Evidence suggests that this is having some effect. In academia, St. John's University now refers to its teams as the Red Storm, and Stanford University's teams the Cardinals; Syracuse University's teams are now simply called the Syracuse Orange. And in professional sports, the Atlanta Braves eliminated "Chief Nok-a-Homa," but few other concessions have been made to Native Americans' protests.

Taken together, families, schools, media, and toys and recreational activities play critical roles in racial socialization and the reproduction of racial inequality. They also contain strong possibilities for interrupting the cycle of the self-fulfilling prophecies that these agents have more commonly perpetuated. While many agents may offer powerful messages that together reinforce racism, people are not powerless to resist them. And therein lies room for change.

Political Socialization

The same socialization agents that teach members of society about "appropriate" and "inappropriate" behaviors and expectations with regard to gender, race, sexual orientation, and class also socialize members *politically*. **Political socialization** is the process through which individuals come to internalize a political identity that defines who they are and how they should behave in the political and economic institutions of society. Individuals develop a lens that shapes their views of how they expect the world to work and what they consider acceptable or even viable politically and economically. The agents that are particularly important in this process are schools, toys and games, and media.

Schools

Sports teams commonly select team names, logos, and mascots projecting images of aggression, violence, and savagery to inspire fear in their opponents. These images often reinforce racist stereotypes, particularly of Native Americans. Here, the Atlanta Braves' mascot, Homer the Brave, bears the image of the savage and uncivilized Native American. Note that other racial and ethnic groups have wielded greater power, which has enabled them to escape such derisive and degrading treatment.

Schools have historically helped transfer cultural values, and that function continues today (Gerstle and Mollenkopf, 2001; Norberg, 2001; Zajda, 2000). In U.S. schools students learn the principles of the U.S. Constitution and Bill of Rights, concepts that facilitate individuals' internalization of values such as the preeminence of private property, individual rights and personal responsibility for one's own fate, and civic obligations and duty to country. Students often begin each day with the Pledge of Allegiance and sporting events with the national anthem, constant reminders of those basic nationalistic values. While in and of themselves these values may not be problematic, the implications of uncritically accepting them may be. These values lead people to believe that the U.S. is a free and open society in which the key to upward mobility and accomplishment is simply individuals' hard work. Thus many people assume that persons who are poor, homeless, illiterate, or powerless have only themselves to blame. The strong implication is that those who may be better off do not have the responsibility to help the less fortunate. If people have successfully internalized these values, they may never question the adequacy of this blaming-the-victim analysis or analyze the role of political and economic institutions in producing such victims (Euben, 1997).

Similarly, textbooks typically portray a sanitized view of American history, which deemphasizes or ignores altogether the most violent aspects of slavery, the carnage of the Vietnam war, the violence by employers and the state against the labor movement, and the genocide of Native Americans in the westward expansion. This cleaner, crisper view of American history urges students to accept as legitimate the continued power and privilege of the few at the expense of the many, because countervailing information that invites critical analysis of that view is not readily available.

Schools teach individuals to revere the electoral process. Through elections for class officers, for example, students learn about their rights and responsibilities as voters, and they learn to value the democratic process as free and open. Along the way, however, they may also learn to accept as normal the highly competitive nature of such a process, as well as notions like "The winner takes all" and "All is fair in love, war, and politics." The process of elections in the context of principles like "one person, one vote" teaches people to validate the rule of politically and economically dominant groups. This is because members of society appear to have participated in selecting that rule, despite the fact that the candidates they choose from are overwhelmingly drawn from the ranks of dominant groups to begin with.

Schools may also impart important information regarding capitalist values of consumerism, through the constant bombardment of students with commercial mes-
pp. 129–131 sages. As we noted in Chapter 5, schools have become infused with corporate ideals, including the role of citizens as consumers. Students quickly learn to accept without question the political economy of capitalism and their need to consume mass-produced products and labels (Brint, 1998).

Competitive school sports prepare students for later physical fitness training, an important aspect of people's lives. But they can also prepare people to accept political decisions involving the nation in wars. Warfare is often seen as just another sporting event characterized by team spirit and "us" against "them." People often accept physical injuries and casualties as normal and justified, and they view as legitimate the notion that "to the winners go the spoils." Wars and competitive school sports even share a common terminology. Teams typically select warlike or aggressive figures or symbols for their names and logos. Competitive team sports may politically socialize people by channeling violence and aggression into an organized setting governed by rules (Dunning, 1993; Wilson, 1992). Thus competitive team sports become part of a "civilizing" process that teaches students it is acceptable to inflict bodily harm on players of the opposing team but not acceptable to do so to neighbors, coworkers, or authority figures. Such a civilizing process becomes easily transferable to situations of war, particularly when both settings share terminology and analytical frameworks.

Toys and Games

The toys and games commonly available reinforce the internalization of dominant ideologies and the acceptance of warfare as a game. Video games are dominated by militaristic themes (including one called Contra, in which a Rambo-like figure single-handedly tries to search for and destroy guerrilla rebels). Real lives, violence, and pain become trivialized into blips on a screen, removing the horrors of war from the players' consciousness and developing the eye–hand coordination necessary for actual participation in high-tech warfare. Even the more realistic graphics on Playstation games maintain a cartoonlike edge that implies a divorce of violence from reality. Although video games may improve eye–hand coordination, that physical development is accomplished in the context of militaristic themes that glorify war as normal and acceptable (Cerulo, 2000). Moreover, as we noted earlier, the gendering of video games as a male activity implies that aggression, war, and violence are "natural" male attributes.

Other toys also tie a political message to play. Almost immediately following the outbreak of the Persian Gulf war in 1991, G.I. Joe "action figures" in desert beige camouflage uniforms began to turn up in toy stores. And just as quickly, Topps, the maker of baseball cards, began selling packets of Operation Desert Storm cards, with pictures of generals and weaponry replacing pictures of star ballplayers. Statistics on individual officers' careers, relative troop strengths, and the capabilities of various weapon systems replaced earned run averages and runs batted in. During the war against Iraq in 2003, department and convenience stores began selling decks of playing cards with the faces of "Iraqi Most Wanted" (identifying Saddam Hussein as the ace of spades). While these cards were originally distributed to American and British troops in Iraq to familiarize them with the faces of "persons of interest," the cards quickly became available as playthings for the general public and implied that Iraqis are violent criminals.

Media

The media are important sources of information for individuals as they seek to make sense of the world around them. Television is probably the most widely used media source of information in the United States. What effect does television have on the development of political identity? How effective is its influence in shaping this identity? Studies show that television can affect viewers' perceptions of what constitutes important issues and who is responsible for these issues (Barnhurst and Wartella, 1998; Iyengar, 1990). Together, these findings illustrate that television can influence how people see the world and their places in it.

While media provide crucial information to viewers and readers, they also tend to present that information from a mainstream point of view. Thus they promote acceptance of dominant political values, including the defense of these values with individuals' lives in war (McChesney, 1999; Parenti, 1998). Reporters cover wars like sporting events, using all the terminology and metaphors of competitive sports, including pep rallies, "up-close and personal" vignettes of "our" various warriors, and nightly score reports of casualties and destruction, as reporters "embedded" with deployed U.S. troops did in the 2003 war against Iraq.

People tend to more readily accept various wars as necessary and legitimate when the media portray other countries' leaders and citizens as evil or subhuman, deserving of destruction. In 1991 President George H. W. Bush repeatedly described the war against Iraq as a war of good against evil. The media frequently noted that the Iraqis "don't value human life the way 'we' do." In 2003, President George W. Bush referred to an "axis of evil" supposedly created by Iraq, Iran, and North Korea. Exposure to such ideological statements, especially on a recurring basis from multiple media sources, enables people to transcend the usual norms against the taking of human lives. The selectivity of media coverage may foster the impression that "we're all in this together," "we'll all benefit equally from our team effort," and "we all agree that this is right and should occur" (MacArthur, 1992).

In addition to socializing people to accept war as legitimate, the media may promote the legitimacy of inequality, domination, and capitalism through the stories they select and the perspective they bring to them. This bias on the part of the media is not surprising, given that many mass media outlets are owned and controlled by large capitalist interests (Hackett and Adam, 1999). For example, the dominant commercial television networks (ABC, CBS, NBC, and Fox) are owned and controlled by major corporate investors (McChesney, 1997): General Electric owns NBC, Disney owns ABC, Viacom owns CBS, and Fox is part of Rupert Murdoch's News Corporation, an international media empire. The significance of the investors' and interlockers' influence over the networks is that people in the United States are far more likely to use television as their source of news than anything else. Only 79.3 percent in the United States read a newspaper, but 93.5 percent watch television (www.census.gov Table 911). In spite of the growth of cable networks offering some competition, the four major commercial networks still dominate in their share of the audience.

Newspapers and magazines are less concentrated than broadcast media, but many of the top print media are owned and controlled by industry conglomerates. Just 10 newspaper conglomerates account for half of the total newspaper circulation in the United States (Knee, 2003). The conglomerates typically own several major newspapers, magazines, and local television affiliates, thereby promoting **homogenization of news.** This means that people are likely to be exposed to a single perspective and a single analysis of very complex stories no matter how many different media individuals select as their sources of news, particularly if these are all owned or controlled by the same conglomerate.

Concentrated control of both broadcast and print media by large corporate interests contributes to political socialization by empowering these interests to determine what is news and how it is interpreted. In a comparative analysis of which major news stories were covered and which were ignored, Herman and Chomsky (1988) documented how media elites censor news to reflect and reinforce corporate and wealthy elites' interests.

The media can also be an important agent in challenging the status quo (Black and Allen, 2001). For example, film footage documenting the excesses of police against civil rights and antiwar protesters in the 1950s, 1960s, and 1970s contributed to growing public intolerance of abuses of power and the problems of racism and militarism in the United States. More recently, journalistic pursuit of charges of sexual harassment lodged against Supreme Court Justice nominee Clarence Thomas in 1992 and Senator Robert Packwood in 1993 contributed to increased public rejection of abuses of power related to gender. And growing reports in 2003 of decades of sexual abuse by the Catholic clergy have similarly prompted public outcries for the need to punish such abuses of power even when the perpetrator is an otherwise revered and trusted religious leader.

Clearly, as the sole legitimate user of force and violence, the state maintains the power to assert and enforce its own interests and to discourage or suppress challenges to its authority and decision making and to the structure of key institutions. Historically, the state in the United States has resorted to use of violence to quash labor unrest and to silence antiwar protests. At other times local police have jailed civil rights, antinuclear, and abortion-rights demonstrators, as well as protestors against the World Trade Organization, to name just a few examples. In China, the state called out the army and used tanks to quell the Student Democracy Movement in 1991. In Israel, the military fires on demonstrating Palestinians seeking political self-determination. Media coverage of such events can serve as an influential vehicle for socializing the public, including potential future critics, to conform to the dominant group's rule.

Together, schools, the media, the state, and the toys and games many people enjoy contribute to political socialization. People often learn to accept and support unquestioningly the existing political and economic structures and to regard the inequalities of privilege and power produced by these structures as right, inevitable, and legitimate. This is not to say that these institutions necessarily conspire to fool people or that individuals are helpless robots with no ability to resist or change what may seem like "thought control." (We discuss how people can become agents for change and resistance in Chapter 10.) The point here is that one of the identities learned through the socialization process consists of who individuals are, where they fit, and how they should behave in the political and economic institutions of society.

CHAPTER SUMMARY

1. While the various agents of socialization are powerful forces in shaping social identities and political consciousness, individuals are not automatically transformed into mindless clones of one another. "Appropriate" behaviors and expectations, as well as resistance to total conformity, are open to a considerable degree of individual interpretation. Individuals' input into the socialization process contributes greatly to a broad diversity of outcomes.

2. Personal variations are apparent in the "appropriate" behaviors suited to one's sex and age group, the challenges people make against class and racial inequalities that they perceive as intolerable, and the resistance many people mount (against great odds) to prevailing political doctrines that serve elite interests. This can be seen in the feminist movement, the gay rights movement, and the civil rights movement. It can be seen as well in the labor movement, in antiwar protests, and recently in the students against sweatshops movement. It is also evident in the militance of senior citizens and people with disabilities in struggles to protect their well-being.

3. People also often change as they learn new things, collect new experiences, and meet new people with different ideas.

4. The process of socialization is not absolute and does not flow in one direction only. It is, in fact, an interactive process (somewhat lopsided because of power differences) between the individual and the various socialization agents, a process typified by conflict and struggle, alterations, and learning.

THINKING CRITICALLY

1. Many agents participate in shaping race, class, and gender identities. Look at the Social Forces/People's Lives reading describing a woman's struggle with the task of selecting a doll for her child. How did her subculture and the dominant, or mainstream, culture interact to help shape her struggle? How did she resolve her conflict? Have you ever confronted a similar conflict over something seemingly simple and harmless? How did you resolve it? How would you analyze her experience from the symbolic interaction perspective and the conflict perspective?

2. Select one of the attitude questions at the beginning of this chapter. How did you answer this question? Now consider these questions: What values does your answer reflect? How did you acquire your attitudes and values? What agents have had a part in teaching you and reinforcing these attitudes, and how specifically did they do this? Are your attitudes the same as or different from those of your friends, your family, your teachers, your religious leaders, or the media? If they are different, how have you managed to ignore the pressures of such agents of socialization?

3. Select a board game other than those discussed in this chapter (some good ones might be Careers, Careers for Girls, Life, Go to the Head of the Class, Couch Potato, and Stratego, but you may think of others). What are the rules and objectives of this game? What race, class, gender, or political socialization messages are contained in those rules and objectives?

4. Examine your gender, race, class, or political identity, and think about some of the agents of socialization that have played an influential role in shaping it. For example, how did your family, your school experiences, your religious training, your peer groups, or the media affect how you see yourself? What factors influenced the socialization experiences you have had? If you are shaping an identity that challenges institutional messages, what factors influenced your ability to resist them?

5. Select a television show or movie and examine the race, class, gender, and political identity messages it contains. Does the show or movie rely on stereotypes, or does it challenge them? Be specific. How would a symbolic interaction theorist, a functionalist, and a conflict theorist analyze this show or movie? What insights might each perspective offer in analyzing the images you see? What limitations does each perspective contain?

KEY TERMS

anticipatory
  socialization, *(159)*
compulsory
  heterosexuality, *(168)*
conflict perspective, *(147)*
degradation ceremony,
  (152)
ego, *(148)*
generalized other, *(146)*
homogenization
  of news, *(179)*
id, *(148)*

imposter syndrome, *(160)*
Liberation Theology, *(155)*
looking-glass self, *(146)*
nature-versus-nurture
  debate, *(144)*
political socialization,
  (176)
reference group, *(153)*
resocialization, *(152)*
second shift, *(161)*
self-fulfilling prophecy,
  (160)

significant other, *(146)*
socialization, *(144)*
socialization agents, *(153)*
sociobiology, *(144)*
superego, *(148)*
symbolic annihilation,
  (157)
symbolic interaction,
  (145)
total institutions, *(152)*

Chapter Seven

Systems of Inequality

In U.S. society, many people are treated as subordinates or inferiors on the basis of their class, race or ethnicity, or gender and are subject to various forms of discriminatory treatment by others. From a sociological perspective, such inequalities are not accidental or distributed randomly but are an integral feature of how society is organized. In U.S. society, **systems of inequality** are constructed around particular attributes—such as one's income and wealth, gender, skin color, sexual orientation, age, and state of able-bodiedness. These systems organize people's access to important resources and opportunities in patterned ways that advantage some and disadvantage others, depending on their status characteristics. Such systems of inequality have far-reaching consequences for the biographies of every member of society.

Sociologists have long been interested in studying and understanding systems of inequality. Karl Marx (1813–1883) drew attention to the processes that produce and maintain economic inequality and poverty in capitalist societies, a concern that is still relevant today. German sociologist Max Weber (1864–1920) was also highly influential in the study of inequality. He encouraged sociologists to analyze societies in terms of their systems of **social stratification,** the ways in which people occupying different social positions are stratified from high to low.

Weber suggested that in any given society social stratification is likely to be multidimensional. The three dimensions of stratification that Weber considered most important are class (possession of property and marketability of skills to generate income), status (social honor or prestige), and power (the ability to dominate or influence others). In Weber's view, the nature and relative importance of these three dimensions may differ from society to society as well as within any given society over time. Weber's notion that social stratification is multidimensional has influenced our approach to analyzing systems of inequality.

In this chapter we examine six systems of inequality, focusing on the United States: economic inequality, racial inequality, gender inequality, age inequality, inequality based on sexual orientation, and inequality based on able-bodiedness. These systems of inequality are human creations or **social constructions** that tend to differ from society to society and in different historical periods. For example, researchers have found that people in many non-Western societies have very different ways of viewing gender and gender relations than is typically the case in the United States, and that in other societies a wide

continued

range of sexual practices—including those one might associate with homosexuality—are accepted as normal (Murray, 2000; Nanda, 1999).

Before looking at the six systems of inequality, we wish to set them in a larger context. Not only are they human creations, but these systems also are organized around differences in power. It is not uncommon for one segment of society to have the ability to set the standards of who or what will be considered "good" or "normal" within a system of inequality, as well as the power to marginalize or impose disadvantages on people who are deemed "bad" or "abnormal."

For example, in male-dominated societies men may reserve certain central social roles for themselves and seek to limit women to other, more marginal roles. In doing so, men decide what role behavior is "normal" for each sex, usually in ways that benefit men. This exercise of male power and its "gendered" outcome are usually justified by an ideology. As used here, **ideology** refers to an organized system of ideas and ways of thinking that may be either critical or supportive of the status quo. In this case we are concerned with ideologies that justify existing systems of inequality.

Ideologies that justify systems of inequality help to keep them going. The ideas they contain typically include the notion that the systems of inequality are necessary and inevitable. When such ideologies are well integrated into the fabric of a society's culture, the inequalities they foster may be accepted by societal members as little more than the "natural order of things." The term **ideological hegemony** has been used to refer to the dominance of a set of ideas governing ways of doing things, to the point where existing social arrangements—including systems of inequality—are treated by societal members as just a matter of "common sense" (Gramsci, 1971; Seybold, 1987).

For example, not very long ago, peoples of European ancestry waged war with indigenous (native) peoples residing in what are now North American nations: the United States, Mexico, and Canada. European colonists and their military forces took away native residents' lands and forced many to live in destitution. The conquerors justified their actions by an ideology that held that European colonists were racially and culturally superior to native North Americans. The latter were viewed and treated as uncivilized "savages" (Smedley, 1999). To this day many native peoples in North America remain socially marginalized and subject to negative stereotypes that can be traced back to ideologies accompanying European colonization (Brown, 2001).

Systems of inequality often give rise to conflict. Some groups seek to bring about social change that will put an end to their mistreatment while groups that are privileged within the system fight to maintain the status quo. People's biographies are strongly influenced not only by their positions in different systems of inequality but also by the presence and outcome of movements for social change. Obviously, if a person is unfavorably situated in a given system of inequality—as is the case for so many people—one way to alter the system is to join or otherwise lend support to such movements.

In the following sections we examine different systems of inequality that directly affect everyone in U.S. society. We address such questions as:

- How unequally are income and wealth distributed within U.S. society?
- Is the system of economic inequality in U.S. society necessary or functional? For whom?

- **What ideas help to justify and rationalize the existence of economic and other systems of inequality, such as those that are based on race, gender, sexual orientation, disability status, and age?**
- **What are some of the effects of these various systems of inequality on those occupying subordinate positions within them?**
- **Are these systems of inequality changing? For the better or for the worse?**

Economic Inequality

One of the enduring features of many societies is **economic inequality,** differences in the wealth and income that families and individuals possess. A great deal of meaning and significance are attached to the possession of such resources, principally because they play a major role in determining how long and how well one will live. For example, people's access to educational opportunities, food and housing, and health care is affected by their location within a system of economic inequality. The position people occupy in a system of economic inequality places them in a particular **class,** a term referring to a segment of the population whose

White settlers at times massacred Native Americans, justifying their acts with the belief that the indigenous people they killed were inferior human beings. In this engraving from 1868, white scouts and some of their Native-American allies carry out a massacre in Idaho.

members are similar in their economic resources. Let us look briefly at the unequal distribution of wealth and income in the United States and the poverty to which this unequal distribution contributes.

Wealth, Income, and Poverty

Wealth is the value of the assets or property that one owns. A small percentage of families owns most of the nation's personally held wealth in the form of corporate stocks and bonds, savings accounts, real estate, cars and boats, and other types of property (Wolff and Leone, 2002). In 1998, the richest 1 percent of the population possessed over a third of all personally owned wealth, and almost half of all wealth if one excluded the asset of owner-occupied housing (Domhoff, 2002).

Wealth is different from **income,** which for most people is money received in the form of hourly wages or annual salaries as well as government benefits such as Social Security, unemployment compensation, or public assistance. Note, however, that wealth may itself generate income, as when stockholders receive dividends and capital gains from corporate stock or when real estate owners profit from rental payments. Wealth, not earnings from employment, generates the majority of annual household income in the most affluent households. In U.S. society, most adults have incomes of some sort, but few own much wealth, particularly income-generating wealth (Phillips, 2002).

The value of one's assets (wealth) minus the value of one's outstanding debts is commonly used as a measure of a person's **net worth.** Members of certain groups in U.S. society that have been systematically deprived of equal opportunities for education, jobs, bank loans, and home ownership, such as African Americans and Native Americans, have average net worths that are extremely low in comparison to that of the white population.

In the United States, there is substantial inequality in the distribution of income, although it is not as extreme as the inequality in wealth holdings. For example, in 2001 the most affluent quintile, or 20 percent of households, received 50.1 percent of the nation's household income; the least affluent received a mere 3.5 percent. Indeed, the bottom 60 percent of households collectively received only 26.8 percent, while the most affluent 5 percent received 22.4 percent (U.S. Bureau of the Census, 2002a:19). People of color, on average, had much lower household incomes than whites and were significantly more likely than whites to fall in the bottom quintiles.

Wealth and income are related in the sense that those with the greatest wealth tend to also receive the highest incomes. Indeed, the top 1 percent of wealth holders received almost 17 percent of all household income in 1997 (Domhoff, 2002). The distribution of both wealth and income has become increasingly unequal in recent decades. The gap between rich and poor has increased, and the rich have literally become even richer (Wolff and Leone, 2002). Often, terms like "two-tiered society" are used to characterize the large and growing gap between the most affluent members of U.S. society and everyone else. In the "Social Forces/People's Lives" reading, *New York Times* columnist Bob Herbert describes some ways in which this gap is expressed in the city of Miami.

Another dimension of economic inequality is the extent of poverty (see Figure 7.1). In 2002, the U.S. Bureau of the Census defined poverty for a family of four (including two children) as an annual income below $18,244 (the amount changes annually and differs depending on family size). That year, 34.6 million people in the United States—most of whom were women and children—lived in poverty. Millions more were living in "near poverty," just above the poverty line (U.S. Bureau of the Census, 2003b). While most poor people in the United States are white, people of color are disproportionately found among the poor (Figure 7.2). Many people manage to climb out of poverty, but they often don't rise very far. For some the climb out is temporary; meanwhile, others keep plunging in. Job losses in recent years, as well as a rise in the number of female-headed households because of marital breakups, have introduced poverty to many middle-class families who had assumed that their economic status was secure (Albelda and Tilly, 1997; Newman, 1999).

The facts about economic inequality and poverty are open to different interpretations. Let us look first at how a functionalist perspective would interpret economic inequality.

Different Perspectives on Economic Inequality

The Functionalist Perspective on Economic Inequality

pp. 10–13 As was discussed in Chapter 1, the foundations of the functionalist perspective were established by early European sociologists such as Émile Durkheim (1858–1917). He and more recent sociologists sharing the **functionalist perspective on economic inequality** held that economic inequality is the result of beneficial forces, and the different positions that people occupy in society receive quite different rewards because this is in the interests of society as a whole (Durkheim, 1964). Thus a functionalist viewpoint might hold that it is not a bad thing that the average chief executive officer (CEO) of a large corporation in the United States receives an annual salary that is more than 400 times that of a typical hourly production worker (Phillips, 2002). Similar, if less dramatic, pay disparities exist throughout the occupational structure.

From a functionalist perspective, attaching different rewards to different positions is "functional," or beneficial to society. It provides incentives for individuals to strive for the most highly rewarded positions. Proponents of this view also argue that the most highly rewarded positions are the most important for the operation of society. It is crucial, therefore, that people who have appropriate talents, and/or who are willing to undergo the necessary training, strive to fill the important positions. Otherwise, the positions could end up being filled by persons who are less competent and society would suffer. Rewarding different positions unequally—in effect, maintaining an ongoing system of economic inequality—is thus seen as necessary and inevitable.

Those sympathetic to the functionalist perspective might argue that the formerly socialist nations in eastern Europe abandoned socialism and moved toward the construction of capitalist economies because their previous economic reward systems

Social Forces/People's Lives

Falling into the Gap

BOB HERBERT

In the United States, the growing income gap between the affluent and everyone else has been particularly noticeable in many of the nation's cities. Millions who are jobless join millions who work one or more low-wage jobs in experiencing poverty and economic insecurity, as indicated by the plight of Miami residents such as Adolfo Jesus Recio, Celestine Hardie, and Naomi Sanchez.

ADOLFO Jesus Recio suffers from asthma, depression and unemployment. His left hand was badly injured in an accident and is now almost useless. He panhandles in the middle of a busy street in the shadow of the downtown Miami skyline.

No one pays much attention to Mr. Recio's hazardous pursuit of a handful of dimes and quarters. We've closed our eyes to poverty in the United States. Government aid these days goes to the plutocrats, and the poor are being left further and further behind.

"I eat from the garbage cans in back of Wendy's and in back of McDonald's," said Mr. Recio. "You have to know what you're doing when you do that. I had a friend a few years ago who died when he ate some food from a dumpster. He was hungry and he ate it. He didn't know they had put poison on it to keep out the vermin."

Mr. Recio pointed toward a highway overpass. "I sleep down there, on a cardboard box under the bridge."

Miami is the poorest big city in the United States—poorer than Newark, poorer than Detroit, poorer than any city with a population of 250,000 or more. Most of the poor are working, and many have more than one job. But the economy is lousy and the city is teeming with immigrants willing to work for extremely low wages, even for pay below the minimum wage. So jobs are hard to find and wages across the board are rock-bottom.

were not unequal enough. That is, under socialism, the relatively modest gap in rewards between the best-paid and worst-paid positions failed to provide sufficient motivation for people to work hard, be productive, and strive to move up, thus setting the scene for economic collapse. Such an analysis would suggest that capitalism is preferable to socialism because capitalism contains vastly greater economic inequalities. However, the picture is more complex than the functionalist thinkers would have it.

The functionalist perspective certainly sounds logical, yet it has long been attacked as an ideology that does more to justify economic inequality than to explain it. In the United States this perspective first formally appeared in sociology journals in 1945, by which time World War II had pulled the nation out of the throes of the Great Depression (Davis and Moore, 1945). During the Depression a quarter of the U.S. labor force was unemployed, poverty was extremely widespread, and sharp economic inequalities prevailed. The functionalist perspective on economic inequality, had it appeared in the Depression years, would have counseled calm acceptance and greater individual striving, as opposed to questioning the system of economic inequality itself.

"People are living on the edge, paycheck to paycheck," said Judith Gatti, director of the Daily Bread Food Bank. She rattled off the categories of people needing food assistance: poor and working poor families, elderly men and women whose government checks are inadequate, mentally and physically handicapped people, battered, women, people struggling with H.I.V. and AIDS, the homeless. She said 43 percent of those helped by the food bank are children.

Over the past few days I met with several people who are working full time and still have trouble feeding themselves and their families. Celestine Hardie is a 49-year-old certified nurse's aide who makes $8.50 an hour working the overnight shift at a nursing home. She then works three hours each morning (at $6.50 an hour) delivering sandwiches for a Subway franchise. She just barely makes it. She keeps her budget from caving in each month by eating at the nursing home and at Subway.

Ms. Hardie said that if she were to receive a windfall of some sort, she'd celebrate by treating her children and grandchildren to a dinner at Red Lobster.

At least Ms. Hardie is working. What is really troubling as you drive or walk around the poorest neighborhoods of Miami are the legions of men and women, many of them young, who are out of work, hungry and filled with the dread of what the next day might bring. A young woman named Naomi Sanchez said her brother had turned to selling drugs and been murdered, and that her best girlfriend had become a prostitute. She said

she was unemployed and was on her way to another friend's house, where she hoped she'd be able to get something to eat.

The poverty in Miami exists in a startling juxtaposition to great wealth. Just a few minutes' drive from the panhandling turf of Adolfo Jesus Recio are the sparkling shores of Miami Beach and the gateway to the pristine environs of Fisher Island, an exclusive enclave that, according to the 2000 Census, is the wealthiest community in America. Fisher Island is off limits to everyone except residents, invited guests and whatever employees are needed to keep them safe and comfortable. It is accessible only by ferry. If Mr. Recio showed up on the dock and tried to board the ferry, he'd be angrily hustled away.

The Miami area is the most extreme example of the economic inequality that is becoming more and more evident throughout the U.S. If the gap between the folks at the top and those at the bottom continues to grow it will at some point undermine the social cohesion of the nation. Anyone who thinks it's a good idea for the pampered elite of Fisher Island to stockpile more and more in the way of luxuries and privilege while increasing numbers of Miamians are going to bed hungry, should think again.

SOURCE: Bob Herbert, "Falling into the Gap," *New York Times*, January 27, 2003, p. A27.

Shortly after the functionalist perspective on economic inequality appeared in the journals, critics assailed it on a number of grounds (Tumin, 1953; Wrong, 1959). The questions the critics asked are still being asked today (Kerbo, 2003):

- Are the most highly rewarded positions indeed the "most important" to society? How could this be proven?
- Do the extremes of enormous wealth and income, juxtaposed to abject impoverishment, have to exist?
- Since the talented at the bottom of the economic ladder necessarily start from a disadvantage, does U.S. society really have an open system of equal opportunity in which all people compete on an equal footing and talent "rises to the top"?
- Is it necessary that some occupations pay millions of dollars per year, while others pay even less than the government-set minimum wage?

Critics of the functionalist perspective on economic inequality have also questioned the role of access to contacts in obtaining jobs: How helpful are contacts in determining a given individual's job opportunities (see the discussion of social pp. 105–107 networks in Chapter 3)? It seems that equal opportunity to compete

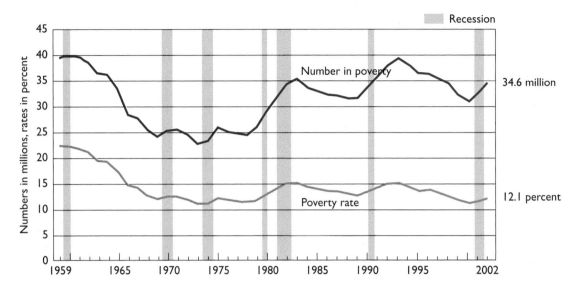

FIGURE 7.1 **Number of Poor and Poverty Rates in the United States: 1959–2002** The extent of poverty in the United States varies depending upon the health of the economy and the availability of decent-paying jobs. The number of people experiencing poverty increases during periods of economic recession and higher rates of unemployment. Note: The data points represent the midpoints of the respective years. (Source: U.S. Bureau of the Census, *Poverty in the United States: 2002.* Washington, D.C.: U.S. Government Printing Office, 2003, p. 3.)

for good jobs cannot safely be assumed. The already economically successful are privy to resources and connections that may then be used to help others get similar jobs, particularly their own friends and family members. In unionized skilled trades and licensed professions members are often able to limit entry or extend it selectively to those of their choosing. Moreover, some trades and professions are able to use their members' collective power to maintain scarcity of their particular skills, and they thus command higher rewards than those in other types of positions.

Physicians, for example, have long been able to use their collective power to restrict the number of accredited medical schools and the number of doctors. They also have been able to choose the geographic areas in which they will practice and whether to serve as general practitioners or specialists. Physicians have thus generated scarcity in relation to demand for their services, which has helped to keep the their average salaries high. In addition, discrimination on the basis of race and sex in medical student admissions has until fairly recently meant that medical students were overwhelmingly white males. Admissions committees often gave special preference to the sons of physicians who were alumni. By putting obstacles to admissions in front of women and people of color, such practices undermined any open system of competition among the talented to enter medicine.

Critics of the functionalist perspective on economic inequality often point out that many jobs that one would think are very important to the operation of society, particularly jobs with significant "caretaking" responsibilities, are little rewarded.

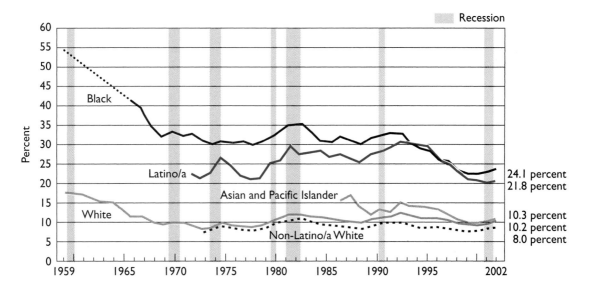

FIGURE 7.2 **Poverty Rates in the United States by Race and Latino/Latina Origin:**
1959–2002   Millions of people in the United States experience poverty regardless of their skin color; however, poverty rates for Latinos/Latinas and African Americans are particularly high compared to the poverty rates for non-Latino/a whites. This situation has existed for many decades.   Note: The data points represent the midpoints of the respective years. Data for Blacks are not available from 1960 to 1965. Data for the other race and Latino/a origin groups are shown from the first year available. Latinos/as may be of any race. (Source: U.S. Bureau of the Census, *Poverty in the United States,* 2002. Washington, D.C.: U.S. Government Printing Office, 2003, pp. 22–27.)

These jobs often involve tasks that families are increasingly unable to perform, especially since most adults today are by necessity full-time participants in the labor force. One need only think of the low pay typically extended to day care workers, those providing services to patients in nursing homes and hospices, and employees in institutional settings serving the mentally ill, recovering substance abusers, and people with serious disabilities. Many caretaking occupations are disproportionately held by women and are stereotypically defined as "women's work" (Albelda and Tilly, 1997). In a society in which the power of males over females continues to be an issue, the tendency to treat women's work as less important than men's may help to account for the gap between such jobs' pay rates and their arguable importance to society.

Finally, critics have suggested that rather than being functional, or beneficial to society, economic inequality leads to a dysfunctional situation. It harms people in innumerable ways: Economic inequality results in a lack of commitment to the larger society by the economically disadvantaged; fosters antisocial behavior such as crime and substance abuse; generates resentments, jealousies, and intergroup conflicts; and can be a very destabilizing force. Economic inequality may especially serve as a source of conflict when it systematically overlaps with skin color, as is the case in the United States (see Table 7.1).

TABLE 7.1 Per Capita Money Income by Race and Latino/Latina Origin: 1980–2000

Year	Current Dollars					Constant (2000) Dollars				
	All Races[1]	White	Black	Asian, Pacific Islander	Latino/a[2]	All Races[1]	White	Black	Asian, Pacific Islander	Latino/a[2]
1980	7,787	8,233	4,804	(NA)	4,865	15,494	16,382	9,559	(NA)	4,865
1985	11,013	11,671	6,840	(NA)	6,613	16,901	17,911	10,497	(NA)	6,613
1990	14,387	15,265	9,017	(NA)	8,424	18,472	19,600	11,578	(NA)	8,424
1991	14,617	15,510	9,170	(NA)	8,662	18,104	19,210	11,358	(NA)	8,662
1992	14,847	15,785	9,239	(NA)	8,591	17,914	19,046	11,148	(NA)	8,591
1993	15,777	16,800	9,863	15,691	8,830	18,557	19,761	11,601	18,456	8,830
1994	16,555	17,611	10,650	16,902	9,435	19,055	20,270	12,258	19,454	9,435
1995	17,227	18,304	10,982	16,567	9,300	19,343	20,552	12,331	18,602	9,300
1996	18,136	19,181	11,899	17,921	10,048	19,825	20,968	13,007	19,590	10,048
1997	19,241	20,425	12,351	18,226	10,772	20,587	21,854	13,215	19,501	10,772
1998	20,120	21,394	12,957	18,709	11,434	21,231	22,575	13,672	19,742	11,434
1999	21,181	22,375	14,397	21,134	11,621	21,893	23,127	14,881	21,844	11,621
2000	22,199	23,415	15,197	22,352	12,306	22,199	23,415	15,198	22,457	12,307

NA, Not available.

[1] Includes other races not shown separately

[2] Persons of Latino/a origin may be of any race.

SOURCE: U.S. Bureau of the Census. *Statistical Abstract of the United States: 2002* (Washington, DC: U.S. Government Printing Office, 2003), p. 440.

A Conflict Perspective on Economic Inequality

A **conflict perspective on economic inequality** would not view it as natural and inevitable. Rather, this perspective would stress that to understand the unequal distribution of income and wealth, one must look at where power in a society resides. In his classic work *Power and Privilege* (1966), sociologist Gerhard Lenski argues that in societies that produce a surplus—more than the minimum needed for basic group survival—the people with power will determine its distribution. In his view, "power determines privilege." In the United States, for example, the distribution of economic rewards is broadly influenced by government policies toward taxation of income and wealth.

In looking at the United States, one might ask:

- To what extent do the wealthy enjoy special tax breaks not available to others?
- Does the system of taxation reduce or simply maintain economic inequalities?
- How much income assistance (if any) is provided to the poor?

When the affluent or their representatives control government, they can use their power to serve the interests of those who are already economically privileged (Domhoff, 2002).

Understanding the relationship between power and privilege can be helpful in understanding movements for change in the formerly socialist nations of eastern Europe. Proponents of a conflict perspective are unlikely to accept the argument that these nations were on the verge of collapse simply because they had too little economic inequality. For example, before its breakup the Soviet Union possessed a highly centralized state-controlled economy. Communist Party leaders put priority on strengthening the Soviet military-industrial complex to compete in the Cold War against the United States and its allies, rather than on producing consumer goods and services needed by Soviet citizens. At the same time, the Soviet state was undemocratic and politically repressive, making it extremely difficult for citizens to express their views or have any impact on state and party decisions directly affecting them.

Top Soviet officials had exclusive authority to shop in special stores offering imported goods to foreigners, rode around in expensive government vehicles, relaxed in luxurious state-owned vacation properties, and used their political connections and social networks to secure preferential treatment for their family members in regard to educational opportunities, health care, and jobs. The visibility of such privilege caused much resentment among Soviet citizens for many years, if only because it contradicted the egalitarian ideas inherent to socialist ideology (Parkin, 1971). From a conflict perspective, people living in the Soviet Union sought its transformation because they could no longer tolerate political and economic injustices that they believed were undermining their ability to live and the quality of their lives. That transformation did not occur simply because the relatively modest gap between the best- and worst-paid Soviet workers stifled worker motivation.

What about economic inequality in U.S. society? Those who interpret economic inequality in the United States from a conflict perspective, as opposed to a functionalist perspective, view this inequality as the outcome of the workings of **capitalism.** In capitalist economies, ownership of a society's means of production is typically in the private hands of a small proportion of the population. In the United States, the enormous income and wealth that is generated by the collective labor of the majority flows disproportionately into the hands of corporate owners. Under the principle of "power determines privilege," top corporate officials, with an eye toward maximizing profits, decide who and how many people will be hired (or laid off), where work will be located (or relocated), and how much (or little) workers' pay and benefits will be.

Keeping workers' wages low helps to keep corporate owners' profits up and the incomes of corporate executives high. In the United States, unemployment, underemployment, economic insecurity, and poverty—or just the threat of these things occurring in one's life—act to push workers into constant competition with one another for jobs or for better paying ones. This competition, in turn, helps to keep wages down. Employers can offer lower wages when the competition for work is intense. From the conflict perspective, economic inequality is fostered by the routine workings of capitalism and, insofar as the state intervenes in this process, it is largely on behalf of those who disproportionately receive its economic benefits and not the average worker.

Indeed, in the years since the formerly socialist Soviet Union dissolved, and Russia has been making the transition to a capitalist economic system, economic inequality has sharply increased in that nation. With most economic activity no longer centrally state-controlled, and economic activity allowed to go loosely regulated,

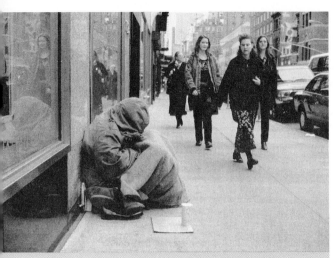

Homelessness is an expression of extreme economic inequality and the poverty to which it gives rise. In urban settings, the more affluent frequently respond to the presence of homeless persons huddled in doorways and on sidewalks with barely a glance.

some Russian citizens have grown extremely wealthy, while others suffer unemployment and poverty at rates never seen under Soviet socialism. Many Russian entrepreneurs have taken advantage of the state's relaxation of control over the economy to operate outside the law, and their quest for ever greater wealth has unleashed a tidal wave of corruption, organized crime, and white-collar offenses. Meanwhile, among those left poor and unemployed in Russia's new capitalist economy, alcoholism, drug abuse, prostitution, suicide, and other social problems have sharply risen.

Similarly, in the United States gross economic inequality means that some members of U.S. society enjoy enormous economic privilege at the same time that millions of impoverished individuals and families experience great suffering. This suffering could be avoided, advocates of the conflict perspective point out, were the state not far more concerned with tax breaks and other forms of "corporate welfare" from which large corporations and the affluent reap great benefits (Glasberg and Skidmore, 1997). As we have noted, some 34.6 million men, women, and children live below the official federal poverty line. Millions more are "near-poor," living just above the poverty line. Many poor and near-poor adults are experiencing unemployment. In addition, many millions of adults work full-time jobs at wages that keep them and their families below or hovering just above the poverty line. The numbers of such workers has gone up markedly in recent years.

As a consequence of the workings of U.S. capitalism, tens of millions of U.S. society's members regularly confront hunger (Schwartz-Nobel, 2002). Millions must deal with lack of affordable housing and homelessness (Mittal and Rosset, 1999). Poverty is a major contributor to serious health problems for millions of people in the United States. Compared with the rates in other industrialized nations, U.S. infant mortality and child death rates are extremely high.

From the conflict perspective, such economic inequality is not "functional" to society. Such inequality exacts enormous costs from persons who experience it, whether a society's economy is capitalist or socialist. Society as a whole loses as well. A vast pool of potential talent is suppressed, as individuals who might make substantial contributions to the well-being of others are caught up in poverty and economic insecurity. They may never have the opportunity to develop or to utilize their natural gifts. Insofar as a system of economic inequality stifles human potential and shortens life spans for some, everyone suffers. The costs of economic inequality to society can be very high, especially when they include increased crime, illness and disease, and social unrest.

Racial Inequality

Relationships between peoples having different physical attributes are often characterized by misunderstanding, tensions, and conflict. Conflict is particularly likely to occur when populations with different physical attributes occupy unequal positions of advantage in the existing system of economic inequality (Steinberg, S., 2001). In systems of **racial inequality**, some groups are subjected to discrimination and exploitation based on their racial "minority group" status, while others are accorded (or accord themselves) privileges denied to minority group members. A **minority group** is comprised of people who share common characteristics (e.g., skin color), on the basis of which they are singled out and subjected to prejudice and discriminatory treatment by others.

The term "minority group" does not denote numbers but indicates lack of status and power within one's society. In South Africa, for instance, blacks far outnumber whites, yet for many years black South Africans were a minority group because the dominant white population structured social institutions to ensure that blacks occupied an inferior status. This system of racial segregation and racial oppression, known as "apartheid," was finally abolished in 1990 after decades of social movement and protest activity and, in the 1980s, international economic and political pressures. In 1994 the first elections open to South Africans regardless of race resulted in the election of a black president, Nelson Mandela, an anti-apartheid leader who the white political regime had imprisoned for 27 years.

The Concept of "Race"

In South Africa, the United States, and elsewhere, the physical trait of skin color has been used by many whites as a criterion of social worth and as an indicator of racial differences. **Race** is a category into which people are assigned based on the social meaning and significance given to certain physical (and sometimes cultural) characteristics of members of a society's population. Although frequently employed as a means of categorizing people, "race" is actually a meaningless concept in biological terms (Gould, 1996). Regardless of superficial physical characteristics such as skin color, people all belong to one human species. Variations in physical traits exist among members of the human species as a consequence of extremely slow evolutionary changes. These changes have evolved in response to differing demands of the various physical environments to which humans have long been exposed. They are also, in part, the outcome of generations of genetic selection as different groups have come into contact with one another.

Thus such features as skin color, hair texture, and shape of the eyes, nose, or lips vary among people whose ancestries lie in diverse geographic locations. Biologically speaking, these varying features do not really depict people of different races. Race is a social concept, not a biological one. Hereditarily "pure" races simply do not exist, and existing systems of racial categorization of people are imprecise and arbitrary (Smedley, 1999).

At times members of a dominant group will define others as racially different based on distinctive cultural characteristics (including language and religion) or their geographic origin. When the criteria for defining a group as being of another "race" is at times biological and at others times cultural or geographic, the fact that races are socially constructed becomes painfully evident. It is not unusual for people use the term "race" to refer to a particular ethnic group. An **ethnic group** consists of persons who share a common culture, which may include a shared heritage, language or dialect, religion, norms, and customs.

Cultural or geographic origin differences may or may not coincide with skin color. But some people have long argued that people in the United States who are of African ancestry are members of a distinct "race" that is biologically and psychologically inferior to that of whites (Gossett, 1997). Until the mid-twentieth century this was widely taken to be a scientific truth. A number of scientists argued that persons of African descent had smaller brains than whites and therefore, by nature, were less intelligent. Even the famous scientist of evolution Charles Darwin stated:

> With civilized nations, the reduced size of the jaws from lessened use, the habitual play of different muscles serving to express different emotions, and the increased size of the brain from greater intellectual activity, have together produced a considerable effect on [whites'] general appearance in comparison with savages. (Quoted in Gossett, 1997:78).

Since they were less intelligent, the reasoning went, African Americans were fit only for the low-level work whites set aside for them. This argument for racial inferiority served as part of a larger ideology justifying the enslavement of African Americans. Later, the same argument was used by racist politicians to justify segregated public education: Mixing the allegedly less intelligent African Americans with whites in the same classroom would harm the progress of the whites.

Michael Omi and Howard Winant favor the term "racial formation" to underscore the social construction of "race" as a concept (1994). **Racial formation** is "the sociohistorical process by which racial categories are created, inhabited, transformed, and destroyed" (Omi and Winant, 1994:55). Designating a particular population a "race" may be a first step toward singling it out for discrimination. The alleged negative characteristics of a group that is racially categorized are often claimed to be rooted in genetics and therefore impossible to change. This type of thinking can lead to **genocide,** the systematic extermination of a group of people by those who consider themselves racially superior.

A society in which the "race" of people is thought to be significant is likely to be racist; there is no other reason for genetic variations in appearance to be of any particular concern. Systems of racial inequality are socially constructed around the false assumption that a link exists between features like skin color and the ways in which people are likely to think or behave. Just as humans cannot change their skin color, this view suggests, neither can they escape what it implies about their social worth.

Personal Racism

Sociologists interested in the ways in which racism is expressed have identified two types of racism, personal and institutional (Feagin and Feagin, 1999) . The first type, called **personal racism,** is racism expressed by individuals or small groups of people. It is an indication of bigotry or prejudice against those deemed "racially" inferior, and it may take such forms as espousing stereotypes based on alleged racial differences, using racial slurs, and engaging in discriminatory treatment, harassment, and even threats or acts of violence.

The distinction between prejudicial and bigoted attitudes, and racist actions informed by the latter, is important. Anyone—including people of color—may harbor racially prejudicial attitudes. But whites are generally much freer to express personal racism by acting on their prejudices, often with abandon and without concern for consequences, a privilege associated with their dominant power position in this society's system of racial inequality.

The view that some people are both racially different and objectionable as a population still exists among many members of the white majority in the United States. This view is reflected in sociologist Joe Feagin's analysis of survey data gathered in the 1990s. Data from one survey, conducted by the University of Chicago's National Opinion Research Center, indicated the following (Feagin, 2000):

- Fifteen percent of whites felt there should be laws prohibiting marriages between African Americans and whites.
- Sixteen percent of whites said that white people should have the right to keep African Americans from moving into their neighborhood.
- Thirty-five percent of whites would approve of a law that said people may sell their homes to whomever they want, even if they choose not to sell to African Americans.
- Forty-three percent said that African Americans should not push themselves where they are not wanted.

Such survey outcomes should be interpreted cautiously, for it is possible that some survey respondents are uncomfortable revealing racist ideas to strangers—in this case, survey researchers—as opposed to friends or neighbors. Thus the survey results may underestimate racial bigotry. In any event, surveys routinely indicate that personal racism is alive and well in the United States.

Racist thinking on the part of individuals is both stimulated and reinforced by pseudo-scientific claims that the capabilities of different "races" are biologically based (e.g., see Rushton, 1997). This notion, of course, requires acceptance of the assumption that biologically distinct races actually exist, which is not the case. In 1994, psychologist Richard J. Herrnstein and political scientist Charles Murray published *The Bell Curve,* in which they argued that there are innate differences in mental abilities along the lines of race. African Americans, for example, were said to be less intelligent on average than whites. Herrnstein and Murray's book was widely reported on in the mass media. Their ideas and the adequacy of their data were overwhelmingly rejected by social scientists as well as biologists, geneticists, and others in the natural sciences (Gould, 1996). Even so, the seriousness with which such ideas are treated by the mass media work to keep alive stereotypes about racial inferiority, and these media stereotypes in turn feed personal racism.

Institutional Racism

As an example of personal racism, recall the horrific 1998 murder in Texas of 49-year-old James Byrd Jr. He was an African American man who was kidnapped by three white men, chained to the back of a pickup truck, and dragged for three miles until he was dismembered ("Life Sentence in Dragging Death," 1999). As outrageous and damaging as expressions of personal racism may be, this form of racism in general has a less far-reaching effect on the life chances of people of color than does the racism that is built into societal institutions, known as **institutional racism.**

An *institution* is a social structure created by people to accomplish certain tasks or perform certain needed functions in society. The economy and the state are examples of institutions. People of color have historically been excluded from key policymaking and decision-making roles in such institutions. This has contributed to institutional racism, whereby the routine everyday operation of societal institutions fosters white privilege and advantage. Institutional racism often operates silently and subtly, through processes that are not immediately obvious and that are difficult to detect and observe (Smith, 1995).

Racism and the Economy

Within the economy, for example, racial discrimination in employment continues to be a major problem. This discrimination helps to keep the income of white households higher on average than those of people of color. A study involving interviews with Chicago-area employers revealed the blatant racist stereotypes and hiring policies of many toward workers of color:

> When they talked about the work ethic, tensions in the workplace, or attitudes toward work, employers emphasized the color of a person's skin. Many believed that white workers were superior to minorities in their work ethic. (Kirschenman and Neckerman, 1991:209–210)

As one employer told the researchers,

> (According to) the energy that they put into their job and trying to be as productive as possible, I would have to put the white native-born at the high end and the Hispanic in the middle and the blacks at the bottom. (Kirschenman and Neckerman, 1991:210).

Employers, acting on these stereotypes, tried to avoid hiring minority workers as a matter of routine. The study found that as a matter of policy they relied on their white employees to refer friends and relatives for job openings, and they regularly placed job advertisements in papers serving particular white communities and white ethnic groups. African Americans or Latino/Latina Americans who somehow made it as far as an interview would often be screened out at that point.

Racial discrimination also affects career opportunities in higher level positions. For example, the federal government's Glass Ceiling Commission investigated the reasons why so few people of color are hired by top management to be executives in large U.S. corporations. According to the commission's findings,

> Color-based differences are inescapable but nobody likes to talk about them . . . The unstated but ever-present question is, "Do they look like us?" . . . Though it is mostly covert, our society has developed an extremely sophisticated, and often denied, acceptability index based on gradations in skin color. It is not legally permissible, but it persists just beneath the surface, and it can be and is used as a basis for decisionmaking, sometimes consciously and sometimes unconsciously. (Quoted in Zweigenhaft and Domhoff, 1998: 110–111)

Institutional racism need not be as direct as in the preceding examples. Indeed, some institutional practices have differential and discriminatory effects on people of color that do not appear to be intentional. Take, for example, seniority rules, often seen by unions as important worker protections. The most familiar such rule is "last hired, first fired." Employers abiding by seniority rules dismiss their most recently hired employees first whenever cutbacks or layoffs occur. Since African Americans, Latino/Latina Americans, Asian Americans, Native Americans, and others who have fought against racial discrimination are often overrepresented among the most recent arrivals in traditionally white-dominated work settings, seniority rules are least likely to protect them from unemployment.

🌐 Racism and the State

Another societal institution, the state, often seems less than aggressive in addressing racism and its consequences or in enforcing laws against discrimination. At the federal level, for example, vast backlogs of complaints regarding incidents of racial discrimination are typical, and many victims believe filing a complaint is useless. Institutional racism by the state often takes the form of neglect or indifference. At times, however, state officials have actively tried to water down or retract existing state policies designed to assist victims of racism (Edsall and Edsall, 1992).

For example, the civil rights movement of the 1960s successfully pressured the state to adopt regulations requiring that employers take **affirmative action** to stop discrimination against people of color, as well as women. Affirmative action meant not only that discrimination in hiring was to cease, but also that employers were to take positive ("affirmative") steps to increase the presence of people of color and women in their applicant pools, thus improving the opportunity for such persons to be considered and hired if qualified. Ordinarily, this required little more of employers than that they widen their advertising of openings and drop discriminatory pre-employment screening practices. Only in some instances, when employers clearly resisted taking such positive steps, were they were temporarily forced to abide by court-ordered hiring "quotas" aimed at breaking down systemic discrimination. Affirmative action policies have had their greatest effect in government employment and, to a lesser extent, in the corporate sector. When implemented effectively, such policies have allowed individuals who had previously been excluded from particular workplaces to learn of opportunities, become part of applicant pools, and often to successfully compete for employment (Reskin, 1998).

Political opponents of affirmative action claim that discrimination in hiring has disappeared and that affirmative action is a form of "reverse discrimination" against whites and males. Its opponents further claim that unqualified workers have been hired simply to meet race and gender "quotas." Even though research by social scientists has shown such claims to be invalid (Reskin, 1998), they continue to be cited by politicians seeking to court white votes by playing on the white majority's frequent misunderstanding of and hostility to affirmative action (Edsall and Edsall, 1992).

Affirmative action policies were a direct outgrowth of the political pressure applied against the state by the civil rights movement of the 1960s and its supporters. But by the mid-1970s that movement had gone into decline, ironically in part due to its successes. When federal legislation outlawed the most blatant forms of racial discrimination, many movement supporters assumed the struggle for racial equality was over. Soon, the state began to do little more than pay lip service to affirmative action, and public support for it eroded as many politicians called the need for it into question. In turn, state pressure on employers to conform to affirmative action requirements waned, and their enforcement has since remained a low priority. In recent years government agencies have shown little interest in even studying the problems of racial (or gender) discrimination in employment.

In the 1980s top politicians routinely distanced themselves from the issue of affirmative action in political campaigns, and some ran openly on platforms decrying "reverse discrimination." The Reagan administration (1980–1988) and the George H. W. Bush administration (1988–1992) were openly hostile to affirmative action, and strict attention to state enforcement of regulations generally declined. In the 1990s, while never pushing affirmative action as an important government priority, the Clinton administration (1992–2000) did fend off calls for its abolition by its harshest critics. The latter included many strong supporters of the George W. Bush administration that followed.

The increasingly uncertain future of affirmative action was, however, dramatically altered in 2003. Despite the public opposition of the Bush administration, in a case involving the University of Michigan (*Grutter v. Bollinger*) the U.S. Supreme Court narrowly ruled in support of the use of affirmative action to achieve student diversity in higher education admissions (Greenhouse, 2003a). This ruling was expected to have a broad effect, for it also indirectly supported the legitimacy of efforts that have been undertaken by a number of major corporations to diversify their workplaces. Growing numbers of firms are coming to realize the economic benefits of having a diverse workforce as they seek to sell goods and services to multicultural domestic and global markets.

In large part, institutional racism by the state is a reflection of the state's racial composition. The fact that whites are in the numerical majority in most parts of the country has meant they can—when they wish—block people of color from high elected office. Moreover, at the top levels of state bureaucracy, where crucial public policy decisions are made, positions are typically filled through political appointment. This has made it very difficult for people of color to rise as high as their talents and accomplishments may merit. Those who do may have to sacrifice a degree of assertiveness about minority interests in return for the employment opportunity they have been afforded by representatives of the white majority.

Recent research on the composition of the nation's "power elite"—those who occupy top positions in government, military, and the corporate world—shows that skin color clearly matters. Prior to the 1960s civil rights movement, hardly any people of color were ever found in such positions. Although evidence suggests that diversity among members of the power elite has increased since then, African Americans and darker-skinned Latinos/Latinas seem to be having the most difficulty gaining admittance into these higher circles of power (Zweigenhaft and Domhoff, 1998).

The state's criminal justice system is also white-dominated. The subject of law enforcement has always been a particularly sensitive one for people of color, due to their mistreatment by the criminal justice system (Mann and Zatz, 2002; Reiman,

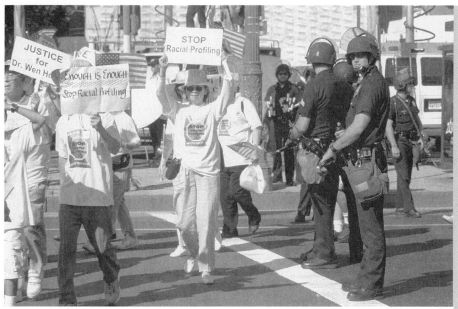

Unlike whites, people of color are frequently subjected to racial profiling, treated with suspicion, and harassed or investigated by the criminal-justice system because they are seen as "different." Asian Americans have found themselves victimized by racial profiling and, like other groups, have actively protested such discriminatory treatment.

2000). Until fairly recently employment discrimination in police departments was rampant. Moreover, even today police departments frequently either ignore charges of police officer misconduct and acts of brutality against people of color or perform internal "investigations" of such charges by police officials with little result. Police have a monopoly over the legitimate use of force, but its misuse has led to mistrust, hostility, and occasionally civil disorder. Acts of police brutality have at times generated violent rebellions in ghettos, in barrios, and on reservations. Police brutality was, for example, an issue in the massive disorders in Los Angeles in 1992 that followed the acquittal of white police officers who had been videotaped beating Rodney King, an African American.

The dominant white majority is also overrepresented among judges, prosecutors, jurors, prison officials, probation officers, and parole board members. People of color are more likely than whites to be arrested and charged with crimes, to be unable to afford bail, and to lack the funds needed to hire an attorney to defend them. People of color are more likely to be found guilty, to receive heavy sentences, and to be denied requests for parole from prison. Once released, they are likely to face very restricted employment opportunities, a situation that sets the stage for possible further involvement with the legal system. Those convicted of felonies are very likely to face permanent loss of their basic political right to vote. For too many persons, going through the criminal justice process is like being trapped in a revolving door (Reiman, 2000).

In documenting the effects of racism, most social scientists have (understandably) looked at its effects on people of color. Yet it is clear that all of society's members—including whites—lose as a consequence of racism, if only because the system of racial inequality stifles the potential accomplishments of millions of people from which everyone could benefit. But in addition, whites are not really "free" in a society in which social significance is accorded to physical traits like skin color. All whites, not just the visible bigots, are limited in the quality of their social relationships with people of color. Whites can find themselves imprisoned by the minority group anger and resentment to which racial inequalities give rise. Even freedom of movement may be affected, insofar as racism-based stereotypes about "dangerous" people guide whites' decisions about where they can safely go and what events they can safely attend. It is worth taking time to imagine how everyone's biography might be greatly altered, and certainly improved, by living in a nonracist society.

Gender Inequality

Just as systems of economic inequality and racial inequality have ideologies justifying their existence, so too do systems of gender inequality. **Gender inequality** stems from the notion that "biology is destiny," that biological differences between the sexes require that the sexes play very different societal roles.

Males and females obviously do differ biologically. Their genetic makeups are not the same, anatomical differences are apparent, and their hormones perform different functions. But how much social importance should one attach to such differences? To answer this question, we must make a distinction between two concepts: sex and gender.

Sex refers to the fundamental biological characteristics that people generally use to categorize persons as either female or male. These characteristics are genetically determined, and are largely related to different potential roles each may play in reproduction. Rarely is there ambiguity as to the sex of any given newborn once the baby's physical traits are established. Moreover, sex differences remain the same from society to society.

Gender, on the other hand, is a social construction, much like "race." Gender refers to the ways of behaving and relating to others that members of society expect of the two sexes; it refers to the different roles that males and females are expected to play. Gender is learned, whereas sex is inherited. As such, the behaviors associated with gender differ in various respects from society to society. For example, in some societies women are expected to be active and aggressive individuals, whereas in others they are expected to be passive and retiring. Indeed, even within societies the role expectations for women may differ—for example, by age, ethnicity, or class (Lindsey and Christy, 1996; Nanda, 1999). And role expectations within societies may change over time.

Nonetheless, males have used the ideology expressed in "biology is destiny" to create and maintain systems of gender inequality in which they dominate. The concept of **patriarchy** is used to refer to such systems. Not only domination but oppression and exploitation are common themes in societies characterized by patriarchy. While undergoing important changes in the last few decades, U.S. society remains very patriarchal. Men and women are not equal sharers of power—whether it be economic, political, or social. This is the case, to greater or lesser degrees, in most societies around the world. The biology-is-destiny ideology hovers over women, justifying male dominance, influencing male–female relationships, and affecting the trajectory of both sexes' biographies.

The Biology-Is-Destiny Ideology

According to this ideology, biological differences between the sexes require that there be a **sexual division of labor,** in which men and women take on responsibility for the tasks that each sex is most capable of performing. Hence, because women bear children, female biology dictates that they are most fit for child rearing and caretaking roles in the home. The home is said to be the best place for those whom nature has decreed the "weaker sex." It is a haven from the rough, competitive world of work and politics in which only men, portrayed as biologically the "stronger sex," are able to excel. Men's role is to provide for their "dependents": women and children.

The ideology suggests that the need for the species to reproduce promulgates yet another important role for women: being sexually attractive. Women thus play an important function when they strive to be, and allow themselves to be, treated as sex objects. This is all in line with nature's grand design.

The biology-is-destiny ideology spills over into the workplace and other institutional arenas outside the home (Lindsey and Christy, 1996). The rigidity of the ideology has eroded somewhat, but most people still accept the notion that there are "men's jobs" and "women's jobs." Few chief executive officers or other top officials of the nation's largest corporations are women (Zweigenhaft and Domhoff, 1998). But most clerks, secretaries, nurses, elementary school teachers, social workers, and domestic helpers are women. Why? According to the ideology, this division of labor simply reflects the basic biological differences between the sexes. Men are equipped to exercise power and function under demanding circumstances. Women are best suited for supportive, caretaking occupations and professions—those that call upon the particular strengths nature has given women.

Critics of the ideology and the restrictions it imposes on women's life chances include feminists and their supporters. **Feminism** refers to the belief that men and women should have equal political, social, and economic rights. Feminists underscore the difference between sex and gender, pointing out that the gender roles accorded women are largely of men's making. Women alone are capable of bearing children, but men are as capable as women of playing a nurturant role. They simply choose to allocate most such tasks to women. Nor is there reason to restrict women to the home out of concern that they are the weaker sex. Given the opportunity, women can fulfill virtually any position in work and politics that is presently male-dominated (recall, for example that during World War II women filled innumerable civilian roles for men who left for the military). Similarly, men are eminently capable of doing so-called women's work in the labor force.

Finally, current social conditions make it clear that women can and must be able to support themselves, instead of functioning as males' "dependents." The millions of women who are unmarried, separated, divorced, or widowed—many with children or others to support—are independent by necessity or choice. The demands faced by these women, for their own survival and that of their families, often cannot be met by the earnings accorded to "women's work" (Albelda and Tilly, 1997).

Feminists also question the notion that women must put priority on making themselves attractive to men in order to ensure reproduction of the species. Standards of beauty and attractiveness tend to be set by members of the dominant gender. Most women are unable to meet these standards, but there are always some who can—or can at least meet them better than others. Thus many women are raised to live in fear of rejection by men and to see other women as threats. Feminists do not see women's role as sex object as natural and inevitable, but as yet another instrument of male domination.

Male Chauvinism and Institutional Sexism

Patriarchy, as a system of gender inequality, finds expression through practices of **sexism.** This term refers to the systematic subordination of persons on the basis of their sex. As with racism, sexism exists both at the level of personal relationships and at the institutional level.

At the personal level, sexism typically takes the form of **male chauvinism.** Men who are chauvinistic express attitudes or behave in ways which suggest that males are superior to females and have a right to insist on females' subordination. Chauvinistic attitudes can range from sexist points of view ("Women are too emotional to be president of the United States") to extreme sexist behaviors ("I wouldn't call it rape—the way she was acting, she was asking for it").

Overt expressions of male chauvinism can be confronted, but such confrontation may sometimes be dangerous in a society in which men hold an unequal share of power. Women who challenge the sexist views and behaviors of a professor or employer, for example, may end up receiving a poorer grade than deserved, being overlooked for a promotion, or being dismissed from work. While feminists and their supporters have pressed the state to provide legal protections for women who are the victims of this type of harassment, it remains widespread.

Institutional sexism fosters male advantage through the routine operations of societal institutions. In the spheres of the economy and the state institutional sexism is pervasive, yet often it is less visible and less open to direct confrontation than male chauvinism. Given its far-reaching impact, institutional sexism is more of a problem than chauvinism—not only for women but for men as well.

Women and the Labor Force

Despite the biology-as-destiny ideology that stresses women's alleged biological proclivity for homemaking and child care, by 2003 some 60 percent of all women over 16 were in the paid labor force (U.S. Bureau of Labor Statistics, 2003). Most were working out of economic necessity, either because they had sole responsibility to provide for themselves (and, in many cases, others) or because their partners were incapable of being the sole providers. Yet by all statistical indicators, women get much smaller rewards on average for their participation in the labor force than do men. This state of affairs is understandable only in light of institutional sexism.

The U.S. labor market is sex-segregated to the point where social scientists commonly use the term *dual labor market* to describe it. Most women hold jobs in which the majority of their coworkers are female. Women are overly represented in jobs that are the least well paying, offer the least security, and have relatively low prestige—clerical work and service occupations (such as waitresses). Conversely, women are underrepresented in the jobs highest in pay, security, and status.

In 2003, the National Organization for Women reported that working women in the United States are on average paid 76 cents for every dollar in wages that men are paid. Rates for women of color are even lower: 66 cents for African American women and 54 cents for Latinas. More than 1 million women work in jobs that pay less than the federal minimum wage (www.now.org). This dual labor mar-

In the dual-labor market in the United States, women are highly over-represented in low-paying jobs such as waitresses. The dual-labor market produces a chronic gap between the average earnings of men and women and places a difficult burden on women who are trying to provide for their families.

ket is not a reflection of educational differences between men and women; women, on average, have the edge over men in years of formal education completed. Rather, the dual labor market is held intact by discrimination in employment, promotion, and pay. By paying less for "women's jobs" than for "men's jobs," and by channeling women into the former, employers use the biology-is-destiny ideology to their own economic advantage.

The struggle of women to improve their standing in the labor market is relatively recent and follows upon similar struggles by people of color to end racial discrimination. But institutional sexism in the economy, like institutional racism, is a routine matter largely because the state does so little about it. Indeed, the state itself is a locus of institutional sexism in employment. Women are poorly represented in the elected and appointed offices that make important policy decisions. They thus have limited power in resolving major issues affecting women's lives. These issues include the level of income maintenance provided to poor female-headed families, government support for affordable day care for working mothers, the need for programs providing universal health care, and the protection of women's reproductive rights (Albelda and Tilly, 1997; Mink, 2002).

Are Males Harmed by Gender Inequality?

Does the system of gender inequality enhance or promote the life chances of men? Do men benefit from patriarchy? Why should society do without the full range of contributions that women can make? The answer is that narrow benefits for some are outweighed by much broader losses for all. Any society in which the opportunities for women—typically half the population—are channeled and restricted is a society that is limited in its development.

Working to change patriarchy would make available a much wider range of biographies for people of both sexes. For example, married men and women with jobs outside the home could each escape the irrational constrictions posed by gender norms when it comes to household work. As it now stands, even when women work outside the home they still perform most of the household chores as well. Employers could reduce the rigidity of bureaucratic work organizations, thereby allowing much more flexibility in both women's and men's job assignments and work schedules. This could better accommodate meeting needs at home. Marital partners would be able to more equitably share the burdens and the joys of child care and other household responsibilities that are now largely considered "women's work."

Were men to significantly increase their contributions to household labor, married women would no longer half-jokingly complain that their daily lives could be improved immensely if only they too had "a wife." As men's roles at home expanded into new arenas of household competence and accomplishment, their female partners would no longer be forced to chafe under a sexual division of labor that so clearly limits their horizons and the uses to which they can put their talents and time. Moreover, were women equitably treated in the labor market, the economic pressure on male "breadwinners" would be less. Their male partners would also be freer to leave unsatisfying jobs or seek additional education in lieu of work, options that are currently inaccessible to many men. Clearly, many men would see tangible benefits from the elimination of patriarchy.

Age Inequality

Aging is a natural biological process to which everyone is subject. There is no reason why older people should be the object of mistreatment, but at times they are. Some cultures interpret aging positively: They respect and venerate elderly persons for knowledge they have accumulated and share with others (Keith, Fry, and Glascock, 1994). The status of elders was extremely high in the United States until the late eighteenth century, when revolutionary turmoil prompted a shift in attitudes toward those occupying traditional roles of authority (Fischer, 1978).

Aging may also be interpreted negatively, as when the elderly are viewed as unattractive, undesirable burdens on society (Falk and Falk, 1997; Nelson, 2002). This interpretation is characteristic of the system of **age inequality** that came to prevail in the United States in the early nineteenth century (Fischer, 1978). This system is organized around the expression of **ageism,** ideas and practices that have negative consequences for persons defined as old.

Old Age as a Social Construction

As with the concepts of race and gender, "old age" is a social construction: Whether and at what age one becomes "old" can be very arbitrary. At times old age is said to commence with the passing of a certain number of chronological years. For example, government agencies have often used age 65 as the start of eligibility for certain benefits, and employers at times offer pensions to workers once they reach age 65. In these cases "old age" is created for the administrative convenience of the organizations.

Physical characteristics associated with aging are also used to arbitrarily define people as old. These characteristics include loss of skin elasticity, wrinkled skin, gray hair or hair loss, and physical frailty. The prevailing ideology of ageism holds that persons with such traits have entered a downward spiral of deterioration. Along with this goes certain assumptions about the ways in which people with outward signs of aging are likely to think and behave. For example, many younger persons mistakenly assume that elders are by definition poor drivers, or that they have little interest in relationships that involve sexual pleasure.

The social construction of old age treats women differently from men. In U.S. society, a youthful appearance enhances a woman's image as a sex object; loss of this appearance devalues women in the eyes of many men. In contrast, as men start to age, they may be described as looking distinguished, a temporary positive assessment that is denied women. Yet even "distinguished" men eventually come to be socially defined as "old men."

Myths and Stereotypes about Elders

The U.S. population is aging. In coming decades there will be rapid growth in the proportion of the population that is 65 and over. This "graying of America" is taking place even while a number of myths and stereotypes about elderly people continue to prevail (see Nelson, 2002). These include the following:

1. *Old people are all the same.* In actuality, elders in the United States are as heterogeneous as the rest of the population. They differ in skin color, ethnicity, national origin, economic status, work experience, sexual orientation, political attitudes, and all the other attributes that differentiate younger people.

2. *Old people are senile.* Senility" is a vague term, often used inaccurately—and pejoratively—in reference to the mental state of older persons. "Senile dementia" is a medical term referring to a decline of mental faculties due to deterioration of the brain. Only a relatively small percentage of elders suffer from this condition. Most anxiety and depression among older people is not only treatable but avoidable, as is the case for the younger population.

3. *Old people are unproductive.* It is true that many older people are not currently active members of the labor force or involved in parenting (although many do take on full- or part-time jobs after retirement or are active grandparents—often even serving as substitute parents for their grandchildren). Younger people tend to be oblivious to the fact that they are the beneficiaries of elders' many years of productive labor in the workplace and home. Moreover, older people make ongoing contributions to societal well-being through volunteer work, participation in religious activities and politics, and support of cultural affairs.

Theories about Aging: Disengagement versus Activity Theory

The myths and stereotypes portraying elderly people as a homogeneous, senile, unproductive, gray-haired mass in a spiraling state of physical and mental deterioration feed into **disengagement theory.** This theory, developed many years ago (Cumming and Henry, 1961), suggests that biological and psychological decline accompanies aging; thus older individuals, in anticipation of death, naturally begin to remove themselves from social roles they occupied during middle age. It is considered natural not only for elderly people to withdraw but also for society itself to disengage from involvement with the elderly.

This mutual withdrawal is presented as necessary, inevitable, and beneficial to all concerned. Persons in a "deteriorating" state escape the pressures of performing a role in the labor force, thereby ensuring a more "successful" old age. Society also benefits by having the opportunity to replace the elderly with younger, more energetic, and presumably more productive workers.

Critics have attacked disengagement theory as an ideology justifying prejudice and discrimination against elders (see, e.g., Levin and Levin, 1980). It counsels elders to abandon the roles they have long occupied, even if both elders and the rest of society may continue to draw substantial rewards from their performance of these roles. Proponents of an alternative view, sometimes called **activity theory,** point out that most people remain healthy and capable of being active into their later years, contrary to the image of decline that is generally presented by those embracing disengagement theory. President Ronald Reagan, who was 77 when he left office, is often cited as an example. Activity theory takes the position that pushing people out of or away from roles they occupied in middle age may actually cause physical and psychological decline that might not otherwise occur, as is often the case with involuntary retirement and other forms of job loss. Nor, proponents of activity theory point out, is it necessarily the case that youth outweighs the advantages associated with years of experience in the workplace.

Areas of Concern for Elders

Many people worry about what lies ahead for them in their later years, and well they should. In the weakening economy of the early 2000s, when many corporations were downsizing and laying off workers, older employees were often among the first ones to go. Firms claimed that they were forced to dismiss older workers whose higher salaries and workplace benefits could not be maintained in economically difficult times, which in and of itself is not illegal. But older workers who are dismissed may well wonder if this is the only or the main reason for their job loss. Although blatant age discrimination may be difficult to establish in such cases, the outcome of such corporate policies is to weaken the ability of older workers to sustain themselves and their families. Given the growing proportion of the labor force that is moving into "old age," subtle forms of employment discrimination along the lines of age are likely are to expand in significance (Gregory, 2001).

Consider, as well, the area of health care. Growing old does not necessarily entail a downwardly spiraling state of health, yet many older people do face increasing health care requirements due to chronic, long-term problems (such as arthritis, high blood pressure, sight and hearing impairments). Some will ultimately require full-time care, although at any time, only about 5 percent of those 65 and older live in nursing homes.

Yet health care costs are high, and government programs such as Medicare do not cover some services. Middle-income people who need long-term nursing home care, and who lack private long-term-care insurance, cannot qualify for nursing home assistance under Medicare until they expend all their assets to the point of poverty. Moreover, the medical profession and its institutions are not adequately oriented toward health needs of the aging. Too few physicians are trained in geriatric medicine; many doctors find the common chronic health problems of elderly people neither interesting nor challenging; physicians often do not accept Medicare patients, preferring the higher reimbursement usually guaranteed with private health insurance plans; and in many parts of the country hospitals and clinics are inaccessible to older persons because of distance or lack of adequate transportation. Finally, for those elders who do ultimately require nursing homes, the number and quality of these facilities remain a national scandal, as do the expenses accompanying even little more than "custodial" care. Ageism, then, is expressed in the ways the state and the nation's health care institutions fail to accommodate the needs of the elderly.

Poverty-level living and income problems are also linked to ageism. Neither the state nor the corporate sector acknowledges a responsibility to assist the elderly to live above the poverty line. Increasing numbers of elderly persons are forced to rely on Social Security benefits for all or most of their incomes, but for many people benefit levels are low and inadequate. Since benefits are keyed to employment and earnings history, persons who have not fared well in the labor market during their adult lives (particularly women and people of color) suffer the most. People who are economically disadvantaged when they are middle-aged are likely to continue to be so.

Moreover, the state has no adequate way of compensating persons who work for firms that fail and who find themselves with broken promises and no pensions. A similar fate awaits those who have invested savings for retirement in banks and insurance companies that experience financial crises or even go bankrupt. Such situations raise fears among many elders, who are understandably very doubtful about the wisdom of some politicians' proposals to "privatize" Social Security by requiring people to partially finance their retirement years through individual investments in the stock market.

These kinds of issues have been taken up by advocates for the elderly population, who are increasingly demanding new government policies and defending existing government programs that presently serve elders' needs. Issues such as pension protection, adequate health insurance, taxation of Social Security benefits, and long-term care loom ever larger as the proportion of the nation's population that is elderly continues to expand. Yet, while elected officials reject the concerns of this sector of the voting population at some political risk, they often push their

Elders are not all the same, nor are they by definition in a state of physical and mental deterioration as they age. Many, if not most, continue to participate in activities they enjoyed in their middle years, such as these elders who are preparing to begin a road race.

elderly constituencies into energy- and resource-draining competition with other groups that similarly need assistance and protection.

In short, the phenomenon of aging is often accompanied by victimization. Older people are subjected to myths and stereotypes, ideological justifications for mistreatment, and other forms of ageism by those who are younger. And they are victimized by ageism through the unresponsiveness of institutions to problems that severely tarnish the so-called golden years of old age. The system of age inequality that has evolved robs elders of their humanity and dignity. It hastens the decline of all too many. Ironically, in the absence of a groundswell of social change, this particular system of inequality awaits us all.

Sexual Orientation and Inequality

Sexual orientation is one of the most important aspects of people's biographies. Matters ranging from who people are likely to choose as a mate to what kinds of protections they are afforded under the law will be influenced by whether people are homosexual, heterosexual, or lean toward one orientation or the other.

Social science research on human sexual behavior indicates that both men and women occupy places on a broad spectrum in terms of their sexual interests and practices, and that there is a great deal of diversity across cultures (Nanda, 1999). Not only is there diversity within U.S. society, but many people move around on this spectrum over the course of their lives. Because of these variations, the terms "homosexual" and "heterosexual" are rather arbitrary categories (Fausto-Sterling, 2000). Only at the far ends of the continuum are individuals exclusively lifelong homosexuals or heterosexuals in terms of both their identity and their behavior.

Interestingly, it was not until the late eighteenth and early nineteenth centuries that the concept of "homosexual" emerged in Europe and the United States (Greenberg, 1988). Individuals who engaged in sexual activities with persons of the same sex were not seen as unique in any way apart from this behavior. This is not to say homosexual practices were widely accepted. Such behavior was condemned by Judeo-Christian religions and prohibited by law.

The concept of homosexuality emerged largely as a result of the medical profession's claim to have "scientifically" established that such behavior was abnormal and pathological, engaged in only by persons who were a separate and different human type (Fausto-Sterling, 2000; Greenberg, 1988). Despite such allegations, which continue today, no one has yet been able to definitively establish any biological or psychological traits (apart from sexual orientation) that differentiate homosexuals from anyone else. The findings from studies attempting to explore the biological foundations of homosexuality remain inconclusive. Whatever the ultimate findings of such studies, there is no reason that they should be used as a basis for defining homosexuality in negative terms.

The Ideology of Heterosexism

The sexual practices many associate with homosexuality have been found in many cultures and historical periods. It is not unusual for practices associated with both heterosexuality and homosexuality to be part of a cultural repertoire (Nanda, 1999). The dominant culture within the United States, however, is supportive of a system of **inequality based on sexual orientation.** As we will discuss, many people condemn those perceived as fitting into the category of "homosexual."

Today, prejudicial attitudes and institutionalized discrimination are widespread against individuals labeled as homosexual. Gay men and lesbians are the daily victims of emotions ranging from disgust to fear to hatred on the part of persons who demand that everyone adhere to the dominant norm of heterosexuality. An ideology called **heterosexism,** which holds that homosexuality is unnatural and immoral, strongly prevails in U.S. society.

Heterosexism affects a large number of people in the United States. Pioneering studies by Alfred Kinsey and others concluded that 10 percent of the U.S. population is predominantly homosexual (Kinsey, Pomeroy, and Martin, 1948; Kinsey et al., 1953). Some argue that this figure is too high; others believe it is an underestimate (see Marcus, 1999). Many persons who have had or continue to have sexual experiences with members of their own sex do not see themselves as homosexual. Many call themselves bisexual, indicating that their lifestyles also allow for heterosexual practices. All these people, as well as their parents, family members, and friends, are affected by heterosexism. Clearly, the system of inequality based on sexual orientation plays a role in the biographies of a substantial proportion of people in the United States.

In a national public opinion poll, 73 percent of the adults surveyed said they know, well or casually, someone who is openly gay. An additional 7 percent know someone who they think is gay (*Los Angeles Times,* 2000). Yet many people continue to accept the myths accompanying the ideology of heterosexism. Many do not want to know about issues of particular importance to homosexuals. Neither the media nor educational institutions have done much to encourage interest, let alone understanding.

Mistaken Notions about Homosexuality

There are many mistaken notions about homosexuality. They include the following (see Marcus, 1999):

1. *There aren't many gay people in the United States.* Since so many gay men and lesbians are forced to hide their sexual orientation, there seem to be far fewer than is actually the case.

2. *Homosexuals are easy to identify.* Many people believe that homosexuals can be identified simply by appearance or gestures. But, in fact, one cannot discern a person's sexual orientation merely by observing him or her.

3. *Homosexuality is caused by mental illness, willful perversity, or recruitment by other homosexuals.* This view ignores the fact that homosexuality is a natural inclination found in virtually every society. Homosexuals generally are mentally healthy, do not choose their sexual orientation, and come to realize their orientation without contact with other homosexuals.

4. *Gay men and lesbians lead unproductive, dissolute lives.* In reality, homosexuals are in all occupations, professions, and callings. As accomplished homosexuals in medicine, the clergy, the arts, education, the military, sports, politics, and

business increasingly refuse to hide their sexual orientation, the productivity and contributions of gay men and lesbians are becoming more apparent.

5. *Homosexuals are terribly unhappy people, because of their affliction.* Rates of substance abuse and suicidal behavior are thought to be higher among homosexuals than within the "straight" population, but this difference very likely reflects the negative treatment homosexuals often experience, not something innate.

6. *Homosexuals are likely to give you AIDS.* Not only is this an erroneous stereotype, but it is dangerous. It ignores the high likelihood of contracting AIDS from those who are not gay. There is no reason to avoid homosexuals (assuming one knows who they are to begin with). It is not possible to contract AIDS through casual contact with homosexuals or, for that matter, heterosexuals.

7. *With proper treatment, people can change from homosexual to heterosexual.* Consider how improbable the reverse assertion seems: "With proper treatment, people can be changed from heterosexual to homosexual." Homosexuality is not an illness. There are no "treatments" that can change people's basic sexual orientation in either direction.

National public opinion polls reveal very mixed attitudes toward homosexuals. Fifty-one percent of adults polled say that gays and lesbians should not be allowed to legally marry, although fewer (46 percent) object to their entering into domestic partnerships that give same-sex couples the same rights and benefits as opposite-sex married couples (Associated Press, 2000). Less than half of those polled support providing Social Security, employer health insurance coverage, and inheritance rights to gay partners (Associated Press 2000). At least a third of registered voters believe that gays should not be allowed to serve openly in the military (Fox News/Opinion Dynamics, 2000). Only 11 percent to 13 percent of adults think that racial minorities, religious and ethnic minorities, and women should not be covered by state hate crime laws but 20 percent would reject applying such laws to homosexuals (Gallup Organization, 1999).

Within a climate of national public opinion such as this, it is understandable that gay men and lesbians not only suffer harassment and discrimination but have few rights to protection under the law. Indeed, many people believe that there are already too many laws that give "special rights" to homosexuals. In a national poll commissioned by NBC News and the *Wall Street Journal* in 1999, some 42 percent of adults felt this way (NBC News/*Wall Street Journal,* 1999). Yet gay males and lesbians deny they want any "special rights" at all. What they do want is the legal rights, protections, and recourse to legal action against discrimination that most other citizens are able to take for granted.

Discriminatory Practices against Gay Males and Lesbians

Many employers discriminate against gay males and lesbians in hiring. Landlords refuse them housing. Insurance companies refuse to provide coverage. Until a 2003 Massachusetts Supreme Court decision ruled otherwise, nowhere in the United States did homosexual couples have the legal right to marriage. Child-custody rights or visitation privileges are often at issue for a gay or lesbian parent. And "gay-bashing" has become a common term, denoting violent attacks on both gay males and lesbians by those seeking to uphold the heterosexual norm. In many settings, such attacks are not recognized as hate crimes; sometimes they are not even investigated.

The fear of violence among gay males and lesbians is not overstated (Sloan and Gustavson, 2000). After the horrendous 1998 murder of Matthew Shepherd, a gay student at the University of Wyoming who was beaten viciously, tied to a rural country fence, and left to die, 68 percent of adults polled stated that an attack such as this could happen in their own communities (CNN/*Time,* 1998). According to the National Coalition of Anti-Violence Programs, a network of 26 organizations that monitor and respond to hate incidents in locales across the United States, rates of violence against people based on their sexual orientation (or their *perceived* orientation) are high, taking forms ranging from harassment and intimidation to assault and even murder (National Coalition of Anti-Violence Programs, 2002).

In the early 1990s the Clinton administration changed Defense Department policy to allow homosexuals to serve discreetly in all ranks and in all military services, a policy reflecting the controversy surrounding the dismissal of many highly talented people found to be gay. While members of the armed forces are not required to reveal their sexual orientation, homosexual conduct remains grounds for dismissal. Even in the absence of such conduct, harassment and violence against those known or thought to be gay remains a serious problem in many military settings. Gay service members have continued to be dismissed at a high rate.

Some Signs of Change

In a milestone action, President George H. W. Bush signed the National Hate Crimes Statistics Act of 1990, which requires the Department of Justice to gather nationwide statistics on crimes motivated by prejudice on the basis of race, religion, ethnic background, or sexual orientation. This was the first time a U.S. president ever signed a bill including sexual orientation as a civil rights concern—and the first time gay rights representatives had ever been invited to the White House for a public ceremony in which a bill was signed into law.

The Hate Crimes Statistics Act was indeed a milestone, yet since its passage in 1990 the National Gay and Lesbian Task Force and other gay rights advocacy groups have complained that inadequate reporting and data-gathering procedures have produced serious undercounting of the numbers of hate crimes based on sexual orientation that actually occur. Moreover, even with the new data produced, the U.S. Congress has resisted adding sexual orientation to the existing law that allows the government to prosecute hate crimes as a federal offense.

Gay men and lesbians are becoming more visible as holders of responsible positions in key institutions. For example, in 1980 fewer than five elected state or local officials in the nation were openly gay. Today, scores of elected officials are known to be gay and the numbers continue to slowly increase. Shortly after assuming office, President Bill Clinton selected a woman who had publicly acknowledged her lesbianism for a key post in the Department of Housing and Urban Development and appointed a gay male with AIDS to his White House staff. President George W. Bush appointed a gay male to head up his administration's initiative to combat

In 2002, Canada's Ontario Superior Court issued an order that legalized same-sex marriages. The couple pictured here are celebrating the issuance of their marriage license in Toronto. Such marriages have not been legal in the United States, but in 2003 the Massachusetts Supreme Court ruled that it was contrary to that state's constitution to bar same-sex couples from marrying.

AIDS. Still, openly gay male and lesbian politicians and top government officials remain unusual enough to invite comment.

Some improvements have been made in the extension and protection of civil rights for gay males and lesbians. A number of individual states have passed laws prohibiting discrimination in such areas as employment and housing. Some states have passed so-called hate crime laws that specifically outlaw and spell out penalties for violent crimes motivated by the sexual orientation of the victim. Yet most states have not passed such laws.

In many large urban centers gay male and lesbian couples now may file at city hall for legal recognition of "domestic partnerships." Vermont became the first state to grant homosexuals the right to enter into civil unions that carry most of the legal rights accompanying heterosexual marriages. As mentioned, Massachusetts courts legalized same-sex marriage in that state in 2003. Some of the nation's newspapers have abandoned their wedding and engagement pages in favor of "celebration" pages, to allow public announcement of same-sex partnerships. Many state and local governments, colleges and universities, and well-known corporations provide insurance coverage and health benefits to same-sex domestic partners of their employees.

The civil rights of gay people may be further transformed in the wake of a 2003 landmark U.S. Supreme Court decision, *Lawrence and Garner v. Texas.* Until the court ruled, consensual homosexual activity in private was a criminal offense in four states, including Texas, under laws prohibiting sodomy. (In nine other states, laws criminalized such consensual sexual acts between heterosexuals as well.) In 2003, the Supreme Court decisively ruled that such laws demean the lives of people who are gay. Speaking for the court, one justice noted that "Gays are 'entitled to respect for their private lives . . . The state cannot demean their existence or control their destiny by making their private sexual conduct a crime'" (Greenhouse, 2003b). The unprecedented Supreme Court recognition of the civil rights of homosexuals in this court case is expected to affect cases involving gay males and lesbians in other areas, from employment to family matters.

Nonetheless, gay males and lesbians still face an enormous amount of oppression informed by individual ignorance and bigotry as well as systemic discrimination. The system of inequality based on sexual orientation has really only begun to come under attack. This means gay people in the United States will continue to be involved with their supporters in courageous struggles to secure recognition and protection of their civil rights (Clendinen and Nagourney, 2001).

Able-Bodiedness and Inequality

In 1990 President George H. W. Bush signed into law a bill that was widely hailed as the most important step taken by the federal government since the 1960s to protect people's civil rights: the Americans with Disabilities Act (ADA). This act was intended to end discrimination against people with disabilities and to foster their participation in the mainstream of economic and social life. The specific areas of discrimination addressed in the act include employment in the private sector, public accommodations, public services, transportation, and telecommunications (Public Law 101-335, 1990).

The term "disability" is open to different definitions and interpretations. The ADA uses the term to refer to any physical or mental condition that substantially limits one or more life activities of an individual. Such life activities include walking, hearing, speaking, seeing, learning, or working. Under this definition, it has been estimated that tens of millions of people with disabilities live in the United States (National Center for Health Statistics, 2002). Figure 7.3 provides some basic information about this population.

Impairments arise from a variety of causes: illness, disease, accidents, environmental hazards, criminal victimization, involvement in war, and problems associated with prenatal development or birth. Persons with disabilities differ in the degree to which they are limited. Some have only one life activity impaired; others are multiply impaired. And people differ in the degree to which their disability is readily visible to others.

People with disabilities face many challenges just living with their conditions, but we are interested here in the system of **inequality based on able-bodiedness,** created and sustained by those without disabilities (Russell, M., 1998; Shapiro, 1993). Again, this system involves persons being victimized by others who are more powerful and who justify their behavior by an ideology based on the alleged inferior attributes of the victimized. In this case the system of inequality is characterized by **ableism,** a system that treats people with disabilities as if they are defective, unwhole, or less than full human beings.

The Ideology of Ableism

The ideology of ableism suggests that the disabling condition is all-encompassing. From this point of view, the objects of attention are not "people with disabilities." The language of the ideology subtly shifts over to talking about "disabled people," a label implying that the disability is the only thing that matters in how they should be viewed and treated (Linton, 1998). The disability becomes a *master status* (see Chapter 3), one that carries a **stigma,** or a negative mark, signifying doubt as to a person's social worth (Goffman, 1963). Those with physical and mental impairments are viewed as if they are members of some other species, one lacking the "normal" interests and concerns that occupy others of their social class, race, sex, age, and sexual orientation. In short, they are seen and treated as disabled first and as people second.

Often the ideology paternalistically suggests that this "separate species" is child-like in nature. Helplessness, dependency, inability to take on responsibility, and need

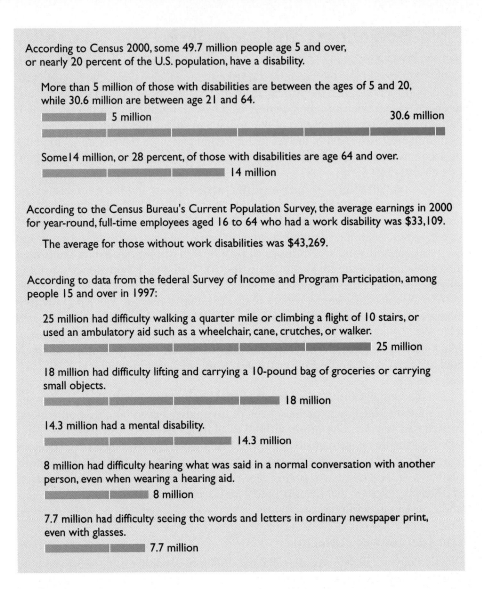

According to Census 2000, some 49.7 million people age 5 and over, or nearly 20 percent of the U.S. population, have a disability.

More than 5 million of those with disabilities are between the ages of 5 and 20, while 30.6 million are between age 21 and 64.

5 million   30.6 million

Some14 million, or 28 percent, of those with disabilities are age 64 and over.
14 million

According to the Census Bureau's Current Population Survey, the average earnings in 2000 for year-round, full-time employees aged 16 to 64 who had a work disability was $33,109.

The average for those without work disabilities was $43,269.

According to data from the federal Survey of Income and Program Participation, among people 15 and over in 1997:

25 million had difficulty walking a quarter mile or climbing a flight of 10 stairs, or used an ambulatory aid such as a wheelchair, cane, crutches, or walker.
25 million

18 million had difficulty lifting and carrying a 10-pound bag of groceries or carrying small objects.
18 million

14.3 million had a mental disability.
14.3 million

8 million had difficulty hearing what was said in a normal conversation with another person, even when wearing a hearing aid.
8 million

7.7 million had difficulty seeing the words and letters in ordinary newspaper print, even with glasses.
7.7 million

FIGURE 7.3 **Facts about People with Disabilities in the United States**
The population of people with disabilities in the United States is not only large, but also diverse in terms of such characteristics as age and the nature of people's disabilities. (Source: U.S. Bureau of the Census, "12th Anniversary of the Americans with Disability Act," *Facts and Figures*, July 12, 2002, p. 1.)

for guidance are assumed to be innate characteristics of people with disabilities. In communicating with such people, the able-bodied often adopt an obviously conjured air of concern and kindness. Their approach is much like the one many people take when they are first introduced to a friend's dog.

On the other side of the coin, many persons are afraid of people with disabilities, so they avoid eye contact and minimize interaction. Some behave as if the disability were catching, but others are simply fearful of what they do not know. Those who are able-bodied may question their own role: If these are "disabled people" (instead of people who happen to have disabilities), how am I supposed to know how to interact with them? What do I do? What do I say? What might the disabled person want from me? Avoidance can be a way of protecting oneself from the unknown and from the fear of embarrassing or stressful social errors that might arise during interactions with members of this "separate species."

In her testimony before the U.S. Senate on behalf of the Americans with Disabilities Act of 1990, Arlene B. Mayerson of the Disability Rights Education Defense Fund described the situation faced by people with disabilities in these terms:

> The discriminatory nature of policies and practices that exclude and segregate disabled people has been obscured by the unchallenged equation of disability with incapacity. . . The innate biological and physical "inferiority" of disabled people is considered self-evident. This "self-evident" proposition has served to justify the exclusion and segregation of disabled people from all aspects of life. The social consequences that attach to being disabled often bear no relationship to the physical or mental limitations imposed by the disability. (U.S. Congress: Senate, 1989:303–304)

Problems Experienced by People with Disabilities

A decade after the passage of the Americans with Disabilities Act, a poll of people with disabilities revealed that they continue to face many serious problems and barriers (National Organization on Disability/Harris Organization, 2000):

- Among people with disabilities aged 18 to 64, only 32 percent were employed full- or part-time, in comparison to 81 percent of those without disabilities. Over two-thirds of those without jobs said they would prefer to be working.
- Those with disabilities are three times as likely as the able-bodied to live in households with total incomes of $15,000 per year or less (29 percent, as opposed to 10 percent).
- Whereas 19 percent of people with disabilities said they lacked adequate health care, only 6 percent of able-bodied persons did.
- While 63 percent of people with disabilities say they are satisfied with life in general, 91 percent of those without disabilities feel this way.
- Only 41 percent of those with disabilities believe their lives will improve in the next several years, and 35 percent expect it to get worse; among the able-bodied, 76 percent expect their lives to improve, and only 8 percent believe their lives will worsen.

Those who are presently able-bodied can, at any time, join the ranks of those who have a disability. Were this to occur, their biographies would radically change as a consequence of this particular system of inequality. Many obstacles to full incorporation of people with disabilities into mainstream society remain. The ADA has drawn criticism from advocates for people with disabilities for doing too little to enable full participation in mainstream societal institutions. The ADA has also been criticized by some politicians and employers for demanding too much in the way of accommodation to people's disabilities. From the point of view of those whose lives are at stake, as with any system of inequality, those inequalities that people have taken the initiative to build, they can equally well take the initiative to pull down (Fleischer and Zames, 2001).

CHAPTER SUMMARY

1. Systems of inequality differ from society to society and change over time. One's life chances will depend not only on the society of which one is a member, but also on one's position in the particular systems of inequality contained within that society.

2. In U.S. society, each individual is situated within a multidimensional matrix composed of six systems of inequality: economic inequality, racial inequality, gender inequality, age inequality, and inequality based on sexual orientation and on state of able-bodiedness. Most people are disadvantaged within one or more of these systems or will be at some point in their lives. People's biographies are shaped and tempered by where they are situated in this matrix.

3. People participate in systems of inequality involuntarily. Individuals cannot exercise control at will over their economic class, ancestry, sex, age, sexual orientation, or state of able-bodiedness.

4. Individuals who are oppressed and victimized within the different systems of inequality often struggle against such treatment, and changes that occur in systems of inequality affect everyone's biographies.

5. Systems of inequality are accompanied by ideologies, or ways of thinking that rationalize and justify them. The ideology justifying a system of inequality is likely to be promoted by those with the power to benefit from it.

6. Wealth and income are unequally distributed in the United States, and poverty is a serious problem. A functionalist perspective views the existence of a system of economic inequality as beneficial to U.S. society. From a conflict perspective, this society's high degree of economic inequality is dysfunctional and harmful.

7. People may act as if "race" and meaningful racial differences actually exist, but race is a social construction rather than a biological reality. The system of racial inequality in U.S. society is expressed through both personal and institutional racism. Institutional racism has a more far-reaching impact on people of color than personal racism.

8. In the United states, a system of gender inequality exists that is justified by the idea that the sexes should play different social roles because "biology is destiny." Male domination, or patriarchy, is supported by male chauvinism and institutional sexism. Whereas patriarchy benefits males in some ways, its elimination would benefit both males and females.

9. Myths and stereotypes about growing old support a system of age inequality in U.S. society that victimizes elders. Proponents of disengagement theory

argue that elders should withdraw from the labor force and other activities for the good of society; however, proponents of activity theory view such withdrawal as harmful and encourage elders' continued contributions.

10. The ideology of heterosexism condemns homosexuality as abnormal and lends support to a system of inequality based on sexual orientation in the United States. Mistaken notions about homosexuality contribute to widespread prejudicial attitudes and discriminatory practices against gay males and lesbians.

11. In U.S. society a system of inequality based on able-bodiedness turns millions of people with disabilities into victims. The ideology of ableism depicts such persons as defective and less than whole. Ableism justifies prejudice and discrimination directed toward those who have physical or mental impairments.

12. The six systems of inequality do not all show signs of weakening. Economic inequality is worsening. Gender inequality has been breaking down much faster than inequality built around sexual orientation. Progress toward eliminating racial inequality may be starting to erode. The prognosis for dismantling the system of age inequality and that involving persons with disabilities is somewhat more promising, at least at this point.

THINKING CRITICALLY

1. Of the six systems of inequality discussed in this chapter, which do you feel has had the most important impact on your own life? How so?

2. While important gains in the dismantling of systems of gender inequality and racial inequality have occurred in the United States, some people would argue that a backlash against further progress for women and people of color is under way. Do you agree? Why or why not?

3. Attitudes toward the rights of people who have disabilities and people who are elderly are more sympathetic and tolerant than attitudes toward the rights of people who are homosexuals. How can you explain the differences in these attitudes?

4. Economic inequality in the United States is worsening, not getting better. Why is economic inequality not a lively public issue, compared with other systems of inequality we described in this chapter?

5. Talented and highly educated women may be pressured to avoid assertiveness and outspokenness in their professional or business lives, lest they be seen as unfeminine. Discuss the effects of such pressures on those who give in to them.

KEY TERMS

ableism, *(217)*

activity theory, *(210)*

affirmative action, *(201)*

age inequality, *(208)*

ageism, *(208)*

capitalism, *(195)*

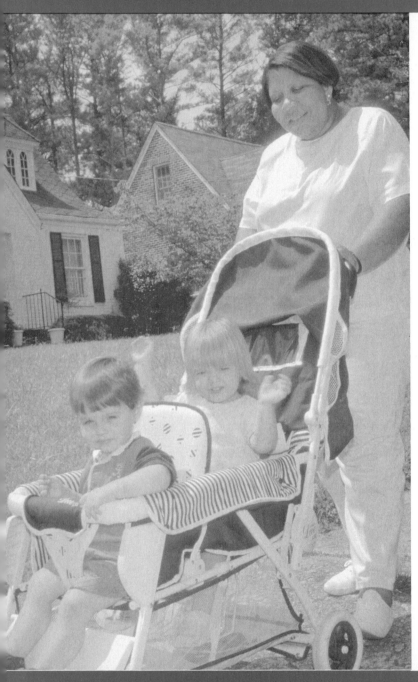

Chapter Eight

Intersections of Race, Class, and Gender

Racism and sexism are among the social forces that shape people's biographies and place limits on the contributions that individuals are capable of making to society. Writing at a time when she was serving as president of Spelman College, a historically black institution, Johnnetta B. Cole commented on her own awareness of racism and sexism:

> My first awareness of race was when I was about three years old, and a little white kid called me "nigger." I lived a good deal of my life more conscious of racism than sexism; for many African-American women of my generation that would be the response. But the women's movement helped raise my consciousness about sexism. Once it was there, the interconnections became clear. ("Race: Can We Talk?" 1991:36)

President Cole's words were directed at two of the six systems of inequality we examined in Chapter 7. In that chapter we discussed the fact that individuals occupy different positions in systems of inequality that are based on class, race, gender, age, sexual orientation, and state of able-bodiedness.

Although we examined each of the six systems of inequality separately in Chapter 7, these systems may be thought of as combining to form a multidimensional matrix or grid (Collins, 2000). Every individual occupies positions in every single one of these different systems of inequality and occupies them all simultaneously. These systems, operating together, shape people's personal biographies. In some systems individuals may be members of the more advantaged or dominating groups; at the same time, in other systems they may be among those who are disadvantaged or dominated. Society cannot be treated as if it were simply divisible into just two groups, such as oppressors and oppressed. That ignores the ways in which individuals may occupy different positions in the systems of inequality that comprise the matrix (Johnson, 2001).

For example, the phrase "white male privilege" is often used to refer to the benefits that European American males receive within systems of gender and racial inequality. But this does not mean that all white males are in a superior position to all other people.

continued

Their class membership is of great importance. In the United States, only a small proportion of white males occupy favorable and dominant positions in the system of economic inequality. The economic resources that are available to the vast majority of white males are highly limited in comparison to those available to upper-class males and also to upper-class females. Many white males can and frequently do experience economic insecurities and exploitation. Indeed, the more unfavorable their position in the system of economic inequality, the more white males objectively have in common with many women and people of color in this regard. Thus males may be dominant within certain dimensions of the matrix but not in others. Figure 8.1 illustrates some of the possible variations in an individual's matrix positions.

The term "intersectionality" is sometimes used to emphasize the fact that different systems of inequality are interconnected (Anderson and Collins, 2004). This interconnection affects how individuals experience these systems. One does not, for example, experience life only as an Asian American, or only as a member of the middle class, or only as a female. At any given moment or situation individuals may find a particular dimension of the matrix to be more salient to their lives than other dimensions, but all persons bear effects of the cumulative lifetime experiences of all the dimensions they occupy in the matrix. Thus an Asian American, middle-class female's everyday or lifetime experiences may vary substantially from those of a person who is the same sex and class but of a different color and ancestry.

Systems of inequality are not static and unchanging. Indeed, these systems often give rise to intergroup tensions and conflicts. At different historical moments, one or another system of inequality may undergo collective protest and resistance by those who experience disadvantage within it. The challenged system may consequently change, thereby altering also the nature of the overall matrix. For example, in the last several decades the civil rights, feminist, and gay rights movements have produced changes in systems of inequality that have in many ways transformed the matrix, changing social relationships, and thus reshaping individuals' biographies across U.S. society.

Viewing systems of inequality as combining to comprise a matrix raises not only the interesting question of how different systems are interconnected, but also the question of why, at times, those who are subordinated within a given system of inequality are divided against one another. As sociologist Allan G. Johnson put it, "Subordinate groups are often pitted against one another in ways that draw attention away from the system of privilege that hurts them both" (Johnson, 2001:55).

For example, some white politicians use rhetoric that pits poor and working-class whites against other low-income people who have a different skin color. Politicians may intentionally do this as they take public stands against affirmative action in employment or subtly stereotype welfare as predominantly serving African Americans. Seeking to attract whites' votes, their rhetoric subtly plays the "race card," dividing people and encouraging those of different skin color to see one another as problems. Consequently, both whites and persons of color may be blinded to the very important difficulties they have in common in terms of class disadvantages. Politicians may use the race card to divert attention away from government's failure to help provide decent-paying jobs, affordable housing, access to health care, and educational opportunities for poor and working-class people, needs that all people have regardless of their racial identity.

In the last decade or so, more and more sociologists have begun exploring the complex and multidimensional matrix of inequality. In this chapter we do so by focusing on several questions:

- What does occupying a privileged position in systems of economic and racial inequality mean for women?
- Does being male confer advantages independent of race or class?
- Has racial inequality declined enough in the United States that we can dismiss race as a significant determinant of one's biography?
- When we use such phrases as "women of color," do we inadvertently ignore diverse experiences and identities among such women?
- What happens when one occupies a subordinate position because of gender and must simultaneously endure the social stigma of disability?

Let us begin with the situation of persons who are clearly members of the dominant group within systems of racial and economic inequality, but not in terms of the system of gender inequality. What does it mean to be white and a member of the upper class, but a woman?

Patriarchy in the Lives of Wealthy White Women

Gender Inequality in the Upper Class

The mass media supply much information about what it means to be a member of the economic upper class. But since class privilege includes the ability to purchase everything from mansions within private gated communities to public relations staff, the accuracy of the picture provided by the media is difficult to know. Television, magazine, and newspaper stories about members of "high society" at times indicate

Economic	Racial	Gender	Sexual Orientation	State of able-bodiedness	Age
Affluent	White	Male	Heterosexual	Able-bodied	Young
versus	versus	versus	versus	versus	versus
Poor	Of color	Female	Gay male, lesbian, bisexual	With a Disability	Elderly

FIGURE 8.1 **Matrix of Systems of Inequality** Each of us exists simultaneously within a number of different systems of inequality, occupying a position of advantage or disadvantage in each of the different systems. Our experiences with these systems of inequality help to shape our individual biographies.

that even those with the greatest class privilege have personal and family problems. Yet the media also show heights of material affluence that presumably provide members of the upper class with much to comfort them in times of trial and tribulation as well as resources to address their problems. Articles in upscale magazines such as *Town and Country* and *Vanity Fair* and occasional television programs that allow a glimpse into the lifestyles and homes of some of the wealthy reveal a material side to life in the upper class that one might associate with royalty.

Yet the popular media are in the business of entertainment, not sociological analysis. A sociological analysis of those who occupy the very highest positions of power in U.S. society reveals that they are not only disproportionately from the upper class (Domhoff, 2002), but that they are also overwhelmingly heterosexual white males (Zweigenhaft and Domhoff, 1998). Moreover, a close examination of gender relations within the upper class reveals striking gender inequality.

Upper-Class Women's Subordinate Gender Roles

Compared with women of other classes, upper-class women may seem to "have it all," but their possessions do not enable them to escape sexism and subordination by gender. Their class membership provides them with enormous security, as does their **white-skin privilege,** a term that refers to the social advantages provided simply by their race (McIntosh, 1992). (Note that white-skin privilege exists for whites regardless of their economic status, as suggested by the "Social Forces/People's Lives" reading.). Nonetheless, the demands that upper-class men place on them to conform to particular gender roles circumscribe upper-class women's life chances.

Nowhere is this clearer than in the data provided by Susan Ostrander (1984), a sociologist who conducted interviews with women of the upper class. Her sample may not be representative of all upper-class women, since it was drawn from one large midwestern city. It consists of women whom she identified through an upper-class acquaintance and who agreed to be interviewed. Nonetheless, her data provide unique insights into the otherwise hidden relations between men and women of privilege.

Ostrander was interested in the roles upper-class women play as wives and mothers, so she interviewed women who were either married and living with their husbands or recently widowed. Most of the women, ranging in age from the mid-thirties to the mid-eighties, were descendants of the oldest families in the city. Their husbands almost all held top positions in major corporations or in family-owned firms in business and law.

The women tended to be highly educated, often at exclusive private liberal arts colleges long patronized by members of their class. By many criteria, women of the upper class are among the most privileged women in the world, and the access to wealth such women have allows them to "have the upper hand in social transactions with other people, especially those outside their own class and racial/ethnic categories"(Kendall, 2002:2). Yet the women Ostrander studied are also caught up in a system of gender inequality which dictates that they subordinate their interests and needs to those of their husbands.

To characterize husband–wife relations among those she interviewed, Ostrander presents the words of four women:

While women of the upper class are in a position of advantage by virtue of being white and wealthy, they still face subordination within the system of gender inequality in which their upper-class male partners play dominant roles.

He expects me to make a nice home to come to, to be a cheery companion, to be ready to go on vacations when he wants to. He expects me to go along with what he wants to do.

My husband has never helped around the house or done anything for the children. If I were starting life over he certainly would.

He wanted to move to the country, and I didn't so we moved to the country.

My husband never asks me what I think. He just tells me how it's going to be. (Ostrander, 1984:37)

In the interviews the women said they were expected to play very traditional female roles, that is, be supportive, nurturant, and compliant to their husbands' needs. While perhaps not typical, the situation described in the following statement, from one of Ostrander's subjects, reveals how far such women might have to go to please:

When he comes home in the evening the house must be perfectly quiet. I've told everyone the phone must not ring after five o'clock. He wants me to be pleasant, pretty and relaxed. I can't dare cry in front of him or show any emotion. I never bring a problem to him, except during forty-five minutes set aside on Sunday mornings for that purpose. I keep a list. (Ostrander, 1984:39)

Upper-class women are expected to run the household (which includes supervising domestic help) and in general take on all home responsibilities that would otherwise distract their husbands from full-time attention to their work. While these women are clearly capable of pursuing their own careers, most do not and many of those who do are likely to wait until their children are grown. Instead, they devote time outside the home to volunteer work, such as serving in leadership and fundraising positions on boards of local charitable and health organizations and in voluntary associations that support music and the arts (Daniels, 1988; Kendall, 2002).

Obviously, upper-class women do not need to work for pay. Not only do their husbands earn substantial amounts, but many of the women have their "own money" from family trusts and inheritances (although most of Ostrander's subjects said that they had given control over their money to their husbands). Even so, an important additional reason why the women do not pursue their own careers is that they need to be available to their husbands at short notice to organize social gatherings, entertain clients, or accompany their husbands on business travel.

The implication is, of course, that any activities these women undertake are, by definition, secondary to the activities of their partners. Indeed, when women of the upper class become too involved and successful in outside volunteer work, their husbands are likely to become jealous and resentful. The husbands see this commitment to something outside the home as a threat to their wives' role.

Ostrander concludes:

> The wives' tasks reflect not only the division of labor, or social differentiation, but also a clear subordination of the women to the men. . . The general mode makes it difficult, if not impossible, for the women to have life agendas independent of the men. (Ostrander, 1984:49)

Ostrander points out one further irony. The women do not have to work for pay, and they often pay other women (cooks, cleaning women, nannies) to perform the bulk of home tasks. Thus the benefits they derive from class privilege over other women subvert inclinations they may have to strongly challenge the gender inequality they themselves simultaneously experience. Being a member of the dominant class plays such an important role in their lives that women of the upper class may well find it difficult to share the heartfelt commitment of many other women to feminism.

Class seems to "trump" gender for women of the upper class, according to sociologist G. William Domhoff. He suggests that the dominant class position occupied by such women leads them to identify their interests as being complementary with those of upper-class men, reflecting "class solidarity between men and women toward the rest of society" (Domhoff, 2002:56). We should also note that insofar as upper-class women's gender subordination aids their husbands' ability to accumulate wealth and exercise power, in effect the system of gender inequality helps to strengthen the system of economic inequality at its very top.

White Women Employers and Domestic Workers of Color

Racial and Class Inequalities in Household Settings

White women of the upper class may tolerate gender dominance in relationships with their husbands. However, their race and class allow them to dominate certain other persons within their households: domestic workers. This capability is also there for middle-class white women who employ domestic help as they attempt to balance housework or child care with careers.

In many cases domestic service in the United States involves a female-to-female relationship between a white, middle- to upper-class employer and a working-class woman of color, either native-born or, as is increasingly the case, an immigrant from Latin America, the Caribbean, or Asia (Chang, 2000; Hondagneu-Sotelo, 2001). Here, racial and class differences are played out through the subordination of one group of women by another, blurring the fact that both experience subordination within the system of gender inequality.

Within most husband–wife households, such activities as cleaning, laundering, caring for children, shopping for necessities, and cooking are still primarily considered "women's work" in the sexual division of labor. But these at-home tasks are not culturally defined as "work" in the same sense as jobs and careers outside the home, and they are not well rewarded even when they are performed as a paid occupation. Women who make a living working as domestics—cleaning other people's homes, doing their laundry, watching their children, running their

Women of color are highly overrepresented among workers engaged in providing private household services such as cleaning and child care. The women who employ these low-paid workers in their homes typically differ noticeably from them by both race and class.

errands, cooking and serving their meals—often do not even receive the legal minimum hourly wage.

Women who are full-time, year-round, private-household service workers have lower median incomes than workers in any other occupational category. In 2001, the median weekly earnings of such workers were only $255 (U.S. Bureau of the Census, 2003). Moreover, the people who employ domestic workers provide them with few, if any, benefits. Employers are unlikely to offer paid sick days, paid vacation days, health or retirement benefits. Some employers do not even pay or withhold required Social Security or income taxes. A study of Latina cleaners and nannies conducted in Los Angeles found that employers were not doing so in many cases because they did not consider work performed in their homes to be "real work," especially if it was part-time (Hondagneu-Sotelo, 1997, 2001).

Women who do domestic work have few job protections, are nonunionized, and may be asked to work under arduous conditions. They are unlikely to get workers' compensation for injuries. Many women who perform such work do not know or fully understand their rights under the law. They may find themselves subjected to treatment ranging from being cheated out of legitimately earned wages to sexual harassment and assault by males in the household. Sociologist Mary Romero (1999) referred to employers' frequent economic exploitation and mistreatment of domestic workers as a little-noticed form of "white-collar crime."

Domestic workers are often hesitant to assert themselves in response to poor treatment by the affluent women who employ them, lest they lose wages that their families desperately need. Women who are immigrants, and particularly those who

Social Forces/People's Lives
White Privilege—Unpacking the Invisible Knapsack

PEGGY MCINTOSH

Regardless of sex or class, members of the white majority possess certain unearned advantages by virtue of their group's position within the system of racial inequality in the United States. In this article, Peggy McIntosh presents many examples of these advantages. She compiled her list as she sought to answer the question "What is it like to have white-skin privilege?" You may wish to add items based on experiences of your own.

THROUGH work to bring materials from Women's Studies into the rest of the curriculum, I have often noticed men's unwillingness to grant that they are over-privileged, even though they may grant that women are disadvantaged. They may say they will work to improve women's status in the society, the university, or the curriculum, but they can't or won't support the idea of lessening men's. Denials which amount to taboos surround the subject of advantages which men gain from women's disadvantages. These denials protect male privilege from being fully acknowledged, lessened or ended.

"White privilege is like an invisible weightless knapsack of special provisions, maps, passports, code-books, visas, clothes, tools and blank checks."

Thinking through unacknowledged male privilege as a phenomenon, I realized that since hierarchies in our society are interlocking, there was most likely a phenomenon of white privilege which was similarly denied and protected. As a white person, I realized I had been taught about racism as something which puts others at a disadvantage, but had been taught not to see one of its corollary aspects, white privilege, which puts me at an advantage.

I think whites are carefully taught not to recognize white privilege, as males are taught not to recognize male privilege. So I have begun in an untutored way to ask what it is like to have white privilege. I have come to see white privilege as an invisible package of unearned assets which I can count on cashing in each day, but about which I was "meant" to remain oblivious. White privilege is like an invisible weightless knapsack of special provisions, maps, passports, code-books, visas, clothes, tools and blank checks.

Describing white privilege makes one newly accountable. As we in Women's Studies work to reveal male privilege and ask men to give up some of their power, so one who writes about having white privilege must ask, "Having described it, what will I do to lessen or end it?"

After I realized the extent to which men work from a base of unacknowledged privilege, I understood that much of their oppressiveness was unconscious. Then I remembered the frequent charges from women of color that white women whom they encounter are oppressive. I began to understand why we are justly seen as oppressive, even when we don't see ourselves that way. I began to count the ways in which I enjoy unearned skin privilege and have been conditioned into oblivion about its existence.

My schooling gave me no training in seeing myself as an oppressor, as an unfairly advantaged person, or as a participant in a damaged culture. I was taught to see myself as an individual whose moral state depended on her individual moral will. My schooling followed the pattern my colleague Elizabeth Minnich has pointed out: whites are taught to think of their lives as morally neutral, normative, and average, and also ideal, so that when we work to benefit others, this is seen as work which will allow "them" to be more like "us."

I decided to try to work on myself at least by identifying some of the daily effects of white privilege in my life. I have chosen those conditions which I think in my case *attach somewhat more to skin-color privilege* than to class, religion, ethnic status, or geographical location, though of course all these other factors are intricately intertwined. As far as I can see, my African American co-workers, friends and acquaintances with whom I come into daily or frequent contact in this particular time, place, and line of work cannot count on most of these conditions.

1. I can if I wish arrange to be in the company of people of my race most of the time.
2. If I should need to move, I can be pretty sure of renting or purchasing housing in an area which I can afford and in which I would want to live.
3. I can be pretty sure that my neighbors in such a location will be neutral or pleasant to me.
4. I can go shopping alone most of the time, pretty well assured that I will not be followed or harassed.
5. I can turn on the television or open to the front page of the paper and see people of my race widely represented.
6. When I am told about our national heritage or about "civilization," I am shown that people of my color made it what it is.
7. I can be sure that my children will be given curricular materials that testify to the existence of their race.
8. If I want to, I can be pretty sure of finding a publisher for this piece on white privilege.
9. I can go into a music shop and count on finding the music of my race represented, into a supermarket and find the staple foods which fit with my cultural traditions, into a hairdresser's shop and find someone who can cut my hair.
10. Whether I use checks, credit cards, or cash, I can count on my skin color not to work against the appearance of financial reliability.
11. I can arrange to protect my children most of the time from people who might not like them.
12. I can swear, or dress in second hand clothes, or not answer letters, without having people attribute these choices to the bad morals, the poverty, or the illiteracy of my race.
13. I can speak in public to a powerful male group without putting my race on trial.
14. I can do well in a challenging situation without being called a credit to my race.
15. I am never asked to speak for all the people of my racial group.
16. I can remain oblivious of the language and customs of persons of color who constitute the world's majority without feeling in my culture any penalty for such oblivion.
17. I can criticize our government and talk about how much I fear its policies and behavior without being seen as a cultural outsider.
18. I can be pretty sure that if I ask to talk to "the person in charge," I will be facing a person of my race.
19. If a traffic cop pulls me over or if the IRS audits my tax return, I can be sure I haven't been singled out because of my race.
20. I can easily buy posters, postcards, picture books, greeting cards, dolls, toys, and children's magazines featuring people of my race.
21. I can go home from most meetings of organizations I belong to feeling somewhat tied in, rather than isolated, out-of-place, outnumbered, unheard, held at a distance, or feared.
22. I can take a job with an affirmative action employer without having co-workers on the job suspect that I got it because of my race.
23. I can choose public accommodation without fearing that people of my race cannot get in or will be mistreated in the places I have chosen.
24. I can be sure that if I need legal or medical help, my race will not work against me.
25. If my day, week, or year is going badly, I need not ask of each negative episode or situation whether it has racial overtones.
26. I can choose blemish cover or bandages in "flesh" color and have them more or less match my skin.

I repeatedly forgot each of the realizations on this list until I wrote it down. For me white privilege has turned out to be an elusive and fugitive subject. The pressure to avoid it is great, for in facing it I must give up the myth of meritocracy. If these things are true, this is not such a free country; one's life is not what one makes it; many doors open for certain people through no virtues of their own.

In unpacking this invisible knapsack of white privilege, I have listed conditions of daily experience which I once took for granted. Nor did I think of any of these perquisites as bad for the holder. I now think that we need a more finely differentiated taxonomy of privilege, for some of these varieties are only what one would want for everyone in a just society, and others give license to be ignorant, oblivious, arrogant and destructive.

(continued)

I see a pattern running through the matrix of white privilege, a pattern of assumptions which were passed on to me as a white person. There was one main piece of cultural turf; it was my own turf, and I was among those who could control the turf. *My skin color was an asset for any move I was educated to want to make.* I could think of myself as belonging in major ways, and of making social systems work for me. I could freely disparage, fear, neglect, or be oblivious to anything outside of the dominant cultural forms. Being of the main culture, I could also criticize it fairly freely.

In proportion as my racial group was being made confident, comfortable, and oblivious, other groups were likely being made inconfident, uncomfortable, and alienated. Whiteness protected me from many kinds of hostility, distress, and violence, which I was being subtly trained to visit in turn upon people of color.

For this reason, the word "privilege" now seems to me misleading. We usually think of privilege as being a favored state, whether earned or conferred by birth or luck. Yet some of the conditions I have described here work to systematically overempower certain groups. Such privilege simply *confers dominance* because of one's race or sex.

I want, then, to distinguish between earned strength and unearned power conferred systematically. Power from unearned privilege can look like strength when it is in fact permission to escape or to dominate. But not all of the privileges on my list are inevitably damaging. Some, like the expectation that neighbors will be decent to you, or that your race will not count against you in court, should be the norm in a just society. Others, like

the privilege to ignore less powerful people, distort the humanity of the holders as well as the ignored groups.

We might at least start by distinguishing between positive advantages which we can work to spread, and negative types of advantages which unless rejected will always reinforce our present hierarchies. For example, the feeling that one belongs within the human circle, as Native Americans say, should not be seen as privilege for a few. Ideally it is an *unearned entitlement.* At present, since only a few have it, it is an *unearned advantage* for them. This paper results from a process of coming to see that some of the power which I originally saw as attendant on being a human being in the U.S. consisted [of] *unearned advantage* and *conferred dominance.*

I have met very few men who are truly distressed about systemic, unearned male advantage and conferred dominance. And so one question for me and others like me is whether we will be like them, or whether we will get truly distressed, even outraged, about unearned race advantage and conferred dominance and if so, what we will do to lessen them. In any case, we need to do more work in identifying how they actually affect our daily lives. Many, perhaps most, of our white students in the U.S. think that racism doesn't affect them because they are not people of color; they do not see "whiteness" as a racial identity. In addition, since race and sex are not the only advantaging systems at work, we need similarly to examine the daily experience of having age advantage, of ethnic advantage, or physical ability, or advantage related to nationality, religion, or sexual orientation.

Difficulties and dangers surrounding the task of finding parallels are many. Since racism, sexism, and het-

are without proper immigration or residency papers, are especially vulnerable to exploitation since employers know they are highly unlikely to complain. Faced with a confusing system of bureaucratic public agencies and courts, often lacking English-language proficiency, and unable to afford legal help, many women fear that contact with government officials will backfire and somehow expose them to immigration or citizenship complications, or that they could even have their children taken away, be jailed, or be deported (Romero, 1992).

Women of color who do domestic work not only must contend with the system of gender inequality that restricts job opportunities for women in general. They are victims as well of the system of racial inequality that operates to "ghettoize" people of color disproportionately into low-wage service occupations. The system of economic inequality places those who are heavily dependent on income from domestic service near the bottom in class terms. Hence women domestic workers of erosexism are not the same, the advantaging associated with them should not be seen as the same. In addition, it is hard to disentangle aspects of unearned advantage which rest more on social class, economic class, race, religion, sex and ethnic identity than on other factors. Still, all of the oppressions are interlocking, as the Combahee River Collective* Statement of 1977 continues to remind us eloquently.

One factor seems clear about all of the interlocking oppressions. They take both active forms which we can see and embedded forms which as a member of the dominant group one is taught not to see. In my class and place, I did not see myself as a racist because I was taught to recognize racism only in individual acts of meanness by members of my group, never in invisible systems conferring unsought racial dominance on my group from birth.

Disapproving of the systems won't be enough to change them. I was taught to think that racism could end if white individuals changed their attitudes. [But] a "white" skin in the United States opens many doors for whites whether or not we approve of the way dominance has been conferred on us. Individual acts can palliate, but cannot end, these problems.

To redesign social systems we need first to acknowledge their colossal unseen dimensions. The silences and denials surrounding privilege are the key political tool here. They keep the thinking about equality or equity incomplete, protecting unearned advantage

*Combahee River Collective: A group of black feminist women in Boston from 1974 to 1980.

and conferred dominance by making these taboo subjects. Most talk by whites about equal opportunity seems to me now to be about equal opportunity to try to get into a position of dominance while denying that *systems* of dominance exist.

It seems to me that obliviousness about white advantage, like obliviousness about male advantage, is kept strongly inculturated in the United States so as to maintain the myth of meritocracy, the myth that democratic choice is equally available to all. Keeping most people unaware that freedom of confident action is there for just a small number of people props up those in power, and serves to keep power in the hands of the same groups that have most of it already.

Though systematic change takes many decades, there are pressing questions for me and I imagine for some others like me if we raise our daily consciousness on the perquisites of being light-skinned. What will we do with such knowledge? As we know from watching men, it is an open question whether we will choose to use unearned advantage to weaken hidden systems of advantage, and whether we will use any of our arbitrary-awarded power to try to reconstruct power systems on a broader base.

Source: Peggy McIntosh, "White Privilege: Unpacking the Invisible Knapsack," in Virginia Cyrus (ed.), *Experiencing Race, Class, and Gender in the United States* (Mountainview, CA: Mayfield Publishing Company, 1993), pp. 209–213. © 1988 Peggy McIntosh. Permission to copy must be obtained from Peggy McIntosh, Wellesley College, MA, 02181. Longer version, from which this is an excerpt, is also available from the author at the above address.

color experience the combined disadvantage of being at the bottom of intersecting systems of racial, economic, and gender inequality.

Women Oppressing Women

Sociologist Judith Rollins conducted some unique research on the relationships between African American domestic workers and white female employers in the Boston area. Rollins used a variety of techniques to gather her data. She interviewed domestics and employers, worked alongside domestic workers in the guise of being their "cousin," drew on her own experiences as a worker in a number of settings, and interviewed personnel at agencies dealing with domestic workers (Rollins, 1985).

While Rollins discovered a variety of relationships between women employers and their domestics, she found that some overall patterns prevailed. Patterns somewhat similar to those she identified have also been documented for employer relationships with domestic workers other than African Americans, such as Latinas from Mexico, Central America, and South America (Hondagneu-Sotelo, 2001; Romero, 1992), as well as Filipinas (Parrenas, 2001). As with our earlier discussion of white women of the upper class, these relationships shed light on the significance of where one is situated within systems of gender, racial, and economic inequality.

In Rollins's view, the close one-to-one interaction, carried out in the physical and social isolation of a private home, can give rise to a type of psychological exploitation. Employers are less concerned with the productivity of household domestics than with their personality traits.

For example, employers expect domestics to express deference—in everything from language ("Yes, Ma'am," "Of course, Ma'am") to behavior toward the employer's property and personal space. This deference must even be paid when the employer expresses attitudes and behaviors not deserving of respect. The domestic worker's deferential behavior toward her female employer reflects their respective positions in the systems of economic and racial inequality. Domestics may be of the same sex as their employers, but race and class differences prevent them from treating each other as equals.

The employer–domestic relationship often also entails dynamics of maternalism. The women employers tend to regard their workers as childlike, in need of motherlike protection, support, and guidance. The maternalistic treatment meted out—giving gifts, offering loans, assisting with reading bills, interceding with travel plans, offering to meet male friends—often must be accepted by domestic workers in the interests of survival. To reject such treatment would be to jeopardize one's job.

One domestic described the situation:

> [My employer] was always offering me bags of stuff. But if it was something I didn't want, I'd thank her, walk out of there, go around that corner and the first trash can I got to, I'd throw it in. But you take it, whatever they give . . . But it was all just more dead weight I had to get rid of. She felt like she was really being nice. (Rollins, 1985:190)

Another woman domestic explained it this way:

> I didn't want most of that junk. But you have to take it. It's part of the job, makes them feel like they're being so kind to you. And you have to appear grateful. That makes them feel good too. (Rollins, 1985:191)

Giving places one in a position of superiority; having nothing to give back except expressions of gratitude relegates one to a position of inferiority. Thus the employers' expressions of maternalism become part of the psychological exploitation domestics must endure.

Rollins believes that the fact that both parties are women intensifies the psychological exploitation. The woman employer, like the domestic worker, holds subordinate status in this society on the basis of sex. Yet employing another woman gives her a position of power that housewives do not usually possess (Rollins, 1985). In this way, the employer can attempt to compensate for the inequalities in power that she experiences in her interactions with her husband.

But the implications of the dynamics between a white, middle-class employer and her domestic servant of color are much broader in Rollins's view:

> The presence of the "inferior" domestic, an inferiority evidenced by the performance she is encouraged to execute and her acceptance of demeaning treatment, offers the employer justification for materially exploiting the domestic, ego enhancement as an individual, and a strengthening of the employer's class and racial identities. Even more important, such a presence supports the idea of unequal human worth: it suggests that there might be categories of people (the lower classes, people of color) who are inherently inferior to others (middle and upper classes, whites). And this idea provides ideological justification for a social system that institutionalizes inequality. (1985:203)

Rollins's research stresses the oppressive aspects of the employer–domestic relationship. Women workers of color often actively struggle, frequently alone, at times in concert with other workers, to resist depersonalization, loss of dignity, and attacks on their self-worth as they go about their work (Dill, 1988; Hondagneu-Sotelo, 2001; Romero, 1992).

In the next section we examine the situation of lower-class African American men, persons who many whites apparently believe are inherently inferior to themselves and of unequal human worth.

African American Men in the Lower Class

When Race and Class Trump Male Privilege

Women of all classes may find themselves caught up in a system of gender inequality, but men too, may be subject to subordination in other systems of inequality. This is clearly the case with regard to African American men (Cose, 2002). Even those black men who have broken through discriminatory barriers, earning success in traditionally "white" occupations and professions, find that race and racism continue to be salient in defining opportunities and day-to-day relations with others (Cose, 1995; Feagin and Sikes, 1994).

All African Americans, regardless of sex or class, must contend with the prevailing system of racial inequality (Bonilla-Silva, 2001). Our focus here is on one particular subset of the African American population: African American men in the lower class who reside in this nation's racially segregated, impoverished, inner-city "ghettos." Their life situations are often so harsh, and their life chances so limited, that such men have been referred to as an "endangered species" (Gibbs, 1988).

The experiences of African American men in the lower class are underscored by the poignant story of Gregory Howard Williams, who grew up as a member of the white middle class for the first 10 years of his life (Williams, 1996). When his parents separated in the 1950s, Williams moved with his father and a brother from their home in Virginia to be near his father's family members in Muncie, Indiana. There Williams discovered that whereas the mother they left behind was white, his father was in actuality a light-skinned African American. His father had been passing for white in Virginia but could not do so in Muncie, where his African American family and ancestry were known. In Muncie, Williams himself was not considered or treated by others as white and was shunned by white adults and children alike. He resided in the racially segregated and extremely poor black community. Growing up as a black male in the lower class, confined to a ghettoized neighborhood, Williams experienced intense white racial prejudice and discrimination that made his impoverished childhood and public school experiences especially harsh and difficult. He ultimately became a college president and is thus an unusual success story. Many other African American men in the lower class experience far less positive outcomes in their personal biographies.

What is happening to African American men in the United States? The following are indicators of what many are experiencing and confronting (Butterfield, 2003; Cose, 2002):

- African American men, including those with college educations, are more than twice as likely as their white counterparts to be jobless.
- Perhaps as many as two-thirds of African American men living in high-poverty neighborhoods of U.S. cities are either underemployed or not in the work force at all.
- African American men have been increasingly less likely to enter marital relationships; only about a third are married.
- African American men are less likely than their white counterparts to attend college; indeed, their college attendance rates have been declining in recent years.
- More African American men are under the control of the criminal justice system than are enrolled in higher education.
- Approximately one in four African American men between ages 20 and 29 is caught up in the criminal justice system—in prison, on parole, or on probation.
- Of all African American men between the ages of 20 and 34, some 12 percent were in jail or prison in 2002, compared to 1.6 percent of white men in that age group.
- The probability that an African American man will be imprisoned at some time during his life is 28 percent, far higher than is the case for white men.
- While rates of illegal drug use are higher for whites, an ever-increasing percentage of arrests of African American men involve drug offenses (e.g., unlawful possession and sale).
- African American men are 6 to 10 times as likely as white men to die from homicide.
- Suicide rates for African American men peak among men in their twenties; for whites the rates do not peak until old age.
- African American men in racially segregated ghetto neighborhoods are less likely to live to age 65 than men in the extremely poor underdeveloped nation of Bangladesh.

Effects of Ghettoization on African American Men

Racially segregated ghettos, while harboring only a small percentage of the nation's total poverty population, constitute almost half of the high-poverty neighborhoods within U.S. cities (Jargowsky, 1998). The dense concentration of low-income people

Children in affluent white suburban neighborhoods often play on elaborate and well-equipped playgrounds. In contrast, children of color who live in impoverished city neighborhoods must make do with whatever objects they can find.

of color in these neighborhood areas renders them highly visible, at the same time as their communities face formidable problems (Wilson, 1996). Severely limited employment opportunities and low-wage jobs for both sexes, but especially for men, make it impossible for many households to avoid poverty. The difficulties associated with living below the poverty line in turn undermine stable male–female partnerships and marriages and create obstacles to getting married in the first place. This then fosters female-headed households, compelling many mothers and their children to rely on a combination of meager public assistance and low-wage jobs, and it negates the role that adult men could be playing as providers and role models in the household (Wilson, 1987).

Poverty also encourages criminal behavior, such as property crime and drug offenses, and in general fosters an overall social climate that can be threatening, stressful, and conducive to impulsive acts of interpersonal violence (Anderson, 1999). The high arrest and conviction rates for black males does not, however, mean their actual rates of criminal behavior are high in comparison to whites of similar class backgrounds. The difference is that unlike white males, African American males are frequently subject to practices of "racial profiling" by police, who often act as if they are an occupying army when patrolling poor black neighborhoods. When members of one particular group are more likely than others to be stopped and searched, and almost automatically considered crime suspects, the probability increases that police will find some reason to make arrests. One outcome is the extraordinary rate of imprisonment of black men, grossly out of proportion to their presence in the U.S. population (Miller, 1996).

The majority of ghetto dwellers abhor the conditions in which they find themselves trapped. Many deeply resent the popular racist stereotype that African American males who live in poor, racially segregated neighborhoods are "dumb, deprived, dangerous, deviant, and disturbed" (Gibbs, 1988: 3). Most ghetto dwellers are deeply concerned and unhappy with the negative features of the climate within which they reside. Coping with problems of living is a constant, unrelenting challenge. But conditions in many communities are such that a significant minority of ghettoized African American males—especially the young—are driven or drawn into behaviors harmful to themselves or others. In part, these behaviors must be understood with reference to the system of gender inequality and ways in which black males experience it.

While undergoing change in recent decades, within this society's system of gender inequality men have long been encouraged to see themselves as the dominant sex. Much of the male claim to dominance rests with their ability to command wages that can contribute in a meaningful way to the support of a family, to earn a "family wage." By placing substantial barriers to doing so in the way of African American men, systems of racial and economic inequality combine to symbolically emasculate them. One important barrier is employer mistreatment or outright rejection. For example, a study of black men in the Los Angeles area found that, in comparison to whites and Latinos, they are not only handicapped in finding employment by residency in high-poverty areas, low levels of education, and connection with the criminal justice system. Far more than others, black men "have been the victims of systematic exploitation or discrimination" by employers (Johnson, Farrell, and Stoloff, 2000:708–709).

Many young African American males in the lower class pursue a sense of empowerment in other ways. For some boys and young men this may mean gang membership, rebellion against the authority of school and law, involvement in the local illegal drug economy, macho posturing, and out-of-wedlock fatherhood (Anderson, 1999). Being a member of the dominant gender, but imprisoned by the treatment one receives due to color and class, may kick off a relentless and at times fruitless search for validation of one's manhood. As the homicide and suicide statistics on young African American males indicate, that search may entail a tragically short life trajectory.

Racism and Middle-Class African Americans

Economic Success in the Face of Racism

A popular stereotype holds that, aside from popular entertainers and athletes, the vast majority of African Americans are inner-city ghetto dwellers or members of the poverty population. Although African Americans are disproportionately represented in lower income brackets in comparison to the proportion of the U.S. population that they comprise, the black middle class is sizable. Almost one-third of all African American families have solid middle-class incomes of $50,000 per year or more. One in seven black families has an annual income of $75,000 or more (U.S. Bureau of the Census, 2003). The more than 2 million adults in these more affluent families tend to be married, middle-aged, employed, and well-educated, and most own their own homes. Most members of the African American middle class are city dwellers (Pattillo-McCoy, 1999), but many live in suburbs or small towns. The black middle class is far better off in income terms than the millions of whites who make up the majority of America's poor. Even so, does being middle class mean that one's racial group membership becomes irrelevant? Do African Americans who occupy professional and executive positions in the labor force face racism?

Academics and public-policy makers have longed debated the alleged **declining significance of race** (Niemonen, 2002; Willie, 1989; Wilson, 1980). Some have argued that most barriers to black advancement have been removed. Whites are less prejudicial in their attitudes, civil rights laws have been passed, and previously closed educational and occupational opportunities have been opened up. One's color, the argument goes, is no longer the key social determinant that it once was in our society. The growth of the black middle class since the 1960s is offered as evidence that the significance of race has declined. More and more African Americans are finding a place in the mainstream of society. Some social scientists even argue that lack of skills and credentials, not racism, is the sole reason for poverty among blacks (Mead, 1992).

In contrast, other social scientists have compiled data which suggest that racism continues to play a significant and determining role in the lives of African Americans, including those who are part of the nation's middle class (Feagin, 2000; Feagin and Sikes, 1994). Critics of the "declining significance of race" thesis hold that not only does racism continue to exist, but that African Americans are denied the unearned "white-skin privilege" that whites possess (Lipsitz, 1998). One of these privileges is the ability to go about one's business secure in the knowledge that one's skin color will not meet with negative reactions or the demeaning surveillance and mistreatment that often accompany racial profiling. Yet, when interviewed, many middle-class African Americans complain of racist treatment by service workers in restaurants and public accommodations, by police officers and strangers on the street, by people with whom they interact at work and school, and by those from whom they seek to rent and buy housing (Feagin, 2000; Feagin and Sikes, 1994).

The negative treatment experienced by African Americans affects their lifestyles and life chances. Racism's cumulative and present-day effects have not only resulted in a smaller proportion of African Americans than whites achieving middle-class status. Due to differences in household wealth and occupational attainment, those African Americans who occupy positions in the middle class are generally in a far more economically fragile and precarious situation than middle-class whites. African Americans are less likely than whites to have achieved the "American dream" of home ownership, and on average possess far less wealth and property (Oliver and Shapiro, 1995).

Racial Segregation of the Black Middle Class

In urban metropolitan areas, housing discrimination (by mortgage lenders, insurers, real estate agencies, property sellers and renters) works to confine many middle-class African Americans to racially segregated neighborhoods. Often these are neighborhoods once occupied and abandoned over time by whites. Frequently, middle-class African Americans find themselves forced to live adjacent to or even in areas that have lost businesses and jobs, spiraled into decline, and developed high rates of poverty, along with all the social problems that often accompany it (Massey and Denton, 1993; Pattillo-McCoy, 1999).

Mary Pattillo-McCoy (1999) spent three years living in and studying "Groveland," a black middle-class neighborhood on Chicago's South Side. She observed many families with nice homes, backyards, and two-car garages. However, while possessing many of the surface privileges of a middle-class lifestyle, these families had to deal with perils that most middle-class whites are able to escape or avoid. The perils stemmed in large part from Groveland's spatial location, segregated away from stable middle-class white neighborhoods but not from low-income and poverty-stricken black neighborhoods with drug and crime problems.

Young Groveland residents in particular were far more likely than youth in typical white middle-class communities in metropolitan Chicago to be exposed to the realities of gang life and drug abuse. Children in Groveland were, at the same time, being bombarded by a consumer culture that romanticized and encouraged emulation of criminal and other outlaw behaviors popularly associated with living in the "'hood." Parenting black children in Groveland thus carried particularly difficult challenges with which most white middle-class parents are unlikely to be burdened (Pattillo-McCoy, 1999).

Sociologist Raymond S. Franklin (1991) argues that many white people in the United States view all African Americans through the same lens that they use to look at black members of the lower class. Whites are strongly disposed to perceive African Americans collectively as less hardworking, less intelligent, more prone to violence, and more likely to prefer living off government welfare benefits than are whites themselves (Gilens, 1999; Rome, 2002). Recent survey data (see Table 8.1) confirm that whites are far more likely to apply these stereotypes to people of color than to themselves.

Franklin believes that such ideas may derive from the fact that African Americans are "overcrowded"—that is, statistically over represented—in the lower class. Racist stereotypes about the character and worth of lower-class blacks, in Franklin's view, cast a "shadow" over African Americans who are middle class. In his words,

> The shadow that is cast and generalized from the economically subordinate portion of the black population determines the attitudes and behavior of all whites toward all blacks, and, specifically, toward the more affluent and educated members of the black population who have class characteristics comparable to their white cohorts. (1991:122)

In other words, middle-class blacks are frequently viewed and treated as if they carried the attributes that whites stereotypically associate with African Americans in the lower class. This may help to explain why, when middle-class blacks begin moving into an all-white middle-class neighborhood, whites begin to move out (Feagin, 2000).

In short, data on the attitudes of the racially dominant white population and the personal experiences of African Americans show that race remains highly significant in the United States. Even as more African Americans have "made it" into the middle

TABLE 8.1 Whites' Trait Ratings of Whites, African Americans, Latinos, and Asian Americans

| | Percentage of White Respondents Applying Trait to: | | | |
Trait	Whites	African Americans	Latinos	Asian Americans
Wealth				
1. Rich	3.4%	0.2%	0.4%	2.1%
2.	10.0	1.4	1.9	11.2
3.	29.8	6.1	5.1	22.8
4.	47.1	25.3	23.4	39.1
5.	7.7	40.1	37.9	16.5
6.	1.7	22.5	26.0	6.8
7. Poor	0.3	4.5	4.9	1.6
Work ethic				
1. Hardworking	6.3%	1.8%	5.5%	10.9%
2.	14.1	4.4	10.5	18.7
3.	25.7	12.5	19.0	26.5
4.	44.4	44.3	41.8	33.2
5.	7.3	22.7	15.9	7.9
6.	2.0	10.5	5.5	2.1
7. Lazy	0.3	3.7	1.8	0.7
Intelligence				
1. Unintelligent	0.1%	1.3%	0.8%	0.4%
2.	1.7	5.4	6.4	2.5
3.	4.2	16.7	16.6	7.0
4.	41.8	49.9	53.1	41.2
5.	27.8	16.7	14.7	21.9
6.	17.5	6.7	5.2	18.8
7. Intelligent	7.0	3.4	3.3	8.2
Violence				
1. Violence-prone	1.2%	5.3%	2.6%	0.9%
2.	4.0	14.1	9.4	3.1
3.	13.2	28.1	25.5	11.6
4.	49.9	37.5	44.8	47.9
5.	17.8	8.6	11.2	20.2
6.	11.3	4.8	4.9	11.0
7. Not violence-prone	2.7	1.6	1.6	5.3

Source: 2000 General Social Survey (authors' calculations), National Opinion Research Center.

class, many whites continue to hold racist stereotypes on the basis of skin color. Despite the advances to which proponents of the "declining significance of race" thesis point, many middle-class African Americans report experiences of discrimination. The biographies of all African Americans are still conditioned today by racial inequality, regardless of their class.

The Importance of Recognizing Women's Diversity

The contemporary feminist movement has long had to confront tensions among its diverse supporters. In recent years, concern with racism has been prominent among these tensions. For more than three decades the feminist movement has been dominated by white, middle-class women and the issues most pressing to them. Tensions have emerged because many women of color have found that the feminist movement has not adequately addressed their felt needs and concerns (Dill, 1983; Guy-Sheftall and Cole, 1995; hooks, 1981). Some scholars and activists have called for a movement that embraces "multiracial feminism," a feminism which focuses on the multiple positions in the matrix of inequality that women occupy, and particularly the central role that inequalities associated with racial ancestry and ethnic heritage play in women's lives (Collins, 2000; Zinn and Dill, 1993).

Even if observers somehow managed to ignore class and other systems of inequality, women of color, by being simultaneously subordinated within the two systems of gender and racial inequality, face challenges qualitatively different from those facing white women or men of color (Spelman, 1988). But it is also important to keep in mind that the phrase "women of color" encompasses in itself a diverse population of women. It includes women from different **ethnic groups,** people who possess distinguishing cultural traits and a sense of community based on their shared heritage (Schaefer, 2004).

Even commonly used ethnic group labels mask a great deal of diversity among women. Latinas, for example, include women who are U.S. citizens of Mexican descent, Puerto Ricans, and immigrants from different Latin nations in the Caribbean as well as Central and South America. Similarly, Asian Americans include women of Chinese, Japanese, Filipino, Asian Indian, Korean, Vietnamese, Cambodian, and Thai ancestry. Native American women come from many different ancestral Indian nations.

The fact that women are not "all the same" should seem like an understatement, given the ease with which our discussion in this chapter has ranged from wealthy white women to women of color who are domestic workers. The tendency of the white-dominated feminist movement to emphasize the common experiences of women has opened it to the charge of **false universalism,** the idea that all women experience life in the same ways (Asch and Fine, 1988). Yet who could experience a relationship more differently than a white woman employer and a female domestic worker of color? Indeed, are there any experiences common to all women that are not somehow tempered by the varying positions that they may hold in the systems of racial and economic inequality? Many scholars believe the answer to be "No" (Amott and Matthaei, 1996).

To illustrate the diversity of experiences and the different challenges that women of color face, we will consider African American women and Chicanas.

Challenges Facing African American Women

The vast majority of African American women who marry or cohabit with male partners do so with African American men. Yet, as we saw earlier, African American males are now being referred to as an "endangered species." A shortage of African American male partners makes it more difficult for many heterosexual African American women to form stable two-parent households (Wilson, 1987). Racism, insofar as it undermines the opportunities and life chances of black men (and women), is of immediate and pressing concern. Many African American women would like to see the feminist movement throw its full weight into the fight against racism and the harm it does to communities of color. In their minds, the feminist movement needs to be much more sensitive to what it means to be both black and female.

At the same time, African American women must deal with how they are treated as women. Their history is unique in comparison to that of other women of color in the United States, for the ancestors of almost all African American women were held in bondage as slaves: legally owned as property, exploited for their labor, and freely sexually assaulted by white males—a dominant group in terms of class, race, and gender (Davis, 1983). Some scholars argue that this historical legacy continues to influence the ways in which many white males perceive and treat African American women (Jewell, 1993). Still today, many feel little reason to respect women of color, subscribing as they do to longstanding racist stereotypes about their morality and sexuality (Collins, 2000; Neubeck and Cazenave, 2001).

African American women must also contend with a system of gender inequality in which they are subordinate to African American males. Disempowered by racial inequality, many African American men seek to compensate through sexist treatment of "their" women. African American women are caught in a quandary: Should they do battle with black men, whose self-esteem and self-worth are already besieged by racism? Or should they be understanding of these men, who are oppressed by racism even as they themselves are oppressed by the men's sexism? These kinds of issues arose in the wake of the controversial 1991 hearings held to evaluate U.S. Supreme Court candidate Clarence Thomas, during which he was charged with sexual harassment by black law professor Anita Hill (Morrison, 1992). Many African American women have come to the conclusion that elimination of the sexism of which they are victims requires combating racism. This is an insight that has not been evident to or widely shared by the white-dominated feminist movement.

Experiences of Chicanas in U.S. Society

The experiences of women of color vary a great deal, both in terms of the women's treatment in their ancestral societies and their treatment in the United States (Amott and Matthaei, 1996). Let us illustrate this point by focusing upon women of Mexican descent, or Chicanas, the largest segment of the U.S. Latina female population. Some of the ways in which Chicanas' experiences and identities as women of color differ from those of African American women will become apparent.

The history of Chicanas can be traced back to the forcible conquest by Spanish invaders of what was later to be named "Mexico" (Almquist, 1989). The Spanish *conquistadores* plundered the territory's indigenous Native American nations, engaged in genocidal massacres of many of their members, and captured or bartered for their women. The Spaniards treated native women as male property and intermarried with them freely. Their offspring, called *mestizos* or *mestizas,* became part of a three-class system of racial inequality in this Spanish colony: Spaniards were at the top, mestizos/mestizas in the middle, and the remaining Native Americans at the very bottom. Important roles that women had often played in the indigenous nations were lost. The goddesses they had worshiped were replaced by a religion oriented around male domination (Almquist, 1989).

For three centuries of Spanish colonial rule the submission of women was promoted by the teachings of Roman Catholicism, the religion of the Spanish invaders. Women were exhorted to emulate the ideals associated with the Virgin Mary—remain pure and celibate before marriage, bear many children and be good mothers when called upon, suffer pain and sorrow with grace and dignity, pursue lives of self-denial, sacrifice, and even martyrdom.

Complementing this principle of *Marianisma* ("Mary-ism"), the cultural norm by which women's behavior was to be judged, was the Spaniards' norm for men called *machismo*. This was a Latino version of the myth of male superiority (Williams, 1990). Men were expected to be strong, sexually virile, and dominant over women while respecting and protecting their honor. Women were expected to be virgins at marriage and sexually faithful afterward, but men's "natural virility" allowed them to routinely have affairs and mistresses. Under Roman Catholicism, women unhappy with this situation could not seek a divorce.

In the mid-nineteenth century the U.S. government precipitated a war with Mexico in order to gain control over rich farmlands and natural resources. Upon winning the war, the government annexed much of what was then Mexico and incorporated this territory's inhabitants and their culture into the United States. The Mexicans who lived there lost control over their properties. The conquering "Anglos" dominated them politically and economically, exploiting their labor when needed and treating them with racist disdain. Most Chicanos/Chicanas today can trace their ancestry to persons living in the annexed area (Acuña, 2000).

Thus Chicanas have long suffered subordination along the lines of race, class, and gender. As persons of Spanish and Native American ancestry, they have been oppressed by their conqueror's acting upon beliefs in Anglo racial, male gender, and European-origin cultural superiority. Chicanas' labor has been and continues to be purchased cheaply (Amott and Matthaei, 1996). Historically, Chicanas have had lower formal labor-force participation than Anglo and African American women, but this has changed dramatically in recent decades. Today, over half of all Chicanas in the United States are in the labor force, principally in the Southwest, where they are over-concentrated in low-paying seasonal jobs and in blue-collar, service, and agricultural settings (Amott and Matthaei, 1996).

Chicanas on average have very limited formal educational credentials. This results from a combination of factors: lack of respect for their cultural heritage and language in Anglo-dominated schools; high dropout rates due to family responsibilities; and, for some, disruptions in school attendance because of family involvement in migrant labor. Their lack of formal education, coupled with racist and sexist employment practices, means that Chicanas are at a serious disadvantage in the job market (Amott and Matthaei, 1996). Moreover, they often find themselves competing for work with other women of color, including Mexican and Central American women who have entered the United States illegally with the desperate hope of finding work.

The cultural traditions of Marianisma and machismo continue to linger among both sexes, but adherence to such traditions varies within the Chicano/Chicana population. This was a key finding in interviews conducted with Chicanas by Patricia Zavella (1987). She found that the inability of men to earn wages that will allow their wives to play their traditional roles have helped alter male–female relations. Increasing numbers of Chicanas have had to go to work to assist in supporting their families. Their entry into the job market has coincided with growth in the service sector of the U.S. economy, which has opened up low-wage job opportunities for these women. Many Chicanas have, in turn, placed pressures on their husbands to take on household tasks, including child care.

Chicanas' participation in work outside the home— work that the family depends on—gives them a sense of empowerment they would not otherwise have in their marital relationships. Zavella found that in some cases this has led to serious conflict between men and women, but in many cases it has contributed to more egalitarian relationships within the home. Her research demonstrates that cultural traditions alone do not determine gender roles; these roles are subject to influences outside the family that may provoke both men and women to negotiate, experiment, and change.

Unlike African Americans, persons of Mexican descent did not become part of the United States through forced migration and enslavement of their ancestors. Chicanos/Chicanas were absorbed through a process

Many Chicana women in the United States toil long hours on farms for low pay in order to help support their families. The backbreaking agricultural work they perform in this country is similar to that performed by millions of impoverished women in Latin American countries.

similar to colonial conquest. While African Americans have long been stripped of their homeland cultures by the dominant white majority, many Chicanos/Chicanas have been able to hold on to language and practices that frequently reflect their dual cultural heritage, Native American and Spanish. Whereas African Americans live an enormous physical and psychological distance from their continent of ancestral origin, persons of Mexican descent live in North America where their ancestors lived; the proximity of Mexico helps strengthen and renew their cultural identity. Thus the challenges faced by Chicanas may seem, and may indeed be, very similar to those faced by African American women, yet the historical and cultural contexts within which Chicanas' and African American women's biographies are forged are not the same. Moreover, as people of color, both groups of women face challenges and operate in contexts that are different from those of white Anglo women.

Special Challenges Facing Women with Disabilities

When Gender and Disability Meet

As we noted in the previous chapter, U.S. society has constructed a system of inequality around people's able-bodiedness. Disabilities include a physical or mental condition that substantially limits one or more life activities, such as walking, hearing, speaking, seeing, learning, and working. People with disabilities have long found themselves the objects of discrimination and marginalization by the able-bodied majority (Russell, M., 1998; Shapiro, 1993).

An estimated 51.1 million people in the United States possess a disability, defined as "a reduced ability to perform tasks one would normally do at a given stage in life." Of these, 60 percent are persons 15 years of age and older who have a severe disability. Almost two-thirds of the latter are between the ages of 15 and 64. (National Center for Health Statistics, 2002; U.S. Bureau of the Census, 2003).

Because people with disabilities are overrepresented in low-income and poverty circumstances, many of them experience subordination in U.S. society's system of economic inequality as well. As we will see, women with disabilities are particularly vulnerable to being poor. In any case, poor or not, such women simultaneously experience subordination within the system of gender inequality. In addition, many simultaneously experience disadvantage within the system of racial inequality. Rates of disability, for example, are higher for Native American and African American women than for white women (Bradsher, 1996).

For many years social science literature concerned with the challenges confronting persons with disabilities assumed either that the sex of such persons was irrelevant or that these persons were males. The idea that women with disabilities might face special problems not faced by able-bodied women or men with disabilities was largely ignored (Quinn, 1994).

Even social movements relevant to people with disabilities were slow to address specific issues of concern to women in this population. Disability-related organizations that have pushed for an end to discriminatory practices and for increased access to the U.S. mainstream (e.g., access to employment and schooling) have tended to be male-dominated. Women's voices have been largely muted within such organizations. The contemporary feminist movement has primarily been concerned with fighting sexism, not ableism. This movement has only recently begun to incorporate concerns unique to women with disabilities.

The relative invisibility of women with disabilities in the United States is clearly beginning to change, and a growing body of data has underscored their plight (Jans and Stoddard, 1999). Yet most people still remain unaware of the special problems these millions of women experience. The impact on the biographies of those forced into subordinate positions on the basis of both their sex and disability is enormous (Frank, 2000).

The Oppression of Women with Disabilities

Women are somewhat more likely than men to have a disability. In addition, women are more likely than men to have the master status of "disabled" thrust upon them by able-bodied members of society. Many women with disabilities cannot escape this master status. Men are more likely to resist its imposition when they can, and to be successful in resisting, because men possess more options and have access to more social roles that it is assumed they can play (Gershick and Miller, 2000).

In a classic article that helped encourage sociological thinking about women with disabilities, Michelle Fine and Adrienne Asch argue that such women often suffer from **rolelessness,** that is, the absence of socially sanctioned roles to fill (1985). This can be clearly seen in the economic arena. Women with disabilities are frequently turned away from aspiring to economically productive roles not only through rejection by employers but also through discouragement stemming from their school experiences and even their own families. Publicly funded rehabilitation and job-training programs provide more services and wage-earning outcomes for men than for women (Fine and Asch, 1985).

In the U.S. system of gender inequality, men are expected to work outside the home, and the occupational reward structure is tilted in favor of "men's jobs." Men with disabilities are thus more likely than women to feel encouraged to aspire to economically productive roles and to seek work. While employment difficulties faced by men with disabilities are common, the situation for their female counterparts is worse. In contrast to the high rates at which able-bodied women, including women with children, have entered the labor force in recent decades, the labor force participation of women with disabilities lags far behind. They are far more likely than men with disabilities to be unemployed or to be working less than full time when they are able to find work. Moreover, even when women with disabilities work full-time, their pay on average is well below that of men, since they are likely to occupy poorer paying "women's jobs."

Thus it should not be surprising that women with disabilities earn less on average than men. Moreover, women are far more likely than men with disabilities to be living in poverty even though the poverty rate for men with disabilities is high. Impoverishment is particularly common for women without partners or others to help support their households. One study found that 73 percent of single mothers with a disability who have children under six years of age live in poverty (LaPlante, 1996). Not surprisingly, a disproportionate percentage of impoverished mothers whose families must rely on welfare have disabilities and are among those from whom recent welfare reform policies have removed the income safety net.

Fine and Asch suggest that the rolelessness handicap extends beyond economic roles to the social arena as well. Our system of gender inequality calls for women to play loving, nurturant, reproductive roles as partners to men, but women with disabilities are widely viewed as unable to do so. They may, for example, depart from the dominant male-generated standards for physical attractiveness. In addition, disability is stereotypically equated with being incapable of handling family and household responsibilities, another unattractive trait to many men. Here is how one never-married woman with disabilities assesses her life:

> If you are not a cripple, you cannot possibly imagine the way the world reduces you to that condition. For a woman, especially, normality, acceptability, and marriageability depend upon looking whole. I have been in leg and arm braces since I was three. Boys never considered me fair game for dating, even though they liked me a lot to pal around with. Teachers never thought it possible that I might accomplish what others could do. Firms that I interviewed with approached me with fear and loathing. I got through because I believed in my inner wholeness, even if my outside leaves a lot to be desired. But the world around me saw a woman without the use of her limbs, without womanliness, without a man, without children. Everything else had a cameo role. (Simon, 1988:220)

Since men can usually determine the terms on which they will interact with women, their rejection of women with disabilities in favor of able-bodied women limits the role options of the former. In comparison to able-bodied women, women with disabilities are less likely to marry and more likely to be divorced. Although far more women than men with disabilities marry, many live without a mate because of divorce, separation, abandonment, or death (Asch and Fine, 1988). Consequently, social isolation is a chronic problem for many such women.

Poor women, particularly those of color, have historically been pressured not to bear children and many have been subjected to involuntary sterilization (Shapiro, 1985). Yet women with disabilities have been treated in this way no matter what their race or class background. It has long been widely assumed that such women cannot mother successfully and thus have no business bearing children in the first place. Many people are surprised that women with disabilities possess sex drives and have "normal" interests and needs that mirror those of the able-bodied population (Lonsdale, 1990). A lack of interest in the challenges faced by women with disabilities leaves the women in a vacuum when seeking appropriate professional advice. In contrast, men with disabilities are unlikely to be discouraged from becoming fathers (it is assumed that they have able-bodied wives to take care of parenting). And what little clinical guidance exists to assist with problems of sexual functioning is principally addressed to men.

Women with disabilities are not immune from sexual abuse, assault, rape, and other forms of serious victimization (Asch and Fine, 1988). Moreover, such women may find it more difficult than women who are able-bodied to extract themselves from exploitative and abusive relationships. The fear of social isolation and their inability to earn a living wage force many women to remain in such relationships, despite the toll on their psychological or physical well-being. While data are inadequate to definitively state that women with disabilities are more likely to experience abuse than other women, evidence does show that those who are abused endure this abuse over longer time periods than women without disabilities (Nosek and Howland, 1998).

Opportunities available to people with disabilities have clearly improved in recent years, and many of those able to do so have become more active participants in mainstream society. The progress made is endangered, however. Conservative politicians, in seeking ways to cut back on the U.S. "welfare state," have attacked a wide range of "entitlements" to protection and assistance, including those that are relied on by women with disabilities. Like others who are subordinated within the U.S. system of economic inequality, people with disabilities are being told to stop looking for government assistance and to instead take individual "personal responsibility" for solution to their plight (Russell, M., 1998). In addition, political conservatives have been attacking the Americans with Disabilities Act of 1990, which was intended to put an end to discriminatory practices. The contemporary feminist movement, which had long ignored the unique problems faced by women with disabilities, may yet prove to be an important ally in the unfinished and embattled disability rights movement.

Unraveling the Matrix of Systems of Inequality

While often referred to as "minorities," together women and people of color make up the numerical majority of U.S. society's members. Much of our discussion in this chapter has focused on this numerical majority. But it is equally important to stress that white males do not all make their way through U.S. society enjoying positions of unchallenged privilege. Being a member of the dominant racial group and the dominant gender does not protect white males from blocked economic opportunities or poverty-level living. Moreover, not only do many white males experience economic insecurity and disadvantage; many are made to suffer because they are gay, elderly, or have disabilities. Their race and sex do not necessarily protect white males from harm imposed by the positions they occupy within other parts of the matrix of systems of inequality.

We have said that all the systems of inequality within the matrix are interconnected. In many ways these systems are also mutually supportive of or dependent on one another. For example, if women of color are successful in combating racism, this can help reduce the sexism to which they are also exposed. The reduction of racism and sexism would help to undermine the system of economic inequality and reduce the overconcentration of women of color who are living in poverty. Overcoming ableism would also improve the economic position of women of color, who are more likely than white women to have disabilities. Understanding more precisely the ways in which aspects of the matrix interconnect, and the implications for individuals' biographies, poses a provocative challenge for sociologists.

The oppressive effects of the matrix of systems of inequality rob society of important contributions from many of its members. U.S. society is thus far less enriched than it otherwise could be in such areas as health care, the sciences, engineering, business, literature, visual arts, and law. This is a situation in which everyone—including white upper-class males—loses.

CHAPTER SUMMARY

1. Each individual simultaneously occupies positions of advantage or disadvantage within systems of inequality organized around differences in class, race, gender, age, sexual orientation, and state of able-bodiedness. The positions each individual occupies in this matrix of systems of inequality are important for many reasons.

2. The positions people occupy in this matrix relative to other individuals and groups affect their life chances and hence their biographies. Changes in the nature of one or more of the systems of inequality that comprise the matrix can have important effects on people's lives.

3. Women are at risk of subordination with the system of gender inequality regardless of their class position. Occupying a dominant position within the system of economic inequality does not allow upper-class women to escape male domination.

4. Women who are privileged by virtue of their class and race may dominate over other women who hold subordinate positions within systems of economic and racial inequality. Women may be oppressed by other women.

5. Being male does not automatically mean one occupies a privileged position in society. The ability of males to dominate can be adversely affected by their positions in systems of racial and economic inequality, as shown through the example of African American men in the lower class.

6. Success in the system of economic inequality can simultaneously be offset by subordination within the system of racial inequality, as is the case for the black middle class. Its members' economic success has not allowed them to avoid experiences of racial segregation.

7. Women do not all have uniform life experiences within the system of gender inequality. Women of color have quite different life experiences than do white women. Experiences also differ between different women of color, such as African American women and Chicanas.

8. Men with disabilities experience advantages over women in dealing with the social stigma of disability. Women with disabilities experience subordination within two systems of inequality: gender inequality and inequality based on state of able-bodiedness.

9. The matrix of systems of inequality has oppressive effects and robs society of the possible contributions of many of its members.

THINKING CRITICALLY

1. As you learned in this chapter, white women of the upper class are subordinate in terms of gender but dominant in terms of race and class. For black men in the lower class, the situation is reversed. What, if anything, do these groups have in common?

2. Some white males feel threatened by advances in education and employment made by women and people of color. Should white males view such gains positively? Give arguments to support your opinion.

3. In discussing some of the problems women with disabilities face, we talked in very general terms about disability itself. What difference do you think the *type* of disability makes in terms of how women are treated? Why?

4. Identify several negative stereotypes about people of color. Include some that are specific to males and others that are specific to females. How are these stereotypes fostered and maintained? What facts contradict them? What functions do such stereotypes play?

5. Discuss the advantages that white-skin privilege provides for whites. How is this privilege affected when one takes into account gender? Class? Able-bodiedness? Sexual orientation?

KEY TERMS

declining significance of
  race, *(241)*

ethnic groups, *(244)*
false universalism, *(244)*

rolelessness, *(249)*
white-skin privilege, *(228)*

Chapter Nine

Deviance, Crime, and Social Control

Through socialization into the commonly shared ideas and practices of a culture, members of society learn the boundaries of acceptable behavior. Sociologists refer to these boundaries as **norms**—standards that define the obligatory and expected behaviors of people in various situations. They are, in effect, rules.

pp. 112–116 As we discussed in Chapter 5, there are different types of norms. These range from *folkways* (the least formal or important norms, involving everyday conventional routines) to *mores* (more formal and important, defining behaviors that absolutely must or must not occur) to *laws* (norms so vital, often to dominant interests, that they are translated into a written legal code and enforced by the state).

Thus norms as folkways may pertain to everyday interactions such as replying "Hi" to a friend's greeting. Norms may, as mores, pertain to behaviors that engender strong and widely held feelings, such as childhood sex play. Or norms may be laws, institutionalized and backed by state power, such as laws prohibiting evasion of taxes. Through the pp. 144–145 processes of socialization, discussed in Chapter 6, people become aware of an enormous number and variety of norms outlining acceptable behavior.

The term **deviance** is used by sociologists to refer to behavior that violates norms held by society's members. Persons whose deviant behavior violates prevailing norms may be seen as being anything from odd or eccentric to annoying, disruptive, or even dangerous to the functioning of society. Since social life is possible only if people generally abide by norms, members of society must develop means of **social control,** that is, means of minimizing deviant behavior (Davis and Stasz, 1990). Some types of behavior, such as destruction of property or violence, must be checked; otherwise, the cooperation among its members that any society needs to function will be jeopardized.

Social control of deviant behavior can be informal, as when a teacher chides a student for misbehavior, or formal, as when an individual is brought to trial in a judicial system. Social control generally calls for the use of **sanctions,** that is, the meting out of punishments or rewards. **Negative sanctions** serve to punish norm violators and to remind others of what could happen to them if they engage in similar behavior. Such sanctions can range from expressions of disapproval by members of one's primary group (family, friends, coworkers) to imprisonment or capital punishment by the state. The nature of the negative sanction depends on such factors as the norm violated, the importance attached

continued

to it, the circumstances under which the violation occurred, the status of the violator within society, and the remorse he or she has shown.

Positive sanctions also serve to encourage conformity, but they do so from a different direction. By rewarding persons who abide by the rules, positive sanctions reinforce their behavior and remind others of the benefits of behaving according to expected norms. The reward one receives for returning a lost wallet to its owner communicates the virtue of honesty over theft. The ceremonies honoring police officers and firefighters who heroically risked or lost their lives in the line of duty remind everyone of the courageous work they do and encourage members of those professions to remain motivated. By seeing what is honored, we can often tell what would bring dishonor. In this case bravery is honored, and by implication expressions of cowardice in the line of duty are condemned.

In this chapter we explore such questions as these:

- Who or what determines that certain people are "deviants"?
- To what degree and in what ways do the ideas of dominant groups play a role in this process?
- Are people sometimes treated as deviant on the basis of attributes other than their behavior?
- Why do people engage in behavior that is considered deviant?
- How "just" is the criminal justice system in its treatment of law violators who differ by race or class?
- Are there circumstances under which deviant behavior may play important functions for society?

The Social Construction of Deviance

How do observers know what deviance is? Does deviance reside in an act itself, or is it defined by society's members? Some have argued that certain acts, such as taking another person's life, are inherently deviant. Other sociologists reject this argument (Becker, 1963). In their view, determining that certain behaviors are deviant is a subjective process and one that tells us something about those making the rules (Orcutt, 1983). According to this view, deviant behavior is *socially constructed.* Let us look at what this means.

For many years sociologists focused their attention almost solely on the deviant and his or her behavior. In the last several decades, however, sociologists have explored ways in which deviance gets defined, or the **social construction** of deviance. Sociologists today readily acknowledge that deviant behavior is always defined with reference to a set of rules, or social norms. One could argue that there is no act in which human beings can engage that is inherently deviant. Social norms must be present. When a person or an act is held to be deviant in the context of a set of norms, the social construction of deviance is taking place. Deviance, then, is relative to time, place, and circumstance. Its determination may be shaped by prevailing power relations in a society (Curra, 2000). What is considered deviant may change over time in a single culture or society or may differ between cultures or societies at a single point in time.

For example, whether taking the life of another human being is defined as deviant depends on the normative context. Killing a bank teller in the course of a robbery would be considered deviant by most people, but not by criminals for whom killing in the course of a robbery is normative. Mass murder is obviously a crime. But seeking out and killing another person—even many persons—may at times receive recognition as a positive accomplishment; an example is the killing of enemy soldiers in war. In contrast, some people are committed to norms, based on religious beliefs or matters of conscience, that hold any killing to be intolerable. As these examples show, judgments made in the context of social norms determine whether deviance exists (Akers, 1985).

If deviant behavior is a social construction, then, in theory, *any* act could be considered deviant by someone. The use of the term "deviant behavior" implies a social process whereby the **label** "deviance" is attached to the acts of an individual or group (Becker, 1963). From this perspective no act is deviant unless people define it as such within the context of norms, be they folkways, mores, or laws.

Does this mean that sociologists believe there is no right or wrong? No—sociologists, like most people, have ethical and moral standards. Saying that deviant behavior is socially constructed is not the same as saying that everything is morally relative and that societal members should be permitted to act however they choose. Sociologists are merely pointing out that a society's members regularly make decisions about what they hold to be right, wrong, moral, or immoral. Indeed, people have to make such decisions to facilitate the functioning of society. For this reason virtually all societies develop some kind of rule-making processes and systems of sanctions, both formal and informal.

If deviant behavior is a social construction, what is considered deviant may vary with time. For example, before 1973, abortion was against the law in many parts of the United States, and this law was widely accepted. People who did not adhere to the law, including both those performing abortions and the women having them, were subject to criminal penalties. Because their behavior violated existing norms as formalized in law, it was considered deviant. Over time, however, views toward abortion changed. More and more people came to the conclusion that women should have the right to make their own decisions about something as personal and private as childbearing. In 1973, the U.S. Supreme Court legalized abortion nationwide through its decision in the case of *Roe v. Wade.* Many people still hold steadfastly to views condemning abortion and disagree with the court's decision, but under the law abortion is no longer defined as deviant.

This example suggests another fact about deviant behavior. There may be little consensus as to whether an act is deviant, and laws may express the normative views of some people but not others. Since the U.S. Supreme Court's decision, groups disagreeing with *Roe v. Wade* have struggled to reverse it. The Court has not acceded to the decision's opponents, but it has allowed individual states to restrict the ease with which abortions may be obtained. Likewise, Congress has come under pressure to deny federal funds for abortions in government health care programs and to prohibit foreign aid from going to family planning programs in underdeveloped nations which offer abortion as an option. This example emphasizes the social construction of deviance: The same act can be considered deviant by some groups and not others.

Only in small, homogeneous societies, where all members tend to share the same norms, is one likely to find considerable consensus as to what behaviors are deviant. Members of larger, more heterogeneous societies, such as the United States, are more likely to disagree about what is deviant. In U.S. society performing or having an abortion is not the only behavior on which people disagree. Consider also using marijuana, driving above the posted speed limit, leaving home (by young people) to join religious cults, engaging in homosexual acts (by consenting adults), and fudging on tax returns. Some people would find one or more of these acts perfectly acceptable, while other people would vigorously condemn them all.

As seen with the example of legalizing abortion, defining deviant behavior may involve struggle and conflict. People may feel very strongly about whether a particular behavior is deviant, depending on the norms by which they believe others should abide. Groups may be at such odds with one another that it is difficult or even impossible to resolve their differences. In the case of abortion, debate in the United States as to when human life begins and differing views over the right of women to control reproduction have forced opposing parties to seek relief in courts and legislatures.

Of course, what is considered deviant behavior differs not only over time and from group to group within a society. The social construction of deviance means that whole societies may also differ in what is considered deviant (Edgerton, 1978). People who go abroad routinely come into contact with the different norms of other cultures. Often it is considered a sign of respect for visitors to adapt to another culture's norms.

At times the need for adaptation even arises in the midst of international conflict. Prior to the war it initiated against President Saddam Hussein's regime in Iraq in 2003, the U.S. government used its military power to wage the Persian Gulf war in response to Iraq's 1990 invasion of Kuwait. To avoid showing disrespect to the gender norms in nearby Saudi Arabia, a U.S. ally against Iraq, female troops stationed at a Saudi air base shortly after the invasion were ordered to remain completely covered at all times despite the severe desert heat. They were also housed in sex-segregated quarters, told to avoid public fraternization with male colleagues, and restricted as to when and where they could drive (Moore, 1990). In the heavily patriarchal (male-dominated) Saudi culture, men commonly suppress public expressions of female sexuality and independence by demanding strict adherence to gender norms pertaining to dress and conduct. (Currently there are signs that limited and slowly progressing liberalization in these cultural practices may be under way.)

In sum, deviance is socially constructed and involves a labeling process. Members of a group, a community, or a whole society may develop norms that make certain behaviors socially unacceptable. These norms take the form of folkways, mores, and laws. Norm violators are labeled deviant and subjected to sanctions intended to minimize such behaviors.

In large, heterogeneous societies, such as the United States, people not only disagree about what behaviors are unacceptable but also possess different amounts of power to define who or what is deviant. In the next section we look at ways in which dominant groups may impose their norms on others.

The Role of Power in Defining Deviance

Although societal members define deviant behavior, doing so is not a simple process of reaching a consensus or measuring the majority public opinion. For each behavior in question, some people's opinions count more than others' opinions. In short, not all individuals and groups possess equal power to determine whether a particular behavior will be considered deviant (Adler and Adler, 1994). In Chapter 7 we saw that some people dominate others within systems of inequality and thus play a strong role in influencing others' life chances. One way to influence people's life chances is to exercise social control over their behaviors. Dominant groups within a society typically have the power to decide what is deviant and what is not.

Writing in his classic work on deviance, *Outsiders,* Howard S. Becker states:

> To the extent that a group tries to impose its rules on other groups in the society, we are presented with a question: Who can, in fact, force others to accept their rules and what are the causes of their success? This is, of course, a question of political and economic power. . . Differences in the ability to make rules and apply them to other people are essentially power differentials. . . Those groups whose social position gives them weapons and power are best able to enforce their rules. Distinctions of age, sex, ethnicity, and class are all related to differences in power, which accounts for differences in the degree to which groups so distinguished can make rules for others. (1963:17-18)

We illustrate Becker's point by using the case of women and deviance.

Norms that Restrict Women

In his provocative book *Labeling Women Deviant* (1984), sociologist Edwin M. Schur suggests that in patriarchal societies many norms function to control women and keep them "in their place." Among those he identifies are *appearance norms* and *motherhood norms.* Control over behavior in such areas, Schur feels, serves "as a capsule statement of what male domination entails" (p. 53). In the last several decades, these norms have been subject to question and change in the United States, and they are held more strongly by some members of U.S. society than others. Still, the continued presence of these norms means that women who depart from them may risk being labeled deviant.

Appearance Norms

In Schur's view, **appearance norms** encourage women to be preoccupied with what are, in effect, male standards of attractiveness. Most women feel an obligation to be concerned about their appearance and are conscious of how they present themselves, not only in the eyes of men but in the eyes of other women (Halprin, 1995). In the United States, commercial advertising has long played a powerful role in stimulating and reinforcing this concern on the part of women (Currie, 1997). Whole industries—such as fashion, cosmetics and beauty aids, diet and weight control, and cosmetic surgery—thrive on it.

Yet the role models for female beauty typically presented in advertising, and in the media in general, cannot be emulated in real life by the vast majority of women.

Women are encouraged to conform to appearance norms, idealized standards of beauty that are created by advertisers and visually reinforced by female celebrities featured in the popular mass media.

No matter how hard they try, most women cannot make themselves resemble those in the annual swimsuit issue of *Sports Illustrated:* young, usually white, long-haired, high cheekboned, blemish-free, and slimly proportioned, with the exception of unusually large breasts (Sutton, 1992). From magazines to Hollywood films to MTV, the mass media present standards of beauty that women compare themselves to and are judged by. In Schur's view, the more a woman falls short of appearance norms, whether by choice or through an inability to conform, the more likely it is she will be labeled as deviant by many males.

Behaviors on the part of women that manifest a preoccupation with personal body shape may reflect the internalization of the appearance norms that Schur describes. Many women try to reshape themselves through cosmetic surgery; they undergo breast implants, facelifts, nose jobs, and liposuction. Diet regimes, health clubs, aerobics classes, and jogging are only in part motivated by health concerns. Some women will risk their health rather than fall short of appearance norms. Some types of artificial breast implants have had serious side effects, and controversy over the adequacy of manufacturers' warnings regarding the safety of breast implants has led to lawsuits (Chapple, 1998). For many women, however, these activities are part of the endless pursuit of the "perfect body" (Glassner, 1988). Obviously, genetics places many limitations on the possibilities for success in this pursuit.

Motherhood Norms

Besides appearance norms, Schur suggests that **motherhood norms** are also directly tied into the system of male dominance (see also Campbell, 1999). Pointing to lesbian couples and heterosexual women (married and single) who choose to be childless, Schur argues that there is no scientific evidence for the existence of a universal, invariant "maternal instinct" in all females that drives them to childbirth and child rearing. In Schur's view, the belief that nature has equipped women with such an instinct is best understood as part of the patriarchal biology-is-destiny ideology (discussed in Chapter 7) that has justified the channeling of women pp. 205–206 into narrow sex-typed roles and responsibilities.

According to Schur, motherhood norms include the notion that "normal" women get married and bear children. Married women who wish to bear children but cannot are objects of sympathy, whereas wives who make it known that they (and their spouses) choose not to bear children may be labeled as deviant by friends, acquaintances, and even family members. *Refusal* to mother is an act that flouts the norm. Women who make this decision may find little social support for it and may be stigmatized as immature, self-centered, and inclined to lead barren, unfulfilled lives.

Men can appeal to motherhood norms to pressure reluctant partners into bearing unwanted children or more children than women really want. Males who have chauvinistic attitudes toward women, or who do not succeed in the traditional role of husband and main breadwinner, may seek to establish or gain recognition of their "manhood" through fatherhood, a situation facilitated by the existence of motherhood norms.

Schur observes that another motherhood norm is the concept of not giving birth out of wedlock. This norm varies in intensity among different groups within society. Given the problems facing African American men that we discussed in Chapter 8, African American women have proportionately fewer choices of male partners of their "race" than do white women, and those who wish to become moth-

pp. 237–240 ▶ ers are more likely to face the prospects of single motherhood. However, the norm may be shifting overall, given the high rates of out-of-wedlock births in recent years, including an especially rapid rise in rates for white females. Such births still often meet with negative evaluations, expressed through pejorative phrases like "unwed mother" and "illegitimate child." Some politicians portray nonmarital births as a breakdown of "family values," which threatens the family as a social institution.

Schur points out that when a birth occurs out of wedlock, it is primarily the woman who is judged to have done something wrong. However, attitudes may be changing on this notion as well. Paternity has come sharply into focus recently because of political clamor over the costs of public assistance for impoverished female-headed families, the need to place more responsibility for child support on fathers from all economic levels, and technological advances that make establishing paternity easier. Still, the fathers of children born out of wedlock are not so routinely condemned as are the mothers. Until recently, many fathers simply disappeared from the picture.

The norm against giving birth out of wedlock pressures women to marry even when they do not wish to. The alternative is to take on the heavy parental responsibilities and economic challenges that often come with being a single mother. Many unmarried pregnant women choose neither marriage nor unwed motherhood; they opt for abortion instead. Obviously, for many in our society abortion itself is a violation of motherhood norms and thus subject to condemnation.

Married women who do not wish to have children and unmarried women who do not want to bear children out of wedlock face hurdles. There is no female contraceptive that is 100 percent effective. Some forms of birth control can pose threats to women's health and safety. Abortion to end an unwanted pregnancy not only remains controversial, but government actions have made access to abortion increasingly difficult for women, particularly those who are poor.

Some women who become mothers unwillingly–whether within or outside marriage—may take out their frustrations on their children; some may engage in child

It is easier for two parents to rear a child than for one parent, but there is no reason the two parents must be of opposite sex. Increasing numbers of lesbian couples are adopting children or rearing children who are born to one or both female partners.

neglect. For such women a new label denoting deviance is waiting: "unfit mother." In Schur's view, motherhood norms not only include the notion that "normal" women marry and have children within marriage but also include expectations that women will strive toward a maternal ideal of self-sacrifice, unconditional love, and nurturance.

Motherhood norms can also make it difficult for women who want to have children outside a conventional marriage. Heterosexual single women who intentionally conceive and give birth may be labeled as deviant. But attitudes toward such behavior are changing, at least with regard to single women with careers. Such change in attitudes may be signaled by the notable lack of controversy over out-of-wedlock births among female celebrities in the entertainment industry, and the tolerant treatment of unwed motherhood on popular television programs. Witness the unwed pregnancies of Rachel on *Friends* and Ellenor on *The Practice*.

Lesbian women who choose to become mothers are viewed as even more deviant than single heterosexual women who do so (Nelson, F., 1999). In a 1993 court ruling in Virginia, a judge awarded custody of a lesbian's baby to its grandmother, reasoning that the lesbian's sexual orientation made her "unfit" to raise the child. Both lesbian and single heterosexual mothers challenge the notion that adequately fulfilling the motherhood role requires dependence on a male partner. The notion that two parents find it easier to rear a child than one parent certainly has merit, particularly since that arrangement may allow for the sharing of the economic burden of running a household and the everyday responsibilities of parenting. However, there is little reason to conclude that the two parents must be of a different sex, or that single women cannot do a fine job as mothers. Many millions have done so. To the degree to which such sentiments are held by other members of society, they pressure women not to choose motherhood outside marriage.

Challenges to the Label "Deviant"

In a patriarchal society, men have the power to make and enforce rules that determine what is "normal" behavior for women. In the United States, in part due to the existence of an active feminist movement for women's rights, that power has been challenged. Appearance and motherhood norms still exist and exert control over women who could become "deviant," but in various ways and in various places these norms have been breaking down (Crane, 1999; Edut, 1998). The feminist movement has inspired many women to depart from gender-based norms that restrict their right to make choices and has encouraged women to capture greater control over their own life chances.

The ability of other dominant groups in U.S. society to attach the label "deviant" to the behavior of those over whom they exercise power has also been under attack. Gay males and lesbians have been fighting against heterosexual-imposed norms that define homosexuality as deviant (D'Emilio Turner, and Vaid, 2000; Smith and Windes, 2000). People of color have been challenging the norm that calls for them to be quietly passive and acquiesce to racist treatment by members of the dominant white majority (Ancheta, 1998; Pinkey, 2000). And people with disabilities have been using political activism to dismantle norms that have excluded them from sharing in activities engaged in by the able-bodied (Charlton, 1998; Shapiro, 1993).

These examples suggest that people may at times resist the label "deviant" that dominant groups attempt to bestow on them. In the next section we look closer at people's resistance to being defined as deviant.

Deviance and Resistance

Thus far in this chapter we have defined deviance as *behavior* that is in violation of social norms. Most sociologists would agree with this traditional definition. We have emphasized that dominant groups may use their power to determine what behaviors will be considered deviant. But power also allows dominant groups to define others as deviant in terms of their very *being*. Thus, being a woman, a person of color, a gay male or lesbian, a person with a disability, an elderly person, or a poor person often means being defined as a deviant by dominant groups, even in the absence of any actual behavior that violates norms.

Deviance as Behavior versus Deviance as Being

Groups with power tend to define themselves as normal and those they dominate as "the other." Arturo Madrid describes what it is like to be defined as the other by dominant groups:

> Being *the other* means feeling different; is awareness of being distinct; is consciousness of being dissimilar. It means being outside the game, outside the circle, outside the set. It means being on the edges, on the margins, on the periphery. Otherness means being excluded, closed out, precluded, even disdained and scorned. It produces a sense of isolation, of apartness, of disconnectedness, of alienation. . . Being *the other* involves a contradictory phenomenon. On the one hand being *the other* means being invisible. . . On the other hand, being *the other* sometimes means sticking out like a sore thumb. What is she/he doing here? (1992:8)

In the "Social Forces/People's Lives" reading, the high school experiences of Dylan N. underscore how painful it can be to be treated as "other."

pp. 118–123 ▶ In Chapter 5 we saw how language can socially construct a definition of who is "normal" through the use of qualifying labels that subtly identify some people as "the other." For example, identifying a political leader as a "gay legislator," a surgeon as a "woman doctor," or an athlete as a "black golfer" subtly suggests that the normal incumbent of these positions is heterosexual, male, or white. In

Social Forces/People's Lives

Attacked for Being Gay

DYLAN N.

A person may be labeled and treated as deviant, not necessarily for violating norms of behavior, but in response to that person's mere being. People who are gay, lesbian, bisexual, or transgender are often defined as "other" and may be the object of horrendous mistreatment. Dylan N. describes the nightmare of trying to be a student in high school where fellow students, as well as teachers and administrators, punished him for the simple fact of being gay.

Dylan N., Nevada

DYLAN N. told his family that he was gay when he was twelve, but that fact came as no surprise to them. "From a young age, I was set aside as different," he explained when we interviewed him in December 1999 in Atlanta, Georgia.

During the first semester of his sophomore year, Dylan appeared on a local public access television program as a participant in a discussion about the experiences of lesbian, gay, bisexual, and transgender students at high school. When word spread among his classmates that he was gay, they subjected him to constant harass-

ment because of his sexual orientation. Some of his peers began to taunt him routinely by calling him a "fag," "butt pirate," "fairy," "homo," "queer," "sissy," "ass licker," "AIDS whore," and other derogatory terms. "It was all part of the normal daily routine," said Dylan.

The verbal harassment escalated almost immediately into physical violence. Other students began spitting on him and throwing food at him.

One day in the parking lot outside his school, six students surrounded him and threw a lasso around his neck, saying, "Let's tie the faggot to the back of the truck."

contrast, when persons holding these positions conform to the assumed statuses of "normal," such qualifiers are neither necessary nor used. Similarly, using the generic term "man" or "mankind" to indicate all of humanity implicitly suggests males are the "normal" human beings and females are the "other."

In addition to language, the very physical structuring of the everyday environment communicates who is a "normal" member and participant of society. When public buildings and classrooms are accessible only by using stairs, bathrooms are accessible only through narrow doors that cannot accommodate wheelchairs, or important signs are posted using only printed words without also using braille, this asserts that able-bodiedness is a requirement of inclusion as a "normal" member of society. The ways in which our society is physically arranged often serve to marginalize people with disabilities as outsiders and deny them the right to fully participate in and benefit from opportunities available to the able-bodied.

Persons who by their being (as the other) or behavior are defined as deviant may be considered "outsiders," a term introduced by Howard S. Becker:

He escaped from his tormentors and ran inside the school. Finding one of the vice-principals, he tried to tell her what had just happened to him. "I was still hysterical," he said. "I was trying to explain, but I was stumbling over my words. She laughed."

The school took no action to discipline Dylan's harassers. Instead, school officials told him not to discuss his sexual orientation with other students.

"Looking back on it, I was so out," he said. "I tried to start GSAs [gay-straight alliances]. Like, I tried to do so much."

After the lasso incident, the harassment and violence intensified. "I was living in the disciplinary office because other harassment was going on. Everyone knew," he said. "It gave permission for a whole new level of physical stuff to occur."

To escape the relentless harassment, Dylan asked for a transfer to another school in the district. When the semester ended, the district placed him in an alternative school for students with poor academic records or behavioral problems.

"The principal [at the alternative school] had a real issue with me," Dylan said. "The principal told me he wouldn't have me acting like a faggot at school. After a semester there, I realized that it was not a place where I could get an education."

Dylan was successful in securing a transfer to a traditional school the following year, when he was fifteen, but school officials again directed him not to discuss his sexual orientation with other students.

The gag rule imposed on him by the school did not protect him from his peers, who learned that he was gay from his former classmates at his first school. "It was the same thing all over again," he said. "They'd push me up against the lockers and call me a fag. They'd chase me around campus in their cars, screaming and yelling 'fag' out the windows." Once, he told us, a teacher walked out of the room while some of his classmates were throwing things at him.

On another occasion, a group of students surrounded him outside the school, punching him, shouting that he was a "bitch," and jeering while security officers stood nearby. When the fight ended, he related, "I was completely bloody. I was bleeding from both lips, my nose, behind my ear."

Dylan tried to return to his second school, the alternative school, but school officials turned down his request to be placed there again. "What they did was they put me in the adult education program. Their justification was, I would be around people who were much more accepting. What they didn't tell me was I would have no chance of getting a high school diploma," he said.

Source: Human Rights Watch, *Hatred in the Hallways: Violence and Discrimination against Gay, Lesbian, Bisexual, and Transgender Students in U.S. Schools* (New York: Human Rights Watch, 2001). Testimonial by Dylan N. for this report available at www.hrw.org.

> But the person who is thus labeled an outsider may have a different view of the matter. He may not accept the rule by which he is being judged and may not regard those who judge him as either competent or legitimately entitled to do so. (1963: 1–2)

Becker thus suggests that outsiders may resist efforts on the part of dominant groups to bestow the label "deviant" or otherwise marginalize them in response to their behavior or on the basis of their being.

Resistance to Being Labeled Deviant for One's Behavior

One of the most familiar settings in which struggles take place over being labeled deviant on the basis of one's behavior is the courtroom. Each year police arrest literally millions of people and charge them with crimes ranging from misdemeanors to felonies. In many cases charges are dropped, but arrests for the most serious offenses result in a court appearance for the accused. There, a battle ensues between the prosecutor, whose job it is to prosecute the case, and the defense attorney, who is intent on achieving a positive outcome for his or her client. The accused does not want to suffer the consequences of being successfully prosecuted and will, through the medium of the defense attorney, resist imposition of the label "criminal." Ordinarily, the higher one's class position, the greater the level of resistance, as individuals in higher positions have more economic resources to bring to bear in financing a defense (Reiman, 2000).

While it is rarely pursued, despite the impression one might gain from sensational cases reported in the media, the "insanity defense" is another example of the struggle over labeling persons deviant whose behavior violates social norms (Robinson, 1996). In this instance, the accused attempts to resist the unwanted label "criminal" by demanding to be given a substitute label: "insane." The goal is to be found not guilty by reason of insanity.

"Insanity" is a legal concept, not a medical one, and individual states differ as to the criteria they use to judge its existence. The defense may argue that the accused was not in his or her right mind when performing the act in question; the prosecution will say that the defendant knew exactly what he or she was doing and knew that it was wrong. Each side is likely to bring in professional psychiatric experts to support its case. While individual cases may receive much publicity, in reality only a tiny percentage of accused criminals attempt an insanity defense. Moreover, of these only a small proportion of the attempts to substitute the label "insane" for the label "criminal" are successful. Judges and juries seem loathe to accept insanity as an excuse for serious crimes, in part because psychiatrists themselves often disagree on diagnoses.

Witness the controversy over the use of the insanity plea in the case of Andrea Yates, a woman in Texas who drowned all five of her small children in 2001. Her attorneys argued that she suffered severe psychosis of postpartum depression and was therefore insane when she killed her children. The prosecutor rejected that argument. Both sides marshaled several psychiatric professionals to argue their point of view on her insanity defense, illustrating the lack of consensus even among the professionals concerning such a diagnosis.

At times, people whose behavior violates social norms are given the label "mentally ill." Once this label is bestowed, through a court process or other routes to diagnosis by mental health professionals, they may find it difficult to ever successfully resist being treated as outsiders (Link et al., 1987). According to sociologist Erving Goffman (1963), such individuals carry a negative social **stigma,** a "damaged identity" by which they are marked by others (Phelan et al., 1997).

For example, persons with a history of mental illness may face rejection by others for such social roles as employee or spouse. Within U.S. society, an element of fear is commonly connected with the idea of associating with the mentally ill, and this frequently results in the avoidance and exclusion of persons so labeled. Even when a person has undergone treatment and no longer has any symptoms of being ill, the label "mentally ill" may remain. Should discrimination interfere with the ability of such a person to enter and perform important roles, the stigmatization may actually contribute to mental illness. This then leads to an "I told you so" attitude on the part of those who would not let the label go (Link et al., 1997).

A similar "looping" process occurs when people are released from prison. Often those released have trouble finding employment because they have been labeled with the stigma "criminal." Employers expect applicants to report criminal convictions, but then they frequently refuse to hire those who do. Seeing little choice if they are to survive, former inmates frequently end up again committing crimes and, if caught, are reinstitutionalized. This pattern is reflected in statistics that show very high rates of **recidivism,** that is, the return to prison of many persons who have already been there. Conviction of persons released from prison for additional criminal behavior simply confirms for employers the wisdom of not hiring those labeled criminal in the first place.

Resistance to Being Labeled Deviant for One's Being

To resist a label like "criminal" or "mentally ill" that is imposed in response to one's behavior is one thing, but to resist being labeled deviant on the basis of one's very *being* is something else again. As we mentioned earlier, certain categories of people are defined and treated by dominant groups as "the other." The dominant group views itself as normal and the other as deviant by definition. Resistance to being labeled deviant often requires that persons who make up "the other" openly question the legitimacy of the dominant group's judgments and assertions about them.

For example, gay men and lesbians who stay "in the closet" do so largely because of the discriminatory treatment they know they otherwise will have to endure, not because they are homosexual. This discriminatory treatment follows a labeling process in which many members of the dominant group—heterosexuals—define homosexuals as unnatural creatures, freaks of nature, and perverts. Gay resistance to being considered the other, as inferiors deserving of oppression, includes questioning the accuracy and legitimacy of the dominant group's stereotypes and assertions. Gay males and lesbians are people who differ from heterosexuals only in their sexual orientation. The stigma of being homosexual is often fought by emphasizing that being different is not the same as being inferior.

Similarly, people with disabilities remain socially and economically marginalized not because of their disability but because of discriminatory and exclusionary attitudes and practices on the part of the able-bodied. People with disabilities are, by definition, considered to be deviant, or the other, by many members of the able-bodied majority. From the perspective of this dominant group, people with disabilities are less-than-whole people. They are missing important physical or mental attributes that would render them decidedly "normal" human beings. Thus the disability rights movement has emphasized the importance of using the term "people with disabilities," as opposed to "disabled people." Such individuals are people first, just like everyone else. What they have in common with the able-bodied is far more significant than the differences associated with a disability. Again, being different is not the same as being inferior.

In the struggle to resist and overcome the label "deviant," some groups defined as the other have been more successful than others. The civil rights movement and the feminist movement have operated for some time and can cite substantial victories.

Have you ever been stopped by the police for the crime of "Driving While Black"? The frustration and humiliation experienced by those suspected of criminal behavior because of their dark skin are common for many people in the United States, including college students. This poster dramatizes what it means to engage in such racial profiling.

Which man looks guilty? If you picked the man on the right, you're wrong. Wrong for judging people based on the color of their skin. Because if you look closely, you'll see they're the same man. Unfortunately, racial stereotyping like this happens every day. On America's highways, police stop drivers based on their skin color rather than for the way they are driving. For example, in Florida 80% of those stopped and searched were black and Hispanic, while they constituted only 5% of all drivers. These humiliating and illegal searches are violations of the Constitution and must be fought. Help us defend your rights. Support the ACLU. www.aclu.org **american civil liberties union**

The disability rights movement is much more recent, but it has made some important strides in combating discrimination, as have groups supporting rights and protections for older persons. The gay rights movement has been somewhat less successful than the others. There is much ignorance about homosexuality and a great many stereotypes about homosexuals. Gay rights activists must also contend with groups who strongly condemn homosexuality on the basis of religious doctrines. But this movement too has had some notable breakthroughs.

In recent years, street demonstrations and court cases have focused on "racial profiling," the practice of targeting people for surveillance, investigation, or arrest on the basis of their race or ethnicity. This is a perfect example of resisting being labeled deviant for reasons other than behavior. It is not unusual for people of color to be stopped on the roads or on the streets and questioned, searched for contraband, or arrested by police even when they have not broken any laws. A person may be treated as a lawbreaker by virtue of fitting a racist stereotype of the "typical" criminal, when the only "crime" committed may be "driving while black" (Harris, 1999; www.aclu.org/profiling).

Racial profiling practices expanded and intensified in the United States in the aftermath of the terrorist acts of September 11, 2001. Muslims and Middle Eastern people in the United States found themselves targeted as suspected terrorists by police as well as by the public. Fears of further terrorist attacks encouraged many members of U.S. society to tolerate the harassment and abuse of Muslims and violations of their civil rights as the price "we" had to pay to be secure. In the year after September 11, the Council on American–Islamic Relations reported almost 1,700 cases of discrimination, intimidation, denial of services, harassment, physical assault, and law enforcement detainment of people who "looked" Middle Eastern or who had Muslim-sounding names (Awad, 2002).

Racial profiling marginalizes people and denies them the basic right of the presumption of innocence until proven guilty. It denies them the right to equal treatment under the law that members of racially dominant groups take for granted. The possible negative consequences of challenging the police or panicked neighbors have proven frightening to people of Middle Eastern ancestry or nationality who are subject to profiling, surely prompting many to remain quiet and docile. Legal actions to combat profiling and mistreatment by U.S. law enforcement and immigration officials have been pursued by national organizations such as the American Civil Liberties Union.

Finally, impoverished people suffer more silently than most who are subject to oppression under the "deviant" label. Despite the large size of the U.S. poverty population—some 34.6 million people in 2002 (U.S. Bureau of the Census, 2003b)—its members are often labeled and treated as "the other" by those who are more affluent. Many view poor people as deviants whose economic circumstances alone are sufficient to call their character into question (Mead, 1992). The large numbers and the diversity of the types of individuals who live under the poverty line, as well as the changing membership composition of the poor as people move into and out of poverty, complicate efforts to organize resistance to this labeling. For many poor people, a sense of fatalism and hopelessness contributes to political stagnation; some accept the dominant view that they are at heart inferior by nature in comparison to their economic superiors. Resistance to being defined as the other and being negatively treated thus is not as visible among poor people as it is among some other marginalized groups.

Crime as Deviance

Whereas deviance is defined as a violation of norms in general, **crime** is a particular form of deviance. It is a violation of a law. As we mentioned earlier in this chapter, laws are the most formal of norms. As such, the term deviance refers to violations of folkways and mores, whereas the term "crime" specifically refers to those behaviors that violate norms encoded in the penal code. Punishments of crimes are therefore commonly harsher and more formalized. But these punishments are not necessarily uniformly applied; patterns of inequality are quite common. We discuss this in greater detail shortly. First, let's explore the importance of class inequality in determining how criminal behavior is defined.

Bias in the Treatment of Different Types of Crime

The Federal Bureau of Investigation (FBI) reports statistics on criminal activity each year in its Uniform Crime Reports (UCR), and how the agency counts such activity is telling. The UCR measures the incidence, arrests, and trends for the violent crimes of murder and voluntary manslaughter, forcible rape, robbery, and aggravated assault. (Figure 9.1 provides an indication of the magnitude of violent crime offenses in the United States.) The UCR also reports on property crimes: burglary, larceny-thefts, motor vehicle theft, and arson. The crimes reported on in the UCR are committed by individuals, and those arrested and convicted of these crimes are disproportionately the poor and the relatively powerless in society (Reiman, 2000).

What is not reported or even counted in the UCR are law violations that are more commonly engaged in by professionals and by corporations, even though these crimes may in fact cause more deaths and injuries and result in greater monetary losses than those individual crimes that are counted. Crimes not reported in the FBI's Uniform Crime Report include such activities as insider trading and securities fraud; deaths and diseases caused by employers' noncompliance with occupational health and safety regulations; medical malpractice resulting in death (including inadequate emergency medical care, lethal prescriptions, or surgical errors related to practicing under the influence of drugs or alcohol); excessive force by police resulting in death; toxic waste dumping; corporate malfeasance; and embezzlement. The failure of the state to report on these crimes creates the impression that crime is something done only by individuals and primarily persons who are poor or otherwise marginal to mainstream society. Nothing could be further from the truth. This becomes especially clear when one examines the case of white-collar and corporate crime.

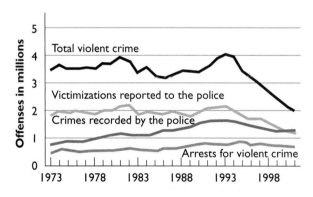

FIGURE 9.1 **Four Measures of Serious Violent Crime: 1973–2001** Violent offenses, while numbering in the millions annually, have been declining. Still, many people do not report their victimization to police and, of those violent offenses that are reported and recorded by the police, many fail to result in an arrest. (Source: U.S. Department of Justice, Bureau of Justice Statistics. Available at www.ojp.usdoj.gov/bjs/.)

The Case of White-Collar and Corporate Crime

While members of dominant groups in society are in a power position to define others as deviant, they themselves may violate norms without necessarily having their own behavior defined as deviant, or they may be sanctioned differently when their acts come to light. As we mentioned, white-collar and corporate crimes committed by the more affluent members of society are not reflected in the Uniform Crime Reports.

White-collar crimes are nonviolent violations of the law by individuals seeking some benefit in the course of their occupations or professions. Such crimes are often committed by people who occupy high-level positions and who thus have access to criminal opportunities that are not available to most workers. For example, in the normal course of doing their jobs, corporate executives are often in a position to enrich themselves at the expense of the firm, consumers, stockholders, or lower level workers in their companies. Among corporate executives, white-collar crimes sometimes take the form of embezzlement, fraud, and insider trading (illegally timing sales or purchase of company stock based on privileged information). Executive treasurers, head bookkeepers, and key accountants who keep track of and control a firm's finances may be in a position to transfer funds from their company into their own accounts, and to hide these transactions for a long time. This is no less a crime than if these individuals broke into someone's home and stole money. Although it often causes great monetary losses, it is not reflected in the Uniform Crime Reports.

One infamous example of very costly white-collar crimes involved an executive in the financial services industry, Michael Milken. In the Milken case of the late 1980s, several brokers engaged in insider trading that provided them with literally millions of dollars in profit while stockholders and many smaller firms suffered billions of dollars of loss. The job of these brokers was to help one company buy another firm's stock to merge the firms. Mergers between major corporations commonly tend to send their stock values soaring, so that anyone holding stock in the firms before they merge stands to make a terrific profit. The law therefore forbids brokers from investing in the firms which they may be helping to merge, because their job provides them with information that could significantly affect the price of the stock and therefore places them in an unfair advantage relative to everyone else. Yet that is exactly what Michael Milken and his cohorts did at Drexel Burnham Lambert, a major securities trading firm. Milken and his cohorts benefited, amassing hundreds of millions of dollars by the time the scheme was uncovered. Milken was prosecuted and fined $200 million, but he was required to serve less than 2 years of a 10-year sentence.

As part of a series of similar revelations a decade later, in 2003 ten of the financial services industry's largest firms were forced by the federal government's Securities and Exchange Commission to agree to pay $1.4 billion in fines and restitution for employee wrongdoing. The SEC found that members of the firms' staffs were providing investors with advice that in some cases was both misleading and fraudulent. The firms involved included such industry giants as Merrill Lynch, Credit Suisse First Boston, and Salomon Smith Barney. According to the SEC, financial analysts in these companies were recommending that investors buy certain stocks, knowing full well that these stocks were unlikely to provide good financial returns. While those who followed the analysts' recommendations to channel their money into these stocks suffered losses, the analysts (and their companies) profited handsomely from handling the investors' accounts. Under the terms of the $1.4 billion settlement, the firms neither admitted nor denied misleading investors (Gordon, 2003).

In recent years, there have been repeated revelations of unethical and illegal actions taking place in corporate suites. The fallout from white-collar and corporate crimes involving top executives has resulted in job losses and significant financial setbacks for many innocent people, such as these former employees of Enron.

White-collar crimes are different from corporate crimes. **Corporate crimes** are violations of the law committed by officers in corporations in the course of setting policy or standard operating procedures that benefit the firm. In effect, the firm itself is the criminal. Examples of corporate crimes include activities such as fraud, toxic waste dumping, stock manipulation, failure to fix known design flaws in products that result in consumer injuries or deaths, and violations of worker health and safety requirements that cause workers to die or get severely injured or diseased on the job. Some of these crimes may be understood in the context of the market environment in which these firms do business (Zey, 1998).

Corporations operate in a market environment that includes competition between firms, the competitive advantages of large corporations over smaller firms, government policies that may actually encourage or enable corporate violations of the law, and the ability of investors to move their investments into and out of corporations quickly if they do not produce immediate and substantial profits every business quarter. Corporate executives are under pressures to produce significant profits to appease stockholders, to successfully compete with other firms in their market environment, and to do so while attempting to comply with the legal constraints under which they are supposed to operate. The environment of the market thus encourages corporate officers to break laws and cut corners to generate quick profits. State policies that reduce government regulation of industries may also pave the way for corporate crimes, insofar as deregulation removes the oversight needed to monitor corporate compliance with existing laws.

An example of corporate crime is provided by the fraudulent standard operating procedures that Bankers Trust Company used throughout the 1990s. The firm convinced customers to become involved in financial deals that generated huge profits for the firm but cost enormous losses for its clients by misrepresenting investment opportunities to them. It enticed customers who lost money to invest in even more complicated transactions, supposedly to help them recover their losses, resulting in even bigger losses for the client and more bank profits. A mass of documents evidenced a "culture of greed and duplicity" at the bank. Said one observer, "Fraud was so pervasive and institutional that Bankers Trust employees used the acronym 'ROF'–short for rip-off factor, to describe one method of fleecing clients" (Holland and Himmelstein, 1995:108).

Sometimes illegal activities represent a hybrid of white collar and corporate crimes, to the extent that they benefit both the individuals involved and the firm. The collapse of Enron in 2002, the biggest bankruptcy in U.S. history, will probably take several years to unravel. But in the immediate aftermath of the announcement of Enron's failure, it became increasingly clear that top-level executives benefited from highly creative and generally unacceptable accounting practices. These practices hid the true, deeply troubled financial picture of this major energy-trading Fortune 500 firm. While continuing to encourage investors (including their own employees) to buy shares of stock in Enron as a solid, very profitable investment, the top executives of the firm were quietly and energetically selling their own shares. Indeed, Enron's rank-and-file workers were explicitly forbidden to sell their shares, which many bought as part of their participation in the company's retirement program.

In contrast to top-level executives who personally made many millions of dollars in this scheme, other Enron workers lost their jobs and in some cases most of their life savings. Meanwhile, Enron's accounting firm, Arthur Andersen, began shredding its Enron-related documents, even after the bankruptcy became evident and after investigations into events began (Sloan, 2002). It will likely take years to sort out how much of what went wrong at Enron was explicitly criminal and how much was a systemic failure of all the usual safeguards against these abuses. But it already appears that at least some of what occurred can illustrate a combination of white-collar and corporate crime.

Explanations for Deviant Behavior

Why do people engage in behavior that violates norms, including those that take the form of laws? How can observers explain deviant behavior? Sociologists and other social scientists have proposed many different types of explanations for such behavior: physiological, psychological, social-psychological, and sociological (Liska and Messner, 1998; Rubington and Weinberg, 1999). Much attention has been focused on why people engage in illegal acts, so our discussion emphasizes criminal behavior more than other forms of deviance.

Physiological explanations argue that deviant behavior is rooted in some type of physical peculiarity or malfunction. Or perhaps the tendency to engage in the behavior in question is inherited and resides in the genes. **Psychological explanations** hold that deviant behavior is an expression of psychological problems or unusual personality traits. Such problems or traits often are said to stem from one's experiences with family members and other persons in a position to influence psychological development.

Social-psychological explanations look at the influence of people's immediate social environment on their thinking and behavior. This environment encompasses not only the family, but also the people with whom one associates in the neighborhood, at school, or in the workplace. While psychological explanations might view deviant behavior as evidence of a personality deficiency, social-psychological explanations often emphasize the role played by peer group influences. Finally, **sociological explanations** examine the ways in which a society is structured and the demands it makes on its members. Such explanations stress that the factors contributing to deviant behavior may lie well outside the control of the individuals and groups engaging in it.

For example, certain forms of mental illness, such as schizophrenia, are thought to be linked to physiological traits. Substance abuse may in many cases be a form of psychological escapism, a way of relieving stress or combating depression. Peers not only may teach novices the skills needed to successfully commit crimes but may provide informal pressures that compel them to engage in repeated criminal acts. A society that fails to deal successfully with economic recessions and the loss of jobs will foster frustration and anger on the part of the unemployed that can be reflected in high rates of partner, spouse, and child abuse. Notice how the discussion here shifted from one type of explanation to another in commenting on the possible causes of different types of deviant behavior.

Obviously, the nature of the explanation that one finds most useful for a particular form of deviant behavior will considerably affect one's approach to solutions. If, for example, higher rates of spouse abuse are "caused" by breakdowns in the economic system such as rising unemployment, then the way to address this deviant behavior is not simply to pass stricter laws and parcel out harsher punishments but also to improve the workings of the economic system.

There is, however, a popular tendency toward **reductionism** when most people think about explanations for deviant behavior. That is, people are quick to reduce explanations for deviance to the psychological or even the physiological level. Thus if some individuals are assaulting their spouses, "something must be wrong with them." Since most people do not abuse their family members, the deviant behavior must stem from defects or deficiencies in the abusers. Sociologists tend to be very leery of reductionist explanations when they are offered dogmatically and without reasonable consideration of other explanatory factors, such as the impact of social group memberships or the effects of societal-level factors. In the next sections we consider different types of explanations for deviant behavior in more detail, providing additional illustrations.

Physiological Explanations

Being deviant in terms of one's behavior implies being different from others in some way. Why, then, could deviants not be different from everyone else in terms of their physiological characteristics? The search for biological traits that would distinguish persons engaging in deviant behavior from everyone else has gone on for a long time and encompassed a variety of behaviors. Some scholars have explored the possibility that the propensity for criminal behavior is inherited. They have even tried to correlate it with physical features, such as racial ancestry, head shape, and body build, or chromosomal differences (Fishbein, 1990). Physiological causes have been explored for other forms of deviance as well, including mental illness, alcoholism, and suicide.

A relationship does exist between physiological characteristics and deviant behavior in some areas. For example, brain damage accompanying aging or alcohol abuse can cause people to act in unusual ways, as in the case of Alzheimer's disease and alcoholic psychosis. Newborns may suffer physiological damage due to their mothers' alcohol and drug use, which can in turn affect their behavior as children or adults. There are indications that for some people heredity may play a role in acquiring an addiction to alcohol (Begleiter and Kissin, 1995). Some perpetrators of violent crimes have suffered from brain damage or tumors to which their behavior may somehow be linked. But for most types of behavior that are considered deviant, physiological explanations thus far have proved inadequate.

While we no doubt will learn more in the future about the relationship between physiological characteristics and behavior, sociologists and other social scientists tend to find reductionist explanations too simplistic and are likely to point to what they leave unexamined. People not only have bodies; they have minds. Explanations for deviant behavior must take into account people's thought processes. People also have friends, relatives, and associates whose behavior bears on their own. Human beings are social animals whose biographies are very much forged by the statuses they occupy within society and by the changing nature of society itself. Even if the involvement of physiology in some expressions of deviant behavior can be scientifically proven, is it not likely that nonphysiological factors have much to do with the behavior as well?

Psychological Explanations

One of the most influential psychological explanations for a wide range of deviant behavior is based on the work of Sigmund Freud (Clinard and Meier, 1992). Freud argued that mental illness stemmed primarily from unconscious conflicts. Depending on their nature, such conflicts could lead individuals to violate social norms.

Following Freud's lead, many psychologists have searched for personality traits that distinguish the deviant from the nondeviant (Clinard and Meier, 1992). For example, whereas some researchers argue that alcoholism is a disease, possibly inherited, and thus best understood in terms of a physiological explanation, others argue that there is such a thing as an "alcoholic personality" with distinct traits. Researchers have even reached a rough consensus on the traits of this personality. Unfortunately, the traits in question can also be found within the nonalcoholic population.

Psychological explanations for deviant behavior often founder because no psychological traits seem to clearly distinguish deviants from nondeviants. For example, mental illness seems to be no more prevalent within the population of known criminals than it is among persons not known to have committed criminal acts.

More broadly speaking, psychological explanations for deviant behavior are limited to inferences or educated guesses about what goes on in the minds of those defined as deviant. Such explanations are at times criticized as reductionist, since often too little attention is paid to the nature and relative importance of social influences on the individual who engages in deviant behavior. While it is very important that researchers continue to study the role psychological factors play in various forms of deviance, sociologists argue that researchers should not do so at the cost of ignoring the possible role of the social environment.

Social-Psychological Explanations

Individuals are constantly aware of the people around them and the fact that these others are conscious of what the individuals are doing in their presence. Social-psychological explanations for deviant behavior are based on people's sensitivity to their immediate social environment. Such explanations suggest that others help shape the behavior that comes to be defined as deviant (Hagan, 1994). Let us look at some examples of social-psychological explanations. Many of these explanations are influenced by symbolic interactionism, an intellectual tradition in sociology discussed in Chapter 1.

pp. 18–19

Differential Association Theory

Sociologists interested in crime and juvenile delinquency often stress the importance of the associates of persons engaging in deviant behavior. One social-psychological explanation for deviant behavior, known as **differential association theory,** posits that individuals learn to engage in deviant behavior by communicating and interacting with those already disposed to do so (Sutherland and Cressey, 1974). Novices are taught the skills and techniques involved in committing crimes and are shown why such behavior is worthwhile, and they are encouraged to adopt others' rationalization for flouting the law.

Take the example of marijuana use. In his now-classic research on how people become users of this drug, Howard S. Becker notes that deviant behavior does not necessarily require a preexisting psychological motivation to engage in the act (1963). Rather, he argues, the reverse can be true: An individual may be urged into certain behavior and only then become motivated to do it again. People are usually encouraged to try marijuana by experienced users with whom they are associating. They may agree to do so simply out of curiosity. Someone who has never used the substance must first be taught the way to use it, the circumstances under which it is best used, and the kinds of sensations to watch for. The novice must also be taught to interpret these sensations as pleasurable.

An individual may have to try marijuana several times with experienced users before learning to enjoy its effects. After the initiation period, these associates may continue to be important in providing access to the substance and sharing in behavior that is ordinarily conducted in secrecy because of its illegality. A person who does not associate with marijuana users, or who associates with people who condemn its use, is unlikely to engage in this particular deviant behavior. Becker's analysis thus underscores the important role group membership can play in encouraging deviant behavior. Explanations that focus only on the psychological characteristics of marijuana users would miss the importance of this factor.

Control Theory

A second social-psychological explanation, **control theory,** suggests that deviance is due to the absence of social control or other external constraints on individual behavior (Costello and Vowell, 1999; Hawdon, 1999; Hirschi, 1969). It assumes that human nature contains flaws that lead people to act in ways that are "bad," and control over these innate tendencies is necessary if society is to function. Those social scientists who favor control theory tend to differ on where the most important sources of control originate.

Containment Theory

In **containment theory,** the sources of control are said to be both external *and* internal to the individual (Reckless, 1961). Containment theory proceeds from this question: Why doesn't much more deviant behavior take place in society? The answer, according to containment theory, is that people encounter both external and internal controls that contain the temptation toward deviance. External controls include community standards for behavior and the institutions that function to uphold them. Internal controls exist within the individual. They result from socialization experiences people undergo through the family, education, and religion, and they supply the individual with self-control capabilities. People who engage in deviant acts are said to do so through a lack of sufficient means of self-control or the absence of clear community standards and social pressures to conform.

Social Reinforcement

A different type of social-psychological explanation suggests that deviant behavior is the result of **social reinforcement.** In this view, humans, as a species, are psychologically motivated to seek out pleasure and avoid pain, but their behavior is directed by past experiences and speculations as to the likely outcomes of future behavior (Akers, 1985). If people feel that the rewards from acts of deviance outweigh the punishments (or potential punishments), they are likely to engage in such acts. From this point of view, people who commit crimes, engage in substance abuse, or take their own lives do so because this behavior has been reinforced in their minds as desirable by the calculus of punishment and rewards. The criminal or substance abuser may have found that the deviant behavior was rewarding enough to be initiated or repeated, whereas the suicide victim may have found that life was punishing enough to be avoided.

Labeling Theory

Finally, **labeling theory** draws attention to how people come to be defined as deviant (as in our earlier discussion of the social construction of deviance). But labeling theory also addresses the social-psychological impact of this label on individuals and its effect on their subsequent behavior. Sociologist Edwin Lemert (1967) made the important distinction between *primary deviance* and *secondary deviance.* With primary deviance, individuals violate a norm and are labeled as deviant by others, but they reject this label as not fitting their self-image. They by and large see themselves as conformists, and the labeling process results in no significant effects on their subsequent behavior. With secondary deviance, individuals violate a norm and are labeled as deviant, but they accept the label and internalize it, thus altering their self-image. Having done so, such individuals assume a deviant role that includes future norm violations. They may in effect become career deviants. This social-psychological explanation points to the possibility that efforts at social control of deviant behavior can actually produce more deviance.

Shortcomings of Social-Psychological Explanations

Social-psychological explanations consider the behavior of people within their immediate social environments. Such explanations explore the nature and relative importance of social influences. Yet social-psychological explanations have critical shortcomings. In the case of differential association, there are many forms of deviance to which the theory does not seem to apply. In most murders, for example, a person impulsively kills a relative, friend, or acquaintance. The murderer usually has never associated with others committing similar acts and has never murdered before.

Similarly, although containment theory may make a lot of intuitive sense, in many instances it sems to be less than useful. For example, a highly successful, middle-aged local business owner—a family man well known and respected throughout his community for his philanthropy and acts of community service—suddenly shoots his equally accomplished and socially involved wife and then takes his own life (Brown, 1993). How does one explain such sudden, seemingly impulsive behavior on the part of someone who by all criteria should be "contained"?

Theories of deviant behavior that stress the importance of reinforcement (through rewards and punishment) lack adequate empirical support. They tend to be applied after the fact: "He must have done that because he found it rewarding." Such theories cannot be used in predicting who is likely to engage in deviant behavior, since people differ greatly in terms of what they are likely to find rewarding.

Labeling theory does not really address why the violation of norms occurred in the first place. And it poses the very difficult challenge of figuring out how and under what circumstances primary deviance becomes transformed into secondary deviance. This social-psychological explanation does have the virtue of drawing attention to the possibility that some people who are labeled as deviant will be propelled into future deviant behavior. But can observers reasonably predict who such people will be?

In general, social-psychological explanations are broader and encompass more factors bearing on deviant behavior than explanations that stop short at the physiological or psychological level. In that sense, proponents of social-psychological explanations are usually able to avoid charges of reductionism. Yet some sociologists argue that social-psychological explanations do not go far enough. They suggest that features of the larger society itself may make deviant behavior "normal."

Sociological Explanations

When individuals engage in deviant behavior, they do so within the context of the particular society in which they live and the ways in which its features affect them. Sociological explanations focus on ways in which such factors may prompt or encourage some individuals to engage in deviant behavior (Hagan, 1994).

Opportunity Structure Theory

Perhaps the best-known sociological explanation bearing on deviant behavior is Robert Merton's **opportunity structure theory** (1957). Merton noted that U.S. society places enormous stress on the pursuit of material success. Indeed, he sees this success as a cultural goal that most people have in common. It is unusual for individuals to say that they have no interest in being better off economically or for privileged persons to express no interest in holding on to or further enhancing their high economic status.

Along with the cultural goal of material success, Merton points out, there are socially approved, legitimate means for pursuing this goal. These include working, saving, and investing. Most people have access to and make use of these means in their quest for material success. But what happens in cases in which the approved means and the cultural goal do not coincide? In Merton's view, the stage is set for individuals to engage in a *mode of adaptation* that can entail deviant behavior.

For example, people may choose the mode of adaptation Merton called *innovation*—they make money illegally. Thus a society whose culture stresses material success, but which offers only some members the means to pursue it, is a society in which one should expect to see deviant behavior in the form of burglaries, robberies, drug trafficking, prostitution, and other types of crime.

Still other people, faced with a gap between the cultural goal of material success and access to the approved means, may reject both. Choosing the mode of adaptation Merton called *retreatism,* they may adopt an alternative lifestyle as a vagrant, pursue altered states of consciousness through substance abuse, or even commit suicide. Retreatism entails removing oneself from a reality that just does not seem workable.

In contrast to retreatism, the mode of adaptation Merton termed *rebellion* involves inventing new cultural goals and new means of achieving them. The goals are likely to be quite different from, or even radically counter to, those that dominate the existing society. Persons who dedicate their lives to revolutionary organizations or transformative social movements (see Chapter 10) are adapting through rebellion.

When a society's culture emphasizes the importance of material success, but there are limited opportunities to achieve it, some people will resort to illegal acts. The U.S. system of gender inequality puts women at a disadvantage in the labor market. Like the woman pictured here, some are driven to accept risks to health and safety by trading sexual favors for money.

Finally, in Merton's scheme of things, the means–goal gap may result in the mode of adaptation he calls *ritualism.* Seeing the goal of material success as hopeless, people abandon it; nonetheless, they go through the motions of working each day, rationalizing that the means are worth pursuing in and of themselves. Since jobs that do not pay well are often also unrewarding in other ways, this can prove to be a rather hollow rationalization.

Merton suggests that since most people are able to utilize socially approved means to pursue the cultural goal of material success, they have little reason to engage in deviant behavior. Yet for others access to these means is problematic. A flawed opportunity structure creates conditions that pressure some people into modes of adaptation that may violate social norms. Much deviant behavior, from this point of view, originates outside the individual's control. Its origins lie in the characteristic features of society itself, such as values promoted by dominant culture and their impact. To reduce such deviance, society itself must undergo fundamental change.

Merton's analysis is very compelling. It provides a larger context for understanding the role of social-psychological factors in producing deviance (Anderson, 1998). Its critics are likely to point out, however, that it does not explain why people adopt any one particular mode of adaptation. Why, for example, in the United States, are there so many thieves and so few revolutionaries? Why do people of affluence, who have access to socially approved means for material success, commit financial crimes? And how can one explain criminal behavior on the part of the extremely well-rewarded executives of large corporations?

Merton's theory seems to contain a bias toward deviant behavior as exhibited by the excluded and downtrodden, while saying comparatively little about deviance on the part of societal elites (Coleman, 1989; Simon and Eitzen, 1990). It is also highly tailored to cultural and social conditions in the United States. Finally, the focus of the model on behaviors does not lend itself to an understanding of those labeled deviant on the basis of their being rather than their actions. Nonetheless, in pointing to the influence of a society's cultural values and structure on its members' behaviors, Merton has greatly enriched sociological thinking about the origins of deviant behavior.

🌀 Deviance and Capitalism

A different, but related, type of sociological explanation for deviant behavior involves the concept of *alienation.* This explanation has its origins in the work of Karl Marx, who we discussed in Chapter 1 as a social thinker influential in ◄ pp. 15–16 the development of the conflict perspective in sociology. Contemporary sociologists borrowing from his ideas can be termed "neo-Marxists" (McGuire and McQuarie, 1994). The focus of the **Marxist theory of deviance** is on the demands that an industrial capitalist society imposes on people (Greenberg, 1993; Taylor, 1999).

An industrial capitalist society is one in which the means of producing goods and services (factories, farms, offices, mines, railroads, communication systems) are privately owned. Ownership tends to be concentrated in the hands of a few, among members of a group called the capitalist class, or *bourgeoisie.* Most people, in order to survive, must work and sell their labor power to members of the capitalist class in return for wages. Marx calls this working-class group the *proletariat.* A problem arises because the self-interests of the capitalist class and those of the working class are in fundamental opposition.

The capitalist class wants to maximize profits in order to expand its wealth and property holdings and further enrich itself. Capitalists thus try to hold wages down to the bare minimum and organize industrial production in cost-saving ways that are often physically and psychologically harmful to their workers. In contrast, the working class wants adequate wages and working conditions. But since its members are not owners of the means of production, this class lacks the power to get its needs met. Consequently, workers experience a sense of **alienation,** or estrangement, from their labor. This is extremely damaging because, in the neo-Marxist view, labor is the principal vehicle through which the human species expresses itself and seeks fulfillment.

Suffering from low wages, sporadic bouts of unemployment, and a sense of alienation, members of the working class are driven into behaviors that are defined as deviant. Crimes of violence, property offenses, and drug crimes are symptoms of the economic oppression and alienation they experience. The structure and workings of society—in this case, its capitalist features—turn the majority of its members into victims. Acting out their alienation from a system that fails to meet their fundamental human needs, members of the working class engage in activities that are harmful to themselves and/or to others (Taylor, Walton, and Young, 1973, 1975).

Neo-Marxists find that this sociological explanation for deviant behavior fits the United States (Hagan, 1997; Quinney, 1979). The U.S. capitalist economy is characterized by chronic unemployment, poverty-level standards of living for the jobless and low-wage families, and workplace alienation, as indicated by worker tardiness, absenteeism, turnover, and acts of sabotage (Sprouse, 1992). Neo-Marxists see economic oppression and alienation as the main reason for the high incidence of crimes of violence, property crimes, and drug offenses at the lower levels of the U.S. class structure. In the neo-Marxist interpretation, capitalists' white-collar and corporate crimes, such as unethical and illegal business practices, are indications that members of the capitalist class also experience a sense of alienation from the economic system in which they participate, even as they accept the logic of capitalism. But they have the most to gain from retaining the system.

Marx argued that workers in industrial capitalist societies, when pushed to the limit, would develop a revolutionary class consciousness and join in social movements to overthrow capitalism. In its place they would construct a "socialist" society in which the workers themselves collectively owned and controlled the means of production. With worker ownership and control, goods and services would be produced to serve the needs of the masses of people, not to enrich the profit of the few. Contrary to what many Marxist analysts have predicted, successful socialist revolutions have not taken place in industrial capitalist societies, such as the United States. Revolutionary movements seeking to build socialism *have* arisen in some underdeveloped, agriculturally-based societies. These movements built socialist economies in such widely different settings as the People's Republic of China, Cuba, and the former Soviet Union. Yet, to varying degrees, deviant behavior has been found to exist in these and other socialist societies.

Thus, while the demands made by capitalism may well drive many people into deviant behavior, clearly the dynamics of capitalism need not always be present for such behaviors to occur. The organization and operation of socialist economic systems may also contribute to deviance, a phenomenon that relatively little sociological research has explored.

Crime and Punishment:
Differential Application of Sanctions

If dominant groups in society have the power to define what is "normal" and what is not, they also have the power to identify those behaviors that are deserving of negative sanctions. Millions of people are sanctioned each year (see Table 9.1). But not everyone who engages in the same behaviors is sanctioned, and not everyone who is sanctioned receives the same kind or degree of punishment. Those who are poor are more likely than the affluent to be detained, arrested, held in jail before trial, convicted, imprisoned, and even executed. This does not mean that poor people are more prone to break laws. One reason for their greater rates of conviction in the criminal justice system is the greater ability of the affluent to afford private attorneys who can devote

TABLE 9.1 Persons under Adult Correctional Supervision: 1990, 1995–2001

Year	Total Estimated Correctional Population[a]	Community Supervision		Incarceration	
		Probation	Parole	Jail	Prison
1990	4,350,300	2,670,234	531,407	405,320	743,382
1995	5,342,900	3,077,861	679,421	507,044	1,078,542
1996	5,490,700	3,164,996	679,733	518,492	1,127,528
1997[b]	5,734,900	3,296,513	694,787	567,079	1,176,564
1998[b]	6,134,200	3,670,441	696,385	592,462	1,224,469
1999[b]	6,340,800	3,779,922	714,457	605,943	1,287,172
2000	6,445,100	3,826,209	723,898	621,149	1,316,333
2001	6,592,800	3,932,751	731,147	631,240	1,330,980
Percent change, 2000–01	2.3%	2.8%	1.0%	1.6%	1.1%
Average annual percent change, 1995–2001	3.6%	3.4%	1.2%	3.7%	3.6%

Note: Counts are for December 31, except for jail counts, which are for June 30. Jail and prison counts include inmates held in private facilities. Totals in 1998 through 2001 exclude probationers held in jail or prison.
[a]Because some offenders may have multiple statuses, totals were rounded to the nearest 100.
[b]Coverage of probation agencies was expanded. For counts based on the same reporting agencies, use 3,266,837 in 1997 (to compare with 1996); 3,417,613 in 1998 (to compare with 1997); and 3,773,624 in 1999 (to compare with 1998). The average annual percent change was adjusted for the change in coverage.

SOURCE: Lauren E. Glaze, "Probation and Parole in the United States, 2001," *Bureau of Justice Statistics Bulletin,* April 2002, p. 1. Available at www.ojp.usdoj.gov/bjs/pub/pdf/ppus01.pdf.

adequate time to aiding clients accused of crimes, in contrast to the poor's reliance on overburdened public defenders. Moreover, judges and many jurors are likely to identify and sympathize with more affluent defendants during trials (Reiman, 2000).

Race is also a critical factor in the differential application of sanctions. Data suggest that people of color are more likely than whites to be arrested, convicted, sent to prison or death row, and executed (Tonry, 1995) (see Tables 9.2 and 9.3). Overall, African American men are imprisoned almost 10 times more often than white men (Human Rights Watch, 2000). In recent years many people of color have been sent to prison for drug offenses. Although white high school students are four times more likely to regularly use cocaine than African American students, African Americans who are arrested on drug charges are one and one-half times more likely to be sent to prison (Centers for Disease Control, 1999).

People of color are also disproportionately represented among those receiving the ultimate punishment: the death penalty (see Table 9.3). Although African Americans comprise less than 13 percent of the total U.S. population, 39 percent of those held under sentence of death and more than 41 percent of the 85 inmates executed in the United States in 2000 were African American (for statistics on capital punishment, see www.ojp.usdoj.gov/bjs/cp.htm). In 2000, of the 18 prisoners held on federal death row, 16 were African American, Latino, or Asian.

TABLE 9.2 Comparison of Sentencing by Race: 2000

	Sentencing Rate (Per 100,000 in population)	Held under Death Sentence (Percentage of total held)	Executed (Percentage of total executed)
African American men	34.6	39.0%	41.2%
Latinos	12.2	8.6	0.0
White men	<0.01	50.6	57.6

SOURCE: www.usdoj.gov/bjs/prisons and www.usdoj.gov/bjs/cp.htm.

The race of the crime victim appears to be an important factor as well: A U.S. General Accounting Office study found that when comparing homicides committed under similar circumstances by defendants with similar criminal histories, the death penalty was "several times more likely" to be imposed when the victim was white than when the victim was African American (www.aclu.org/death-penalty/race.html). Most chilling is the fact that DNA testing increasingly reveals an apparent rush to judgment clouded by racism that all too often sends innocent men of color to death row. As of 2000, at least 100 people had been exonerated as a result of DNA testing, and the majority of these have been African American and Latino (Alter, 2000).

People of color are likely to be required to post bail bonds substantially higher than those required of whites in order to obtain their freedom while they await trial. This is the case even for people who commit the same crime and who have similar criminal histories. Such practices occur despite the fact that no evidence exists to support the claim that people of color are more likely to flee before being brought to trial. One study found that in the case of drug charges such as possession or sale of illegal drugs, African Americans and Latinos/Latinas paid average bail bonds that were four times greater than those paid by whites charged with similar law violations (Houston and Ewing, 1991, 1992).

This discriminatory pattern of setting bail bonds reverberates throughout the trial and sentencing process. National studies have found that people accused of crimes who are held in jail prior to trial because they cannot afford to post bail tend to receive longer sentences than defendants who are able to do so. Being jailed can impede the accused's ability to adequately participate in the preparation of his or her defense. It may also create the impression that the accused is guilty (Houston and Ewing, 1991). Since people of color are more likely than whites to be unemployed or disadvantaged in the labor market, and are disproportionately found among the poor, a system based on ability to pay bail imposes a greater burden on them whether they are guilty or innocent. In large measure, this means that the right to the presumption of innocence until proven guilty—with all its symbolic and practical implications—is compromised for people of color and the poor.

Furthermore, in some states, the civil liberties and rights of convicted felons are not only limited while they are imprisoned but may continue to be denied long after

TABLE 9.3 Executions and Other Dispositions of Inmates Sentenced to Death, by Race and Latino/Latina Origin: 1977–2001

Origin[b]	Total under Sentence of Death, 1977–2001[c]	Prisoners Executed		Prisoners Who Received Other Dispositions[a]	
		Number	Percent of Total	Number	Percent of Total
White	3,316	422	12.7%	1,250	37.7%
Black	2,784	263	9.4	1,000	35.9
Latino/Latina	550	52	9.5	140	25.5
All other[d]	104	12	11.5	34	32.7
Total	6,754	749	11.1%	2,424	35.9%

[a]Includes persons removed from a sentence of death because of statutes struck down on appeal, sentences or convictions vacated, commutations, or death by other than execution.
[b]White, black, and other race categories exclude Latinos/Latinas.
[c]Includes persons sentenced to death prior to 1977 who were still under sentence of death on December 31, 2001 (8), persons sentenced to death prior to 1977 whose death sentence was removed between 1977 and December 31, 2001 (372), and persons sentenced to death between 1977 and December 31, 2001 (6,374).
[d]Includes American Indians and Asians.

Source: Tracy L. Snell and Laura M. Maruschak, "Capital Punishment, 2001," *Bureau of Justice Statistics Bulletin,* December 2002, p. 11. Available at www.ojp.usdoj.gov/bjs/pub/pdf/cp01.pdf.

prisoners have served their sentences and paid their debt to society. Twelve states deny convicted felons the right to vote indefinitely, thereby limiting their lawful participation as citizens of their own nation. African American men in particular suffer this fate, since they are disproportionately represented among those convicted. Nationally, one in seven African American men are barred from voting; in states that carry out such penalties after time has been served, the rate is one in four (Katz, 2000).

Taken together, these data indicate the power of dominant groups not only to determine who and what is deviant, but also to mete out differential sanctions to people committing the same infractions. Patterns of racial inequality suggest that the criminal justice system operates as a powerful social control mechanism, one that serves to punish people of color more harshly than whites. Labels and stigmas of conviction and imprisonment can follow a person long after time has been served. This compounds pre-existing patterns of inequality, creating great difficulty for individuals who have been caught up, fairly or unfairly, in the system at one point in their lives to resist the label thereafter.

Note that major corporations and top-level executives who commit crimes are in a better position than the average worker to avoid the imposition of the label of deviance on their behavior, and to thus evade punishments and stigma (Reiman, 2000). Even when those engaging in white-collar or corporate crimes are caught and punished, the sanctions are typically not as harsh as those suffered by persons convicted of the types of crimes of violence and property crimes found in the Uniform Crime Reports. The sentences imposed against executives who break the law commonly involve monetary fines, which, even when substantial (as in the case of

Michael Milken), are far less damaging in their impact than the smaller fines levied against the poor.

Convictions for white-collar and corporate crimes often carry less prison time than convictions for those in the Uniform Crime Reports, and imprisonment typically takes place in minimum security prisons where amenities and treatment of prisoners are far better than in medium or maximum security prisons. White-collar and corporate felons seldom lose their right to vote permanently, their crimes are not punished by the death penalty, even when large numbers of individuals lose their lives as a result of their offenses. Executives who break the law are free to return to the political participation in which they can influence the laws that bind them and the sanctions they receive should they violate them.

Between 1992 and 2001, federal prosecutors pursued criminal charges against 525 of 609 corporate executives identified by the Securities and Exchange Commission as having committed offenses. Of those charged, 142 were found guilty of a crime. Only 87 of those found guilty served any time in jail, and most of them served only a few months. Ironically, in many instances those forced to make restitution for their high-level financial crimes can legally claim much of it as a tax writeoff (Smith, 2002).

Do Societies "Need" Deviant Behavior?

Virtually all societies, however they may differ from one another, contain behavior that comes to be defined as deviant. In light of this fact, some sociologists have suggested that perhaps societies *need* deviant behavior. Rather than viewing deviant behavior negatively, perhaps one should see it as functional to society. This **functionalist theory of deviance** was first put forth by the French sociologist Émile Durkheim (1964). Durkheim's importance to the more general functionalist perspective in sociology was addressed in Chapter 1.

pp. 12–13

Durkheim pointed out that deviance is found not merely in poorly organized, unstable societies. Rather, the best of societies (using whatever criteria one wishes) contain deviant behavior. Crime of one sort or another, for example, can be found everywhere. According to Durkheim, the occurrence of crime is actually a service to society; the anger and dismay crime generates function to bring people together and strengthen their solidarity as a group. The deviance reminds people of their commonly shared morality. As a sociologist who was interested in the bases of social order, Durkheim saw deviant behavior as contributing to societal stability. Without periodic opportunities to collectively condemn unwanted behavior, reinforcing social order would be difficult. In effect, deviant behavior functions as an internal threat against which societal members must rally.

Sociologist Kai Erikson elaborated on Durkheim's thoughts in *Wayward Puritans* (1966). Erikson uses the term "boundaries" to refer to the norms that evolve in human groups:

> Human behavior can vary over an enormous range, but each community draws a symbolic set of parentheses around a certain segment of that range and limits its own activities

within that narrower zone. These parentheses, so to speak, are the community's boundaries. (p. 10)

Since the boundaries, or norms, are not always apparent, undergo change, and yet still must be internalized by new group members, some way must exist to demonstrate what they are. In Erikson's view, deviant behavior serves this function:

> The deviant is a person whose activities have moved outside the margins of the group, and when the community calls him to account for that vagrancy it is making a statement about the nature and placement of its boundaries. It is declaring how much variability and diversity can be tolerated within the group before it begins to lose its distinctive shape, its unique identity. (p. 11)

Thus Erikson sees the actions of *policing agents* as important in demonstrating where a group's norms, or boundaries, lie. Policing agents take many forms and include criminal justice systems, the psychiatric profession, military institutions, and religious bodies. These agents, confronting people who wander outside society's boundaries, show everyone where the boundaries are.

Erikson points out that much of what observers call "news" in the mass media concerns deviant behavior and its consequences. Many of the programs that appear on entertainment television also focus on deviant behavior. In recent years much "reality" programming has centered on police activities, most wanted criminals, and unsolved crimes. Erikson's argument is that the mass media play an important role in reinforcing societal norms by showing people repeatedly testing them and policing agents enforcing them.

Erikson suggests that deviant behavior is so important to societal stability that society actually encourages it. The failure of prisons to rehabilitate and of mental hospitals to cure actually ensures a steady supply of deviants who will violate norms, generate activity on the part of policing agents, and regularly reinvigorate the majority's sense of the boundaries of socially acceptable behavior. Indeed, the segregation of deviants into such institutions ensures their continued alienation from society. Moreover, while institutionalized, deviants have the opportunity to learn new styles and techniques of norm violation from one another, an education that may assist some in pursuing a "career" of deviant behavior (Erikson, 1966).

Erikson's ideas do not address the sources of the behavior that violates norms, but these sources are a major concern of sociologists. Moreover, his argument that deviance may be beneficial, or functional, to society does not address the enormous harm done by many deviant acts. But he does force observers to think about whether a minimal degree of norm violation by a society's members is unavoidable if that society is to operate successfully. Accepting Erikson's ideas might cause one to view deviant behavior as a phenomenon that makes important contributions to society.

The logic of Erikson's views regarding the important functions that deviance may play within society may be extended to the practice of labeling other societies as deviant. Demonizing other societies, a common political practice, creates an "us versus them" mentality that often defines "us" as normal and "them" as evil, less civilized, and less deserving of existence. Political and military elites in the United States and elsewhere frequently identify and portray other societies ("them") as external threats. What functions does this play for society? For one, it can encourage societal members to at least temporarily suspend norms against killing so that participation in wars becomes a civic duty around which people across society will unite. The demonization of other societies as threats may also function to distract societal members from the failure of their government to address serious social problems (e.g., unemployment, poverty). External threats can make society's rank-and-file members feel dependent on their government for information about and protection from these threats, thus reinforcing the ability of political elites to retain political power even as serious domestic social problems persist.

Deviance and Social Change

Deviant behavior may be viewed as serving important functions from yet another perspective. People may intentionally violate norms to draw attention to societal conditions that they consider wrong and to bring about or increase pressures for social change. History is filled with examples of people "going against the system" even at the cost of enormous sacrifices of their livelihoods or even their lives.

As participants in the U.S. civil rights movement, many social activists violated norms and risked negative sanctions as they sought to end racial segregation and other discriminatory practices (Williams, 1987). Consider the importance we now attach to the historic refusal of a Montgomery, Alabama, seamstress, Rosa Parks, to give up her seat in a segregated city bus to a white man. On the day this occurred in 1955, the norms governing appropriate behavior for African Americans in the nation's South included a detailed and intricate body of rules of interracial etiquette (Doyle, 1971). African Americans, for example, had to enter the front of the bus to pay and then had to go back outside and enter the rear of the bus to sit in the "colored only" section. Violators of such rules, some of which were unspoken while others were written into law, invited harsh sanctions from members of the dominant white majority.

Mrs. Parks's action led to her arrest, which sparked a major boycott of public transportation and local white-owned businesses in Montgomery by members of the African American community. The boycott proved successful. The buses were de-segregated. The Montgomery bus boycott demonstrated to the nation that segregation could be fought by collective grassroots action. From that point on norms governing black–white relations underwent a sustained attack, including an all-out assault on such common features of everyday life as "whites only" restrooms, schools, bus station entrances, water fountains, cemetery sections, phone booths, motels, blood banks, lunchrooms, movie theater seats, swimming pools, and beaches.

By the early 1960s African Americans and their supporters, including many whites, were flagrantly contesting the norms of racial segregation through peaceful, racially integrated marches, boycotts, and sit-ins across the South. Groups such as the National Association for the Advancement of Colored People, the Congress of Racial Equality, the Student Nonviolent Coordinating Committee, and Dr. Martin Luther King's Southern Christian Leadership Conference provided leadership, legal assistance, and other resources to help advance what had become a major social movement.

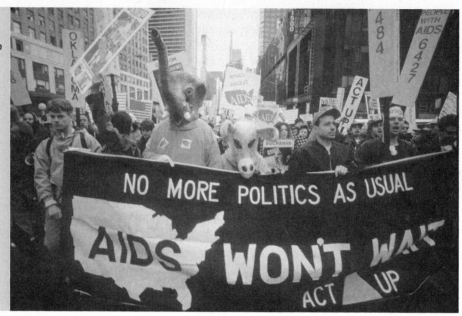

Deviant behavior can be used as a force for social change, as when non-violent protestors break the law in the course of staging marches and demonstrations. The militant protests of the gay rights movement and its allies helped to spur greater federal government action in the face of the enormous health care needs of people with AIDS.

Many southern civil rights workers and other supporters of the movement were targeted for negative sanctions, such as harassment, loss of jobs, and threats or acts of violence directed against themselves and their families. Widely condemned acts of racist terrorism occurred, including a church bombing in Birmingham, Alabama, that killed four African American children, and the murder of three young civil rights workers in Mississippi (a black state resident and two white New Yorkers). These acts were the response of whites who felt their world shattering as the civil rights movement, building on its day-by-day successes, overturned laws permitting racial segregation.

The civil rights movement helped inspire others to violate norms, question injustices, and engage in deviant behavior to challenge "business as usual." The feminist movement, the disability rights movement, and the gay rights movement are but three examples. Within the gay rights movement, an organization known as ACT UP became concerned with the slowness of AIDS research and drug trials and angered over the high costs of drugs used to delay the onset of AIDS. ACT UP achieved results through dramatic demonstrations during the 1990s that harassed and embarrassed government and pharmaceutical industry officials (Shepard and Hayduk, 2002).

But not all change requires a group protest or a broad social movement. Sometimes an individual willing to take risks for what he or she believes in can have an important impact. Even if the person is unsuccessful in bringing about change, efforts in this direction can inspire others. A good example is that of **whistle-blowers** within corporate or governmental settings. These people, at great risk to their jobs and career chances, speak out to the mass media about such issues as unsafe corporate practices, unethical and illegal acts, wasteful spending, fraudulent policies, corruption, and incompetence (Glazer and Glazer, 1999; Miethe, 1999).

For example, in the early 1990s a technician at Tennessee's Oak Ridge National Laboratory, a federal nuclear facility managed by Martin Marietta Energy Systems, appeared on a CBS news program to "blow the whistle" about suspiciously high rates of cancer among the laboratory's workers. The technician himself had recently undergone treatment for colon cancer. In his view, the cancers were caused by unsafe working conditions that exposed workers to dangerous radiation. Managers at the facility retaliated by assigning the technician to "a room filled with toxic and radioactive chemicals" and ordering him "to perform useless work there" ("Whistle-Blowing," 1993). He ultimately won a legal action requiring compensation for the way he was mistreated by the laboratory's managers. Through his whistle-blowing deviance, the technician was also successful in helping to draw attention to the issue of worker health and safety at nuclear facilities in the United States. The dangers of radioactive contamination and pollution for people working in or living around such facilities has since become a major public health issue.

More recently, Sherron S. Watkins, a former vice president at Enron Corporation, became a whistle-blower when she told both the chief executive of Enron and the firm's auditor at the accounting firm of Arthur Andersen about serious and illegal irregularities in Enron's accounting procedures. She termed them "an elaborate accounting hoax . . . I am incredibly nervous that we will implode in a wave of accounting scandals," she wrote to Kenneth Lay, Enron's chief executive officer (Pellegrini, 2002). She also told Congress and helped launch an investigation into what quickly became arguably the largest, and most scandalous and criminal, corporate bankruptcy in U.S. history. As thanks for her whistle-blowing, Watkins was treated like an outcast and publicly vilified by her employers in the press.

Watkin's experience in the aftermath of her whistle-blowing is not unusual. Often a battle for credibility emerges when the whistle-blower's superiors attempt to cast discredit on the disclosures and tarnish the whistle-blower's reputation (Hilts, 1993). The whistle-blower's actions violate norms that call for organizational loyalty, communication only through proper channels, and maintenance of confidentiality of internal information. Such actions reverberate in the executive suite. What if all employees got it into their heads to act like this? Hence employers are likely to engage in social control through negative sanctions to eliminate this deviant behavior.

CHAPTER SUMMARY

1. Whether or not behavior is considered deviant depends on the norms that people develop and use to judge others. Negative and positive sanctions are used to exercise social control over deviant behavior. Norms and social control over deviance are necessary for any society to function.

2. Deviance is a social construction. In a heterogeneous society, what is considered deviant will differ from group to group and may change over time. Norms also differ from society to society.

3. Deviance involves a labeling process. The distribution of power in society helps to determine which behaviors and whose behaviors will be labeled as deviant. The label of deviant may carry a negative social stigma, one that is difficult to shed.

4. Not all labeling of people as deviant involves their behavior. People may be labeled deviant simply because they are seen to differ in their characteristics from a dominant group in some way. Dominant groups tend to view those they dominate as "the other," as people who have characteristics that render them deviant by their very being.

5. Since dominant groups frequently impose the "deviant" label on people who do not want it (e.g., because it portrays them as inferior people, because it leads to unjust treatment), the labeling process often encounters resistance. The more powerful the group doing the labeling, the more difficult resistance becomes.

6. Sociologists have long been interested in why deviant behavior, particularly crime, occurs. Explanations that focus principally on physiological or psychological shortcomings of those who engage in deviant behavior have been of limited value. Most people engaging in deviance are similar to those not engaging in such behavior.

7. Social-psychological explanations examine the influence of one's immediate social environment on deviant behavior. Sociological explanations focus on how people's behavior is affected by group memberships and features of society over which they may have little control. Sociologists explore ways in which societal conditions (e.g., blocked economic opportunities, class inequalities) may be conducive to or encourage some types of deviance.

8. The presence of deviant behavior in all societies (although societies often differ on what behavior is considered deviant) raises the issue of whether societies "need" deviance. Some argue that deviance is functional to society, since norm violations remind people of what the norms are, thus encouraging social stability and order.

9. Societies may benefit from those groups and individuals who rise up and deviate from norms that support harmful and unjust social conditions. Harsh inequalities and abuses of power may call forth counteractions and social movements.

10. From the revolutionary to the whistle-blower, people at times challenge what those more powerful would prefer be considered normal. Such forms of deviant behavior can produce social change, even while entailing significant risks for those seeking to alter the status quo.

THINKING CRITICALLY

1. Discuss the role played by power in definitions of what behavior will be considered deviant. Are people who have power or who are otherwise privileged able to "get away with" behaviors that might be considered norm violations if engaged in by others? Why? Give examples.

2. We pointed out that what is considered deviant may differ from society to society, given that societies have different norms associated with their cultures. On the basis of other courses you have taken, experiences of your friends and family members, or observations you have made while traveling, discuss some examples of these differences and speculate about why they exist.

3. In Chapter 5 we discussed subcultures. Subcultures often have their own norms, which differ in various ways from those that prevail elsewhere in society. Are there norms that must not be violated within the college student subculture? What are they? What happens to people who violate them, and why?

4. Are there circumstances in which you have felt that you were defined and treated as deviant simply on the basis of who you are rather than because of your behavior (e.g., on the basis of your sex, class, race or ethnicity, sexual orientation, age, or state of able-bodiedness)? How did you feel, and why? How did you respond?

KEY TERMS

alienation, *(280)*
appearance norms, *(259)*
containment theory, *(276)*
control theory, *(276)*
corporate crime, *(272)*
crime, *(269)*
deviance, *(255)*
differential association theory, *(276)*
functionalist theory of deviance, *(285)*
label, *(257)*
labeling theory, *(277)*

Marxist theory of deviance, *(280)*
motherhood norms, *(260)*
negative sanctions, *(255)*
norms, *(255)*
opportunity structure theory, *(278)*
physiological explanations, *(273)*
positive sanctions, *(256)*
psychological explanations, *(273)*
recidivism, *(267)*

reductionism, *(274)*
sanctions, *(255)*
social construction (of deviance), *(256)*
social control, *(255)*
social-psychological explanations, *(273)*
social reinforcement, *(277)*
sociological explanations, *(273)*
stigma, *(266)*
whistle-blowers, *(288)*
white-collar crime, *(271)*

Chapter Ten

Social Change and Social Movements

Societies and cultures rarely stand still. They are frequently involved in a process of change, slow or rapid, incremental or radical. Social scientists have always been fascinated by the rapid changes that accompanied the Industrial Revolution in the mid- to late nineteenth century. Radical changes generated by political revolutions such as those in France, Russia, China, and Cuba are also a source of great interest to social scientists. Probably of greater interest to most people living today are the changes that have occurred in their own lifetimes. Just ask your grandparents how different the world is today than when they were your age. Ask them about such things as dating rituals, sexual mores, child–parent relations, race relations, technology, and transportation. Ask your parents about the tremendous social changes ushered in by the feminist movement, the civil rights movement, the students' rights movement, and the antiwar movement during the 1960s and 1970s. And you yourself may already be aware of how everyday life has dramatically changed since September 11, 2001. Consider, for example, how different it is now to get on a plane, work in a skyscraper, check out a book on explosives from the library, or simply open an unsolicited piece of mail. Some of the questions these changes inspire include:

- What is social change?
- Why does it occur?
- How does it occur?
- What forces and factors affect the direction and magnitude of social change?
- Are all social changes as dramatic as revolutions?
- What are the consequences and ramifications of social change?
- Does social change provide advantages and benefits to some and not to others?
- What is the impact of social change on various groups in society and on global relations?
- Is social change inevitable, or can people affect social change?

The Meaning of Social Change

When sociologists talk about **social change,** they are referring to significant variations or alterations in social structures and cultures over time. Social change may occur on varying levels and in varying degrees of intensity. For example, **social reforms** are adjustments in the content of cultural patterns of behavior or normative systems, adjustments that do not fundamentally alter the social structure. Alterations in U.S. minimum-wage laws—for example, requiring that employers increase the wages of the lowest paid workers—do not change the structure of society: Corporations remain in control of the production of goods and services, and federal laws are still made by Congress. **Social revolutions,** on the other hand, are fundamental and radical upheavals of existing social structures. Revolutions sometimes involve bloody battles between identifiable organizations of armies, but this is not always the case. The Industrial Revolution, for example, fundamentally altered the processes of production and the power and control workers had over those processes, and therefore it changed institutions, roles, and statuses (Evans, 1999; Gutman, 1977; Thompson, 1966). But it did not occur on a battlefield between clearly organized armies. The battlefield was the shop floor in the factories, and the conflict was initially between individual workers and owners (although, to be sure, the struggles in the labor movement that emerged many years later were at times quite bloody).

It is also useful to consider that some social change is **manifest**—it is largely recognized and intended. In many cases a large or powerful group (not necessarily a majority) deliberately and consciously organizes a movement for change. For example, the colonists began the American Revolution to gain independence from Great Britain. The feminist movement arose when women began pressing for social, political, and economic equality. Similarly, the civil rights movement emerged out of a collective, concerted effort by many people to confront and challenge racism in the United States.

Other social change is **latent**—it is largely unrecognized and unintended. For example, the baby boom that occurred in the United States after World War II was not recognized until it was well under way. It produced a demographic "bubble" that had many consequences. Schools became overcrowded when that age cohort entered the education system, and the situation prompted a national scramble to build more schools and hire more teachers. Competition for jobs intensified as baby boomers entered the labor market, and by the 1980s unemployment and underemployment had become a greater possibility for more people. Baby boomers became a political force in the late 1960s and early 1970s when they participated in several social movements. The antiwar movement hastened an end to the Vietnam war. Critical analyses of the war, the military draft, and the political process raised by the antiwar movement also prompted a lowering of the legal voting age from 21 to 18. The growing feminist movement gained women more access to higher education and better jobs. In turn, the new opportunities for women had the unintended consequence of reducing birth rates in the United States. When baby boomers retire early in this century, they will impose great demands on the Social Security system. At that time the labor force will be much smaller and perhaps be unable to support those demands without major reforms in public policy.

Explaining Social Change

How do sociologists explain social change? Is it a natural, inevitable phenomenon? How much effect can people have on it? Is a society's social change propelled by forces within that society, or do external forces contribute to changes in all societies? What are the forces of global social change? Are these forces neutral and natural, or are they social constructions in response to the interests of particular groups?

Sociologists generally agree that whether it is manifest or latent, social change is an ongoing process; it is not a singular, discrete event in a vacuum of time and place. The discussion of the baby boom indicated that an initial social change may set the stage for later changes. Beyond this fact, there is wide disagreement over how to explain social change. Several theoretical perspectives attempt to explain it as a normal, natural force that is part of a stable social system. But another perspective views conflict as the key catalyst for social change.

Cyclical Theory

Some sociologists see social change as a natural cycle in the rise and fall of social systems. This analysis is called **cyclical theory** (Pareto, 1963; Sorokin, 1957). In this view, societies are likened to an organism. Every society is presumed to pass naturally and inevitably through the same age phases that individual biological organisms (particularly the human being) pass through: infancy, childhood, adolescence, adulthood, old age, and, finally, decay and death. Oswald Spengler (1926) argued that each phase lasted a definite and predictable length of time for all societies. He suggested that all societies possess an internal biological clock determining their natural life span, which he believed to be a millennium (1,000 years).

However, some societies have lasted beyond a millennium (such as Egypt, China, and India) and others seem to perish "prematurely" (such as the Union of Soviet Socialist Republics, which lasted slightly more than half a century). Even when a society perishes, whether it is, in fact, dying a "natural" death from old age is questionable. The division of Germany into the Federal Republic of Germany (FRG) and the German Democratic Republic (GDR) after World War II was a political act taken by the Allied countries to ensure that Germany would never again be an international threat. And the reunification of these two countries into a single Germany in 1989, effectively causing the demise of the GDR and FRG as independent nations, was also a political, not a natural, development.

Spengler's cyclical theory also leaves little room for an examination of the effect of external forces on a given society's life span. For example, it ignores the role that invasion, war, annexation, exploitation, or genocide inflicted by other societies may play in hastening a society's death. More recent cyclical analyses of social change have sought to correct this limitation by examining societies' rise-and-decline patterns as part of a global system. For example, in his book *The Rise and Fall of the Great Powers,* Paul Kennedy (1987) argued that some societies rise economically and politically while others around them decline, in large part because the ascending societies ultimately conquer the faltering ones. This type of rise-and-decline cycle is influenced by a society's economic production, its fiscal strength, and its military strength. Rising states tend to capitalize on technological developments to enhance and increase production, which increases taxable wealth. This in turn provides the state more funds to support military expansion, which facilitates the ability of rising states to conquer declining states.

Although Kennedy's analysis does recognize external factors that may affect societies' cycle of social change, it overemphasizes military conquest as an important factor in the rise and decline of states. Consider Japan's successful competition in the global market of the 1980s. Japan had capitalized on technological innovations to increase production, but it did not invest the state's revenues in military expansion, and it did not militarily conquer anyone. Moreover, in the 1980s the Soviet Union failed to exploit technological innovation effectively as it was investing a great deal of its state revenues in military expansion, and it declined without being militarily conquered. Both cases call Kennedy's analysis into question.

Evolutionary Theory

Other sociologists favor an **evolutionary theory** to explain social change. They share cyclical theory's assumption that societies are like organisms, but evolutionary theory likens social change to Darwin's notion of biological evolution. Societies go through a natural series of stages based on increasing complexity, propelled toward higher, more advanced, and developed states of existence. Thus evolutionary theory favors a notion of progress, wherein each new stage of development is more advanced than the one before. All societies are believed to progress through the same stages in the same order while evolving into ever-higher forms (Comte, 1966; Durkheim, 1964; Fei and Ranis, 1997). But whereas cyclical theory sees the death of a society as the natural end to the social life cycle, evolutionary theory makes no such presumption. Some societies might die off, but only as a result of "natural selection." Recent analyses argue that this natural selection is governed by a society's cultural inheritance of technological innovations, which permits a society to command greater control over its environment. Only those societies that invest in technological innovation will survive (Lenski, Lenski, and Nolan, 1991; Lopreato and Crippen, 1999). That is, the "fittest" societies survive. Sociologists call this last argument **social Darwinism.**

The problem with social Darwinism is that it does not analyze the ways societies might differ in their access to information and technology or the role conquest plays in the demise of societies. Furthermore, evolutionary theory's presumption that all societies must pass through the same stages in the same order, and that each successive stage is necessarily more advanced, denies the unique histories societies may have. It assumes that all societies have access to the same resources to achieve the same levels of evolution. Its implicit use of Western nations as models of "advanced" societies denies the possibility that non-Western societies may be advanced as well. Social Darwinism does not address the possibility that societies may have "advanced" by taking advantage of resources from the "less advanced" societies. We will return to this issue shortly.

Equilibrium Theory

Other sociologists believe social change naturally occurs as societies become more and more complex. The increasing complexity demands greater and greater specialization of social structures and social roles. This analysis, called **equilibrium**

theory, shares cyclical and evolutionary theories' analogy of society as a biological organism (Alexander and Colomy, 1990; Ogburn, 1964; Parsons, 1951). Societies are likened, for example, to the human body, in which the circulatory, digestive, endocrine, and musculatory systems are interdependent. Each system requires the functioning of all the others in order to function adequately itself. Any disturbances or alterations in one of these bodily systems prompts adjustments in the others so that the body as a whole remains in equilibrium. Like an organism, social systems are seen to have a natural tendency toward stability. When a disturbance or change occurs in one sector of a social system, the great interdependence of sectors prompts changes in all other sectors to accommodate the initial change and achieve stability in the overall system (Parsons, 1951). From the viewpoint of equilibrium theory, social change entails a series of minor adjustments, rather than fundamental alteration of the structure of society.

The problem here lies in the question of the source of disturbances or changes in particular sectors of the social system. What causes such changes to occur in the first place if all the parts are integrated and harmoniously in balance? And if stability is the normal state of existence for a social system, how do sociologists explain radical social change like revolution?

Equilibrium theory is imprecise in its notion of "social system," a central concept. Just what constitutes a social system is unclear: Is it a neighborhood, a city, a nation? If the social system were to be defined as a nation, how do observers take account of the economic interdependence today that in fact creates a world-system? If one nation changes its trade relations, for example, the change affects other nations. Economic recessions in one nation can have painful economic and political repercussions in others. Thus one of the difficulties of equilibrium theory is its neglect of the possibility that changes may come from outside the social system.

Finally, equilibrium theory emphasizes how order and stability are maintained, but it ignores conflict. Critics question the failure of equilibrium theory to discuss the role that conflict and power differentials may play in destabilizing society (e.g., Gouldner, 1970).

Marxist Theory

In contrast to theoretical perspectives focusing on change as gradual and natural, another one sees conflict as a normal, constant state of affairs that makes change a regular feature in all social structures. Sociologists refer to this view as **Marxist theory.** What causes conflicts to erupt and generate social change?

Karl Marx and Friedrich Engels (1848/1967) referred to the ongoing process of social change as the **dialectic.** Every social structure begins as a **thesis,** or its current (temporary and momentary) state of existence. But every state of existence contains serious fundamental contradictions and crises which commonly intensify until challenges to the status quo erupt. The challenge is called the **antithesis.** The conflict that accelerates between the thesis and antithesis eventually must resolve itself into what Marx and Engels called the **synthesis.** The synthesis is a wholly new social structure carrying some elements from the thesis and some from the antithesis. This new structure eventually becomes normalized as a new thesis that carries its own contradictions and crises, prompting the dialectic process to continue.

For example, Marx and Engels argued that every social structure of production has inherent contradictions and antagonisms, and conflicts percolate between two classes, those who own the means of production (**capitalists**) and those who do not (the **proletariat,** or workers). Sharp class antagonisms in a capitalist system arise because of contradictions between social production, in which goods and services are produced by groups of workers cooperating together, and private ownership of a firm's productive resources by the capitalists. While capitalists pay workers a wage for their labor, workers are producing far greater wealth than the value of their wages. The difference between what workers are paid and the wealth they create is profit for the capitalist. Capitalists are constantly looking for ways to increase their profit at the workers' expense. Conflict takes the form of continual organized struggle between the proletariat and the capitalists over the fruits of workers' labor. An antithesis to capitalism occurs when workers' organized struggle produces a fundamental change in ownership of the means of production and captures control over all the wealth produced. Marx believed that the conflict between capitalism and the struggle for worker ownership would produce socialism as its synthesis. For Marx, social change is thus the outcome of an ongoing process of class struggle between these two groups. Marx saw the entire history of humanity as the history of such class struggles.

According to this analysis, order in society comes about only with conflict and change. Hence conflict is not necessarily a negative, destructive force. Marx and Engels saw conflict as a positive, restructuring force, a prerequisite for social change and progress.

While Marxist theory may respond to many of the limitations of other theories of social change, it does not explain social stability. If conflict and change are natural features of social structure, how is social stability possible? Is it not possible for social change to occur without conflict?

In sum, these theories of social change offer quite different explanations for how and why individual societies may change. Each also implies some explanation for unequal development throughout the world. Is the modern world-system, marked by unequal economic growth and development, a sum total of each nation's individual social change processes, or is each nation an element of a larger, more globally interrelated process? We now turn to this question.

Modernization, Development, and Underdevelopment

Evolutionary theory implies that social change entails progress and that all societies must follow the same path in their development. Poor nations are presumed to need to embrace the values and imitate the experiences of industrialized Western nations in order to become modernized and civilized (Harrison, 2000; Hoselitz, 1960; Rostow, 1960). The poverty of some nations and their failure to modernize are attributed to their failure to adopt the "appropriate," "progressive" Western values and ways of doing things. **Modernization theory,** a global version of the culture-of-poverty analysis (see Chapter 5), argues that the value systems of poor ◀ p. 124

nations interfere with their development and modernization. Such nations are therefore "less developed" or "more primitive" than the "developed" nations.

Many industrialized nations may have exported their contemporary goods and modern technologies to poor nations. While these goods and services may help poor nations better address pressing basic needs, that they do not produce these themselves is not enough to explain why they are poor in the first place. To understand clearly why a particular nation is poor, rather than dismissing it as primitive because it has a different value system, is important.

The Meaning of Development

Critics have questioned the meaning of development implied in modernization theory (Frank, 1967; Todaro, 1989). A high level of development is frequently defined as an advanced degree of urbanization and industrialization, characterized by the use of state-of-the-art technology and the generation of large amounts of wealth. This definition is simply a description of the West; it is based on the ethnocentric assumption that Western nations are the most highly evolved.

Furthermore, during the 1950s and 1960s many underdeveloped nations became more industrialized and increased their manufacturing production rates. Urbanization, including some electrification and sewer systems, increased, and commercial transportation systems emerged in some places. Yet the standard of living for most people in these nations did not improve (Seers, 1969). This contradiction between the growth of urbanization, industry, and wealth production on one hand and the stagnation of poverty on the other called into question the conventional meaning of development. It showed that development benefited some people but not others in these nations. Moreover, such extremes of inequality could be found in the "developed" nations of the West as well. How, then, do observers measure development?

Studies frequently measure development in terms of kilowatt-hours of electricity used per capita and the amount of wealth a nation produced, or its gross domestic product per capita. These measures are reflections of urbanization and industrialization. The problem here is that such measures simply average out the wealth produced and the electricity consumed over the entire population, thereby skirting the important question of distribution: Does everyone in the population receive an equal amount of the wealth produced? Arriving at only one statistic for an entire population implies that distribution is equal. An aggregate measure, such as gross domestic product per capita, can be used to compare the overall wealth of nations but ignores regions of poverty, patterns of inequality, and hunger and homelessness that exist even within so-called developed countries. Similarly, it allows observers to define countries such as Haiti or the Philippines as less developed while overlooking their regions of wealth and their elites.

Some critics suggest replacing the definition of development with a definition of **basic needs** (Basu, 1996; Streeten, 1981; Sundaram, 1996; Wood, 1986). Using this definition, observers would look at how evenly the basic goods and services needed for survival are distributed within the entire population. Basic needs are measured in terms of health (such as life expectancy at birth and infant mortality rates), education (such as literacy rates and the proportion of the population age 5 to 14 enrolled in

Contradictions between the growth of urbanization, industry, and wealth on the one hand and deep poverty on the other stand in stark contrast in cities like this one in underdeveloped nations.

school), food (a proportion of minimum daily requirements for human survival), water supply (the percentage of the population with access to clean water), and sanitation (the percentage of the population with access to sewers and other sanitation facilities). The basic-needs approach to development makes it clear that even nations like the United States would have difficulty being defined as fully developed.

Critics also have argued that modernization theory looks at individual nations as if they existed in a vacuum, focusing only on internal dynamics and value systems as causal factors for development. This ignores international power dynamics and global historical processes. Each nation has occupied a particular structural position and played a particular role in the development of the world-system. As we discussed in Chapter 3, a world-system is an international structure pp. 47–49 organizing the production, distribution, and consumption of goods and services. In that arrangement, peripheral nations are generally poor, providing primary goods for production and cheap, unskilled, exploitable labor for huge multinational corporations to manufacture goods and services that are then sold mostly to consumers in the wealthier, more powerful core nations. Peripheral nations are clustered in Africa, Latin America, and Asia, while the core nations are concentrated in western Europe and North America, Japan, and Australia. Nations therefore have different sets of experiences, histories, and social and economic structures, not by choice or value system but by virtue of their relationships with other nations, relationships marked by differential power and privilege (Frank, 1967; Wallerstein, 1974; 1997). For example, by the late seventeenth century India's economy was more advanced than economies in Europe. India had a large, thriving manufacturing sector that produced many luxury commodities, including textiles such as silk and cotton. Yet by the end of the eighteenth century India's economy, particularly its manufacturing sector, had declined significantly because Great Britain destroyed India's textile industry by flooding India with cheaper British-made cotton in an effort to eliminate competition for its own textiles (Griffin, 1979). Therefore, India's status as an underdeveloped nation resulted not from its own "primitive" value system but, rather, from its inequitable trade relationship with a more powerful industrialized nation.

Poor or peripheral nations are thus not simply at a stage of development and modernization already experienced by industrialized nations, and industrialized nations did not at one time take the same path now traveled by peripheral nations. Rather, peripheral nations are **underdeveloped nations.** That is, their historically disadvantageous relationships with more powerful industrialized or core nations have imposed severe limitations on development opportunities. Industrialized countries today were never *underdeveloped:* They did not face exploitation by stronger economies and thus severe restrictions on their access to opportunities and resources for development (Frank, 1967). Such structured national inequalities continue to deepen as the world enters the new millennium because of centuries of entrenched world-system relations (Chase-Dunn, 1998; Chase-Dunn and Hall, 1997).

Dependency and Development

We may understand the historical dynamic of underdevelopment by examining three different types of relationships (often referred to as forms of dependency) between nations: trade dependency, dependent development, and debt dependency.

🌐 Trade Dependency

In his historical analysis of the world-system, Wallerstein (1980) traced the outcomes of trade-dependency relationships. **Trade dependency,** which dominated the world-system between the fifteenth and nineteenth centuries, is characterized by limited numbers of trade partners for peripheral nations. Typically, a peripheral nation would be colonized by a core nation and focus its productive activities on a limited number of commodities, usually mineral and agricultural products. This was the case, for example, in the sixteenth and seventeenth centuries, when England economically colonized Ireland and took its wool to produce textiles. Peripheral nations sent the raw materials to the core colonizers and imported more expensive finished consumer goods from these same colonizers. Initially this arrangement may have been useful to the peripheral nation, because it was able to concentrate limited economic resources on a few activities, rather than trying to produce everything it needed. The peripheral nation also had a guaranteed market for its primary commodities.

In the long run, however, this arrangement hurt the development of peripheral nations (Delacroix and Ragin, 1981). Since its economic activity was concentrated on the production of a limited number of basic goods, the peripheral nation developed a distorted economy rather than a diversified one. Its economy could not absorb economic shocks from trade disruptions, extreme weather patterns, and changes in consumer demands in the core. For example, if a peripheral nation focused on sugar crops and coal, it was not able to withstand a decrease in sugar consumption in the core, destruction of the sugar crop from a season of floods, or shifts in the core from the use of coal to other energy sources. Loss of the market for its goods would seriously damage the entire economy of the peripheral nation. In a nation with a diversified economy, shocks to one industry can usually be offset by the health of other industries. Therefore, a nondiversified economy produces a structural blockage to development in the periphery.

Trade dependency creates other economic troubles. Primary commodities are cheaper than finished consumer goods. Trading relatively cheaper primary commodities for more expensive finished goods creates an imbalance of trade for the peripheral nation, because it often pays for the finished goods with the relatively low earnings generated by its exports. Throughout the world-system there has been a drain of money and resources away from the periphery to the core, which has seriously harmed the peripheral nations' ability to support their own development. The one notable exception to this trend appears to be the oil-producing nations. But these nations have operated together for many years in a cartel (the Organization of Petroleum Exporting Countries, OPEC), so together they have greater control over the supply and price of a basic commodity everyone needs for production. They also trade with many global partners rather than with a few. They therefore do not suffer the restrictions imposed by trade-partner concentration.

Finally, researchers have found that trade dependency deepened income inequalities between urban and rural areas, between elites and masses, and between men and women within peripheral nations (Bornschier and Chase-Dunn, 1985; Scott, 1995). Local elites in the periphery often cooperated with core elites to control trade arrangements, the benefits of which were rarely redistributed equally throughout the peripheral nation. Income inequalities also were aggravated because male elites from the core typically awarded the trade routes to men in the periphery (Boserup, 1970; Papanek, 1979). Moreover, males in the periphery were often charged with the more lucrative cash-crop farming, mining, and manufacturing for trade, while women were left with the responsibility of subsistence farming to feed the local population (Deere, Humphries, and deLeal, 1982). For example, women in South Africa and Lesotho increasingly worked the farmlands by themselves, while the men in their families were drafted to work the mines (Mueller, 1977). In Latin America, corporations sought out Peruvian and Colombian men to work in the factories, while women were recruited into agriculture (Deere and deLeal, 1981).

Unequal power relationships within the periphery allow elites to own and control most of the fertile land, a situation that continues today. They decide what will be grown on it and what market the crops will go to. Wealthy landowners typically grow cash crops and luxury items for export and elite consumption (such as sugar, coffee, and cocoa) rather than food needed for landless workers' and their families' survival. As a result, most workers are poor and many suffer chronic hunger and malnutrition, which are often misunderstood as a problem of overpopulation. Poverty and hunger in the periphery is, more accurately, a product of the lack of local control over the land by the masses. Thus inequitable trade relations between the core and periphery reach into the everyday lives of individuals in the periphery, particularly the peasants, the rural dwellers, and women. Their lives are impoverished not because they have not adopted the values of the West but because elites in their countries and in core nations maintain trade relationships that principally benefit themselves.

Dependent Development

By the 1930s, having successfully rebelled against colonial domination, peripheral nations such as Brazil, Mexico, and India attempted to resolve the problem of the resource drain and the unequal benefits accompanying trade dependency on the core. One strategy was to substitute locally produced goods for imported goods (**import substitution**) and to manufacture goods for sale abroad (**export processing**). This dual strategy is referred to as **dependent development,** because peripheral and semiperipheral nations' efforts at development are focused on dependency on private (usually corporate) actors from the core. These peripheral nations attempted to bring about economic development with focused and planned foreign investment in certain manufacturing sectors. This investment would enable them to employ local workers in a more diverse economy and to manufacture the consumer goods they previously imported, thereby reducing the cost of the goods. Peripheral nations encouraged corporations from the core to invest in them by promising a low-wage, exploitable labor force, inexpensive natural resources, and large markets.

The real effects of dependent development began to solidify by the 1960s. In their cross-national statistical analysis of 103 countries between 1965 and 1977, Bornschier and Chase-Dunn (1985) found that in the short run the flow of investment capital to build new plants and the generation of new jobs in the factories did stimulate the local economy. So, too, did the increase in construction activity on peripheral nations' roads, railways, airports, sewage and electrification systems, schools, and housing required by corporations.

In the long run, however, the presence and dominance of these corporations aggravated underdevelopment. First, most profits earned locally by the corporations flowed back to core nations, where the companies were headquartered. Furthermore, rather than bringing in outside money, the core-headquartered corporations often used local capital, depriving local entrepreneurs of an investment source (Muller, 1979; see also DeOliver, 1995). Bornschier and Chase-Dunn found that income inequality remained high in peripheral nations because any profits that did not drain back to the core were concentrated in the hands of the local elites.

Export-oriented factories more recently emerged in electronics, pharmaceuticals, and apparel in the Philippines, Mexico, Sri Lanka, Hong Kong, and other areas. Employers hire women rather than men because they are seen as a more docile, cheaper labor force. However, researchers have found that wages at such jobs are typically insufficient to support the women workers and their children. Women who receive wages lack benefits or protective legislation (Enloe, 1989; Ponniah and Reardon, 1999). In fact, the economic situation for many women in peripheral countries has deteriorated to the point where they must often work a daily "triple shift" combining employment in factories with bartering and street trade and the work of managing the household (Dickinson, 1997; Hossfeld, 1988; Ward, 1990). Researchers have found that both trade dependency and dependent development have increased

Multinational corporations commonly employ young women in poverty-stricken nations because they view them as a cheaper and more docile labor force that is less likely than male workers to challenge the sweatshop conditions and human rights violations in the factories. The women shown here toil in a microelectronics factory in the Philippines.

hunger and infant mortality rates throughout the periphery (Shen and Williamson, 2001; Ward, 1984). World-system trade relations favoring core corporations have helped impoverish women and children in peripheral nations and altered their life courses, their family relations, their work, their economic and social status, and their very survival.

How do these core–periphery trade relationships affect individuals who live in the more privileged and powerful core nations? The relative wealth of the core does not insulate residents there from the effects of these core–periphery economic arrangements (Massey, 2002). Workers in the core lose jobs, partly because core corporations relocate factories to the periphery and partly because inexpensive goods from peripheral nations flood core markets and compete with more expensive domestic goods. As core manufacturers go out of business, unemployment rises. Competition for low-wage jobs in the core may be heightened with the influx of jobless immigrants from peripheral nations whose quest for survival leads them to the core. Workers' lives in the core, then, are affected by world-system trade relations. Many people in the core suffer from the increased unemployment; some lose their homes because they cannot maintain mortgages, and some experience poverty, hunger, and even homelessness.

Indeed, the North American Free Trade Agreement (NAFTA) was supposed to reduce the negative consequences of the unequal global trade relations between the United States, Canada, and Mexico by stimulating job growth and prosperity for everyone in North America. Yet only five years after its passage in 1996, NAFTA had succeeded in destroying hundreds of thousands of production jobs in the United States, because corporations moved them just across the border to the subcontracting production zone in Mexico where wages were much lower (Cypher, 2001). Although NAFTA was supposed to stimulate wages in Mexico to rise to meet those paid to workers in the United States, workers' wages in both nations have instead dropped significantly (Cormier and Targ, 2001; Wallach and Sforza, 1999). This illustrates how the core is not immune to the effects of core–periphery trade relationships.

Ironically, the very conditions producing the deterioration of the lives of women, children, and the poor in the periphery may also increase the possibilities of their resistance to these unequal relationships. People working under similar oppressive and exploitive circumstances have begun forming networks of organizations within and between regions, which may help to pave the way to global workers' and feminist movements (Bacon, 2001; Compa, 2001; Moghadam, 1999). For example, women in Mexico's *maquilladoras* have increasingly mobilized and at times organized strikes against their employers. Given the close location of the production area to the United States, struggles for unionization are likely to draw attention and participation from U.S. organized workers who recognize the need for solidarity among all workers in North America and beyond.

Debt Dependency

Governments in peripheral countries have sought to boost development with international aid and loans from core nations and international development agencies such as the International Monetary Fund, the World Bank, and the Organization for Economic Cooperation and Development. Sociologists call reliance on loans for development **debt dependency.**

Unfortunately, in the 1970s and 1980s many underdeveloped nations found that declines in the value of the goods they produced and exported eroded their incomes and their ability to pay the high interest on their bank debts (Debt Crisis Network, 1985). Increasingly, peripheral nations were forced to take out new loans from private banks in the core nations simply to pay off their old debts. Loans that should have helped with development now only helped the profitability of private banks in the core.

Studies have shown that while loans initially stimulate development, over time they impair development (Glasberg and Ward, 1993; Sharma and Kumar, 2002). This is not surprising. Money that is borrowed at increasingly higher interest rates to pay off old debt drains more and more money from the peripheral nation. Because the vast majority of private banks providing the loans are headquartered in the core nations, the interest paid is not reinvested in the periphery. By the early 1980s, a chronic debt crisis existed throughout the peripheral world, a crisis that was particularly pronounced in Latin America and that continued into the new century. For example, by 1999 Argentina's debt rose to $140 billion, and 70 percent of its government budget had to be devoted to debt service payments (www.jubilee2000uk.org). That left precious little for the state to devote to any development projects or to social needs, prompting massive social unrest and political upheaval that continued into 2003 in response to rising hunger and malnutrition.

When peripheral nations reach the point where they are unable to continue to pay the interest on their debt, private banks refuse to provide new loans to pay off the old ones. At this point, the International Monetary Fund (IMF) steps into the breach. The IMF is an international organization of nations that is supposed to provide temporary help to poor nations trying to overcome economic obstructions to development. When these nations run the danger of bankruptcy or default of massive, crushing debt, the IMF's role is to push them to restructure their economies to focus on market-oriented policies, thus making investment once again attractive to private banks and core-based corporations. The IMF does this by imposing a standard austerity program on the ailing peripheral economy in return for the promise of economic assistance.

The austerity program typically includes (1) devaluation of the recipient nation's currency, making its money worth less; (2) a decrease in the amount of money the peripheral nation spends on social welfare, including subsidies for consumer goods, and the elimination of price controls; (3) an increase in control of labor unions, including the suppression of labor strikes for better working conditions and higher wages; (4) an increase in the amount of money the peripheral nation allocates to military spending (to help enforce the austerity program by suppressing labor strife, food riots, and insurrections and to secure the general political climate for core corporations' investments); (5) a decrease in or elimination of state control of industry, including the selling of state-owned industries to wealthy groups of individuals or corporations; (6) a sharp reduction of imports and increase in manufacturing for export; and (7) a dramatic increase in the amount of money the peripheral nation devotes to paying off its debt (Debt Crisis Network, 1985). The IMF's rationale is that this program will force peripheral nations to keep their expenditures down while they pay off their debts and their economies get healthy once again.

Unfortunately, the track record of the IMF's austerity program is not impressive. Several case studies have documented how the austerity program contributes to political unrest sparked by the meager availability and unaffordability of basic resources (Auvinen, 1996; Walton, 2001), damages prospects for development (Weeks, 2000), and helps drain even more capital from the periphery and semiperiphery to the core (see also Bienefeld, 2000; Sidel, 2000).

We have already noted the alarmingly high proportion of Argentina's government budget that is earmarked for repayment of its debts. The nation's newspapers are dominated almost daily with the heartbreaking stories of children dying from malnutrition, with no relief in sight. The IMF gave the national government a reprieve in 2003 by postponing a scheduled repayment of $141 million, but it merely postponed the problem. The national economy continued its free-fall because of the crushing debt that continued to mount almost daily. Indeed, the IMF's own austerity program contributed to the crisis by insisting as a condition for continued support, that Argentina increase its profits from exports in order to pay off its debts. Argentina is the fifth largest exporter of agricultural products in the world, but more than half its population lives below the poverty line, and the malnutrition and starvation rate among its children has skyrocketed. Food is plentiful in Argentina, but not for its residents. The need to repay its loans has come to dominate its budget as well as its policies, skewering social welfare in return (http://archives.here-now.org).

Peripheral nations' debts to private banks are thus being paid off at the expense of the poor, the workers, women, and children, the very groups that did not benefit from previous efforts to develop (Miller, 1997). The real winners in the economic restructuring imposed by the IMF are the wealthy elites in the periphery and corporations and private banks in the core.

This discussion of trade relationships, dependent development, and debt dependency shows that development is *not* simply a matter of poor nations following the steps to modernization taken by industrialized nations. Nor are peripheral nations simply in an earlier stage of development long surpassed by industrialized nations. Rather, the historical role of peripheral nations in the world-system has meant that they have had to follow a path the industrialized nations have not. Underdevelopment is best understood within a global context of private profit generation, rather than as a problem of improper societal value systems. Underdevelopment is a *political* process and a public issue involving economic and military power differentials. It is not simply a problem of national cultural dynamics or a matter of slow, inevitable progression toward development through the adoption of more "modern" values.

Debt dependency in peripheral nations has caused economic devastation as these countries attempt to pay off their crushing debts to private banking corporations by redeploying limited resources away from social services. Here, a starving young Argentine woman holds her child as she begs for money in front of a bank.

Creative strategies to address the problems of underdevelopment, crushing debt burdens, and global inequality have begun to link these problems with global environmental issues. **Debt-for-nature swaps** are arrangements in which debt-ridden governments agree to purchase or set aside land to conserve as state-owned parks and to protect their natural resources in exchange for a debt cancellation. The first such swap occurred in 1987 between Bolivia and Conservation International, a private U.S. organization that had purchased Bolivia's debt from Citicorp Bank. Conservation International agreed to pay off the debt in exchange for Bolivia's promise to protect almost 4 million acres around the Beni Biosphere Reserve. Nineteen other, similar debt-for-nature swaps have been arranged since 1987. By 2000, such arrangements canceled $1.5 billion in underdeveloped countries' debt while preserving valuable natural resources (www.napa.ufl/edu/2003news/debtnature.htm). And while most have entailed Latin America's rainforest areas, such as those in Ecuador, the Dominican Republic, and Costa Rica, swaps have also been arranged for land in the Philippines, Nigeria, Madagascar, Zambia, and Poland (Lugar and Biden, 1998).

These swaps underscore the interdependence of nations in the global economy as well as in the environment, and they highlight the possibilities for change in the politics of underdevelopment. Such arrangements must be approached with caution, however, to prevent the larger global power structures from using the desperately needed economic help as leverage to reassert corporate dominance, heighten existing gender and class inequality, and subvert popular struggles against elite advantage (DeBoeck, 2000; Hamilton, C., 1995; Turner and Craig, 1995). This is because the more advantaged participants in these arrangements can potentially insist on conditions beyond protection of the environment in exchange for debt relief.

Technological and Social Change

Many contemporary observers view technological innovation as the generator of social change. What is the role of technology in processes of social change? Where do technological developments come from? Why do some technologies develop and not others? Is technological development a neutral process, wherein "necessity becomes the parent of invention"? Who determines the meaning of necessity, and who decides what is necessary? Who benefits and who is hurt by technological development?

Energy Production

Among the more visible differences between core and peripheral countries' development is the greater availability of advanced technology in the core. Many people have been taught that the Industrial Revolution was a time marked by a sudden explosion of inventions that revolutionized production processes and everyone's lives, generally in a positive way. New technologies improved people's lives and made society more progressive. Those who argued against the increasing reliance on technology were often criticized as being old-fashioned or standing in the way of progress.

We learned that **inventions**—new practices and objects developed out of existing knowledge—"happened" because necessity dictated their development. For example, the steam engine was invented because people needed a large source of power to modernize industry. But who decides that a particular invention is needed? Who supports the development of particular inventions as solutions to problems? Why are some inventions developed, and others not (even though they may, in fact, be needed)?

For example, why is the technology for nuclear power generation and energy production based on the burning of fossil fuels so well developed, while the technology for solar energy remains relatively primitive and inefficient? The answer may lie in who benefits and who is hurt by society's continued dependence on certain kinds of energy production. Nuclear energy and fossil fuels are nonrenewable energy sources: They are based on resources that are mined or extracted from the ground (such as coal, petroleum, and uranium). Society cannot use the resources indefinitely without depleting them, and it cannot turn them into energy without the technological help provided by energy corporations and utility firms.

Solar energy, wind energy, and geothermal energy are based on renewable resources. Consumers can indefinitely derive energy from these resources as long as the sun shines fairly regularly, the winds blow, and Earth's surface continues to retain warmth. These resources still require some technological aid in delivering their energy to consumers in usable forms, but energy corporations and utilities need not be relied on to provide them. Once the technology is in place, the resources are self-sustaining in their delivery of energy.

Clearly, then, energy corporations and utilities have a stake in using their considerable economic power and resources to sponsor research to invent technologies that rely on nonrenewable sources of energy. These same companies purchased several patents for useful solar technologies from independent developers in the 1970s and then never used them (Reece, 1980). Now, major energy corporations like BP Amoco carefully control the development of solar technologies to ensure that even if renewable energy is produced, people will remain dependent on them (Berman and O'Connor, 1997). This is not an option readily available to nonelites, given the level of economic and power inequality between large corporations on the one hand and consumer and community groups on the other. Were consumers to have access to those technologies that rely on renewable sources of energy and that therefore challenge substantially the dominance of energy corporations and utilities, they might be independent of the energy corporations and the utilities after the initial construction of facilities. Large corporate interests benefit greatly from society's dependence on them as providers of energy; everyone loses a great deal from their ability to turn that reliance into expensive (for consumers) and profitable (for them) energy production.

Technological Change and the Labor Process

Framing the analysis of technological development and social change in terms of who benefits and who is hurt also points to the rise of the factory during the late 1800s and early 1900s as a major *social* change rather than as an inevitable, neutral result of technological progress. Prior to the eighteenth century, individuals manufactured many consumer goods in their homes, using manual labor, a system often referred to as **cottage industry.** They sewed clothing, cobbled shoes, built furniture, and created pottery using their hands and simple tools. This system allowed them to determine how long they worked on any given day, which days they worked, how much they produced, what they produced, and to some extent how much money they made. While capitalists provided them with the materials for making goods on order, the workers could determine how to maximize use of the materials, and they often kept the remnants to make goods for themselves or to sell to other buyers. Thus the cottage industry system gave workers control over the work process and some power over distribution of the profits of their labor. This changed when production shifted to factories. Why did this change occur if workers stood to lose so much?

The conventional view is that factories developed in response to the invention of the steam engine as a central source of power. The steam engine was too expensive and too large for individual cottage industries to use. It was simply cheaper, according to this view, for workers to gather together under one roof and share use of the new centralized source of power. This would seem to make sense, until one examines research on forces leading up to the development of both the factory and the steam engine.

Through his historical analysis of industry in the United States, Dan Clawson (1980) clearly establishes that there was a terrific struggle from the mid-eighteenth century to the late nineteenth century between workers in the cottage industries and capitalists wishing to exert greater control over the work process. Capitalists were dismayed by workers' retention of remnants of materials that the capitalists had paid for and by workers' sometimes erratic work hours. And they were displeased that workers could determine what the capitalists would pay for production. To gain greater control over the labor process, capitalists built factories and tried unsuccessfully to coerce workers into them. Workers were well aware that they stood to lose much by giving the power of managing the work process to the capitalists. Capitalists countered by using the coerced, unpaid labor of prisoners, slaves, and orphans in the

By telecommuting to work from home, employees can save money on gas, lunch, and perhaps child care, as well wear whatever they want. On the other hand, such work is a form of technological cottage industry, where workers labor in isolation, deprived of the social and political contacts with other workers that might foster collective action.

factories. The use of such an inexpensive labor force began to erode the cottage industries' ability to compete with the factories' economy of scale, volume of production, and lower priced commodities. Poverty and lack of alternatives eventually forced the cottage industry workers to join the workers already in the factories.

All this took place *before* the introduction of the steam engine. Prior to the late eighteenth and early nineteenth centuries the factory merely gathered the workers together under one roof, but the technological aspects of the production process remained essentially the same as before the development of the factory. It was *after* the factory took hold that the steam engine was introduced and became a technological justification of the factory. What workers lost in control of the work process capitalists gained. The capitalists could determine the commodities produced, the way they were produced, the hours and days worked, and the wages earned. The introduction of the steam engine, then, was stimulated by the conflict between workers and capitalists over control of the production process and the resultant profits. Use of steam power firmly tilted that struggle in favor of the capitalists, rationalizing the social change in production that had already taken place.

Currently, the rise of personal computers has ironically recreated the isolation of the cottage industry as an increasing number of workers (especially women) telecommute to work for corporate employers from home, but without the element of worker power and control over the work process previously held by workers before the Industrial Revolution. That isolation decreases the likelihood that telecommuting workers will be able to communicate and develop informal peer groups, develop a sense of common bond, and organize against management.

Technology and Reproductive Issues

While most analyses of social change brought about by technology focus on its effects on work and production, the area of human reproduction has also seen profound technologically generated changes (Baker, 2000; Franklin and Ragone, 1998; Lay et al, 2000). Technological developments such as fetal monitors can measure the heart rate of the fetus and thus determine whether the fetus is in distress during labor. Such devices are quite useful in increasing the chances of a healthy, live birth. But critics note that they have also given more control over the birthing process to doctors and technicians. One alarming indicator of this shift is the number of cesarian births over the last decade. After slowly declining in the early 1990s, the rate of cesarian section births is once again on the rise, so that more than one-fifth of all births in the United States are now delivered through surgery (Neergaard, 2000:A1; Rowland, 1992). The American College of Obstetrics and Gynecology noted that doctors' habits rather than medical necessity were a major factor producing the increase, an assessment that suggests the power of doctors to use technology and impose their interests over and above those of the mother and the child in the labor and birth process.

Some would argue that the increase in cesarian section deliveries represents greater knowledge about health and safety for both the mother and the baby. However, physicians' increasing reliance on fetal monitors and other technologies to justify interventions like cesarian deliveries may be based on more compelling incentives. Because cesarian sections are surgery, they are expensive, and the surgeon can count on being paid by the mother's health insurance company. The combination of insurance coverage and the profit motive in organized medicine has prompted technological developments that invest greater control of the birth process with doctors and less with women.

Technology has also altered the process of conception and pregnancy, thereby throwing society into a storm of controversy over several ethical issues. Some technologies increase the chances for sex preselection in conception and may reinforce cultural patriarchal notions of males as a "preferred" sex (Stearney, 1996). Amniocentesis can identify genetic defects in a fetus, revealing conditions such as Down syndrome, Tay-Sachs disease, sickle cell anemia, and a host of other genetic abnormalities. It can also identify the sex of the fetus. Critics have long argued that such information could lead to the abortion of a fetus that happens to be the "wrong" sex or have unwanted disabilities. And, since many societies value males more strongly than females, there is an increased danger of abortion of female fetuses simply because they are females (Gill, 1998; www.nytimes.com/2002).

The abortion of "defective" fetuses, or those with potential disabilities, also raises an issue: When is a defect life-threatening, and when is it simply a departure from social constructions of the "perfect" human being? While the technology of procedures like amniocentesis may be useful in early identification of fetal genetic disorders and infections in order to promote treatment, that same technology holds great potential for abuse. It allows people to identify and destroy fetuses that fail to conform to the culturally dominant image of perfection—a human being with no genetic, physical, or mental "defects." Technological innovations in reproduction (including the human genome project that is mapping human genetic material) have also opened the door to genetic engineering (Ho, 2000; Mehlman and Botkin, 1998). This may help doctors to correct gene mutations that produce life-threatening conditions and diseases, but it also introduces the chilling potential of eradicating populations who are determined by members of the dominant groups to be undesirable on the basis of a wide variety of criteria (Roberts, 1997).

In vitro fertilization has increased the chances of becoming parents for infertile couples or those who have had difficulty establishing a pregnancy. This technology is not readily available to those who can't afford the high costs of such care (Merchant, 1996). The class inequality issues this raises are also apparent in that reproductive technology has made it possible for a couple to hire a third party to carry the fertilized egg, give birth to the child, and then turn it over to them for parenting. Observers refer to the person who carries the fertilized egg and gives birth as the

surrogate mother (although there are some controversies concerning the very definition and identification of who is the mother, who is the surrogate, who is biological, etc.).

The technology of in vitro fertilization raises several thorny issues concerning class dynamics. Poor women could be contracted to carry and deliver babies for middle-class and wealthy couples. Poverty could create a situation in which poor women "rent out" their wombs, much like poor and working-class families during the early twentieth century rented out rooms in their homes to lodgers to help pay the rent. Such a situation has the potential for seriously exploiting the surrogate.

Surrogacy contracts also enable brokers to control the lives of the surrogates, both economically and socially. The contract typically specifies behaviors that are strictly forbidden (such as drinking, smoking, drug use, and dieting) and those that are required (eating healthy foods, taking vitamins, getting plenty of sleep, and avoiding risky activities, which may include certain kinds of jobs). Like the workers in the factories Dan Clawson studied, surrogate mothers become workers who can be carefully controlled by those who stand to profit a great deal from that control.

Clearly, the main beneficiaries of surrogacy are the lawyers who broker such contracts. Surrogacy brokering is a highly lucrative business, aided by the development of reproductive technologies that raise ethical and social questions. Meanwhile, poor and working-class women and people of color can be hurt in these arrangements. Consider that they are paid for a full nine months of their lives (and *not* merely for eight hours per day, five days per week) and factor out what they are getting paid per hour; even at a wage of $10,000, they are poorly paid.

Moreover, surrogates' bodies undergo the physical risks of any pregnancy, and they are often emotionally battered by the process of giving birth and then having the baby taken away in fulfillment of a contract. Although it may be relatively easy to agree to be a surrogate in exchange for more money than many of these women can earn in a year, it is not always so easy to adhere to the contract.

Surrogacy also raise gender issues. For example, the contracts are commonly developed between the adoptive father and the surrogate mother. What is the role, then, of the adoptive mother? Which of these women is the "mother"? Which one has the right to participate in determining the fate of the child? What is the relationship between the two women, and between each of them and the adoptive father? This uncertainty of the women's respective roles gives the adoptive father greater power in the contractual arrangement.

This discussion illustrates the tremendous changes in human reproduction that have been brought about by technological developments. But it also highlights the fact that cultural change has lagged behind the technology. Although science enables these changes to occur, social and cultural processes have not yet determined whether they *should* occur or how to deal with their effects if they do. This implies that social change is not just a process made possible by technological inventions and innovations; it is also a political process.

Technological Innovation, Power, and Inequality

Technology is not a neutral force. It is driven by many factors, including profit motives and vested interests in control over such processes as work and reproduction.

Technology is not necessarily the natural response to necessity; it is a social and political response to necessity as defined by those who stand to benefit most from its development and who have the power and the economic resources to support such development.

Technological developments frequently affect individuals' daily lives, enhancing some aspects and restricting others. For example, factory technology meant that workers would no longer be able to control their work or their earnings. Their life choices became more restricted as they lost control of the work process. Similarly, while reproductive technology may enhance the chances that infertile couples can have babies, it also increases the medical establishment's control over reproduction and can aggravate class, gender, and racial inequalities.

Ironically, technological developments that enhance the power of the already privileged may also introduce unintended benefits to the *disadvantaged*. For example, while the rise of the factory concentrated power in the hands of capitalists, it also made the production process more efficient than it had been under the cottage industry system. More goods were available to more people at lower costs than previously was the case. The rise of the factory also stimulated the rise of the labor movement, which enabled workers to collectively resist capitalists' greater control and exploitation. Since workers were now engaged in the work process under one roof, they could more easily communicate and develop common viewpoints, common strategies for resistance, and more strength in their combined organized efforts to challenge capitalists' power.

Social Movements

Our discussion of technology and social change so far implies a top-down view of social change: Elites define issues and needs, direct resources to address those needs, and produce changes consistent with their interests (Figure 10.1). But are people little more than captives of dominant groups' seemingly overwhelming power to guide and govern technological and social changes, or can they affect the direction and the content of social change? Since social change is a human, social construction, humans do have the ability to affect how societies change. Social change does not just happen like the weather. What people do alters the content of social structures and sometimes alters the very structures

FIGURE 10.1 **Necessity Is the Parent of Invention? Top-Down Social Constructions of Social Change** Inventions don't just happen. In society, elites commonly decide what is needed based on their own interests; they then use their power and control over important resources to determine which inventions and technologies will be developed. This is a "top-down" approach to change.

FIGURE 10.2 **Social Change from the Bottom Up: Social Change as a Political Process** Social change may come not only from elites who dominate the direction of technological developments but also from subordinates. In systems of inequality, those who are among the oppressed may actually influence social changes by combining their efforts in social movements that apply pressure to elites and institutions to produce changes that address the needs and interests of the oppressed. This is social change from the bottom up.

themselves. How do people affect social change, if so much is made to happen by and for the already privileged? Must individuals always adjust to the changes dictated by people who are powerful and advantaged, or are there options to counter those forces? Can change be stimulated from the bottom up?

The key to these questions is found in collective, organized action. Individuals are fairly powerless by themselves to challenge the social changes introduced by the powerful and advantaged members of society. One voice alone may not be heeded or even heard. However, organized, collective efforts by many similar-minded individuals have historically posed formidable challenges to the powerful, even if they have had variable success (Figure 10.2). For example, when factory owners introduced machinery into the stocking industry in Great Britain in the nineteenth century, workers collectively rebelled by smashing the machinery they saw as displacing their labor (Rude, 1964, 1985). Although the rebellion only temporarily postponed the introduction of the new machinery, it represented collective action taken to resist the use of technology that benefited factory owners but hurt workers.

We call persistent, organized, collective efforts to resist existing structures and cultures, or to introduce changes in them, **social movements.** They often permit the less powerful members of society to effectively challenge and resist the more powerful members. Social movements thus may offer organizational opportunities for producing change from the bottom up within societies. Social movements also sometimes allow the relatively powerless to affect intersocietal relations. For example, the U.S. antiwar movement during the 1960s and early 1970s increased the pressure on the United States to redefine and end its military role in Vietnam. The impact of the antiwar movement in that instance had lasting effects on U.S. military relations: the War Powers Act restricted the ability of future presidents to militarily intrude into other countries' internal affairs. Social movements, then, can be the vehicle through which individuals working together may be able to address issues that otherwise seem too big, too daunting, and overwhelming to them.

Types of Social Movements

Social movements differ in the types of change they pursue and the amounts of change they aim for (Aberle, 1966) (see Figure 10.3). For example, **redemptive**

Type of change sought:	**Amount of change sought:**	
	Total	Limited but Specific
Individuals	Redemptive	Alterative
Society	Transformative	Reformative

FIGURE 10.3 **Types of Social Movements**   Differences in social movements may be based on dimensions such as degree of change and type of change they seek to achieve. This chart diagrams four different types of social movements along these two dimensions.   (Source: David Aberle, *The Peyote Religion among the Navajo* (Chicago: Aldine, 1966).)

movements attempt to change individuals, not society. Many redemptive movements are religious movements seeking to convert individuals. Evangelists who preach on television and Jehovah's Witnesses who knock on doors to talk to people are engaged in similar attempts to convince individuals to convert from sinful pursuits to Christianity.

Alterative movements also seek changes among individuals. But whereas redemptive movements seek total changes, alterative movements focus on limited, specifically defined changes. Students against Drunk Driving (SADD), an organization of high school and college students, for example, seeks to convince other students to resist the peer pressures to drive under the influence of alcohol or other drugs. SADD has chapters throughout the country, but it does not try to change society. Rather, it focuses on trying to alter the behaviors of individual students.

On the other hand, Mothers against Drunk Driving (MADD) is a **reformative movement,** in that it aims to change society. This nationally organized group actively lobbies for strict national and state legislation criminalizing driving under the influence of alcohol. What MADD seeks is a limited, specifically defined change in societal norms, not just in the behavior of individuals.

Similarly, the AARP (formerly the American Association of Retired Persons) is a reformative movement comprising more than 32 million members over the age of 50. The AARP lobbies legislators for better legal protection of the rights of the elderly, and it informs the rest of society about those rights through education, advocacy, and service in the community. The AARP also engages in voter registration drives and voter education campaigns, and it presses for attention to health care and quality-of-life issues that concern older persons. The AARP's goal is not to radically change the structure of society but to reform institutional politics and change societal norms toward treatment of the elderly.

The goal of **transformative movements,** like that of reformative movements, is change in society. But while reformative movements work toward limited, specific changes, transformative movements seek total change in society. Revolutions are good examples of transformative movements. Their goal is radical and total change of the social structure, resulting in a society that is completely different from the existing form. The Cuban revolution of the 1950s, for example, worked to overthrow the dominating capitalist social structure that produced gross inequalities of wealth, power, and privilege and to replace it with a socialist structure that favored collective production for the common good rather than for individual wealth.

This typology is useful for differentiating many social movements. It is, however, limited because not all social movements seek change; some work to preserve the status quo. Indeed, social movements that achieve once-sought changes may shift to protect these changes from efforts to repeal them. For example, antiwar activists who helped eliminate the military draft system in the United States in the 1970s are now faced with the prospect of opposing efforts to change from an all-volunteer military to a new military draft system in support of antiterrorism programs. This new role as protector of the status quo makes it difficult to classify the movement within the typology.

Some movements may begin as one type of movement in the typology but may morph into another type over time, as underscored by this new role of the antiwar movement. For another example, Mothers against Drunk Driving began as an alterative movement focused on discouraging individuals from operating a motor vehicle after consuming alcohol; it has recently become more of a reform movement as it shifted toward efforts to influence federal and state policies criminalizing drunk driving.

Within large social movements several types of movements (based on their goals and strategies) may coexist. For example, the feminist movement actually consists of several different movements (Ferree, Lorber, and Hess, 1999). The liberal feminist movement, articulated by organizations such as the National Organization for Women (NOW), is a reformative movement. Its goal is to integrate women better into existing political, social, and economic institutions, thereby increasing the equal participation of women in society. Such organizations do not question or challenge the existing social structures; they challenge the discrimination against women that occurs within those structures. Their efforts, therefore, focus on legislative lobbying, anti-discrimination suits in the courts, and public education and consciousness raising.

In contrast, the radical feminist movement defines men as the enemy and seeks to change existing institutions viewed as patriarchal. Marriage, in particular, is seen as an oppressive institution for women; radical feminists seek to redefine the structure of family to eliminate the traditional restrictive roles that inhibit women's development as independent individuals. For example, families of women living together to support one another and perhaps their children do not include men and are not based on male-dictated and gendered divisions of labor. Radical feminists, then, support one another's individual resistance to oppressive institutions. While the ultimate goal is to have so many women resist that the existing institutions change, radical feminists work primarily to convince individual women to alter the social structures of their personal living arrangements. In this sense radical feminists may be understood as involved in a form of redemptive movement.

Marxist or socialist feminists, however, see capitalism as the enemy rather than men per se. In their view, both men and women are victims of a system that exploits people for the benefit of the capitalist class. The conflict between men and women is viewed as a false wedge driven within the working class by the capitalist class to divide and conquer it and reduce the possibility that male and female workers will organize to challenge capitalism. Socialist feminists, then, do not seek greater integration of women into the political, social, and economic institutions of society, as do liberal feminists, since that would only legitimate the existing system of oppression. Similarly, they do not define men as the enemy, as do radical feminists, because that would divert energy and attention away from the real problem of capitalism as an oppressive social structure. The goal of socialist feminists is to have women and men recognize sexism as a vehicle of capitalist oppression and join forces in working toward a socialist society. The elimination of sexism requires the elimination of capitalism first. Socialist feminists, then, represent a transformative movement; they seek total change of society.

When a social movement consists of several types of movements, the diversity usually stems from disagreements among the participants on the definition of the source of a problem or on the strategy most appropriate for change. That much said, however, the question still remains of how social movements develop in the first place. Why do social movements occur, and how do grievances of individuals translate into efforts to bring about social change? The fact that societies are interdependent leads to another question: Do social movements in one society have implications for individuals elsewhere?

Explaining Social Movements

🌐 Absolute versus Relative Deprivation

Karl Marx and Friedrich Engels (1848/1967) argued that the working class and the capitalist class would eventually become so polarized that the workers would suffer immiseration, or **absolute deprivation:** They would be unable to purchase the simplest means of survival. According to this analysis, as the capitalists became richer because of their control over the labor force and work process, the workers would be forced to work longer hours at low wages just to support their own subsistence. When the workers became so poor that they were immiserated, Marx and Engels argued, they would collectively revolt to overthrow the social structure that caused their oppression. That is, revolutions, as organized resistance movements designed to challenge and replace existing social structures with new ones, would be provoked when the workers became intolerably impoverished.

The immiseration thesis is often used to frame popular media analyses of the civil rights movement in the United States. According to these analyses, the civil rights movement was touched off by a single act of resistance: When Rosa Parks finally could not take the intolerable conditions of racist oppression, she refused to give her seat on a Birmingham, Alabama, bus to a white man. The use of immiseration, or absolute deprivation, theory in this instance points to one of the limitations of that thesis: Not all social movements are prompted by economic deprivation. Rosa Parks may have suffered from extreme or even absolute deprivation of civil rights, but the fact that she was employed suggests that she had at least a minimum, if not middle-class, ability to purchase what she needed for basic survival.

Some sociologists criticize the use of this thesis on still other grounds. James Davies (1962, 1969, 1974), for example, argued that revolutions historically did not occur when conditions reached an intolerable or absolute low. Rather, he noted, such organized rebellions occurred in response to **relative deprivation.** Davies argued that people's understanding of deprivation is *relative* to conditions around them, conditions they expect, or conditions that previously existed but no longer do. People revolted when a gap opened, over time, between the conditions that they expected and the conditions that actually existed (see also Klandermans, Roefs, and Olivier, 2001). Davies's relative deprivation thesis can apply to economic as well as social and political conditions.

For example, people's expectations may gradually rise, but real conditions may gradually improve too, even if they don't quite reach expectations. In Davies's view, revolutions will not occur until real conditions begin to deteriorate somewhat relative to expectations. In this instance, real conditions do not need to deteriorate to the point of immiseration, as Marx and Engels believed; it is sufficient, according to Davies, that real conditions simply get slightly worse while expectations continue to slightly rise.

In a similar case of relative deprivation, expectations for improved conditions may rise sharply, and real conditions may also rise sharply but not quite enough to reach expectations. Revolutions will not occur until real conditions plateau while expectations continue to rise. In this instance, real conditions need not deteriorate at all; it is sufficient that real conditions stagnate while expectations continue to increase.

Finally, expectations for improved conditions may be on a sharp increase, and real conditions may be on an equally sharp incline of improvement. In this instance, revolutions will occur when expectations for improved conditions rise more sharply than real conditions. It is not necessary for real conditions to deteriorate or even stagnate; for revolutions to occur, it is sufficient, even in the face of vastly improved real conditions, that expectations dramatically increase relative to real conditions.

Resource Mobilization

Critics of both the absolute deprivation and the relative deprivation explanations argue that they imply a spontaneous combustion of social dissatisfaction. The theories presume that at a given time conditions will become absolutely intolerable, or the difference between expectations and real conditions will suddenly become intolerable, and a large group of people will revolt. This analysis ignores the question of resources. No matter how intolerable conditions become, people usually do not revolt unless they have access to resources to support their organized social movement activity. They need human resources to articulate their frustration and formulate a strategy for response; leadership to organize and mobilize others; tangible resources, such as financial backing, to spread the word, support endangered or jailed participants, and communicate widely with other potential supporters; and networks of other groups of people or existing organizations to support movement efforts (McCarthy and Wolfson, 1996). Thus revolutions and other social movements are unlikely to occur in the absence of supportive resources and the ability of people to mobilize and apply them when political opportunities arise to create disruptions (Meyer and Staggenborg, 1996), regardless of how pronounced the feelings of absolute or relative deprivation might be. Sociologists refer to this explanation of social movements as **resource mobilization theory.**

In his study of the civil rights movement, Aldon Morris (1984, 1999) found, on the basis of extensive interviews with activists and participants, that resource mobilization was the best explanation for growth and success of the movement. Morris concluded that African Americans everywhere did not suddenly and simultaneously get frustrated enough to rebel. He documented how leaders in several African American organizations mobilized resources and combined their organizational efforts to become a powerful collective force in challenging segregation and other forms of racial discrimination in the United States.

As we noted, popular media accounts of the civil rights movement often ascribe its beginnings to a single incident, Rosa Parks's seemingly spontaneous refusal to give her seat on the Birmingham bus to a white person. Morris documents that Parks was, in fact, an active member, and the first secretary, of the local National Association for the Advancement of Colored People. She had been arrested several times before that incident for the same action. Rosa Parks's famous act of rebellion was part of an organized, conscious resistance movement rather than an isolated, spontaneous reaction to racism. She herself insisted, "My resistance to being mistreated on the buses and anywhere else was just a regular thing with me and not just that day" (Morris, 1984:51).

Whereas many popular accounts personalized the civil rights movement in the charismatic leadership of Martin Luther King Jr., Morris demonstrated that the movement was much greater than one person. Reverend King was simply the most visible and stirring articulator of the issues, a person able to galvanize and mobilize great numbers of individuals. But the civil rights movement was actually the result of the collective efforts of the National Association for the Advancement of Colored People (NAACP), the Southern Christian Leadership Conference (SCLC), the Student Nonviolent Coordinating Committee (SNCC), and the Congress of Racial Equality (CORE), as well as African American churches, white religious organizations, labor unions, student organizations, and local small businesses. Their combined efforts mobilized vast resources in support of the movement. Instead of having to organize individuals in support of civil rights, the leadership was able to tap into existing organizations of people, communication networks, and monetary resources to quickly and effectively organize boycotts, marches, voter registration drives in hostile southern states, and acts of civil disobedience such as sit-ins at lunch counters.

Morris's analysis of the civil rights movement illustrates how social movements can use resource mobilization to empower people who are powerless, disadvantaged, and largely disenfranchised from the mainstream. Against overwhelming odds, the civil rights movement managed to reform a discriminatory social structure and alter rigidly racist cultural values that had denied African Americans basic civil rights.

Doug McAdam (1982, 1988), who also studied the civil rights movement, noted the role of the state as a factor in the rise and fall of social movements. For example, elimination of racist barriers to blacks' voting enhanced the likelihood of electing well-placed sympathetic elites such as John F. Kennedy and Lyndon B. Johnson. However, McAdam emphasized that federal support for the goals of the civil rights movement came only in response to insurgency and violent and nonviolent acts that subverted civil order. Similar findings on the role of the state in social movements, particularly in response to insurgent disruptions, can be seen in analyses of other movements, such as the labor movements in Brazil and South Africa (Seidman, 1993) and the antinuclear movements in the United States and Germany (Joppke, 1993; Meyer, 1993).

The civil rights movement has achieved only partial success in eliciting affirmative action, equal employment opportunity, and desegregation legislation. But even that much was unlikely to have occurred in the absence of the pressure applied by the organized, collective efforts of the movement (Lawson, 1990). And although the legislation represents only official policy changes and does not always alter actual practices, it is important to note that the movement has been less active in the past three decades. Indeed, a conservative white political backlash has opposed affirmative action and other policies that would challenge white racial privilege (Omi and Winant, 1986; Pincus, 2000; Staples, 1995). The movement may have to reemerge, mobilizing resources and galvanizing the politically, socially, and economically disenfranchised to continue the progress toward racial equality begun between 1950 and late 1960s.

In fact, the civil rights movement seems to have begun reawakening. For example, several organizations and groups, including the NAACP and the Rainbow Coalition, picketed the National Football League's 1994 Super Bowl game in Atlanta, Georgia, because the stadium unfurled the Georgia state flag at the game. The flag at the time included a replica of the Confederate flag, which many see as a strong historical symbol of racism. The state of Georgia was put under considerable pressure to change its flag before the 1996 Winter Olympics in Atlanta, under the scrutiny of the world. It wasn't until 2003 that the state capital unfurled the new state flag, without any replica of the Confederate flag. More recently, South Carolina agreed, after a long public boycott and intense public pressure, to remove the Confederate flag from atop the state house. It remains a focus of struggle, however, as the state continues to fly the flag on public common areas. Civil rights groups have also actively protested police brutality and racial profiling as well as racial bias in voting procedures in the 2000 presidential election. What is important here is that the increased willingness to articulate such concerns and to demand change indicates a renewed spirit in the civil rights movement and the potential for recapturing lost momentum.

If social movements require the mobilization of organizations and other resources, how do the poorest groups in society get their needs addressed? In their comparative study, *Poor People's Movements* (1977), Frances Fox Piven and Richard Cloward argued that only insurgency and mass rebellions like strikes and riots brought concessions from elites for poor people. Forming and dealing with organizations, they argued, sapped energies, diverted attention, co-opted the poor

The civil rights movement has reawakened in part in response to protests against the Confederate flag flying atop the South Carolina Statehouse. Here, a demonstrator is removed by a state trooper after interrupting a rally of pro-Confederate flag supporters in 2000.

into nonthreatening actions, and promoted the false perception that the political system was fair and responsive to their needs. According to Piven and Cloward, insurgency emerges from the mass discontent and disruption of everyday life produced by poverty and deprivation. Thus their analysis of poor people's movements (such as the welfare rights, the unemployed workers', the industrial workers', and the civil rights movements) implicitly used a deprivation model to explain how the poor and powerless wrested change from elites: The poor rebelled, rioted, and staged strikes in massive eruptions of insurgency sparked by discontent and deprivation.

Piven and Cloward rejected a resource mobilization explanation of poor people's movements. However, Jenkins and Perrow (1977), in their study of the migrant farmworkers' movement (1946–1972), demonstrated that resource mobilization was critical to the efforts of the United Farm Workers in the late 1960s and early 1970s to win the right to unionize and secure decent working conditions. The lack of resources was a key factor in the failure of the earlier National Farm Labor Union in the late 1940s and mid-1950s. Both organizations of migrant farmworkers had outside leadership, derived initial organizational sponsorship from outside their communities, and used insurgency tactics like strikes and boycotts. But widespread *sustained* support from a coalition of liberal organizations neutralized elite resistance to the farmworkers' insurgency in the late 1970s and led to the right to unionize for migrant farmworkers. Jenkins and Perrow concluded that discontent was not enough to ignite the insurgency and the successful challenges of the migrant farm-workers' movement. Persistent organizational support from outside groups that had access to resources and devoted them to a group that had little was the critical difference between success and failure.

Resource mobilization, organization, and political opportunity appear to be critical as well to the increasing activism of the welfare rights movement. For example, the Kensington Welfare Rights Union (KWRU) organized a variation of the civil rights freedom riders in their national bus campaign in 1998 to gather testimonials from those harmfully affected by welfare reform. The group presented thousands of these to the United Nations, demanding a human rights violation investigation. The KWRU remains highly visible and active. It has launched a Poor People's Economic Human Rights Campaign, participated in demonstrations at the Republican and Democratic national conventions in 2000, organized a Poor People's World Summit to End Poverty, and maintains a website on the Internet (www.kwru.org) to disseminate information (Baptist, Jenkins, and Dillon, 1999; Cress and Snow, 2000).

We can also see evidence of resource mobilization in the disability rights movement, which has been organized, vocal, and visible since the 1980s in the United States as well as elsewhere around the world (Cooper, 1999; Hayashi and Okuyhira, 2001; Neath and Schriner, 1998). "Disability" covers a wide range of conditions, including hearing and visual impairments, motor function limitations, mental disabilities, diseases such as AIDS and cancer, and physical appearances that depart from cultural definitions of "normality", such as obesity, harelips, dwarfism, and facial disfigurement (Stroman, 1982). Such a diversity of conditions could have easily led to a splintering of the disability rights movement into separate powerless organizations, each attempting to apply pressure for legislative reforms addressed to its own constituency. Instead, more than 80 different national disability organizations joined forces in the United States to form the Consortium for Citizens with Disabilities to press successfully for passage of the Americans with Disabilities Act of 1990. This act makes full and equal participation in U.S. society more accessible to people with disabilities. The consortium elicited the support of other organizations such as the American Federation of Labor and Congress of Industrial Organizations (AFL-CIO) and the American Civil Liberties Union (ACLU). Simple acts of discontent and insurgency would not have been enough to get results for people who are so marginalized. The mobilization of the vast resources of many organizations, both within the wide-ranging community of people with disabilities and outside it, was critical.

Students today are often stereotyped as apathetic and selfish, particularly when compared with the baby boom generation of politically active students of the 1960s and 1970s. But as the "Social Forces/People's Lives" reading shows, there is a great deal of evidence to suggest this stereotype is wrong. In the past decade alone, students have been key in mobilizing resources to affect globalization of the economy. In particular, the United Students against Sweatshops has had an impressive impact on corporate use of sweatshops in peripheral countries to produce licensed products like sweatshirts, t-shirts, and other apparel with universities' and colleges' names and logos. It has organized on campuses around the country, staging sit-ins and demonstrations at college administrative offices, holding petition drives, and organizing boycotts. Its efforts have succeeded in forcing schools to withdraw from lucrative licensing contracts with corporations like Nike until the corporations agree to eliminate production of their goods in sweatshop conditions and submit to monitoring of conditions by the Workers Rights Consortium, a watchdog group that is independent of industry influence (Featherstone, 2000). This success has been repeated in scores of colleges and universities around the country, including some of the biggest National Collegiate Athletic Association (NCAA) schools. The students against sweatshops movement has also accomplished something that was far more difficult to find in the movements of the 1960s and 1970s: coalitions between students and organized labor (Cooper, 1999). Student coalitions with labor as well as with faith communities were also apparent in the organized protests against the World Trade Organization in Seattle, Washington, and in Washington, D.C., in 1999 and 2000 (Nichols, 2000).

Similarly, students forged alliances with the workers who clean campus buildings in the Justice for Janitors movement. Students demonstrated and staged sit-ins at campus administrative offices at colleges and universities all around the country in 2001 to demand living wages and health benefits for janitors who had been paid below-poverty wages. A three-week standoff between students and administrators at Harvard University resulted in an agreement to raise wages and provide benefits to janitors there. Similar demonstrations and agreements have occurred at several other campuses, and many more are continuing the struggle (Bacon, 2000; Cooper, 1999; McKean, 2001).

Clearly, students are not all apathetic, but rather many comprise a highly active and important element in social movements affecting not just local, selfish concerns but global, world-system issues faced by far less privileged people around the world and at home. And that activism holds encouraging signs for further student participation in social movements: research suggests that when students participate in one social movement activity they tend to be more likely to influence the formation of new campus organizations devoted to activism (Van Dyke, 1998).

External Forces

Most explanations for social movements look at the internal dynamics of individual societies, but societies do not exist in a vacuum. Forces supportive of social movements or against them can come from outside a given society (Tilly, 1998). For example, we just noted the effect the student movement against sweatshops in the United States has begun to have on conditions of production around the world. An organized international boycott and disinvestment campaign against corporations doing business in and with the white minority apartheid government in South Africa helped advance the defeat of that racist structure. And as noted earlier in this chapter, debt crises have prompted the imposition of IMF-sponsored austerity programs in many underdeveloped countries. In their cross-national comparative analysis of countries with debt crises, John Walton and Charles Ragin (1990) found that the likelihood of political protest was enhanced by increased external pressures for countries to adopt the austerity programs. Such external pressures also increased the

Joe Hill Goes to Harvard

JANE MANNERS

Many observers who witnessed the visible activism of students in the turbulent 1960s and 1970s often lament the apathy and lack of interest about social issues among today's younger generation. This reading challenges that assumption, describing the current surge in student activism that has galvanized around issues of inequality in the political economy. Students are not just thinking globally; they are indeed also acting locally.

ON May 8 twenty-three jubilant, grubby Harvard students left the offices of university president Neil Rudenstine after a twenty-one-day sit-in, the longest in Harvard's history. The students had demanded that the university pay its workers what the City of Cambridge had determined was a living wage—now the minimum for all municipal employees—$10.25 an hour. A university committee had ruled against a similar proposal a year earlier, but this time, after the sit-in drew three weeks of coverage critical of the university in the local and national media, the administrators gave ground, agreeing to reopen serious discussion.

Several commentators pointed out the incongruity of privileged Ivy Leaguers taking up such a blue-collar cause, but what the coverage often missed was that the Harvard sit-in was part of a growing movement on U.S. campuses emerging from a burgeoning alliance between student activists and organized labor.

A significant factor in the Harvard students' victory was the support of local and national unions. The carpenters' local and the Boston office of the progressive, union-backed group Jobs With Justice organized a community march in support of the students. The dining-hall workers' union, itself in the middle of contract negotiations, listed amnesty for the student protesters among its demands and twice held rallies outside the president's office. In the last week of the sit-in, AFL-CIO leaders, including president John Sweeney, staged a 1,500-person

intensity of the protests. Walton and Ragin found that although deprivation and hardship of living conditions certainly contributed to people's grievances, these were not strongly related to the protests.

Feminist movements focused on improving the well-being of women in individual nations are increasingly becoming more global in their perspective and their efforts. Networks of women's rights organizations throughout the world, with the help of resources like the Internet, are helping to shape a more international feminist movement, applying pressure on governments and international agencies to secure women's political and human rights, access to education and health care, and access to jobs. They also work to raise consciousness among women locally about their rights (Ferree and Subramaniam, 2000).

The gay rights movement has similarly organized forces across national boundaries, linking many national gay rights organizations in North America, South America, Asia, Europe, Australia, and Africa in the International Gay Association (IGA).

rally at Harvard, and AFL-CIO lawyers helped shape the students' final agreement with the administration.

Across the country, according to Jobs With Justice, living-wage campaigns are now active on at least twenty-one college campuses, and those at Wesleyan and the University of Wisconsin/Madison have already claimed victories. Meanwhile, students elsewhere are working on related campus labor issues, like outsourcing, benefits and organizing nonunion workers—not to mention the catalyzing cause of sweatshops. The AFL-CIO's student outreach program, Union Summer, has played a key role in turning simmering concerns on campus about sweatshops, globalization, the decline in real wages and the growing gap between rich and poor into effective campaigns. Union Summer, which was part of Sweeney's platform when he was campaigning for the AFL-CIO presidency in 1995, gives 200 interns—mostly, but not exclusively, college students—a small stipend and a few days' training in labor history and organizing, and then sends them out for monthlong stints with labor campaigns around the country.

After a month talking with people who work twelve-hour swing shifts and support a family on $6.50 an hour, the students often feel that returning to sheltered college life is no longer an option. "It was a transformative experience for me," says Dan Hennefeld, a Harvard graduate who's now employed by the garment and textile workers union, UNITE, and who attended the first Union Summer in 1996, after his freshman year. "It made me want to be in the labor movement," he says. When Hennefeld got back to Harvard that fall, he helped start a group called the Progressive Student Labor Movement, which became the driving force behind the recent sit-in (three of the organizers were also Union Summer grads).

The nearly 2,000 graduates of Union Summer have played a major role in spreading awareness of labor issues on campus. In addition to those at Harvard, student labor leaders at Duke, Brown, Georgetown and the universities of Tennessee, Connecticut and Wisconsin are all Summer alums. To make room for an increasing number of applicants, the AFL-CIO is offering three specialized, ten-week internships this summer: Seminary Summer for future religious leaders (mostly seminarians, novices and rabbinical students), Law Student Union Summer and International Union Summer, now in its second year, which places a few college students in organizing campaigns in such countries as Egypt, Mexico and Sri Lanka. During their brief stints the interns are schooled in organizing techniques and tactics. "I'm blown away by how smart and focused the student leaders today are," says Paul Booth, currently assistant to the president of AFSCME [American Federation of State, County, and Municipal Employees] and one of the writers of the 1962 Port Huron Statement of the Students for a Democratic Society. And, he adds, they've taken to heart an essential principle of today's campus activism: organizing campaigns around the school itself. Students understand, Booth says, that "they ought to be getting the institutions they relate to to do things that are meaningful."

Source: Jane Manners, "Joe Hill Goes to Harvard," *The Nation*, July 2, 2001.

The IGA helps movement organizations join forces, share experiences and information, and support one another's national agenda for gay male and lesbian civil rights. The gay rights movement has also organized in solidarity with other groups' movements, including those of women, labor, and people of color, drawing on shared experiences of oppression and the shared desire for change. For example, in a cross-national analysis of gay rights movements, Barry Adam noted that the Mexican Gay Pride Day activities offered support to the people of El Salvador in their struggle for self-determination and, in return, the Farabundo Marti National Liberation Front in El Salvador gave its support to the international gay rights movement (1987:165). Similarly, the International Lesbian and Gay Association has gained status as a consulting organization with the Economic and Social Council to address human rights violations in member nations in the European Union (Sanders, 1996). Thus external resources may combine with internal resource mobilization to provoke and sustain social movements across national boundaries.

1. Social change is not simply a neutral, natural life force in societies. It is, rather, a political process that involves organized struggles between the powerful, advantaged segments of society, on the one hand, and the disadvantaged and disenfranchised segments, on the other. People with power and privilege are often in a better position to define the content and direction of change in a way that preserves and enhances their power and privilege.

2. Development is similarly a political process, marked by unequal historical relationships among nations in a world-system. Countries are not on a continuum from advanced to less developed, as if all countries mature through a single series of steps to modernization. Rather, some countries are *underdeveloped* because they have historically been thrust into a disadvantaged position by other countries that have dominated them through colonization or military intervention, or by other means exploited their resources and drained their economies.

3. Technological innovation as a force of social change is also the product of power inequalities: Dominant groups are in the best position to define technological needs according to their own interests. Technological innovations tend to enhance the power and control of dominant groups over the less powerful, whether the technology pertains to the workplace or to such personal affairs as human reproduction. However, despite the strong sense that power inequalities direct social change in order to reinforce and reproduce those inequalities, people are not entirely powerless to affect this process.

4. Social movements are the means through which the less powerful, the disadvantaged, and the disenfranchised can challenge and alter the status quo. And they may even be organized across national boundaries to produce larger, stronger movements with access to greater resources than otherwise possible. What, then, do processes of social change mean for individuals' daily lives?

5. New technologies are introduced almost every day. Many of them make individuals' existence easier or more comfortable, such as air conditioners, dishwashers, refrigerators, and cars. Yet these same technologies help to deplete nonrenewable resources, including fossil fuels, and pose waste disposal and even pollution problems.

6. Some technologies make work safer, such as robots that perform dangerous jobs. Those same technologies, however, may also cost workers their jobs as machines displace human labor. Educational technologies introduce the problem of unequal access to information, as personal computers, copy machines, and fax machines become increasingly central to the education process. Those of you who are unable to afford your own personal computers or word processors know that writing papers and other assignments is more difficult and time-consuming for you than for students who have this equipment.

7. Reproductive technologies are making it possible for many women to conceive and give birth who might otherwise not have had the chance. But the cost of such technologies means that the hope they offer for fertility is available only to

relatively affluent women. And these technologies are also contributing to a continuing battle over women's control of the birth process. Women today may have a greater chance than their mothers had to have a baby, but they will need to be highly assertive with their doctors and midwives to have the pregnancy and birth experience they want.

8. In addition to technological changes, global changes in trade and production also alter people's existence. World-system relationships that affect development in Latin America, Asia, and Africa also affect people in countries like the United States. When corporations shift production to poor countries to take advantage of inexpensive labor, consumers in the United States may be able to purchase clothing and electronics more cheaply than before. But they may also find that their jobs disappear as a result of that shift.

9. Once it becomes clear that social change is a political process rather than an inexorable neutral force, people become more empowered to participate in that process. Individuals have generally found it very difficult to combat oppressive forces, but organized groups of individuals have had greater success in resisting social arrangements and institutions they saw as oppressive. This means that you have the potential to participate in the process of social change, from the social organization of the classroom to the institutional arrangements of the economy and the state.

THINKING CRITICALLY

1. We often feel powerless as individuals against the institutions of society. Yet sometimes individuals do alter how they are affected by institutions. Consider the students in the "Social Forces/People's Lives" reading. How did students manage to instigate change? What resources did they marshal on behalf of the issues that concerned them? Did they, in fact, do this alone? Which theory of social movements best explains this reading?

2. Select a recent technological innovation and discuss how it might alter society. How might it make life easier or better? What might be some of the limitations or problems generated by this technology? Now consider: Who would benefit from this technology, and who would be hurt? Why? How might this technology alter your life?

3. The early 1990s saw the breakup of the Soviet Union into separate, independent countries. How has this dramatic social change in eastern Europe affected the United States? How has it affected your daily existence? What does this suggest about the sources of social change?

4. Select a social movement (such as the nuclear freeze, gay rights, disability rights, women's rights, labor, pro-choice, anti-abortion, or fundamentalist movement or some other movement of your own choosing). Examine the successes and setbacks of this movement. What factors might account for its successes? What factors might account for its setbacks? Who benefits and who is

hurt by the movement's successes? How? Which theory of social movements best explains this movement?

5. Compare your daily life with that of your parents or grandparents at your age (it might be useful and interesting to talk with them if possible and to talk to both males and females). How is your life different from theirs? Why? How is it similar? How might gender or class explain some of these differences and similarities? Which theory of social change or social movements might explain the differences or similarities?

KEY TERMS

absolute deprivation, *(317)*

alterative movements, *(315)*

antithesis, *(297)*

basic needs, *(299)*

capitalists, *(298)*

cottage industry, *(309)*

cyclical theory, *(295)*

debt dependency, *(305)*

debt-for-nature swaps, *(307)*

dependent development, *(303)*

dialectic, *(297)*

equilibrium theory, *(296)*

evolutionary theory, *(296)*

export processing, *(303)*

import substitution, *(303)*

inventions, *(308)*

latent social change, *(294)*

manifest social change, *(294)*

Marxist theory, *(297)*

modernization theory, *(298)*

proletariat, *(298)*

redemptive movements, *(314)*

reformative movements, *(315)*

relative deprivation, *(318)*

resource mobilization theory, *(319)*

social change, *(294)*

social Darwinism, *(296)*

social movements, *(314)*

social reforms, *(294)*

social revolutions, *(294)*

surrogate mother, *(312)*

synthesis, *(297)*

thesis, *(297)*

trade dependency, *(301)*

transformative movements, *(315)*

underdeveloped nations, *(301)*

Chapter Eleven

The State and Capital

Consider the effect the institutions of the state and the economy may have on you. Perhaps you or someone you know has been called to serve in the war in Iraq. Whose interests are served when someone like you goes to war? Or perhaps someone you know needs financial assistance in order to survive day to day. Where does such assistance come from, and who decides if it is available and how much individuals receive? Who decides who gets to make such decisions on your behalf? Do you get to participate in deciding who will make policy affecting your life? These kinds of questions suggest that two of the most powerful institutions affecting individuals' biographies are the state and the economy.

The term **state** refers to the organization of political positions and the structure of political relations in society. The state, then, as an institution, is different from government, which refers to the politicians who occupy positions within the state. As individual politicians come and go, the **government** may change specific policies or views, reflecting individuals' personal styles, perspectives, party affiliations, interests, and so forth. However, the structure of political relations—electoral processes, policy-making processes, relations between the government and corporations, labor, consumers, and others—remains intact regardless of the individuals who occupy positions within the institution of the state.

The **economy** comprises the structures, relationships, and activities that produce and distribute wealth in society. Both the state and the economy are quite influential in shaping individuals' opportunities and their places in the larger society. These institutions do not operate in isolation from each other but, rather, intersect in various ways to affect peoples' lives. In the United States as well as most Western industrialized nations, the economy is a capitalist one: The means of production (or *capital*) are privately owned, as are the profits these generate. But the process of production is largely performed by workers, who neither own the means of production nor the wealth and the profits their labor produces. Note that this arrangement of the economy is not universal; not every nation adopts this approach to production and distribution of wealth. Moreover, not all states respond to the economy in the same way. Some states claim to adopt a position in which the state maintains a "hands-off" approach to the economy; the United States, for example, attempts to let the marketplace rather than legislation control the economy

(continued)

and economic actors. Other states may take a much more activist role in participating in the economy, regulating and controlling the markets and economic actors. Such is the case in nations like China and Cuba.

The varying ways that economies may be arranged, and the ways the state may participate or not participate in these arrangements, suggests the need to explore several questions:

- What is the nature of the relationship between political and economic institutions within a capitalist society?
- Can a society in which economic ownership is concentrated in relatively few hands function democratically?
- Is the state a neutral arbiter among competing interests, legislating in the common good?
- What is the relationship between the military, the state, and private capital?
- In what ways do the needs of owners and controllers of capital clash with the fundamental needs of workers or of the poor, and with what results?

This chapter explores how sociologists use different perspectives to examine these questions. In particular, we focus on the corporate economy in this chapter; we emphasize the role of labor in the economy more specifically in Chapter 12. Thus here we look at voting patterns in the United States and at the way the institutions of the state and economy affect how well voters can influence their elected leaders in government. We also examine the relationship among workers, private corporations, and the state and consider how this relationship affects the functioning of government. In short, we discuss various ways in which the state and the economy intersect. Finally, we consider an example of how these relationships can affect people's daily existence by examining welfare reform of the 1990s: How has the relationship between the institutions of state and economy shaped social perceptions about poverty and the development of social policy that addresses this issue?

The Relationship of State and Economy

The discussion of the relationship between the state and the economy begins with an understanding that these institutions are not completely isolated from one another. The state must often legislate economic actors and relationships in order to avoid chaos and economic crises. So, for example, Congress may enact legislation to regulate wages, taxes, banking and stock market practices, and labor relations to prevent devastating economic depressions. These sorts of legislation are examples of how the state and economy intersect and overlap. That intersection often operates in ways that privilege one set of interests over others, creating systems of structured class inequality. Sociologists refer to the intersection of the institutions of state and economy as **political economy.**

There are three major forms of political economy: capitalism, socialism, and communism. **Capitalism** is a political economy characterized by an arrangement of production in which workers cooperate to produce wealth that is then privately owned by whoever hired the workers. Workers own their labor power and are paid a wage to use their labor to produce wealth; capitalists own or control the means of production, and therefore own the wealth that workers produce using these means. The state is structured on the assumption that individuals generally bear the responsibility to provide for their own basic needs, and that employers have the legitimate right to own the wealth produced by workers. Inequality becomes based in part on whether one is an owner of the means of production or an owner only of labor power. The system of structured class inequality based on ownership of the means of production often intersects, as well, with gender and race inequalities. Clearly, this is the political economy that dominates the United States and most if not all of the core countries of the world.

Compare this to the political economy of **socialism.** Here the production of goods and services relies on social cooperation between workers to create wealth and workers are paid a wage in exchange for their labor—as they are in a capitalist economy. But where the means of production under capitalism are privately owned, under socialism these are more likely to be owned or controlled by the state. The state thus becomes the owner and controller of the wealth produced, with the power to determine its distribution. Systems of structured inequality in this political economy may still be class-based, as they are under capitalism, but that inequality is more likely to be moderated by the state in its provision or subsidization of basic goods and services for all. In such a system, for example, the state often becomes a provider of health care, housing, food, and income support when employment is unavailable. This does not mean that class inequality is nonexistent or that it does not intersect with other systems of inequality, such as gender, religion, or ethnicity and race. But the stark gaps between wealth and poverty that are common under capitalism are less likely to be found under socialism because of the state's activist role in providing for basic needs. Cuba is a familiar example. Variations of the socialist political economy can be found in Sweden and Norway, often referred to as "social democracies" or "mixed economies" since they contain elements of both capitalism and socialism.

In the political economies of **communism,** workers must still cooperate to produce the goods and services needed, but the means of production are collectively owned by the workers themselves. In this case, since ownership of the means of production guarantees ownership of the wealth produced, the workers are in a position to determine its distribution. Clearly, the decision-making process of the distribution of wealth may invite the creation of structured systems of inequality, as criteria must be used to determine who gets what. Karl Marx envisioned a distribution formula whereby wealth would be distributed from each according to one's ability to produce for the group as a whole, and to each according to one's need regardless of ability to produce (although he was not specific about how to evaluate either ability or need). Israeli kibbutzim are small-scale examples of a communist political economy where wealth distribution is in part determined by time commitment to the collective: Those who have been living in the kibbutz longest receive the greatest benefits. Structured inequality in this instance becomes a function of longevity and loyalty to the collective. This does not mean that other systems of structured inequality do not matter; gender as well as race, ethnicity, and religion are still likely to intersect with length of time one has been a member of the kibbutz in determining distribution of wealth.

Kibbutzim in Israel essentially operate as communist societies. Work is performed collectively, and the benefits resulting from that work are shared collectively.

These political economy types are more like ideal types than actual, discrete systems. Most real world examples are hybrids of these types. The United States, for example, is often understood to be the prototypical example of the capitalist political economy, but the state still has at various times taken an activist role in subsidizing basic needs or in participating in the functioning of the economy. And there are many worker-owned production facilities (like Joseph Industries, Inc., a forklift parts manufacturer in Streetsboro, Ohio, that is entirely worker-owned) and worker cooperatives (like the Moosewood Inn, in Ithaca, New York) in the United States. Similarly, the former Soviet Union has often been identified as the prime example of the communist political economy, but the workers there did not own the means of production or control the wealth they produced. Indeed, the state owned the means of production and workers were paid wages in exchange for their labor, making the former Soviet Union's political economy more one of "state capitalism" than pure communism. The point here is that differences between political economies are more likely to be differences of degree than of actual type.

In this chapter we focus on the capitalist political economy in order to explore how this political economy may affect individuals' lives. Other political economic structures produce their own latent institutional consequences and systems of inequality. An understanding of how a capitalist political economy may affect people's lives will help shape similar questions regarding how other political economic structures may do so for people in other nations. What, then, is the relationship between the state and the economy in a capitalist political economy?

There are two basic views of the relationship between the state and the economy, particularly in a capitalist, democratic society: pluralism and power elite theory. One sees the state and economy as separate institutions whose relationship is minor at best, and the other sees the state and economy as fused in significant ways.

Pluralism

Some sociologists argue that the state and the economy are two entirely separate institutions. They generally presume that the economy is a neutral institution governed by its own "laws" of the market, such as supply and demand, and they focus their analyses of the state on how political structures affect people's lives and how individuals may affect the political process. The economy and the state are not seen as linked in any significant way. Sociologists call this theory of the state **pluralism.** There are two strands of pluralist thought: group pluralism and elite pluralism.

Group Pluralism

According to advocates of the theory of **group pluralism,** democratic society is composed of a wide variety of groups which develop around specific needs or interests (Truman, 1951). These **interest groups** compete to get their goals met, and none of them is omnipotent or more powerful than any other. Individuals engage in political activity through these groups to affect the workings of government. People may choose to belong to one or more of these interest groups, and many very likely belong to several. Each of these groups pressures the state in order to get its needs met. In doing so, the groups compete against one another, often making conflicting demands on the state. Examples of interest groups include the National Rifle Association, the American Medical Association, the National Association of Manufacturers, the American Banking Association, the Teamsters Union, the National Organization for Women, the National Association for the Advancement of Colored People, and the AARP (formerly called the American Association of Retired Persons).

In this view, the state acts as a neutral referee, weighing and balancing competing demands, evaluating the legitimacy of each, and ultimately making policy in the common good of society. In this way, the state ensures a balance of power between many groups, thereby lending stability to society. That stability is also ensured by several other characteristics of democratic political systems. For example, a balance of power may occur between the interest groups, because none of them is strong enough to win whatever it wants each time. This leads groups to form alliances with one another on a variety of issues. These alliances are likely to shift and change as focal issues change, and this prevents permanent alliances from becoming entrenched and too powerful. Groups also realize that each has a sort of veto power over the others. If any group did attempt to thwart the interests of the others, the others would form an alliance against the transgressor. This interaction among groups is said to ensure the common good of society as a whole. Moreover, since members of society are likely to belong to several interest groups, the overlapping memberships create pressures that dilute each group's powers. Interest groups must compromise with others to avoid losing members who may find the conflict between their various memberships too great.

Group pluralists further believe that society is balanced and stable because everyone agrees on the basic rules governing interest group competition. This means that when people have an interest or a goal they want the state to address, they approach the state through democratic procedures, including elections, petitions to legislators, and lawsuits filed in the courts. Adherence to these procedures ensures legislation in the common good.

Society is also stabilized by the existence of *potential* interest groups. When existing interest groups do not address the needs or interests of people, or when the state ignores people's interests, individuals may mobilize to form a new active interest group and enter into the democratic process of appealing to the state. The possibility of such a mobilization prevents existing groups from ignoring the interests of others.

Critics argue that group pluralists tend to treat all existing groups as if they had the same relative strength and power. But some groups have access to greater resources than others, some are larger in membership than others, and some represent more powerful constituencies. Moreover, some important interests have historically been weak and disregarded in the democratic process, such as those of children, the homeless, undocumented workers, people of color, and the poor. It is difficult to argue that all groups, both existing and potential, are equally powerful when some groups have consistently had great success in obtaining many of their goals while others have had little success.

Group pluralists would counter this criticism by arguing that the reason some groups seem more successful is that their interests and objectives are more consistent with the common good. However, the meaning of this term is unclear. Who defines the common good? Is it possible that what the state defines as the common good may hinder or eliminate the ability of some groups to have their objectives met? What are the social background characteristics of those who define the common good? Pluralists assume that the state is neutral and that individuals within that institution make decisions impartially. Their analysis assumes that governmental officials have no interest group ties of their own.

Critics of group pluralism also take issue with the notion of potential interest groups. How can the power of potential groups be gauged if they do not yet exist? How can the effectiveness of potential groups in altering or modifying the behavior of existing groups or elite politicians be analyzed? Existing interest groups and elected officials may, indeed, worry about challenges from ignored interests, but how much do they worry, and how much does that concern alter their pursuit of their own objectives?

Finally, critics often argue that group pluralists overemphasize groups and ignore the important role that elites play in society. It is difficult to ignore political elites in democracies, where they assert great influence over how individual voters cast ballots for individual candidates. How can we explain the role of these elites in a pluralist model of the relationship between the state and the economy? Are these elected political elites separate from economic elites?

Elite Pluralism

Where group pluralists emphasize the importance of competing interest *groups,* advocates of **elite pluralist theory** emphasize the swirl of competing political *elites* in the electoral process. Politicians, as political elites, compete for people's votes in the same way that consumer products compete for their dollars. Just as competing interest groups are balanced by the need for cooperation and alliances, competing candidates are balanced by the fact that various constituents ignored today may be needed tomorrow for coalitions and support. So politicians must legislate in the common good because their own political fate is in the hands of voters. If elected officials do not pay attention to certain interests, they run the danger of being voted out of office by angry constituents. If they ignore issues of concern to people who do not regularly participate in the electoral process, politicians still run the danger of being voted out of office when those individuals become politically active (Lipset, 1960; Pinderhughes, 1987).

For example, elected officials have consistently ignored or attacked the interests and needs of the gay community. In response, gays have become increasingly

Although pluralists argue that elites are held in check by the electoral market place, critics note that not all of the elites in power are elected. These auto workers are trying to stem the flow of jobs from the United States to Mexico stimulated by NAFTA. Although they may elect their political representatives, they do not elect the corporate leaders who determine whether they will continue to have jobs.

active politically. They have organized and mobilized their resources in the electoral process to replace unsympathetic elected officials with more supportive candidates. In the 1970s there were fewer than 5 openly gay elected officials in the United States; by 2002 there were 228 (www.victoryfund.com).

Critics of elite pluralism have argued that while this perspective presents a picture of how people might like to think the state and democracy work in the United States, it still does not explain the persistence of serious social problems such as racism, poverty, sexism, suppression of political dissent, and homelessness. If the system is balanced by the need for politicians to heed the interests of their constituents, why do so many people feel left out? Why do so few people vote? Pluralism does not adequately account for the many people who are not politically well represented or involved.

Furthermore, elite pluralists suggest that voting is the way in which people can hold elites whose decisions fundamentally affect their lives accountable. But how do they hold nonelected elites accountable? The decisions of economic elites—corporate chief executive officers, banking officials, and the like—affect people's livelihoods in the most basic ways, including whether someone will have a job or get a mortgage to buy a house. Since they are not elected, how can people hold them accountable for their decisions? And, more to the point, are political elites and economic elites separate groups of elites? Or are they one and the same?

Power Elite Theory

According to the pluralist model, power is diluted by the dynamics of countervailing interests and competing elites so that no one group is omnipotent. Power is dispersed across a wide array of interest groups and across a large number of political elites. On the other hand, C. Wright Mills (1957) suggested in his book *The Power Elite,* that power is concentrated in a select, or elite, group of individuals. Their advantaged position of power ensures that their interests will prevail over all others. Pluralism focuses on the electoral and interest group processes as they relate to policy making by the state. The assumption is that the state and the economy are separate institutions. In contrast, **power elite theory** examines some of the ways the institutions of the state and the economy intersect or are fused. Unlike pluralists, these theorists argue that the state cannot be neutral, because of the common interests and views of the **power elite** (Mills, 1957). The power elite are those people who fill the key leadership positions of three main institutions: the state, the corporate economy, and the military. The power elite is composed of relatively few members who hold common interests and share a similar worldview because they come from similar backgrounds of class, education, religion, social milieu, and so forth.

Mills argued that the members of the power elite tend to be unified by three related processes: class identity, co-optation, and the interchangeability of the institutional elites. **Class identity** results from the common life experiences of members of the elite, which give them a sense of being members of an exclusive group. Members of the power elite have usually attended the same few prestigious private prep schools and Ivy League colleges, hold common memberships in exclusive social clubs, live in affluent communities, and travel in cliques. Their children tend to marry one another, thereby sealing wealth and power between families (Domhoff, 2002). In this way they are unlikely to confront views held by members of other classes that challenge those they share. They are unified in their beliefs about what is best for society and how the world works, because these beliefs are constantly reaffirmed by their class peers.

That shared arena of interaction extends into the boardroom, where these same elites are likely to sit on several corporate boards of directors together. Overlapping memberships on corporate boards not only provide a common point of view among corporations, but also reinforces elites' shared interests and adoption of a normative system shaped by corporate ideals and goals.

Co-optation involves the socialization of prospective and new members of the elite so that they come to share the worldview of the power elite. That is, individuals who aspire to elite positions must be willing to adopt the prevailing worldview and ideology held by the existing elite, who select new members into their circle of privilege. Only those who share that ideology will be selected. Once selected, new members of the elite become surrounded by that ideology, and they further internalize it.

Finally, the power elite are unified by their **interchangeability** across three major institutions: the state, the corporate economy, and the military. Changing from a position of power in one institution to another is not uncommon among those at the pinnacle of power. This mingling of leadership blurs any sharp distinctions in experience, perspective, ideology, or worldview such leaders may have. For example, Alexander Haig Jr. was a president of United Technologies (a major defense contractor), a former four-star general in the U.S. Army, and secretary of state under Ronald Reagan (1981–1982). George Shultz, president of the Bechtel Corporation (another major defense contractor), was Reagan's secretary of state (1982–1989) as well as a previous secretary of the treasury and secretary of labor (Dye, 1990:91).

More recently, President George W. Bush was an executive with Harkin Energy, an oil corporation. Vice President Richard Cheney was the chief executive officer of Halliburton Oil Company from 1995 until 2000 and the secretary of defense from 1989 until 1993. Donald Rumsfeld, the secretary of defense under President George W. Bush, served as the chief executive officer of G.D. Searles, a major pharmaceutical corporation. He also served as chairman of the RAND Corporation, a major military think tank. And Secretary of State Colin Powell was an army officer, National Security Advisor from 1987 to 1989, and served as director in AOL Time Warner as well as Gulfstream Aerospace and General Dynamics, both major Department of Defense contractors (Dye, 2002). (Table 11.1 presents additional examples of former cabinet members and their institutional ties.)

Mills argued that the interchangeability of elites among the three most powerful institutions results in a fusion of views among leaders. They do not develop viewpoints and interests specific to one institution. When the power elite switch hats from one institutional realm to another, they bring with them their prejudices, their beliefs, and their interests. No seriously divisive viewpoints are expressed, then, among leaders. There is only one viewpoint, expressed by one group of people: the power elite. Thus the interests of Halliburton, the Pentagon, and the White House become fused into one set of common interests, each supporting and realizing benefits from the war initiated against Iraq in 2003.

If one accepts that there is a power elite, what effect do its members have on the relationship between the state and the economy? According to some social scientists, their influence occurs through the actions of the "military-industrial complex." What is the military-industrial complex? How does it affect the state and the economy?

The Military-Industrial Complex

The **military-industrial complex** is composed of the uniformed military, the aerospace-defense industry, the civilian national security managers, and the U.S. Congress (Hooks, 1991; Pilisuk and Hayden, 1965). Each of the components of the military-industrial complex works to advance its own interests while simultaneously promoting and reinforcing the interests of the others (Abdolali and Ward, 1998; Jones, 2001).

What does each of these components want? The uniformed military needs to maintain—and preferably expand—its capability to wage war. Its massive budgets enable it to conduct public relations campaigns portraying military goals as patriotic and justified (Herman and Chomsky, 1988; Wagner, 1989).

An even more influential component of the military-industrial complex is the corporate sector, particularly the large aerospace-defense industry. This industry supports military expenditures because it benefits from huge procurement contracts. In 2001, for example, U.S. military contracts totaled $149 billion, 35 percent of which went to just 10 U.S. corporations (http://web1.whs.osd.mil/peidhome/rocstat/p01/fy2002/top100.htm; www.census.gov/Press-Release/www/2002/cb02-54.html). Such sizable contracts guarantee substantial profits without the risks of the free market. After the end of the Cold War in the late 1980s, Congress reduced the growth of the military budget. However, the reductions did not return the military budget

TABLE 11.1 Institutional Ties of Former Cabinet Members, 1973–2001

Secretaries of State

Henry Kissinger (1973–1977)   Project director, Rockefeller Brothers Fund and the Council on Foreign Relations

Cyrus Vance (1977–1980)   Member of the board of directors, IBM and Pan American World Airways; trustee, Yale University, the Rockefeller Foundation, and the Council on Foreign Relations; secretary of the army under President Lyndon Johnson

Alexander M. Haig (1981–1982)   President, United Technologies Corp.; four-star general, U.S. Army; Supreme Allied Commander, NATO forces in Europe

George P. Shultz (1982–1989)   President, Bechtel Corp.; director, General Motors, Borg-Warner, and Dillon, Read & Co.

James A. Baker III (1989–1992)   Houston attorney with oil industry interests

Warren Christopher (1993–1997)   Law clerk for U.S. Supreme Court Justice William Douglas; partner, O'Melvany & Meyers; director, California Edison, First Interstate Bancorp, Lockheed; chairman of the board of trustees, Carnegie Corp.

Madeleine Albright (1997–2001)   Member, Council on Foreign Relations

Secretaries of Treasury

William E. Simon (1974–1977)   Director, Federal Energy Office; senior partner, Salomon Brothers

Michael Blumenthal (1977–1979)   President, Bendix Corporation; vice-president, Crown Cork Co.; trustee, Princeton University and the Council on Foreign Relations

G. William Miller (1979–1981)   Chairman and chief executive officer, Textron Corp.; partner, Cravath, Swaine & Moore; director, Allied Chemical and Federated Department Stores; chairman, Federal Reserve Board

Donald T. Regan (1981–1985)   Chairman of the board and chief executive officer, Merrill Lynch & Co.; vice-chairman, New York Stock Exchange; trustee, University of Pennsylvania and the Committee for Economic Development; member, policy committee of the Business Roundtable

James A. Baker III (1985–1989)   See above

Nicholas Brady (1989–1993)   Chairman, Dillon, Read & Co.; director, Purolator, NCR, Georgia International, ASA, and Media General

Robert E. Rubin (1995–2001)   Chairman, Goldman Sachs; trustee, Carnegie Corp.

Secretaries of Defense

James R. Schlesinger (1973–1977)   Director, Central Intelligence Agency; chairman, Atomic Energy Commission; research associate, RAND Corporation

Harold Brown (1977–1981)   President, California Institute of Technology; member of the board of directors, IBM and the Times-Mirror Corp.; secretary of the air force under President Lyndon B. Johnson

(continued)

SOURCE: Thomas R. Dye, *Who's Running America? The Bush Restoration* (7th ed.) (Upper Saddle River, NJ: Prentice Hall, 2002), pp. 74–77.

to pre–Cold War proportions. More important, Congress began to reverse these reductions by 1997, and by 2001 the total Department of Defense budget had grown to almost $300 billion, more than any year since 1980 (www.statab.gov: Table 491). Even more money was added to wage the 2003 war against Iraq. This is a pattern that is unlikely to be reversed any time soon, given the concerns expressed by the Bush administration over threats allegedly posed by countries like Syria, Iran, and North Korea and by overseas terrorist organizations such as al-Qaeda. In such a politically charged environment, many corporations that enjoyed highly profitable defense contracts during the Cold War still benefit hugely from military expenditures, and are likely to continue to do so.

The civilian national security managers support military spending because they view U.S. national security as requiring access to global resources and markets. They also develop foreign policy with that requirement in mind. These government officials are influenced heavily by their backgrounds in large corporate firms. Many have ties to the influential private-sector Council on Foreign Relations (CFR), whose concerns include corporate interests abroad. In 2000, 70 percent of the top 100 industrial corporations had at least one officer serving as a member of the CFR (Domhoff, 2002:85), as did 21 of the top 25 banks and 16 of the top 25 insurance companies. Not surprisingly, then, civilian national security managers' views on national security and foreign policy are consistent with those of corporate leaders.

Finally, members of Congress consistently grant the military a large proportion of the federal budget because doing so creates jobs for their voting constituents both in the military (on its hundreds of bases) and in the aerospace-defense industry (www.statab.gov: Table 494). Furthermore, since members of Congress tend to be affluent, they are likely to be stockholders in major American corporations, including aerospace-defense contractors. And so are their major campaign contributors (Domhoff, 2002). The positions that representatives take, then, on defense spending may affect both their own personal wealth and their chances of getting reelected.

The primary interest unifying these components of the military-industrial complex is the protection of private profit making. For close to 50 years, U.S. military expenditures and foreign policy had been fueled by Cold War fears of communism.

More recently, they have been influenced by fears that underdeveloped countries will restrict or eliminate U.S. access to crucial resources. At the same time, thousands of U.S. corporations have opened production facilities abroad, particularly in underdeveloped countries. But those countries characterized by widespread poverty and oppression are vulnerable to revolutions and popular support for socialist economic systems. These systems threaten capital-accumulation interests, because they may institute state control of production, nationalize industries, and restrict employers' exploitation of labor. Vast military expenditures have been devoted, then, to securing the political environment in which U.S. corporations operate abroad. This protection has often extended to U.S. military and paramilitary (e.g., CIA) interventions in other countries, such as Chile in the 1970s, Nicaragua in the 1980s, Iraq in 1991 and 2003, and the Balkans in the late 1990s.

Why are private capital-accumulation interests so important to the state? In 2002, the top 500 corporations employed more than 10 percent of the total U.S. labor force. And they produced revenues of $7.4 trillion, more than the combined gross domestic products of Japan and Germany (www.fortune.com/fortune/fortune500/giants.html). These firms are clearly at the center of the nation's economic well-being. When they succeed in growing and in generating profits, the economy avoids stagnation, recession, or, worse, depression. Thus, as former secretary of defense and General Motors chairman Charles E. Wilson once said, "What is good for our country is good for General Motors and vice versa."

In order to grow, many major firms must expand their operations beyond the shores of the United States. When firms operate production and trade facilities in other countries, sociologists call them **multinational** (or **transnational**) **corporations.** Most of the money such corporations have invested abroad has gone to the economies of developed countries where American corporations provide manufactured goods. The remaining investment capital has gone to Mideast countries rich in petroleum and to underdeveloped countries, where corporations can capitalize on inexpensive, nonunionized labor, lax or nonexistent environmental and labor laws, and various tax breaks. Since U.S.- based multinational corporations' earnings from their foreign operations account for 50 percent or more of their annual earnings, they want to be sure that the environment in which such earnings are produced is secure. Thus the economic well-being of the United States depends significantly on U.S. corporations' ability to do business abroad.

Not coincidentally, the ability of these firms to operate in other countries also gives them access to—and often control over—critical raw materials. These resources, needed in aerospace-defense industries, are often inaccessible or expensive to mine in the United States. Therefore, it is in both the economic and the military interests of the state to secure the safety of U.S. corporations that procure these materials in other countries and enable them to continue operations in times of political unrest.

The global expansion of U.S. capital-accumulation interests has been aided, then, by congressional willingness to provide tax dollars for military expenditures and by the foreign policy devised by civilian national security managers. These managers, typically drawn from business and finance circles, formulate foreign policy that is consistent with the need to protect corporations' foreign operations. For example, U.S. national security managers have supported economic and military aid to underdeveloped countries. Economic aid often requires the recipients to purchase goods and services from U.S. corporations. Military aid similarly requires the recipients to purchase military equipment and supplies produced by the U.S. aerospace-defense industry (Bixby, 1992). This arrangement has enormous economic consequences for U.S. corporations: In 1997, sales of U.S. arms and weapons systems to both underdeveloped and industrialized nations exceeded $31.8 billion, almost 60 percent of the world export market (www.fas.org).

The Gulf Wars

The power of the military-industrial complex was exercised forcefully in 1991, when the United States entered into the Persian Gulf war against Iraq. Ostensibly, American intervention after Iraq's invasion of Kuwait was based on the need to maintain U.S. access to Kuwait's vast oil reserves. Yet U.S. national security managers had previously notified Iraq's Saddam Hussein that Iraq could settle its disputes with Kuwait in any manner that it saw fit. Why, then, did the United States, with the approval of Congress, go to war against Iraq?

In the aftermath of the war, it became clear that the big winners were the components of the military-industrial complex. One was the Raytheon Corporation, the manufacturer of the Patriot missiles, which became a military symbol of U.S. strength and resolve. The profits of Exxon and other oil corporations increased by an amazing 75 percent in the first weeks of the war (Hayes, 1991). This is because the war created a disruption in oil production, thereby allowing U.S. oil corporations to sharply raise their prices. Other big winners included the military, which was facing vast budget cuts at the end of the Cold War against the Soviet Union. Finally, among the major winners were members of Congress whose home districts benefited economically from the military buildup and the prospects of future orders for military hardware from several Mideast countries. Clearly, President George H. W. Bush benefited from the Gulf war as well. His approval rating in the United States reached the highest point in his presidency, boosting his political capital a great deal. People in the United States and abroad perceived him as a strong, nononsense president and international leader. Many in the media characterized the 1991 Gulf war as an end to the "Vietnam syndrome," wherein political leaders in the post- Vietnam era hesitated to become involved in international conflicts for fear of strong criticism and resistance in the United States. All components of the military-industrial complex, then, benefited handsomely from massive expenditures connected with the war with Iraq, even if the poor, the hungry, the homeless, the working-class unemployed, women, and schoolchildren in the United States, as well as nonelites in Iraq and Kuwait, did not.

Given these strong corporate—especially oil—interests tied to the first Bush administration, it is not surprising to find the United States aggressively at war against Iraq in 2003. Some argue that a war against Iraq was necessary for world security because of that country's previous use of chemical and biological weapons against the Kurds in 1991 and its supposed pursuit of nuclear weapons of mass destruction in 2002. However, no such weapons have been located, even after toppling Saddam Hussein and his administration. Moreover, a similar case could be made for the need to protect the world against weapons of mass destruction produced by North Korea,

The military-industrial complex benefits each of its components by fusing their interests; sometimes members of the elites of the various components overlap, as has been the case with the Halliburton Corporation, the Texas-based construction and engineering company. Pictured here is Dick Cheney, who was the Chief Executive Officer of Halliburton from 1995 until 2000, the year he was elected Vice President of the United States. Notably, Halliburton was given a highly lucrative contract to redevelop Iraq after the war there in 2003.

a state that has withdrawn from an international nuclear disarmament treaty and announced an expansion of its nuclear arsenal, yet none has been made. One difference between these two countries is that Iraq controls huge oil supplies needed by the United States and the industrialized nations in which its multinational corporations have investments, and North Korea does not. Notice that Halliburton Corporation has alone been awarded the highly lucrative contract to rebuild Iraq in the aftermath of the war. And remember Halliburton's substantial connections to the George W. Bush administration.

A Power Elite Analysis of the State–Economy Relationship

The discussion of the military-industrial complex illustrates the kinds of insights one can develop by using the power elite perspective. In contrast to pluralists, power elite theorists suggest that the state is not neutral or independent but is heavily influenced by capital and corporate interests. Voting processes simply make the existing state *appear* legitimate; they channel people's energies into activities that appear to empower them but do not fundamentally challenge elites' interests. Electoral politics also distract people's attention from an understanding of the relationship between the state and the economy and therefore create the false security of believing that the state legislates for the common good.

Note also that the power elite are typically white male Protestants educated at prestigious institutions. Analyzing the power elite in 2000, for example, Thomas R. Dye (2002) found that only 10 percent of the top 7,314 economic and political institutional positions in the power elite were filled by women; and people of color were almost nonexistent among the power elite, where African American representation was generally restricted to high-level government positions but not chief executives in major American corporations. Dye also found that 54 percent of the corporate elite and 42 percent of the state elite were graduates of the 12 most exclusive private universities (p. 148). And more than two-thirds of the institutional elite were members of exclusive social clubs; more than one-third belonged to one or more of the most prestigious of these clubs. Together, these data suggest a strong race, class, and gender bias among the power elite.

Given the combined processes of co-optation and class identity, evidence of an overwhelmingly white, male, relatively affluent network of individuals mentoring, supporting, and promoting new elites much like themselves is not surprising. Yet evidence suggests this network is not powerful enough to be entirely closed; it is possible for someone outside the network to break into elite ranks. Although few women currently hold executive-level positions in the powerful institutions of society, the expectation that more women will hold these positions in the future is reasonable. However, in spite of the limited progress of women and people of color in their representation among the power elite to date, even less progress has been made in terms of class. The power elite remain firmly drawn from among the most economically privileged in society (Zweigenhaft and Domhoff, 1998).

The evidence of increasing diversity in the power elite, however small thus far, points to a weakness in power elite theory: Mills mistakenly attributed a sense of omnipotence to the elite and therefore overlooked the dynamics of struggle and conflict identified in Chapter 10 that can affect the composition of the power elite. For example, the civil rights and feminist movements combined to open some opportunities for cooptation into the elite previously unavailable to anyone but white males.

Mills also assumed that the three main power elite institutions are equally significant, but he provided no evidence supporting this equality. Moreover, he provided no concrete analysis of how the main institutions of society operate together to produce an omnipotent institutional structure. Nonetheless, he opened up a lively debate with pluralist sociologists over power and its exercise at the national level.

Voting: Who Participates?

Most people are not central actors in the power elite. How, then, do nonelites participate politically? Pluralists emphasize the importance of elections and voting. However, power elite theorists point out that while voters may elect some of the power elite, they do not elect the leaders who run the corporate economy and the uniformed military. Voters have no way to hold these elite leaders accountable. Pluralists assume that everyone agrees on how people are to behave politically and that the only acceptable means of affecting government is through electoral politics. But the norms of political behavior are determined by the people in power and the people who benefit most from the existing system. For example, regulations defining who may vote, based on residence qualifications, are determined by Congress, which is disproportionately populated by persons who are relatively advantaged. One must have a permanent address in order to qualify to vote. Thus the homeless are not allowed to participate in selecting the leaders whose decision making will affect their lives. Electoral politics may channel certain issues and problems into a controlled institutional arena, but what happens when elites consistently ignore some issues?

In any case, voters in the United States turn out in notoriously low numbers. As you can see in Figure 11.1, voting participation rates have steadily declined from an all-time high of around 63 percent in the 1960 national elections. By the 2000 presidential election, only 54.7 percent of the eligible voters actually participated (a slight improvement over 1996) (www.census.gov/population/socdemo/voting). Participation rates are even worse in state and local elections. In fact, among industrialized capitalist democracies only Switzerland has a lower voter participation rate

FIGURE 11.1 **U.S. Voter Turnout: 1932–2000** Voting is supposed to be the means by which we hold our elected leaders accountable, yet rates of voter participation in national elections since at least 1932 indicate that citizens do not flood the voting booths to make their opinions matter. Why is turnout so low? Did you vote in the last election? Why or why not? (Source: www.census.gov/population.socdemo/voting)

than the United States (Wattenberg, 2002). What do such poor voter turnouts in the United States mean?

Pluralists argue that the low rates indicate the population is satisfied with the existing leadership and feels no need to participate. When the electorate becomes dissatisfied, they argue, it will mobilize and vote to unseat the unsatisfactory political elites. To pluralists, then, low voter turnout rates suggest that the system is working and that voters are happy with the current state of affairs.

Table 11.2 shows the characteristics of persons who vote. Such data make the pluralist interpretation difficult to accept. Overwhelmingly, the highest turnout rates occur within the higher income, higher education, and higher occupational status groups. And whites, as a group, tend to turn out more than people of color. One might interpret these data as evidence that people who benefit most from the status quo are more likely to participate in electoral politics than people whose interests are ignored and who are thus disadvantaged by it.

Some pluralists counter that it is good that the better educated are the most likely to vote, since they are more likely than the poorly educated or illiterate to make intelligent choices and are not likely to be exploited by political extremists (Banfield and Wilson, 1963). Some also argue that the language skills of highly educated people and the political skills entailed in high-status occupations easily translate into the skills required to participate effectively in electoral politics. Others argue that political participation (particularly those activities that go beyond voting) requires a great deal of time, money, and energy—resources that the poor and working class are not likely to have in great quantities (Lipset, 1960).

Critics of pluralism point out that the electoral system is set up to *discourage* some people from participating. Registration and voting procedures raise mechanical obstacles to participation by the poor, the working class, and the poorly educated. Indeed, registration rates for African Americans and Latinos/Latinas, as well as the poor, lag behind those of whites and more affluent groups. Deliberate bureaucratic obstructions that hinder efforts to register racial and ethnic minorities and poor people include states' failure to deputize registrars or to set up registration posts at satellite locations and the lack of bilingual registration and election forms. In addition, the confusion associated with absentee ballots (for students, migrant workers, and military personnel), poorly phrased and confusing legalistic jargon on referenda, confusing appearances of ballots (such as the infamous "butterfly" ballots in Florida in the 2000 elections), hostility at registration and voting sites toward voters of color, and endless primaries all serve to reduce participation rates among those groups (Piven and Cloward, 2000).

Taken together, these analyses of differential participation suggest that, for numerous reasons, the

TABLE 11.2 Characteristics of Voters: 2000

Characteristic	Percentage Voting
Education	
Less than 8th Grade	26.8%
Some high school	33.6
High school graduate	49.4
Some college	60.3
Bachelor's degree or higher	72.0
Labor force status	
Employed	55.5%
Unemployed	35.1
Occupation[a, b]	
Managerial, professional	79.0%
Technical, sales, administrative support	68.0
Service occupations	52.2
Precision product, craft, repair	53.6
Farming, forestry, fishing	54.2
Operators, fabricators, laborers	46.4
Income	
Under $5,000	28.2%
$5,000–$9,999	34.7
$10,000–14,999	37.7
$15,000–24,999	43.4
$25,000–34,999	51.0
$35,000–49,999	57.5
$50,000–74,999	65.2
$75,000 and over	71.5
Race/ethnicity	
White	56.4%
African American	53.5
Latino/Latina	27.5
Sex	
Male	53.1%
Female	56.2

[a]www.census.gov/population/socdemo/voting/cps1998.
[b]These data are for 1992; the Census Bureau did not report out this characteristic for 2000.

SOURCE: www.statab.gov, Table 401.

advantaged are more likely to vote than the disadvantaged. Yet an examination of who does *not* vote reveals that nonparticipation cuts across all categories, including the more advantaged groups—substantial segments of even the most advantaged groups still do not vote. And even greater numbers refrain from other forms of political participation as well. What does such nonparticipation mean?

A likely explanation for variation in the social background characteristics of nonvoters is that a wide variety of people within the existing political system exhibit a great deal of disaffection and alienation (Boggs, 2000; Conway, 2000; Harrigan, 2000). When Marx spoke of **alienation** as an overwhelming sense of normlessness, powerlessness, and meaninglessness, he was referring to workers' estrangement from their work (Marx, 1844/1964; see also Seeman, 1959). But alienation can also affect people's political behavior. Electoral politics simply does not address the interests or needs of many people. Why, then, should they vote? In a 1999 public opinion survey, more than one-fourth of the respondents agreed that "it doesn't make much difference how I vote because all politicians are pretty much alike" (Hart and Teeter/NBC/*Wall Street Journal,* 1999; see www.publicagenda.org/issues). A 1999 survey suggested one reason people might think voting makes no difference is because they lack confidence in the leadership of elected officials. More than half of the respondents indicated that they trusted elected officials in Washington to "do what is right . . . only some of the time" (www.publicagenda.org). Census data also indicate a similar erosion of confidence in leaders: By 1999 between one-fifth and two-fifths of respondents said they had "very little confidence" in government, Congress, and political parties (www.statab.gov: Table 398).

In addition, many people may feel alienated from electoral politics because voting occurs in the political process long after many important decisions have already occurred without their participation. Most people neither participate in selecting party candidates nor get to determine the campaign issues. And the candidates from whom they may choose on election day bear such strong similarities to each other that they present very little difference, either in their social background characteristics or in their ideological positions.

Political alienation is not the same thing as **apathy.** When people are apathetic, they do not care what the outcome is. When people are politically alienated, they care about the outcome but feel that the system is neither fair nor just. Why are people alienated? They are alienated in part because the way the system actually works is not the way they were taught that it is *supposed* to work. Modern political history has contributed to voter alienation. The Vietnam era imbued a generation with the realization that elected officials could conduct a war against the wishes of vast segments of the population. Government misconduct—Watergate in the Nixon era and the Iran–Contra affair of the Reagan administration—as well as the Whitewater investigation and sexual scandals of the Clinton administration and, more recently, questions surrounding vote counts in the Bush–Gore presidential election in 2000—indicated to voters that political elites are less trustworthy and ethical than one would like to believe. Thus, although people are taught that voting is the means by which they can hold elected officials accountable, and that voting is the exercise of power, their experiences suggest that voting is not necessarily an effective way to control political elites or to get them to address their concerns.

Critics of pluralism point out that the electoral process involves far more than simply voting. Campaign formation, candidate selection, and the party agenda are important aspects of the electoral process that occur before anyone enters the voting booth in November (Domhoff, 2002). The participants at these early stages of the electoral process are likely to be persons already advantaged by the system as well as active members of one of the two major parties. Party candidates have typically come up through the ranks of the party organization. The party is not likely to champion outsiders and challengers to the system because they have not invested loyalty, time, money, energy, and work in the party organization.

Moreover, the huge expense of running a campaign usually means that aspiring candidates will try to articulate positions that attract the support of powerful interests. For example, Bill Clinton received the enthusiastic support of the computer industry in his 1992 presidential campaign after he forcefully advocated developing an expansive "information superhighway." The computer and communications industries stood to gain huge profits from such a project. Thus political elites are most likely to listen and respond to the interests of privileged groups, particularly corporations and affluent individuals, during candidate selection and campaign planning.

Even when third-party candidates, expressing interests ignored by candidates representing the two major parties, emerge, voters often are discouraged from voting for them. In a two-party system where the winner takes all, voting for third-party candidates may rob votes from one of the major candidates and throw the election to the more objectionable of the two. Indeed, notice the energy that the Democratic Party invested in discouraging Green Party voters in the 2000 presidential election. The Democrats noted that a vote for Ralph Nader would take votes away from the Democratic candidate, Al Gore, and therefore strengthen the likelihood that Republican George W. Bush would be elected. That threat reminded many voters to stay away from Nader and vote for Gore. It may very well have also discouraged alienated citizens from participating altogether.

The 2000 presidential election also may have alienated voters, especially people of color, because of the unusual circumstances in Florida. Thousands of ballots, particularly in voting districts with heavy populations of people of color, remained uncounted because the use of cardboard punch ballots produced unclear results when "chads" (the piece of cardboard that gets pushed out to select a candidate) did not fully break off. Many ballots in these districts were designed in a side-by-side butterfly fashion that did not clearly align chads corresponding with candidates, thus confusing voters. And many people of color complained that they were harassed by police as they waited in line to vote, or were told by election monitors that they were at the wrong voting district and could not vote there. Together, the irregularities in Florida caused a long delay in declaring a presidential winner there for weeks while the courts attempted to deal with the problem. Ultimately, it was the Supreme Court, not the voters, that decided the winner in Florida. In a very tight presidential race, Florida's electoral votes would determine the outcome of the national election; in essence, the Supreme Court appointed the president by declaring a winner of the state. Many voters became quite cynical in the aftermath of the 2000 elections, a cynicism that could easily translate into political alienation.

We can also see inconsistencies between the objectives of privileged voters and those of the masses in the kind of legislation that is passed. For example, Richard Hamilton (1972) found that during the 1950s and 1960s, most people in the working and middle classes in the United States supported the expansion of federal social welfare programs. Yet legislators consistently opposed efforts to expand such programs. Then, too, polls indicated that 63 percent of people in the United States

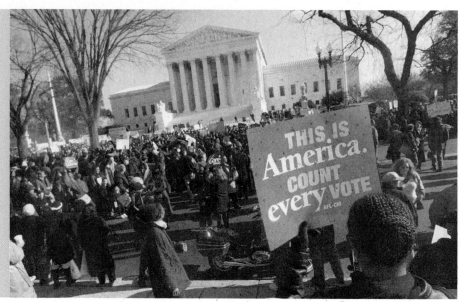

Controversies over how ballots were counted in Florida in the 2000 presidential election drew widespread protests from voters. Here, a large crowd of demonstrators demands adherence to the democratic principles that define the political process in the United States—that every ballot submitted be counted.

favored the equal rights amendment (ERA) to the U.S. constitution, which would prohibit discrimination on the basis of sex. Yet the ERA was not passed because constitutional amendments require ratification by two-thirds, or 38, of the nation's state legislatures, and only 35 states were willing to approve it (*Time,* 1982a, 1982b).

The class bias of elected officials also dilutes the power of voting. Members of the nation's political elite tend to come overwhelmingly from economically advantaged backgrounds (Dye, 2002; Zweigenhaft and Domhoff, 1998), partly because it is very costly to prepare for and run large campaigns. Once elected, these privileged persons are not likely to be sympathetic to the views of the disadvantaged, such as the poor, the homeless, and other groups considered marginal in U.S. society.

Our discussion of the limits of electoral politics suggests that the state and the economy are not actually separate, distinct institutions. What is the relationship between these two institutions in a capitalist system, and how does it affect individuals' daily lives?

The State and Capitalist Society

The discussion of the power elite and the analysis of the military-industrial complex suggest significant ways in which the state and the economy operate together in a society dominated by corporate interests. Sociologists do not necessarily agree, however, on the nature and meaning of their intersection. In *The Communist Manifesto,* Karl Marx and Friedrich Engels (1848/1967) argued that "the executive of the modern state is but a committee for managing the common affairs of the whole bourgeoisie," the bourgeoisie being the capitalist business owners. Their observation has become a centerpiece of debate among various sociologists, who have engaged a spirited argument over what Marx and Engels meant: Why and how might the state manage the common affairs of capitalists? Three main theories of the state have wrestled with this question: business dominance theory, capitalist state structuralist theory, and class dialectic theory.

Business Dominance Theory

Business dominance theory extends the analysis of power elite theory by arguing that the state is not a neutral arbiter of the common good because the capitalists either "capture" the state or dominate it to use it as their instrument (Miliband, 1969). Capitalists may capture the state and take control of it by entering key leadership positions in Congress, the White House, and the Cabinet (Dye, 2002; Useem, 1984). Or they may dominate the state by using campaign financing to gain favored access to and applying pressure on elected officials (Clawson, Neustadtl, and Weller, 1998). Capitalists may also greatly influence the state by filling positions in key advisory, regulatory, or policy committees, such as the Council on Foreign Relations, a nationally influential private organization that advises the president and Congress on foreign policy (Burris, 1992; Domhoff, 2002).

Business dominance theorists argue that the state is not free of **capitalist interests,** that is, individuals and organizations that benefit from amassing and maintaining private profits. Business dominance theorists note that the people making decisions in the name of the state are either capitalists themselves or politicians who may be beholden to them because of their massive campaign contributions. This analysis implies that the capitalist mentality of individuals who fill key governmental positions determines the role of the state in capitalist society.

Capitalist State Structuralist Theory

Advocates of **capitalist state structuralist theory** agree with business dominance theorists that the state is not a neutral arbiter of the common good (Jessop, 1990; Poulantzas, 1973). But they take issue with the focus on individuals. Structuralists argue that an economy based on capitalism *forces* the state to shape its policies in ways that are consistent with capitalist interests because the fate of the state rests on the economy's health. The state needs to collect taxes for social programs to discourage unrest and make its existence legitimate in the eyes of the citizenry. But it must often legislate in favor of capitalist interests rather than social programs because to do otherwise would be to damage the health of the economy on which the state depends (O'Connor, 1987, 1996). The state, then, is not simply subject to the whims of individual political leaders; the needs of the corporate capitalist economy forces the state to legislate in ways that support private profit making at almost any cost or risk economic collapse. Therefore, changes in personnel in political offices do not alter the types of decisions that the state makes. State decisions will be consistent with the interests of capitalists, regardless of who is elected to fill state offices.

The influence of the economic structure on the legislative process can be seen in laws passed by the state that ostensibly control the capitalist sector but may in fact function to advance its interests. For example, a law deregulating the banking industry in 1982 prompted pronounced concentration of that industry into fewer banking institutions as larger banks could now take over smaller ones. The legislation also spawned the savings and loan (S&L) crisis of the late 1980s. **Deregulation** is the process of removing or significantly relaxing government restrictions on industries. In the case of the banking industry, deregulation removed the structural and legal constraints that kept large commercial banks and smaller S&L institutions from competing against each other by limiting them to do business in different markets. Previously, S&L institutions had been legally restricted to providing low-cost home mortgages and offering low interest rates on deposits. Following deregulation, the two types of financial organizations began to compete against each other, to the decided advantage of the large commercial banks. To attract depositors from the commercial banks, S&L institutions offered dramatically higher interest rates on deposits but continued to collect low rates on old mortgages. This meant they were bringing in less money than they were paying out. In addition, deregulation permitted S&L institutions to engage in speculative investments that had previously been prohibited. These investments, particularly in real estate, crashed in the late 1980s, causing many S&Ls to go bankrupt. And there were now far fewer field supervisors to regularly audit the S&L institutions' books to ensure that prudent investments were being made. The lack of supervision encouraged a great deal of fraud to occur in the industry as standard operating procedure (what Calavita and Pontell, 1991, called **collective embezzlement**).

Before long the unwise speculative investments and the shortfalls between high-interest payouts on deposits and low-interest incomes on mortgage loans caught up with the S&L institutions; a massive national crisis erupted in the industry (Glasberg and Skidmore, 1997). Many S&L institutions failed and had to close, leaving the government to cover their debts in the largest government bailout of private corporations, and the first government bailout of an entire industry. The costs to taxpayers have proven to be immense.

This saga of the S&L collapse illustrates how laws passed by the state to deregulate the banking industry resulted in further concentrating the industry in fewer hands (particularly large commercial banks). This unfettered concentration of banking business advanced the interests of the largest members of the industry at the expense of working people (who relied on the S&Ls for affordable mortgages) and taxpayers (who had to pay for the bailout).

Class Dialectics and the State

Some sociologists challenge both the business dominance theorists and the structuralists on the grounds that they tend to focus on relations between elites in the state and in the economy and fail to examine how these relations affect the rest of society, especially the working class. Sociologists using a **class dialectic perspective** focus on the dynamics of conflict between the working class and the capitalist class. They point to how this conflict at times results in compromises in state policy, some of which may not be in the best interests of capitalists (Levine, 1988; Quadagno and Meyer, 1989; Wysong, 1993). They ask, If the state is captured, controlled, or influenced either by members of the capitalist class itself (business dominance theory) or by the structure of the capitalist economic system that favors them (capitalist state structuralist theory), how is it possible to periodically get legislation passed that favors workers or that disadvantages capitalists? For example, how is it possible to have laws guaranteeing workers the right to form unions and collectively bargain with capitalists? How is it that there have been policies increasing social welfare expenditures and expanding social welfare programs, such as the New Deal in the 1930s and the War on Poverty in the 1960s?

Class dialectic theorists argue that the state is the arena in which class struggles are played out. Social welfare programs (such as unemployment insurance, income support programs, food stamps, Medicare, and Medicaid) and the legal protection of workers' rights (such as the right to collective bargaining and laws protecting worker health and safety) are outcomes of prolonged struggles in that arena. According to class dialectic theorists, these outcomes actually exemplify the state's willingness to address working-class interests in order to protect capitalist interests.

For example, during the late 1800s and early 1900s, workers in the United States began to press forcefully for the right to unionize. They faced serious challenges and concerted opposition by capitalist interests. Capitalists fired workers who were active in organizing attempts and hired private police and paramilitary forces to beat and shoot striking workers. Sometimes, as in the cases of the Pullman railway workers' strike in 1893 and countless coal miners' strikes (particularly in the 1930s), the state sent in armed troops to quash workers' organizing efforts (Sexton, 1991). The state used various methods to undermine and discredit labor leaders. In a glaring case, Joe Hill, a leader of the International Workers of the World, was arrested for committing a murder that no one had witnessed. Although no evidence ever connected Hill to the murder, he was convicted and eventually executed in 1915 for the crime (Foner, 1965).

At the same time, deplorable working conditions and oppressive treatment made socialism an increasingly attractive alternative for many workers. Under socialism, workers would control their working conditions. Much debate occurred within Congress and among capitalists. Capitalists abhorred collective bargaining with workers' unions, but the threat of socialism was even more repugnant. Many understood that socialism would become much more attractive to workers who were denied the right to unionize. Collective bargaining came to be seen as the lesser of two evils. Finally, with the grudging approval of many elites in the corporate community, Congress passed the Wagner Act in 1934, guaranteeing workers the right to unionize (Weinstein, 1968; Zinn, 1980). Thus workers' struggles with capitalists were fought out in the arena of the state, with the state acting not as an unbiased judge but as an advocate for the long-run interests of the capitalist class. The business dominance and capitalist state structuralist perspectives would find it difficult to explain the state's behavior in these situations, unlike the class dialectic perspective.

The State and Political Economy: New Federalism and Welfare "Reform"

We have seen that the state may be viewed as the central arena in which struggles between the interests of labor and those of capital accumulators are acted out. Organized struggles in the 1950s and 1960s succeeded in gaining many civil rights, anti-poverty, education and job training, and health programs. But since the late 1970s the state has restructured the economy more straightforwardly in favor of business interests and to the disadvantage of labor, as well as the poor, women, children, and people of color. Two key restructuring projects were the New Federalism of the 1980s and welfare reform of the 1990s.

New Federalism

What came to be called **New Federalism** was based on the conservative political philosophy that the federal government should be involved only with taxation and national defense; all else, particularly social welfare programs, should be the responsibility of state and local governments. Under New Federalism battles previously won by disadvantaged groups would have to be fought again in the future.

New Federalism began quietly in the late 1970s under President Jimmy Carter. The state responded to an ailing economy by lowering federal social welfare expenditures, reducing the burden of taxes on the wealthy to stimulate increased saving and investment, and relaxing or eliminating federal regulation of corporations. The goal of New Federalism was to regulate the economy to the advantage of businesses, particularly large corporations. The assumption was that firms would reinvest their increased profits to improve productive capacity, thereby creating new jobs. President Ronald Reagan greatly expanded this approach, which came to be called **supply-side,** or **trickle-down, economics.** Its supporters argued that benefits to capitalists would trickle down to benefit labor, so that eventually everyone would benefit from New Federalism. "A rising tide lifts all boats" was the supply-siders' motto.

In practice, though, some ships sank. Tax cuts instituted under President Reagan in the 1980s greatly benefited the wealthy and large corporations. Meanwhile, the economy continued to suffer, increasing the ranks of the poor, the hungry, and the homeless. While their needs grew, some social welfare and entitlement programs originally designed to catch economic victims in a federal safety net were slashed; others' eligibility requirements were redefined to reduce the number of people the programs served (Abramovitz, 1996).

Critics decried the New Federalism as a "mean season" attack against the welfare state and a massive attempt to dismantle it (Block et al., 1987; Piven and Cloward, 1982). The effect of the state's twist on Robin Hood could be seen on the individual level. Overall, the economic distance between the nation's wealthy and poor widened to a gap unseen since the Great Depression in the 1930s. As Figure 11.2 shows, the average family income of the poorest 20 percent of the U.S. population declined by 10 percent between 1967 and 2000, while the average family income of the wealthiest 20 percent increased during the same period by 13.2 percent. More strikingly, the average family income of the wealthiest 5 percent increased more than 20 percent (U.S. Census Bureau, 2001). New Federalism had succeeded in redistributing income from the poorest to the wealthiest.

New Federalism particularly impoverished women, even as their share of jobs in the labor force increased. During the 1980s, women's share of poverty increased quite dramatically because the vast majority of new jobs created were minimum-wage, part-time service-sector jobs with no benefits. A mother of three who worked full-time, year-round at the minimum wage would be unable to earn enough on her

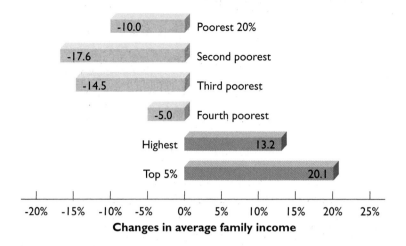

-10.0	Poorest 20%
-17.6	Second poorest
-14.5	Third poorest
-5.0	Fourth poorest
13.2	Highest
20.1	Top 5%

-20% -15% -10% -5% 0% 5% 10% 15% 20% 25%

Changes in average family income

FIGURE 11.2 **The New Federalism and Changes in Average Family Incomes: 1967–2000** The New Federalism of the 1980s and 1990s included major cuts in the tax burden for the most affluent members of U.S. society, as well as cuts in budgets for programs providing assistance to the poor. The result was a substantial shift in the distribution of income from the poor and middle classes to the affluent so that the rich got richer and the poor and middle classes got poorer. How did this happen? (Source: U.S. Census Bureau Current Population Reports (P60-213), "Money Income in the United States: 2000.")

own to rise above the federal poverty line. Working part-time guaranteed that both she and her children would be entrenched in poverty, be hungry, and possibly be homeless. If she did not have a wage-earning partner, a mother was likely to face impoverishment. Single-parent families increased from 13 percent of the total number of families in 1970 to 29.7 percent in 1992, and most of these were female-headed. The median family income of married couples increased 9 percent between 1980 and 1993, but the median income of female-headed households actually declined by 1.7 percent (U.S. Bureau of the Census, 1994). Thus, while the overall rate of poverty in the United States in 1993 was 15.1 percent, the rate of poverty among female-headed families was an astounding 35.6 percent (compared with a rate of 16.8 percent for male-headed families) (U.S. Bureau of the Census, 1994).

New Federalism also disproportionately hurt people of color. The poverty rate for whites in 1993 was 12.2 percent, but the rate for African Americans was 33.1 percent and for Latinos/Latinas, 30.6 percent (U.S. Bureau of the Census, 1994). According to the Bureau of Labor Statistics, African Americans were more than twice as likely as whites to be unemployed in 1992, and Latinos/Latinas were almost twice as likely. The gap between African Americans and whites in terms of wealth and median family income widened, regardless of education levels.

People with disabilities were also targeted by the New Federalism. The federal government reduced its financial responsibilities by redefining eligibility standards and reformulating the budgeting for disabilities programs. For example, greater financial responsibility for the education of children with disabilities was shifted to states and local communities, whose already-strapped budgets could not make up the shortfall of federal contributions. By 1984 the federal share of community-based services for people with disabilities had dropped to 7 percent, down from 45 percent, leaving state and local governments to make up the difference. In 1984, some 70 percent of total public spending on community-based services for people with disabilities came from state-level funds. Income maintenance programs for people with disabilities declined 2 percent between 1985 and 1987 (Castellani, 1987:43). Clearly the federal safety net had gaping holes through which the poor and people with disabilities could easily fall.

Meanwhile, the New Federalism benefited corporations quite well without producing the much-heralded expectation of benefits for the working class. Deregulation of industries, relaxation of antitrust laws, and huge tax windfalls for corporations were supposed to increase productivity and new jobs. Instead, they fueled more than a decade of merger mania. Between 1980 and 1988 the total value of corporate mergers and acquisitions "exceeded two thirds of a trillion dollars" (Phillips, 1990:172). Mergers and acquisitions do not increase productive capacity or stimulate the production of new jobs. They simply reshuffle who owns the existing production facilities. In fact, mergers often entail job loss, as the acquiring firm tries to streamline operations to help pay off its debt. Although the number of jobs lost through mergers is not well documented, AFL-CIO secretary-treasurer Thomas Donahue testified before Congress that an estimated 80,000 union jobs were lost as a direct result of mergers and another 80,000 as an indirect result (*National Journal,* 1989). His estimate is conservative, since it does not include the number of nonunion jobs lost through mergers. Corporations were using their increased profits from New Federalism policies to buy one another out, not to create new jobs. The rising economic tide was not lifting all ships. Only the largest corporations were rising; smaller businesses were capsizing. Between 1985 and 1992, there were 533,000 small-business failures, a significantly larger number than in previous years (Federal News Service, 1993).

These attempts to dismantle the welfare state continued through the 1990s under welfare reform.

Welfare Reform

The Personal Responsibility Act of 1996, more familiarly known as "welfare reform," dramatically changed how public assistance is administered and gave individual states far greater flexibility in determining how such programs would be implemented. Key provisions in the national policy included a sharp reduction in benefit amounts as well as reductions in length of time over a lifetime recipients would be permitted to collect benefits (the act established a national limit of five years, but 22 states have since instituted far more stringent time restrictions). Recipients must find paid employment in order to continue to be eligible for assistance (Beaulieu, 1998). These reforms were based on the stereotype of the lazy "welfare queen," who continued to live off the public dole indefinitely, refusing to work, having more children in order to increase her benefits, and acting as a financial drain on public resources (Sidel, 2000). That stereotype, however, never matched the reality. Relatively few recipients ever remained very long on welfare (over 70 percent received welfare assistance for less than two years, and only 8 percent remained on welfare for over eight years); the average family size of welfare recipients, at two children, was no larger than the average middle-class family size, and more than 75 percent of welfare recipients had three children or fewer; and most welfare recipients were not lazy people who refuse to work, but instead were women who had lost jobs or who worked at low-wage jobs that failed to provide income above the poverty level (U.S. Department of Commerce, Bureau of the Census, 1999; Seccombe, 1999). These facts did not dissuade those in Congress who were intent on further dismantling social welfare programs.

When welfare reform was implemented, the number of people on public assistance or welfare declined sharply. This decline was ascribed to the success of the program in weaning those who had grown dependent on the state by forcing them to get jobs. But questions remain: Where did these former welfare recipients go? Are they off the welfare rolls because they are now gainfully employed? Has welfare reform thus significantly reduced poverty? The answer apparently is "no." Many former recipients have simply run out of benefits, but they have been granted no opportunity to complete education or training programs to secure decent jobs. Others have jobs, but these are minimum-wage or low-paying jobs which often carry few or no benefits (Abramovitz, 2000; Casey, 1998). The Urban Institute found, for example, that 61 percent of welfare recipients had jobs after leaving welfare, but they were earning a median wage of $6.61 per hour, and fewer than one-fourth of them had medical benefits from their jobs (Gault and Um'rani, 2000).

Evidence from individual states confirms the finding that welfare reform is not reducing poverty, even if it is reducing the number of people receiving welfare assistance. The Wisconsin Works (W-2) program reduced welfare roles by half in three years, but most participants have remained in poverty: One-fourth of those who left welfare returned for cash assistance, and half of those who found jobs are earning so little they remain below the poverty line (www.legis.state.wi.us/lab/reports/01-7full.pdf). A mother of two working full-time, year-round at a minimum-wage job simply does not have enough income to move her family above the poverty line, and the loss of benefits such as medical care compounds the poverty. Other former recipients have simply disappeared out of the system, perhaps to the streets among the homeless.

Among the hardest hit by welfare reform have been women of color and their children. This is partly because Latinas and African American women "are more vulnerable to poverty than white women," having higher rates of both poverty and unemployment. Researchers attribute this racial disparity to educational disadvantages and both gender and racial discrimination by employers (Gault and Um'rani, 2000:2). Many states have compounded the likelihood of continued poverty among former welfare recipients, particularly among women of color and children: In their enthusiasm for welfare reform, they have failed to inform recipients and the working poor who leave welfare that they or their children are still eligible for programs like Food Stamps, Medicaid, and housing assistance (Houppert, 1999).

Evidence strongly indicates, then, that welfare reform and the significant cuts in antipoverty programs under the New Federalism have served to intensify poverty,

The welfare reforms of the 1990s may have "ended welfare as we know it" but did not appreciably end poverty. Many families, such as the one pictured here, may have left the caseloads of welfare agencies around the country, but that does not mean that they have found gainful employment (or any employment at all). While women of color and their children have been disproportionately harmed by welfare reform, whites remain the largest single group among the poor.

particularly among women, children, people of color, and people with disabilities (Schram and Beer, 1999). Programs such as welfare reform and the New Federalism are based on the assumption that the capitalist economy has the ability to solve social problems like poverty. However, an economy that increasingly offers minimum-wage service work with no benefits as the only real option to the poor, and which does not seriously address discrimination in employment and education opportunities, is in no position to reduce structural economic inequality (Blau, 1999; Eitzen and Zinn, 2000; Huber and Kosser, 1999).

Dismantling the Welfare State?

As much as the New Federalism and welfare reform have clearly contributed to a growing gap between rich and poor, between men and women, and between whites and people of color, it is important to note that these policy changes do not necessarily represent a dismantling of the welfare state. This is because these programs together constitute only one part of the welfare state, namely **social welfare.** Two other components of the welfare state remained largely untouched or even enhanced under the New Federalism: gilded welfare and corporate welfare.

Gilded welfare involves state policies and budgetary expenditures to redistribute wealth from the poor and working class to the middle class and the affluent. These include Social Security, Medicare, federal income tax deductions for home ownership and local property taxes, dependent children tax deductions, and home business tax deductions. While much of media and public attention has focused on social welfare expenditures, the fact is that gilded welfare spending far outweighs social welfare spending. For example, during the 1990s the federal government spent an annual average of more than $1 trillion on gilded welfare programs but only $117 billion on antipoverty programs (U.S. Bureau of the Census, 1999). This means that social welfare spending represented slightly more than 9 percent of the total spending on social and gilded welfare. Despite the media and popular perceptions that social welfare is a drain on the federal budget, it certainly appears to be a very small slice of that pie.

Even more expensive have been the corporate welfare expenditures. **Corporate welfare** encompasses the state policies and expenditures that redistribute wealth to corporations and the affluent by directly or indirectly subsidizing, supporting, rescuing, or otherwise socializing the cost and risk of investment and private profit making. These include subsidies to industries such as agriculture, tax abatements, depreciation allowances for equipment, Department of Defense spending that provides guaranteed markets at noncompetitive prices, and corporate bailouts. The "Social Forces/People's Lives" reading illustrates some of these elements of corporate welfare.

Taken together, the corporate welfare programs are an enormous slice of the federal budget. For example, the bailout of the savings and loan industry in the late 1980s represented a massive federal commitment of taxpayers' money to subsidizing the risks of profit making in private savings and loan institutions and rescuing those that had failed as a result of investing in junk bonds and real estate speculation. The bailout itself was a major increase in corporate welfare: Although the federal government has bailed out more than 400 individual corporations since World War II (Lockheed and Chrysler among the largest), it had never before agreed to bail out an entire industry. And while previous bailouts were limited to fixed amounts over a clearly defined and relatively short time period, the savings and loan bailout occurred with no discussion of a limited dollar amount or a limited time period. This was, in fact, the first time any corporate entity was bailed out with a "blank check"— and what a blank check it has been. The program has not concluded its bailouts but has thus far cost at least $250 billion, with estimates that the total cost could reach as high as $500 billion (Glasberg and Skidmore, 1997). Comparison of this expense of a single corporate welfare program with the entire budget of 1990s antipoverty expeditures, at a mere $117 billion, clearly shows that the welfare state for the affluent and nonneedy is, indeed, alive and well, and growing every day.

What occurred during the 1980s and 1990s was not as much a dismantling of the welfare state as a redistribution of resources from social welfare to gilded and corporate welfare. Indeed, the huge state expenditures devoted to corporate welfare programs suggest that, far from dismantling the welfare state, the New Federalism has expanded the welfare state—targeting corporate and gilded welfare rather than social welfare. The state has never been neutral in the struggle between capitalist interests and those of workers, the poor, women, people of color, ethnic minorities, people with disabilities, and children. New Federalism and the attacks on social welfare it unleashed succeeded in promoting legislation and budgeting practices that unabashedly favored capitalists and redistributed wealth from the poor and workers to the wealthy and corporations. Even conservatives like Kevin Phillips (1990; 1993) could not argue that this was in the common good.

Aid to Dependent Corporations

CHUCK COLLINS

Much of the mainstream media, and governmental policy as well, have treated welfare as an undeserved handout to the poor. However, as this reading illustrates, it is not just the poor who receive governmental aid to subsidize their existence. Welfare is also extended to the affluent, in ways that are less visible but no less a subsidy than Temporary Assistance to Needy Families. The author refers to these programs as "wealthfare." Why is wealthfare treated differently from welfare, in both the press and governmental policy?

IN 1992 rancher J. R. Simplot of Grandview, Idaho, paid the U.S. government $87,000 for grazing rights on federal lands, about one-quarter the rate charged by private landowners. Simplot's implicit subsidy from U.S. taxpayers, $261,000, would have covered the welfare costs of about 60 poor families. With a net worth exceeding $500 million, it's hard to argue that Simplot needed the money.

Since 1987, American Barrick Resources Corporation has pocketed $8.75 billion by extracting gold from a Nevada mine owned by the U.S. government. But Barrick has paid only minimal rent to the Department of the Interior. In 1992 Barrick's founder was rewarded for his business acumen with a $32 million annual salary.

Such discounts are only one form of corporate welfare, dubbed "wealthfare" by some activists, that U.S. taxpayers fund. At a time when Congress is attempting to slash or eliminate the meager benefits received by the poor, we are spending far more to subsidize wealthy corporations and individuals. Wealthfare comes in five main varieties: discounted user fees for public resources; direct grants; corporate tax reductions and loopholes; giveaways of publicly funded research and development (R&D) to private profit-making companies; and tax breaks for wealthy individuals. . . .

Tax Avoidance

The largest, yet most invisible, part of wealthfare is tax breaks for corporations and wealthy individuals. The federal Office of Management and Budget (OMB) esti-

mates that these credits, deductions, and exemptions, called "tax expenditures," will cost $440 billion in fiscal 1996. This compares, for example, to the $16 billion annual federal cost of child support programs. . . .

The tax code is riddled with tax breaks for the natural resource, construction, corporate agri-business, and financial industries. Some serve legitimate purposes, or did at one time. Others have been distorted to create tax shelters and perpetuate bad business practices. . .

Depreciation on equipment and buildings, for example, is a legitimate business expense. But the "accelerated depreciation" rule allows corporations to take this deduction far faster than their assets are wearing out. This simply lets businesses make billions of dollars in untaxed profits. . .

One particularly generous tax break is the foreign tax credit, which allows U.S.-based multinational corporations to deduct from their U.S. taxes the income taxes they pay to other nations. . . While in many cases this credit is a valid method of preventing double taxation on profits earned overseas, the oil companies have used it to avoid most of their U.S. tax obligations. Until 1950, Saudi Arabia had no income tax, but charged royalties on all oil taken from their wells. Such royalties are a payment for use of a natural resource. They are a standard business expense, payable *before* a corporation calculates the profits on which it will pay taxes.

These royalties were a major cost to ARAMCO, the oil consortium operating there (consisting of Exxon, Mobil, Chevron, and Texaco). But since royalties are not income taxes, they could not be used to reduce Exxon and friends' tax bills back home.

When King Saud decided to increase the royalty payments, ARAMCO convinced him to institute a corporate income tax and to substitute this for the -royalties. The tax was a sham, since it applied only to ARAMCO, not to any other business in Saudi Arabia's relatively primitive economy. The result was that the oil companies avoided hundreds of millions of dollars in their American taxes. Eventually the other oil-producing nations, including Kuwait, Iraq, and Nigeria, followed suit, at huge cost to the U.S. Treasury.

In contrast to the ARAMCO problem, many corporate executive salaries should not be counted as deductible expenses. These salaries and bonuses are often so large today that they constitute disguised profits...

Chicken McNuggets and Other Vital Matters

Taxes are but one form of wealthfare. Subsidized use of public resources, as with J. R. Simplot's grazing and American Barrick's mining, is also widespread. Barrick's profit-making was allowed by the General Mining Law of 1872...

In a manner similar to the mining situation, the U.S. Forest Service under-charges timber companies for the logs they take from publicly owned land. The Forest Service also builds roads and other infrastructure needed by the timber industry...

Agriculture subsidies typically flow in greater quantities the larger is the recipient firm. Of the $1.4 billion in annual sugar price supports, for example, 40% of the money goes to the largest 1% of firms, with the largest ones receiving more than $1 million each.
The Agriculture Department also spends $110 million a year to help U.S. companies advertise abroad. In 1992 Sunkist Growers got $10 million, Gallo Wines $4.5 million, M&M/Mars $1.1 million, McDonalds $466,000 to promote Chicken McNuggets, and American Legend Fur Coats $1.2 million...

The government also pays for scientific research and development, then allows the benefits to be reaped by private firms. This occurs commonly in medical research. One product, the anti-cancer drug Taxol, cost the U.S. government $32 million to develop as part of a joint venture with private industry. But in the end the government gave its share to Bristol-Myers Squibb, which now charges cancer patients almost $1,000 for a three-week supply of the drug.

Who Is Entitled?

Beyond corporate subsidies, the government also spends far more than necessary to help support the lifestyles of wealthy individuals. This largess pertains to several of the most expensive and popular "entitlements" in the federal budget, such as Social Security, Medicare, and the deductibility of interest on home mortgages. As the current budget-cutting moves in Congress demonstrate, such universal programs have much greater political strength than do programs targeted solely at low-income households.

While this broad appeal is essential to maintain, billions of dollars could be saved by restricting the degree to which the wealthy benefit from universal programs. If Social Security and Medicare payments were denied to just the richest 3% of households this would reduce federal spending by $30 to $40 billion a year—more than the total federal cost of food stamps. Similarly, mortgage interest is currently deductible up to $1 million per home, justifying the term "mansion subsidy" for its use by the rich. The government could continue allowing everyone to use this deduction, but limit it to $250,000 per home. This would affect only the wealthiest 5% of Americans, but would save taxpayers $10 billion a year.

Progressive organizations have mounted a renewed focus on the myriad handouts to the corporate and individual rich. One effort is the Green Scissors coalition, an unusual alliance of environmental groups such as Friends of the Earth, and conservative taxcutters, such as the National Taxpayers Union.

Another new organization, Share the Wealth, is a coalition of labor, religious, and economic justice organizations. It recently launched the "Campaign for Wealth-Fare Reform," whose initial proposal targets over $35 billion in annual subsidies that benefit the wealthiest 3% of the population. The campaign rejects the term "corporate welfare" because it reinforces punitive anti-welfare sentiments. Welfare is something a human society guarantees to people facing poverty, unemployment, low wages, and racism. "Wealthfare," in contrast, is the fees and subsidies extracted from the public by the wealthy and powerful—those who are least in need.

Source: Chuck Collins, "Aid to Dependent Corporations" *Dollars & Sense* 1 (May/June 1995), pp. 15–17, 40.

1. Political and economic institutions intersect in very powerful ways in the United States, a capitalist society dominated by the presence of large corporations.

2. The state hardly seems to be a neutral arbiter, balancing competing demands of various interest groups and legislating in the common good. Rather, it is a very active participant in class struggles and frequently legislates in favor of capital-accumulation interests.

3. At times, when groups of the disadvantaged press for change, the state finds ways to incorporate their demands as long as capitalist interests are not adversely affected. Indeed, reforms may serve to legitimize and stabilize the capitalist system.

4. Even voting, which would seem to be the mechanism by which everyone, regardless of race, gender, income, occupation, or education, could participate in the political economy, does not appear to level the playing field. Participants in the political process are disproportionately likely to be individuals who are already advantaged by the existing political economy, and their participation increases the likelihood of protecting and maintaining their advantage relative to others.

5. The state is not able to escape the influence of capital-accumulation interests. To undermine capital accumulation is to undermine the country's (and maybe the world's) economic health. The state is therefore constrained to make policy decisions from a very limited range of options.

6. However, perceptions of what is a viable option for a given problem can be influenced by the process of class struggle. That is, conflict between the relatively advantaged and disadvantaged members of society can often redefine problems and solutions so that new ways of understanding issues can develop. For example, there is a growing welfare rights movement in the United States, which has begun to mobilize and organize around the problems of welfare "reform" and its attacks against the poor.

7. Further, there is a rising coalition of labor and faith communities struggling to get all employers to pay their workers a living wage. Allies from a variety of walks of life are forming common bonds and are encouraging harbingers of social challenge and social change. They attempt to counter the ways the state responds to its constituents, particularly those who have received fewer advantages and resources at the state's disposal.

THINKING CRITICALLY

1. Consider the issue of corporate welfare described in the "Social Forces/People's Lives" reading. Why is corporate welfare treated differently than social welfare for the poor, both in the press and in government policy? What factors and forces entered into this social construction of need?

2. Look in the newspaper for a situation that currently or potentially involves the presence of the U.S. military in a foreign country. What is at stake in that country for the United States? Whose interests are likely to be served by the military's presence, and why? Identify the components of the military-industrial complex, and analyze what each has at stake in this particular case. What effect might U.S. military involvement in this situation have on you?

3. Select an issue that is currently controversial (such as the North American Free Trade Agreement, reform of the welfare system in the United States, health care, abortion rights, or gun-control legislation), and sort out the various interests that are likely to be affected by that issue. Consider the different ways that such a controversy might be resolved. Whose interests are served and whose interests are hurt by each possible outcome? How are you likely to be affected by each outcome? How might you affect the outcome?

4. The Supreme Court currently includes two women and one African American. Does their inclusion alter the kinds of decisions made by the Court, as opposed to the decisions of an all-white, all-male Court? Why or why not? Suppose *five* of the Supreme Court members were women or people of color. Would that change the decisions made? Why or why not? What if the Chief Justice were a woman or a person of color?

5. Does the existence of the military-industrial complex, the power elite, and the dominance of the state by business mean that nonelites are powerless? Why or why not? What can you point to as evidence of nonelite power or powerlessness?

KEY TERMS

alienation, *(348)*

apathy, *(348)*

business dominance theory, *(351)*

capital interests, *(351)*

capitalism, *(332)*

capitalist state structuralist theory, *(351)*

class dialectic perspective, *(352)*

class identity, *(338)*

collective embezzlement, *(352)*

communism, *(333)*

co-optation, *(338)*

corporate welfare, *(359)*

deregulation, *(352)*

economy, *(331)*

elite pluralist theory, *(336)*

gilded welfare, *(358)*

government, *(331)*

group pluralism, *(335)*

interchangeability of elites, *(338)*

interest groups, *(335)*

military-industrial complex, *(339)*

multinational (transnational) corporations, *(342)*

New Federalism, *(354)*

pluralism, *(334)*

political economy, *(332)*

power elite, *(338)*

power elite theory, *(338)*

socialism, *(333)*

social welfare, *(358)*

state, *(331)*

supply-side (trickle-down) economics, *(354)*

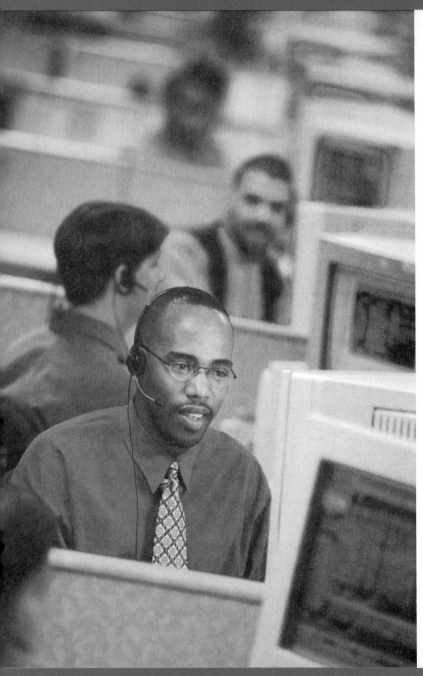

Chapter Twelve

Work and Production

When you graduate from college, do you expect your income to be better than, worse than, or the same as that of your parents when they were at that stage of their lives? What about your lifestyle? Are you likely to purchase your own home before you are 30 years old? Will you be able to afford to send your children to college? Will you be able to afford adequate health care? Where will you be economically in the next 20 years? The next 30? During the 1960s, a college degree was almost a guarantee of security and upward mobility. Now, that security is less certain. What has changed in the last 40 years or so to alter the meaning of a college degree in the work world?

Since the late 1970s, people in the United States have begun to feel that they are working harder but falling further behind in their standard of living and their economic well-being. In a 2000 survey by Public Agenda 2000, almost half of the respondents worried that "the strong economy would turn sour in the near future" (www.publicagenda.org/issues). In that same survey, 60 percent said they did not earn enough money to live the way they wanted. And an increasing number of middle-class workers are finding their jobs becoming less stable, more insecure every day (Newman, 1999; Rubin, 1996). More and more couples, particularly those with children, are finding that both partners must work full-time to be able to afford the basic necessities of their lives (Uchitelle, 1999; 2000). Poverty rates remain stubbornly high. But if work is the antidote to poverty, and if we're enjoying one of modern history's most robust and prosperous economies, riding a rising tide that lifts all boats, how can this be? The question of what happened to the American Dream is linked to the labor process and its place in the economy. It should be examined from several perspectives:

- What is the current structure of work and the economy in the United States?
- How and why has that structure changed in recent decades, and what effect do the changes have on individuals?
- Who benefits and who is hurt by these changes?
- What role have labor unions played in fostering or mitigating changes in the structure of work and the economy?
- Are people helpless victims of the economy as an institution, or are there prospects for change that offer promise to workers?

The Meaning of Work

To answer these questions requires a careful definition of the meaning of work. Generally, **work** refers to any activity "that produces something of value for other people" (U.S. Department of Health, Education, and Welfare, 1973). This activity can involve both paid and unpaid labor. That is, people need not be paid for their production of something of value for it to be considered work. Moreover, their efforts need not be readily visible to anyone else, publicly recognized, or performed outside the home to be considered work. As long as these activities produce something of value for someone else, they have engaged in work. So work includes paid labor (usually performed outside the home, but not necessarily) that takes place in what sociologists often refer to as the **formal labor market;** unpaid labor (both voluntary and involuntary, but excluding domestic labor), performed in the **informal labor market;** and **domestic labor** (work done to maintain the home and family, usually unpaid) (Glazer, 1987:249).

Many sociological studies have examined the relationship between work done in the formal and informal labor markets as well as domestic labor. Most of these studies note that women far more frequently than men work in two or more of these sectors (Nelson, 1999). Men more commonly work in the formal labor market, typically outside their homes. Even when women work full-time in the formal labor market, they are still primarily responsible for the domestic labor at home. Working full-time in the formal labor market does not seem to appreciably alter the domestic division of labor. Hochschild and Machung (1997) refer to the domestic labor responsibilities facing women at the end of a full day in the formal labor market as the **second shift.** This situation may be changing somewhat in some households; but the overall pattern still indicates that when women enter the formal labor market, the total amount of time they spend each day at work (both in the formal and domestic labor spheres) increases substantially, while for male partners the total amount of time spent each day at work remains essentially the same.

Some middle-class and upper-middle-class women respond to the pressures of the second shift by transferring the domestic labor that must be done into the formal labor market. The typical arrangement is for white middle- and upper-class women to hire poor immigrants or women of color to care for their children, clean their homes, and cook their meals (Ehrenreich and Hochschild, 2003). This arrangement does provide employment for poor women, but it also highlights the assumption that such work belongs to women. Class advantage allows some women to shift the burden of gender exploitation to other, less advantaged women, whereupon they also exploit class and racial inequalities (see Chapter 8). pp. 230–237

Women are more likely than men to work in the informal labor market, engaging in the invisible unpaid labor of volunteer work and bartering (Stone and Harvey, 2001). Bartering may involve the sharing of car rides, child care, and errand running with other women. The volunteer work done by women may be an important aspect of community as well as an aid to the careers of many women's partners (Meadows, 1996). It can involve working in local libraries, schools, and museums and developing charitable resources for the less fortunate in a community. Although women's volunteer work can build visibility, social networks, and contacts vital for their husbands' success at work, it is often devalued as unimportant in large part because it is unpaid.

In many cases, participating in the informal labor market is imperative for women living in poverty if they and their families are to survive. Many poor women must participate in all three spheres of labor every day. The following is a description of a typical day for a woman in Peru:

> Soledad, age thirty-five, with three children and a husband who works occasionally as an electrician, rises at 4 A.M. . . . She eats a stale bun with tea and packs her merchandise for the hour and a half long ride from Villa El Salvador to the centre of Lima . . . She is one of the thousands of *ambulantes* or street vendors who crowd the capital's major commercial districts, hawking cigarettes, candy, magazines, lottery tickets, cheap clothing, trinkets for tourists. Before leaving around 5:30, she wakes up her teenage daughter, Manuela. She will serve breakfast for the family and make sure that her two young brothers will arrive on time at the morning shift at the local primary school. Fourteen-year-old Manuela will do some school work, but most of her morning will be spent cleaning and washing clothes at the water spigot in the shack which adjoins the house. Sometimes, she will share these tasks with her mother during the evening hours . . . Soledad will return home sometime after noon with her morning's earnings. In her "free moments" she also knits sweaters on consignment. Since [her husband] lost his job three months ago, her work brings in the household's only regular income. Around 1:30, Soledad and Manuela will pick up the family's most important daily meal at a *comedor popular.* It is one of some 800 communal or "popular" kitchens which function in Lima today. The weekly fee is modest because Soledad, like the other women who organised the *comedor,* combine resources and take turns preparing the meals for the dozens of families served by it. Some of the women work at the *comedor* in the mornings. Soledad spends one afternoon a week cooking the snacks which will be distributed in the evening. But she is distracted and worried about what her younger children may be up to—no one is at home . . . On Monday afternoons, Soledad and two of her neighbours from the local "Glass of Milk Committee" will go to the municipal depot to pick up their weekly ration of powdered milk. It will be distributed free by other members of her committee . . . The daily struggle to ensure her family's survival adds up to an eighteen-hour work day . . . She says, "I feel tired all the time." (North, 1988:12)

Soledad's incredible day describes what is referred to as the **triple shift:** a daily juggle of work in the formal, informal, and household labor spheres (Hossfeld, 1988). Soledad's story occurred more than a decade ago, yet little has changed in rural Peru. Moreover, although Soledad lives in a peripheral nation, many women in the United

The task of juggling paid labor with domestic labor commonly defines the day of many women in the United States. The woman shown here appears to be pressed for time as she gets herself ready for work, chatting on her cell phone—perhaps with her employer or a client—while simultaneously getting her young child ready for the day.

States similarly labor a triple shift, juggling paid work in the formal labor market, unpaid housework, and the informal labor of carpooling, child care, and volunteer work connected with their children's schools and after-school activities.

The income people get from their participation in the formal labor market affects their ability to meet such basic needs as food, clothing, shelter, education, fuel, transportation, health care, and income for retirement. Looked at more broadly, labor market participation affects individuals' life chances. It is important, then, to examine the formal labor market: How is it structured, and how does its structure produce differential experiences by race, class, and gender? In this chapter we explore the formal labor market structure and how it has changed over the past 50 years. We examine how some burdens of the changes, such as unemployment, get distributed. We also investigate the effect of these changes on wages and on the status of the middle class. And we discuss the prospects for further change.

▌The Structure of the Formal Labor Market

The formal labor market in the United States is made up of different sectors: agricultural, goods-producing, and service sectors. In 2000, some 75.5 percent of the employed population worked in the service sector, compared with only 22.1 percent in the goods-producing sector (manufacturing, mining, and construction) and 2.4 percent in agriculture (www.statab.gov: Table 596). Workers in agriculture tend to be paid minimum wage; the work is seasonal, prompting many workers to migrate from region to region to follow various growing seasons. Although some migrant farmworkers have unionized, their working conditions tend to be unstable because of the seasonal nature of their work and the uncertainty of weather conditions.

Workers in manufacturing and mining are more likely than farmworkers to be unionized, although, like farmworkers, the majority are not. Compared with agricultural work, the work in this sector tends to be less seasonal and more secure, be better paid, and have greater benefits. However, even in this sector, job insecurity is not uncommon, since factories and mines shut down production when the economy is slow or when corporations merge or shift production outside the United States.

Less than 14 percent of all U.S. workers are unionized, and workers in the service sector are the least likely to be unionized (U.S. Department of Labor, Bureau of Labor Statistics, 2000). Workers in jobs such as nurses aides, child care, retail, fast food, convenience stores, and janitorial services tend to be paid minimum wage (or less, if they are high school or college students), have few, if any, health and retirement benefits, and work part-time. Jobs in this sector are growing faster than those in either of the other two sectors. Research on the effects of employment sectors on earnings challenges the functionalist view (pages 189–193) that earnings of individuals simply indicate that some jobs are more important than others and that some individuals make greater investments in their training and education (Davis and Moore, 1945). The structure of labor markets appears to differentiate earnings according to gender and race/ethnicity, regardless of education level or skill (England, Thompson, and Aman, 2001). A closer examination of the formal labor market helps explain why this might be the case.

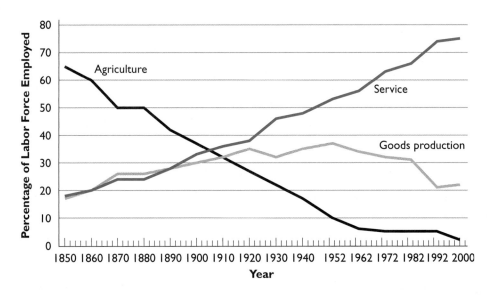

FIGURE 12.1 **Distribution of Employment by Activity Sector: 1850–2000**
The U.S. economy has undergone dramatic changes since the mid-1880s. How do these changes affect workers? How might they affect your own life chances after you graduate from college? (Sources: U.S. Department of Labor, *Monthly Labor Review* 107 (April, 1984); U.S. Department of Labor, *Employment and Earnings* 36 (November, 1989) and *Employment and Earnings* 42 (January, 1995); www.census.gov/statab, Table 596.)

The Changing Structure of Paid Work

The structure of the formal labor market in the United States has changed over time. Look at Figure 12.1: In 1910, the formal labor market was almost evenly distributed among the agriculture, manufacturing and goods-producing (including mining and construction), and service sectors. By World War II, this distribution had shifted dramatically; employment in agriculture continued to decline, while employment in manufacturing and service work continued to increase. After 1952, service employment kept climbing as both manufacturing and agricultural jobs fell. Currently, employment in the agricultural sector is shrinking almost to extinction, as food production in the United States falls increasingly under the control of major food-processing corporations. The service sector is growing by leaps and bounds: three-fourths of U.S. workers today are employed in this sector. And manufacturing activities are dramatically declining, with little more than one-fifth of the U.S. labor force engaged in manufacturing (www.statab.gov: Table 596).

Strikingly, between 1970 and 1990 the greatest job growth was in involuntary part-time work (i.e., jobs people accept in the absence of full-time opportunities, even when they prefer or need to work full-time). Such jobs increased by 121 percent,

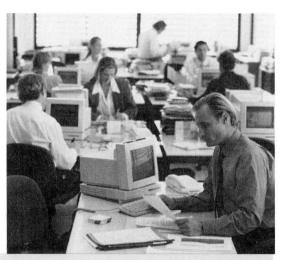

Agricultural employment in the United States has sharply declined since the mid-1800s, largely because of the mechanization of farm labor. While agricultural employment is at an all-time low, service-sector employment has skyrocketed in the structural transformation of the economy. The sharp rise in service-sector jobs has in some ways imitated the work conditions of manufacturing jobs. Here, office workers are crowded into small work areas, much like an administrative sweatshop.

while total employment grew by only 54 percent (Folbre, 1995). What is the significance of the dramatic increase in involuntary part-time work? Until very recently, most workers were hired by employers and placed in jobs under that employer. By the late 1990s, the trend was increasingly toward temporary workers hired to perform projects and then let go when the projects were completed. This shift was signaled in 1996 when AT&T announced the layoff of more than 40,000 workers, along with the intention of hiring many of them back as consultants and temporary workers on specific projects. These layoffs included everyone from low-level supervisors to high-level managers. AT&T insisted it was not laying off workers—it was conducting a "force management program" to reallocate its human resources by examining the skills of its work force and deciding which people to assign to current projects. Those not invited back were simply "unassigned" (Andrews, 1996). The company proudly presented its decision as the wave of the future for all corporations: "We have to promote the whole concept of the work force being contingent . . . [giving rise to a society that is increasingly] jobless but not workless" (Andrews, 1996:D6).

The Economic Policy Institute found that almost one-third of the workers in the United States (around 30 million workers) now "toil in temporary, contracted, self-employed, leased, part-time, and other 'nonstandard' arrangements," known as **contingency work** (Cook, 2000:15). Temp agencies, which hire temporary and part-time workers and lease them out to corporations for project work, themselves now employ almost 3 million workers. Jobs with temp agencies account for one-fourth of all new jobs created since 1984. And these workers are not restricted to temporary clerical work: "Contingent jobs are embedded in every sector of the economy, affecting workers of all collars. Their diverse ranks include high-tech software engineers and office workers; janitors, taxicab drivers and chicken catchers misclassified as independent contractors; adjunct college professors; and home healthcare workers" (Cook, 2000:15). Even colleges and universities are adopting this corporate shift toward contingency workers in their increasing reliance on adjunct faculty to teach courses for a fraction of the cost of full-time faculty (Noble, 2001).

Why is this shift toward contingency work so attractive to corporations, and what does it mean to workers? Contingency work typically falls through the cracks of worker-protection laws and is not subject to unemployment insurance benefits to which employers must contribute, making such workers more easily exploitable. Contingency workers also represent an attractive cost-saving device for employers, since such workers average $100 less than their more permanent counterparts in weekly take-home pay. In addition, few contingent workers receive health care or retirement benefits. Only one-fifth of contingency workers have employer-provided health insurance and retirement benefits, compared to more than half of all noncontingent workers who do receive such benefits (Cook, 2000). And where manufacturing and mining workers (previously the majority of the work force) tended to be unionized, service workers in general and contingency workers in particular are not. This represents a decided political advantage to employers, whose temporary work force is not currently organized to resist the power of their employers and whose individualized, competitive isolation reduces the opportunities for the kinds of communication networks that used to encourage worker consciousness.

Causes of the Structural Transformation of the Economy

What has caused this structural shift and transformation of the economy? Sociologist Beth A. Rubin points to **globalization,** the "processes that create a global network of interdependent actors and activities that are unconnected to a specific place or national economy" (1996:5). The dramatic pathbreaking developments in *technology,* particularly in microelectronics, have spurred the development of an increasingly *global economy* and the acceleration of increasing *capital mobility.* In turn, globalization has encouraged *deindustrialization* (Anderson and Cavanagh, 2000; Eitzen and Zinn, 1989a: 2). Let's look at these forces one at a time.

Technology

Just as the steam engine fueled the Industrial Revolution, the computer microchip has spurred the latest structural transformation of the economy. Notably, the stimulant for both inventions was not need per se, but the need of affluent and powerful owners of the means of production to gain greater control over and profit from the production process.

The microchip is capable of storing, retrieving, and manipulating mountains of data quickly and accurately. Information can instantaneously be transmitted from one computer to another halfway around the world. Engineers and architects can anticipate and correct design problems quickly on computer screens, rather than spending months on costly experiments only to discover serious product defects. And microchips have enabled computerized robots to increase productivity in manufacturing. While these robots eliminate many tedious, boring, low-paying, and hazardous jobs, they also unfortunately displace human labor rather than create jobs (Aronowitz and DiFazio, 1994; Rifkin, 1995). Similarly, use of online and distance learning modules permanently displaces an increasing number of full-time faculty from the academic market (Noble, 2001). Thus microchips and the technological advancements they foster have served to increase productivity, but at the cost of eliminating many higher paying manufacturing and professional jobs.

The Global Economy

In addition to the destruction of manufacturing jobs, the microchip has contributed to the shift toward a global economy. The speed and accuracy of information processing between computers around the world enables managers in the United States to run production processes abroad. Prior to the development of the microchip, the sheer distance separating North America from the other continents essentially protected U.S. manufacturers from international competition for the large markets within the United States. Enormous breakthroughs in transportation and communication have reduced that protection, and products from abroad now easily compete with domestic products in U.S. markets (Dolbeare, 1986).

The success of that competition can be measured by the decreasing profits of manufacturers in the United States. Many U.S. corporations have responded to the competition by stepping up the level of automated production, destroying jobs but increasing productivity. Other corporations have wrung concessions from workers, such as lower wages, moratoria on pensions, decreases in health benefits, and increases in layoffs. In addition to wringing such concessions from workers, corporations have gained many concessions from the localities or states in which they were located. These concessions include tax benefits, eased environmental and land use restrictions, and sometimes actual cash payments or land donations. Such concessions are attractive to firms and used as incentives for firms to stay in a given location, but the costs are borne primarily by workers, whose taxes are likely to increase or whose municipal or state budgets become squeezed by the loss of corporate taxes. When these benefits are used up, corporations often move anyway, sometimes leaving the United States entirely for greener pastures in Mexico and beyond.

Capital Mobility

The globalization of the economy is related to a third force in the restructuring of the U.S. economy: capital mobility, the ability to move money and assets. Banks and manufacturers may move both financial and production resources at will anywhere they choose. They have increasingly chosen to merge their assets with other corporations and to relocate their plants abroad and invest outside the United States.

Investment Abroad

Over the past 50 years, investment abroad by U.S. corporations has grown dramatically, from $16 billion in 1950 to $4.9 trillion in 1998 (www.census.gov). Indeed, many of the largest U.S. corporations receive a significant proportion of their revenues from their investments abroad (*Business Wire;* 2001; http://ptg.djnr.com). So

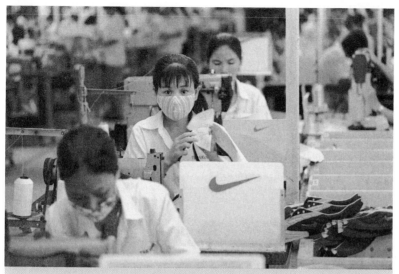

Hundreds of thousands of manufacturing jobs in the United States have been exported to poor nations, particularly those in Southeast Asia and Central America, where workers are paid pennies per day and where worker health and safety regulations and workers' rights to collective bargaining are nonexistent. Here, workers in a Nike factory in Asia wear cloth face masks as their only protection against breathing in deadly textile dust.

much of their production and revenue has shifted outside the United States that such firms are routinely referred to as multinational or transnational corporations.

Why have these corporations invested so heavily abroad? Part of the reason is that labor in other countries, particularly in the underdeveloped nations of Latin America and Asia, is nonunionized and cheaper than labor in the United States. Moreover, underdeveloped countries tend to have fewer and more lax environmental and worker health and safety regulations. Thus production is inexpensive, if not safe and responsible. Decisions to invest abroad have the consequence of exporting U.S. production jobs.

The historic North American Free Trade Agreement (NAFTA) of 1994 was supposed to help open the political borders separating the United States, Canada, and Mexico, smoothing the way for cheaper and easier trade between the three countries. Eliminating trade barriers such as tariffs, and allowing corporations to engage in production and sell goods in all three countries as if they were one, would, in theory, result in prosperity, more jobs, and an improvement in environmental standards throughout North America. Five years later, evidence showed that NAFTA enhanced capital mobility for corporations but provided little else. For example, while NAFTA supporters insisted that the treaty would produce 200,000 new jobs in the United States annually, the fact is that "hundreds of thousands of U.S. jobs have been lost" (Wallach and Sforza, 1999:7). This is because under the treaty, 40 percent of U.S. exports to Mexico are actually parts to be assembled by low-wage workers at U.S.-owned plants. The products then return to the United States as finished consumer goods, causing a huge U.S. trade deficit with Mexico. Trade deficits commonly produce layoffs because they indicate heavy importing that is not offset by sufficient exporting. So, not only are U.S. workers' jobs being exported to Mexico with the help of NAFTA; those jobs that remain here are jeopardized by trade deficits.

Moreover, not only have almost a quarter of a million workers in the United States lost their jobs as a result of NAFTA, but companies that promised to create new NAFTA-stimulated jobs have not fulfilled that promise. A survey of firms that made such promises in 1993 found that almost 90 percent had failed to make good on those promises by 1999, and many had already relocated production to Mexico (Wallach and Sforza, 1999). And although one promise of NAFTA supporters was that it would stimulate increases in wages for workers in Mexico and therefore reduce the motivation for illegal immigration to the United States, workers in Mexico are no better off than U.S. workers under NAFTA. Although jobs are fleeing from the United States to Mexico, and Mexican productivity has increased by 36.4 percent, Mexican wages have declined 29 percent. Workers in Mexico's *maquilladora* production centers average weekly wages of $55.77, one reason that "60 percent of the Mexican labor force lives below the poverty line" (Wallach and Sforza, 1999:7). So what was promised as an economic boon to everyone has provided advantages primarily to corporate elites in the United States. Notably, as low as wages are in Mexico, they are still higher than wages paid to workers in China. Multinational corporations are now relocating production from Mexico to China (Ramirez, 2003). This underscores the ease with which these firms can scour the globe seeking the cheapest wages.

🌐 Runaway Shops

U.S. corporations often decide it is profitable to relocate production and service facilities elsewhere within the United States in addition to overseas. Both forms of relocation are often referred to as **runaway shops.** The pattern has been that manufacturing corporations close plants in the North and Midwest (the "frostbelt"), where labor unions have historically been strongest, and move production to the South and Southwest (the "sunbelt"), where unions have been nonexistent or weak (Rifkin and Barber, 1978). By 2001, only 7.2 percent of workers in the sunbelt were represented by unions, compared with 18.3 percent of workers unionized in the frostbelt (www.statab.gov, Tables 608, 639). Often, such a move gives corporations the opportunity to further automate production, eliminating even more human labor.

Indeed, something of a bidding war has waged over the past two decades among states vying for plants to be relocated in their communities. That bidding war can be quite costly: States and cities may offer corporations gifts of land, long moratoria on taxes (many of which are lowered to attract business), infrastructural development (such as roads and schools), and lax regulations. For example, when Pennsylvania wanted to attract Norwegian global engineering and construction firm Kvaerner ASA to relocate a shipbuilding enterprise there in 1997, the state offered the company a $307 million economic incentive package. It cost the state $323,000 per job to create a mere 950 jobs, none of which paid anywhere near this figure (Barlett and Steele, 2001). Politicians have engaged in this expensive, seemingly irrational bidding war because they fear the consequences of having to explain to voters why they did not try to attract jobs to their states.

Such costs raise the issue of who the winners and losers are in the domestic re-location of production facilities. The communities where plants shut down relied on their presence for jobs and economic security; thus runaway shops are clearly not to their advantage. But whether the recipient communities are winners either is equally questionable. Some states and cities have begun to recognize that the bidding war does not work to anyone's advantage: New York City, New York State, New Jersey, and Connecticut have agreed to stop advertisements designed to entice producers to pull up stakes and relocate. And the National Governors' Association works to explore similar ways to curb corporate relocators' power to instigate costly giveaways by states that can hardly afford them, all for the dubious distinction of creating relatively few jobs (Schwartz and Barrett, 1992).

Mergers

U.S. corporations also move investment capital into **mergers** with other corporations. That is, they invest in the purchase of other firms. The flurry of mergers or takeovers over the past two decades has been called **merger mania.** As Figure 12.2 shows, the number of mergers per year grew from 1,719 in 1985 to 9,599 by 1999. Corporate purchases of other firms are quite expensive: The total cost of the mergers in 1999 was $3.4 trillion, up from $149.6 billion in 1985 (www.statab.gov: Table 742). These purchases take away from funds that might otherwise be invested by firms in production. In some cases, investing in a merger rather than in productive

FIGURE 12.2 Mergers and Acquisitions: 1980–1999   Since 1980, mergers between large corporations have accelerated so that fewer corporations are producing or providing the goods and services people use. What consequences might this have for the economy, both in the United States and worldwide? What consequences might it have for workers, consumers, and local communities?   (Source: www.census.gov, "Mergers and Acquisitions," Table 882.)

capacity can lead to corporate revenue losses that, in effect, greatly increase the price of the merger. The importance of such investment decisions can be seen in the 2000 merger between America Online (AOL) and Time Warner. That merger created the largest media conglomerate in the United States, worth more than $350 billion. But less than two years later, the merged company was posting massive losses, until its value plummeted to $50 billion. Shareholders lost 45 percent of the combined value of the merged firm, and the chief executive officer Richard Parsons announced the company's strategy of cost control, signaling significant layoffs (Szalai, 2003; *Washington Times,* 2002).

Mergers help restructure the U.S. economy by increasing concentration in corporate America, so that the country's productive capacity is increasingly being owned and controlled by fewer hands. This means less competition among fewer producers and higher prices for consumer goods. Increasing concentration of productive capacity also gives corporations greater power advantages over workers and the state. They find it easier to wring concessions from workers and to elicit favorable tax policies and relaxation of state regulations. Finally, mergers tend to eliminate jobs because the acquiring firm seeks to reduce duplication and to streamline its merged operations (Russell, 1987). Merger mania, then, has been a strong factor in restructuring the U.S. economy.

Deindustrialization

As we pointed out earlier, since World War II, the economy has witnessed increasing growth in its service sector. At the same time, manufacturing activities are being shifted to the work force in poorer countries (Collins, 1998). As a result, plants in the United States are increasingly becoming empty. Either they are shutting down or the workers are simply assembling imported parts into finished goods, rather than manufacturing the parts themselves and then assembling them. Social scientists refer to this process of declining domestic manufacturing activity as **deindustrialization.**

The increasing reliance on imported manufactured goods and parts has greatly affected workers in the United States. Some workers have lost their jobs (and health and retirement benefits) too close to retirement age to be retrained and hired elsewhere. Other workers have relocated their families in hope of finding new jobs, only to discover that thousands of others had the same idea. What looks like a promising local job market can easily become glutted with dislocated workers in search of employment.

Some economists and politicians argue that the dislocation of workers, while admittedly uncomfortable, is temporary. As the economy undergoes its normal readjustments, new jobs will inevitably be created to replace those lost to deindustrialization. Unfortunately, research shows that more jobs have been lost than created and that the new jobs tend to pay less than the old jobs that were destroyed (Heintz, Folbre, and the Center for Popular Economics, 2000; Zweig, 2000). The evidence suggests that the new jobs created in the service sector have not filled the void left by deindustrialization.

In addition to permanently dislocating workers, deindustrialization can have devastating consequences on whole communities. Towns and cities that once prospered while heavily or exclusively reliant on a single company (or a single industry) find themselves facing increased poverty and loss of population when the company moves or closes (Brady and Wallace, 2001). The effects of a shutdown can reverberate throughout the community. Small businesses that once relied on the now-unemployed workers go bankrupt; industries that once supplied goods and services to the now-closed main employer lose business and thus must themselves shut down and lay off their own employees; and municipal services that once relied on income and property tax revenues must be cut back or eliminated altogether, including things like police and fire protection, sanitation removal, schools, and hospitals.

The effects of shutdowns on individuals is often devastating as well:

> Jeff, who is 50, lost his job at Rapp Digital almost two years ago, making him one of 21,000 computer-industry professionals in New York City to have been let go since the end of 2000 . . . [H]e had three months of severance—plenty, he thought, to get him to his next position. The three months went by, then four, then five, then six . . . "Once it hits a year, . . . there's no reason to believe it's going to be any better this time next year." [Jeff's wife finally tells him that he must find a way to contribute financially or move out.] Now, working at the Gap at $10 an hour, it takes Jeff two and a half weeks to earn what he used to make in a day at Rapp Digital. . . [A]fter "the year-and-a-half-long process of dehumanization," as Jeff calls it, he's happy to have any job . . . Jeff's outplacement [a service provided by Rapp Digital when they laid him off] proved to be little more than a halfway house between full-time employment and full-time unemployment . . . [S]ix months after being let go, he filed for personal bankruptcy protection. . . "Shame is . . . about who or what you are or what you are not . . . I felt guilty about losing my job and shame about not being able to support my family." (Mahler, 2003: 46–48, 66, 70)

This worker's saga is not unique; it might just as easily describe the scores of similar stories that continue to emerge throughout the United States (Binkley, 2001; Dandaneau, 1996; Thomas, 1997).

Changing Corporate Organizational Structure

Why has it been possible for corporations to engage in decision making that produces deindustrialization, plant relocation, and the globalization of labor and production? The answer lies partly in the changing organizational structure of firms. Most companies were once owned and controlled by a single proprietor, who often resided in the community or close by, but firms now are owned by stockholders and controlled by managers and bankers. The change began in the late 1800s, when owners needed to raise capital to expand; they had the choice of either taking out loans and incurring debt or selling shares of ownership, or stock, in their firms. When an owner sells shares in the firm, the company structure expands to include a board of directors and potentially thousands of shareholders. Since the sales of stocks were dispersed among thousands of independent shareholders, corporate managers were able to control a corporation by owning as little as 5 percent of its stock (Bell, 1973; Berle and Means, 1932). Burnham (1941) termed this turn of events the **managerial revolution,** in which ownership and control were presumably separated, with control over corporate decision making accruing to professional managers. Critics, however, have noted that while it may be true that the sale of corporate stock separates ownership and control, shares are not as widely dispersed as previously thought. Wealthy families and banks retain the largest proprietary interests in most firms, since they hold the greatest number of shares (Mayer, 2001; Mintz and Schwartz, 1985).

The stock market increasingly looms as an important factor motivating what corporations do. This is because, in addition to the interests of financial institutions as major stockholders, corporate chief executives themselves have strong vested interests in their firms' stock performance. Increasingly, chief executives' compensation is derived less from salaries (which are taxable at the highest levels as income) than from lucrative stock options. They have the option of purchasing huge blocks of stock in their firms at below-market prices, with the option of selling those shares if they wish when the asking price is highly favorable. The idea is to tie the executives' personal fortunes with those of the firm, thus motivating them to do whatever is in the best interest of the company on the assumption that this means making the firm more profitable.

Unfortunately, executive compensation has clearly shown no positive correlation with profits in the past few decades. By 2002, when the Standard & Poor's stock prices averaged a loss of 23.4 percent and corporate profits suffered a 4 percent decline, chief executives posted a 6 percent increase in their compensation (www.afl-cio.org/corporateamerica/paywatch). Higher compensation, then, does not necessarily mean a more profitable or productive firm, but it does show a strong link to stock market performance. Since executives' compensation is primarily tied to the performance of their company's stock, they become motivated to make decisions that will increase the value of the stock, even if those decisions will not make the firm more profitable. Moreover, such decisions do not necessarily enhance workers' job security. For example, mergers between large firms are widely considered to be likely to increase the value of a stock, even if they do not increase productive capacity or preserve jobs. More significantly, announcements of massive worker layoffs typically have the effect of driving up the value of shares of stock in the short run because they mean huge savings in wages for the firm; yet layoffs may harm the economy overall by stimulating recessions and decreasing the ability of consumers to afford goods. One observer went so far as to call such executives "corporate killers," suggesting that "Wall Street loves layoffs" (Sloan, 1996:44). No less an observer than *Business Week* wondered in a 1997 cover story if "executive pay. . . [is] out of control . . . Don't confuse a bull market [a market in which stock prices tend to rise] with managerial genius" (Reingold, 1997:cover).

How does the separation of ownership and control, and stock prices as a force in corporate decision making, promote plant relocation and deindustrialization? Companies that are controlled by financial institutions, corporate managers, and large stockholders are not necessarily tied to the local community where the plants operate; these interests often reside elsewhere and may have little allegiance to the local community. Thus the controlling interests of firms become an important force in the structural transformation of the economy.

In addition to undergoing a change in their ownership and control structure, corporations are no longer the individual, competitive firms they once may have been. Instead, the vast majority of the largest firms (referred to as the Fortune 500, because of their inclusion in *Fortune*'s annual list of the 500 biggest corporations) are connected through **interlocking boards of directors,** created by economic elites who sit on multiple corporate boards. The strongest corporate interlockers are economic elites from the largest commercial banks. With large commercial banks acting as central figures in these corporate networks and the stock market acting as a major motivating force in chief executive and board decision making, boards of directors—not surprisingly—treat the corporation as an organization of chunks of financial assets to be bought and sold or relocated rather than as a staple in the local community and an organization that has mutual obligations and responsibilities. Corporate boards of directors may be more concerned with keeping their firms' cash flows, stock values, and dividends high. Corporate interlocking directorates, then, may support plant relocations, shutdowns, and deindustrialization because the interests of shareholders in the firm (including chief executives, financial institutions, and affluent investors) are privileged over the interests of stakeholders (including workers, consumers, and the communities in which firms do business).

Economic Restructuring and Labor-Management Changes

Some observers blame U.S. workers for the loss of jobs in the nation's manufacturing and goods-producing sector. They argue that high wages paid workers have made U.S. firms noncompetitive relative to the wages in other industrial countries. Many U.S. corporations have used this rationale to justify relocating production to other countries. However, the evidence shown in Figure 12.3 comparing workers' wages in the United States and its industrialized competitors does not support this viewpoint. In 2001, workers in the United States received average hourly wages comparable to those of workers in Japan and lower than the wages of workers in Germany. In U.S. dollars, workers in the United States received $20.32 per hour, while workers in Japan earned $19.59; in comparison, workers in Germany received $22.86 per hour (http://stats.bls.gov).

Only a comparison of the hourly wages of U.S. workers to those of workers in South Korea, Mexico, and Brazil reveals a decided advantage for foreign competitors from an industrialized country. In 2001, Korean, Mexican, and Brazilian workers earned considerably less than U.S. workers. Thus the evidence does not support the argument that the U.S. economy has become noncompetitive in international markets simply because workers in the United States have been paid too well relative to their counterparts in competing countries.

A more important factor in explaining the restructuring of the U.S. economy away from manufacturing is the power structure of business. It is managers, not workers, who determine the placement of factories and the level of hiring to be done; management decides its own compensation, as well as whether to invest the firm's cash flow in expansion and modernization of existing plants or in purchases of other firms. Indeed, as we pointed out, many of the largest firms have spent significant proportions of their investment capital on mergers and acquisitions, instead of upgrading facilities and production processes. In the early 1990s, General Motors announced that it had to lay off 75,000 workers because of serious declines in the market value of its stock. Executives implied that the workers themselves were the

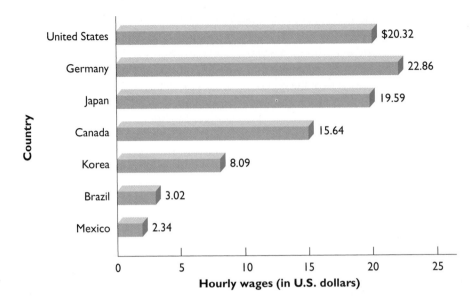

FIGURE 12.3 Hourly Wages for Production Workers in Selected Countries: 2001 While many believe that workers in the United States do not compete with workers in other industrialized nations because they demand excessive wages, this figure suggests that such an analysis is at best oversimplified. What else might cause jobs to be exported? (Source: http://stats.bls.gov Bureau of Labor Statistics "International Comparisons.")

cause; however, poor managerial investment decisions, inordinately high compensation of management, and refusals over decades to update its U.S. facilities have been the main causes of GM's troubles. Yet managers did not suffer the extensive layoffs, loss of income, or loss of pension security that workers did. Unfortunately, workers are the more visible and easily blamed "causes," and they become the greatest victims.

In contrast, despite the declining profits of manufacturing in the United States, corporations' chief executive officers (CEOs) have continued to prosper. Between 1965 and 1979, increases in the annual pay of U.S. production workers and the total compensation for CEOs were roughly parallel. The wages/compensation of workers as a proportion of that of chief executive officers ranged between 3.5 and 4 percent, or 25 to 1. However, from 1980 on, workers' pay increases slowed considerably, while the compensation of CEOs soared (Phillips, 1990:181). Total compensation of CEOs continued to increase sharply in the 1990s, unabated by declines in corporate profitability. By 2000, the ratio of chief executive officers' compensation to wage workers' income was 400 to 1 (www.epinet.org/books/swa2000/surprising).

How has this growing gap between workers' pay and CEO compensation been possible? Part of the answer relates to the power structure of work organizations in the United States. Workers' wages are determined either by management alone or through negotiation between management and unions in collective bargaining, but CEOs' compensation is determined by a corporation's board of directors (who are often elected by shareholders). The CEO is typically a member of the board and thus is in a position to greatly influence his or her own compensation.

Another factor that heavily contributed to the rise in CEOs' compensation through the 1980s and 1990s was the restructuring of tax codes under the Reagan administration. That restructuring encouraged executives to shelter much of their compensation in ownership of their firms' stocks, which were not taxed as heavily as income. Since stock values increased dramatically in the 1980s and much of the 1990s, CEOs' total compensation soared to unprecedented heights, even as the CEOs were laying off tens of thousands of workers and demanding that workers give up benefits included in their labor contracts. Thus, while workers' salaries and purchasing power have at best risen little as a result of economic restructuring, those of CEOs have increased remarkably, regardless of the condition of their firms or the general economy (Abowd and Kaplan, 1998; www.aflcio.org/corporateamerica/paywatch/pay).

Technological changes, the globalization of the economy, increasing capital mobility, and deindustrialization have combined to generate a structural transformation of the U.S. economy that differentially affects labor and management. Exactly how has this transformation affected the daily lives of workers? We now turn to an examination of some of its effects.

Economic Structural Transformation and Inequality

Taken together, the transformation of the economy has accentuated inequality in U.S. society. This becomes clear in an examination of these effects: (1) structural unemployment and underemployment, (2) the shift of the formal labor market from manufacturing to service work, and (3) the declining income generated by the remaining jobs in the formal labor market (Eitzen and Zinn, 1989b).

Unemployment

One indicator of the overall effect of deindustrialization and the permanent restructuring of the economy is unemployment. Between 1979 and 1983, a trend of job losses because of plant closings emerged, with almost 12 million workers permanently dislocated from their jobs. Close to 5 million of these job losses were due to plant closings; the rest were caused by the elimination of jobs or shifts, the lack of enough work to sustain the existing work force, or business failures (Mishel and Simon, 1988: 27; U.S. Department of Labor, 1985). That trend continues: In 2000 alone, 3.1 million workers were permanently dislocated, 49.4 percent of them because of plant closings (www.statab.gov: Table 590). These figures suggest that deindustrialization and the unemployment it generates have escalated since the 1980s. Unemployment in the United States generally deepened from the end of World War II through the early 1990s, rising from a rate of 3.9 percent in 1947 to 7.5 percent in 1992. By 2001, however, the unemployment rate hit one of its lowest points since World War II, falling to 6.0 percent of the total labor force (www.statab.gov: Table 567). That rate began to creep upward again in 2003, but it is still relatively low.

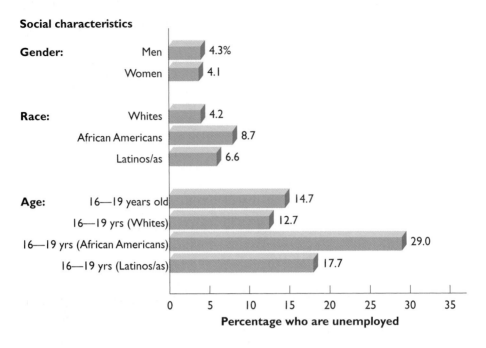

Social characteristics

Gender:
Men 4.3%
Women 4.1

Race:
Whites 4.2
African Americans 8.7
Latinos/as 6.6

Age:
16—19 years old 14.7
16—19 yrs (Whites) 12.7
16—19 yrs (African Americans) 29.0
16—19 yrs (Latinos/as) 17.7

0   5   10   15   20   25   30   35

Percentage who are unemployed

FIGURE 12.4 **Unemployment Rates by Race, Gender, and Age: 2001**   While unemployment is on the rise for all groups in the United States, it does not strike the working population randomly. On the basis of the data in this graph, which people do you think are more likely to lose their jobs? Why do these unemployment patterns occur?   Note that the Bureau of Labor Statistics did not report out comparable data for Asian Americans or Native Americans. (Source: www.bls.gov)

Interpreting this as a signal of the end of the ravages of the current economic structural transformation might be tempting. But look deeper, at the patterns describing *who* the unemployed are, and examine the issue of underemployment.

In 2000, teen unemployment was 13.1 percent (www.statab.gov: Table 598). Because teenage workers tend to be less experienced and less skilled than older workers, they are often hired for unskilled or semiskilled work. Unskilled work is frequently the first to be dislocated by automation.

Even more telling is a breakdown of unemployment by gender and race, as shown in Figure 12.4. Women's unemployment rates were higher than the rates for men until 1995, after which their rates became the same or lower than those of men, a pattern that now continues (www.statab.gov: Table 598). But this parity is, paradoxically, a result of continued sex discrimination. Men have had greater employment in manufacturing, precisely the sector that has suffered the most severe job losses. Women, on the other hand, have had greater employment opportunities in the service sector, which has shown pronounced increases in employment.

Racial and ethnic comparisons of unemployment show a more marked pattern. Unemployment rates for African American workers have consistently remained more than twice the rates for white workers. Latino/Latina workers have fared only slightly better, with rates of unemployment consistently running more than 50 percent higher than those of white workers. The unemployment rates for African American and Latino/Latina teenage workers have shown equally alarming patterns relative to white teenage workers: Teenagers of color are more than twice as likely as white teenage workers to be unemployed (www.statab.gov: Table 598). A large part of this consistent difference in unemployment rates by race is the result of past pp. 197–204 ▶ and present-day institutional racism (see Chapter 7).

This analysis of unemployment is based on the official rates of unemployment reported by the U.S. Bureau of Labor Statistics. But these rates have come under criticism for *underreporting* the real rates of unemployment. This is because of the way the Bureau of Labor Statistics defines and counts unemployment. Persons must be considered "attached to the labor force" in order to be counted as active participants in the labor market. Anyone who has been out of the labor force and has not been actively looking for a job in the previous four weeks is not counted as unemployed. Thus people who have become discouraged and have ceased looking for work are not included in the official statistics on the unemployed. Nor are those who work at least one day per week at a part-time job, even though they would like full-time work. Including all the uncounted people who want to work in the formal labor market but who cannot find employment would almost double the real rate of unemployment beyond the official rate reported by the government (Mishel, Bernstein, and Schmitt, 2001).

The state determines eligibility for federal benefits for the unemployed on the basis of definitions and counts established by the Bureau of Labor Statistics. Persons who are attached to the labor force and lose their jobs through no fault of their own are supposed to be provided for under the federal unemployment insurance program. However, the percentage of the unemployed who actually receive unemployment insurance payments has declined since World War II. In 1999, only 37.2 percent of those who could not find employment were receiving benefits or payments from the program (www.statab.gov: Table 537). This is in part because many of the unemployed could not find new jobs before their entitlement period expired. Others did not work long enough before losing their jobs to qualify for unemployment benefits. Still others worked only seasonally or part-time and thus did not qualify for such benefits. Moreover, the payments provided by the program cover no more than 50 percent of the wages earned during employment and ordinarily continue only for a period of 26 weeks.

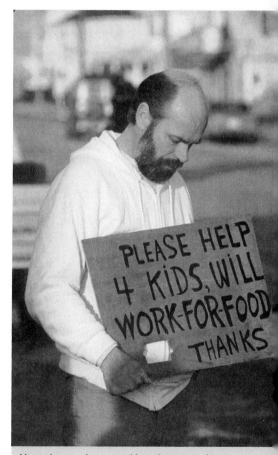

Unemployment, hunger, and homelessness no longer represent an alien or remote existence for middle-class families in the United States. Many middle-management workers, as well as administrative and manufacturing workers, have been "downsized." Some, like the man pictured here, have been forced to take to the streets to beg for work, food, or shelter.

Economic structural transformation has, then, caused unemployment for significant numbers of U.S. workers in recent decades. Throughout this period most workers have still been employed. What has happened to them?

Underemployment and Declining Income from Existing Jobs

Beyond structural patterns of unemployment, and perhaps more significant in the new century, is the problem of underemployment, a phenomenon that is hidden by the historically low unemployment rates that especially marked the 1990s. **Underemployment** refers to the situation in which individuals are employed at jobs that do not fully utilize their skills, that pay less than a living wage, or that do not offer opportunities for full-time employment. We have already discussed the problem of the sharp increase in involuntary part-time employment as a significant trend in the 1990s. And we have already noted the dramatic rise in contingency work as the wave of the future. Part-time and contingency work that are involuntary are examples of underemployment, which is likely to increase as a regular feature of the labor market in the coming decades.

Additionally, the growth of the service sector contributes in large measure to low wages as an element of underemployment. This is because service sector jobs are frequently minimum wage. For example, 79.1 percent of retail sales workers are paid low wages, as are 81.4 percent of food service workers and 71 percent of personal service workers (Kim, 2000). Low wages mean that people who hold such jobs, even if they work full-time, will not rise above the poverty line. Take, for example, the case of a worker at a convenience store who works 40 hours per week for a full 52 weeks a year, at the 2001 federal minimum wage of $5.15 per hour. That person will earn $10,712 annually before taxes. Considering the fact that the poverty line for a family of three (a single adult with two dependent children under the age of 18) was $14,494 in 2002, this worker will clearly not earn enough for his or her family to rise out of poverty (www.census.gov). Once taxes are taken out of this worker's paycheck, the family's situation will be much worse. This is clearly a case of underemployment: This person is working full time but is stuck in the position of being a member of the "working poor." The "Social Forces/People's Lives" reading describes in human terms how the increasing dominance of minimum-wage service jobs in the economy translates into real, everyday struggles to secure a roof over one's head. By 2000 more than 3.5 million U.S. workers were working two or more jobs simply to make ends meet (www.statab.gov: Table 586).

Although there has been a net increase in the number of jobs created in the United States since the late 1970s, these new jobs do not compensate for the income that workers lost as jobs shifted from manufacturing to services. Weekly earnings in the goods-producing sector averaged $690 in 2000; in comparison, weekly earnings in the service sector averaged $496 that same year (www.statab.gov: Table 607). Thus the greatest job growth is occurring in the sector that pays lower wages. The average annual compensation rate in the shrinking industries is more than $13,000 greater per year than the compensation rate in the expanding industries. Jobs in goods production average an annual compensation of $52,443, whereas service-sector compensation averages only $39,266 (www.statab.gov, Table 615). Why is there such a gap in compensation for work in different sectors?

Part of the answer may be unionization. Workers in the service sector (with the notable exception of government workers) are unlikely to be represented by unions. Evidence shows that the collective bargaining that unions engage in typically succeeds in raising workers' wages and benefits, including health and pension coverage (Krecker and O'Rand, 1991; www.statab.gov: Table 638). Thus the much greater average annual compensation in the more unionized goods-producing sector is not surprising. Jobs in the service sector are three times more likely than those in goods production to pay the minimum wage of $5.15 per hour, and many such jobs are only part-time, seasonal, or temporary work. Part-time workers typically do not receive health or pension benefits. Indeed, in 2001, some 37.6 percent of full-time workers were not included in group health coverage at all, and 48.5 percent were not included in a pension plan (www.statab.gov: Table 627).

Another problem is that the value of the minimum wage has sharply declined since 1978. The minimum wage in 2000 could purchase only three-fourths of what it could purchase in 1978. This is because the minimum wage, which is established by Congress and is rarely adjusted for inflation, has not kept up with the cost of living (www.statab.gov: Table 624). As we noted earlier, workers who labor full-time, year-round on minimum wage cannot earn enough income to rise above the poverty line. In fact, the poverty rate for full-time, year-round workers over the age of 15 has increased since 1973, so that 3.1 percent of these workers were in poverty by 1999. Full-time workers headed up 18.7 percent of all poor families in the United States in 1999, and part-time workers headed 35.6 percent of poor families (www.statab.gov: Table 686). Work, then, is not necessarily the simple antidote to poverty. Even working full-time, year-round is not a guarantee that one will not be poor, especially if one works, as do so many people in the United States, in the low-wage jobs that predominate the service sector.

Gender, Racial, and Ethnic Inequality and the Labor Market

Look at the racial, ethnic, and gender distribution of workers between sectors and within sectors; notice the patterns of inequality that changes in the labor market have only accentuated. Since World War II, female labor-force participation rates have increased more sharply than those for males (Bianchi and Dye, 2001). But men and women do not necessarily secure employment in the same kinds of jobs, and they do not receive equal compensation for the work done (Bose and Whaley, 2001; Steinberg, 2001). In 2000, women held more than 62 percent of the jobs in the service sector, where, as previously noted, wages are often very low. Men, in contrast, are far more likely to be employed in goods production, where wages are much better (www.statab.gov: Table 596). Women were especially concentrated in clerical and service jobs, holding over 90 percent of the jobs in nursing and dental hygienics, sewing and stitching, child care and early childhood education services, secretarial and reception work, bookkeeping, and bank tellers. On the other hand, men were concentrated in higher paying jobs, holding over 90 percent of the jobs in fields such as logging, construction work, mining, auto mechanics, plumbing and pipefitting, firefighting, engineering, and airplane piloting and navigating (www.statab.gov: Table 593). These data suggest that there is a **segmented labor market** wherein women and men compete in different labor markets for different jobs (Rosenfeld, 1980). The

Nickel and Dimed

BARBARA EHRENREICH

According to public policy and cultural lore alike, work is the antidote to poverty. One can avoid poverty simply by getting a job. But most jobs are now in the service sector, where wages are typically very low, with few or no health or retirement benefits. Barbara Ehrenreich tried working at several such jobs to see what it meant in real terms to try to live on a minimum-wage paycheck. This reading, excerpted from her book *Nickel and Dimed,* illustrates how it is that people can be poor, hungry, or homeless even though they may work full time.

THIS job shows no sign of being financially viable. You might imagine, from a comfortable distance, that people who live, year in and year out, on $6 to $10 an hour have discovered some survival stratagems unknown to the middle class. But no. It's not hard to get my coworkers talking about their living situations, because housing, in almost every case, is the principal source of disruption in their lives, the first thing they fill you in on when they arrive for their shifts. After a week, I have compiled the following survey:

Gail is sharing a room in a well-known downtown flophouse for $250 a week. Her roommate, a male friend, has begun hitting on her, driving her nuts, but the rent would be impossible alone.

Claude, the Haitian cook, is desperate to get out of the two-room apartment he shares with his girlfriend and two other, unrelated people. As far as I can determine, the other Haitian men live in similarly crowded situations.

Annette, a twenty-year-old server who is six months pregnant and abandoned by her boyfriend, lives with her mother, a postal clerk.

Marianne, who is a breakfast server, and her boyfriend are paying $170 a week for a one-person trailer.

Billy, who at $10 an hour is the wealthiest of us, lives in the trailer he owns, paying only the $400-a-month lot fee.

The other white cook, Andy, lives on his dry-docked boat, which, as far as I can tell from his loving descriptions, can't be more than twenty feet long. He offers to take me out on it once it's repaired, but the offer comes with inquiries as to my marital status, so I do not follow up on it.

Tina, another server, and her husband are paying $60 a night for a room in the Days Inn. This is because they have no car and the Days Inn is in walking distance of the Hearthside. When Marianne is tossed out of her trailer for subletting (which is against trailer park rules), she leaves her boyfriend and moves in with Tina and her husband.

Joan, who had fooled me with her numerous and tasteful outfits (hostesses wear their own

significance of such a segmented labor market can be seen in comparative incomes: Female-dominated jobs pay median annual incomes ranging from $16,980 for child care workers to $56,770 for dental hygienists, while the median annual incomes in male-dominated jobs range from $27,240 for logging equipment operators to $99,400 for airline pilots, copilots, and flight engineers (http://stats.bls.gov).

clothes), lives in a van parked behind a shopping center at night and showers in Tina's motel room. The clothes are from thrift shops.*

It strikes me, in my middle-class solipsism, that there is gross improvidence in some of these arrangements. When Gail and I are wrapping silverware in napkins— the only task for which we are permitted to sit—she tells me she is thinking of escaping her roommate by moving into the Days Inn herself. I am astounded: how she can think of paying $40 to $60 a day? But if I was afraid of sounding like a social worker, I have come out just sounding like a fool. She squints at me in disbelief: "And where am I supposed to get a month's rent and a month's deposit for an apartment?" I'd been feeling pretty smug about my $500 efficiency, but of course it was made possible only by the $1,300 I had allotted myself for start-up costs when I began my low-wage life: $1,000 for the first month's rent and deposit, $100 for initial groceries and cash in my pocket, $200 stuffed away for emergencies. In poverty, as in certain propositions in physics, starting conditions are everything.

There are no secret economies that nourish the poor; on the contrary, there are a host of special costs. If you can't put up the two months' rent you need to secure an apartment, you end up paying through the nose by the week. If you have only a room, with a hot plate at best, you can't save by cooking up huge lentil stews that can be frozen for the week ahead. You eat fast food or the hot dogs and Styrofoam cups of soup that can be microwaved in a convenience store. If you have no money for health insurance—and the Hearthside's niggardly plan kicks in only after three months— you go without routine care or prescription drugs and end up paying the price. Gail, for example, was doing fine, healthwise anyway, until she ran out of money for

estrogen pills. She is supposed to be on the company health plan by now, but they claim to have lost her application form and to be beginning the paperwork all over again. So she spends $9 a pop for pills to control the migraines she wouldn't have, she insists, if her estrogen supplements were covered. Similarly, Marianne's boyfriend lost his job as a roofer because he missed so much time after getting a cut on his foot for which he couldn't afford the prescribed antibiotic.

My own situation, when I sit down to assess it after two weeks of work, would not be much better if this were my actual life. The seductive thing about waitressing is that you don't have to wait for payday to feel a few bills in your pocket, and my tips usually cover meals and gas, plus something left over to stuff into the kitchen drawer I use as a bank. But as the tourist season slows in the summer heat, I sometimes leave work with only $20 in tips (the gross is higher, but servers share about 15 percent of their tips with the busboys and bartenders). With wages included, this amounts to about the minimum wage of $5.15 an hour. The sum in the drawer is piling up but at the present rate of accumulation will be more than $100 short of my rent when the end of the month comes around. Nor can I see any expenses to cut. True, I haven't gone the lentil stew route yet, but that's because I don't have a large cooking pot, potholders, or a ladle to stir with (which would cost a total of about $30 at Kmart, somewhat less at a thriftstore), not to mention onions, carrots, and the indispensable bay leaf. I do make my lunch almost every day—usually some slow-burning, high-protein combo like frozen chicken patties with melted cheese on top and canned pinto beans on the side. Dinner is at the Hearthside, which offers its employees a choice of BLT, fish sandwich, or hamburger for only $2. The burger lasts longest, especially if it's heaped with gut-puckering jalapeños, but by midnight my stomach is growling again.

So unless I want to start using my car as a residence, I have to find a second or an alternative job.

*I could find no statistics on the number of employed people living in cars or vans, but according to a 1997 report of the National Coalition for the Homeless, "Myths and Facts about Homelessness," nearly one-fifth of all homeless people (in twenty-nine cities across the nation) are employed in full- or part-time jobs.

Source: Barbara Ehrenreich, *Nickel and Dimed: On Not Getting by in America* (New York: Henry Holt and Company, 2002).

What happens when men and women do the same job? If differences between men's and women's median annual incomes were attributable to the differential work they do, one should expect to find no gaps between incomes when men and women do the same jobs. However, the data suggest otherwise. Regardless of whether a job is performed predominantly by women or men, women tend to earn less than men. In

2001, women earned 66.7 percent of the salaries paid to men in managerial jobs, 88.9 percent of men's income in engineering jobs, 77.4 percent of that in protective services, and 70.7 percent of that in machine operation. Even in female-dominated jobs such as sewing machine operation, women still averaged only 90.1 percent of the salaries of their male counterparts; they also averaged 94.9 percent of male elementary teachers' salaries and 87.9 percent of male registered nurses' wages (note that there were too few men in the other female-dominated jobs to even make a comparative assessment of their wages) (http://stats.bls.gov). Thus, even when men and women perform work in the same job category, men's income is higher. And this is the case in both female-dominated and male-dominated jobs. Why?

Examining job categories more closely reveals that they frequently contain a hierarchy of statuses, all of which are categorized as the same job. Take the occupation of baker. Female bakers are typically employed in supermarkets and similar establishments, where baking entails popping premixed dough into the oven. In contrast, men are more likely to be bakers in the traditional sense, employed in bakeries, restaurants, and catering services, where baking involves measuring and mixing ingredients specified in a recipe to create fresh-baked goods. Reskin and Roos (1990) found that exploring such gender discrepancies in the status hierarchy of job categories offered a powerful insight into wage discrepancies.

Differences in earnings also exist along racial and ethnic lines. Table 12.1 shows patterns of such disparity in earnings. Whites typically earn considerably more than workers of color. Notably, the hours required to attain these earnings are not necessarily the same: workers of color tend to work more hours than white workers, suggesting even greater wage disparities by race than comparative median weekly earnings indicate (Mishel, Bernstein and Schmitt, 1997).

In addition to wage differentials based on race, ethnicity, and gender, a **glass ceiling** faces women and people of color in promotions, particularly to managerial levels in corporations. Such workers may rise to middle-management levels but rarely are promoted to the highest executive levels (Albelda and Tilly, 1997; Maume, 1999; Walters, 1996). According to a study by the U.S. Department of Labor (1991c), the glass ceiling is lower for people of color than it is for women, but neither advance very frequently into the higher ranks of management. One reason for this ceiling is that corporate recruitment and promotion practices tend to rely on word-of-mouth referrals and networks rather than on executive search and referral firms. Thus an informal mentoring system in which white male executives recruit, train, and refer other white males for promotions tends to lock women and people of color out of the system.

The Department of Labor study also found that career-enhancing projects, educational opportunities, and credential-building assignments were often less accessible to women and people of color in corporations (a situation probably

TABLE 12.1 Median Weekly Earnings by Sex and Race: 2001

	Men	Women
Whites	$785	$584
African American	567	479
Latino/Latina	611	480
Asian American	818	622

Note: no comparable data on Native Americans are available

Source: www.ewowfacts.com/chapter03/20d.pdf.

related to the restricted informal mentoring system). Finally, women and people of color did not always benefit from the protection of Equal Employment Opportunity Commission regulations aimed at combating discrimination. Accountability and compliance with such regulations were carefully monitored at lower levels but were highly lax for senior-level executive positions and managerial positions involving decision making. Taken together, the forces of informal mentoring, accessibility to career-building opportunities, and lack of compliance with equal employment opportunity rules at higher levels in the corporation produced the glass ceiling for women and people of color. This glass ceiling helps depress their median annual income figures relative to those for white males in the United States.

Furthermore, research has shown that job displacement caused by plant closings and industrial reorganization hits women and people of color harder than males and whites (Pastor, 2001). For example, rates of unemployment and duration of unemployment are greater for women and African Americans than for men and whites. The consequence of differential job displacement and types of employment, combined with wage discrimination based on gender and race, and ethnicity, is that women and people of color are more likely than males and whites to be poor. In the United States in 2001, the poverty rate for women was 22.3 percent, compared with the rate of 17.3 percent for men. The rate for whites was 9.9 percent, whereas the rate for African Americans (22.7 percent) and Latino/Latinas (21.4 percent) was more than twice that for whites (www.census.gov); the poverty rate for Native Americans, averaged over three years between 1998 and 2000, was 25.9 percent (www.firstnations.org).

The social implications extend beyond individual workers. Families certainly are affected. Female-headed families are more than five times more likely than married-couple families to be poor. The poverty rate for female-headed families was 26.4 percent in 2001, compared with only 4.9 percent for married-couple families (www.census.gov). Even within these categories, there are stark racial differences, as shown in Table 12.2. Asian American families tend to have poverty rates similar to those for white families; but African American and Latino/Latina families, whether married-couple or single-headed (male or female), are as much as three times more likely than white families to be poor (unfortunately, the Census Bureau did not report out comparative data for Native American families). Moreover, the workfare provisions of welfare reform that require women receiving public assistance to take any job reinscribe gendered and racialized patterns of poverty. This is because the jobs available are most often menial, low-wage service-sector jobs in such settings as convenience stores and other retail outlets and fast-food restaurants. This means that poor women are likely to be locked into dead-end, low-paying jobs with little chance of breaking that cycle, by order of the state. The economic structural transformation in the United States has not only accentuated racial and gender inequalities; it has also contributed to the disproportionate impoverishment of women and children, particularly those of color.

The Declining Middle Class

The economic structural transformation of the United States has also contributed to the erosion of the nation's middle class. For the first time in history, downward mobility has been greater than the upward mobility many have come to take for

TABLE 12.2 Families Below the Poverty Level: 2001

Families	Poverty Rate (%)
All families	9.2%
Married-couple families	4.9
Male householder, no wife present	13.1
Female householder, no husband present	26.4
White families	7.4%
Married-couple families	4.5
Male householder, no wife present	11.7
Female householder, no husband present	22.4
African American families	20.7%
Married-couple families	7.8
Male householder, no wife present	19.4
Female householder, no husband present	35.2
Latino/Latina families	19.4%
Married-couple families	13.8
Male householder, no wife present	17.0
Female householder, no husband present	37.0
Asian American and Pacific Islander families	7.8%
Married-couple families	6.6
Male householder, no wife present	9.1
Female householder, no husband present	14.6

Source: www.census.gov/hhes/poverty/poverty01.

granted (Newman, 1999). Until now, members of each succeeding generation have generally been able to exceed the lifestyle their parents could afford. Now the current generation of workers is struggling just to match that lifestyle. In a 1999 poll, 38 percent of the respondents believed that it was harder to become affluent in the U.S. today than it used to be (www.pollingreport.com/workplay).

The **middle class** is loosely defined as a category of people whose income places them above the poverty line but below the wealthiest fifth of the population. It may also be conceptualized by lifestyle. Ehrenreich defined the middle class in terms of home ownership, the ability to send one's offspring to college, and "the ability to afford such amenities as a second car and family vacations" (1986:50). Probably the most visible and telling indicator of the decline of the middle class is home ownership. In 1980, some 65 percent of American households owned their own homes; in 2000, the figure was 67.4 percent. There has been no overall decline in home ownership, but a breakdown by age reveals serious decreases in ownership among certain groups. For younger Americans the prospect of owning a home is becoming dimmer: Between 1980 and 2000, the home-ownership rate for people younger than 35 years old fell from 51.6 to 40.8 percent, and the rate for those between the ages of 35 and 44 declined from 71.2 to 67.9 percent (U.S. Department of Commerce,

1993; www.statab.gov: Table 956). Clearly, home ownership, a key feature of the American Dream, is getting more difficult for younger generations to obtain.

The ability to send their offspring to college has also begun to elude more and more members of the middle class: "For a family with 1985 earnings equal to the median national income, keeping a child in a four-year private college or university would have taken 40 percent of that income, up from 30 percent in 1970" (Phillips, 1990:22). By the end of the 1990s, even sending a child to a state university or public college had become increasingly costly and therefore less affordable for many middle-class families. At the same time, government support per student for college education has stagnated (Collins and Yeskel with United for a Fair Economy, 2000). The combination of rising college tuitions and fees, rising home purchase prices, and the replacement of higher-paying manufacturing with lower-paying service jobs has seriously eroded the lifestyle of the middle class. Its downward mobility has been described by sociologist Katherine S. Newman (1999) as a "fall from grace." Indeed, if you recall the description of Dana's family situation pp. 4–5 ▶ at the opening of this book, it is evident that at the center of much that troubled this family was its fall from grace resulting from deindustrialization and downsizing.

The structural transformation of the economy has thus made the American Dream less and less possible, for the first time in history, for many members of the middle class. Earlier manual labor job paths to upward mobility for members of the working class and the poor either have permanently disappeared or have undergone serious income erosion. The changing structure of the economy has meant that many white-collar workers and professional and managerial workers are finding themselves unemployed for the first time. In the past, economic woes generally hit blue-collar and unskilled workers while others were largely spared. Now even persons with college degrees and good skills are joining their more traditional brethren on the unemployment, food-stamp, and soup-kitchen lines, a situation that may make middle class victims of the structural transformation of the economy more sympathetic to the plight of the poor as they begin to share common deprivations.

Prospects for Change

Clearly, a major contributing factor to problems of deindustrialization and the structural shifts of the formal labor market is the lack of control by labor and communities over the work process. That is, the power structure of the corporation, in which decision making, which is strongly influenced by shareholders' interests and which occurs at the top of the organizational hierarchy with little or no input from workers, has greatly affected work and workers in the United States and abroad. To change this, any strategies for change must confront that power structure. One possible vehicle for confronting such a formidable structure in order to increase labor control is labor unions. As social movement organizations, unions historically mobilized the critical resource of workers' collective labor power to affect the power structure of work in the formal labor market to their advantage. While unions' strength has significantly declined in recent decades and their ability to mobilize collective resources has consequently been far less effective than in the decades following World War II, some evidence suggests a resurgence of labor movement activity.

Unions provide definite benefits for workers. They have had a positive impact on wages, benefits, health and safety on the job, and the like. However, deindustrialization and global relocation have meant a loss of jobs in manufacturing, the very sector where unions had made the greatest inroads in organizing workers. Labor unions have lost significant ground since 1960 in the proportion of the labor force they represent, with membership declining from a high of greater than 35 percent of the U.S. work force to a low of 13.5 percent in 2000 (www.statab.gov: Table 637). Evidence suggests that this may be changing, though. The numbers of new union memberships are on the rise even as the proportion of workers in the total work force who are represented by unions remains low. The reason for this seeming contradiction is that the total number of workers in the formal labor force itself is growing faster than the increase in the number of workers in unions. Therefore, the proportion of unionized workers seems to indicate that workers are continuing to disregard organized or collective bargaining as a viable strategy. The actual rise in union membership, however, suggests otherwise. Indeed, a 2001 Associated Press poll on labor unions found that 61 percent of respondents approve of labor unions, and half of the respondents said that they sympathize with workers in recent labor disputes. What might account for this turn of worker support for and participation in the labor movement?

Several strategies and approaches to change in unions as social movement organizations are beginning to occur. First, elections in the Teamsters Union in the early 1990s brought in a leadership devoted to reform, symbolizing the new image of greater honesty sought by unions. The Teamsters have eliminated perquisites for union executives: Gone are the union limousines, special jets, and luxury condominiums in Puerto Rico, as well as the unlimited paid vacations anywhere in the world for union executives. The image of less privileged union executives, along with greater democratization of unions, promises to improve workers' sense of participation in union decision making and to enhance their perception that unions are functioning in their interests.

Unions are also increasingly coming to recognize the need to organize workers globally (Williams, 1999). It is no longer useful for workers in the United States to be unionized if their counterparts in other countries are not. Corporations can simply exploit the differences in pay and work conditions to undermine workers' standard of living both here and abroad. Unions are beginning to take corrective action. For example, telephone technicians in New England went on strike against Northern Telecom, a company based in Canada, and the strike lasted for months. The company was not inclined to bargain with the New England workers until the Communication and Electrical Workers of Canada supported them at the bargaining table. Within days, the New England strike was over, to the satisfaction of the workers. The lesson here: Since the division of labor has become globalized, workers must also globalize their union representation. This suggests that U.S. workers should stop seeing their counterparts in other countries as rivals and competitors.

In addition to organizing workers across national borders, much organized international activism has mobilized around the problem of sweatshops in peripheral pp. 303–305 countries (see Chapter 10). Pressure is mounting to force multinational corporations to comply with international standards of worker health and safety, if not living wages. Such efforts at the very least hold the potential to regularize work conditions regardless of where production takes place, so that corporations have less incentive to transplant jobs abroad.

Another way in which unions can make an impact is by organizing workers who have not been unionized, particularly in the nongovernment service sector. That sector is the least unionized of the formal-labor-market sectors. Service workers in the state sector, on the other hand, are among the most unionized of the service workers, and as a result they enjoy better wages and benefits, better working conditions, and somewhat better job security than service workers in the private sector. While union representation in manufacturing has seriously eroded, representation among government workers had increased to 42 percent by 2000 (www.statab.gov: Table 638). Similar progress in organizing labor can be made with service workers in the private sector. Indeed, several unions have begun energetic organizing efforts among janitors, hotel and restaurant workers, secretaries and clerical workers, nursing home workers, and the like.

In fact, the very thing that undermined organized labor in the 1970s and 1980s has, ironically, become important for the new century of unionization. The ability to globally relocate or automate manufacturing jobs severely damaged the effectiveness of one of the most powerful weapons labor had: the strike. But the structural transformation of the economy from goods production to services holds tremendous promise for a resurgence of the efficacy of the strike. Unlike goods-producing jobs, service-sector jobs (e.g., those in janitorial services, nursing home services, convenience stores, hotels and restaurants, and delivery services) are not as geographically mobile. Services are typically provided in local settings for the most part and therefore are difficult to relocate by employers seeking to avoid unionization. For workers in an organized service sector, going out on strike can be quite effective in forcing employers to negotiate living wages, decent and safe working conditions, health and retirement benefits, and perhaps even profit or power sharing. The unionized workers at the United Parcel Service (UPS) demonstrated this in 1997, when they won a landmark strike against their employer (Cockburn, 1997). UPS workers, represented by the Teamsters Union, managed to gain agreements from UPS management to convert 10,000 part-time jobs to full-time jobs at twice the hourly pay rate; to increase workers' wages by 15 percent over five years for full-time workers and up to 35 percent for part-time workers; and to discontinue plans to drop out of the union's pension program (Magnusson et al., 1997:29). No other union had succeeded in gaining such beneficial contract provisions in more than two decades. The fact that the jobs of local delivery service workers cannot be exported to another country, combined with the mobilization of workers' collective power to strike as a resource, gave these workers an advantage not experienced by labor in some time.

In addition to a renewed sense of energy in the American labor movement, some promising changes have occurred in corporate worker–management relations. One such change has been the introduction of **employee stock option plans,** or **ESOPs,** in which managers set up ways for workers to purchase shares of stock in their own companies. This approach provides workers with a share of the profits their labor

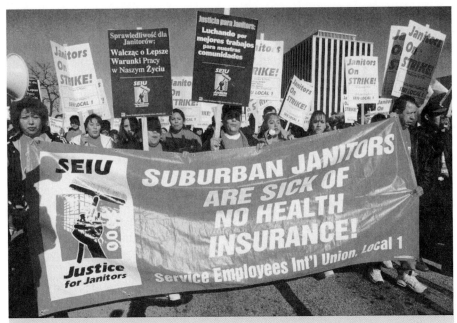

Ironically, the same structural shift toward service-sector employment that has profoundly hurt the American labor movement has in fact begun to reenergize it. This is because service work is harder to export than are manufacturing jobs, because service work is often performed at the actual place of service. This has begun to empower service workers. These demonstrators in the Justice for Janitors movement strike for better work conditions, wages, and benefits.

helps create and may motivate them to become more productive (Ford, 1988). More than 11,000 firms in the United States now provide ESOPs to over 10 million workers (Rosen, 1998). Such a strategy may be quite lucrative for workers, especially during periods when the stock market is highly robust. But profit sharing does not mean power sharing—workers under ESOP plans still do not share in the decision making that affects their jobs, the work process, or the work environment (Logue, 1998). Such decisions remain in the hands of chief executive officers and boards of directors, whose decisions are likely to continue to be more strongly influenced by managerial and ownership interests, not the needs of workers. And while increased values in stocks may certainly be advantageous to workers holding significant shares of stock in their firms, decisions that produce such increases can also mean the loss of workers' jobs (through downsizing, job export, etc.).

Some strategies offer promise for workers to gain more control over or voice in corporate decision making. For example, by 2000 there had been approximately 3,000 employee-owned companies employing almost 3 million workers in the United States, almost all of which were employee or community buyouts from prior owners (as opposed to start-ups). Many of these plants or companies were about to be shut down and their operations relocated elsewhere (National Center for Employee Ownership; Varano, 1999). The buyouts often succeeded through coalitions of community, labor, and, at times, religious organizations and municipal governments (Hodson and Sullivan, 1990:166–167; Logue, 1998). Sometimes such buy-outs are financed with workers' pensions or employee stock option programs (Ford, 1988). When workers pool their stockholdings in the company, they may have enough capital or clout to buy out at least the plant in their community, thereby preserving jobs and the plant's productive capacity. Once a buyout is completed, the plant may be converted to a **worker cooperative,** which is entirely owned and operated by the workers themselves (MacLeod, 1997; Pencavel, 2002). In the typical worker-owned cooperative, not only does the entire work force of the company own the firm; decisions, including the selection of managers, is commonly done democratically, with each worker having one vote; and all share in the profits generated by their collective efforts (Delaney, 1996; Estey and Bowman, 2000). This ensures that ownership and operation remain locally controlled and eliminates the possibility of a runaway shop. While not all were buyouts of existing firms by workers, there are currently more than 250 worker-owned cooperatives thriving in the United States (Locker and Stone, 2000).

As intriguing as worker-owned buyouts may be, however, caution must be used. As with other corporations, when financial institutions provide major loans or sit on the firm's board they may exercise considerable clout over owners' decision making. This can compromise owners' power to determine their firm's future, whether they are worker-owners or more traditional professional corporate managers.

Federal programs sometimes offer other useful strategies for communities and workers to prevent runaway shops. For example, the federal Community Reinvestment Act (CRA) offers local community organizations an opportunity to challenge banks' tendency to "disinvest" in the local community. Banks frequently take the deposits from their branches in local communities and reinvest that finance capital elsewhere, often supporting plant relocations. Bank mergers tend to reinforce patterns of disinvestment in the local community. The CRA provides local community organizations an opportunity to challenge banks' practices when a bank is attempting to open inter-city branches or to participate in an interstate merger between banks, because these expansions require federal approval. One factor that can affect that approval is community reinvestment. Therefore, a CRA challenge can potentially hinder banks' expansion plans and therefore can prompt negotiations between the local community and the bank, frequently resulting in greater bank commitments to invest in local and regional development (Fitzgerald and Meyer, 1986). Successful CRA challenges of banks' decisions have resulted in more than $1 trillion reinvested back into previously severely underserved low- and moderate-income communities since 1977 (www. enterprisefoundation.org/policy/crasummary), a shift the Federal Reserve credits with the effectiveness of the legislation (www.federalreserve.gov/boarddocs/speeches/ 1998). These highly encouraging results, however, are just a beginning: Banks continue to deny mortgage loan applications from African Americans and Latinos/Latinas at twice the rate as applications made by whites (www.innercitypress.org/cra).

These developments suggest positive possibilities for workers to become a stronger force in the reshaping of the U.S. economy. And unions are now poised to play a more significant role in reducing gender and racial inequalities than they have in the past. If unions, as workers' own bases of power, are to grow once again, they must organize across national borders and into previously nonunionized labor sectors like the service sector and contingency work. And they must seek to include more women and people of color among their members. Unions therefore must address the issues and concerns of such workers in order to attract them as members. Through unions, women and workers of color may be able to gain a stronger voice in what happens to them in the formal labor market.

CHAPTER SUMMARY

1. Several factors have worked to devalue college degrees and what they can do for people who attain them. Moreover, higher education (when it can be obtained) no longer guarantees upward mobility.

2. The changing structure of the economy and of the formal labor market is reducing workers' control over decisions affecting their jobs and their participation in the economy. The consequences of that restructuring most negatively affect lower level workers and the poor, women, and people of color—that is, those who have historically been disadvantaged in the formal labor market.

3. The changing structure of the economy has resulted in increasing inequality. The gaps between rich and poor, between men and women, between whites and people of color have steadily widened.

4. The most recent phase of the structural transformation of the economy has hit the middle class and managerial workers, those who until recently enjoyed comparatively secure, protected positions and opportunities for upward mobility.

5. The changing formal labor market suggests that the economy is hardly a neutral force devoid of politics. Power imbalances enable some in the economic hierarchy to make decisions that benefit themselves but adversely affect others. Workers can protect themselves by actively seeking a greater voice in decisions that affect the economy, their communities, and their jobs.

6. Work occurs not only in the formal labor market but in the informal labor market and in the unpaid domestic labor sphere as well. Work in these three spheres is differentially distributed along racial, ethnic, class, and gender lines: The poor and the working class, women, and people of color are much more likely to engage in a triple shift than the wealthy, men, and whites. People who are already advantaged are better able to delegate responsibility for the work done in the household and in the community to the less advantaged. Perhaps strategies can be formulated to more equitably distribute work in all three spheres, and ways devised to better reward both paid and unpaid labor.

THINKING CRITICALLY

1. Consider the "Social Forces/People's Lives" reading describing Barbara Ehrenreich's experiences in low-wage jobs. Since she had a job, how can her situation be explained? What does her story suggest about the structure of work?

2. We discussed Reskin and Roos's observation that broad job categories contain discrete occupational status hierarchies. Select a job category and analyze the occupational status hierarchies that it might include. Which of these occupations might pay more, and why? Who is more likely to have each of these occupations? What does this suggest about the distribution of earnings?

3. Consider the division of labor in your family. Outline the various jobs that each member does, and identify whether these are done in the formal, the informal, or the unpaid domestic labor markets. Which of these markets does each family member *primarily* work in? Is there a balance between labor markets for all members, or do some members work primarily in one market? What might explain the distribution of work in your family? For example, is gender an important factor?

4. Think of industries or corporations that left or ceased operations in your state or community. Why did they leave or close? How did these shutdowns affect your local community? Your state? Your family or the families of those you know? What could the community and/or the state do to avoid the loss of industries or to reduce the effects of their loss?

5. The North American Free Trade Agreement (NAFTA) allows free movement of goods, services, and production between the United States, Mexico, and Canada. This means that corporations in the United States may elect to produce goods in any of the three countries without incurring import tariffs (taxes) on goods produced outside the United States. Who is likely to benefit and who is likely to be hurt by NAFTA, and why? What might those who may be hurt by NAFTA do to protect themselves from possible disadvantages of the trade agreement?

KEY TERMS

contingency work, *(370)*
deindustrialization, *(376)*
domestic labor, *(366)*
employee stock option
  plans (ESOPs), *(393)*
formal labor market,
  (366)
glass ceiling, *(388)*
globalization, *(371)*

informal labor market,
  (366)
interlocking boards of
  directors, *(378)*
managerial revolution,
  (377)
merger mania, *(375)*
mergers, *(375)*
middle class, *(390)*

runaway shops, *(374)*
second shift, *(366)*
segmented labor market,
  (385)
triple shift, *(367)*
underemployment, *(384)*
work, *(366)*
worker cooperative, *(395)*

Education

In the United States, most people spend a substantial part of their childhood and young adulthood in school. More than 84 percent of adults age 25 and older have completed a high school education, and 26 percent have completed four or more years of college (U.S. Bureau of the Census, 2003). Even persons who drop out of school at the earliest legal opportunity (age 16 in most states) may have been in school for 10 or 11 years. Participation in schooling is a near-universal experience for members of U.S. society. Thus, it is appropriate to ask what role educational institutions play in shaping people's biographies.

pp. 10–12   Viewed from a functionalist perspective (see Chapter 1), U.S. society's system of education serves many important purposes. It plays a major role in the socialization of society's children and youth, supplementing the socialization provided by other major social institutions, such as the family and the mass media. Access to education contributes to the ability of adult citizens to participate effectively in a political democracy. Broadly speaking, by exposing young people to the dominant cultural heritage and many of the skills they will need to function as adults, schools contribute to the continuity and stability of society as a whole. For such reasons, many people place a great deal of faith in education as a social institution.

Indeed, education has come to be seen as the answer to many of this society's most serious problems—from eliminating poverty to maintaining the United States' competitive advantage over other industrial nations in the global economy. Unfortunately, it is clear that the U.S. system of education, as it is presently functioning, is not making such problems disappear. Consequently, over the last couple of decades a cacophony of voices has arisen calling for change in the education system. Specially appointed commissions and government agencies have issued numerous reports critical of education in the United States. One of the most influential and widely quoted reports, *A Nation at Risk,* contained this harsh assessment:

> The educational foundations of our society are presently being eroded by a rising tide of mediocrity that threatens our very future as a Nation and a people. . . If an unfriendly foreign power had attempted to impose on America the mediocre educational performance that exists today, we might well have viewed it as an act of war. As it stands, we have allowed this to happen to ourselves. (National Commission on Excellence in Education, 1983)

Most criticisms of the U.S. system of education have focused on unsatisfactory levels of student academic achievement, as measured by standardized tests, which often fall short of those of students in other major industrialized nations. For example, U.S. students

(continued)

test comparatively poorly in mathematics and science, two areas crucial to technologically advanced societies. Solutions offered by critics to combat this perceived mediocrity in U.S. education have included mandatory testing of teachers for competency, greater parental involvement in schools, increased course requirements and graduation prerequisites, and an extended school year or day. Shortcomings in student achievement are seen primarily as the outcome of inadequate effort on the part of students, their families, and school staff.

Such reasoning undergirds the No Child Left Behind Act that the U.S. Congress overwhelmingly passed and President George W. Bush signed in 2002 (www.nochildleftbehind.gov). The cornerstone of this legislation is federally mandated, annual standardized testing of students in every state in the nation. The assumption is that more intensive testing of students will improve school performance. All U.S. students will be periodically tested on their reading, math, and science skills. Results will determine whether individual schools are making adequate progress toward student proficiency. Those schools that "fail," whose students are not making measurable gains, may be subject to sanctions.

Proponents of the act argue that this "tough love" approach will prove to be especially effective for improving underperforming schools in low-income urban and rural areas, where average performance on standardized tests is below that of more affluent communities. Others doubt that such a testing-based strategy will lead to any real improvement in schools located in low-income communities (Orfield and Kornhaber 2001). In this opposing view, without a federal and state government commitment to providing massive infusions of new teaching resources and upgraded physical facilities, failing schools will probably be able to do little but narrow their curricular and classroom practices to try to "teach to the test." Under such circumstances, unequal educational opportunities and unequal outcomes of schooling for children of the poor and nonpoor will simply continue.

Whatever the merits of this act, putting government pressure on schools to improve students' academic performance clearly overlooks key features of education that sociologists have found to play an important role in student failure and success. In passing legislation intended to correct student performance that is below par, politicians ignored how such phenomena as economic, racial and ethnic, and gender inequalities may affect student learning. Acknowledging the significance of these phenomena would require solutions for inadequate student performance that go far beyond demanding that students, families, and school staff simply try harder. These solutions would include attacking systems of inequality.

In this chapter we explore such questions as the following:

- How do societywide systems of economic, racial and ethnic, and gender inequality influence the social institution of education?
- Does education attack systemic economic, racial and ethnic, and gender inequalities, or does education function to reproduce these inequalities?
- How do children's educational opportunities differ in poorer urban, rural, and small-town communities compared to more affluent communities?
- What is the relationship between education and upward social mobility for U.S. society's members?
- What are the prospects for enhancing equality of educational opportunities?

Family Background, Education, and Life Chances

Imagine two young people, both 15 years old. The first is named Christopher Lane Bond—"Kip" to his friends. His father is a successful corporate attorney with a Yale law degree, and his mother, a graduate of Smith College, is a part-time editor for a publishing firm. Kip has never attended a public school, even though those in the affluent, predominantly white suburb where his family lives are said to be excellent. Instead, through the sixth grade, Kip went to a private day school near his home, and he is now a resident student at a private college preparatory school in another state.

Kip's parents are proud of the outstanding quality of the education he is receiving in the all-male prep school. Ivy League–educated teachers and staff provide each boy with a great deal of personal attention. His parents expect that when he graduates, Kip will attend an elite private college such as the institutions from which they both graduated. There, Kip will mingle with persons from similarly enriched educational backgrounds, choosing courses from a full range of offerings in the arts and sciences. He will participate in the fraternity system, polishing his social skills and developing future social contacts and connections. Ultimately, Kip wants to move on to a prestigious law school and a place in his father's firm. The social networks he develops through his educational experiences and his family will enhance the probability of Kip's economic and social success.

Then there is the other young person, Michele Josephine Mendez—"Josey." Her father works for a large frozen-food company, where, for the last 20 years, he has

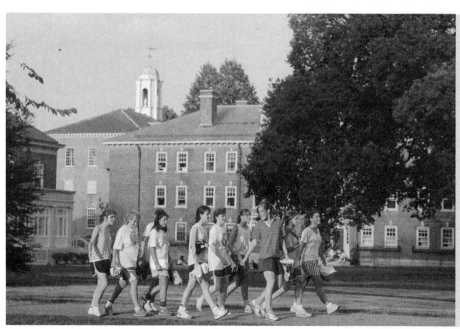

Youths who attend well-financed, high-quality private schools, such as these teens crossing the campus of an elite college preparatory academy, have a distinct advantage over others when it comes to competing successfully for admission to top-ranked colleges.

operated machinery at the loading dock. A high school dropout, this is the best job he can find. Josey's mother works as a hairstylist in a local salon, using skills she learned at a beauty academy after graduating from high school. Knowing how easy it would be for Josey to drop out of the large public school she attends, they have kept a tight rein on her. Josey's parents do not want her to end up on the streets like many of her peers in their low-income neighborhood.

The situation at Josey's high school is bleak. The facilities are outmoded, and the building is run-down. Shortages of books and supplies, overcrowded classes, episodes of violence, chronic drug abuse, and frazzled teachers are common. Even though it is clear that Josey is not learning very much, her parents hope conditions at the school will not lead her to drop out before graduation. When she graduates, Josey's parents expect that she will look for work to help the family pay bills. Josey's father thinks that after graduation she should try to take some evening computer programming courses at an inexpensive local community college to avoid ending up stuck in a dead-end job like "the old man."

Kip and Josey underscore an important issue: unequal educational opportunity in U.S. society. Agents of socialization such as schools and the mass media encourage us to think of our society as a **meritocracy,** a system in which rewards come to people on the basis of their individual merit. The concept of meritocracy assumes the existence of equal educational opportunity, for without it the system would obviously be unfair. With equal educational opportunity, success or failure becomes more a matter of individual responsibility. If Kip and Josey receive equal educations, but one goes on to a successful career and the other does not, we might think that the unsuccessful one is less able or motivated. But Kip and Josey, by virtue of being born into quite different levels of the system of economic inequality, also start the competition from very different vantage points. Kip is ahead from the beginning—the playing field is tipped in his favor. In fact, the resources available to each are so different in type and amount that their individual talents may have relatively little to do with where each one ends up.

The Importance of Cultural Capital

More broadly speaking, Kip and Josey have been endowed with very different amounts of "cultural capital" due to their respective class positions. **Cultural capital** refers to material and nonmaterial cultural goods that are socially valued, such as education, high family social status, and social skills. These goods can usher individuals into positions in which they will have social leverage over others in society (Bourdieu and Passeron, 1991). With the cultural capital that he is accumulating, Kip will be welcomed through doors of prestige and privilege that Josey will have little chance of even finding. Moreover, Kip and Josey have unequal amounts of "social capital" (see Chapter 4). The class-based social networks in which pp. 105–107 they and their families participate vary sharply in the degree to which they interact with others who can help with opportunities to pursue success.

Clearly, the class level of a family is an important source of its children's cultural capital. Class position helps determine a family's purchasing power as a "consumer" of education, just as it determines a family's ability to consume other goods and services, from autos to health care. The consumer power of the affluent is quite a bit greater than that of the poor and working class, and the quality of education that they are likely to be able to consume is not the same for each population group.

The resource of family income helps determine where children, such as Kip and Josey, spend their years in elementary school and high school. A family's economic circumstances dictate where it can afford to reside, and the relative affluence of a community ordinarily dictates the amount and quality of resources found in its public schools. In the United States both federal and state governments provide financial assistance to local school systems. School budgets, however, still depend heavily on money raised by local property taxes.

In an affluent suburban community such as that in which Kip's family lives, residents often own expensive single-family homes on large lots and have two or more family vehicles. Even modest taxes on valuable property can generate a lot of money for their children's public schools. In a poorer community such as the one in which Josey's family lives, the comparatively lower value of the property in the community, and the inability of many people to pay high taxes, produces tax revenues that are often insufficient to meet the educational needs of children attending the local schools. This situation exists not only in many cities, but also in numerous small towns and rural areas.

Affluence not only allows some families to live in property-rich communities and send their children to well-financed, resource-endowed local public schools. It may also allow people like Kip's parents to send their children out of the local community altogether to attend private college preparatory schools. Today such schools usually try to achieve some diversity in their student enrollment, yet they often remain exclusive institutions that function to reinforce the advantageous life chances of the upper social and economic classes (Zweigenhaft and Domhoff, 1991). The high-quality education provided to a relatively select group of children by private prep schools makes their graduates attractive candidates for admission to the prestigious colleges that are a steppingstone to top-ranked graduate and professional schools (Cookson and Persell, 1985).

Family income is clearly linked to the probability that a high school graduate will attend college. The National Student Loan Program reported that in 1970 only 46 percent of high school graduates from the lowest income families (less than $25,063 annually) attended college, compared to 79 percent of graduates from the highest income families (over $74,584 annually). By 1997, college participation rates for both populations had increased (to 53 versus 89 percent), but the gap in college attendance had grown from 33 to 36 percent (www.nslp.org).

Family income not only helps determine whether a student will go on to attend college. It also has an impact on the type of institution that high school graduates will attend. The divergent educational trajectories that Kip and Josey are likely to enter upon high school graduation are not uncommon. The children of the affluent are much more likely than those from low-income backgrounds to attend four-year colleges or universities. When low-income students do go to college, they are far more likely than the affluent to attend a two-year or community college. Moreover, students like Josey who attend community college are far less likely to go on to later complete a four-year college degree than students like Kip, who start their college careers in a four-year school.

Students from less affluent socioeconomic backgrounds do not necessarily fail to go on to college because they are less able than those who do. Social scientists have found that students from affluent families who have low measured intelligence are *more* likely to attend college than students from low-income families who have high measured intelligence (Kerbo, 2003). A discrepancy between indications of ability and college attendance also exists if one looks at academic achievement rather than measured intelligence. The National Student Loan Program reported that in 1996, two years after graduating from high school, 78 percent of high-achieving graduates from low-income families were in college. In contrast, 97 percent of the high-achieving graduates from high-income families were in college, as were 77 percent of the lowest achievers from such families (www.nslp.org).

The discrepancy in college attendance arises partly because affluent families are better able to help pay for their children's college education, but aspirations for college attendance also differ for people from different class backgrounds (Kerbo, 2003). These aspirations are influenced by one's socialization experiences in the family, in school, and with peers. Students from affluent families are more likely than others to *expect* to go to college, and they are also the ones whose families are most capable of affording to send them.

Indeed, the costs of college tuition have been increasing while the availability of student financial aid, other than debt-generating loans, has failed to keep up with the increases. According to the National Center for Public Policy and Higher Education, public higher education has become less affordable for all but the most affluent families. In 2000 the average low-income family with a child attending a public four-year college or university had to pay 25 percent of its annual income for tuition, up from 13 percent in 1980. Tuition costs at public community colleges are much lower, but they also doubled in that 20-year period. Many students from poor and working-class backgrounds begin college but are forced to quit due to financial hardships; many more are deterred by the costs and do not enroll at all. In periods of economic slowdown or recession, when jobs become scarce and layoffs occur, declines in state tax revenues force public institutions to raise tuition to meet their expenses. At the same time, low-income families are the ones likely to be hurt most by a poor economy, making it even more difficult for them to afford the increased tuition (National Center for Public Policy and Higher Education, 2002).

Students from low- and middle-income families are most dependent on loans to pay their college costs and have the highest ratio of student debt to family income, yet their families are least able to help them pay the loans back. Their debts on graduation have been increasing. The average debt of college seniors from low-income families went from $7,629 in 1989 to $12,888 in 1999. While college has grown ever more expensive for everyone, the most affluent obviously find it easily affordable. In fact, between 1980 and 2000, there was no increase in the percentage of family income paid out for tuition among the 20 percent of families with the highest incomes, as they alone experienced significant income gains in that period (National Center for Public Policy and Higher Education, 2002). Such families are, of course, most able to afford to send their children to elite private colleges, where tuition is substantially higher than at public institutions. A study of the nation's 146 most selective colleges and universities found that only 3 percent of the freshmen come from the bottom quarter of families ranked by income, and only 10 percent come from the bottom half (Savage, 2003).

Unequal Life Chances

The fact that Kip and Josey have unequal educational opportunities, and thus will have different educational experiences and attainments, will affect their life chances. Kip's law school degree and Josey's computer programming certificate will open up quite different occupational and earning opportunities. Kip and Josey will labor in vastly different realms and garner vastly different rewards.

We know that those with a bachelor's degree typically earn much more annually than those who have only graduated from high school or who have completed some college but have no degree. For example, in 1999 persons with a college degree received on average almost 100 percent more annual income than persons with a high school diploma (Kerbo, 2003). But when one factors in gender, the gap in earnings between the college completers and noncompleters widens further. In 2000, women with some years of college (Josey's father's hope for her) had median annual earnings of $21,597. In contrast, men with at least a bachelor's degree had median earnings of $42,292 (National Center for Education Statistics, 2002a). Thus Josey's likely future earnings disadvantage will not only be a consequence her attaining less education than Kip, but it will also be an outcome of her subordinate position in U.S. society's systems of gender and economic inequality.

In this section we emphasized the importance of family economic background in determining one's ability to gain access to and take advantage of educational opportunities. In the next sections we look at ways in which systems of economic, racial, and gender inequality affect the nature and quality of education that schools provide to students in the United States. Differences in school experiences can have a significant and lasting impact on individuals' personal biographies.

Class Inequality and Schooling

Much research has focused on the relationship between education and the class structure of U.S. society (Lucas, 1999; Meier et al., 1989; Oakes, 1985). Although many people think of education as the "great social equalizer" and a vehicle of upward social mobility, evidence suggests a different reality. Sociologists have accumulated evidence that the U.S. education system both reflects and contributes to class inequality.

Tracking in Schools

Schools may best be viewed as **gatekeepers,** functioning to keep people at or near the class position of their families of origin. Of course, many people have overcome the obstacles and risen above squalid conditions, but by and large these admirable individuals are exceptions. Despite the billions of dollars spent on education in the United States each year, class inequality continues, and most people end up living in pretty much the same way as their parents. How do schools succeed in performing this gatekeeping function?

In the 1960s, some sociologists argued that class position of the family was the key determinant of a child's achievement in school. A massive, federally funded study by sociologist James Coleman (1966) provided data in support of this view. However, other sociologists took issue with Coleman's research (Bowles and Gintis, 1976; Dougherty, 1981), asserting that schools tend to treat low-income students *differently* from their more affluent counterparts. Today, while not denying that families also play some role, sociologists believe that the nature of the experiences that schools themselves provide for low-income children has an important impact on their academic performance.

One of the most important phenomena investigated in recent years is the system of tracking found in U.S. public schools (see Goodlad, 1984; Lucas, 1999; Oakes, 1985). **Tracking** involves the placement of students in classroom learning situations and school programs that are supposed to be geared to their individual abilities and learning potential. The practice originated early in the twentieth century, when urban public school systems sought ways to reorganize their curricula to accommodate a growing and increasingly heterogeneous school population. Today, in tracking systems stemming from the practices begun at that time, students are placed in homogeneous "ability groups" with others who have been determined by teachers and counselors to have similar learning potential. Virtually all students experience some form of ability grouping during their years of schooling (Lucas, 1999).

Most elementary schools have *in-class* ability grouping (Asher, 1992). For instance, a student may be assigned to sit with certain classmates who will read books of a similar level of difficulty during reading period. By the upper grades, tracking usually takes the form of *between-class* ability grouping (Slavin, 1990). In some cases a student may travel with a set of peers through a year-long curriculum, or track, entirely separate from the track of another set of peers. Most middle and high schools have some system of tracking, although the systems vary in the degree to which they are formalized (Asher, 1992; Lucas, 1999).

In high school, students may be assigned to a track labeled "college preparatory," "general," "vocational," "special," or "alternative." Even when overarching track designations are not formally present in a school, courses are typically organized to correspond to different levels of ability. The tracking is still there; it is simply less visible (Lucas, 1999). College preparatory courses may be labeled "high honors," "honors," and "advanced." Non-college-oriented courses may be labeled "basic," and "remedial." Schools serving primarily children of the affluent are likely to offer more college preparatory courses, for example, in science and mathematics (Spade, Columba, and Vanfossen, 1997). The content of courses offered, and the value each carries toward earning points that will determine a student's graduation class ranking, are ordinarily quite dissimilar.

Negative Aspects of Tracking

Educators who defend tracking claim that it is the most effective and efficient way of teaching students and justify it as being in students' interests. Here is how proponents defend ability grouping:

In essence, the argument in favor of ability grouping is that it will allow teachers to adapt instruction to the needs of a diverse student body and give them an opportunity to provide more difficult material to high achievers and more support to low achievers. The challenge and stimulation of other high achievers are believed to be beneficial to high achievers. (Slavin, 1990:473)

Yet, in recent years, tracking has grown quite controversial, as evidence of its effects on students have accumulated. A substantial body of research suggests that track placement can have *negative* effects on students (Fischer et al., 1996; Hallinan, 1994). These effects have led some to call for the abolition of tracking (Loveless, 1999).

Tracking may do the most harm to low achievers and is thought to be a factor in delinquent behavior and dropping out of school. Children and youths are generally aware of their standing compared with that of other students in the tracking system. When students are consistently placed in low-level reading groups or in a collection of known "gut" courses in which little is expected of them, they are likely to develop a negative self-image, low motivation to achieve, and limited aspirations for the future (Gamoran and Berends, 1987). Schooling can become a humiliating and alienating experience when every day one must take one's place at or near the bottom of a system of stratification built around a school staff's judgment of who has the ability to learn what. In summing up research literature on the negative effects of tracking, sociologist Harold Kerbo notes that tracking "tends to separate children by class background" and "works to reinforce class differences" (Kerbo, 2003:405).

Looking at the backgrounds of students in different tracks, for the most part children and youths whose families are middle-class or higher dominate the college preparatory tracks or their course equivalents, while children of poor and working-class families are by and large clustered in the lower tracks and courses for the "less able" (Glazer, 1990; Oakes and Guiton, 1995). Examining the backgrounds of college freshmen enrolled in four-year institutions, Table 13.1 indicates that family income and education level are highly correlated with the academic rigor of the high school track in which the freshmen were participants. Who makes such track placement decisions, and how?

Teachers play a major role, as do guidance counselors, particularly in the middle and high school years. Two factors are thought to operate in the decision-making process. The first is subjective: biases about abilities and appropriate expectations for children of different class origins and skin color (see Irvine, 1990). African American, Latino/Latina, and Native American children are disproportionately assigned to the lower tracks. School staff may be influenced by a child's home circumstances, dress and physical appearance, language, behavior both in and out of the classroom, and their experiences with his or her parents and siblings. Such "measures" may have little or nothing to do with a child's ability to learn. But when school staff believe they do, a **self-fulfilling prophecy** is likely to be set in motion p. 29 (Rist, 1970, 1973). In Chapter 2 we reviewed experimental research indicating that teachers' positive expectations can have a significant impact on students' intellectual growth (Rosenthal and Jacobson, 1968a, 1968b). School staff may

TABLE 13.1 Nature of High School Curriculum Track Taken by Beginning Students Enrolled in Four-Year Institutions of Higher Education, by Selected Student Characteristics

Selected Characteristic	Core Curriculum or Less[1]	Midlevel[2]	Rigorous[3]
Total	31.0%	50.3%	18.7%
Sex			
Male	32.5%	47.5%	20.1%
Female	29.9	52.5	17.6
Race/ethnicity			
Asian/Pacific Islander	26.9%	42.1%	31.0%
Hispanic	34.3	49.5	16.2
Black, non-Hispanic	41.6	50.3	8.1
White, non-Hispanic	29.0	51.4	19.7
American Indian/Alaskan Native	—	—	—
Family income in 1994			
Low income	39.6%	45.6%	14.8%
Middle income	30.8	51.6	17.6
High income	24.5	48.4	27.1
Parents' highest education			
High school or less	39.4%	51.2%	9.4%
Some college	32.7	54.3	13.0
Bachelor's degree or higher	25.7	49.3	25.0
Derived SAT combined score			
Lowest quartile (400–790)	49.0%	49.1%	1.9%
Middle quartiles (800–1090)	29.7	55.7	14.7
Highest quartile (1100–1600)	15.0	40.8	44.1
Free or reduced-price lunch eligibility at high school			
0–4 percent	24.7%	48.2%	27.1%
5–24 percent	32.6	50.6	16.7
25 percent or higher	37.4	51.4	11.2

—Sample size too small for a reliable estimate.

[1] Core curriculum includes four years of English, three years of social studies, three years of mathematics, and three years of science.

[2] Midlevel curriculum exceeds core curriculum, but is less than rigorous. Includes at a minimum one year of a foreign language, geometry, algebra I, and three years of science including two of the following courses: biology, chemistry, or physics.

[3] Rigorous curriculum includes four years of English, four years of mathematics (including precalculus or higher), three years of a foreign language, three years of social studies, three years of science (including biology, chemistry, physics), and at least one advanced placement (AP) class or test taken.

Note: Details may not sum to 100 due to rounding.

SOURCE: U.S. Department of Education, National Center for Education Statistics, *High School Academic Curriculum and the Persistence Path Through College* (Washington, DC: NCES, 2001), p. 10.

likewise "create" low achievement simply by making tracking and course enrollment assignments that carry with them low expectations for students' performance.

A second factor that comes into play in determining placement is the use of standardized achievement and IQ (intelligence quotient) tests. Despite widespread acknowledgment of the inadequacies of such tests and the cultural biases known to accompany their use (Gould, 1996), they continue to be used. One problem with standardized tests is that they tend to reflect the advantages associated with a privileged class background (Fischer et al., 1996). The resources affluent families can make available to their children from an early age give the children greater exposure to the types of knowledge and skills these tests measure. It is the affluent family that is most capable of providing enriched daycare and nursery school experiences; the stimulation of travel; educational games and a home computer; expensive books, magazines, and videos; and support for lessons and hobbies. Children from poor and working-class families generally lack such resources and, on average, perform less well on achievement and IQ tests (Lareau, 1989).

The conclusion typically, but erroneously, drawn from such test results is that poor and working-class children are less able and less motivated, and thus belong in a track that will demand less of them. Moreover, since in U.S. society children of color are disproportionately found in the poor and working-class populations, and on average test less well than the more affluent white population, children of color are more likely to be in classes in the lower tracks (Glazer, 1990). As a consequence of tracking, students within a racially mixed school building may well experience racial segregation along curriculum lines (Meier et al., 1989).

Tracking, then, results in very different sets of educational experiences for children from different socioeconomic classes. Jeannie Oakes (1990) explored the impact of tracking in mathematics and science, two areas of importance to the highly technological U.S. economy. Using survey data from 1,200 schools and 6,000 teachers, Oakes found that low-track students tended to have less qualified math and science teachers, lower quality texts and laboratory equipment, less active and engaging classes, and fewer opportunities to take college preparatory math courses. She also found that the proportion of low-track math and science classes increased with the proportion of children of color in a school. Thus opportunities to learn math and science differed along both class and racial lines. Familiarity with math and science is increasingly important for finding a decent-paying job. But, as one social scientist put it, "The lower track is training for the blue-collar jobs of the '50s. Those jobs are gone" (Glazer, 1990:749).

Tracking leads to quite different trajectories for youths from different class backgrounds. Those from more affluent families, having been exposed to the appropriate subject matter in the college preparatory track (Oakes, 1985, 1990), are likely to go on to a four-year college or university, with prospects for a white-collar job or postgraduate professional training. Because of their family incomes, they generally are able to afford expensive higher education. In the last couple of decades even middle-class families have had increasing difficulty securing the economic resources needed to pay for college (National Center for Public Policy and Higher Education, 2002).

The Gifted Classes

FRANCES LEFKOWITZ

Students from poor and working-class families enrolled in public school programs for the "gifted and talented" are far fewer than those from more affluent families. Those from low-income backgrounds who are selected for such programs often feel out of place and left to wonder if they belong in gifted classes. They may doubt whether they have what it takes to succeed in comparison to their economically privileged peers, many of whom treat enrollment in gifted classes as a birthright. Frances Lefkowitz describes her own sense of alienation as a student, which she struggled valiantly to overcome.

I HAVE nothing to say about the politics of poverty, what causes it and what it causes and how to make it go away. I can only tell you what poverty does to a person. It gets inside you, nestles into your bones, and gives you a chill that you cannot shake. Poverty becomes you—it shapes what you see and taste and dream—till there is no telling where you stop and poverty begins. To be poor is to live in denial—not the denial of professional counselors and self-help books, which is an avoidance of some truth too painful to admit, but denial in its most literal sense: you must say no to yourself constantly. Being poor means stripping down to the essentials, and there's not much a person really needs to survive— bread, cheese, blankets, a little black-and-white TV, some toothpaste, soap, pencils, a library card. In and of itself, it isn't bad not to have things, and if all of us lived this way, there would hardly be anything wrong with it at all. To be poor is one thing; to *know* that you are poor is

another thing altogether. That is when poverty becomes poison.

In my junior high school, an L-shaped, four-story stucco building with a yard covered in blacktop and painted with white and yellow lines, I got transferred into what was then called the "gifted classes." It was there that I met people, not just characters on TV or in the movies, but real people who were gifted in every sense of the word—gifted with homes and meals and stereos and cars and vacations, and gifted also with a faith in the rightness of the world and their place in it, a faith that was, and still is, foreign to me. Until my second semester of seventh grade, my world was full of kids like me: Kids whose parents were struggling to keep them fed, clothed, in school, and out of trouble. Kids who arrived accidentally or too soon, who spent a lot of time on their own, scheming and scamming to get by, just like their parents. Kids who zipped up their blue-hooded

In contrast, children from working-class and poverty-level families, who have been routed into and through non-college-bound tracks, end up with quite different destinations (Rose, 1989). They are most likely to go directly into the labor market, where they compete with others who possess limited skills, or to two-year community colleges or technical schools that are not selective in their admissions criteria (Brint and Karabel, 1989; Herideen, 1998). In such colleges and schools, they may gain credentials that will enable them to enter a paraprofessional position or skilled manual trade. Earning even these credentials may take time, for these students are sweat shirts on a damp Saturday morning and stuffed their dirty clothes into a pillowcase and lugged it down the street to the Laundromat. Kids who made their own lunches and were sent to Safeway with booklets of orange-and-white food stamps to buy milk or tuna fish or a quarter pound of bologna from the meat counter, and who kept their fingers crossed that the cashier would have a heart and give them real change back instead of the coupons for fifty-eight or thirty-five or twenty-two cents.

Then suddenly I was plopped into the middle of these gifted classes filled with the middle classes—kids, mostly white, many Jewish, who wore braces and were driven to and from school by their parents and who brought homemade lunches in crisp white paper bags, not oversized and wrinkled brown bags left over from carrying home a half gallon of milk and a loaf of bread, but bags bought in a package expressly for the purpose of packing school lunches. Every morning they picked up these bags, plump with promise, from clean tile counters. Then at lunch, they brought them outside to the benches in the yard, rather than sit inside the cafeteria, where the rest of us were eating hot lunch for free or a reduced price, our parents having filled out the requisite forms, putting the right numbers into the right blanks. The gifted kids ate outside, with the clean smell of fog and eucalyptus, and got first dibs on the handball court, and left portions of their lunches—half a sandwich, a baggie of raisins—for the seagulls who flew up from Ocean Beach and hovered above the schoolyard, waiting until the bell rang and we ran inside for class.

The first lesson of the Gifted Program was that money made you smart: poor kids went to the regular or the dumb classes; rich kids went to gifted. There also appeared to be some connection between race and smarts; I was white, so I could pass, could slip by and seem to fit in with the gifteds, even if I didn't. The San Francisco Unified School District used to send its no-

tices home in English, Spanish, Chinese, and Tagalog, so the color line was far from black and white, but it was there nonetheless. I had a social-studies teacher—also coach of the public-speaking club I had joined—who once told me how she wouldn't let a black girl in her class go to the "baffroom" until she could say it properly. She told me this as a joke between two people of the same color and, she assumed, class. But all I could feel was the pressure of a full bladder and the fear of peeing my pants in front of thirty kids as a teacher taunted me for reasons I didn't understand.

What happens to a poor white girl who gets transplanted into the gifted classes? A girl whose way of thinking is based equally on logic and emotion, whose affinity for schoolwork, like her younger brother's affinity for sports, could be traced in part to the void left by a recent divorce, which split up not only the parents but also the three children? At first I wonder if a mistake has been made. My confidence, the sassy way I hold my own against my brothers and the boys in the neighborhood, leaks out of me like water from the bottom of a potted plant. In class, I don't raise my hand or join the discussion; I'm not even sure what the others are talking about. Is it possible they are speaking a different language? Like an exile from another country, I don't know where to sit at lunchtime, don't know what to do when my old friends—the ones I used to cut school with and go smoke in the bushes or steal lip gloss from Woolworth's—call me "traitor" as we pass each other in the hallway.

Eventually, my curiosity, my creativity, and my yearning for praise take over. One day during a spelling bee, I am one of only two students left standing, and it dawns on me that I am as smart as these gifted kids.

Source: Frances Lefkowitz, "The Gifted Classes," *The Sun* 325 (January 2003), pp. 17–18.

often forced to attend school part-time; neither they nor their families may be able to afford the costs of full-time school attendance.

Students assigned to lower tracks in high school are less likely than other students to stay through graduation or otherwise experience school success (Fischer et al., 1996). Young people who drop out are in the weakest position in the labor market and are likely to remain so throughout their adult working years. In 2000, some 11 percent of persons between the ages of 16 and 24 had not completed high school and were not enrolled in school. As would be predicted from the greater

TABLE 13.2 Percentage of High School Dropouts among Persons 16 to 24 Years Old, by Race/Ethnicity: 1970, 1980, 1990, 1995, 1999

Year	White	Black	Latino/a
1970[1]	13.2	27.9	—
1980	11.4	19.1	35.2
1990	9.0	13.2	32.4
1995[2]	8.6	12.1	30.0
1999[2]	7.3	12.6	28.6

—Data not available.

[1] White and black include persons of Latino/Latina origin.

[2] Because of changes in data collection procedures, data may not be comparable with figures for earlier years.

SOURCE: National Center for Education Statistics, *Digest of Education Statistics, 2000* (Washington, DC: U.S. Government Printing Office, 2000), Table 106.

representation of students of color in lower level tracks, the percentage of dropouts was lowest among whites, at 6.9 percent, while the rate for African Americans was 13.1 percent and the rate for Latinos was 27.8 percent. Latinas and African American females had lower dropout rates than their male counterparts (National Center for Education Statistics, 2002b). Data from selected years prior to 2000, found in Table 13.2, show a similar pattern.

Over the last several decades, U.S. society has experienced the phenomenon of *credential inflation* (Collins, 1979). The high school diploma and more recently the bachelor's degree have steadily lost value as credentials for employment. More people than ever before have college degrees and even graduate degrees today and consequently find themselves pitted in intense competition for advancement. In response to the rising number of diploma and degree holders, employers have slowly increased the educational requirements for entry-level jobs. Being a high school dropout today means facing a future of very limited life chances.

In sum, the tracking system within education, buttressed by the fact that families in different class positions bring different resources to bear on behalf of their children, shapes individuals' biographies. Students with the potential to learn and make important contributions are more likely to be encouraged in school if they are from families of higher class position. The class bias that ignores and suppresses the potential of people from poor and working-class backgrounds deprives everyone in society of the contributions they could otherwise make. The gatekeeping role played by education is a major factor supporting the perpetuation of economic inequality and differences in the distribution of life chances within society as a whole.

Although the focus in this section was on class inequality, we noted that African American, Latino/Latina American, and Native American students from low-income families are disproportionately represented in lower level tracks and ability groupings, and they are more likely to drop out of school than white students. In the next section we address ways in which the system of racial inequality in the United States has affected and continues to affect the quality of education available to students of color. We begin with a look at racial segregation in education.

Racial Inequality and Schooling

Until a landmark U.S. Supreme Court decision in 1954, it was perfectly legal for towns and cities in the United States to maintain separate schools for white children and children of color. Southern states routinely practiced segregation of students by race. The segregation of African American children was part of the "Jim

Crow" strategy southern whites used to uphold the position of racial superiority they had enjoyed during the era of slavery (Williams, 1987). Millions of children of color, many of whom are adults today, went through racially segregated schools, which were typically less well funded, staffed, and equipped than those available to whites in the same communities. In cases where maintaining dual systems of schooling was too expensive because there were only a few children of color, these children were bused long distances to segregated schools in other communities. Legal segregation has long been outlawed, yet public education remains highly segregated along color lines.

De Jure and De Facto School Segregation

In 1954, after decades of legal struggles by civil rights groups, the U.S. Supreme Court ruled that racially segregated schools denied children of color equal rights under the law. This ruling, rendered in *Brown v. Board of Education of Topeka* (Kansas), pulled the legal foundations from under the U.S. educational version of South African apartheid. The Court ordered offending school districts to dismantle racially separate systems and to abolish segregationist policies "with all deliberate speed." The Supreme Court ruling met with a great deal of state and local resistance, however. **Desegregation** (ending segregated public school systems) remained rare in the southern states for another 10 years, until Congress passed the Civil Rights Act of 1964. That act gave the executive branch of the federal government the power to initiate lawsuits against school systems that refused to desegregate and the power to cut off their federal financial assistance.

The federal government's attack against segregated schools was aimed primarily at the southern states, where racial separation was written into law and was therefore known as **de jure segregation.** Once this legalized segregation was ended, southern schools ultimately became the least segregated in the nation (De Witt, 1992). This remains the case, even though segregation of southern schools is on the increase: In 1988–1989, some 44 percent of African American children were in predominantly white schools in the South; by 1991–1992, the figure had dropped to only 39 percent ("New Era of Segregation," 1993). The drop has continued, so that southern schools are now the most rapidly segregating of those in any region (see Schemo, 2001).

In the Northeast, Midwest, and West, schools were segregated largely because of the racially discriminatory policies of real estate agencies and bank mortgage lenders as well as the informally enforced, self-segregation of neighborhoods by white landlords and homeowners. This is known as **de facto segregation.** Unlike the case in the South, school segregation was not authorized by law, but local school boards—typically all-white—often helped create and perpetuate segregation by the ways in which they located new schools and drew boundaries. Relatively little federal government pressure to desegregate was exerted on these school systems outside the South. Rather, initiatives to break down segregation took the form of an occasional court order and voluntary local plans.

While U.S. society has been growing more racially and ethnically diverse, since the mid-1960s the school systems attended by children of color in the Northeast, Midwest, and West have become increasingly segregated. Today, children in these regions frequently attend schools that have few, if any, members of other racial and ethnic groups, much like the racially segregated neighborhoods they live in. De facto segregation is most noticeable in metropolitan areas where predominantly African American and Latino/Latina school systems within central cities are surrounded by suburban school systems that are predominantly white (Orfield, Eaton, and Jones, 1997).

According to a study by the Harvard University Civil Rights Project, 70 percent of African American children attended schools predominantly made up of children of color in 1998–1999, up from 63 percent in 1980–1981. Among Latinos/Latinas, 76 percent were in such schools in 1998–1999. The study found that schools in the state of New York were the most racially segregated in the United States, followed by schools in Michigan, Illinois, and California. Moreover, most children of color are economically as well as racially segregated in their schooling. According to Gary Orfield of the Civil Rights Project, "A map of schools attended by the average black or Hispanic student would almost perfectly match a map of high-poverty schools" (Schemo, 2001).

Private church-related schools, such as Roman Catholic parochial schools, are even more racially segregated than public schools. Church-related schools make up 80 percent of all private schools in the United States. Harvard's Civil Rights Project found that 48 percent of black children in Catholic schools and 44 percent of children in other private religious schools are attending "highly segregated" institutions, meaning that less than 10 percent of those attending the schools are white. In contrast, 34 percent of African American children attend public schools that are "heavily segregated" (Schemo, 2002).

A landmark 2002 U.S. Supreme Court decision allows public funds to be used by states to give "vouchers" to low-income children who wish to transfer out of public schools. The vouchers could be used toward the costs of attending private schools, including religious schools (Frahm, 2002). Vouchers are similar to a check, but they are no educational panacea for most poor children of color who live in racially segregated communities. Vouchers typically cover only a portion of private school costs, and schools must be willing to accept both the children and the vouchers. Children from the very poorest families are unlikely to have the extra money needed to make use of vouchers. When those children whose families can afford to use the vouchers transfer to private schools, the student bodies they abandon will be even more economically disadvantaged on average. Ironically, the relatively few low-income children of color who are able to use vouchers to enroll in private schools may not escape racial segregation, given such schools' color composition.

Segregation and Central-City Fiscal Crises

De facto school segregation in public and many private church-related schools reflects prevailing patterns of local housing segregation. Discrimination in the rental or sale of housing has been illegal nationwide since the 1960s. Nonetheless, informal discrimination in banks' mortgage-lending policies and on the part of home insurers, as well as bias in housing owners' and realtors' sales and rental practices, have subtly channeled African Americans and Latino/Latinas into certain residential areas within cities. As these areas have grown and extended, one result has been "white flight" (the relocation of white Anglo residents) into outlying suburban communities. Often these are communities that historically have not tolerated the presence of African American or Latino/Latina families. Tragically, even today the residents of many communities make residents of color feel unwelcome.

Given that people of color are disproportionately represented among the poor and low-income working class in central cities, many cannot afford the high housing costs in outlying white communities. Moreover, even those who can afford to relocate often must weigh the difficulties and costs of commuting back to central-city jobs. Some parents of color may worry about how they will replace the local support network of family and friends that helps with child and elder care when they are at work. All must consider how they and their children will be received and treated in the new community. The difficulties many families face in moving to predominantly white communities outside central cities—from racial discrimination to the issue of their own resources—reinforce segregated living patterns. Because public education systems in the United States tend to be organized around local or neighborhood schools, which parents generally prefer, residential segregation readily translates into racially separate schooling.

The U.S. population has undergone significant changes in composition in recent years, due both to natural population growth and to immigration policies that have made it easier for people from Latin America, the Caribbean, and Asia to enter the United States and gain U.S. citizenship. Because of this, public school enrollments of children of color have been growing rapidly. In 2000, children and youths who are African American, Latino/Latina American, Asian American, and Native American accounted for approximately 39 percent of the total enrollment in the nation's public schools, up from 22 percent in 1972 (National Center for Education Statistics, 2002a).

Many people of color live in the nation's major cities where urban fiscal crises have squeezed budgets for education and other community services. The aging and deterioration of central-city housing, combined with the loss or shutdown of businesses and manufacturing plants, has left cities across the United States with a weakened property tax base. Their fiscal situations have been exacerbated by cutbacks in federal aid that state governments have not been able or have been unwilling to offset. Most cities' budgets are stretched to the limits, as residents have the need not only for education but for health care, police protection, and income assistance programs. Too often the funds available for public education fall far short of what is needed to adequately staff and equip city schools. While money alone does not create quality education, many city schools are so starved for funds that they lack even the most rudimentary supplies. Other urban school systems face student educational deficiencies and needs that are far greater than those typically found in more affluent communities, spend more than the latter in per-pupil expenditures, and still find that the funds available are nowhere near enough to do the job.

The result is what education critic Jonathan Kozol calls *Savage Inequalities* (1991). Kozol is referring to those inequalities that characterize the gap between the quality of public education cities can afford to provide and the quality more affluent towns and suburbs can afford. Differences in resources affect the educational opportunities of students who must attend these schools, no matter what their skin color. Kozol's research on the differences between well-financed and poorly financed

Many students in the United States attend public schools that are under-financed, overcrowded, and understaffed, and where it is difficult for them to get a quality education. The children pictured here are forced to learn in a portable classroom that does not even have enough seats to accommodate them.

schools across the country vividly illustrates the outcomes of spending inequities. He found that poorer schools tend to be physically dilapidated, overcrowded, understaffed, and ill-equipped with textbooks and supplies. Kozol even found science laboratories with no science equipment. In Kozol's view, the overall effects of attending such schools on children's educational opportunities, level of performance, and sense of self-esteem are extremely negative. The disproportionate enrollment of children of color in poorly financed, economically and racially segregated schools thus contributes to their limited life chances.

Unequal Educational Opportunity and Rural Schools

The savage inequalities that Jonathon Kozol describes extend to other sectors of U.S. society as well, often restricting the life chances of children in rural areas and small towns. We are stressing problems facing urban school systems in this chapter, yet almost one in three public school students live in rural communities or in towns with populations of 25,000 or fewer. Indeed, in some 20 states, mostly in the South, Appalachia, northern New England, and the Great Plains, over a third of all students go to rural schools (Beeson and Strange, 2003).

In many small towns and rural areas, high rates of poverty among families and children are a serious problem. An estimated 2.5 million children live in rural poverty, and in many of the nation's counties the poverty rate exceeds 35 percent (Save the Children, 2002). Taken as a whole, rural areas and small towns are predominantly white. In 2000, however, over 50 percent of rural children living in poverty were children of color. According to one report, "In rural areas, roughly 33 percent of Hispanic children, 37 percent of African American children, and 44 percent of American Indian children lived below the poverty line" (Save the Children, 2002). There is a high incidence of racial segregation in rural education, particularly in the "Black Belt" states of the South, in heavily Mexican American areas of Cali-

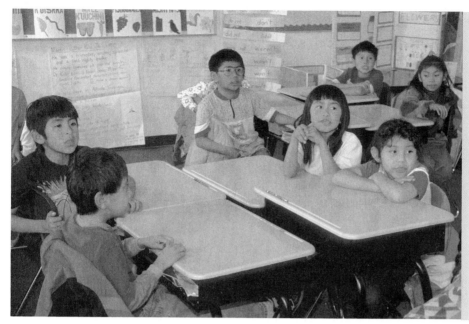

Children living in isolated rural communities, many of whom come from low-income families, often attend schools that have few resources, offer limited educational opportunities, and are racially segregated. These Native-American children attend school on a rural reservation.

fornia and the Southwest, and on Native American reservations. Dropout rates tend to be even higher in rural than in urban school districts.

Like urban areas, rural areas and small towns are faced with inadequate and frequently inequitable state school funding policies. On a per-student basis, less money tends to be spent on schools in such locations. Many small-town and rural communities are economically depressed and incapable of levying sufficient taxes to significantly improve educational conditions. Children on isolated tribal reservations often attend schools with extremely limited resources. Increasingly, rural students are being forced to attend large regional consolidated schools, often commuting long distances and up to three hours a day, because their local communities cannot afford to support their own education facilities. Local education needs go unmet in part because rural communities and small towns often lack the political clout necessary to get legislatures and the U.S. Congress to adequately address their children's lack of educational opportunities.

Racial Inequalities within Schools

The internal environments of schools play an important role in limiting opportunities for children of color (see Hallinan, 2001). In a variety of ways a school's environment—including its staff composition, patterns of teacher–student interaction, and curricular opportunities—can prove inhospitable to learning.

School Staffing

Consider, for example, the staffing of public schools. By and large, whites disproportionately populate the staff of the nation's public schools: 84 percent of public

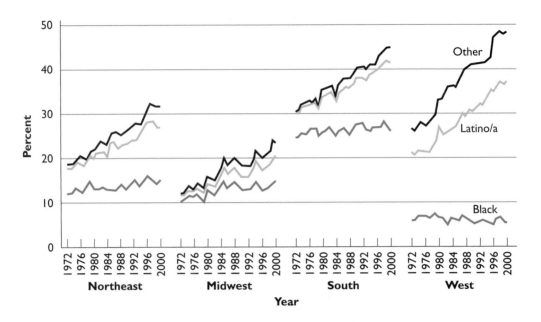

FIGURE 13.1 **Percentage of Public School Students Enrolled in Grades K–12 Who Were Children of Color, by Region, 1972–2000** The U.S. public school population is increasingly diverse, with children of color making up an ever-increasing proportion of students from kindergarten through high school. The rise in the numbers of Latinos/Latinas is especially notable. (Source: National Center on Education Statistics, *The Condition of Education, 2002* [Washington, D.C.: U.S. Government Printing Office, 2002, p. 45])

school principals are white, as are 91 percent of teachers (National Center for Education Statistics, 2001). These percentages do not reflect the student composition of U.S. public schools which, as shown in Figure 13.1, have contained growing proportions of children of color in all regions for the last few decades (nationally, whites make up only 69 percent of the public school student population). The U.S. societal system of racial inequality often discourages interracial relationships, and many white school staff lack knowledge and harbor stereotypes about people of color. White staff members can find it difficult to comprehend the needs and capabilities of children of color, to interact effectively with them, and to fashion educational programming that will maximize their individual learning potentials. In part this is also an outcome of the inadequacies in the higher education and training that school staff members themselves receive (Irvine, 1990).

Jeannie Oakes studied three California high schools and found that students were being channeled into different tracks on the basis of racial stereotypes held by teachers and counselors: Even when their scores on standardized tests were identical, Asian Americans were far more likely to be placed in high-track classes than Latinos/Latinas. Oakes is quoted as saying:

Even where language was a problem for both Asian and Hispanic groups, some [school officials] would say, "The Asian kids will work together and make sure each other learns . . . and we can't depend on Hispanic kids to do that." The trouble is that there are stereotypical judgments made about groups that then are applied to most children who belong to that group, whether or not it may be true in that individual case. (Glazer, 1990:750)

School staff make decisions that often have the effect of providing children of color with an education that is different from and inferior to that provided to white children. Students of color are, for example, more likely than whites to be in low-ability classes for the non–college bound (Oakes and Guiton, 1995). They are also underrepresented in gifted and talented programs (Ford, 1998) However, they are overrepresented in other, less desirable statuses. According to Marion Wright Edelman of the Children's Defense Fund,

Once a black child enters public school he or she is twice as likely as a white child to be held back a grade, three times as likely to be placed in classes for the educable mentally retarded [EMR], and twice as likely to be suspended from school. . . A white child is twice as likely to be placed in a class for gifted students as in an EMR class; a black child is almost three times as likely to be placed in an EMR class as in a class for gifted students. (1988:144–145, 154)

In addition, as noted earlier, a higher proportion of students of color are channeled into low-level high school tracks labeled "general" or "vocational," as opposed to "college preparatory" (Applied Research Center, 2001).

The problems that children of color face in obtaining quality educations are often further subverted by the indifference and even hostility of school staff to student–staff cultural differences that may exist.

Cultural Differences

Jacqueline Jordan Irvine (1990) has explored factors that may help explain the problem of African American achievement in public schools. One of the main factors she addresses is that of **cultural synchronization**, the match between the cultural characteristics of students and the culture of their school environment. Irvine argues that African Americans share common cultural traits deriving from their African ancestry and from their history of racial oppression as a people in the United States (see also Kochman, 1981). These cultural traits are not possessed by the dominant "Eurocentric" majority (white Americans of European ancestry). In Irvine's words,

Because the culture of black children is different and often misunderstood, ignored, or discounted, black students are likely to experience cultural discontinuity in schools, particularly schools in which the majority, or Eurocentric persons, control, administer, and teach. . . This lack of cultural sync becomes evident in instructional situations in which teachers misinterpret, denigrate and dismiss black students' language, nonverbal cues, physical movements, learning styles, cognitive approaches, and worldview. When teachers and students are out of sync, they clash and confront each other, both consciously and unconsciously, in matters pertaining to proxemics (use of interpersonal distance), paralanguage (behaviors accompanying speech, such as voice tone and pitch and speech rate and length), and coverbal behavior (gesture, facial expression, eye gaze). (1990:xix)

Researchers and educators point out that conflicts arising from lack of cultural synchronization between African American children and school staff occur most notably in schools serving children from poor, racially segregated city neighborhoods where residents are socially isolated. In poverty-stricken sections of New York City, for example, teachers and students have grappled and clashed over African American students' use of nonstandard English (Lee, 1994). Whereas many students are, in effect, "bilingual" and can switch back and forth between the two, others do not possess skill in the use of standard English. Linguists have noted that the nonstandard English used by African Americans reflects remnants of West African languages used by slaves. However, it is often dismissed with little respect by teachers. Under such circumstances, many students use it intentionally as a form of resistance to school authority and as a badge of in-group ethnic and class identity (Lee, 1994).

While acknowledging the presence of cultural differences, researcher John Ogbu (1991) argues that the academic performance of African Americans as well as other people of color must be understood in the context of how they came to be incorporated into U.S. society, their history of discriminatory treatment, and the patterns of adaptive behavior they consequently adopted. To use his terms, **immigrant minorities** have come to the United States voluntarily. Examples include many immigrants from Asia, the Caribbean, and Latin America. On average, their children tend to do better in school than the children of **involuntary minorities** such as Native Americans and African Americans, groups who were incorporated into U.S. society through colonization, conquest, or slavery.

Ogbu believes such differences in academic performance are due to a variety of factors. Immigrant minorities usually possess a positive social identity rooted in their original homeland. They have reason to be optimistic about their future life chances when comparing the opportunities before them to those they left behind. They rationalize that the problems they often face in this country—with language, discriminatory treatment, employment, housing—are temporary, and they expect to overcome such problems with time and effort. Immigrant minorities tend to trust members of the dominant group and the institutions that it controls and seek ways to use its institutions for their benefit. In sum, immigrant minorities are likely to possess a positive worldview and hopes for the future that affect their children's orientation toward schooling and may be reflected in academic performance.

In Ogbu's view, African Americans' history and contemporary life experiences have encouraged many to adopt a negative worldview and to be cynical about their future life chances. The social identity of African Americans is less likely to be positive than that of immigrant minorities, given their long history of oppression and denigration by the dominant white population. African Americans often find optimism about their life chances hard to come by, for the problems in living they face often look and turn out to be permanent. Their experiences with members of the dominant white majority and the institutions it controls generate wariness and distrust.

Ogbu suggests that under conditions of poverty and racial isolation in a segregated community, many African American children have difficulty believing that societal rules for self-advancement will work for them. They may doubt that schooling will produce any worthwhile payoff and that going to school will provide them with the cultural capital they need to "make it" outside their community. Affected as well by teachers' low expectations for their success, many students place little value on academic performance. Those who do value schoolwork often have to deal with ridicule by their more alienated peers (see Fordham and Ogbu,1986). This lack of faith in the benefits of schooling appears to be especially acute for African American boys, based on problems in living that they see many of the adult males in their communities experiencing.

Ogbu thus gives a much broader interpretation of the academic performance of children of color, suggesting that a group's history, position in U.S. society's system of racial inequality, and worldview contribute to how its members interact in the school setting. This may help explain why groups differ in their experiences with school and why many African Americans and other students of color have difficulty with their academic performance. In the absence of mutual respect between students and school staff, the school environment is likely to be one of tension and even conflict. Staff members then focus their energies on maintaining order and control, and opportunities for students to learn are lost.

The in-school experiences of children of color can also be affected by how white school staff react to the community politics accompanying desegregation. For example, African American parents and students in Selma, Alabama, protested the placement of many black children with high test scores in the lowest tracks (Glazer, 1990). Despite the fact that the Selma school system was 70 percent black, over 90 percent of black students were tracked low. Observers suggested that such tracking practices started in the early 1970s, when Selma public schools finally desegregated, as a way of persuading middle-class white parents to keep their children in the local public schools. While Selma ceased to maintain separate schools for blacks and whites, its school system *resegregated* students within schools through racially biased track placements.

Selma is not unusual in this respect. Other school systems have segregated students by race within schools to help reduce many middle-class whites' antipathy toward having their offspring attend school with children of color. Kenneth Meier and his colleagues (1989) studied 174 large central-city school systems. They confirmed other researchers' findings: African American students were more likely than white students to be in lower level tracks. But they also found that school systems in which whites were concentrated in the higher tracks experienced less white flight. In their view, racially biased tracking practices, while harming the educational opportunities of many children of color, had become a means by which public school officials were able to stem the flight of middle-class white families from central cities.

Given the high degree of competition for jobs today, being disadvantaged in terms of educational credentials amounts to losing the competition before it begins. Moreover, lack of school success feeds into the discriminatory hiring practices of many employers. Such employers can reject people of color for being educationally unqualified, thereby hiding the blatant racism involved in rejecting them for their skin color. Indeed, one way employers may minimize the probability that persons of color will qualify for jobs is to arbitrarily inflate the educational credentials required for the positions. (Federal affirmative action policies, minimally enforced in recent years, originated to prevent such discriminatory employer practices. See Reskin, 1998.)

Racism remains a central open wound within U.S. society as a whole. Many may wish it were not so, but U.S. schools have not escaped or proved to be a haven from U.S. society's system of racial inequality. Education, as one of many white-dominated and controlled social institutions, needs to be purged of racism as much as any of the others.

Gender Inequality and Schooling

Thus far we have been discussing education as if a student's gender was of no real significance. However, given that a system of gender inequality also exists in U.S. society, we should expect to find evidence of it in schooling. Evidence shows that males and females are treated very differently in school and that their differential treatments affect educational opportunities along gender lines (Sadker and Sadker, 1994; Wellesley College Center for Research on Women, 1992). As we will see, the nature of the treatment school-age girls experience structures and skews the directions in which their learning proceeds and adversely affects their sense of competence and self-esteem. In brief, girls are not encouraged to explore and develop their full potential and range of talents as much as are boys. This lack of encouragement is greatly exacerbated for girls who are simultaneously disadvantaged in other systems of inequality, such as girls who have a disability (Rousso and Wehmeyer, 2001).

Suppressing Female Students' Potential

Ample research exists to show that boys receive far more teacher attention in school at all grade levels, no matter what the sex of the teacher (Sadker and Sadker, 1994). This is not simply because males demand more attention; teachers actively solicit males' responses more frequently within the classroom. When teachers express more interest in, and give more positive feedback to, contributions from boys, they create an environment that encourages boys to be actively engaged in the learning process while girls become passive and restrict their involvement (Wellesley, 1992).

Some researchers argue that differential treatment by teachers can lead to **learned helplessness** in female students, whereby they lose confidence in their own abilities and are less likely to persevere in schoolwork that is difficult and challenging (Parsons et al., 1982; Wellesley, 1992). Girls may thus abandon some of the more difficult academic courses and programs for which they are actually well qualified.

For example, many people have commented on the relative absence of girls in advanced mathematics and science courses that college-bound students might profitably take (Raffalli, 1994). Jones and Wheatley (1989) point out that there are gender differences in attitudes toward science as well as differences in achievement in science by sex. Achievement differences are especially notable in chemistry, earth and space science, and physics. Differences in attitudes toward science start as early as elementary school; differences in achievement start to show up when students reach adolescence (Jones and Wheatley, 1989). Since no one has demonstrated that innate sex differences in science-related skills or aptitudes exist, social scientists interpret such attitudinal and achievement differences as outcomes of the ways in which males and females are treated.

Jones and Wheatley (1989), along with many others, argue that schooling often fails to encourage girls to be interested and involved in science and may actively discourage them. In observations of 30 physical science and 30 chemistry classrooms, Jones and Wheatley found that 93 percent of the wall posters and displays used males as the dominant scientific figures. Teachers in these classrooms were more likely to call on male students and to ask males to volunteer to conduct experiments and demonstrations. Female students were more likely to be relegated to the role of observers. Finally, teachers' use of language and examples showed that "teachers continue to sex type science occupations and reinforce the traditional role of the woman as the homemaker" (Jones and Wheatley, 1989).

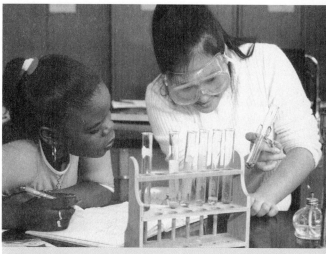

School teachers and staff members often fail to encourage girls who are capable of pursuing advanced academic programs and career goals in the sciences. These girls, intent on solving a chemistry problem, are less likely than their male classmates to carry their interest in science on to the college level.

The results are a school environment that leaves many girls uncomfortable pursuing the skills necessary for a career in science. The National Council for Research on Women reported that girls of high school age have less confidence in their mathematics skills than do boys, and that boys outperform girls at higher math achievement levels. Moreover, girls are said to be "alarmingly absent" from advanced placement classes in computer science, demonstrating "reticence about a technology that seems to them largely devoted to the interests of boys" (Thom, 2001). By the time they complete high school, girls with an interest in science are less sure about their career goals in this area than are boys. The Council noted that the first year of college is a time when women disproportionately abandon their plans for a science major (Thom, 2001).

At present, women outnumber men in college attendance. But women and men are not equally well represented in all the various majors and fields of study. For example, women are highly underrepresented in engineering and other technical fields that require an in-depth science and math background (Thom, 2001). Instead they are more likely to find their way into education or the humanities, fields in which such a background is not necessary. Thus women who graduate from college tend to end up in programs leading to jobs that are less well paid than those of men, and this is reflected in annual earnings differences in Figure 13.2.

In 2000, women received 76 percent of the 108,168 bachelor's degrees awarded in education, but only 18.5 percent of the 72,555 bachelor's degrees awarded in engineering (U.S. Department of Commerce, 2003). Although this is a major advance from the 0.004 percent of the engineering degrees they received in 1959–1960 (National Center for Education Statistics, 1992), women are still a long way from parity with men in this technical field.

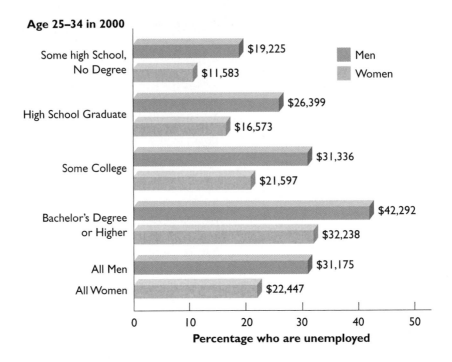

Age 25–34 in 2000

Some high School,
No Degree — Men: $19,225 / Women: $11,583

High School Graduate — Men: $26,399 / Women: $16,573

Some College — Men: $31,336 / Women: $21,597

Bachelor's Degree or Higher — Men: $42,292 / Women: $32,238

All Men: $31,175
All Women: $22,447

Legend: Men, Women

X-axis: 0 10 20 30 40 50

Percentage who are unemployed

FIGURE 13.2 **Median Annual Earnings of Male and Female Workers, Age 25–34, in 2000** On average, women aged 25 to 34 have lower incomes than men, even when they have completed equivalent years of schooling. This is partly because women are more likely than men to be enrolled in educational programs that do not lead to the more highly paid skilled jobs and professions. (Source: U.S. Department of Commerce, Bureau of the Census, *March Current Population Surveys, 2001.* Available at www.census.gov.)

The research on science classrooms addresses an aspect of the educational environment thought to bear on girls' self-esteem: the way in which women's contributions to society are handled in the formal curricula. There have been definite improvements in recent years, but curricula still heavily focus on the contributions of men in such subjects as English and social studies. Observing that girls' self-esteem goes *down,* not up, as they progress through school, researchers have postulated that curricular bias and insufficient attention to the contributions that women make are part of the reason:

> Lowered self-esteem is a perfectly reasonable conclusion if one has been subtly instructed that what people like oneself have done in the world has not been important and is not worth studying. (Wellesley, 1992:67)

Not all students, as we saw earlier, are bound for college or are channeled into college preparatory programs or tracks in public high schools. Most high schools have vocational education programs that serve both male and female students who are likely to enter the labor force directly upon graduation. Again, treatment is different for the two sexes, despite laws prohibiting discrimination in vocational education programs (Wellesley, 1992). Girls tend to be clustered in programs that prepare them for low-paying, dead-end, traditionally female jobs (such as secretarial work and food services), whereas boys are concentrated in programs that point toward skilled trades and occupations (such as woodworking and engine repair) in which monetary rewards and opportunities for mobility are likely to be higher.

Female teachers predominate in the courses girls take in home economics, consumer skills, health care, and office practices, whereas male teachers are most likely to supervise the boys whose presence dominates courses in industrial arts, agriculture, and technical occupations. Moreover, high school placement efforts and policies do not work to break down the resistance women face when attempting to enter areas of pp. 385–389 the labor market that men have tended to monopolize (see Chapter 12) (Wellesley, 1992).

In 1972 Congress passed legislation barring sex discrimination at institutions that receive federal funds. Title IX of the Education Amendments of 1972 states, "No person in the United States shall, on the basis of sex, be excluded from participation in, be denied benefit of, or be subjected to discrimination under any program or activity receiving Federal financial assistance." Title IX pertains not only to the formal curriculum but also to athletic activities, another arena in which one's potential and range of talents may be cultivated and displayed. Here again, while there have been some efforts to address discrimination, problems remain.

For example, only about 30 percent of high school girls participate in athletics, while almost twice as many high school boys do so. Despite an 847 percent increase in female high school sports participation since Title IX was enacted in 1972, it is estimated that girls still receive 1.1 million fewer chances to play high school sports than boys (King, 2002). Within high schools there tends to be far less interest in and enthusiasm for girls' sports than for boys' sports. Ironically, many girls participate in pep clubs and cheerleader squads whose activities help validate this situation (Eder and Parker, 1987). The bias in athletics parallels the bias in the formal curriculum, in that women's contributions are less well acknowledged and valued.

The imbalance in men's and women's sports participation continues at the college level. In high school, the more than 6 million boys and girls who play sports vie for fewer than a half million college-level sports openings. Most of these openings are filled by males. The number of women participating in college sports has risen from less than 30,000 prior to Title IX to more than 150,000 today, but women still have 30 percent fewer sports slots to compete for. And, not surprisingly, men's sports also receives the greatest proportion of college sports expenditures. For example, men receive $133 million more annually for athletic scholarships (King, 2002). Critics argue that such treatment of women athletes is fundamentally unfair and in violation of Title IX of the Education Amendments; however, the federal government has been slow to move aggressively against sex discrimination in school sports. It is estimated that 80 percent of schools and colleges are still not in compliance with the law (King, 2002). Meanwhile, Title IX has opponents who claim that efforts to expand women's sports have begun to hurt sports for men and who have sought to reduce the requirements of Title IX. Thus, over 30 years later, controversy continues to surround this federal legislation.

The School and Teenage Pregnancy

Today's teenagers become sexually active at an early age. The average age of first intercourse is estimated to be 16 but, increasingly, many children are sexually active even earlier. Among high school seniors surveyed in 2001, only 3.6 percent had sexual intercourse before age 13. However, among ninth graders surveyed that same year, 9.2 percent had done so. Almost a quarter of the ninth graders were sexually active at the time of the survey. Data for 2001 indicated that, overall, 48.5 percent of male high school students and 42.9 percent of female students had experienced sexual intercourse, and over 33 percent of high school students in general were currently sexually active (Centers for Disease Control, 2002).

Teenage pregnancy has become a widespread phenomenon and a problem of major importance. Indeed, the United States has a higher rate of early childbearing than almost any other industrialized society, although the U.S. rate has fallen somewhat in recent years. In 1990, teenagers were responsible for 31 percent of the 1,165,000 live births to unmarried mothers. By 2000, this had fallen to 27.9 percent of 1,347,000 births (U.S. Department of Commerce, 2003). This downward trend is thought to reflect a combination of a leveling off of teenage sexual activity and increased teen contraceptive use. In 2001, some 46 percent of high school students said they'd had sexual intercourse, compared to 54 percent in 1991; the percentage of students using condoms went from 46 in 1991 to 58 in 2001 (Centers for Disease Control, 2002).

Even with this slight downward trend in teenage pregnancy rates, it clearly is not uncommon for girls to confront the challenge of motherhood while in high school (and even in junior high school or middle school). Schools shortchange girls and narrow their life chances by the ways in which they handle teenagers who become pregnant. Many of these girls face discrimination within school, both while they are pregnant and after they have their children. School staff may exert little effort to have the girls continue attending school, making them feel like second-class citizens whose presence somehow contaminates the rest of the student body (Wellesley, 1992).

Girls who drop out of school are more likely to go on to bear a child out of wedlock than those who stay enrolled (Upchurch, Lillard, and Panis, 2002). Yet, once pregnant, many in-school students then drop out. One study found that for 72 percent of teenage girls who had both conceived a child and dropped out, the conception had preceded the dropout (Polit and Kahn, 1987). Such data led researchers to conclude that "the single best-documented consequence of an early pregnancy is a truncated education" (Polit and Kahn, 1987:133). However, other research qualifies this conclusion. Girls who have children while enrolled in school, but who remain in school, are just as likely to graduate as those who do not become pregnant. But girls who become pregnant and drop out of school are less likely than the others to graduate (Upchurch, Lillard, and Panis, 2002). Sociologists do know that half of the families headed by female school dropouts live in poverty (Polit and Kahn,

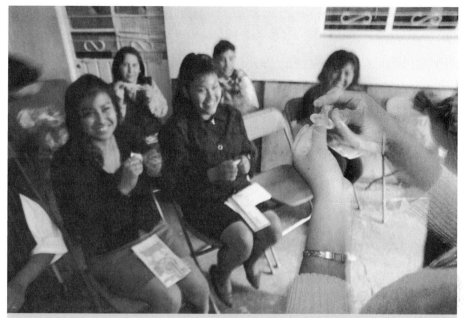

High teen pregnancy rates in part reflect the failure of many U.S. school systems to provide comprehensive sex-education programs. The young women in this photo are fortunate to have a comfortable and receptive environment in which to ask questions about safe sex and contraception.

1987). The boys who father these schoolgirls' children generally do not have similar negative consequences of pregnancy on their life chances.

Clearly one of the contributors to high rates of premarital pregnancy and premature motherhood is the failure of most schools to fill the vacuum in students' sex education. Their own sense of sexuality is of central interest to young people and poses many important issues for them, yet schools suppress discourse and thus knowledge about it (Fine, 1992). Parental ambivalence and opposition, often on religious grounds, have helped keep comprehensive sex education programs out of public education. Thus many girls have little or no knowledge of contraception and safe sex practices or hold erroneous beliefs such as the notion that it is not possible to become pregnant at first intercourse. Although abortion is not an acceptable option for many girls, others who would exercise this difficult choice may find abortion unaffordable or lack access to an abortion provider.

There is no evidence that sex education programs "cause" young people to become sexually active who are not already so. For many years it has been known that adolescents who are sexually active are more likely to take precautions against pregnancy if they have been exposed to a comprehensive sex education program (Zelnick and Young, 1982). The failure of so many schools to deal with this important topic is especially harmful for girls since they must deal with both pregnancy and possible parenthood. Finally, inadequate sex education contributes to the spread of AIDS and other sexually transmitted diseases, some of which frequently go undetected by those affected because of poor dissemination of information on risk factors and symptoms as they occur in women.

Sexual Harassment in Schools

Schools contain many of the same dynamics in gender relations that exist in the larger society, including sexual harassment. The harm to those victimized is such that one researcher refers to sexual harassment as "gendered violence" (Stein, 1995). Sexual harassment in schools has been declared by the courts to be illegal under federal antidiscrimination legislation such as Title IX (discussed earlier in connection with gender and sports). Court cases in which students have sought redress for sexual harassment—from both teachers and staff, as well as from other students—have made headlines. Yet the harmful nature of student harassment of students has long been ignored, and the damage done to girls by sexual harassment has typically been made light of and often dismissed by (predominantly male) school administrators who feel that "boys will always be boys."

Sexual harassment begins as early as grade school, where it has been found to have a harmful effect on girls' sense of self-esteem (Murnen and Smolak, 2000). Insofar as male students are permitted to get away with such behavior, "the clear message to both girls and boys is that girls are not worthy of respect" (Wellesley, 1992: 73). This message has been communicated to girls through other aspects of their school experience as well.

Gaining accurate knowledge of the extent of sexual harassment is difficult, because it is a sensitive subject, difficult to define, and invites varying interpretations. The first survey undertaken of the harassment experiences of students in grades 8 to 11 found that sexual harassment in schools is widespread (Barringer, 1993; Frahm and Barger, 1993; see also Kopels and Dupper,1999). In this survey, sexual harassment was defined to students as "unwanted and unwelcome sexual behavior which interferes with your life."

Four out of five of the students polled, including boys, said they had experienced some form of harassment; the most common forms (in rank order) were being subjected to sexual comments, jokes, gestures, or looks; being touched, grabbed, or pinched in a sexual way; being intentionally brushed up against sexually; and being shown, given, or left sexual pictures, photographs, illustrations, messages, or notes. Most of the harassment occurred in school classrooms and hallways. One in four of those victimized never told anyone. While most harassers were other students, one-fifth of the victims reported being harassed by teachers, custodians, coaches, or other members of the school staff.

The survey found that boys were more likely to be harassers and girls were more likely to be victims. Two-thirds of the boys surveyed, compared with 52 percent of the girls, said they had harassed other students. Conversely, 65 percent of the girls, compared with 42 percent of the boys, said they had been touched, grabbed, or pinched in a sexual way. Moreover, the effects on girls were found to be greater: 70 percent of girls but only 24 percent of boys said they were "very upset" or "somewhat upset" when the harassment happened. Female students were far more likely to say the harassment led to their not wanting to go to school, not wanting to talk in class, finding it hard to pay attention, making a lower grade on a test or in a class, finding it hard to study, and thinking about changing schools (Barringer, 1993).

The sex-biased interactions among peers also include harassment of male and female students perceived to be homosexual. In the survey mentioned above, almost 25 percent of the boys and 10 percent of the girls said they had been called a homosexual; this was the form of harassment boys found most upsetting. In a news account accompanying details of the survey, a student described a nightmare of chronic harassment by his peers:

> "If I had the option, I wouldn't have gone to school after the second day of sixth grade," said a 16-year-old Connecticut boy who endured years of taunts from classmates who called him gay. The boy, who said he is not gay, received mocking invitations from other boys to have sex. He was tickled, pinched, tripped, beaten and called a "fag," he said.
>
> Once, he said, "a guy screamed out across the street, 'Oh. By the way, I will be attending the orgy tomorrow night." (Frahm and Barger, 1993: A6)

Boys called homosexuals may be told that they are "acting like a girl." When boys condemn other boys as "fags" or "queers," their homophobic comments typically include reference to alleged female traits, to which nothing but negative attributions are made. The message once again is that there is little about being female that is worthy of respect. Homophobia directed at girls seems almost contradictory, as it typically contains accusations of excessive masculinity (the stereotypical derogation of lesbian women as "bull dykes"). Such harassment makes it clear that females have no business appropriating "male traits." The underlying, unspoken premise can be phrased by male harassers in this way: If even lowly females can be like us, what does it mean to be male? School personnel who permit such harassment, whether through lack of vigilance or as an outcome of their own homophobia, lend support to a system of inequality in which the status of being female is further denigrated.

Since this first study of sexual harassment in schools, other studies have confirmed its findings that harassment is widespread. However, there is much more consciousness of harassment as being a problem than was the case a decade or so ago (American Association of University Women, 2001). This consciousness is no doubt aided by the knowledge on the part of school authorities that they can be sued for failure to act on complaints. Sexual harassment on the basis of sexual orientation, however, still does not seem to be taken sufficiently seriously by school authorities. In its interviews with students who are lesbian, gay, bisexual, or transgender, Human Rights Watch (2001) found the treatment to which students reported being subjected to be so serious as to constitute violations of their human rights under international law. These studies of sexual harassment have also revealed the widespread extent to which many students—regardless of sexual orientation—are being made miserable daily due to physical and psychological bullying by other students. Some victims of bullying have responded to constantly being picked on, ridiculed, or harassed by taking their own lives or, in some instances, the lives of other students and school staff.

Thus the institution of education in the United States rather systematically shortchanges female students by linking the quality of their educational experiences to the societal system of gender inequality. Women's biographies are subtly shaped by the structure of their school experiences. In many subtle and some not-so-subtle ways, girls are told that they are second-class citizens best suited for the sex-typed roles awaiting them in a male-dominated society. Rather than liberating women from patriarchy, education tends to cave in to patriarchy's influences.

Legal Challenges to Unequal Educational Opportunity

The portrait of education presented here has emphasized the role it plays in reinforcing and perpetuating the status quo—in this case, existing systems of economic, racial, and gender inequality. In this sense sociologists say that education plays a "conservative" function in society (Henry, 1963), as it helps conserve what already exists. Put another way, education contributes to the **social reproduction** of systems of inequality, facilitating their continuance over time (Bourdieu and Passeron, 1991). These systems are strengthened to the degree to which members of society accept class-biased, racist, or sexist treatment within educational institutions (Oakes et al., 2002).

As other chapters have noted, however, these systems of inequality breed tensions that often result in challenge to the system. One of the most important vehicles of challenge is a court of law. Social science research can play an important role in documenting the harm being done by different systems of inequality and the processes through which this harm occurs. Such data have at times been of great assistance to people trying to inform and persuade the courts of injustices to be corrected, although courts do not always heed the information (Chesler, Sanders, and Kalmus, 1988).

One would think that systems of tracking—insofar as they provide students from different class backgrounds with markedly different educational treatments—would be subject to challenge in the courts (Welner and Oakes, 1996). Courts have mandated changes in school system policy in those cases where racial segregation was obviously part of the reason for instituting a tracking system and children were denied equal rights to education on the basis of their race. However, the courts have been reluctant to act in cases where race cannot be shown to be involved, but where tracking apparently functions in ways that deny poor children equal educational opportunities. Judges may also be genuinely puzzled over how or whether it makes sense to change educational practices that are so firmly tied into U.S. society's system of economic inequality. Hence tracking within schools will continue until some new legal bases or vantage points are devised from which to challenge it.

Similarly, de facto segregation of central-city schools has been relatively impervious to legal challenge. Recent Supreme Court actions have made such challenges extremely difficult. People who seek change through the federal courts must be able to demonstrate that the segregation occurred deliberately; that is, they must show that the school system intended to create racially homogeneous schools (Orfield, Eaton, and Jones, 1997). Meanwhile, as we noted earlier in this chapter, the racial segregation of schools is progressively worsening.

While federal courts are not offering much help in ending de facto segregation today, efforts to use state-level courts have likewise proven ineffective. The public schools in the city of Hartford, Connecticut, provide an example. Hartford schools serve largely African American and Latino/Latina students from poor and working-class families, whereas school systems in the surrounding suburbs are predominantly white and middle class. In 1993, a group of white, African American, and Latino/Latina parents filed suit against the state. In *Sheff v. O'Neill,* they argued that their children's rights to equal educational opportunities, guaranteed by the Connecticut state constitution, were being denied. They claimed that not only de facto racial segregation but economic segregation as well were having damaging effects on the educational opportunities available to Hartford children.

In 1996 a state court found on behalf of the complainants and required the Connecticut governor and state legislature to take steps to address this situation. Yet, in keeping with the general climate of indifference among political elites regarding racial segregation of city school systems, steps taken by the state to desegregate the schools were minimal. Racial segregation of Hartford's schools—a city identified in the 2000 U.S. Census as having the second-highest poverty rate of any in the nation—has actually increased since the suit was brought. While the complainants finally decided to settle the case with the state in 2003, the solutions to which the parties agreed are unlikely to make significant inroads into the racial and economic segregation of Hartford's school children for many years, if at all.

The situation regarding sex discrimination in education is a little more promising. Although education is highly segregated along the lines of race and class, males and females are at least educated side by side for the most part. Nonetheless, the many problems identified in this chapter remain. These problems continue to be attacked today because sex discrimination remains a major public issue. Women are not allowing this issue to fade away, and efforts to combat sex discrimination through the courts, legislation such as Title IX, and the media continue unabated.

CHAPTER SUMMARY

1. As a key social institution, education performs many functions. One important function served by education is its contribution to the socialization process, preparing children and youth to participate effectively in society as adults. Education can be an important source of cultural capital.

2. Society is often said to be a meritocracy, and educational achievement is commonly seen as one of the routes to success. Yet the likelihood of college attendance is less a function of intelligence or academic achievement than of family income. The class position of a high school graduate's family affects not only the probability of college attendance but the type of institution that he or she will attend.

3. Many young people are not achieving well in school, as numerous studies have made clear. Some observers argue that students, teachers, and parents need to put more effort into achieving academic success. Few link students' failure to

achieve to the ways in which the U.S. systems of economic, racial, and gender inequality are affecting their education.

4. Research by sociologists demonstrates that children's educational opportunities and performance are influenced by the positive or negative treatment they receive in school. The treatment of students has been found to differ along the lines of family economic background, as well as skin color and sex. Negative treatment and low expectations for certain categories of students can create a self-fulfilling prophecy by leading to lower levels of achievement.

5. Schools in essence serve as gatekeepers. Educational practices such as ability grouping and tracking channel students into different curricula (e.g., academic versus vocational), often along the lines of class and race. Racially segregated schools and the inadequate financial resources available to central-city, small town, and rural school systems hinder the educational opportunities available to many low-income children and youth. Low levels of achievement and high dropout rates are the result.

6. Male-oriented school curricula and classroom gender biases operate in ways that narrow the horizons and suppress the academic and career potential of female students, for example, by discouraging many from pursuing study in advanced mathematics and science. Girls' academic potential is also negatively affected when schools fail to address the needs of those who become pregnant or when sexual harassment is allowed to go unchallenged.

7. Court actions aimed at attacking unequal educational opportunity have met with some successes in addressing racial and gender inequalities in the U.S. educational system, although much still needs to be done. Whether use of the courts will lead to improving opportunities for low-income students whose class position places them in a situation of educational disadvantage is less clear.

THINKING CRITICALLY

1. Compared with that of Kip and Josey, how would you characterize the cultural capital to which you have access? What can this cultural capital do for you? What is the relationship between your cultural capital and the likelihood that you will someday occupy a position at the very top of the class structure?

2. Discuss what is meant by "credential inflation." Are there occupations or professions that you think require far more in the way of educational credentials than is really necessary? Identify them, and discuss the reasons for this situation. What are the ramifications?

3. Despite legislation and court decisions, public schools today are highly segregated along racial lines. Discuss the arguments for racial and ethnic diversity in public education. Why don't these arguments outweigh the resistance to taking whatever steps are necessary to end segregation?

4. Have you ever been subjected to sexual harassment in a school setting? What were the circumstances? What was its impact on you? What did you do about it?

Why? Do you think that more attention should be paid to combating sexual harassment in schools? If not, why not? If so, what steps do you think should be taken?

5. Thinking back on high school, how would you characterize the class backgrounds of students you know who dropped out? What academic "tracks" were they in? Did they go to college? How do you think their lives will differ from yours 10 years from now, assuming you complete a college degree? Why?

KEY TERMS

cultural capital, *(402)*

cultural synchronization, *(419)*

de facto segregation, *(413)*

de jure segration, *(413)*

desegregation, *(413)*

gatekeepers, *(405)*

immigrant minorities, *(420)*

involuntary minorities, *(420)*

learned helplessness, *(422)*

meritocracy, *(402)*

self-fulfilling prophecy, *(407)*

social reproduction, *(430)*

tracking, *(406)*

Health

Imagine being afflicted with a progressively debilitating disease for which there is no known cure. The disease, which affects the central nervous system, can cause blindness, incontinence, paralysis, muscle spasms, dizziness, numbness, and slurred speech. Each time symptoms flare up, they may become more severe. Now imagine that a new drug has come onto the market that may actually slow the course of the disease. Wouldn't you be eager to begin using it immediately? But what if the drug was so expensive that you could not afford to buy it? What if your health insurance did not cover its high costs? What if other people with the same disease, who are not nearly as ill as you, were able to gain immediate access to the drug while you could not? If such a situation were to arise, you would probably conclude that you are part of a health care system that falls far short of meeting your needs.

This situation is real; it reflects some of the difficulties many people in the United States face in obtaining a drug treatment for multiple sclerosis. Some 350,000 people have multiple sclerosis (MS), which most often strikes young people, particularly women, between the ages of 20 and 40. In the early 1990s, a genetically engineered drug, Betaseron, which showed promise in slowing the course of MS, was introduced (Lewis, 1994). But to recoup research and development expenditures and financially reward its private investors, the new drug's manufacturer charged about $10,000 for a year's supply. Many MS patients and their families did not have health insurance. For others, insurance would not cover the expense. Few could afford to pay for it out-of-pocket.

Despite its high cost, the demand for Betaseron quickly exceeded the initial supplies. Consequently, its manufacturer held a lottery to determine who would receive the drug and when. Persons suffering the most advanced stages of MS were excluded from the lottery, as those with advanced MS had not been included in the experimental trials establishing the effects of the drug. Some 67,000 people with lesser, but varying, symptoms of MS entered the lottery. Winners began receiving the drug, but other entrants were told they would have to wait 18 months or more to be eligible to receive it, a period during which their health could well undergo further irreversible decline. Almost 4,000 other people with MS—some of whom were not eligible for the lottery—by luck or social connections managed to become part of research projects that prestigious medical institutions were conducting on Betaseron, and thus they bypassed any wait (Lewis, 1994). Betaseron remains in use, but even today many people with MS lack access to it. The price of the drug to patients remains in the range of $10,000 per year, making it unaffordable to many; some health insurers continue to resist covering the costs.

(continued)

This situation is a small, but symbolic, expression of the problems many people face when they confront the health care system in the United States. As we shall see, health issues are directly linked to social, economic, and political features of a society. If access to high-quality health care is not available or is inequitably distributed, the health status of many members of society will be adversely affected.

In this chapter we address several questions:

- How can one assess the health status of a society's members?
- How does people's health status differ in various parts of the world?
- What is the health status of people in the United States, one of the wealthiest nations in the world?
- What role do systems of economic, racial, and gender inequality play in people's access to quality health care and in their health status?
- What kinds of chronic problems and shortcomings fuel public concern over the adequacy of the U.S. system of health care?
- What alternatives could improve this system?

These difficult questions must be pursued if people's life chances are to be protected and enhanced.

Assessing Health Status

What is the meaning of "health"? From one point of view, **health** can be defined simply as the absence of illness or disease. This view may be called the **medical model** of health, and it is the model that has come to prevail in many Western nations, including the United States. The medical model is the principal point of reference for the U.S. **health care system,** which includes practicing physicians and other medical professionals; the settings in which they practice (clinics, hospitals); the universities, research centers, and manufacturing corporations that create new drugs and medical technologies; and the organizations that regulate health care and help consumers purchase it (government agencies, insurance firms). When it is guided by the medical model, a health care system focuses on responding to the problems of individuals who present themselves to it. The system is largely skewed toward *curative,* rather than preventive, activities.

The medical model provides a very narrow, and in many ways inadequate, definition of health. A broader and more adequate conception would define health as the condition that exists when people are free to use their mental and physical capabilities to the fullest extent possible. Anything hindering people's human capabilities, physical or mental, would be viewed as contributing to poor health (Sen, 2000). A health care system built around such a definition would obviously need to respond to medically treatable problems. But in defining health much more broadly, such a system would be largely directed toward *preventive* and *protective* activities.

For example, besides immunizations and other disease-prevention medical measures, a preventive health care system might place high priority on ensuring that everyone in a society had access to:

1. Adequate food, water, clothing, shelter, and hygiene.
2. Jobs with wages and benefits sufficient to permit an adequate standard of living and the education and training necessary to perform these jobs well.
3. A guaranteed minimum income above the poverty line for those who cannot, for reasons beyond their control, be employed.
4. Safe, flexible, low-stress workplace conditions.
5. Affordable, high-quality child care and elder care for households that need it.
6. Adequate vacation and leisure time to engage in individual and group recreation.
7. A natural environment cleansed of and protected against toxic and other harmful polluting substances.
8. A social environment unmarred by the threat or reality of warfare, criminal assault, and other forms of violence.

A health care system aimed at protecting and enhancing human capabilities would be primarily **proactive,** aimed at enhancing people's collective well-being, rather than primarily **reactive,** aimed at responding to individual cases, as is the case with the medical model. Unfortunately, aside from a few notable exceptions such as the health care system of Sweden (Twaddle, 1999), most societies have failed to organize their health care systems around a preventive model.

Because of the prevalence of the medical model, the most widely used indices of health status relate to illness and death, rather than to how well people are exercising their human capabilities. Among these measures is **life expectancy**—the average number of years a group of people all born in the same year are expected to live. This statistic can vary greatly from society to society. In 2001 life expectancy in Italy was 76 years for men and 82.5 for women, but in Sierra Leone it was only 42.7 years for men and 48.6 for women (U.S. Central Intelligence Agency, 2001).

Another frequently used measure of health status is the rate of **infant mortality**—infant deaths in the first year of life, expressed in terms of the number of infant deaths per 1,000 live births. Again there is wide variation worldwide. In 2001 the infant mortality rate was 124 infant deaths per 1,000 live births in Somalia but only 5 per 1,000 in Canada (U.S. Central Intelligence Agency, 2001).

Finally there is the rate of **maternal mortality**—the deaths of mothers as a consequence of pregnancy and birthing, expressed as the number of mothers who die per 100,000 infants born. The variation is once more quite extreme. In 1996 the rate was 96 maternal deaths per 100,000 infants born in the Philippines but less than 2 per 100,000 in Norway (United Nations, 2001).

Obviously, these measures assess only very crudely the health status of any given society's members. The statistics do not, for example, reveal anything about the different rates of life expectancy, infant mortality, or maternal mortality at different class levels of a society. They provide no insight into why these rates vary among nations. Social scientists find interpretation of such statistics a complex task. Nations differ greatly in their fundamental social, cultural, geographic, political, and economic characteristics. They also differ in that their data gathering, record keeping, and reporting are not conducted with equal efficiency. Health-status statistics therefore have somewhat limited value and must be used with caution. With this in mind, we will look at how the United States is doing with regard to the health status of its population.

Health Status of People in the United States

Compared with most of the world's nations, the United States measures up well on the health-status indicators we have been discussing. Indeed, the U.S. population has undergone a marked improvement in its health status since the early part of the twentieth century. Persons who were born in 1900, for example, could expect to live only about 47 years. For those born in the United States today, average life expectancy is 77 years (National Center for Health Statistics, 2001).

The vast life expectancy gains in the United States since 1900 have occurred only in part because of advances in the field of medicine. Improvements in diet, personal hygiene practices, and housing conditions have played a key role. Perhaps most important have been improvements in public health and sanitation policies. Medical advances have, comparatively speaking, played a relatively minor role in increasing average life expectancy (McKinlay and McKinlay, 1990).

The most important medical development of the previous century was the ability to immunize against or treat common infectious diseases that frequently resulted in death. Such diseases—from tuberculosis to influenza—cause far fewer deaths in the United States today (though they remain important factors in mortality rates for the nation's poor). Spared from life-threatening infectious diseases, and living on average much longer than in the past, older Americans today are most likely to succumb to cancer or heart disease (see Table 14.1).

For life expectancy at birth to have dramatically gone up, the infant mortality rate had to come down. Again, the statistics for 1900 and today provide a sharp contrast. At the beginning of the twentieth century 143 infants died for every 1,000 born live in the United States. By the end of the 1990s the infant mortality rate had dropped to about 7 per 1,000. Similarly, the maternal mortality rate has dramatically dropped. In 1915 some 610 mothers died for every 100,000 infants born live in the United States, a statistic found only in underdeveloped nations today. Now the number is down to 8.

Both infant and maternal mortality rates have been reduced in part by the same kinds of improvements in nutrition, sanitation, and so on, that have increased life expectancy. Moreover, advances in prenatal, neonatal, and obstetric medical practices have aided infants and mothers. Advances in obstetrics, coupled with changes in abortion laws, have also made it easier for women to detect problems and end pregnancies that could have been life-threatening.

The maternal mortality rate in the United States dropped precipitously after the U.S. Supreme Court's 1973 *Roe v. Wade* ruling legalizing abortions. It went from 21.5 maternal deaths per 100,000 live births in 1970 to 9.4 in 1980 (U.S. Department of Health and Human Services, 1992). The maternal mortality rate dropped further to 8.2 in 1990, but in 1999 it spiked back up to 9.9 (U.S. Bureau of the Census, 2003). Recent Supreme Court actions permit individual states to impose restrictions that have made it more difficult for women in some states to obtain abortions. Further restrictions on women's legal right to choose abortion could lead to greater increases in the maternal mortality rate.

Despite the promising trends in the United States since the early part of the twentieth century, the health status of people in this society remains a cause for public concern. Good health is not equally distributed within the U.S. population, any more than are wealth and income. We take this issue up in the next sections, examining why systems of economic, racial, and gender inequality are important to people's health status within U.S. society. Here we note that the United States, which spends more money per capita on health care than any other nation in the world, compares unfavorably with many less affluent nations on measures of health status. Many western European nations, for example, have lower rates of infant and maternal mortality, and people born today in those nations have longer life expectancies than people born in the United States.

Infant mortality rates are greatly reduced when children receive basic preventive health care, including early immunization against diseases. This baby is clearly not enjoying the immunization experience, but is much more likely to remain healthy as a result of it.

Although numerous factors account for health-status differences between the United States and other nations, two stand out. First, as we saw in Chapter 7, the distribution of income in U.S. society leaves many individuals and families ill-equipped to afford basic necessities. All major industrial capitalist nations have income inequalities, but the United States has a higher degree of income inequality than many others, including the United Kingdom, Canada, Germany, Italy, Sweden, the Netherlands, Australia, Spain, and Japan (Kerbo, 2003). Second, unlike governments of other major industrialized nations, the U.S. government does not consider health care a right of citizenship and does not provide a national system of health care for all of its people. The importance of the combination of these two factors for the health status of the U.S. population will become clear in the next sections.

pp. 188–189

Class Position and Health Status

The U.S. government does not routinely collect and disseminate data on mortality rates (death rates) and other health-status indicators by class position (although it does do so by race, sex, and age). Nonetheless, researchers have been able to definitively link health status to class inequality in the United States and elsewhere. For example, Wilkinson (1996) found that the health status of people is better in those nations with comparatively lower levels of economic inequality. Given the fact that the distribution of wealth and income has been growing more unequal in the United States in recent years, the nature of the correlation between class position and health status should be of great public policy concern (Navarro, 1990, 1991).

Class Differences in Health Status

The limited data that the federal government compiles on class inequality and health are revealing. For example, survey data on people's assessments of their own health status indicate considerable differences among income categories. In interviews of a

TABLE 14.1 Deaths by Major Causes: 1960-2000   (Age-adjusted death rates per 100,000 population.)

Year	Heart Disease	Cancer	Cerebrovascular Diseases	Chronic Lower Respiratory Diseases	Accidents	Diabetes Mellitus	Influenza and Pneumonia	Intentional Self-Harm (Suicide)	Chronic Liver Disease and Cirrhosis	Assault (Homicide)
1960	559.0	193.9	177.9	12.5	63.1	22.5	53.7	12.5	13.3	5.2
1961	545.3	193.4	173.1	12.6	60.6	22.1	43.4	12.2	13.3	5.2
1962	556.9	193.3	174.0	14.2	62.9	22.6	47.1	12.8	13.8	5.4
1963	563.4	194.7	173.9	16.5	64.0	23.1	55.6	13.0	14.0	5.4
1964	543.3	193.6	167.0	16.3	64.1	22.5	45.4	12.7	14.2	5.7
1965	542.5	195.6	166.4	18.3	65.8	22.9	46.8	13.0	14.9	6.1
1966	541.2	196.5	165.8	19.2	67.6	23.6	47.9	12.7	15.9	6.5
1967	524.7	197.3	159.3	19.2	66.2	23.4	42.2	12.5	16.3	7.5
1968	531.0	198.8	162.5	20.7	65.5	25.3	52.8	12.4	16.9	8.1
1969	516.8	198.5	155.4	20.9	64.9	25.1	47.9	12.7	17.1	8.3
1970	492.7	198.6	147.7	21.3	62.2	24.3	41.7	13.1	17.8	9.0
1971	492.9	199.3	147.6	21.8	60.3	23.9	38.4	13.1	17.8	9.8
1972	490.2	200.3	147.3	22.8	60.2	23.7	41.3	13.3	18.0	10.0
1973	482.0	200.0	145.2	23.6	59.3	23.0	41.2	13.1	18.1	10.2
1974	458.8	201.5	136.8	23.2	52.7	22.1	35.5	13.2	17.9	10.5
1975	431.2	200.1	123.5	23.7	50.8	20.3	34.9	13.6	16.7	10.2
1976	426.9	202.5	117.4	24.9	48.7	19.5	38.8	13.2	16.4	9.2
1977	413.7	203.5	110.4	24.7	48.8	18.2	31.0	13.7	15.8	9.2
1978	409.9	204.9	103.7	26.3	48.9	18.3	34.5	12.9	15.2	9.2
1979	401.6	204.0	97.1	25.5	46.5	17.5	26.1	12.6	14.8	9.9

(continued)

TABLE 14.1 (continued)

Year	Heart Disease	Cancer	Cerebrovascular Diseases	Chronic Lower Respiratory Diseases	Accidents	Diabetes Mellitus	Influenza and Pneumonia	Intentional Self-Harm (Suicide)	Chronic Liver Disease and Cirrhosis	Assault (Homicide)
1980	412.1	207.9	96.4	28.3	46.4	18.1	31.4	12.2	15.1	10.5
1981	397.0	206.4	89.5	29.0	43.4	17.6	30.0	12.3	14.2	10.1
1982	389.0	208.3	84.2	29.1	40.1	17.2	26.5	12.5	13.2	9.4
1983	388.9	209.1	81.2	31.6	39.1	17.6	29.8	12.4	12.8	8.4
1984	378.8	210.8	78.7	32.4	38.8	17.2	30.6	12.6	12.7	8.1
1985	375.0	211.3	76.6	34.5	38.5	17.4	34.5	12.5	12.3	8.0
1986	365.1	211.5	73.1	34.8	38.6	17.2	34.8	13.0	11.8	8.6
1987	355.9	211.7	71.6	35.0	38.2	17.4	33.8	12.8	11.7	8.3
1988	352.5	212.5	70.6	36.5	38.9	18.0	37.3	12.5	11.6	8.5
1989	332.0	214.2	66.9	36.6	37.7	20.5	35.9	12.3	11.6	8.8
1990	321.8	216.0	65.5	37.2	36.3	20.7	36.8	12.5	11.1	9.5
1991	313.8	215.8	63.2	38.0	34.9	20.7	34.9	12.3	10.7	10.1
1992	306.1	214.3	62.0	37.9	33.4	20.8	33.1	12.1	10.5	9.6
1993	309.9	214.6	63.1	40.9	34.5	22.0	35.2	12.2	10.3	9.8
1994	299.7	213.1	63.1	40.6	34.6	22.7	33.9	12.1	10.2	9.4
1995	296.3	211.7	63.9	40.5	34.9	23.4	33.8	12.0	10.0	8.6
1996	288.3	208.7	63.2	41.0	34.9	24.0	33.2	11.7	9.8	7.8
1997	280.4	205.7	61.8	41.5	34.8	24.0	33.6	11.4	9.6	7.3
1998	272.4	202.4	59.6	42.0	35.0	24.2	34.6	11.3	9.5	6.7
1999	267.8	202.7	61.8	45.8	35.9	25.2	23.6	10.7	9.7	6.2
2000[1]	257.5	200.5	60.2	44.9	33.9	24.9	24.3	10.3	9.5	5.8

[1]Preliminary data.

SOURCE: U.S. Bureau of the Census, *Statistical Abstract of the United States, 2002* (Washington, DC: U.S. Government Printing Office, 2003), p. 79.

TABLE 14.2 Self-Assessment of Health: 1997

Selected Characteristic	Current Health Status [Percent distribution, (standard error)]		
	Excellent/ Very Good	Good	Fair/Poor
Total	63.9 (0.34)	24.7 (0.28)	11.5 (0.21)
Sex			
Male	66.1 (0.46)	23.4 (0.40)	10.5 (0.30)
Female	61.8 (0.43)	25.9 (0.37)	12.3 (0.27)
Age			
18–44 years	73.6 (0.39)	20.8 (0.35)	5.6 (0.19)
45–64 years	58.5 (0.64)	26.9 (0.55)	14.6 (0.42)
65–74 years	43.3 (0.91)	33.2 (0.83)	23.5 (0.78)
75 years and over	35.5 (0.97)	35.2 (0.93)	29.3 (0.95)
Race/ethnicity			
White non-Hispanic	66.0 (0.39)	23.5 (0.32)	10.6 (0.23)
Black non-Hispanic	54.0 (0.88)	28.2 (0.78)	17.9 (0.73)
Other non-Hispanic	63.8 (1.79)	27.8 (1.64)	8.4 (0.88)
Hispanic	59.0 (0.86)	28.8 (0.75)	12.2 (0.61)
Education			
Less than 12 years of school	38.0 (0.74)	34.3 (0.71)	27.7 (0.65)
High school graduate/GED recipient	57.7 (0.59)	29.2 (0.54)	13.1 (0.39)
Some college	68.2 (0.58)	23.7 (0.54)	8.2 (0.32)
Bachelor of arts or science degree/graduate or professional degree	80.6 (0.54)	15.2 (0.48)	4.2 (0.26)
Family income			
Less than $20,000	46.9 (0.61)	29.9 (0.50)	23.2 (0.49)
$20,000 or more	70.0 (0.37)	22.7 (0.34)	7.3 (0.20)
$20,000–$34,999	57.9 (0.71)	29.2 (0.67)	12.9 (0.48)
$35,000–$54,999	69.3 (0.71)	23.5 (0.63)	7.3 (0.39)
$55,000–$74,999	76.6 (0.81)	19.0 (0.75)	4.3 (0.38)
$75,000 or more	80.8 (0.74)	16.5 (0.70)	2.7 (0.30)
Poverty status			
Poor	45.7 (0.96)	30.3 (0.81)	24.0 (0.75)
Near poor	51.6 (0.78)	30.1 (0.65)	18.3 (0.56)
Not poor	71.3 (0.40)	21.9 (0.36)	6.9 (0.21)

SOURCE: Centers for Disease Control and Prevention, "Summary Health Statistics for U.S. Adults: National Health Interview Survey, 1997," *Vital and Health Statistics*, Series 10, No. 205 (May 2002), p. 53.

sample of the U.S. adult population, 81 percent of individuals in the most affluent households ($75,000 and over in family income) reported that they were in excellent or very good health in 1997 (see Table 14.2). In contrast, among those in the lowest income households (under $20,000) only 47 percent had such a positive self-assessment. Strikingly, only 3 percent of the best-off households reported fair or poor health, in comparison to 23 percent of the economically worst-off (Centers for Disease Control, 2002).

The correlation between class position and health status suggested by such self-assessments receives further support from federal inquiries into the degree to which people believe their daily activities are restricted by illness, injury, or impairment. Persons in middle-class to affluent households report the fewest restrictions, while those in the lowest income households report the most (U.S. Centers for Disease Control, 2002).

Class differences are also evident when people are asked whether they have a usual source of health care. Some 27 percent of adults aged 18 to 64 who live in poverty report they have no usual source of care, in comparison to only 14 percent of the non-poor (National Center for Health Statistics, 2001). Given their often negative health status self-assessments and their lack of a regular source of care, it is not surprising that members of poor families spend more time than the nonpoor being treated in hospitals. In 1999, families with incomes under the poverty line required 993 days of care per 1,000 population, whereas the nonpoor required only 292 days of care per 1,000 population. (National Center for Health Statistics, 2001).

One of the handful of federal investigations of mortality rates by class was undertaken in 1986 and focused on heart and cerebrovascular diseases. The mortality rate for heart disease was found to be more than twice as high for persons employed in blue-collar jobs (as operators, fabricators, and laborers) as it was for those working in higher paying white-collar positions (as managers and professionals). The findings for class position and cerebrovascular disease pointed in the same direction (Navarro, 1990).

Another federal study of mortality rates linked to class inequality was released in 1993. It showed that for people aged 25 to 64, death rates among those with incomes of less than $9,000 per year were *triple* the rates for people with incomes of $25,000 per year or more (Kerbo, 2000). Other federal studies in the 1990s found that rates of death from lung cancer and from diabetes are two and a half times as high for men with incomes under $10,000 per year as for men with incomes of $25,000 or more (National Center for Health Statistics, 1998). There is little doubt that infant mortality rates are highest among the poor, as are death rates for children in general. This then also contributes to lowered life expectancy for those who find themselves in positions at or near the bottom of the U.S. class structure (National Center for Health Statistics, 1998).

Reasons for Class Differences in Health Status

Why are the poor more likely than the affluent to suffer serious health problems and have shorter lives? Some might think that poor people simply choose not to take care of themselves. But the fact is that members of the poverty population confront a daily environment containing many more health threats than the environment of the more affluent. Features of their workplaces, community settings, neighborhoods, and living quarters put people who are impoverished at particular risks for health problems (Williams and Collins, 1995).

Many adults who live in poverty, and even more of those who live just above the official government poverty line, hold full-time or part-time jobs. These jobs often involve physically taxing, stressful, and hazardous labor. Men and women holding low-wage jobs in agriculture/forestry/fishing, manufacturing, construction, transportation/utilities, and wholesale and retail trade have high occupational injury rates. In addition, many workers (particularly in manufacturing) are routinely exposed to toxic fumes and substances that can cause both acute and chronic illnesses and diseases. While not all were low-income, 3.8 million U.S. workers suffered disabling occupational injuries in 1999 alone. More than 5,000 work injuries resulted in deaths that year (U.S. Department of Commerce, 2003).

Low-wage workers often lack the power to improve health and safety conditions in the workplace, although unions and community groups have struggled successfully to bring an end to some of the most blatant abuses. Still, much remains to be done. A tragic reminder of this involved chicken-processing workers in North Carolina. Such work is grueling and injurious; chicken processing workers are, in fact, three times more likely to be injured on the job than other workers in North Carolina. Common injuries include carpal-tunnel syndrome, an extremely painful condition affecting the nerves of the wrists, which stems from repetitive work on the processing line (Diebel, 1993). A fire at Imperial Food Products in Hamlet, North Carolina, in 1991, caused 25 deaths and injured 56 workers. As described in one press account,

> With the fire raging, many workers died attempting to flee through emergency exits, which were chained shut—supposedly because workers were stealing chickens. The dead left bloody footprints where they'd tried to beat down the fire doors in desperation (Diebel, 1993).

Despite such horror stories and the workers' struggles to put an end to them, health and safety standards and provision for their enforcement continue to remain a problem in many individual states, particularly for nonunionized, low-wage workers.

Features of their community settings, neighborhoods, and living quarters also contribute to health problems among poor people. Older buildings, in which the poor are likely to live, may have health dangers associated with asbestos and lead paint, insects and rodents, and deficient heating and electrical systems. Skyrocketing rental costs have forced many low-income families to double or even triple up in apartments and houses. The overcrowding of dwellings magnifies stress and facilitates the spread of infectious diseases.

Individuals and families who are homeless are particularly vulnerable to illness, accidents, and violent episodes because of their constant exposure to life on the streets. And homeless shelters pose the danger of contracting a communicable disease such as tuberculosis. Indeed, a rise in tuberculosis rates in the United States, after decades of near-eradication of the disease, has paralleled the rise in the number of homeless.

Poverty-stricken households often lack enough to eat. The federal government uses the term "food secure" to describe those households that "have access at all times to enough food for an active healthy life, with no need for recourse to emergency food sources or other extraordinary coping behaviors to meet their basic food needs" (U.S. Department of Commerce, 2003:127) In 2000, using this definition, over 11 million households—or 10.5 percent of all households—were food *insecure.*

Well over a quarter of these food-insecure households contained people who were hungry (U.S. Department of Commerce, 2003).

Without adequate food, people lose their ability to resist or to regain health after falling ill or experiencing serious injury. Dietary deficiencies can lead to malnutrition, which has been associated with anemia, tuberculosis, and osteoporosis. Pregnant women who do not eat adequately are likely to give birth to low-weight babies, who often suffer mental retardation and other disabilities. Low birth weight has also been directly linked to a higher likelihood of infant mortality. Malnutrition frequently undermines the health of the elderly, as well as children.

Some members of the poverty population suffer from living amid conditions of violence. For example, poverty conditions contribute to the high rate of homicide in the United States. In low-income sections of many cities, some residents—children as well as adults—resort to deadly weapons to protect themselves and to handle conflicts with others. Most killings are impulsive; they are individual acts involving a single victim, usually a family member, friend, or acquaintance. Yet other homicides are more organized. Youth street gangs may periodically engage in armed warfare with one another, and local drug dealers may commit murder to safeguard their activities and control the competition. Often, homicide victims are innocent bystanders to gang members' "drive-by killings" or to shootouts from drug deals that have "gone bad." Government policymakers have come to view the high rate of death by homicide in the United States as a major public health issue.

Illegal drug abuse is widespread throughout the U.S. population, regardless of people's class position, but the sale and use of crack cocaine, heroin, and other addictive drugs is endemic in some poverty-stricken urban neighborhoods. The sale of such drugs (including sales to buyers from outlying towns and suburbs) often goes on openly, making some city neighborhoods resemble "drug bazaars." City hospital emergency rooms routinely treat drug users who become ill. Many users accidentally die from drug overdoses. Others contract diseases from sharing needles and syringes; rates of acquired immune deficiency syndrome (AIDS) are high for intravenous drug users. The human immunodeficiency virus (HIV) responsible for AIDS is often passed by male drug users to female sexual partners, who, if they become pregnant, may transmit HIV to their fetuses. Hospitals serving poor communities treat not only the newborns who are HIV-positive and may develop AIDS but also the babies born to women who are substance abusers. The latter

The sharing of needles and syringes by drug users has contributed to the spread of the virus that causes AIDS, and many users have died as a consequence. In areas of high drug traffic, used and discarded injection equipment can pose a health threat to those who come into contact with it—user and nonuser alike.

infants' exposure to drugs, including alcohol, prior to birth can impair their health and ability to thrive.

Finally, as will be discussed later in this chapter, the U.S. health care system has failed to provide adequate services to tens of millions of low-income people who are without adequate health insurance coverage. Poor people often find that the care they need is inaccessible and unaffordable. Consequently, they are more likely than the more affluent to be without the care they need altogether or to postpone seeking it at great risk to their health.

Taken together, self-assessments of people's health status, inferences that can be drawn from official statistics on the distribution of illness and disease, and people's differential exposure to unhealthful work and living environments indicate that class position helps shape people's health status in the United States. Middle- to upper-class people are far less likely than those with low incomes to be exposed to a high volume of health risks and are better able to afford and gain access to health care. The more affluent are thus more likely to be healthy.

The system of economic inequality in the United States is interconnected with the system of racial inequality. It is thus important to ask specifically about the health status of people of color, who are disproportionately represented in U.S. society's low-income population. How is their health status any different from that of whites?

Racial Inequality and Health Status

By most health-status indicators, people of color are, in general, worse off than whites in the United States (U.S. Department of Health and Human Services, 1998b). But it is important to draw attention to the fact that differences in health status along the lines of race are often *also* differences influenced by class. One cannot make sense of racial differences in health status, for example, without understanding how different populations are distributed in the class structure. On average, the incomes and wealth holdings of African Americans, Latino/Latina Americans, Native Americans, and some segments of the Asian American population are well below those of whites. People of color are also overrepresented in the lower reaches of the class structure. We have noted that the economically disadvantaged—whatever their skin color—are more likely than the affluent to have health problems.

Two health-related issues that pertain specifically to people of color must be addressed. First, does the daily experience of being a person of color in a society in which racial inequality is so prevalent have a negative impact on one's health? Second, are people of color offered inadequate health care services *because* of their race? Let us briefly examine some illustrative data concerning race and health status.

The most comprehensive data available from federal government sources compare whites with African Americans. A good starting point is infant and maternal mortality rates. We have seen that infant mortality rates in the United States are higher than those in many other major industrial nations. But *within* the United States, infant mortality rates differ sharply by race. The rate for whites in 1999 was 5.8 infant deaths per 1,000 live births; for African Americans it was 14.6 per 1,000 (National Center for Health Statistics, 2001). Low weight at birth, a risk factor linked with infant mortality, occurred in 13 percent of all live births to African American mothers but in only 6.6 percent of births to white mothers. Finally, maternal mortality also differs sharply by race in the United States. In 1999, over 25 African American mothers died per 100,000 live births, compared to 7 white mothers (U.S. Bureau of the Census, 2003).

Life expectancy figures are likewise strikingly different by race. For example, a white female born in 1999 could expect to live to 79.9 years of age, while the life expectancy for African American females was 5.2 years less. For males, the difference is even more extreme. White males born in 1999 could expect to live 74.6 years. African American males could look forward to only 67.8 years of life, or 6.8 years less than whites (National Center for Health Statistics, 2001).

Apart from the impact of class position on people of color, does racism have its own impact on health? How does one account, for example, for findings indicating that among the children of African American college-educated parents, infant mortality rates are almost twice as high as the rates among babies of similarly educated white parents (Schoendorf et al., 1992)? It would appear that something harmful is happening to African Americans on the basis of their race and not simply their class.

A number of explanations are possible (U.S. Department of Health and Human Services, 1998). Higher rates of infant mortality may be related to the accumulated and compounded social stresses many African American women endure as they function in a system of racial inequality. Such stresses can be experienced in white-dominated educational institutions, places of employment, or even in everyday social interactions. Or the higher infant morality rates may be related to the residential racial segregation experienced by many urban-dwelling African Americans, pp. 241-243 ▶ including—as we saw in Chapter 8—members of the black middle class. Many African Americans reside in communities where medical facilities providing quality prenatal, postnatal, and well-baby care are few and overburdened.

Perhaps racial discrimination in employment opportunities for college-educated African Americans, something not experienced by whites, hampers their access to jobs that come with adequate health insurance and with pay that allows them to afford the health care needed. To some extent, racial discrimination is reflected in the lower average incomes for African American college graduates in comparison to their white counterparts. Or perhaps the higher rates of infant mortality relate to the toxicity of living environments in which many African Americans reside. Evidence suggests that hazardous waste facilities and other sources of pollution are disproportionately concentrated in or near communities of color (Bullard, 1997). These are the kinds of questions that challenge social scientists as they attempt to sort out the relationship between racism and health status.

A second issue is whether there is racism in the health care system itself. Are people of color less well served by this system than whites, simply on the basis of race? In a comprehensive report prepared for the U.S. Congress in 2002, the Institute of Medicine found that on average people of color tend to receive health care of a lower quality than that received by whites. This is the case even when their income level, health insurance, and severity of health conditions are comparable. Among the causes identified were bias, stereotyping, and prejudice toward people of color on the part of health care providers. Some, such as Latinos/Latinas and Asian immigrants, were also found to face barriers to health care because providers are at times not responsive to language and culture differences.

In addition to problems in obtaining access to the health care system, people of color are often left out of drug testing trials and access to state-of-the-art experimental drugs that could help them. AIDS, for example, is having a devastating effect on the health status of communities of color; deaths from AIDS are much higher among African Americans and Latinos/Latinas than among whites (National Center for Health Statistics, 2001). Yet researchers have found that African Americans and Latinos/Latinas who are infected with the virus from which AIDS develops are only half as likely as whites to participate in clinical trials of promising experimental drugs. Some people of color may choose not to participate out of lack of trust in the (predominantly white) medical research establishment. However, the disparities suggest systematic exclusion by researchers (Gifford et al., 2002).

In sum, the disproportionate presence of people of color in the lower levels of the U.S. class structure has a negative impact on their health status. However, one's location in the system of racial inequality may affect one's health, both in combination with or independently of one's class position. The day-to-day treatment of people of color by members of the dominant white majority and by institutions it controls, including the U.S. health care system, contributes to health-status differences along the lines of skin color. As we will see, the system of gender inequality in the United States also plays an important role in influencing one's health status.

Gender Inequality and Health Status

The U.S. health care system has long been male-dominated—from physicians to researchers to executives and administrators. Although still underrepresented, women are increasingly moving into such central positions in the system. In many medical school entering classes, for example, the proportion of men and women is now similar. At the same time as this shift has been under way, the contemporary feminist movement has encouraged women to speak out against gender biases and shortcomings in how the health care system treats them.

As we saw in Chapter 12, women are on average in a weaker posi- ◄ pp. 385–389 tion in the labor market than men. They are more likely to be unemployed, employed in temporary jobs, or employed part-time. Women are less likely than men to occupy positions that offer adequate employer-provided health insurance, even when they work full-time. This situation most adversely affects women who are living alone, as well as women who are the sole or principal wage earners for their families. Many of these women have experienced loss of a partner through divorce or death.

Because female-headed households are more likely to be poor than are male-headed or dual-headed households, single women raising families face serious problems in affording and gaining access to health care. Many low-income female-headed households are forced to rely on the government-sponsored health care program known as Medicaid, which serves impoverished individuals and families. The limitations and shortcomings of this program, discussed in the next section, leave those who are eligible for it chronically underserved.

Biases and shortcomings in the health care system's treatment of women contribute to the problems women face in getting adequate care (Ratcliff, 2002). Research bearing on women's health problems has chronically lacked adequate researcher interest and funding. For years women were largely excluded as research subjects in studies sponsored by the federal National Institutes of Health (NIH). This exclusion has had serious implications for women's health status. For example, in 1990 researchers reported findings showing that heavy consumption of coffee was unrelated to increased risk of heart attacks and strokes. All of the 45,600 subjects were men. The effects of heavy coffee consumption on the health of women—helpful, harmful, or none at all— went unaddressed. What *is* known is that one-tenth of women aged 45 to 64 have some form of heart disease, that heart disease is the number-one cause of death among women, and that more women than men die from their first heart attack (U.S. Department of Health and Human Services, 1998) .

Criticizing such bias in research procedures, one U.S. senator observed:

> Drugs are developed with incomplete data on metabolic differences between men and women. Diseases are studied without an understanding of the effects of hormones and reproduction. Even preliminary animal studies are usually done only with male rats. (Cimons, 1990: A20)

In responding to researchers' claims that the use of male research subjects is justifiable because women's bodies are more "complicated" than men's, one critic stated:

> Saying that women's bodies are complicated is saying that there is a norm out there and that norm is the male body. It's such blatant sexism. ("Our Bodies, Their Selves," 1990)

Access to affordable, quality health care — whether for themselves or for their children — is difficult for the many women who are heads of low-income households. This mother endures a long wait for her child to be seen and treated by the staff of a public health clinic.

Sexism in the health care arena also means that there are health problems pertaining to women on which comparatively little research has even been done. One example is osteoporosis, which afflicts some 25 million elders in U.S. society. This is a highly preventable condition involving loss of bone tissue, which leaves thin bones that are vulnerable to fractures (usually affecting the wrist, hip, and spine). Twice as many women as men over the age of 65—one in three women—develop osteoporosis. Although the condition is associated with 1.3 million bone fractures annually, resulting in physical disability, suffering, and substantial expense, until recently relatively little money has gone toward research and education on this major public health problem.

In response to criticisms by the feminist movement and public outcries over such matters, Congress passed legislation directing the National Institutes of Health to allocate far more resources to research on key women's health issues. In 1991, NIH launched the largest federally-funded study ever conducted on women's health, the Women's Health Initiative. The initiative has set in motion new research on the causes and most effective treatment of illnesses affecting millions of women, including various types of cancer, heart disease, and osteoporosis. In this type of research, findings are slow in coming, but useful knowledge for women should be available from the initiative in the next decade.

In 1993, Congress passed legislation requiring that NIH ensure that researchers have appropriate representation of women in their clinical drug trials. However, evidence suggests that researchers have yet to improve the gender balance of those selected to participate in clinical trials and are still doing little analysis of their data by sex. One review of drug trial outcome studies published between 1994 and 1999 in an influential medical journal found that on average only 24.6 percent of those participating in the published studies were female, and that data analysis by sex took place in only 14 percent of the studies (Ramasubbu, Gurm, and Litaker, 2001).

We have seen that the health status of people in the United States varies along the lines of class, race, and gender. Part of the explanation for these differences in health status rests with inadequacies in the U.S. health care system itself. In the next section we discuss some of this system's features.

The U.S. Health Care System

The United States spends more money on health care each year than any other nation in the world. Yet, as we saw earlier in this chapter, it compares poorly to many other industrialized nations on commonly used measures of health status such as life expectancy and infant mortality rates. In this section we look at inadequacies in the U.S. health care system that help account for this.

Inadequacies in Health Care Coverage

The U.S. health care system does not embrace all of this nation's citizens. The United States is alone in this regard among major industrial nations, such as Canada and those in western Europe. Other nations provide either a system of national health insurance or a system of national health services that covers everyone. Coverage is provided regardless of an individual's employment status or income. People in these nations are not denied care because they cannot afford it. Health care is considered a right. In U.S. society, on the other hand, health care is treated like any other commodity in a market economy: you get what you are able to pay for.

Unlike other major industrial societies, in U.S. society access to the health care system is heavily tied to an individual's place of employment. In 2002, slightly over 60 percent of the U.S. population was covered under some type of private health care insurance coverage through employers (Pear, 2003). However, few states actually require employers to provide such insurance and many employers, especially smaller firms, fail to do so. Only 30.8 percent of those with jobs in a workplace with fewer than 25 employees were part of a employer-based health insurance plan in 2002, as opposed to 68.7 percent of those in workplaces with more than 1,000 employees (Pear, 2003). Even when employers do offer health insurance, the coverage and costs to employees vary widely. For example, sometimes an employee's dependents are included in a plan offered by employers; sometimes they are not. Policies vary in the range of health problems they cover, the nature and extent of services allowed, and the allocation of insurance expenses between employer and employee.

With rising health care costs, insurance rates have gone up dramatically in recent years. To cut company costs, employers have responded by demanding that employees accept less comprehensive coverage and take on more of the burden of paying for their insurance. Thus those who receive health insurance through their employers have been experiencing growing out-of-pocket health care expenses, the equivalent of a decrease in pay. Moreover, millions are covered by insurance that is inadequate in the event of catastrophic illness. In such an event, many workers have no choice but to exhaust all their assets and go into heavy debt to pay medical and hospital bills. The fear of losing health care benefits puts pressure on employees to think twice about moving to other jobs. Worse yet is the fear of how one will cope with health problems in the event of job loss.

In 2002 some 43.6 million people under age 65—including 8.5 million children—had no health care insurance at all for the entire year (Pear, 2003). (Persons age 65 and older are eligible for Medicare, a government program discussed later.) Millions more lacked coverage at one or another point during the 2002 calendar year. For the most part, the uninsured are low-income working people and their families. Some uninsured workers are employed by small firms that do not provide health insurance benefits; others are self-employed and simply cannot afford the high costs of purchasing private insurance. Many others without insurance are unemployed, moving between jobs, or searching for their first jobs (new college graduates included). The 43.6 million people who were uninsured in 2002 were usually ineligible for the two main government-financed programs of health care, Medicare (for the elderly and people with disabilities) and Medicaid (for persons who are extremely poverty-stricken).

People who lack insurance but do not qualify for one of the government programs often put off seeking health care unless and until a problem becomes acute and disabling. Many uninsured children and adults rarely if ever even see a dentist, despite advanced tooth decay or gum infection. Pregnant women do without prenatal care, and infants and children in families without health insurance have little contact with doctors. Adult wage earners are reluctant to lose badly needed income by taking time off from work to see a doctor when they do not feel well, and they may have no way to pay for a doctor's treatment in any event. Symptoms of health difficulties (unexplained bleeding, chest pains) that would immediately send more affluent, well-insured individuals to doctors tend to be ignored or downplayed in importance. Consequently, the health problems of the uninsured often go unaddressed until they end up in a state of extreme distress in overcrowded, understaffed hospital emergency departments.

Many people assume that those without health insurance end up getting the care that they need one way or another. However, this is not true. The National Academy of Sciences's Institute of Medicine has investigated some of the consequences of not having health insurance coverage. The Institute found that every year more than 18,000 people die prematurely due to the lack of insurance; almost half of them are in the 55–64 age range. When uninsured persons with serious health problems such as breast cancer, hypertension, and infection with HIV do get care, it frequently occurs later than it does for those with health insurance. Such delays can be fatal. Those without insurance are also likely to get too little care, poorer care, and to become ill and die sooner than the insured (Hadley, 2002; Institute of Medicine, 2002a).

In an effort to meet some of the health care needs of the elderly, the federal government began the health insurance plan called Medicare in 1965. Medicare covers more than 30 million people age 65 and older and another 3 million people with disabilities. The program has proved to be a lifesaver for people who otherwise would have to go without health care, but it is not comprehensive enough for many elderly people. Medicare does not pay the full costs of care, and the services it does cover are limited. For example, Medicare policies allow payment for only a limited number of days of hospital care and physician visits.

Medicare also does not help the elderly meet the expenses of prescription drugs, whose prices have been skyrocketing in recent years. It remains to be seen whether federal Medicare reforms enacted in 2003 will be helpful in this regard. Rising out-of-pocket health care expenses pose a burden for older people who have chronic health problems and who often exist on fixed incomes. Out of economic necessity, increasing numbers of elders (and others) are crossing the borders into Mexico or Canada in search of less expensive prescription drugs, or they order drugs from abroad over the Internet. In most cases the drugs being purchased are of high quality, but in some instances elders are putting themselves at risk. U.S. pharmaceutical companies, among the most profitable firms in the U.S. economy, have advocated placing restrictions on such importation of lower-priced medicines, even those they themselves manufactured. Medicare reform legislation in 2003 appears to support the companies' position.

Some elders are victims of "patient dumping," prematurely discharged by hospitals because their health insurance does not adequately cover costs. Many are affected by Medicare's restrictions on payment for long-term skilled nursing-home care, important to the very old and their families. Such practices and restrictions may put adult children who must "parent their parents" under a great deal of stress and expense; they frequently must provide their parents with home care while juggling employment and child-rearing responsibilities. Most of the caretaking responsibility usually falls upon the shoulders of daughters. While elders may have some money of their own, nursing-home care is extremely expensive and relatively few elders have private long-term-care insurance. Medicare policies force the elderly to spend down their personal financial assets to the point of poverty in order to become eligible for government assistance in paying for full-time, long-term care.

Medicaid is the other major government health care plan. It was begun as a cooperatively financed venture by federal and state governments in 1965 to help the poor, especially impoverished families with children that qualify for cash welfare assistance. Yet today, as a consequence of various rules, regulations, and cost-containment policies, less than 40 percent of those living under the official poverty line are covered by Medicaid. Moreover, as the nation's welfare rolls have fallen in recent years, so have the Medicaid rolls (albeit nowhere near so dramatically). In many individual states, poor families have been allowed to believe erroneously that without welfare eligibility they cannot receive Medicaid when, under federal law, the two programs are supposed to operate separately. People who meet established criteria for economic need are legally entitled to Medicaid assistance, no matter what their eligibility for welfare.

Those in poverty who are covered by Medicaid often find the coverage to be very inadequate (Abraham, 1994). For example, by law only limited set fees will be paid by government to physicians for the services they provide to Medicaid patients. Since these payments tend to be about half of what the physicians customarily charge, many doctors have a policy of simply not taking Medicaid patients—adults or children—even if they are seriously ill. Families are put into the position of either begging for care or hunting until a willing physician can be found. Either way, necessary care may be delayed. Moreover, each individual state sets its own standards for the depths of poverty that must be reached before persons are eligible for Medicaid. Thus people living well below the poverty line may still be considered "too well off" to qualify, a stance adopted by many state governments to help slow their share of rising Medicaid costs. Turned away by health care providers or deemed ineligible by state-run Medicaid programs, millions of impoverished men, women, and children find themselves without the health care they need.

Over half of the poverty population consists of women and children. People of color are also overrepresented in poverty. These are the categories of people who are most likely to have either no health insurance or—if they are "fortunate"—the inadequate coverage provided by Medicaid. The fact that people living in other major industrialized nations experience lower rates of infant mortality and longer life expectancies reflects the failure of the U.S. health care system to serve all its citizens.

Health Care: A Market Commodity

Other inadequacies of the U.S. health care system stem from the treatment of health care as a commodity to be bought and sold in a market system. In the United States, physicians have long been independent entrepreneurs. Much of the cost of their medical education is subsidized by taxpayers through government grants to medical schools and government-subsidized student loans. Nevertheless, new doctors still find themselves burdened with substantial educational debts, the high costs of starting up and maintaining a new practice, and ever-increasing payments for malpractice insurance. Indeed, patients' successful lawsuits against physicians have increased the costs of insuring a medical practice to the point where some physicians, including specialists in higher risk areas such as obstetrics and surgery, have left the profession.

Doctors also expect to receive personal incomes high enough to compensate for the effort and sacrifices associated with their chosen profession. Most do what astute businesspeople have always done—locate in, and cater to, that segment of the market that is likely to be most financially stable and lucrative. For many physicians, the preferred market location is where people reside in relatively affluent, and well-insured, households.

Physicians tend to migrate to urban metropolitan areas and their sprawling suburbs. In such communities, they can affiliate with high-quality medical facilities whose services more affluent households can afford. But this also means that people living in isolated rural areas of the country, in small towns, and in the nation's racially segregated and poverty-stricken ghettos, barrios, and reservations, go underserved.

In a new health care development, which some call "concierge" or "boutique" medicine, some doctors reserve their services for the highly affluent. These physicians provide care only to those who are able to spend thousands of dollars a year beyond their private health insurance premiums. Boutique doctors select patients based on their ability to pay and give them on-call, pampered treatment. In comparison to other doctors, these physicians see far fewer patients, spend more time with each of them, routinely call upon the most expensive diagnostic tools and tests, and provide highly personalized one-on-one follow-up care (Friedman, 2002). Doctors going this route may rationalize that in this way they can use their training to provide the very best of care, yet this emerging "wealth care system" dramatically illustrates how the health care system is linked to economic inequality.

The market effect on health care delivery also is seen in the ever-increasing tendency toward specialization within the medical profession. This tendency, under way since World War II, is expressed in the declining proportion of newly trained doctors who go into general practice or family medicine. In part, specialization is a function of the generation of new knowledge and advanced technology. But it can also be understood as one way in which physicians have sought to capture and control the most profitable shares of the market for their services.

When physicians become specialists they in effect limit the degree to which they are in competition with other physicians for patients. Specialization also allows physicians to command high levels of compensation for unique services. As shown in Table 14.3, in 1998 physicians in family or general practice had annual net incomes averaging $142.5 thousand, while those specializing in surgery averaged $268.2 thousand (U.S. Department of Commerce, 2003) Whereas the total number of doctors in the United States has grown substantially in recent decades, increased specialization among them has actually reduced the number of primary care physicians, doctors who provide routine and continuing care and who know when it is necessary and appropriate to refer patients to more expensive specialists.

What do people do if they are among are the tens of millions of uninsured or underinsured, have difficulty paying for health care, put off seeking care as long as possible, and then find that private doctors are either uninterested in providing service or are simply inaccessible? For many low-income people, the hospital emergency department has become a substitute for the primary care physician, and a desperate one at best. But the emergency department is likely to see patients whose conditions are more serious precisely because these are people who have not been seen by a primary care physician. Ill and suffering adults and children wait for hours while life-and-death cases—severe burns, gunshot wounds, drug overdoses, car accident injuries—receive first priority.

Rapid, impersonal, assembly-line processing by harried and over-worked emergency department staff contrasts sharply to the treatment that private physicians provide to the more affluent. Poor people who must be hospitalized often find them-

TABLE 14.3 Mean Net Income of Physicians by Specialty: Selected Years

Specialty	Mean Net Income (in Thousands)					
	1985	1990	1995	1996	1997	1998
All physicians	$112.2	$164.3	$195.5	$199.0	$199.6	$194.4
General/family practice	77.9	102.7	131.2	139.1	140.9	142.5
Internal medicine	102.0	152.5	185.7	185.7	193.9	182.1
Surgery	155.0	236.4	269.4	275.2	261.4	268.2
Pediatrics	76.2	106.5	140.5	140.6	143.5	139.6
Obstetrics/gynecology	124.3	207.3	244.3	231.0	228.7	214.4

SOURCE: U.S. Bureau of the Census, *Statistical Abstract of the United States, 2003* (Washington, DC: U.S. Government Printing Office, 2002), p. 108.

selves shunted off to crowded, overburdened, public charitable institutions where, because of strained budgets, the quality of care may not be the best. In some instances, uninsured people have been refused admission by upscale private hospitals and have been taken by ambulance to several different hospitals until one agreed to admit them. Those treated but not hospitalized are offered little in the way of routine follow-up care. Unless one is well-insured and able to take care of the bills, encounters with the health care system can be confusing, alienating, and dehumanizing (Abraham, 1994).

Managed Care

The U.S. health care system's adherence to market principles has also been underscored in recent years by the phenomenon of "managed care." Under **managed care,** large health insurance companies set strict limits on the types and amounts of services for which they will pay when an insured patient has a particular health problem. This system was introduced by the health insurance industry in the 1990s with the rationale that it would help contain rising health care costs, which have nonetheless continued to rise. Meanwhile, health insurance companies have come under criticism that managed care does little more than reduce services to the insured in order to keep insurers' profits high (Kleinke, 2001).

Patients, for example, may face limits in the kinds of diagnostic tests their insurance companies will pay for, as well as in the nature and length of the treatment allowed by insurers (e.g., the number of days of hospitalization). Doctors must abide by each individual insurance company's patient treatment rules if they wish to be reimbursed for their services. This, in effect, puts many doctors in the position of working for the patients' insurer, rather than the patient. Doctors who believe a certain test or treatment would be best, in their professional judgment, often have to spend time arguing—sometimes futilely—with insurance company representatives, who often are not doctors themselves. Treatment delays and regimens dictated by insurance company rules not only frustrate doctors, but put additional stress on patients and can have serious negative health consequences. The "Social Forces/ People's Lives" reading describes how treatment delays threatened the life of a six-month-old child and then left him permanently disabled.

Social Forces/People's Lives

A Baby's Struggle

GEORGE ANDERS

In the United States, those fortunate enough to have health insurance are frequently required by insurance companies to enroll in a managed care plan. Critics of managed care argue that such plans too often pay insufficient attention to individual health care needs in favor of enforcing profit-enhancing company rules. Managed care systems have at times resulted in tragedy, as in the case of Lamona Adams's six-month-old son James. Lamona and her husband sued the insurance company and a jury found it guilty of medical negligence, resulting in a multimillion-dollar out-of-court-settlement. But does money make up for what the managed care system did to James?

THIS wasn't the way Lamona Adams wanted to spend the night. Resting her infant son on her shoulder, she paced to the edge of her garage and peered into the darkness, looking for the first sign of the headlights of her husband's car. It was 4:35 A.M. on a chilly March morning. All the other houses on Fireleaf Way were dark and still. Families in Fairburn, Georgia, were enjoying a few more hours of sleep before Saturday began. . .

But Lamona Adams was already wide awake and very worried about her six-month-old son. What had started the day before as a moderate fever was steadily worsening. She had skipped work on Friday and taken the boy to the doctor, who recommended giving him Tylenol every four hours. That had helped for a while. By nighttime the Tylenol wasn't subduing his fever anymore. At 3:30 A.M., Lamona had awakened to find her son, James III, feeling unusually hot, panting and moaning. His temperature: 104 degrees Fahrenheit.

Alarmed, Lamona called her health plan's after-hours hotline at 3:50, asking what to do next. That was standard procedure for her; like millions of other Americans, she belonged to a "managed-care" plan, which required members to have most medical treatment approved in advance and to use only the most cost-effective doctors and hospitals if they wanted their bills covered. Only if a grave emergency arose were those restrictions waived.

It took a few minutes for Lamona's health plan, Kaiser Permanente, to log in the baby's symptoms and relay information from an operator to a nurse, from the nurse to a doctor, and then back to the nurse again. But by 4:05, word had come back: take the baby to the emergency room of Scottish Rite Children's Medical Center.

"That's the only hospital I can send you to," the hotline nurse added.

"How do we get there?" Lamona asked. She and her husband had moved to Georgia just a few months earlier and were still learning their way around.

"I don't know," the nurse replied. "I'm not good with directions." Rather than guess, the nurse passed along the hospital's phone number and suggested that Lamona call for directions herself.

For the next 20 minutes, Lamona hurried to get ready. She phoned her husband, James Jr., who was working as a night security guard, and implored him to come home at once. She called Scottish Rite and got directions. . . A few minutes later, she saw the first flicker of her husband's headlights. As her husband arrived, Lamona jumped into the back seat of their Plymouth Acclaim, holding the baby.

Her husband asked for directions, and she gave them. They had to drive three miles to reach Interstate 85 just south of Atlanta, then travel north on I-85 for more than 30 miles—past downtown Atlanta and on to the northern outskirts of the city. After that a junction, west six more miles on I-285, and about another mile on local streets. . . In the back seat of the car, Lamona kept looking into her baby's eyes, trying to reassure herself about his illness while making the baby aware that his mother was very close. For the first two thirds of the drive, the boy blinked back at her. As the car continued north, his eyes fell shut.

"Budé!" his mother snapped, calling her child briskly by a favorite nickname. "Budé!" The boy's eyes opened again. Lamona leaned forward and told her husband, "James, hurry!" The father accelerated as much as he dared, and he began to grow nervous too. A few minutes later he realized he had shot past the junction for I-285, the road leading toward Scottish Rite.

"I don't care, just go, go, go!" Lamona replied. They spotted a large blue "H" road sign, directing them to a closer hospital. As they neared the exit, the boy's eyes closed again. A few moments later his heart stopped. At 5:29 A.M. the parents pulled into the parking lot of Kennestone Hospital at Windy Hill. Lamona bolted out of the car holding her son and ran into the emergency room, crying, "Help my baby! Help my baby!"

A nurse grabbed the infant and gave two breaths of mouth-to-mouth resuscitation. A pediatric "crash cart" was wheeled into the area, stocked with emergency equipment designed to save a baby's life. Nurses and doctors began a whirlwind of rescue measures—inserting breathing tubes into baby James, beginning cardiopulmonary resuscitation and administering two doses of epinephrine, a powerful hormone and heart stimulant. As they started to work on the inert baby, his head lifted, then thudded against the emergency-room cot. . . .

When she heard that thud, Lamona Adams screamed. She fell to her knees and, by her own account, became hysterical. Hospital employees took her arms and escorted her to the hospital's nearby chapel. A nurse came in and tried to soothe her. A few moments later her husband arrived, with grim news. "It doesn't look good," he said. "They've got all these tubes in him." Unable to move, Lamona stood in the chapel, praying, again and again, "Don't take my baby, God."

After nearly 20 minutes of resuscitation efforts, Kennestone's nurses reported the first sign of a renewed pulse. By 6 A.M. the baby's heartbeat was steady enough that CPR could stop. But blood tests showed that he was still profoundly sick, with carbon dioxide levels far above normal. Even more ominously, the original cause of his fever remained undiagnosed. Doctors administered antibiotics in the hope that they would help; they learned a day later that his body was ravaged by a potentially fatal infection: meningococcemia.

At 7 A.M. Kennestone's doctors decided to transfer the Adams baby to Scottish Rite, the hospital he originally was headed for, which could do far more for gravely ill children. This time, at last, an ambulance carried the boy. At Scottish Rite swarms of specialists clustered at the boy's bedside around the clock for days. Neurologists, surgeons, infectious-disease experts, and others tried to assess the damage. It was clear that antibiotics were subduing his fever and that the hospital could keep the infant alive for at least a few days. But the doctors' early assessments were full of foreboding. Meningococcemia had already caused vast, perhaps devastating, damage to little James. He was immobile and unresponsive. The blood flow in his hands and feet had essentially ceased.

One of the doctors, James Jose, began talking with the parents about whether it might be appropriate to withdraw life support at some stage. The crucial question, he said, was how badly the boy's brain had been damaged. Could he still see? Would he ever be able to move? To speak? To read? Even if his brain had withstood the double trauma of meningococcemia and heart stoppage, further crises lay ahead. Little James's skin had begun to turn black at his extremities, as blood cells and tissue died. It was clear that if he did survive, his ruined hands and feet would have to be amputated. . .

Two months later James III had recovered enough to be discharged from Scottish Rite. His physical wounds had healed with incredible speed, as is generally true for babies. Scar tissue had formed at his extremities, cushioning the previously exposed muscle and bone. As his bandages came off, he began to move about in his hospital crib, smiling at his parents when they came to visit. He was not quite nine months old—too young to realize how different he was from any other child his age. In a whispered moment, a Scottish Rite doctor confided to the parents that only a tiny child could be so determined to live.

Back in Fairburn, the Adamses put their family life back together as best they could. Lamona kept her civilian job with the army, if only to secure health insurance for her little boy. Her husband quit his job to spend more time at home with his son and to handle the boy's frequent appointments with doctors and therapists. In the parents' hours at home together, away from the stares of strangers who didn't understand what had happened to the boy, they built their own sanctuary. . .

Source: George Anders, *Health against Wealth: HMOs and the Breakdown of Medical Trust* (Boston: Houghton Mifflin, 1996), pp. 1–5.

Managed care has undermined the morale of many doctors, undercut their ability to function independently as trained professionals, and created increased paperwork and administrative costs in their private practices. The costs are in turn passed on to patients. Managed care has also led to complaints that even patients with costly private health insurance often receive inadequate care, and are more likely to be put at risk of preventable suffering and premature death. Although there have been calls for the federal government to step in and act to protect "patient rights, " the balance of power over control of health care nationally is tilted toward the health insurance industry with its huge political campaign contributions and army of lobbyists, not patients and their doctors (Lundberg, 2002). There is consequently little end in sight to managed care, short of a social movement aimed at health care reform more generally in the United States.

The Corporatization of Medicine

In yet another trend within the health care system, large private firms have been entering the health care delivery field in a search for profits. This trend, termed the **corporatization of medicine,** has served to move health care away from the traditional approach of independent private practice by an individual physician (Light, 1989; Starr, 1982). Corporatization also represents a move away from the provision of services by nonprofit health care clinics, hospitals, and other health care facilities that focus on providing services, and whose main financial concern is only that income come close to matching expenses (Kleinke, 2001; Lundberg, 2002).

Corporatization of medicine represents a market-driven approach to providing health care. Clinics, hospitals, nursing homes, and home health services are increasingly being bought or established by private investors seeking to provide services for profit. Ever-larger investor-owned firms run such facilities as chains, much like department stores and fast-food restaurants (and, we might note, funeral homes). Physicians themselves have become increasingly involved as owners and participants, understandably attracted by the lucrative returns such firms promise in a nation that spends hundreds of billions of dollars on health care each year (Robertson, 1999).

The main danger of the concentration of health care services in the hands of large investor-owned corporations is that these firms may place a higher priority on making profits than on properly serving local communities. Firms can avoid providing to the general public services that are incompatible with their profit goals (such as emergency medicine), including health care to low-income populations whose health insurance status and ability to pay for services may be highly limited. The specter of private investors reaping financial benefits from the selective servicing of people's illnesses is not an attractive one. Moreover, such market-driven practices do not bode well for improving the well-being of those who are being inadequately served or not served at all by the present health care system.

The U.S. health care system is currently undergoing strains stemming from two developments: the AIDS/HIV epidemic, one of the most dangerous and costly health care problems in recent years; and the aging of the population, which is bringing ever-increasing demands for health care by growing numbers of elders. If the U.S. system of health care does undergo significant reform in the near future, it may be spurred along by these two phenomena. Let us examine some of the challenges posed by each of these developments.

Strains on the U.S. Health Care System

The Impact of AIDS

AIDS was unknown as a health problem prior to 1981. It rapidly became a **pandemic,** a disease that can be found throughout the world. The most concentrated outbreaks of AIDS at present appear to be located in parts of South and Southeast Asia, Subsaharan Africa, and Latin America and the Caribbean. However, the U.S. population is greatly affected.

In the United States, between 1981 and 2001, the U.S. Centers for Disease Control recorded 816,149 cases of AIDS. Almost 468,000 people with AIDS died in that period (www.cdc.gov). In addition, counting those alive and diagnosed with AIDS, almost a million people in the United States are presently estimated to carry the human immunodeficiency virus (HIV) by which AIDS is spread. Approximately 40,000 new infections occur annually (Okie, 2001).

In nations outside the United States, the picture is extremely frightening. According to the United Nations Programme on AIDS (www.unaids.org), as of 2002 some 21.8 million people had died worldwide—4.3 million of them children under 15 years of age. In the year 2002 alone, 3.1 million people died. Over 14 million children under age 15 have been left orphaned by the deaths of parents due to AIDS. At present, 42 million people are living with AIDS. In 2002, some 5 million more people were newly infected with the HIV virus, including 800,000 children. Of all regions of the world, Subsaharan Africa is most intensely devastated by the epidemic,

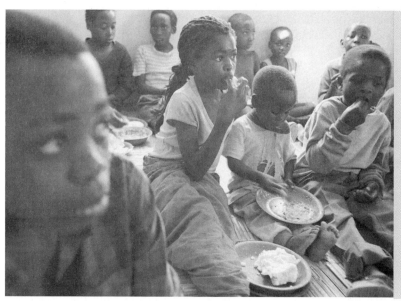

In many African nations, increasing numbers of children are being orphaned because their parents have become victims of the AIDS epidemic. The children pictured here are being fed and cared for at an orphanage. They are fortunate not to be living homeless in the streets like many other African orphans are forced to do; however, the bleak future of these children is reflected in the sadness of their faces.

having 29.4 million living AIDS cases. All such estimates may be conservative, since many AIDS cases may go undiagnosed or misdiagnosed in underdeveloped nations, where health care facilities serving those residing in city slums and in rural areas are especially poorly equipped and understaffed.

AIDS is affecting a wide range of people in the United States. Those with AIDS include heterosexuals, homosexuals, and bisexuals; women and men; whites and people of color; adults, teenagers, children, and infants. Although stereotyped in the past as a "gay disease," in reality HIV and AIDS are well established in the general heterosexual population. People in the United States have become infected with the HIV virus as a result of little more than a single episode of unprotected sex, the sharing of a needle, a transfusion of infected blood, or birth with an HIV-positive mother. The characteristics of patients in the United States who have been diagnosed with AIDS are shown in Table 14.4.

As AIDS has taken on epidemic proportions within the United States, the health care system has simultaneously faced the task of searching for a cure and caring for the many thousands who have been struggling against this disease. Although no cure or preventive vaccine has been found, important breakthroughs have occurred in the discovery of drugs that slow the appearance and initial severity of AIDS symptoms. Such drugs, along with regular medical care, are necessary to extend the lives of people with AIDS. But treatment is extremely expensive. For example, in the United States the average annual cost of treating a patient who is HIV-positive is $18,300. The total cost of treating people with AIDS and with HIV is estimated at $7 billion in the United States each year (U.S. Agency for Healthcare Research and Quality, available at www.ahcpr.gov).

Many AIDS patients have no private health care insurance, either through employers or purchased on their own and must rely upon assistance under Medicaid. Since the medical bills can be substantial, and physicians are unlikely to treat individuals for whom they will receive limited, if any, compensation, people with AIDS are often forced to depend on the charity of public hospitals. These hospitals tend to lack the funds and facilities needed to keep up with the continuous demands placed on them by the constant health problems of the poor, no less persons with AIDS.

Even those who are well-employed and covered under private health insurance at the time AIDS enters their lives may face problems. When AIDS patients become too ill to work and must leave their jobs, they eventually usually lose their health insurance. The cost of purchasing insurance on one's own is ordinarily prohibitive. An individual health insurance policy with a private insurer can cost $4,500 a year or more, depending on the comprehensiveness of the coverage desired. But, regardless of cost, firms that sell health insurance are not likely to be willing to insure individuals who have been diagnosed with AIDS. Paying for treatment on their own, such persons may have to spend their way down into abject poverty—only then are they possibly eligible for assistance from Medicaid.

Physicians, nurses, and others involved directly with patients have been engaged in debate over their professional responsibilities toward people with AIDS. Some are unwilling to work with AIDS patients at all, noting possible risks to themselves and their other patients. Some, however, have taken on the care of AIDS patients as a

TABLE 14.4 AIDS Cases Reported by Patient Characteristics: 1981–2001

Characteristic	1981–2001 Total	2001
Total	816,149	43,158
Age		
Under 5 years old	6,975	(NA)
5–12 years old	2,099	(NA)
13–19 years old	4,428	(NA)
20–29 years old	133,725	(NA)
30–39 years old	362,021	(NA)
40–49 years old	216,387	(NA)
50–59 years old	66,060	(NA)
60 years old and over	24,453	(NA)
Sex		
Male	670,687	31,994
Female	145,461	11,164
Racial/ethnic group		
Non-Latino/a white	343,889	13,237
Non-Latino/a black	313,180	21,031
Latino/a	149,752	8,209
Asian/Pacific Islander	6,157	430
American Indian/Alaska Native	2,537	194
Transmission category		
Males, 13 years and over	666,026	31,901
Men who have sex with men	368,971	13,265
Injecting drug use	145,750	5,261
Men who have sex with men and injecting drug use	51,293	1,502
Hemophilia/coagulation disorder	5,000	97
Heterosexual contact[2]	22,914	2,213
Heterosexual contact with injecting drug user	9,821	549
Transfusion[3]	5,057	105
Undetermined[4]	57,220	8,909
Females, 13 years and over	141,048	11,082
Injecting drug use	55,576	2,212
Hemophilia/coagulation disorder	292	9
Heterosexual contact[2]	35,660	3,205
Heterosexual contact with injecting drug user	21,736	937
Transfusion[3]	3,914	113
Undetermined[4]	23,870	4,606

NA, not available.

[1] Includes persons with characteristics unknown.

[2] Includes persons who have had heterosexual contact with a bisexual male, a person with hemophilia, a transfusion recipient with human immunodeficiency virus (HIV) infection, or an HIV-infected person, risk not specified.

[3] Receipt of blood transfusion, blood components, or tissue.

[4] Includes persons for whom risk information is incomplete (because of death, refusal to be interviewed, or loss to followup), persons still under investigation, men reported only to have had heterosexual contact with prostitutes, and interviewed persons for whom no specific risk is identified.

SOURCE: U.S. Bureau of the Census, *Statistical Abstract of the United States, 2002* (Washington, DC: U.S. Government Printing Office, 2003), p. 120.

personal crusade, risking physical and emotional burnout as they struggle to keep people alive in the hope that a cure will be discovered.

Of late, the number of new cases of HIV infection and AIDS in the United States has declined somewhat and leveled off. As a staff member of the U.S. Centers for Disease Control put it, "The development of highly effective drugs to control HIV produced those declines, but the leveling-off in reported cases and deaths suggests that the treatments have reached most Americans who know they are infected and who have good access to medical care." In short, despite the efforts of the health care system many people do not know they are infected and, of those who do, many cannot get care. She went on to warn that further progress in fighting AIDS "is in serious jeopardy" (Okie, 2001).

People with AIDS tend to be young. Death rates from AIDS are highest for persons between the ages of 35 and 44 (National Center for Health Statistics, 2001). HIV infection is rising among women, whose infection rates have been low in comparison to those of men. The strain that those with HIV infections and AIDS are placing on the U.S. health care system is compounded by the demands being placed on it by society's elders.

The Impact of the Aging Population

Aging is accompanied by a variety of chronic health conditions, some of which are disabling. Given that the proportion of the U.S. population that is 65 or older is projected to dramatically increase in the coming years, the number of elderly persons placing demands on the health care system is expected to escalate quite rapidly.

As people age, they are vulnerable to a host of problems: heart conditions, rheumatism and arthritis, vision and hearing problems, and numerous other maladies. One of the most serious health conditions, and one for which there is currently no cure, is Alzheimer's disease. A leading cause of death for the elderly in the United States, Alzheimer's involves the physical deterioration of the brain. As the brain deteriorates, people with Alzheimer's become progressively disabled—emotionally, cognitively, and physically. More than 100,000 elders die from the disease each year, many after lengthy and costly care in hospitals and nursing homes.

As more people in the United States live longer, increasing numbers are being diagnosed with Alzheimer's disease, particularly those living to 85 and older. As the age demographics of U.S. society change, Alzheimer's disease has been taking on the dimensions of an epidemic. Currently 4 million people are affected by the disease; but without effective intervention, as many as 14 million people may be affected by the year 2050 (Cowley, 2002).

Most elderly persons with Alzheimer's disease are cared for at home, rather than in a hospital or nursing-home setting. But they pose a major burden of responsibility for partners, who are usually elderly themselves, or for their middle-aged offspring, who may be struggling to care for their own children at the same time. Whoever does the caretaking faces enormous demands. The physical and emotional stress accompanying caretaking can undermine the health of people who are well, causing them to need care themselves.

The need for quality, affordable nursing home or other care facilities to meet the health care demands of the aging population is real and growing. At present,

How to provide for the increasing numbers of elders who will need nursing-home care is becoming a major issue in the United States. The quality of nursing-home care shown here, where staff members encourage elders to be mentally and physically active consistent with their capabilities, is unaffordable to the millions of older people who lack private long-term care insurance.

some 1.6 million people reside in nursing homes, including many elders who have Alzheimer's disease. Not all of the nation's 17,000 nursing homes provide adequate care, and elders who must rely on this care are frequently exposed to personal indignities and mistreatment. Nursing-home care can cost more than $50,000 per year. Indeed, one of the principal reasons so much home care of the elderly occurs is the failure of Medicare, the government health plan for those age 65 and older, to provide adequate coverage for those who need long-term care in an institutional setting. Again, like AIDS patients who need treatment under Medicaid, it is often necessary for the elderly to divest themselves of all their savings and assets before they can be eligible for care under this government program.

Private long-term care insurance is available for purchase, but its cost can be prohibitive for those who wait for their later years to seek it. For many younger people, long-term care insurance for future old age is not only an added expense; it is a luxury for those who lack or can barely afford adequate health insurance coverage for themselves and their families in the present. In the absence of a national health care policy, the health care prospects awaiting the millions of people in the United States who will turn 65 in the next several decades, and who may live to experience Alzheimer's and other serious diseases, are not encouraging.

Fixing the U.S. Health Care System

Many people believe that the U.S. health care system needs to undergo a fundamental change—or even complete rebuilding. In too many cases, people's health care needs are going unmet, and they suffer or die unnecessarily. Yet agreement on the directions to go is almost nonexistent. Let us briefly outline some ideas on how the system could be fixed (National Issues Forum, 1992).

One idea is to keep the existing system and look for ways to make it better. Advocates of this position suggest that the U.S. health care system is the envy of much of the world. The system allows people a great deal of freedom to choose their own physicians and to take advantage of constant advances in technology. The costs of health care are, however, rising far too rapidly. And more could be done to provide some health insurance coverage for the more than 15 percent of persons under age 65 who lack any health insurance at all. Thus it has been suggested that all elements of the health care system cooperate in searching for ways to reduce waste, eliminate duplication, and contain administrative costs. In addition, government could make more use of tax incentives to encourage smaller firms to provide some health insurance coverage for their employees. Such measures, it is argued, will lead to a more affordable and more inclusive health care system without radical changes being made.

A second idea more directly addresses the plight of those without adequate coverage. It also involves substantial changes in the ways in which health care is provided. Under this idea, the government would *require* employers to provide private health insurance coverage to all employees and their families. All other persons would be eligible for expanded versions of government programs (such as Medicaid) from which they are now excluded. Employers would be encouraged to channel their employees into health care programs that promise to help keep costs down. Such measures, it is argued, will address the need for all citizens to have some basic coverage while minimizing the burden on taxpayers. Clearly, however, government would play a greater role in this approach than in the first set of proposals mentioned.

A third idea, which calls for much more ambitious reform, is modeled after the health care system operating in Canada. The U.S. government would guarantee health care for all citizens as a matter of right, and this would be paid for with new taxes. Under what is called a **single-payer plan,** employers and employees would no longer have to pay money to the approximately 1,500 private insurance companies that currently provide health care coverage. The federal government would initiate strict controls over health care fees (a policy that physicians initially strongly resisted in Canada) and prescription drug costs. It would streamline administrative procedures by having all bills submitted to it for payment. Advocates of this plan note that it allows everyone to receive the health care he or she needs, regardless of ability to pay. The plan also separates health care from one's employment status, since the government would make the same health care benefits available to everyone, whether employed or not. Health care would become an entitlement, to be called upon when needed. Advocates of this idea argue that it would make sense within such a system to strongly promote preventive care, since this would save taxpayers a great deal of money in the long run. The role of government would be greatest in this third proposal.

The prospect of a universal, tax-supported health care system inevitably raises the question of how comprehensive it would be. Can the United States afford to provide every citizen with all the health care services that are now available to the wealthy and well-insured? Or will it be necessary to reach a consensus on the conditions under which certain services will be provided, in effect rationing services that are extremely expensive or likely to be in short supply?

After all, some might argue, there must be outer limits to what can be spent on health. Other areas, from schools to highways, require heavy expenditures too that cannot go ignored. And don't all nations' health care systems practice some type of rationing in the face of limited resources? For example, in most health care systems people may be placed on a waiting list for surgery that is not considered urgent. In nations with the technological capabilities for organ transplants, rationing occurs whenever surgeons decide who will receive replacement organs as they are harvested from donors.

It is important to stress that debate about changing the existing system of health care in the United States, and the kinds of changes that should occur, takes place within a particular political and economic context. The United States is a class-divided capitalist society in which the most affluent exercise a disproportionate amount of political power. Those who profit from the present health care system—particularly the pharmaceutical and medical technology industries and the health insurance industry—employ powerful lobbying and public relations firms to work on their behalf. They are capable of spending a great deal of money to make sure that the changes adopted are not against their collective self-interests. When proposals for health care system reform were put forward by President Bill Clinton's administration in the mid-1990s, the health care industry's congressional lobbyists and its public relations firms successfully mobilized enough opposition to head off the proposed changes.

In the absence of a strong groundswell of grassroots sentiment and widespread political activism, fundamental changes in the U.S. health care system are not likely to occur. Minor reforms that seek to minimize some of the worst features of the status quo seem more likely. Because of the powerful special interests that profit from the current health care system, the medical model will no doubt continue to play the dominant role in shaping any adopted reforms. It will be a challenge to move to a more proactive model of health care, one designed to remove conditions that prevent people from using their mental and physical capabilities to the fullest extent possible.

The present U.S. health care system both performs miracles and excludes people, saves lives and allows unnecessary suffering and premature deaths. Recognition of these kinds of inadequacies and contradictions may yet stir demands for change and reform. The nature of the reforms that occur will impact the biographies of everyone.

CHAPTER SUMMARY

1. The overall health status of members of U.S. society has benefited from significant progress since 1900. Improvements in such standard measures as infant and maternal mortality rates, as well as life expectancy, have been rapid and substantial.

2. Despite this progress, many other nations are doing better than the United States on measures of health status—even though the United States spends more money on health care than any other nation. At the same time, the world's underdeveloped nations, in which the vast majority of Earth's population resides, are doing much worse than the United States.

3. Since the United States is one of the richest industrialized nations in the world, it is important to ask why it does not fare better on measures of overall health status. Much of the answer lies in the way the U.S. health care system is organized. Rather than recognizing health care as a right of all citizens, health care has been relegated to the level of a commodity. If you need health care, you may purchase it if you have enough money.

4. Since health care can be very expensive, and since wealth and income in the United States are so unequally distributed, many people cannot afford health insurance coverage or pay for needed care on their own. Tens of millions of people lack private or employer-provided health insurance, and government programs fail to fully meet the health care needs of those eligible for them. Higher-than-necessary rates of infant mortality and lower-than-necessary rates of life expectancy in the United States are a reflection of a health care system that does not provide for all of U.S. society's members.

5. Access to health care is not only affected by the U.S. system of economic inequality, which leaves millions unable to afford health care. Racial and gender inequalities also affect people's health status. The health status of people of color is, on average, poorer than that of whites, and racial bias has been found to exist within various sectors of the U.S. health care system. The system also contains gender biases that have adversely affected the nature and quality of health care available to women.

6. With health care treated as a marketable commodity in the United States, rather than a right, corporations have come to play a major role in shaping the health care system. Health insurance companies are increasingly involved in the management of care. Their "managed care" policies have failed to reduce rapidly rising health care costs and have been criticized as interfering with physicians' ability to adequately treat their patients. Health care delivery has also been undergoing a process of corporatization, leading to adverse effects when the pursuit of profit trumps the provision of needed health care services.

7. Currently, the operation of the U.S. health care system is strained by the demands being placed on it by two developments. The system is being asked to respond to the needs of substantial numbers of persons infected with HIV and those who have contracted AIDS, an incurable disease. It is also strained by the health problems of U.S. society's growing population of elders, including the increased number of persons who have Alzheimer's disease.

8. Most people believe that changes are needed in the U.S. health care system, but there is little consensus on what these changes should be. Ideas vary as to the degree of reform and rebuilding that is necessary and the role that government should play in an altered health care system. Corporations and others who profit from the existing health care system will struggle against proposed changes that

may adversely affect their interests. Meaningful improvements may require a groundswell of grassroots sentiment and widespread political activism.

THINKING CRITICALLY

1. Throughout this chapter our focus has been on physical health and not mental health. How important do you think it is that the U.S. health care system address the mental health of society's members? In your own view, in what ways does the current system fall short? What changes do you think should be made, and why?

2. For many years the U.S. medical profession has resisted any type of national health care system, even though the health status of people in the United States falls short of that in other major industrialized nations. Why do you think this is the case?

3. What types of problems with the existing health care system have you encountered? Were these problems somehow linked to your class position, race, or gender? How so? What do you think it would take to eliminate such problems?

4. Discussion of health care reform generally assumes that large, private insurance companies must continue to play a central role in the U.S. health care system. Critics argue that the profit-seeking orientation of such companies drives up health care costs; they point out that the Canadian system, in which private insurers do not play a role, is much less expensive to administer. What keeps private companies in the picture in the plans for U.S. health care reform?

5. If you and all your family members were, like over 40 million other persons in the United States, without any health insurance coverage at all, what problems would you confront? How would you deal with them?

KEY TERMS

corporatization of medicine, *(458)*
health, *(436)*
health care system, *(436)*
infant mortality, *(437)*

life expectancy, *(437)*
managed care, *(455)*
maternal mortality, *(437)*
medical model, *(436)*
pandemic, *(459)*

proactive health care system, *(437)*
reactive health care system, *(437)*
single-payer plan, *(464)*

Chapter Fifteen

Families

Consider the various images of families shown on television over the years. In the 1950s television program *Leave It to Beaver,* the mother is a full-time homemaker, the father works at an office in an unspecified occupation, they have two children, and they live in a comfortable suburban home. In *The Honeymooners,* a full-time homemaker is married to a bus driver, they have no children, and they live in a cramped, working-class walk-up apartment in New York City.

By the 1970s and 1980s these images began to change. *The Brady Bunch* showed a "blended" family—a mother with three daughters from a previous marriage now married to a father with three sons from a previous marriage. *Kate and Allie* were two single mothers who lived with their children in one apartment and functioned as a family. *My Two Dads* depicted a family of two gay men raising a daughter. In *The Cosby Show,* mom and dad both had lucrative and satisfying professional careers; their five children lived with them in a large city brownstone house, although at various times the children moved out or returned to their parents' home with spouses and offspring. In *Punky Brewster* the family consisted of a young foster child and the elderly man who adopted her. And *Roc* showed a working-class African American family of a young, dual-occupation couple living with the husband's elderly father and unemployed brother in a single household.

During the 1990s, the images continued to change. In *Blossom,* a single father raised his children alone. In *Murphy Brown,* a single, successful professional woman decided to maintain her pregnancy and raise her child alone. In *The Golden Girls,* four aging women, including one woman's mother, lived together in a Florida condominium.

By 2000, *Everybody Loves Raymond* introduced a family of three young children living with their full-time homemaker mother and full-time sportswriter father. Grandparents and an uncle lived next door, but the distinction between their households was blurred, as if there were not two separate households but one simply connected by a corridor of backyard.

These television families are a limited array of the various forms that the institution of the family may take. Despite their variety, all are, in some fashion, families. Your own family situation may differ significantly from the families seen on television. What, then, is a family? In this chapter we examine the meaning of "family" by examining the following questions:

- What family forms prevail in the United States, and why?
- What factors make some forms more advantageous than others?

(continued)

- **Who benefits and who is hurt by different family forms?**
- **Does the variety of family forms, and the troubles afflicting many families, mean the family is breaking down as an institution?**

Beyond being aware of the forms families may take, understanding the dynamics among family members and the forces that might affect those dynamics is important. In this chapter we explore the factors that can create problems and stress for families. We consider how developments in other institutions affect the creation, alteration, and dissolution of family ties. For example, we examine the roles the state and economy play in encouraging and rewarding some family forms but not others.

Let's turn first to the meaning of family.

Defining Family

In 1949, George Murdock defined family, on the basis of an analysis of nearly 500 societies, as "a social group characterized by common residence, economic cooperation, and reproduction" (1949:1). Murdock's definition, which he believed to be universally applicable to all societies, stated that a family consisted of "adults of both sexes, at least two of whom maintain a socially approved sexual relationship, and one or more children, own or adopted, of the sexually cohabiting adults" (1949:1). He believed this family form was widespread because it was functional to society: It fulfilled societal needs. This definition reflects the functionalist theory of family, which emphasizes the role of the institution of family in addressing the functional imperatives of societal survival (see Chapter 3). These include reproduc- pp. 62–64 tion to replace lost members of society, protection of societal members, transmission of cultural information to new members through socialization, and motivation of societal members to perform expected roles (Ogburn and Tibbits, 1934).

While many sociologists accept Murdock's definition, others criticize it for what it omits. For example, it does not include the realities of many family forms today: single-parent families, married couples without children, gay male and lesbian couples, multigenerational families without sexual relationships, and elderly couples with no children. It also excludes cohabiting couples, both heterosexual and same sex.

Murdock's definition of family seems to confuse *family*—defined by a set of principles determining relatedness—with **household**—a common residential unit in which related and nonrelated individuals may live (Andersen, 1990; Ferree, 1990). However, a family and a household are not necessarily the same thing. For example, in pre–Civil War United States, slaves contributed to a slave owner's family as an economic unit and were often considered part of the household, but they were not accepted as legitimate family members according to the conventional definition (Jones, 1987). Consider, too, the case of children of a divorce, who may live in a separate household with only one of their parents but often still consider *both* parents to be their family.

Sociologists who accept Murdock's functional definition of family often recognize that there may be different types of family, based on the role it plays for the individual, and they have differentiated families on the basis of biological factors. **Families of orientation** are the families into which individuals are born or adopted; **families of procreation** are those into which individuals marry and in which they often produce their own offspring. This differentiation of family by the biological role it plays for the individual assumes that most individuals will marry into a heterosexual relationship that will likely produce offspring.

But this is a very shaky assumption. Many people enter into cohabitation relationships, both heterosexual and homosexual, and a growing number of couples (both married and cohabitating) are choosing not to have children. Many gay males and lesbians increasingly refer to their relationships with their partners and their partners' relatives as **families of choice,** reflecting a family form not defined by biology (Cody and Welch, 1997; Stiers, 2000). In this form, family is defined by stable relationships based on shared economic and emotional ties in one or more households.

Sociologists have also differentiated between nuclear and extended families. A **nuclear family** is composed of two parents and their offspring living together. The classic example is the family on *Leave it to Beaver.* An **extended family** includes the nuclear family plus other members of one or both parents' families of orientation (e.g., grandparents, aunts and uncles, and siblings). TV examples are the families in *Everybody Loves Raymond, Roc,* and the later years of *Cosby.*

Some sociologists link these types of family to social class. The nuclear family typifies the middle class, because the breadwinner earns enough to support the family without the financial help of other family members; the extended family is more commonly found among the working class and poor, since several generations or members of the same generation tend to live together out of economic necessity. Such a differentiation of family forms continues to confuse households with families. It is also historically inaccurate: Many middle-class families in the 1950s and 1960s in the United States lived in some form of extended family (particularly those including two married members, their children, and one or more grandparents) (Litwak, 1965). As will be shown later, many still do today.

Research also indicates some racial and ethnic differences in the prevalence of extended families. Although most families in the United States, regardless of racial or ethnic group, are "maintained by a married couple or by a single parent with children" (Taylor, 1998:25), African Americans are twice as likely as whites to live in extended families that "transcend and link several different households" (Farley and Allen, 1987:168; see also Kane, 2000). Similarly, Latino/Latina (Perez, 1998), Native American (Yellowbird and Snipp, 1998), and Asian American families (Nakano Glenn and Yap, 1998) are more likely than white families to be structured as extended families. Discrete ethnicities exist within each of these socially constructed racialized categories, but one thing they have in common is the likelihood that extended family structure derives, in part, from cultural histories and experiences, including racism, immigration, resettlement, internment, and exclusion in the United States. But far from being dysfunctional, these extended family forms manifest strong family-centered values and norms, egalitarian domestic divisions of labor, and adaptable family roles (Kane, 2000). Extended families may thus operate as structures that reflect resilience of the family in the face of institutional challenges (Taylor, 1998).

For example, extended families among Vietnamese Americans serve as a structure for rebuilding and reconstituting families disrupted by migration after the Vietnam war. The evacuees of the first wave of immigrants tended to be among the Vietnamese elites, who settled in the United States. Those who fled after 1975 tended to be poorer, and they fled to asylum in neighboring countries in Asia where they were placed in refugee camps and often waited as long as two years to be resettled to countries like Canada, Australia, China, and the United States. As individuals arrived from these interim arrangements, they joined the earlier arrivals, who took in both kin and nonkin in an attempt to reconstruct families within their community (Kibria, 1998).

Cultural familial norms may encourage extended families. For example, Native American, Latino/Latina, and Asian American cultural norms often define adult children as responsible for the care of aging parents (Phua, Kaufman, and Park, 2001). The wider community becomes part of the familial network of kin and nonkin, thereby contributing in part to the greater likelihood of extended family structures.

Extended family forms may also be a response to the economy (Aaron et al., 1999). While white families' household income tends to derive primarily from the incomes of one or both partners of a marriage, African American families' income is more likely to be based on the combined incomes of both partners, adult children, and extended relatives. Given the lower average annual earnings of African Americans compared with those of whites, there are clear economic pressures to pool relatively limited financial resources as a means of escaping extreme poverty.

Economic pressures are contributing to a general resurgence of extended families in the United States. Many middle-class families with aging parents are returning to a form of extended family. As reliable, adequate nursing-home care becomes increasingly expensive and inaccessible to the middle class, elderly parents are moving in with their children. Family Caregiver Alliance estimates that one-fourth of all U.S. households is caring for an elderly family member (www.caregiver.org). This is creating a **sandwich generation** of adults caring for both elders and children. In the United States, 40 percent of the 22 million people caring for their elderly parents are simultaneously raising children (Feyerick, 1998). Notably, women are typically the caretakers, regardless of whether the elderly parent is hers or her partner's (Guberman, 1999; Velkoff and Lawson, 1998). In 2002, more than one-fourth of the adult U.S. population provided care for an individual who was disabled or chronically ill, including parents and partners (National Family Caregivers Association, available at www.nfcacares.org).

Furthermore, as housing costs soar and when shifts in the economy make decent-paying jobs scarce even for college graduates, an increasing number of middle-class offspring return home as adults to live with their parents (Zhu, Yang, and Liu, 2002). In 2000, some 56 percent of young men 18 to 24 years old and 43 percent of young women in the same age group were living with their parents, up from a total of 42 percent in 1960 (Fields and Casper, 2001; U.S. Bureau of the Census, 1992). So the extended family appears to be widespread within the population, reflecting a variety of social and economic circumstances.

Nearly half of all marriages end in divorce, and most divorced people remarry. Within five years after divorce, 58 percent of white women have remarried, as have 44 percent of Latinas and 32 percent of African American women (Bramlett and

Although the nuclear family is often assumed to be the "normal" family form, there is in fact a wide diversity of family forms. Here we see examples of just three of the types of families that are common in the United States: gay couples with children, adoptive families, and extended families in which grandparents may be raising their children's offspring.

Mosher, 2001; www.census.gov/statab: Table 117). Many remarriages involve partners with children from previous marriages, creating an increasing number of **blended families** consisting of two new partners and their respective children. When these new marriages produce children as well, they create a family consisting of stepsiblings, half-siblings, stepparents, and parents. Joint-custody arrangements between divorced parents can mean that marriage to a new partner does not necessarily sever the relationship between a parent and his or her children. Thus the children may live primarily with one parent but also remain part of the other parent's household. The blended family, like the new extended family, challenges the conventional definition of family since it often involves several households.

Finally, new technologies in reproduction have introduced the prospect of a variety of combinations and arrangements involving biological providers of sperm and egg, carriers of fetuses, and providers of custodial care of offspring. Such relationships became evident through painful legal dramas involving custody battles over children born as the products of "surrogate" mothers and those with whom they had contracted to carry the fetus. They have also gained attention when celebrities are involved, exemplified by the family created by film director Julie Cypher and rock singer Melissa Etheridge, two lesbian mothers whose two children were fathered by sperm donated by rock legend David Crosby.

How, then, can "family" be defined and still capture the wide diversity of forms which constitute that institution? A critical definition based on that offered by Carol D. Stack (1974:31) can be useful because it reflects a variety of situations, including those contoured by race, class, and gender: **Family** is an organized, ongoing network of kin and nonkin who interact daily, sharing economic and household responsibilities and obligations, providing for domestic needs of all members, and ensuring their survival. The family network may span several households that may be based on biology or on choice.

▌Diversity of Family Forms

Given that the family may be structured in different ways at different times, which forms of the family are most prevalent in the United States today, and why? As shown in Figure 15.1 (based on data for 2000), the conventional understanding of the nuclear family—a breadwinning father, a full-time homemaker mother, and two or more young offspring living in the same residence—describes less than 7 percent of U.S. households (www.census.gov/statab: Table 53). More than twice as many households consist of two income-earning married adults and their children. Married couples with no children total more than one-third of U.S. households. Single-parent households are also common. Among these, female-headed households are more than four times more frequent than male-headed households (www.census.gov/statab: Table 61). Unmarried cohabiting couples are also on the rise. Since 1970, the number of unmarried couples living together without marriage has increased more than 600 percent. By 2000, cohabiting couples totaled 5.3 million of over 104 million documented households (www.census.gov/statab: Tables 54, 60, 61, 579). Unfortunately, the Census Bureau does not have data for other household arrangements, such as

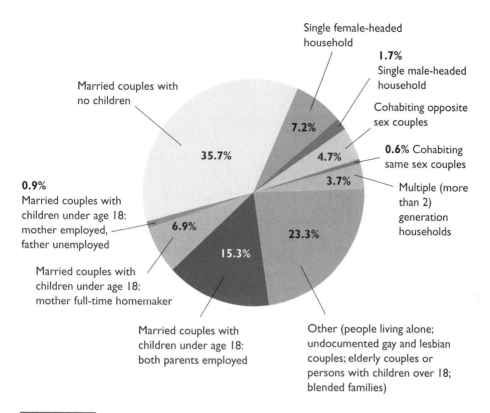

Single female-headed household

1.7%
Single male-headed household

Cohabiting opposite sex couples

Married couples with no children

7.2%

35.7%

4.7%

0.6% Cohabiting same sex couples

3.7%

Multiple (more than 2) generation households

0.9%
Married couples with children under age 18: mother employed, father unemployed

6.9%

23.3%

15.3%

Married couples with children under age 18: mother full-time homemaker

Married couples with children under age 18: both parents employed

Other (people living alone; undocumented gay and lesbian couples; elderly couples or persons with children over 18; blended families)

FIGURE 15.1 **Proportion of Family Forms in the United States: 2000**
Contrary to the stereotype of the "typical" family as a married couple with children living at home, families are actually quite diverse in the forms they assume. What is the structure of your own family? (Source: www.census.gov/statab Tables 53, 54, 60, 61, 579; Tavia Simmons and Grace O'Neill, *Households and Families: 2000.* U.S. Census, 2000 Brief. Washington, DC: U.S. Dept. of Commerce.)

blended families. However, despite these limitations, the data indicate that the conventional nuclear family is no longer the typical U.S. family.

Are the proportions of family types similar for white, African American, and Latino/Latina families in the United States? According to Figure 15.2, in 2000 white and Latino/Latina families were more likely to be two-parent households than were African American families. African American families were more likely than either Latino/Latina or white families to be headed by single mothers with no husband present. Wives in African American married-couple families were also more likely to work in the formal labor force than were white wives (www.census.gov/statab: Table 578). Let's take a closer look at the diversity of family forms in the United States.

Family Forms: Cultural Choice or Institutional Response?

In a controversial speech given in 1992, Vice President Dan Quayle argued that single-parent families were largely responsible for much of what was wrong in the United States. He insisted that "appropriate" family values call for a two-parent

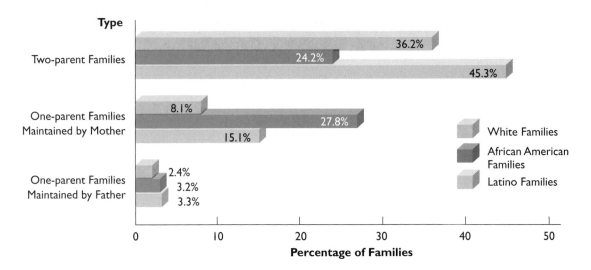

FIGURE 15.2 **Family Forms by Race: 2000** The prevalence of various family forms varies by race in the United States. What factors might affect this variation? (Source: www.census.gov/statab Table 55)

family, in which one of the parents (presumably the mother) assumes primary responsibility for taking care of the children. He urged a return to such family values as the answer to most social problems.

This attitude suggests that family forms other than the traditional nuclear family structure represent conscious choices on the part of individuals or reflect different cultural norms within the population. But what about institutional forces that might influence the form some families assume? Institutional forces may not only be responsible for diversity in family forms but they may also influence the interpersonal dynamics and individual experiences within these forms (Allan and Crow, 2001).

Reasons for the Rise in Single-Parent Families

Several forces help account for the growing number of single-parent families, primary among them being divorce and unwed motherhood.

⊙ Divorce

Many single-parent families are the result of divorce. The annual per capita divorce rate in the United States in 2002 was 40 percent, (www.cdc.gov/nchs/data), up from the rate of 35 percent in 1970 (www.census.gov). What factors contribute to the increase in divorce?

Divorce has become easier to achieve since 1970 with the advent of **no-fault divorce** laws in many states. Prior to this legislation, couples were required to demonstrate that one of the partners was responsible for the destruction of the marriage, usually on the grounds of adultery or severe mistreatment. Under no-fault divorce laws, attribution of blame for misconduct is no longer necessary in order to dissolve the marriage. One or both partners may simply apply to the courts for a divorce by citing irreconcilable differences. Such a significant change in legal requirements for divorce indicates substantial changes in society's values and cultural norms regarding marriage, the declining influence of religious institutions, and the increasing influence of the state in family affairs.

Economic conditions may also contribute to the divorce rate. Participation in the formal labor market provides some women with greater economic independence from their husbands, thereby making divorce a more viable option. A weak economy, including high rates of unemployment and inflation and a significant decline in the value of wages, may introduce serious stresses into a marriage. The forces of economic stress contributing to divorce affect some groups more than others. Divorce rates (as well as rates of marital separation and abandonment) are highest among the lowest income groups (Neubeck and Neubeck, 1997).

Unwed Motherhood

Divorce is not the only factor contributing to single-parent families. Many such families *begin* with a single parent. Unmarried mothers accounted for 33.2 percent of all births in the United States in 2000, up from 4 percent in 1950 (www.census.gov/ statab: Table 74). Almost one-fifth of all never-married women in the United States in 1998 became mothers, up from slightly more than 15 percent just a decade earlier (www.census.gov/statab: Table 82). Part of the reason for this increase is that cultural sanctions against out-of-wedlock births are changing. Less often today do people refer to children of unwed mothers as "illegitimate." And an increasing number of affluent, over-30 single women are choosing to have babies without plans of marriage. However, apart from this trend, teenagers constitute a significant, but declining, group among unwed mothers. What accounts for a high rate of births to single females, especially teenagers?

One factor is that girls have become capable of reproduction at increasingly younger ages, in part because of improved nutrition and health. An earlier onset of menstruation means that a greater percentage of females are able to become pregnant. In the late 1990s, the proportion of teenagers who were sexually active had declined from the high rates noted in 1990, but these rates still remain high. According to the Alan Guttmacher Institute, more than half have had intercourse by the time they turn 17 (www.agi-usa.org). Although such teenagers may have access to contraceptives, many do not use them. In 1999, some 27 percent of sexually active young unmarried females did not use contraceptives during their first intercourse (www.agi-usa.org). Many pregnancies result from the female's first sexual experiences, when use of contraceptives is often neglected.

Why do so many teenagers neglect using contraceptives? Part of the problem is lack of knowledge and misinformation concerning birth control and pregnancy. Sex education in the public schools takes place to some extent, but it is mired in controversy. The programs often fail to provide information about what leads to pregnancy and how to use and obtain contraceptives. Some parents fear that such information will only make teenagers *more* sexually active. But studies have found that sex education does *not* increase the rate of sexual activity among teenagers, and it may actually increase the probability that those who are sexually active will use contraceptives (Grunseit et al., 1997).

Religious and state institutions may also discourage use of contraceptives. The Roman Catholic church, for example, does not approve of contraceptive use by anyone. Whereas most U.S. married Catholics tend to ignore the church's disapproval, teenagers who are active members of the church may be discouraged from using this protection. State and federal laws restrict access to certain types of contraceptives (birth control pills, diaphragms, and intrauterine devices) by requiring a physician's prescription. Since many teenagers are reluctant to admit sexual activity to a family doctor, or are unable to afford to see one, they may have limited access to prescribed contraceptives. Planned Parenthood and other clinics offer free exams and contraceptives, but they are not always easily accessible to teenagers (especially in rural areas). Thus policies of such institutions as education, religion, and the state contribute to the high rates of teenage pregnancy and single parenthood.

In addition, gender socialization and cultural notions of romantic love may contribute to teenage pregnancies (Finlay, 1996). Traditional gender roles assume male aggression and sexual expertise and female docility and sexual purity. These gender roles often suggest that a "good girl" does not *plan* for a sexual encounter (Kisker, 1985). Guilt over sexual activity, coupled with the **cultural myth of romanticism,** may thus lead some females to avoid contraception. Being prepared for sexual intercourse by having contraceptives amounts to admitting that one is sexually active; but a female's sexual activity may be understood or excused if she was "swept off her feet" in the heat of a romantic moment. For teenaged males, cultural norms of masculinity and machismo are likely to discourage use of condoms (Castro-Vasquez, 2000). In this way cultural definitions of gender-specific appropriate behaviors contribute to single parenthood.

Reasons for the Rise in Other Nontraditional Family Forms

Institutional and cultural arrangements may also encourage the growth of other nontraditional family forms in the United States. For example, the lack of paid family-leave policies and government-supported child care programs may encourage multihousehold extended families. Other countries, such as Sweden, use income tax revenues to provide for parental leave from employment during the first year of a child's life, with minimal loss of income for the parents who elect to take such leave. Many governments in Europe at least partially support daycare facilities for children over the age of one, thereby ensuring adequate institutional support for parents who must work outside the home but do not want to jeopardize the care and education of their children (Ferber, O'Farrell, and Allen, 1991). In an economy where many hold low-wage jobs, both partners in a traditional nuclear family must earn incomes just to survive or to achieve a standard of living above poverty. Living in an extended family where child care help is available may be necessary. Poverty among the elderly, particularly women, may prompt the need for an extended family to provide elder care.

Rising divorce rates have sent many women to work to provide for themselves and their children. But wage inequalities in the formal labor market mean that many women, especially those who are the sole providers for their families, will struggle to avoid poverty and many will not succeed. The lack of affordable dependent care for young children, persons with disabilities, and the elderly means that many families (and most often women) have to turn to help from kin. For example, the U.S. Bureau of the Census found that in 1999 more than one-fourth of infant and toddler children whose mothers were employed in the formal labor market were cared for by relatives other than their parents; 20.8 percent of these children were cared for by their grandparents (www.census.gov/population). Clearly, then, varying family forms to some extent respond to such institutional forces as the dynamics of the economy and state policies in addition to diversity in cultural norms, rather than merely reflecting individual choice.

The deployment of troops to the Middle East in 2003 has also focused attention on the issue of institutional forces prompting nontraditional family forms. When individuals who are part of two-parent families are deployed far from the family household, single-parent families are, at least temporarily, created. When the soldier activated for duty is the mother, the father may be thrust for the first time into an extended experience of the double shift more commonly juggled by women. When single parents are deployed, new considerations of child care are needed, as illustrated in the "Social Forces/People's Lives" reading. Grandparents may suddenly find themselves functioning as full-time primary caretakers of their grandchildren. Divorced parents may need to rearrange custody agreements. And if the unthinkable should happen and the deployed parent never returns home, these temporary arrangements may very well become permanent.

Does the diversity of family forms mean that the institution of the family in the United States is in a state of crisis? Not necessarily. The impact of powerful institutions such as the economy make the traditional nuclear family untenable for many people. Yet other family forms and variations develop to ensure the survival and well-being of societal members. The institution of the family is not breaking down, but it is undergoing substantial change and adapting to challenges created by the manner in which other institutions like the economy and the state operate. The latent functions of these institutions are likely to prompt adaptive strategies in the institution of the family. Whether all the changes are for the good is a matter of considerable debate and a worthy subject for social science research.

Poverty and Families

Institutional forces not only influence family forms but also affect the experiences of families, as seen most clearly in the different patterns of poverty seen in Chapter 12 (Table 12.2). The U.S. Bureau of the Census found that in 2000, single-parent families, especially those headed by a female, were far more likely than married-couple families to be poor. And families of color were more likely than white families to be poor. Why do such patterns exist? How can these be explained in the context of the current economic climate?

p. 390

Social Forces/People's Lives

When Parents Are Soldiers

ADAM PIORE

Most families in the United States juggle the demands of family life and the labor market. The pressures this creates often contribute to the diversity of family forms discussed in this chapter. This reading describes how the jobs of people in the military can be especially challenging to efforts to balance work and family life, particularly when children are involved. What happens when one or both parents are in the military and are activated and deployed in a war? How does this alter the family form? How does it alter the roles played by different family members? Do other jobs have a similar effect on families?

MASTER Sgt. Sue Harper stands in her kitchen clutching a drawer so tightly her knuckles turn white. Oblivious to the dinner chatter in her dining room, the rail-thin blonde with the ponytail and glasses presses a telephone to her ear. "Master Sergeant Harper, sir. I was told to check in every couple of hours," she says. After a moment, she hears what she was hoping for. "Well, good! Thank you, sir." Harper hangs up, relieved. There will be no deployment to Turkey tonight. Instead, she can sleep at home in the same bed with her 12-year-old daughter, Maria, on the Kaiserslautern military base in Germany. From her smile, you'd think she won the lottery. But this simple reprieve is better than money. Harper is a single mom, and living alone with Maria has forged an unusually strong bond between mother and daughter. Saying goodbye is never easy; saying goodbye as she heads off to war is almost more than Harper can bear. "Every parent feels they are the only person who understands their kid and can do things for them," says Harper, 39, a public affairs officer with the 21st Theater Support Command, a logistics unit. "I worry that other people just won't get her like I do." Then she asks the question that haunts her most: "What if I don't come back?"

These are lonely times for parents like Harper. Those familiar media images of husbands and wives bidding each other tearful farewells on docks and airfields

tell only part of the story. According to the Pentagon, the number of single moms and dads in the military has nearly doubled since the last gulf war from 47,685 in 1992 to almost 90,000 today. Despite the dramatic increase, however, the Pentagon has no special programs in place for them. Military officials aren't even sure why the numbers are up. "That's not something we could speculate on," says Lt. Col. Cynthia Colin, a Pentagon spokesperson. "We recruit people, and the people in the military reflect society."

While there are no hard data to explain the jump, it's clear that jobs in today's much smaller forces are more demanding than in the past. Between 1992 and 2002, the military shrank from about 1.8 million to 1.4 million active-service members; those who remain have seen their burdens increase. "Certainly, frequent deployments and long separations are challenging for marriages," says Shelley MacDermid, a professor and co-director of the Military Family Research Institute at Purdue University. "One hypothesis is that as the tempo has gone up, it's been harder to stay married."

Raising a child in the military—moving from base to base, surviving on a paltry government salary—has never been easy. But life as a single military parent these days poses special challenges. The prospect of war brings agonizing choices: How to explain to your child the need to leave? How much to reveal about the danger ahead? Perhaps most difficult of all: What to do with your kids while you're gone?

For Sgt. Shala Gatson, 24, also stationed in Germany, the solution lay about 5,000 miles away. In January, Gatson delivered her two young sons, Cori, 7, and Dashon, 5, to her ex-husband (and Dashon's father), Elton, in Alexandria, LA. Because the army doesn't pay the cost of flying children back to the United States, Gatson, a supply specialist also with the 21st who makes roughly $2,000 a month, had to borrow from friends to come up with the $800 airfare. During the all-too-brief time with his mother in Louisiana, Dashon one day nonchalantly asked, "Mama, are you going to die?" "No," she told him. "I'm going to do my best to come back. Mommy has to go and protect the other people from the bad guys. Mommy is going to go work on computers." After she left, the boys struggled to adjust. They were happy to be spending time with Elton, but their mother was ever in their thoughts. "My mama is fighting a war," Cori told his teacher one day, "and after the war we're all going back to Germany."

Harper chose to bring a friend from Arkansas to Germany to care for Maria. Theresa Snuffer, or "Ms. Theresa," is a silver-haired former stay-at-home mom whose husband served five tours in Vietnam. She understands the needs of children like Maria. "I don't think a kid should be uprooted," says Snuffer, who arrived in Europe last month. "It's OK for summer vacation. But during the school year, they should be around their own things." In addition to a tight-knit group of military neighbors to help Snuffer look after Maria, there is a school staff experienced in handling deployments. In recent weeks counselors at Kaiserslautern Middle School have been gathering the names of students whose parents are deploying. They will be watching for several telltale signs. "Some children start acting out," says counselor Harriet Scofield. "We often see grades falling, uncompleted homework. Other children will start having problems with peers, picking arguments."

Ironically, the increase in the number of single parents in the military may be in part the result of recent Pentagon successes. In 1989, Congress created a new network of mostly five-day-a-week child care centers for parents in the military, and offered subsidies based on family income. The moves made the military a more viable career option for all parents, singles and couples alike. Still, there are gaps. Child care is usually available only weekdays from 9 to 5 and soldiers are fined if they are late picking up their kids. More broadly, no consideration is given to the special needs of single parents. "We have a lot of different people in different situations," says the Pentagon's Colin. Providing more assistance for single parents being sent to the gulf is "really not feasible," Colin says. "It would just be way too much work. Each situation is different, depending on where you are stationed and what your situation is. Some people might live near a grandparent. Others may live in another country."

While they were still together in Germany, Sue and Maria made the best of it. Maintaining the ordinariness of life, the little daily rituals, seemed to bring the most comfort. There were dinners at their favorite restaurant, Alt Landstuhl, where waitresses still wear traditional German costumes, and where Maria and her mother like to order "the grossest things" on the menu. "That's how I fell in love with snails," says Maria. In those precious final days, special events took on new meaning. In an auditorium festooned with balloons, men and women in camouflage sat among students for an awards ceremony that was likely to be the last school event many of the parents would attend for a long time. Maria was called to the stage three times: for good citizenship, for making the honor roll and, most important, for winning the school competition in the National Geographic Geography Bee. She received a medal on a ribbon and placed it squarely over her mother's shoulders. Sue won't be able to attend the regional finals, to be held this month, but for a little while, at least, things were as they should be. Mother and daughter shared a moment of celebration together, and Iraq and the looming thunder of war seemed far, far away.

Gatson and Harper finally shipped out to Turkey the last week of February. It was easier for Gatson—by the time she left, she could barely stand the sight of her sons' rooms. "The house is so empty," she said. "Nobody fussing, nobody coming in and saying, 'How you doing?'" Harper found it difficult. Every morning before school, she said a tearful goodbye, never knowing if she would be there when Maria came home. Finally early one morning a little past 4 A.M., Harper kissed her sleepy daughter and slipped away.

SOURCE: Adam Piore, with Arian Campo-Flores, "Single Parents in the Armed Forces Face Some Special Problems as They Ship Out for the Gulf," *Newsweek*, March 17, 2003, pp. 52–53.

The Effect of State Policies

Wage inequality creates more difficulty for single women of all racial and ethnic groups than for married couples and men to provide for their families and rise above poverty levels. For the same reason, African American and Latino/Latina married couples and single parents find doing so more difficult than their white counterparts. The inadequacy of the minimum wage means that even when a father works full-time, year-round, he may not earn enough to provide adequately for his family. His spouse must also participate in the formal labor market. Even when both parents work, the family may be unable to remain above poverty. Unfortunately, most social welfare programs that provide assistance to the poor are specifically designed to aid *single mothers* and their children, a policy that discourages partners from remaining together during serious economic hardship.

State policy may, on the other hand, improve rather than aggravate the economic circumstances of some families. Although African American and Latino/Latina families are more likely than white families to be poor, not all families of color are poor. In fact, the number of African American and Latino/Latina middle-class families has grown since 1990 (www.census.gov/statab: Table 736). Such growth suggests that state programs aimed at providing equal educational opportunities and prohibiting discrimination in employment have had some impact.

Other research demonstrates the effect of state policies on the economic well-being of various family forms. Federal economic policies of the 1970s and 1980s that reduced support for women and children, as well as welfare reform of the 1990s that eliminated women's and children's entitlement to public assistance, exacerbated the **feminization of poverty,** in which an increasing proportion of the poor are female-headed families, particularly those headed by women of color (Roschelle, 1999). The term "feminization of poverty" has been commonly used in the mass media to describe the increased presence of women in poverty, but its use may erroneously imply that women have either chosen to be poor (e.g., by electing to stay on welfare to remain home with their children) or somehow brought poverty on themselves (e.g., by leaving their marriages). An increasing number of observers prefer instead to refer to the **pauperization of motherhood,** a concept that more accurately points to the *institutional* forces that have impoverished women (Amott, 1993; Folbre, 1985).

The state may also contribute to the pauperization of motherhood. In the 1990s, state welfare reform programs harmed impoverished single mothers and their children, especially those of color, by imposing impossibly short time limits on eligibility for public assistance, while rewarding two-parent middle-class families with tax deductions for having dependent children and giving tax credit for child care expenses. The state, then, can play an influential role in determining the economic viability of various family forms. Under certain state policies, family forms other than the traditional two-parent nuclear family may be economic liabilities.

The Effect of Marital Dissolution

Marital dissolution provides another glimpse into the economic effect of institutional forces on family forms. Most marriages are dissolved either by divorce or by death of

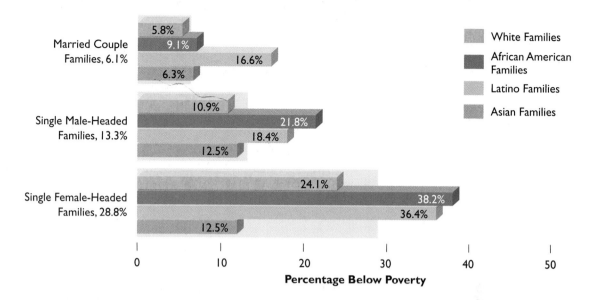

FIGURE 15.3 **Poverty and Family Structure, 2002** Patterns of poverty show that married-couple families have the lowest risk of being poor than single-parent families. The risk of poverty is greatest for single-mother families, particularly African-American and Latina families. Why might this be the case? (Source: www.bls.census.gov)

one of the partners. Research shows that in both cases, women tend to suffer long-term negative economic consequences that men are less likely to face (Bartfeld, 2000; Shelton and Dean, 2001). Poverty rates for women, for example, have a strong tendency to be higher after divorce than during marriage (www.census.gov), and female-headed households have a much greater tendency than male-headed households to be poor (see Figure 15.3). Studies have found a serious erosion in women's standard of living following divorce (Hanson, McLanahan, and Thomson, 1998).

In contrast, marital dissolution tends to *improve* men's standard of living when they have relied on their partners for less than one-fifth of their predivorce household income (McManus and DiPrete, 2001), suggesting that traditional divisions of labor are economically more dangerous for women than for men. While women's ratio of income to needs drops by at least 50 percent following divorce (Burkhauser and Duncan, 1989), the ratio for men substantially increases, even after deductions for child support and alimony (Peterson, 1996). Why does this happen? Research suggests that institutional forces are at work here, particularly in state policies and labor-market practices (England, 2000). For example, on the assumption that women are more appropriate caregivers than men, courts tend to award women physical custody of children in a divorce, thereby reducing the economic responsibility fathers must bear. Even when courts order that fathers pay child support, few fathers comply fully, particularly after the first year. In 1997, only half of the women awarded child support payments by noncustodial fathers actually received full payment

(Garfinkel et al., 1998); about one-fourth of these fathers simply refused to pay (www.acf.dhhs.gov). In any case, the amounts of the payments tend to be less than the actual costs of raising children (Pirog-Good, 1993; Seltzer, 1989). In addition, gender inequalities in the formal labor market help generate greater incomes for husbands than for wives (Koretz, 2001). Together, these factors produce a situation after divorce in which "men retain a larger share of the family's income, while their economic needs decrease more than their income" (Holden and Smock, 1991).

Indeed, research indicates a trend toward greater economic interdependence in marriage, in which the incomes of both partners are crucial for the family's economic well-being. In such arrangements, divorce is likely to produce a lower standard of living for both men and women when the marriage dissolves (McManus and DiPrete, 2001). This research underscores the fact that gendered divisions of labor in marriage produce economic consequences in the aftermath of a divorce: traditional gendered divisions of labor in which the woman is a full-time (unpaid) homemaker are likely to produce far harsher economic hardship for her than when she is employed in marriage. Men's increasing reliance on women's earnings in marriage means they will likely feel the loss of their wives' contributions in divorce.

The extent of a woman's decline in economic status after divorce seems to be related to class and race (Molina, 2000). The greatest economic decline following divorce occurs for women whose predivorce family incomes were highest. Research also indicates that women of color suffer declines in income after divorce that are more significant than those of white women (Duncan and Hoffman 1985; Stroup and Pollock, 1999). The factors that seem to intensify the negative economic consequences of marital dissolution for women appear to be related to gender roles in traditional nuclear families and to wage inequities based on sex and race in the formal labor market (Shelton and John, 1999).

Research demonstrates that the economic effects of widowhood are often just as disadvantageous for women as divorce. Poverty rates for women tend to increase following the deaths of their husbands (Hungerford, 2001). And while higher prewidowhood incomes may offer greater protection from postwidowhood poverty, one study found that women in higher income groups were more likely to suffer a significant decline in their ratio of income to needs than women whose prewidowhood incomes were lower (Holden, 1990).

The age of the wife at the onset of widowhood significantly affects her chance of poverty, with widows younger than 60 more likely to fall into poverty (Burkhauser, Holden, and Feaster, 1988; Zick and Smith, 1986;). This is because many insurance policies award greater benefits to an older widow and because younger widows with children may face restrictions and inequalities in the formal labor market (Holden and Smock, 1991). Also, federal Social Security policy tends to penalize younger widows with no children; they are not eligible for the survivor benefits normally extended to children, and they are too young to collect Social Security benefits themselves (Holden, 1990; Holden and Smock, 1991).

Some husbands may provide their surviving wives with protection from possible poverty through their pension funds, but only if the husbands are vested (i.e., they have paid into the insurance for a long enough period of time, usually 5 to 10 years). However, some pension funds do not extend any benefits to the surviving spouse;

others may offer only a one-time lump-sum payment; and still others may deny the surviving partner any benefits until such time as the deceased would have become eligible to collect benefits as a retiree (Holden, 1990; Holden and Smock, 1991). Provisions that deny benefits altogether for widows or delay benefits for younger widows push women into poverty at the time of widowhood. In addition, while husbands may try to protect their partners from poverty in widowhood through private life insurance, research shows that they tend to seriously underinsure themselves (Auerbach and Kotlikoff, 1987).

Certain state policies can aggravate the economic disadvantages women confront. For example, the state may not adequately enforce child-support payments or allow for the timely transfer of property following the death of a partner. Even Social Security policy continues to contribute to gendered inequality because there is still a gender gap in spouse and widow benefits that does not take into account the unpaid labor of homemakers (Meyer, 1996). And private-sector policies (such as wage inequalities, insurance policy inequalities based on age, and inadequate pension provisions) add to the institutional forces that penalize women in such circumstances.

Poverty in Nontraditional Families

For workers who have adopted a nontraditional family form, state policies and economic forces also affect their benefits and thus their families' economic well-being. Some policies, for example, penalize families that are based on cohabitation rather than marriage. Gay male and lesbian couples, as well as cohabiting heterosexual couples, often find that employers will not cover their partners under their health insurance policies or as pension and life insurance beneficiaries. Similarly, individuals in such relationships are frequently denied the legal right to participate in decision making concerning care and continued life support of their partners in times of serious illness.

Some of this may be changing, however. Several states now recognize gay and lesbian civil unions, thereby extending the economic and legal benefits of marriage to such couples (Silverman, 2000). Dozens of municipalities, including Hartford, San Francisco, Seattle, and Tacoma Park, recognize relations between cohabitants as legitimate and, upon application, will certify them as licensed domestic partnerships, much like licensed marriages. A few cities, including Atlanta, extend medical insurance coverage to "domestic partners" of their employees. Moreover, a small but growing number of corporations recognize the legitimacy of cohabitation in their policies. Ben and Jerry's Homemade, Inc., extends the same benefits, including health and pension benefits, to cohabitants that married partners enjoy at the firm. The Lotus Development Corporation has a domestic partners plan for gay male and lesbian couples (but not for heterosexual cohabitants) enabling them to receive family benefits. The firm's reasoning behind its homosexuals-only plan is that heterosexuals can marry to receive family benefits, whereas, gays and lesbians cannot. By 2003, more than 5,800 employers offered domestic partner benefits, including over 200 Fortune 500 corporations and more than 5,000 smaller private firms, nonprofit agencies, unions, colleges, and governmental employers (www.hrc.org). Such policies may help prevent poverty in nontraditional families in the event of a serious illness or retirement.

Family Dynamics and Family Issues

We have been discussing ways in which the economy and state can affect the well-being of families. Those institutions can also affect relationships between family members. For example, China maintains a 20-year-old state policy mandating one-child family structures in an attempt to reduce the population growth rate. Families that restrict themselves to one child are given preferences for jobs and promotions, housing, education, and health care; those who do not comply are typically denied access to these rewards and resources and may also find that subsequent children are not covered by state-sponsored services, including health and education. Since cultural values privilege males over females, China's state policy creates an incentive for female infanticide, female-child abandonment, and abortion of female fetuses as couples strive for their one and only child to be male. Over time the one-child policy reverberates throughout the culture as it reshapes family structures and dynamics, as the concepts of siblings, cousins, nieces, nephews, aunts, and uncles evaporate because these statuses eventually lose their social meaning. It also poses challenges to families that have traditionally relied on a network of children in the extended family to care for aging parents. When two only-children marry, they alone become responsible for four aging parents having no other siblings to help shoulder that burden (Lev, 2000). China's one-child family policy, then, illustrates the impact that state policy can have on family structures and dynamics.

How do institutional forces affect the internal dynamics of families in the United States? How do state policies and changes in the U.S. labor market affect the domestic division of labor? How do state policies and the economy affect violence within families? And how might state policy affect reproductive and parenting rights of young women, gay males and lesbians, and people with disabilities?

Family Violence

"The family" is often idealized as providing a safe, satisfying and secure "haven in a heartless world" (Lasch, 1977). Unfortunately, this is not always the case. All too often the family is an arena in which people experience severe violence. One common assumption is that only the mentally ill physically abuse their spouses or children and that such abuse occurs only in poor families. However, research challenges these beliefs. Approximately four million women are seriously assaulted by their partners each year, and nearly one in three women are assaulted by their partners at least once in their relationship (www.apa.org; www.stopfamilyviolence.org). In 2000 in the United States, more than 876,000 children were victims of abuse, most at the hands of one of their own parents; more than 1,000 children died of abuse and neglect (www.surgeongeneral.gov).

Reports of elder abuse increased 150 percent over the 10-year period between 1986 and 1996, an increase that significantly exceeded the 10 percent increase in the older population. In 90 percent of the cases where the abuser was known, perpetrators of elder abuse were family members; two-thirds of these were adult children or spouses (www.aoa.dhhs.gov/Factsheets/abuse). Almost one-third of the murders of people aged 65 and older are now committed by a family member (www.apa.org), and most of the victims are women with chronic illnesses or disabilities (www.surgeongeneral.gov). Although *reported* rates of family violence are highest among low-income people, violence is, in fact, widespread and common in families of all income levels (Anderson, 2000; Tower, 1996). Mental illness has been linked to only 10 percent of acts of family violence.

If poverty and mental illness are not the principal causes of family violence, then what else might be? Gelles and Straus (1988) noted that family violence is not a new phenomenon. They suggested an interactionist perspective, focusing on the intimate interactions between the individuals involved. Violence, they argued, is related to the institution of the family itself, for it is a structure that puts individuals in close and constant contact with one another. Such a structure is likely to foster emotionally intense relationships simply because of the unrelenting proximity of family and household members who may use "biographical ammunition" against one another. Since the relationships within families are very intimate and interaction is frequent, tensions heighten as individuals know better than people outside the family which emotional buttons to push.

Constant contact may also increase the chances that some household members will become easy or convenient targets against whom other members unleash their everyday frustrations. The roles given to family members according to their age and sex also play a part in domestic violence. For example, conflicts between children and adults, or husband and wife, may reflect power differences and may be a natural outcome of family roles built around age and gender inequalities. Using violence to resolve conflicts may also derive from social and cultural influences that encourage or reinforce violence. Many violent abusers were themselves abused or observed abuse in their families. Such experiences may lead them to see violence as an acceptable and normal way to resolve conflict. Furthermore, books, television, movies, and videos

Assault and battery and other forms of physical violence are often treated by police as a private family affair when it occurs in a domestic setting behind closed doors. However, an increasing number of state and local police departments have begun to treat violence committed behind closed doors by an intimate or partner as they would treat acts of violence occurring on the streets between strangers. The severe injuries suffered by this woman at the hands of her partner illustrate vividly the violence that can occur in the privacy of one's home.

often treat the use of force as an understandable and acceptable form of behavior. Violence is a standard component of media entertainment, including sports. And the national jubilation that accompanies military victories such as the U.S. defeat of Iraq in 1991 and 2003 relates the use of violence to heroic acts and often directly or indirectly links this behavior to maleness. Gelles and Straus concluded that the combination of direct and indirect socialization experiences contributes to an atmosphere in which many forms of family violence are viewed as "normal" violence, because they are accepted and given legitimacy in the larger culture.

Another problem is that much family violence in the United States occurs out of public view. People in the United States value their privacy, so physical violence and abuse within the family are far less subject to public scrutiny and control than the same behaviors in many nonfamily settings. For example, it is not acceptable for a teacher to beat a student, an employer to beat an employee, or a religious leader to abuse followers. Thus the use of physical violence against another person in most institutional settings outside the family is construed as assault and battery. But within the family, violence is often viewed as a way for parents to discipline their children or as an adjunct to everyday marital conflicts. The hesitation of courts and local police to interfere in domestic disputes can leave family victims of physical violence unprotected and reinforce the legitimacy of violence as a means of coping with or resolving conflicts.

Power Differentials in the Family

A conflict perspective offers some insight into why family violence takes on the patterns it does. Why are children, the elderly, and women most often the targets of abuse in families? The answer may lie in the question of power inequality. The structure of families carries gendered and age-based power inequalities that may contribute to family violence. In particular, children and the elderly are physically less powerful than their abusers and typically do not have decision-making power in the family. Where children are concerned, the state enforces that power inequality in its recognition of parental rights to determine child rearing and in the relative rarity of its willingness to recognize the rights of children seeking emancipation from parental control. Further, Gelles and Straus noted that power differentials in the home were one of the most important factors affecting spouse abuse and violence (see also Anderson and Umberson, 2001). "The risk of intimate violence is the greatest when all the decision making in a home is concentrated in the hands of one of the partners. Couples who report the most sharing of decisions report the lowest rates of violence" (Gelles and Straus, 1988:92). Thus gender roles that reinforce power differentials, vesting males with greater power and control in decision making, contribute to the likelihood of domestic violence.

Analyzing domestic violence in terms of internal family power structures offers new insights into gender relations. For example, observers on all sides of the controversy concerning family violence agree that although women do sometimes batter their partners, the vast majority of batterers are men. Indeed, a woman typically attacks only in self-defense, either hitting back after an attack against her or striking first because she has been victimized before and believes she will be seriously assaulted if she does not (Kimmel, 2000). Why should this gendered pattern of violence exist? Conventional explanations suggest a biological or psychological answer, which might suggest that men are simply more innately aggressive than women. But such explanations do not address why men are more likely to vent their frustrations and anger against their female partners than against other potential targets, such as male friends and colleagues or male authority figures. Nor do they address why stress on women is not as likely to escalate into physical violence against male partners. A conflict perspective suggests the importance of issues of dominance and power differentials based on gendered social structures (Gordon, 1988; Merry,

2002). Men more commonly attack women because women are more often socially perceived as subordinate, weaker, and less likely to strike back. In a society whose dominant culture supports the notion that men are "naturally" more powerful and dominant and in which most social institutions are dominated by men, it is likely that domestic violence by men will be accepted as unfortunate but "normal."

Sources of Stress in Families

The gendered and age-based power differentials in families provide a structural context in which expressions of frustration and stress become directed at the least powerful members of the family: women, children, and the elderly. Gelles and Straus pointed to the many sources of mounting stress confronting families in the United States that may contribute to violent behavior. The ravages of poverty and unemployment increase stress in families. Reported rates of violence tend to be highest among poor families (Benson et al., 2000). However, violence is not restricted to poor families alone. Stress factors other than poverty afflict higher-income families, including performance of household responsibilities while balancing two jobs or careers, lack of adequate day care for children, responsibility for aging or ailing parents or dependents with disabilities, and conflicting schedules. Let's examine these stresses and their effects on the family.

Many families depend on two incomes to provide a middle-class standard of living. In a 2002 survey, 56 percent of the respondents felt they did not earn enough money to live the way they wanted (www.roperweb.ropercenter.uconn.edu). In another survey that same year, 35 percent of the respondents reported that they did not have enough money for basic necessities in the past month (www.roperweb.ropercenter.uconn.edu). Moreover, respondents in a 2001 poll indicated that they do not believe this is likely to change any time soon: 56 percent said they thought economic conditions in the United States were getting worse (Public Perspective, 2001:45). Such anxieties concerning the stability and health of the economy suggest a threat of erosion of people's ability to maintain their standard of living, and that anxiety (or, in an age of increasing layoffs, perhaps an all-too-real situation) often drives both partners in a two-parent middle-class family to enter the paid labor market.

Changes in the work force and the increasing frequency of dual-income couples has led to another, sometimes stressful situation: women earning higher salaries than their partners. In a society that grants the male status for being the family provider, this situation creates **status inconsistency** in which one's claims to power and deference based on some statuses are not consistent with other statuses. Status inconsistency can also occur when one's educational attainment is much greater than one's occupational status, a source of stress for both men and women. This stress becomes increasingly likely in an economy in which decent-paying jobs are relatively scarce and competition for them is high. It can also occur when corporations downsize and fire middle-level managers, engineers, and other professional and technical personnel, who often then must take lower paying jobs (Hautzinger, 2003). Researchers suggest that men's attempt to reassert dominance and privilege in the face of such stresses is related to family violence (Anderson, 1997).

How do two-earner families cope with domestic responsibilities? When both parents work, they frequently arrange their employment schedules so that they can take shifts caring for their children. While such an arrangement reduces the expense of day care, it also means that the parents rarely see each other. This arrangement produces stress because it severely reduces the partners' ability to interact as a couple and their ability to interact together with their children as a family (Presser, 2000). Such stress is likely to intensify for some families in the United States, since recent trends show an increase in part-time, low-wage employment (see Chapter 12). pp. 369–371 This suggests potential for a rise in the three-income family, in which one parent takes one job while the other moonlights at two.

Most families know how stressful it is to balance employment with child care. Yet the high expense of daily child care, and the relative scarcity of adequate care facilities, can only add to the stress of families. Child care difficulties become particularly acute in single-parent families, where something of a vicious cycle occurs. Single-parent families tend to have lower incomes relative to two-parent families, and the parent has greater difficulties securing and paying for adequate child care that would enable him or her to maintain a job. In 2000, the annual cost of care for a four-year-old in a child care center averaged $4,000–$6,000, with some centers charging $10,000 and more per year. Child care for younger children costs more. The Children's Defense Fund noted that these costs in urban areas are higher than the average annual tuition rates of public colleges in 49 states, and in some cities the cost of child care was twice the cost of college tuition (Schulman, 2000). Low-income families typically pay between 5 and 15 percent of their incomes on child care, while higher income families typically spend an average of less than 5 percent of their incomes. Single-parent families spent higher proportions of their family incomes for child care, on average, than two-earner families (www.urban.org). Of course, higher quality child care arrangements cost more than less-than-adequate child care.

In the absence of good alternatives, low-income families and single-parent families have little flexibility in the care they can choose for their children. Almost 46 percent of the children whose parents work in the formal labor force are cared for by relatives, usually grandmothers (www.census.gov/population/socdem/child). This arrangement, while cheaper than daycare centers, may create family conflict, since it extends the dependence of grown children on their aging parents even as they are now raising their own children. It also imposes burdens on older caretakers, who may be less able to meet the demands of child care.

Many families in all classes suffer the added stresses of caring for elderly relatives or family members with disabilities. Most of the elderly with disabilities are cared for by their families and friends (Department of Health and Human Services, 1999). The stress of such caregiving can be seen in a variety of ways. More than 55 percent of the caregivers in a Department of Health and Human Services study reported having trouble sleeping through the night because of the added responsibilities of caregiving. Most also reported stress resulting from the limits caregiving imposed on their privacy and free personal time, and from the relentless attention required by the care recipients (see also Chisholm, 1999; Singleton, 2000).

Nursing-home care, which may reduce some of the stresses of caregiving, does not free family members from responsibilities. They visit relatives in nursing homes, and many often assist with chores such as laundry, shopping, financial management,

management of medical appointments, and supervision of nursing-home care. And such care is expensive: The average annual cost of nursing-home care per person in 2000 was more than $52,000, and some states averaged as much as $80,000 per year (The American Association of Homes and Services for the Aging, available at www.aahsa.org; www.ltcfeds.com). Such costs influence families to assume greater and greater burdens of at-home care for the elderly, including the elderly with disabilities. Family Caregiver Alliance estimates that one-third to one-half of all elder caregivers are employed in the labor market. The struggle to juggle mounting family responsibilities, compounded by the demands of elder care and work outside the home, eventually forces about 12 percent of the caregivers to quit their jobs to devote themselves full-time to providing care for elderly family members (www.caregiver.org). This may ease the time crunch for the caregivers, but they pay a price—significant loss of family income. In the absence of adequate, affordable nursing care facilities, caring for elderly family members can easily become a major source of family stress, contributing to increasing family violence in homes at all income levels. Clearly, families in the United States face a variety of serious pressures. Any one or any combination of these pressures could raise a family's stress level so high that violence becomes increasingly possible. Violence, then, is not something that occurs only in poor families or in families where mental illness prevails.

Stress in and of itself is not a sufficient explanation for family violence. The pattern whereby men are the ones most likely to use violence against less powerful or weaker members of the family, particularly women, children, and the elderly, suggests the significant role of the structure of power differentials. Men don't hit women, children, and the elderly because they are simply stressed out; they hit them when they are stressed out because they can. Men don't typically hit their boss when they're stressed, or their neighbor or the police in their neighborhood. Stress certainly may play a role in family violence, but structural power differentials provide vulnerable targets. Family violence, then, is not a personal problem of poor judgment; it is a public issue produced by structural and cultural arrangements. This analysis suggests a route to change that doesn't depend on psychological explanations. To reduce domestic violence, particularly as it victimizes women, it is crucial to address gendered power differentials.

Prospects for Change: Reducing Family Violence

Taken together, the research on family violence indicates important influences that the culture, the state, and the economy have on the production of family violence. But research also provides encouraging insights into the role these factors may play in *reducing* that violence. For one thing, where previous generations accepted family violence as a matter of course, current cultural norms in the United States no longer support such tolerance. This may be due at least in part to several decades of strong public education efforts and policy initiatives and pressures by childrens' and family rights advocates (Strauss, 2000). Simply put, what happens behind closed doors is not necessarily a private family matter beyond the reach or jurisdiction of the law if it involves violence.

Although income alone is not associated with family violence, the stress triggered by the struggle to survive is an important factor. Since limited economic means to support a family is a stress factor associated with family violence, the lower rates of domestic violence found among those in a healthier economic environment are not surprising. The warning signal in the new century is the nation's growing gap between rich and poor. While unemployment rates in the 1990s were among the lowest in the United States since World War II, more people were working in service jobs at low wages with few if any medical or pension benefits and little job security. At the end of the 1990s, unemployment rose. The economic vise that squeezes an increasing number of families increases the likelihood of rising rates of domestic violence. Improving wages, benefits, and employment security are important measures for reducing domestic violence.

Some observers have cited the competing demands facing dual-occupation families as a stress factor that can lead to violence; some research suggests otherwise. Women may sometimes derive a greater sense of self-worth from juggling multiple roles simultaneously, while men may benefit from being less pressured about the family's financial well-being and from having more opportunities to care for and spend time with their children (Gerson, 1993). This finding calls into question analyses emphasizing psychological stress as an explanation for family violence. Indeed, female participation in the paid labor force may reduce power differentials based on income contributions within the family and therefore may reduce the potential for family violence. Providing more support for women's participation in the paid labor force could be an important way to reduce family violence.

Other social changes have contributed to women's empowerment in the home. Women no longer need to resign themselves to abuse. In the last several decades, women have had an increasing number of alternatives such as programs and shelters for both abuse victims and their children. Although these projects still cannot support all who need them, their increased availability encourages women to realize that abuse need not be tolerated. Moreover, women's increased participation in the formal labor market provides them with an economic alternative to reliance on an abusive partner for financial support.

Despite encouraging findings that family violence may be declining, however, recent studies suggest that the incidence of intimate partner violence (Tjaden and Thoennes, 2000) and child abuse (www.acf.dhhs.gov/programs; www.calib.com/nccanch/pubs/factsheets) remain alarmingly high. That much said, greater insight into the social and economic roots of domestic violence are helping to point to more effective avenues for prevention, intervention, and treatment (Healey, Smith, and O'Sullivan, 1998). Most states now have laws mandating that teachers, health practitioners, and social workers report cases of suspected child and partner abuse. Findings of abuse often lead to mandatory arrest of adult abusers and enrollment in a treatment program. More of these programs are needed, even as their increased availability has helped many family members to address domestic violence.

Legal mandates for protection of abuse victims are far from perfect, however. A false accusation by an ignorant or vindictive teacher, for example, can tear a family apart. And given what is already known about racial and class assumptions in evaluating children in the classroom, the chances are strong that even a well-meaning teacher may define poor families and families of color as abusive. Moreover, laws governing child abuse frequently tread a fine line between legal protection for abuse victims and civil liberties concerning parental rights and the right to privacy. All too often these laws still offer inadequate protection for victims of domestic violence; conversely, children in poor families and families of color may be removed from families unnecessarily (Roberts, 2001).

The same cultural and institutional factors that can greatly influence the acceptance of family violence can also serve to reduce that violence. Hence policies that reinforce a healthy economy, that challenge conventional and unequal gender roles, and that provide social and economic supports to abuse victims are important for curbing and perhaps eliminating violence within families.

Reproductive and Parenting Rights and Issues

The choice to reproduce is largely understood to be a private matter, but for some families this decision is controlled or limited by the state, as our earlier discussion of China's one-child policy indicates. In such cases, the tension between the institutions of state and family affect decision-making dynamics between family members. For example, some people with disabilities must struggle against state laws or state agencies that interfere with their decision to bear and raise children. State agencies may encourage sterilization of people with severe mental or physical disabilities or refuse to extend social welfare benefits to children born of parents with disabilities (Brady, 2001; Kallianes and Rubenfeld, 1997).

Several myths prompt this social and legal resistance to reproduction and parenting by people with disabilities. These myths include the notions that disabilities are inherited or contagious, that the presence of persons with disabilities is depressing and should not be inflicted on the children, and that physical mobility is critical for adequate child rearing (Shaul, Dowling, and Laden, 1985). None of these myths are supported by evidence. The vast majority of physical disabilities are not inherited. Even those that are inherited do not necessarily cause offspring to lead less-than-full lives. People often base assumptions about the limitations posed by disabilities and the fear of their inheritance on the false notion that people with disabilities are by definition unhealthy or sick. But most of those who have disabilities do not see themselves in that way; disability is viewed as the master status more by able-bodied observers than by persons with disabilities themselves. People with disabilities tend to focus their lives, much as everyone else does, on the demands posed by work, family, and achieving a productive and full life. Finally, many people with physical disabilities and mobility restrictions are able to raise children through creative adjustments to the challenges posed by the disabilities (Shaul, Dowling, and Laden, 1985). Institutional supports, such as access ramps to buildings and streets, wheelchair-accessible public transportation, and braille notations in public areas, can make these adjustments easier. Thus any restrictions posed by physical disabilities for raising children appear to be based more on cultural assumptions and the failure of the state to provide institutional supports than on any intrinsic limitations posed by the disabilities themselves.

Many with disabilities find they must struggle against state laws and agencies in order to preserve and protect their rights to parent. Although state laws and agencies often assume that persons with disabilities are unable to provide children with proper care, many with disabilities creatively adjust to their disability to become competent parents. The woman in this picture demonstrates that she is fully capable of enjoying playtime with her son.

Another reproductive rights issue involves the right to end unwanted pregnancies. State-imposed restrictions on this right can affect decision-making processes between family members. For example, some states, such as Pennsylvania, have restricted access to abortions for minors. The laws in such states require parental notification when teenagers seek abortions and parental permission before they can receive abortions. These laws may pose problems for teenagers whose pregnancy is the result of incest or rape. Incest victims, for example, may face extreme danger in seeking permission for abortion from an enraged incestuous father. Thus these laws can contribute to an increase in family violence.

On the other hand, the Food and Drug Administration's 2000 approval of RU-486 (the "morning-after pill"), requiring only a physician's prescription, has the potential to greatly enhance women's access to greater control over their own bodies, especially in areas with few or no clinics or physicians who can perform abortions. Whether such a prescription falls under the age restrictions imposed in states with parental consent laws for abortion remains unclear .

Research on child rearing shows no difference in parent effectiveness between lesbian or gay parents compared to heterosexual parents (Allen and Burrell, 1996). Yet gay males and lesbians often confront cultural resistance to their roles as parents (Clarke, 2001). Moreover, they frequently find that the state interferes with their rights to parent. In custody battles, the courts often resist the right of gay male and lesbian parents to retain custody of their children, regardless of their parenting abilities. Most custody decisions are made in state domestic relations courts, where the judge (rather than a jury) acts as factfinder and determines what is in "the best interest" of the child. Whereas some state statutes require the demonstration of the existence of harm to the child in order to wrest custody from the parent, other statutes allow the judge to consider *future* potential harm to the child. In the latter situation, the bias of the judge regarding the "fitness" of gay males and lesbians to parent becomes a major influence in custody determinations (Lofstrom, 1998). Even so, some indications suggest that gay and lesbian parents are winning significant custody battles. Most states no longer routinely deny custody or visitation rights of parents simply because of their sexual orientation (www.aclu.org).

Some adoption agencies have allowed gays and lesbians to adopt openly gay adolescent children, but only when the child has expressed "a clear and definite sense of his or her sexual identity" (Raymond, 1992:119). Such a requirement limits the possibilities of children who need caring adoptive homes, since "clear and definite" sexual identities tend to occur relatively late in adolescence (on average, age 17 for men and age 22 for women). Adoption agencies may erroneously assume that gay males and lesbians can be effective parents only of gay children, thereby focusing solely on the sexual identity of the prospective adoptive parents and ignoring the possible parenting talents they may have.

These statutes, agency practices, and legal precedents challenge conventional definitions of family and parent. But they also highlight the role of the state and of social service agencies as institutions influencing the outcome of issues such as reproduction and parenting rights. The outcomes of these critical public issues affect family forms and family dynamics as the state punishes some and rewards others on the basis of their conformity to dominant views on what comprises the "normal" family form.

Contradictions between Work and Family

Conflicting demands between participation in the formal labor market and family responsibilities may produce tensions in two-parent households, particularly for women (Coltrane and Adams, 2001; Worley and Vannoy, 2001). When family responsibilities mount, adding care of the elderly, for example, to child care and housework, women generally must balance them with the demands of work in the formal labor market. A 1999 survey of the effect of elder care responsibilities on caregivers found that 7 percent quit their jobs to care for elderly family members; about 40 percent reduced their work hours; 40 percent took time off from their jobs without pay, with an average annual loss of almost $5,400; and, sooner or later, 85 percent rearranged their work hours (U.S. Department of Health and Human Services, 1999). Since caregivers are most often women, the demands of caregiving mean an added hurdle for women in the workplace, damaging not only their chances for promotions and salary raises, but perhaps their very livelihood.

Balancing work and family care of both elders and children commonly besets women more than men, and the competing demands can affect a woman's livelihood. One study describes a woman who tried working reduced hours in order to care for her small child, only to find her boss implying that she may not have her job for very long under this arrangement. She noted, "If I go back [to my job] full time pretty soon, I'll be okay. But if I keep this up much longer, I won't be. I may already be out. My boss says, 'You're walking alone right now. You're not committed here'" (Hochschild and Machung, 1989:91). Another woman in the study, struggling with the needs of her young child (who had an ear infection) and her job, felt the pressure to reconcile the conflict by quitting her job: "I'm on the verge of quitting . . . I'm supposed to go on a business trip tomorrow, and I have a strong urge to say, 'I'm not going.' . . . The worst thing I could possibly do [at work] is to acknowledge that my children have an impact on my life" (Hochschild and Machung, 1989:95–96). Sometimes a woman's attempt to balance the competing demands of work and family threatens or restricts her livelihood (Budig and England, 2001; Maume, 2001), contributing to the glass ceiling limiting many women's career advancement opportunities and to women's lower wages. Such stresses are also structured into welfare reform policies that demand single mothers work but provide little help in meeting child and home responsibilities.

Why do the demands of work and family collide as they do, and why do women bear the brunt of that antagonism? Although African American women and white working-class women have a long history of working outside the home for pay (Eisenstein, 1983), the world of the formal labor market was, until the end of World War II, largely defined as a male domain, and women's work was said to belong in the home. The formal labor market has been slow to recognize the permanent presence of women in the labor force, and employers have failed to take steps to ease the contradictions between women's roles on the job and their roles at home. Few state policies help reconcile those contradictions; policies like welfare reform make them worse.

The same assumptions about women's and men's "appropriate" roles in the labor market also affect the division of labor in the family. After a full day in the formal labor market women frequently come home to work full-time on domestic responsibilities, what Hochschild and Machung (1989) refer to as the *second shift*. Families use a variety of strategies to deal with these conflicting demands, but most of them disadvantage women. Some women are pressured to quit their jobs or reduce their hours in order to maintain the household, conventionally defined as women's responsibility. Others attempt to negotiate shared responsibilities within their families, with mixed and often unsatisfactory results. At the very least, such attempts frequently create tensions within the family. Men often resent being asked to assume greater domestic responsibilities.

Some progress toward redefining household responsibilities is occurring so that men share these burdens as partners with women. For example, research shows that men are beginning to spend more time engaged in parenting than previous generations (Levine, 2000), often in spite of pressures from employers not to

As more and more women (including women with very young children) enter the formal, paid labor market, the stress of juggling the contradictory demands of work and family will eventually mean that an increasing number of men will have to redefine their own roles in the family's domestic division of labor. The man shown here is tackling the daily task of styling his daughter's hair. As more men take on such chores, the household division of labor will become more egalitarian.

do so. Other research demonstrates the positive benefit of this change for the social and emotional development and well-being of both daughters and sons (Warner and Steel, 1999). But there is still a long way to go before the notion of the second shift applies to men as well as women.

Of course, the gender inequalities in balancing home and work demands do not necessarily reflect all families in the United States. Research shows that these inequalities are less pronounced among African American couples than white couples. Part of the reason for this may be that African American women have historically been more likely to participate in the formal labor market than white (particularly middle-class white) women. African American families may be more likely to view such participation as a matter of course and as an economic fact of life, and therefore they are more likely to have adjusted to sharing responsibilities more equitably (John, Shelton, and Luschen, 1995). Research also shows that egalitarian divisions of household labor being more likely in African American families is not simply a function of economic necessity. Compared with white families, African American families maintain this pattern regardless of the woman's employment status, income, and gender role values (Ross, 1987). However, despite these greater levels of egalitarianism, African American women, like their white counterparts, remain responsible for most of the traditionally female-relegated household chores like cooking, cleaning, and laundry (Broman, 1988).

A few changes slowly occurring in the workplace are beginning to address the tension between work and family. For example, an increasing number of firms have been instituting **flextime** to allow workers to maintain full-time job status while sharing more responsibilities at home (Glass and Estes, 1997). Some flextime programs enable workers to arrive at their jobs earlier or later than is customary, as long as a full workday is put in. Other arrangements allow employees to work 10-hour days, with three days off to care for family. These flextime arrangements are available to both men and women, facilitating greater sharing of the demands of work and family. However, evidence indicates that affluent professionals use flextime most often (Sharp, Hermsen, and Billings, 2002). For a variety of reasons, flextime is less viable for others. Some have jobs that are not time-flexible and cannot be altered, such as teaching or shift work. Others simply don't have the power to negotiate such options with their employers. For example, according to Cynthia Fuchs Epstein (1993), many law firms provide flextime, and even emergency child care assistance, for women attorneys but not for legal secretaries. Even unionization is not a guarantee of access to flextime. Factors such as gender of membership and leadership affect whether or not unions negotiate work-family benefits like flextime (Gerstel and Clawson, 2001). Thus flextime arrangements have great potential for easing some tensions between work and family responsibilities for both men and women, but their implementation has been less than perfect and still needs much work.

Some corporations are beginning to recognize that it is in their best interest to pay attention to the difficulties of workers balancing work and family. Prompted by the United Auto Workers Union, Ford Motor Company now has an ambitious program to develop 30 Family Service and Learning Centers providing round-the-clock child care (including care for mildly sick children and children whose parents may work the midnight shift), summer camp, tutoring, and activities for teens after school as well as retirees. Notably, these services are available to all workers, not just to elite executives. And Ford is not alone: other companies, such as IBM and JC Penney, are joining their ranks in developing programs to address the needs of all workers to balance work and family (Greenhouse, 2001).

Other firms are offering **catastrophic leave policy,** which allows workers to donate unused paid time off (such as sick leave, vacation time, and personal leave time) to fellow workers facing family crises (Taylor, 2003). This policy fosters a strong sense of community among workers helping each other balance work and family demands with the support of their employer. And the employer benefits from avoiding lost productivity and perhaps lost trained and experienced personnel. However, in most cases it is fellow workers, not the employer, who are making the principal sacrifice.

Future Trends

So far, this chapter has discussed ways that institutions such as the state and the economy are influential factors affecting the family. Not only do these institutions influence the diversity of family forms observed in the United States; they also affect the relationships between family members as well as the economic and social well-being of the family. Thus the great diversity of families does not necessarily indicate a breakdown of traditional values and of the healthy family in the United States; rather, it indicates the broad variety of ways that people cope with pressures from the state and the economy. Since these institutions are such important influences on the family, what future policies are needed to ensure the efficacy of the family, regardless of the form it takes?

One way to answer this question is to examine the experiences of other countries. Many European countries spend freely on social welfare programs that support the family. Many European countries also provide family leave benefits through national health insurance programs, unemployment insurance, or special parental leave programs. Employers themselves do not directly pay workers on leave; instead, the state provides parents with pay while they are on leave to care for newborn infants. State payments relieve small employers of an economic burden. Importantly, many of these programs provide leaves for fathers as well as mothers. Of course, the taxpayer ultimately pays for such programs, but the existence of these programs and the willingness of most citizens to pay for them clearly indicates that the well-being of the family is a political and social priority.

In addition, the gendering of roles continues to define parenting as a woman's job. Congress passed the Family and Medical Leave Act in 1993, giving men in larger workplaces the legal right to take unpaid time off from work to care for a newborn. Some men decline to exercise this right because they simply cannot afford to lose the income even temporarily. But many others remain at work for fear of ridicule, of being passed over for promotion, or even of losing their job (Levine, 2000). One South Carolina state trooper reported that when he requested time off to care for his newborn daughter, his supervisor told him, "A man's job is to work, not stay home with the kids" (Ligos, 2000). An Ivy League professor requesting parental leave was told he would never get tenure if he took such time off. And a human resources manager at a major corporation admits that he advises men to take vacation time and sick leave instead of parental leave to avoid the stigma on their permanent record. But in firms where senior executives have set a positive example by taking parental leave themselves, more men have been found to follow their lead and do likewise. This suggests promise for change over time. The state has put into place a legal right to parental leave (even if unpaid at present); economic institutions may play a key role in translating that right into practice by setting nurturing executive behavioral norms that challenge traditional gendered work and family roles.

European countries differ a great deal in the benefits they provide. Sweden offers the most generous benefits: If both parents have been gainfully employed, both may share 270 days of parental leave at 90 percent of their regular salary. They are not required to use all their parental leave at once; rather, it can be spread out over the first four years of the child's life and can be used to care for a sick child. Parents are entitled by law to the same position they had prior to taking parental leave or to an equivalent position (U.S. Department of Health and Human Services, 1985). At the other end of the continuum are Greece and the Netherlands, where maternity leaves are mandated for 12 weeks (Ferber, O'Farrell, and Allen, 1991).

Despite their diversity, all family leave policies in Europe are more generous than those provided in the United States, where, despite new laws, leave is still provided only on a voluntary and limited basis by many private (especially small-business) employers. Typically, such leaves are unpaid and do not necessarily ensure that parents will still have their jobs when they are ready to return to work. The lack of state support for paid parental leave, coupled with the scarcity of affordable, adequate daycare facilities, undermines the ability of U.S. families to maintain a middle-class standard of living while caring for their children. The European approach is not perfect, however. It does not provide family leave policies for workers to care for sick partners or elderly family members. In the face of inadequate affordable nursing-home care, and with increasing numbers of families assuming the care of sick or elderly family members themselves, such programs are clearly needed.

In the area of child care, many European countries provide greater state subsidies for facilities than the United States does. However, like the United States, no European country fully subsidizes child care, and none provides adequate, affordable care for *all* children from infancy on. Thus child care remains a source of the tension between family and work, both in Europe and in the United States. In an increasing number of families, single parents and both parents in two-parent families must earn wages in order to survive economically, and they clearly need state support to help pay for child care. The alternative would be state income assistance that allows parents to work less, but no country places that much value on family caretaking responsibilities.

CHAPTER SUMMARY

1. Individuals commonly live in structures they refer to as families. Basically, a family is an organized, ongoing, and enduring network of people whose daily interactions provide for the needs and survival of members, regardless of age

or gender. Family networks may be confined to a single household or stretch over several households and may be defined by biological ties as well as by ties of choice. They contain one or more adults and may or may not include children.

2. Despite cultural and media depictions of the conventionality of the nuclear family (consisting of two children and two opposite-sex parents, with the female parent as full-time homemaker-mother and the male parent as sole provider), the typical U.S. family is quite different.

3. According to U.S. Bureau of the Census figures, the most common family form in the 1990s was the dual-earner family. This is partly because the economy necessitates that both partners work in the paid labor force in order to maintain even a modest middle-class standard of living.

4. Several types of family are frequently found. Single-parent families (especially female-headed households) have become increasingly common, in part because of relatively high divorce rates and unwed parenthood. Many couples, both heterosexual and homosexual, set up households and maintain a marriagelike relationship despite the absence of state endorsement of that relationship. Finally, given the disruptive dynamics of the economy, it is not unusual to find multigenerational households or families that extend over several households.

5. The structure of institutions like the economy and the state greatly influence the structure of the family in the United States. These institutions differentially reward or support various family forms. Dual-earner families often have an economic advantage over single-earner families, depending on the amount of income each earner gets. For example, a married male executive making over $200,000 per year can clearly support a wife and three children on the basis of that income alone, whereas a husband and wife working at minimum wage will barely be able to manage. Given the growth in low-wage service sector jobs and involuntary part-time work, many dual-earner families have difficulty providing for themselves.

6. Pressures from the economy can introduce stress factors that encourage such dynamics as family violence. State policies have different effects. Most policies tend to favor two-parent families and males. The failure of the state to adequately support daycare or elder care causes fewer stresses on two-parent families in which one parent earns enough money to support the entire family, thereby enabling the other parent to remain home and care for dependents. Health insurance and retirement benefits that are extended only to dependents or partners in state-sanctioned relationships adversely affect cohabiting couples, both homosexual and heterosexual.

7. Patterns of institutional discrimination in the labor market reward some family forms and disadvantage others. For example, income differences based on gender mean that female-headed households suffer poverty more than male-headed households or two-parent households. Income differences based on race mean that Latina and African American female-headed households are likely to be less advantaged than white female-headed households.

8. Institutional influences from the economy and the state are likely to affect the internal dynamics of various family forms. For example, when families are characterized by power inequalities, particularly those based on age and gender, family violence is most likely to occur as pressures on families increase. The stress of trying to maintain a single-parent family is increased under conditions of low pay; the stress of insufficient income is likely to be heightened when state policies do not support dependent care, health care, and so forth, in all family forms.

9. Violence can readily occur even in dual-earner families, particularly when the wage earners work part-time and/or at minimum-wage jobs. Even in families of higher income, family violence can be precipitated by increased stress generated by the economy, such as the fear of losing one's job or the necessity of working additional hours to maintain one's position. In a society in which aggression and violence are culturally acceptable, especially for males, stress becomes manifested through violence against the least powerful family members.

THINKING CRITICALLY

1. Families do not exist in a social vacuum: social institutions can affect family forms as well as their daily experiences. What effect does the state have on family structures? How does the dominant definition of family affect families whose structures depart from that definition? Consider the families in the "Social Forces/People's Lives" reading in this chapter. From what dominant norms do these families depart? How would you define the structure of these families? What effect does the state have on their structure? On your own family?

2. An old African proverb suggests that it takes an entire village to raise a child. What does this mean? What institutions and people might be important for raising a child? Think of your community or state. What supports exist for child rearing? What is lacking? Now think of your own family. What people or institutions besides your parents participate or have participated in raising you or your siblings? What does the African proverb suggest about the definition of family?

3. Look at the wedding-announcements section of a newspaper. What sorts of information are included in these announcements? Are there racial, class, and gender differences in the information or the way it is provided? What is not included in the information given? What social message might the existence of wedding-announcement sections be promoting? What social arrangements are *not* being promoted?

4. In 1993, advances in reproductive technology enabled several postmenopausal women in Europe to bear children. What implications does this ability have for the definition of family? How might it alter the structure and dynamics of families? What are the advantages and disadvantages of bearing children late in life? What are some social implications of this technology and the changes it might bring?

5. How would you define the structure of your own family? What factors influence that structure? Consider who performs each of the various roles of provider and homemaker: What are the sources of family income, and who contributes the income? Who handles the household responsibilities? What factors influence who performs these roles? Have the structure and division of labor in your family always been the same as they are now? If not, what prompted the change?

KEY TERMS

blended family, *(474)*

catastrophic leave policy, *(498)*

cultural myth of romanticism, *(478)*

extended family, *(471)*

families of choice, *(471)*

families of orientation, *(471)*

families of procreation, *(471)*

family, *(474)*

feminization of poverty, *(482)*

flextime, *(497)*

household, *(470)*

no-fault divorce, *(476)*

nuclear family, *(471)*

pauperization of motherhood, *(482)*

sandwich generation, *(472)*

status inconsistency, *(489)*

Chapter Sixteen

Religion

Since the Industrial Revolution, humanity has become ever more knowledgeable and sophisticated in its collective scientific and technological capabilities. The evidence for this is all around. Some products of science, such as medicines and machinery, help make our lives longer and easier; other products, such as toxic wastes and nuclear weapons, threaten everyone's health or even people's very existence.

Sociologists, theologians, and others have commented on the sharp contrast between the rational, calculating style of thinking required by modern science and the reliance on faith that has traditionally accompanied the belief systems of many religions. Some have argued that the great wave of modern scientific and technological advances has eroded the significance of religion as a framework for viewing or interpreting the world. The term used to characterize this process is *secularization,* which simply refers to a decline in the significance of religion in people's lives. We return to this concept later in the chapter.

Yet for people throughout the world—whether they reside in core, semiperipheral, or peripheral nations—religion is often of great significance even today. Consider the following:

- In Poland, political rule by the Communist Party is overthrown by Solidarity, a prodemocracy social movement receiving implicit support for its efforts from the Pope, a Pole, and other leaders of the Roman Catholic Church.
- In Bosnia, Muslims are terrorized, hunted down, raped, tortured, and massacred by Serbs, many of whom are members of the Eastern Orthodox Church, in a wave of "ethnic cleansing."
- In fundamentalist strongholds, some Muslims interpret Islamic teachings in ways that justify organized terrorist attacks on their own and other nations' governments, attacks that extend to the crimes against humanity that occurred in the United States on September 11, 2001.
- In Northern Ireland, Roman Catholics and Protestants engage in violence against each other, including terrorist bombings and assassinations.
- In India, the political domination, economic adversity, and social persecution experienced by the Sikh religious minority contributes to the emergence of a militant Sikh religious movement and terrorist attacks aimed at Hindus and the Hindu-controlled state.
- In China, police and military forces harass, beat, and detain religious adherents who gather to worship in private homes or other places not registered with the government, driving underground those who practice what the government considers "unauthorized religions."

(continued)

505

- In the United States, conservative Christian religious leaders and media televangelists call on their followers to oppose the teaching of moral relativism and evolution in public schools, condemn legalized abortion, reject pleas for acceptance and equal rights by gay males and lesbians, and demand that candidates take positions on these issues in state and national political campaigns.

These phenomena, all of which have received mass media attention, suggest that religion has a dramatic impact on the biographies and life chances of people across the globe. Religion can play a key role in the emergence and perpetuation of serious social tensions and conflicts, both within and between societies. It can also be a catalyst for large-scale social change.

While less newsworthy, religion can also be an important component of the shared cultural values that contribute to stability and harmony among members of a society. In the United States, groups such as the Mennonites, the Amish, and the Society of Friends (or Quakers) serve as models of the ways in which religion can inform a lifestyle of cooperation and nonviolent actions. Even when there is more than one religion within a society, harmony may prevail on the basis of societal members' willingness to accept or at least tolerate religious diversity. This is certainly the case in the United States, despite periodic expressions of intolerance such as hate crimes involving anti-Semitism against Jews.

Yet, one may wonder about the strength of this tolerance in the United States, given the mistreatment and even violence that many Muslims (and so-called Middle-Eastern-looking people) experienced in the wake of the events of September 11. In this instance, acts of individual religious intolerance have been accompanied by a governmental "war against terrorism" in which religion plays a role. This "war" has included religious and racial profiling of Muslims and persons of Middle Eastern nationalities or ancestry. Many such persons—including international students—have been subjected to "voluntary" questioning by law enforcement authorities, while others have been subjected to arbitrary arrest and detention in jail without clearly defined charges, access to family members or legal assistance, or even trials.

In this chapter we address a number of questions:

- What is religion?
- Why is religion universal in human societies?
- What functions can religion be said to play?
- In what ways can religion contribute to societal harmony and stability?
- In what ways can it contribute to conflict?
- What are the characteristics of religion in the United States?
- What links exist between religion in the United States and class, race, and gender?
- Is there a general worldwide trend toward secularization?

Before we address these questions, it is important to stress that by bringing the sociological imagination to bear on religion, sociologists do not aim to prove the validity of their own religious beliefs or to disprove the validity of any others. For example, determining whether there is a higher power or an afterlife is beyond the scope of sociology. These are not matters that can be pursued through sociological research. Rather, sociologists are interested in religion because it is a universal social institution that affects people's thinking and behavior. In short, sociologists are interested in understanding the social significance of religion.

What Is Religion?

Sociologists have reached a broad consensus about the meaning of religion. **Religion** has the following characteristics (Johnstone, 2001):

1. Sociologists regard religion as essentially a group phenomenon. While religion is certainly a very personal matter, and while many people pray, contemplate, or meditate in solitude, religion typically is shared with other people. In the United States expressions of religion include rituals involving family and friends in the home; church, mosque, or synagogue services; revival meetings; and the appearances of ministers from television's "electronic churches," communicating to vast viewing audiences. In each case, religion is a collective experience.

2. Religion is concerned with the sacred. In his studies of religion, French sociologist Émile Durkheim made a distinction between the **sacred**—objects, beings, and situations considered so special as to inspire awe, reverence, or fear—and the **profane**—ordinary objects, beings, and situations that are a routine part of everyday life. When Muslims make a pilgrimage to Mecca in Saudi Arabia, where Islam had its origins, or when Christians take communion to commemorate the body and blood of Jesus Christ, they are expressing reverence for the sacred.

3. Religion is commonly concerned with the supernatural. People may hold certain things or matters as sacred because they associate them with higher forces, powers, or beings. Such supernatural elements, while not readily observable, are believed to play a role in the workings of the universe. For example, people may believe that there is one god **(monotheism),** as in Judaism, Christianity, and Islam; that there are many gods and goddesses **(polytheism),** as in Hinduism; or that spirits can be found in other people or in the natural environment **(animism),** as is the case with many African and Native American groups.

4. Religion, then, is characterized by a body of beliefs. The beliefs typically include a systematic set of accepted facts concerning the sacred and the workings of the supernatural. This body of beliefs provides a set of norms to guide the thinking and behavior of the group's members. Hindus, for example, hold to a doctrine of reincarnation, which views the life span as endless. People are born and eventually die, but they return to exist in a different life whose nature and level of good fortune or suffering depend on their actions in the earlier life. Muslims and Christians believe that God's judgment of a person's actions can condemn the person to eternal suffering in hell or eternal bliss in paradise or heaven. Jews who follow the teachings of the Torah (the first five books of the Old Testament) believe God has designated Jews as a chosen people to show others how to live in God's image.

5. The norms accompanying religion prescribe and sanction a particular set of practices. Religions typically involve the conduct of a set of rituals, dictated by or otherwise linked to the body of beliefs members share. Rosh Hashanah, a high holy day in celebration of the Jewish New Year, is a festival accompanied by the blowing of the ram's horn, a rite said to celebrate God's handing down of the teachings contained in the Torah. Unlike most Christian churches, the Seventh-Day Adventists observe Saturday as the day of rest and worship, believing it to be the original Sabbath day and the one observed by Christ and his apostles. Some fundamentalist Protestant groups handle rattlesnakes and drink poisonous strychnine in the course of their religious services, believing themselves protected from harm by God.

6. Finally, religion provides group members with moral prescriptions. In accordance with their accepted system of beliefs, group members embrace a morality that dictates "good" and "bad" ways of thinking and behaving. The moral prescriptions function much like social norms in that they act as a form of social control. Members must avoid the bad or suffer the consequences of perhaps offending a deity or creating disharmony with a higher power. The Roman Catholic clergy warn against committing serious "mortal sins" that violate the Ten Commandments (e.g., "Thou shalt not kill"). Violating these commandments denies a person admission to heaven. Buddhists, who follow the teachings of the Buddha—the "Enlightened One"—are exhorted to abstain from destroying life, stealing, impurity, lying, and alcohol if they wish to transcend this world and enter the absolute peace of nirvana.

In sum, religion exists when a social group embraces a body of beliefs and practices that are concerned with the supernatural and the sacred, and encourages its members to conduct themselves in accordance with moral prescriptions associated with these beliefs. Clearly, religion can take many different forms. In the next section we examine some ways in which sociologists categorize religions.

Forms of Religion

Sociologists generally characterize religions as sects, churches, cults, or denominations (McGuire, 1992). These categories are models. No one religious group necessarily fits perfectly into any one of the categories. But they provide sociologists with a way to think about the differences and similarities among religious groups, which often vary along such lines as size, openness to membership, doctrine, degree of commitment expected, authority structure, and relationship to the larger society (Johnstone, 2001).

Churches, Sects, Denominations, and Cults

The term **church** is used in a generic sense to refer to religions whose membership is open to everyone. Persons are often born into church membership. Churches are somewhat conservative institutions in that they exist comfortably with and within the prevailing order, functioning in cooperation with the state and other social institutions. Indeed, the membership of churches includes people who hold key positions in such institutions and are themselves supportive of the church. Thus churches tend to be part of the prevailing social order.

Internally, church organization is hierarchical, with substantial authority over religious affairs granted to trained clergy. Churches view their own doctrines as the only legitimate ones, hold a position of religious dominance to the point of monopoly, and actively discourage competitors. They can be quite large, encompassing the population of an entire society or set of societies. The Roman Catholic Church in medieval Europe fit these characteristics closely. Although some religious groups in the United States, including the contemporary Roman Catholic Church, exhibit many churchlike characteristics, none exercises the level of dominance called for in this definition. The major religious groups in the United States, as will be discussed shortly, are perhaps best categorized as denominations.

A **sect,** in contrast, is a religious group formed by people in protest of their social environment, including other religious groups. Sects thus tend to exist, to varying degrees, in a state of negative tension with the larger society. Sects typically are small and are organized along informal democratic lines that maximize members' involvement. The membership of sects is more exclusive than that of churches, which essentially consider all persons or citizens to be eligible for full membership. Groups such as the Mormons and the Jehovah's Witnesses have many sectlike characteristics.

Sect members consider themselves to have been specially selected for salvation; as members of an elect group, they pride themselves on being the "true believers." Their insistence on doctrinal purity often leads them to revive doctrines associated with an earlier religious group; accordingly, they dismiss any other doctrines as wrong. Lay members play a major role in sect leadership, and new members are formally admitted through a process involving religious conversion or adult baptism. Sects demand strict membership conformity to their teachings regarding moral principles and behavior.

A **denomination** is a religious group that lacks the level of societal dominance that defines a church. Denominations seek to coexist with other religious groups. This requires that denominations accept the legitimacy of—or at least be willing to tolerate—other groups' doctrinal claims. Like churches, denominations generally accept the status quo and experience little tension with the larger society. Most of the major religious groups in the United States today are considered denominations, such as the Lutherans, Methodists, Presbyterians, Episcopalians, Roman Catholics, American Baptists, and Orthodox, Reform, Conservative, and Reconstructionist Jews (McGuire, 1992).

Finally, sociologists use the term "cult" to refer to some religious groups. Among members of the general public this term has taken on negative connotations since the early 1970s because of such developments as the "brainwashing" charges made against religious groups like the Hare Krishna and the Unification Church; the horrifying mass suicide and murders involving the Reverend Jim Jones and over 900 members of the People's Temple in Guyana in 1978; the controversial 1993 tragedy in which religious leader David Koresh and his community of more than 80 Branch Davidians suffered death from fire and government agents' gunshots in Waco, Texas; and the 1997 mass suicide of 39 members of the Heaven's Gate cult near San Diego, California.

As sociologists use the term, however, a **cult** is simply another form of religious group. Like denominations, cults are willing to live with or tolerate the religious claims of other groups. At the same time, cults retain a sectlike negative tension with their social environment. The cult, like the sect, emerges as an alternative to dominant ways of thinking and is a form of dissent against religious mainstream doctrines. However, the dissent is typically far less encompassing and rigid than it is in sects, and cult adherents may even simultaneously participate in other religious groups or share in other groups' belief systems.

Unlike the sect, the cult does not call for going back to original doctrines, but often organizes its beliefs around *new* revelations or rediscoveries of forgotten doctrinal lore. Cults, more than other religious groups, may be organized around a leader who is believed to have special insights or gifts pertaining to the supernatural and the interpretation of truths. While many cults are short-lived, some go on to thrive and eventually take on the characteristics of a denomination, as in the case of Mary Baker Eddy's Christian Science and Elijah Mohammed's Nation of Islam, popularly called the Black Muslims (Johnstone, 2001).

Official versus Nonofficial Religion

The discussion of forms of religion has focused on what some sociologists call **official religion,** involving organized religious groups such as those to which we referred above. But many people—including many who are adherents of an official religion—hold to beliefs and engage in practices that depart from the religious norms of such groups. Such beliefs and practices may be thought of as expressions of **nonofficial religion,** also often termed *popular* or *folk* religion (McGuire, 1992). Nonofficial religious beliefs and practices are part of many people's lives, but they are not authorized by or under the control of organized religious groups.

Nonofficial religion takes a wide variety of forms. Many people are followers and fans of the popular religion provided by independent evangelists and religious entertainers who appear on radio and television. Others follow charismatic "New Age" spirituality figures or "gurus." Such media personalities provide inspirational messages to huge audiences. They seek to stimulate and guide spiritual thinking among those exposed to their media-savvy skills of persuasion, but they do so outside the auspices of official religion (Frankl, 1987).

Nonofficial religion also includes everyday folk practices that reflect common superstitious and magical beliefs, such as carrying special charms and amulets, avoiding walking under ladders, throwing salt over one's shoulder, and knocking on wood for luck. Many people believe in a world of the unknown that is responsible for paranormal occurrences, those that go beyond what people typically understand to be reality. Some people claim, for example, that they or others have detected spirits or ghosts, communicated with deceased persons, or traveled out of their bodies. Others believe in unseen laws and forces that govern the predictive powers of palmistry and astrology, faith healing, or the practice of witchcraft. All these practices may be considered expressions of nonofficial religion.

From a sociological perspective, nonofficial religion may be different from official religion, but it is not inferior to it. Indeed, as mentioned earlier, persons may readily hold to both. Sociologists view both official and nonofficial religion as socially significant and worthy of study. Nonofficial religion, for example, can provide important roles for women (palm or tarot card reader, faith healer, astrologer, medium, witch), in contrast to official religion, which often excludes women from key positions and responsibilities. Women's celebration of "feminist spirituality," discussed later in this chapter, is an important form of nonofficial religion that offers an alternative to the male domination found in most organized religious groups in the United States.

As seen in Figure 16.1, adherents to various religions number in the billions. The institution of religion, in one form or another, has existed in virtually all known societies. But why? We address this question in the next section.

1. Christianity: 2 billion
2. Islam: 1.3 billion
3. Hinduism: 900 million
4. Secular/Nonreligious/Agnostic/Atheist: 850 million
5. Buddhism: 360 million
6. Chinese traditional religion: 225 million
7. Primal-Indigenous: 150 million
8. African Traditional and Diasporic: 95 million
9. Sikhism: 23 million
10. Juche: 19 million
11. Spiritism: 14 million
12. Judaism: 14 million
13. Baha'i: 6 million
14. Jainism: 4 million
15. Shinto: 4 million
16. Cao Dai: 3 million
17. Tenrikyo: 2.4 million
18. Neo-Paganism: 1 million
19. Unitarian-Universalism: 800 thousand
20. Rastafarianism: 700 thousand
21. Scientology: 600 thousand
22. Zoroastrianism: 150 thousand

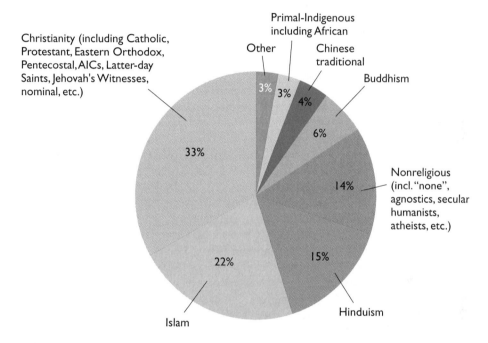

FIGURE 16.1 **Major Religions of the World by Number of Adherents**
Not only do the adherents to religion number in the billions worldwide, but the religions with which people are associated are numerous. Christianity draws the largest number of adherents among the world's major religions, followed by Islam and Hinduism. (Source: Available at www.adherents.com/Religions_By_Adherents.html. Pie chart is copyright 2002, www.adherents.com.)

Why Is Religion Universal?

Some sociologists have posited that religion exists because it helps meet people's psychological needs. Others have suggested that religion—like other key social institutions—serves vital functions for society, such as contributing to the order and stability that are necessary for a society to operate. Let us examine different views on the functions of religion.

Psychological Functions

Explaining the existence of religion as a means of serving certain psychological needs of humanity requires assumptions about just what these psychological needs are, a topic that is certainly debatable. One might argue, for example, that religion helps people explain various important events that occur in their lives—from weather and environmental changes to loss in war to childbirth and death. The causes of many events and situations that inspire awe, terrify, or generate great joy may be beyond the boundaries of rational understanding for the people who experience them. Religion may help people "make sense" of such events. For example, three-quarters of U.S. adults polled at a time when people were trying to cope with fears and anxieties following the horrific attacks of September 11, 2001, said they felt closer to their God or supreme being that year (*Time,* Cable News Network, 2001).

Consider the phenomenon of suicide. In the United States more than 30,000 persons take their own lives annually, according to official government statistics on the recorded causes of deaths (U.S. Bureau of the Census, 2003). Sadly, these statistics are widely believed to underestimate the actual numbers of suicides. Despite many decades of research by social scientists and others, the reasons people kill themselves still remain highly speculative. The official doctrines of some religions, such as Roman Catholicism, tend to view the act of suicide negatively. But religious clergy may help persons most directly affected by a suicide to understand and accept the event, may endow the death (and the life) of the deceased with meaning, and may assist the bereaved in the grieving process. In this way, religion may provide people with an understanding of events not otherwise understandable.

Religion may also provide answers to fundamental questions about human existence that can be anxiety-provoking: Where did I come from? Why am I here on this Earth? What is the meaning or purpose of my life? What happens to me (or my soul or spirit) after I die? Religious belief systems offer guidance in answering such questions, giving meaning and purpose to people's lives, especially when they are suffering. Indeed, the system of beliefs characterizing a religion often psychologically sustains people who are struggling to change the shape of their world (and thus of the world of those who will follow them).

Any debate about what the universal psychological needs of humanity are, and how religion meets these needs, would have to take into account the fact that some people are not religious or reject religion. **Atheists** deny or disbelieve the existence of a god or gods. **Agnostics** deny or disbelieve the possibility that people can know that a god or gods exist. This suggests either that people have no universal psychological needs or—perhaps more likely—that people may at times construct or adopt nonreligious belief systems that function to meet some of the kinds of needs we have been discussing.

The doctrine of the Communist Party of the former Union of Soviet Socialist Republics is sometimes cited as an example. The party officially outlawed religious expression and persecuted such groups as Jews. Yet the party's members embraced a very encompassing nonreligious belief system regarding the revolutionary origins, changing nature, and future of Soviet and world socialism. This belief system presumably provided answers to many of the party members' questions about conditions in the Soviet Union and elsewhere, justified their own existence, and helped provide them with a mission in life.

Ultimately, the beliefs and actions of the Communist Party proved unable to cope with the fundamental dissatisfaction of growing segments of the Soviet Union's population, and the political domination of the party entered its dramatic decline. But for a brief historical period, it can be argued, a belief system other than that provided by religion met important psychological needs of many people in that nation. During this same period, other citizens of the Soviet Union hid their religiosity and moved their outlawed religious practices underground. Since the Communist Party's fall from power and the breakup of the Soviet Union, many people in the newly independent republics have been openly practicing their religions.

Social Functions

While acknowledging the probable significance of religion in helping meet people's psychological needs, sociologists seeking to explain why religion exists have been more interested in addressing its social significance. This involves looking at the possible functions that religion plays in society and the benefits that accrue to society as a whole, or to particular groups within society, from its presence. Two approaches to religion, the functionalist and the Marxist, will be used as illustrations. These approaches are informed, respectively, by the more general functionalist and pp. 10–12, 14–15 conflict perspectives in sociology that were discussed in Chapter 1.

⬤ A Functionalist Approach to Religion

Earlier, we mentioned the French sociologist Émile Durkheim, who, in drawing a distinction between the sacred and the profane, emphasized the importance of the sacred as a key element of religion. Durkheim's *Elementary Forms of Religious Life* (1954), which first appeared in print in 1915, has had an important influence on sociological thinking about religion from a functionalist perspective.

Durkheim was fascinated by the fact that religion, in one form or another, seemed to be a feature of all societies. He explained its universal presence by hypothesizing that religion made important social contributions. In the absence of religion, societies would fall into disorder and decline. Durkheim's approach thus posited that religion was "functional" to society as a whole. Let us briefly examine his logic.

Durkheim believed that a system of moral values serves as the cement that binds the individual members of a society together. A society cannot operate unless its members live in relative harmony and cooperation with one another to accomplish all the tasks necessary for its survival. Therefore, people must agree on what they will consider "good" and "evil" behavior. Religion provides a society's members with a system of moral values that help define and discourage deviant behavior within the society. Without such a system of values, individuals would be likely to behave in ways that would bring them into conflict with one another, thus undermining social order and threatening societal survival.

According to this view, commonly held beliefs, as expressed and reaffirmed through religious practices, bring people together, remind them of their shared identity, and strengthen their interpersonal bonds. The rituals surrounding important life events—such as baptisms, confirmations, bar and bat mitzvahs, weddings, and funerals—contribute to group solidarity. The traditions of religion remind people that

Religious rituals such as marriage ceremonies bring people together and remind them of the beliefs and values they hold in common. Here, surrounded by family and friends, a bride and groom make their marital vows under the chupa, a marriage canopy traditionally used in Jewish weddings.

they share a history and, by implication, possess the opportunity to share a common destiny. In times of hardship and disappointment, religious rituals can ease despair and provide a sense of hope that energizes the group and keeps it going until times get better.

Durkheim based much of his thinking about the functional nature of religion on his knowledge of non-Western preliterate societies. He recognized that his ideas were not as applicable to industrial societies of his day, which were characterized by outbreaks of crime and other forms of deviant behavior, as well as civil disorder and labor unrest. In Durkheim's view, the influence of traditional religion declined in industrializing societies. As such societies grew in size, heterogeneity, and complexity, societal members had more difficulty in holding on to a commonly shared set of moral values. The increasingly interdependent division of labor, which he thought was an important element of the modern industrial order, could not maintain harmony and stability. Thus Durkheim championed the forging of revitalized systems of morality that would increase the stability of industrial societies (Durkheim, 1964).

Durkheim's functionalist approach to religion describes how religion may contribute to societal cohesiveness and solidarity. But his analysis ignores one key factor: societal inequalities. Some would argue that in many societies religion plays an important role in justifying or legitimizing, and thus perpetuating, the unequal distribution of power. Let us consider this argument in more detail.

A Marxist Approach to Religion

Karl Marx was just as interested in the social problems associated with industrializing societies as was Durkheim. But the interpretation Marx gave to the origins of such phenomena as civil disorder and labor unrest was very different. Durkheim, in adopting a functionalist perspective that emphasized the importance of order in society, held that social instability and class conflict arose from the loss of a shared set of moral values with industrialization. Marx, proceeding instead from a conflict perspective, believed that class conflict was a natural outcome of capitalism, the economic system around which industrialization was organized in Europe and the United States.

In Marx's view, class conflicts were not only natural but also inevitable. Inter-class warfare would ultimately lead to a revolutionary overthrow of capitalism by the working class and thus to the creation of a new economic system organized around production to meet the needs of workers. He called this new system "socialism." Understanding what capitalism was doing to them, many workers realized the desirability of joining with others to struggle against the capitalist class. In Marx's terminology, these workers possessed **class consciousness.**

Yet not all workers thought at this level. Many members of the working class possessed what Marx called **false consciousness.** They failed to understand that the sources of their collective alienation and misery—and the limitations on their life chances due to bouts of unemployment, poverty, poor housing, hunger, and ill health—lay with the capitalist economic system to which they sold their labor power. Instead of condemning capitalism, the victims of false consciousness tended to blame themselves for their hardships, to think their suffering was a matter of bad luck or fate, or to believe that it must somehow be a part of God's master plan.

To Marx (1964), religion was a form of false consciousness. Many Christian churches, for example, preached acceptance of one's life burdens because they were simply God's will. One might suffer in this life, but by observing the moral prescriptions accompanying the church's system of religious beliefs, it was possible to be rewarded in the afterlife. In Marx's view, this way of thinking led workers to look for happiness after death rather than to create happiness now by changing the society in which they were living and in which their children would live.

Marx believed that religion functioned to benefit the capitalist class. It counseled members of the working class to go along with the capitalist economic system, a system that redistributed wealth upward and left workers very little in return for all their labor. It was in this sense that Marx referred to religion as a drug, in this case "opium":

> Religion is the sigh of the oppressed creature, the sentiment of a heartless world, and the soul of soulless conditions. It is the opium of the people (Marx, 1964).

In Marx's view, workers in capitalist society who possessed false consciousness would suffer until they developed class consciousness—casting aside religious and other beliefs that undermined the potential for change.

Religion, Social Control, and Social Conflict

From Marx's perspective, religion helps to legitimize systems of inequality. Societal elites may use religion to exert control over potentially disruptive or rebellious groups, such as the working class. On the other hand, sometimes religion provides groups with ideas that inspire them to struggle against inequalities and resist unjust treatment by elites. In this section we examine ways in which religion can play a role in maintaining social control as well as in generating social conflict.

Religion and Social Control

Sociologists influenced by Marx's ideas on religion point out that people in power often urge the powerless to embrace religious beliefs that portray the existing unequal situation as natural and just. In many societies, a dominant religion performs exactly this function. Its belief system mutes and blunts social conflict to the advantage of the privileged. In effect, religion acts as a form of social control.

For example, Christian doctrines provided the basis for belief in the divine (God-ordained) right of kings to rule, legitimizing the power of the monarchy during the European feudal era. Early Protestants, such as the puritanical Calvinists, held to religious doctrines that interpreted material success and the accumulation of business assets as a sign that one was among God's chosen people and destined for heaven; those who were poor, despite their hard work, could only try harder and accept God's decision as to their destination. Hindu religious doctrine maintains a hierarchy of castes in part by forbidding followers to change to a higher caste than the one into which they were born, lest they come back in their next lives at a much lower level of existence. In South Africa, missionaries of the Dutch Reformed Church helped build a religious justification for racial apartheid by preaching that white minority rule is part of God's plan and converting many black Africans to this belief.

When one group of people is conquered by another, use of military force is often only the first step in their subjugation. As in the case of black South Africans, the religions of the native peoples may be replaced by that of the conqueror. European colonial powers often used Christianity as a key part of their strategy to control indigenous populations. Mexico is a case in point. Mexico City was once the site of Tenochtitlán, the capital city of the Aztecs. After the Spanish colonial forces conquered the Aztecs in 1521, they systematically tore down Aztec religious temples and destroyed or buried other material evidence of the Aztec religious belief system. The grand Roman Catholic Metropolitan Cathedral in Mexico City's main square was built by the Spanish on the site of razed Aztec temples; it stands today as a symbol of the long history of Spanish colonial rule.

Over the course of centuries, throughout Mexico and the rest of Latin America, the military put down rebellions while the Catholic Church proselytized and sought to convert and baptize as many members of the indigenous population as possible. The peoples of Latin America were confronted by the sword *and* the cross, a powerful combination that enabled the occupying colonial powers to undermine the autonomy and traditional beliefs of native groups. Clearly, however, the social control functions of religion are not always wholly successful. For example, the military continues to play an important role in protecting the system of political and economic inequality found in most Latin American nations. And indigenous groups have in many instances held on to traditional religious beliefs and practices, sometimes expressing them in secrecy, reflecting centuries of resistance to efforts by dominant groups to impose other religions on them.

Although this may seem contradictory, religion at times inspires groups to actively challenge the status quo, often in order to end perceived injustices. Rather than a contradiction, though, this is really a matter of how religious leaders and their followers choose to interpret the basic doctrines. For example, the mass media drew widespread attention to the Taliban's interpretation of Islam, which the male-run group used to harshly subjugate the women of Afghanistan. At the same time, other Islamic groups strongly denounced that interpretation as inconsistent with Islamic teachings.

Similarly, in the example given earlier, the Roman Catholic Church played a major role in supporting the system of economic inequality that benefited wealthy landowners in Latin America. Yet, as we will discuss shortly, a "Liberation Theology" movement emerged within the church in parts of Latin America, and some clergy and church members have been interpreting Catholic doctrine as requiring vigorous challenges to patterns of inequality there. Thus religious groups may interpret their doctrines in ways that support the status quo or that support social change. We next examine some examples of these change-oriented groups.

Religion and Social Conflict

Religion is not always a system of beliefs that can be used to justify the status quo. Religion can, in contrast, be a source of inspiration for oppressed peoples to struggle against inequality and injustice. In this section we look at

In his art, the celebrated twentieth-century Mexican muralist Diego Rivera often critically depicted those with power and authority, including those with religious authority, as is demonstrated here in his mural The Constitution.

ways in which religion has played a role in societal conflict that arose in connection with issues of social justice and human rights.

Church Involvement in the U.S. Civil Rights Movement

In the antebellum (pre–Civil War) period, some white churches in the United States were important defenders of slavery. Later, as in South Africa (Villa-Vicencio, 1978), many white churches in the United States accepted or actively backed racial segregation (Jaynes and Williams, 1989). Yet white churches ultimately played an important role in the struggle to overturn segregation during the civil rights movement of the 1950s and 1960s. Many white churches joined with African American churches in supporting civil rights activities in this period, even while other white churches, most prominently in the South, continued to support segregation (Morris, 1984).

African American churches and individual black clergy were at the forefront of the civil rights movement from the beginning. These churches supplied an already organized constituency of activists, trained leaders, financial assistance, political savvy, and important moral and spiritual support (Lincoln and Mamiya, 1990). The churches also served as major points of mobilization for meetings and demonstrations and helped feed and house traveling civil rights workers from various political organizations and religious groups. Black women, as well as black men, played valuable leadership and supportive roles (Barnett, 1993). Realizing the importance of the African American churches, segregationist whites attacked hundreds of them during the civil rights era. Fires and bombings destroyed many church buildings (as they did again in the 1990s).

African American clergy forged important ties and coalitions with one another and with their white counterparts. Alliances with white clergy were possible because in the post–World War II period some of the largest white religious groups slowly began to denounce segregation (Jaynes and Williams, 1989). One of the most important organizations to come out of racially integrated coalitions was the Southern Christian Leadership Conference (SCLC), formed in 1957.

The SCLC, which was dominated by African American clergy, gained acclaim under the activist leadership of the Reverend Dr. Martin Luther King Jr. (Blumberg, 1991). It played a significant role in attacking ideas of white racial supremacy and dismantling racial segregation by helping to organize freedom rides, sit-ins, and protest marches across the southern states, as well as the historic "March on Washington" on August 28, 1963, at which Rev. King delivered his famous "I Have a Dream" speech.

Religious participants in the SCLC, and in the civil rights movement more generally, held that reward in the afterlife requires people to treat one another nonviolently and with justice while on Earth. They viewed racial segregation—a system of injustice often enforced by violence—as contrary to God's will and believed it was one's religious duty to oppose it. Such beliefs also helped inspire many black and white South African clergy and churches to struggle against racial apartheid. South African leader Bishop Desmond Tutu, like Martin Luther King Jr., was awarded the Nobel Peace Prize for his role in nonviolent struggles for racial equality.

◉ Liberation Theology: The Case of Latin America

Liberation Theology in Latin America provides yet another example of religion acting as an agent to challenge inequality. In this case a segment of the Roman Catholic Church has helped mobilize its followers in a struggle to close the huge gap between the rich and the poor that exists in much of Latin America.

Latin America, as we noted earlier, was conquered and colonized with the help of the Roman Catholic Church. Over the centuries colonial powers, especially Spain and Portugal, drained the vast wealth and natural resources of this region. When the various Latin American nations finally achieved independence, they were among the poorest and most underdeveloped nations in the world. The colonial powers' withdrawal left intact a system in which masses of people lived in poverty, while a relatively small group of landowners and other capitalists had great wealth that they had been able to accumulate under the protection of the colonial state. This economic and political situation continues to characterize much of Latin America today.

The origins of Liberation Theology are thought to lie with a meeting of dissident Latin American Catholic bishops in Medellín, Colombia, in 1968, where the bishops condemned all forms of institutionalized violence, including poverty and economic exploitation by employers. Their ideas were given form and popularized by Peruvian priest and theologian Gustavo Gutiérrez in *A Theology of Liberation* (1973). His focus was liberation of the poor as a class from their position of oppression. In Gutiérrez's view, this liberation requires a society built around the principles of socialism.

Proponents of **Liberation Theology** have criticized traditional teachings of the Roman Catholic Church and the role of the church in Latin America, demanding that it end its historic support of the existing order and cease teaching that people should simply resign themselves to their fates and hope for rewards in the afterlife. Gutiérrez believed that the church must side with the "poor of this world—the exploited classes, despised ethnic groups, and marginalized cultures" (1983:37). It cannot be neutral, a position that allows economic exploitation and poverty to continue.

The governing hierarchy of the Roman Catholic Church, headquartered at the Vatican, has not welcomed Liberation Theology (Gismondi, 1988; Scherer-Warren, 1990). The theology calls for political activism in the face of inequalities, and its groundings in Marxist class analysis call for the Catholic Church—traditionally conservative and antisocialist—to take a position on the political left.

Since the 1980s the Church's governing hierarchy has actively sought to restrict the activities and influence of bishops and priests advocating Liberation Theology, and many have been dismissed, transferred, and silenced. At the same time, debates have broken out among some Liberation Theology proponents over the necessity of socialism as opposed to the possibility of reforming capitalism to aid the poor. Thus, for a variety of reasons, the movement has been slowed.

While less is heard about Liberation Theology today, its ideas remain popular among poor people in Latin America, home to almost half of the Catholic Church's worldwide membership. Its teachings have provided the foundation for *comunidades eclesiáis de base* (local community-based churches) that serve important religious, social, and economic needs of the rural and urban poor, and that have helped to support struggles for social and economic justice. Resistance to church efforts at repression of Liberation Theology has made Latin American folk heroes of some of its most outspoken proponents among the Catholic clergy, such as Bishop Samuel Ruiz of the Mexican state of Chiapas.

🌐 The Falun Gong Movement in China

Participants in China's Falun Gong consider themselves to be involved in a spiritual movement, and they tend to resist others' categorization of Falun Gong as a cult or even a religion. Persons from any religious orientation can simultaneously participate in Falun

In China, practitioners of Falun Gong have been subjected to harassment, imprisonment, and allegedly even torture and death. In 1999, the Chinese government banned expressions of participation in this spiritual movement, including the group practice of physical exercises shown here.

Gong, and its adherents present themselves as part of an informal spiritual movement that lacks a membership list. Established in China in 1992 by Li Hongzi, the movement claims to have 100 million members, 60 million of whom reside in China, although these numbers cannot be verified. The Chinese government claims the numbers are much smaller (http://religiousmovements.lib.virginia.edu).

Religion in China has traditionally included a focus on health, and Falun Gong's cultivation of practices involving physical stretching, slow movements, and meditation is consistent with this tradition. People come together in groups to practice, frequently in public places. Hierarchy and clergy take no part in these practices or in the movement overall. Participants are encouraged to acquaint themselves with the teachings of Li Hongzi, which have been published in book form. The focus of his teachings is on individuals' personal development, in terms of body, mind, and spirit. The exercises or practices are intended to move individuals to higher levels in this regard.

The Chinese government is a highly centralized, top-down, nondemocratic government in which the Communist Party plays the central governing role. The party adheres to an atheist doctrine and is intolerant of religious freedom within China. Moreover, it is threatened by the free association of people in groups over which it lacks political control. The seemingly spontaneous and voluntary gatherings of Falun Gong participants are considered politically suspect by Chinese authorities, as are those of other spiritual or religious groups. In the 1990s the government continually attempted to disrupt and curb not only Falun Gong, but other groups as well, in a government "antisuperstition" campaign (www.amnesty.org).

In 1999 more than 10,000 participants in the Falun Gong movement responded to government harassment and repression by holding a silent, nonviolent surprise protest in front of Beijing's Communist Party headquarters. The Chinese government pointed to this protest as proof that Falun Gong is politically organized and not simply a set of informal spontaneous spiritual gatherings. The government officially banned Falun Gong (and other "heretical organizations") in 1999 and launched an intensive campaign of media and propaganda efforts denouncing it as a dangerous cult. The government has harassed, arrested, and imprisoned participants, some of whom have disappeared after imprisonment or are known to have died. International human rights groups such as Amnesty International have charged the Chinese government with violating international human rights law by imprisoning Falun Gong participants or sending them to labor camps without trial, and even with subjecting them to torture (www.amnesty.org).

The Chinese government has been denounced by groups and nations worldwide for religious intolerance and for its violations of the human rights of its citizens, including freedom of expression and association. In the face of government repression, many people in China continue to practice Falun Gong. This spiritual movement, whether intentionally or not, has dramatically exposed the draconian antidemocratic stance of China's leaders to world condemnation at a time when China seeks to become accepted as a leading world power and trade partner. It remains to be seen whether religious freedom or political repression will win out in China, but Falun Gong provides yet another demonstration of the ways in which religion, however defined, can create tensions bearing on social change.

🌐 U.S. Religious Groups and Current Social Justice Activity

The foregoing examples illustrate some ways in which religion may play a role in social change, in some cases helping to inspire people to challenge religious or civil authority that supports the abuse of power. In recent years, religious groups from a variety of denominations have taken active roles in addressing social and economic justice issues within the United States (Alpert, 2000). Some religious groups have supported the "living wage" and antisweatshop movements for fair treatment of workers or have taken a stand against poverty and harsh welfare reform policies. Still other groups have aided communities confronting issues of environmental racism or raised questions about capital punishment and racial discrimination in its administration.

A 2000 poll by Princeton University's Survey Research Center found that over three-quarters of U.S. adults feel that "religious groups should take a more active role in raising awareness about racial discrimination, giving poor people a voice in public affairs, protecting the environment and promoting a greater sense of community responsibility" ("Survey Assesses Public Role of Religion," 2000). Yet, whereas some religious bodies are quite active and responsive to their members' desire for involvement on such issues, many others are clearly not. Even those religious bodies that are active may limit their activities and avoid questioning the status quo. A church may engage in charity or help to feed the poor but have no interest in asking why people are poor in the first place or in antipoverty social movements. Comparison of the conditions under which religion serves a social change function with those under which it largely is indifferent to or justifies existing inequalities is an interesting area of research for sociologists.

Religion in the United States

Religion plays a major role in the lives of people in the United States. The evidence for this lies in data on people's affiliation with organized religious groups, participation in religious services, exercise of religious beliefs, and prayer behavior. Religion may even influence how people view the nation and its purpose or mission. Religion also tends to reflect existing systems of economic, racial, and gender inequality in the United States. Let us discuss these features of religion in more detail.

The United States as a Denominational Society

Although statistics on religious preference are somewhat limited in their detail, they do provide a rough picture of the U.S. population's orientation. According to the U.S. Bureau of the Census (2003), in 2000 most adults named one of the major denominational families as their religious preference: Protestant, 56 percent; Catholic, 27 percent; and Jewish, 2 percent. Another 5 percent were classified as "other," and 8 percent of those polled did not identify a preference. Over the last few decades the percentage of Protestants has slipped slightly. However, while Protestants outnumber Roman Catholics in terms of actual membership in religious bodies, membership in the Roman Catholic Church far surpasses that of any *single* Protestant denomination in the United States.

The United States has been called a **denominational society** because it is characterized by religious pluralism, rather than the presence of a dominant church (Greeley, 1972). In addition to the major denominational families, well over a thousand different religious groups have been said to exist in the United States (Melton, 1989). Scholars cannot reach a consensus on the number of religious groups in U.S. society, given their disagreements over the definition of "religious group" (www.religioustolerance.org). Suffice it to say that there are many such groups. The emergence and coexistence of denominations, sects, and cults are facilitated by constitutionally guaranteed rights to freedom of association and freedom of religion and by a historic consensus that one's religion is a personal and private matter. Thus in the United States most people tend to tolerate even groups whose beliefs and practices seem unusual or extreme.

Civil Religion in the United States

The diverse collection of religious groups exists within a larger cultural context that sociologist Robert Bellah (1967) has called **civil religion.** According to Bellah, a set of widely held beliefs, akin to a national religion, holds that the nation and its institutions, particularly its political institutions, are under the special favor of God. Civil religion is said to provide the nation with an ideal view of itself and to promote national cohesion among heterogeneous groups. It is accompanied by its own rituals, through which people reaffirm commitment to their nation and its divine mission (McGuire, 1992).

Thus members of U.S. society pledge allegiance to "one nation, under God." Money carries the phrase "In God We Trust." Memorial Day ceremonies celebrate the sacrifices of the deceased with prayer, while presidential inaugurations call upon God to bless and guide the newly elected leader. The notion that the United States exists for purposes ordained by God, and is carrying out God's will, was a major theme in justifying U.S. participation in World Wars I and II. Politicians portrayed the Korean war and the Cold War against the Soviet Union and its allies as wars against "godless communism." In the nation's history, many immigrants have come seeking relief from religious persecution, a fact used to support the view that the United States is the "Promised Land." When political dissenters desecrate "sacred" symbols—for example, by burning the flag in acts of protest—they are considered "heretics."

Religious Participation and Belief

Religion has long been and continues to remain a strong social institution in U.S. society. One can see the strength and social significance of religion today, for example, in the highly charged political debates that take place over issues such as legalized abortion, the death penalty, the availability of sex education and contraceptives in public schools, whether schools should teach theories of evolution or creationism, and the rights of gay males and lesbians to marry. Religious groups are usually major participants in debates on these controversial issues, and they often influence public policy.

Key indicators of religious activity provide evidence that religion is important in the lives of millions of people in the United States. In a 2000 survey of adults reported by the U.S. Bureau of the Census (2003), about two-thirds said they belonged

TABLE 16.1 Religious Preference and Church Membership and Attendance in the United States: 1980–2000

Year	Religious Preference (%)							Church/ Synagogue Members (%)	Persons Attending Church/ Synagogue (%)[1]
	Protestant	Catholic	Jewish	Orthodox	Mormon	Other Specific	None		
1980	61%	28%	2%	(NA)	(NA)	2%	7%	69%	40%
1985	57	28	2	(NA)	(NA)	4	9	71	42
1990	56	25	2	(NA)	(NA)	6	11	65	40
1995	56	27	2	1%	1%	5	8[2]	69	43
1996	58	25	3	1	1	3	9[2]	65	38
1997	58	26	2	1	1	4	8[2]	67	40
1998	59	27	2	2	1	4	8[2]	70	40
1999	55	28	2	1	2	2	10[2]	70	43
2000	56	27	2	1	1	5	8[2]	68	44

NA, Not available.

[1] Persons who attended a church or synagogue in the last seven days.

[2] Includes those respondents who did not designate.

SOURCE: U.S. Bureau of the Census, *Statistical Abstract of the United States, 2002* (Washington, DC: U.S. Government Printing Office, 2003), p. 56.

to a church or synagogue, a figure that has not varied much in the last few decades. Membership, of course, is not the same as attendance, which is somewhat lower. In this same survey, 40 percent said they had attended religious services in the previous week. As seen in Table 16.1, this figure has also been relatively stable over the years. However, the actual attendance rates may be much lower than that reported by pollsters (Hadaway, Marler, and Chaves, 1993). People may want to appear more religious than they are.

But membership and attendance are only part of the picture. Polls pertaining to beliefs also point to the importance of religion in people's lives. For example, in a 2001 poll of U.S. adults, 61 percent said that religion is very important in their lives; 25 percent said it is fairly important; and only 14 percent said it is not very important (*Los Angeles Times,* 2001). In that same poll, almost 94 percent of adults said they believe in God, while 2 percent said they don't know, and only 4 percent said they do not believe. In other polls conducted in 2000, three-fourths of U.S. adults polled believe that Satan or the devil exists (Princeton Survey Research Associates, 2000), and almost three-fourths believe there is a life after death (National Opinion Research Center, 2000).

In 2000, some 77 percent of U.S. adults polled said they pray at least once a week and 56 percent said they pray at least once a day (National Opinion Research Center (2000). Prayer is a slightly more common behavior among women than men, and it is also somewhat more likely to be engaged in by African Americans than whites. More than a decade ago, Andrew M. Greeley, a sociologist and priest, examined patterns of prayer behavior over time and believes that, by this single measure, people in the United States may be becoming more, rather than less, religious ("Talking to God," 1992).

Sociologists have found correlations between membership in major denominational families such as Protestants, Catholics, and Jews, and a variety of different attitudes and behaviors. Dramatic differences have been found when, for example, it comes to topics such as homosexuality, abortion, and divorce. Just as striking, however, are differences in attitudes and behavior *within* such major religious denominations. Members of some religious groups are quite conservative on these and other issues while others are far more liberal or tolerant (Johnstone, 2001). Within the major denominations, the degree to which different religious groups emphasize the importance of serving one's self through religiosity (i.e., using religious adherence to gain eternal salvation in the hereafter) versus the importance of religiosity as a vehicle for social service (i.e., using religion to address pressing social problems such as poverty and discrimination) varies significantly. The point to be made, however, is that people's religious group affiliations and beliefs can have a strong impact on how they think and act, which simply underscores the fact that religion—as a social institution—shapes individual biographies in important ways.

Class, Race, Gender, and Religion

Religion, like other social institutions, reflects, and in some cases reinforces, systems of inequality that prevail across U.S. society as a whole. In this section we explore some of the links between religion and class, race, and gender.

Religion and Class

Different religious groups tend to draw more members from some social classes than from others. Using such indicators of class position as income level, educational attainment, and occupational prestige, sociologists find that people who are Jews, Episcopalians, and Presbyterians tend to be among the more occupationally successful and affluent members of society, while those who belong to the Southern Baptist Church, the Nazarenes, and Churches of God are more likely to occupy positions in the lower and working classes (Roof and McKinney, 1987).

Moreover, the mode of religious expression favored by people tends to differ by class. According to Stark and Bainbridge (1985), more affluent people are more likely than the poor to be church members, to attend church, and to participate in church ritual observances. Poor people are more likely than the more affluent to pray in private, to hold strong beliefs based on the doctrine of their religion, and to have highly intense religious experiences. Membership and participation in religious bodies are also accompanied by varying degrees of social prestige, and the affluent may use membership in the "right" church to make a statement about their higher social status. Religious affiliation may also contribute to a person's social group identity and social networks, insofar as it brings individuals into contact with others who are likely to be similar in class position. One's position in the class structure, then, may determine the meaning of religion and the rewards and other outcomes that come with participation.

Religion and Race: The Case of African Americans

Earlier we pointed out that white churches in the United States historically chose to ignore, and in some cases actively supported, racial segregation. Many religious groups did not become actively involved in antiracism activities until the era of the civil rights movement. But the widespread activism of the civil rights era has retreated into history, and the movement's goal of complete societal racial integration has been only partially achieved (Orfield and Lebowitz, 1999). As we have seen in other chapters, in a variety of subtle and not-so-subtle ways, racism and racial segregation are still very much alive.

A major characteristic of religion in the United States today is the separation of African Americans from whites in practices of religious worship (Jaynes and Williams, 1989). In contrast to other arenas of life in which racial desegregation has occurred since World War II (such as places of employment and higher education), most U.S. churches tend to be either predominantly white or predominantly black. A generation ago, Rev. Martin Luther King, Jr. observed that Sunday morning at 11 A.M. is "the most segregated hour of the week" (Vischer, 2001), an observation that largely holds true today. The degree of racial separation in religious worship is revealed by a study based on 1998 data on U.S. church membership. It found that 69 percent of U.S. religious congregations are almost all-white, and another 18 percent are almost all-black. Only a small percentage of congregations in the United States could be considered racially integrated (Vischer, 2001).

This separation is only partly a matter of differences in accustomed and preferred ways of worshiping. It reflects past and present effects of racial discrimination, current patterns of residential segregation along racial lines, and denominational loyalty (Jaynes and Williams, 1989). Within a society in which racial inequalities continue to exist, many African Americans may not want integrated churches that mean no more than worshiping in a time, place, and manner largely determined by white people. Black churches provide a comfortable social space for those who need to escape, for at least a few hours a week, interracial interactions that remind them that they are members of a "minority group" in white-dominated U.S. society.

Many African Americans worship at black churches that are part of denominations to which their families have belonged for generations, such as the African Methodist Episcopal Church, in which 2.5 million people hold membership (U.S. Bureau of the Census, 2003). Some 80 percent of African Americans who are church-affiliated belong to one of seven major black denominations.

The black church has always been an important social institution for African Americans, for it is one of the few institutions in the United States over which they can exercise control and in which they can conduct themselves autonomously. The church has served a number of functions for African Americans. Besides providing a key forum for religious expression, the black church has been an important center of community social life, group communication, and information exchange. The black church also has served important economic functions for African Americans, providing charitable aid to the needy, support for the ill, and assistance with burial costs. It has played an active role in education of black children, in many cases raising funds for and operating schools. Finally, the black church has been central to political activity on the part of African Americans, providing an environment within which people can develop useful political skills and from which they can act collectively against racism and segregation. As we discussed earlier, mobilization of people and finances by black churches was crucial to the success of the civil rights movement.

Black churches continue to serve many of these important functions. For millions of African Americans today the black church remains a place of respite from a society in which "race" matters.

Religion and Gender

Like race and class, gender plays a role in religion in the United States. Judaism, Christianity, and Islam tend to be patriarchal in orientation, with adherents worshiping a male God or father figure. These religious traditions have historically accorded men a higher spiritual status and more important religious leadership roles than women. Moreover, elements of their belief systems have been used to legitimize female subordination (Haddad and Esposito, 2001; Renzetti and Curran, 1992).

Orthodox Jews comprise a small, but significant, segment of the U.S. Jewish community. In the Orthodox Jewish tradition, men engage in communal worship, daily prayer, and religious studies; women attend to the religious training of children and the maintenance of religious rituals in the domestic realm. Orthodox women may not serve as rabbis, and at synagogue services the women sit behind the men and cannot take part in significant rituals. Religious laws prohibit married women from bequeathing property to others without their husbands' consent. Whereas men can divorce women, women are not free to divorce men. Beliefs and practices bearing on gender are somewhat more egalitarian among Conservative Jews, and much more so among Reform Jews and Reconstructionists. Among the latter, women may participate fully in services and a growing number are serving as rabbis.

Within Christianity women have traditionally been relegated to a secondary status. Some observers trace the rationale for this back to the writings of St. Paul, which can be used to justify gender subordination. For example:

> Let the wives be subject to their husbands as to the Lord; because a husband is head of the wife, just as Christ is head of the Church, being himself savior of the body. But just as the Church is subject to Christ, so also let wives be to their husbands in all things. (Ephesians 5:22–24)

Among Christian denominations the degree to which patriarchy plays a role varies, just as it does among Jewish denominations. Its presence is strong in fundamentalist Protestant denominations that tend to be guided by literal interpretations of the Bible. At times it manifests itself publicly, as in the large all-male religious gatherings organized by the Promise Keepers, a Protestant group that some feel is seeking to uphold male supremacy within the family. But the Roman Catholic Church, by far the largest of the Christian religious groups in the United States, is also heavily invested in doctrinal rules affecting male–female relations.

Under Catholic doctrine sex before or outside marriage is prohibited, and within marriage sexual intercourse is to take place only for the purpose of procreation. Births are to occur only within marriage. The use of artificial methods of birth control is outlawed, as is abortion. Marriage is a sacrament, and divorce is not recognized as legitimate. The norm of heterosexuality is emphasized; gay males and lesbians may be Catholics in good standing as long as they do not engage in homosexual behavior, which is sinful.

Growing acknowledgment of the existence of gay priests and lesbian nuns began to contribute in the 1980s to debate within the church over its doctrine regarding homosexuality (Curb and Manahan, 1985; Grammick, 1989). Until then, there was little discussion of the fact that some clergy members themselves were violating church doctrine. Similar debates over homosexuality and homosexual clergy have also been occurring in many other religious denominations (Ostling, 1991; Sheler, 1990). But in recent years numerous media reports and lawsuits have made the Catholic Church a main focus of attention on matters of sexual behavior involving clergy.

The Roman Catholic Church has been rocked by revelations regarding a small percentage of priests who have engaged in sexual behavior with other adults, with underage youth, and even with children. Some of this behavior on the part of priests has involved violations of criminal laws protecting children against sexual abuse and molestation. It has involved minors of the opposite sex, as well as minors of the same sex. There have been some accusations of sexual abuse of nuns. Such revelations have occurred both in and outside the United States. Only a portion of the sexual misconduct seems to involve homosexual priests, and the debate around homosexuality has broadened to include such issues as how the Catholic Church recruits and counsels its clergy, its obligations to report sexual offenders to the authorities, how it deals in general with the subject of sexuality, the desirability of allowing priests to marry, and the limited roles currently permitted women within the official church hierarchy.

From the Pope to the parish priest, the most important Catholic religious leaders are male. Nuns play a supportive and auxiliary role through church institutions such as schools, hospitals, and social services organizations. Unlike other Christian denominations, and some Jewish denominations as well, the Catholic Church has remained inflexible in its position of prohibiting females from performing the religious roles of male clergy.

Islam is the fastest growing religion in the United States, and it may soon be larger in membership than Judaism as the nation's largest non-Christian religion. This rapid growth is primarily the consequence of immigration from nations heavily populated with Muslims (people who believe in Islam), many of whom are from eastern Europe, the Middle East, Asia, and Africa. Growth has also occurred through increased numbers of converts to Islam, particularly among African Americans. Like Christianity and Judaism, Islamic religious doctrine is subject to a variety of interpretations by religious leaders and adherents.

In some nations (e.g., Iran, Pakistan, Sudan), most Muslims adhere to a conservative interpretation of Islam that is highly patriarchal and has a major impact on male–female roles and relationships (Imam, 2001). For example, women may be

The number of followers of Islam has been increasing in the United States, and Islam is now the nation's fastest growing religion. Here, Muslims of all ages, wearing both contemporary and traditional dress, gather in a mosque to pray.

restricted in their dress, the nature and range of activities in which they are permitted to participate outside the home, and in their legal and political rights vis-á-vis males. Under the most conservative doctrinal interpretations of Islam, men are the heads of their households, and women are to be obedient to their wishes. Women are expected to bear children for their husbands and confine themselves to duties as wives and mothers within the home, while men fulfill religious obligations, serve as breadwinners, and engage in political activities. Women are prohibited from entering mosques, and most religious rituals involve only males. Female confinement to the home in part reflects a moral issue. Some Muslims believe that women are so sexually alluring to men that it is best to keep them hidden away. Women may not travel without an appropriate male companion, generally a relative. When appearing in public, they must dress modestly; many Muslim women use a veil and drape themselves to hide their faces and figures. Women may face punishments for violating these rules. Since September 11, 2001, Muslim women wearing head scarves and veils in the United States have frequently been among those whose appearance arouses suspicion among non-Muslims, as discussed in the "Social Forces/People's Lives" reading.

In those nations where such highly conservative interpretations of Islam prevail, patriarchy has been subject to criticism by feminists and others, especially since Islamic practices elsewhere have allowed for much more gender equity and even the advancement of women to positions of political leadership (Afkhami, 1997). Muslim women living in the United States find that conservative and patriarchal interpretations of Islam do exist in the Muslim community, but to nowhere near the extent in some other nations. Immigrant women often enjoy many fewer religion-generated restrictions and more opportunities for involvement in Islamic religious activities than in their nations of origin (Braude, 2000).

Earlier we mentioned the concept of nonofficial religion, beliefs and practices that depart from those of organized religious groups. Influenced by their own dissatisfactions with the treatment of women by official religion, informal groups of women across the United States have begun to create and experiment with beliefs and practices based on principles of "feminist spirituality" (Christ and Plaskow, 1992; Plaskow and Christ, 1989). **Feminist spirituality** revolves around ecological sensitivity and the view that people are part of nature and its cycles; images or symbols of the divine, such as the Goddess, that derive from and speak to female experiences; and close interpersonal bonding and sharing of power with others as equals (Martin, 1993).

The principles of feminist spirituality promote positive views of women. In Judith G. Martin's words,

The primary source of feminist spirituality is *women's experiences*—their experiences of joy and anguish, of connectedness and alienation, of anger expressed and confidence restored; experiences that teach us to attune ourselves to the waxing and waning of opportunities; experiences that simultaneously help us appreciate how our lives are woven into the process of creation and the events of history, and how holistic participation in them liberates by bringing us into touch with our deepest selves. (1993:118)

Often, gatherings coincide with particular cycles of nature or important historical events. Women create their own rituals at these gatherings, which may include inspirational readings, storytelling, music, and prayer or meditation. Participants at times borrow from or reinterpret aspects of existing religious traditions (MacNichol and Walsh, 1993).

In sum, a variety of links connect religion to patterns of economic, racial, and gender inequality in the United States. Religious groups and places of worship tend to vary in their class composition. Many places of religious worship are largely racially segregated. Most African Americans, for example, are members of predominantly black churches. And religious doctrines often place strictures on the roles deemed appropriate for women. The latter situation has been undergoing some change in recent years. Yet the emergence of gatherings of women practicing feminist spirituality suggests that official religion in the United States still does not treat women as equals to men or speak adequately to women's spiritual needs.

The Secularization Thesis: A Reexamination

In the introduction to this chapter we mentioned the concept of **secularization,** referring to a decline in the significance of religion in people's lives. For many years social scientists and other social thinkers accepted the *secularization thesis,* which predicted that religion would progressively play a less important role in societies around the world. Religious institutions would come to exercise less control over people's thinking and behavior, as other institutions (science, education, the state) increasingly took over functions traditionally performed by religion.

The secularization thesis can be traced back to some of the original contributors to sociological thinking about religion. As we have seen, Marx believed that religion was a form of false consciousness. It would, he believed, be cast aside as more and more people came to understand that they could transform their existence here on Earth by making radical changes in capitalist society. To Durkheim, the increasing size, heterogeneity, and complexity of industrial societies were undermining religion, as they made it more and more difficult for societal members to cling to a shared set of moral values. Finally, the German sociologist Max Weber believed that modern societies were increasingly becoming organized around large-scale bureaucratic organizations that emphasized human rationality, calculability, and efficiency. This approach superseded traditional modes of thinking and thus diminished the role of religion in the conduct of daily life.

Influenced by such thinking, for many years social scientists accepted the idea that "reason" would progressively vanquish "superstition" and religious beliefs would be replaced with knowledge generated by science and technology. "God Is Dead" became a popular slogan in the 1960s to symbolize the assumed ascendance

Social Forces/People's Lives

Silence as Self-Protection

FAISAL MOHYUDDIN

Freedom of religion is constitutionally protected in the United States, yet the years since September 11, 2001, have underscored the fragility of the protection extended to persons who are or are thought to be Muslims. The profiling, harassment, and detention of innocent people whose religious affiliation sets them apart from the majority has not only proved threatening, but has frightened many onlookers into silence simply to avoid victimization. Faisal Mohyuddin, a graduate student at Northwestern University, comments on his experiences with how many Muslims have been perceived and treated since 9/11.

WHEN my article "I am a Muslim and I am an American" appeared in the Daily Herald last September, I did not expect the piece to initiate a still-unfolding conversation regarding the experiences of American Muslims in the post-September 11th era.

The article attempted to alleviate some of the anti-Islamic sentiments that have long lingered in the American psyche, sentiments exacerbated by the attacks of a year ago. I wanted readers to reconsider how Muslims are perceived and treated.

I wrote about my sister because I wanted to show how close to home these misinformed suspicions of Muslims reverberated. She was already accustomed to strange looks from people for wearing a headscarf, and many readers worried that my mention of her in the article made her an even greater target for anti-Islamic sentiments and possible harassment.

After Sept. 11, being called "terrorist" or "Osama bin Laden" became disturbingly commonplace. It is difficult to gauge how much of the additional harassment

of the secularization process over religious faith. Proponents of the secularization thesis took the position that "science is expected to make religion implausible."

In recent years the secularization thesis has undergone a major reexamination by social scientists, largely because the predictions of religion's demise have simply not proved true (Shupe, 1990). Sociologists have concluded that secularization is not a master trend occurring around the world in a unidimensional manner; the situation is much more complex (Berger, 1999; Haynes, 1998). As two sociologists explained, commenting on the possible extinction of religion:

> There is growing evidence to indicate that such forecasts were premature . . . This is not to deny the dramatic secularizing forces in the world. But in the United States and around the world, the religious factor is thriving. Religion has not disappeared even in those societies that have sought vigorously to suppress faith and organized religion. (Shupe and Hadden, 1988:viii)

was caused by my article, but I became more cautious about what kinds of information about my family and myself I shared with others.

Most Muslims will testify that the intolerance experienced by my sister and the types of caution I exercised continue to infiltrate daily lives. In trying to claim America as our home and prove the virtuousness of our faith, Muslims have learned to expect responses infused with anger, suspicion and mistrust.

Too often in the past 12 months it has been acceptable in America to openly express anti-Islamic attitudes. Muslims have been asked to step off airplanes because others find them "dangerous-looking."

The fact that more than a hundred Muslim and Arab foreign nationals remain in federal detention centers for alleged "links" to terrorism indicates that these attitudes pervade even the highest levels of our government.

Never have American Muslims tried to work so hard to prove the authenticity of our Americanness. We fly American flags, march in Fourth of July parades and participate in multiple-faith services. Many have enlisted in the armed forces.

Because our efforts often yield little success, many American Muslims have adopted silence as the most effective self-protection. We have learned to stay quiet because no matter what we do, people still see our beards, turbans, headscarves and skin colors.

Most of us remain silent because we are afraid to criticize what we see America doing; we know that our disagreements will connect us—despite our protests— to terrorism and extremism.

In response to my article, many readers wrote and called claiming that I was defending the terrorists— though I clearly denounced them in the piece—and paving the way for more violence. Most readers, however, responded to my article positively, thanking me for taking the risk of speaking up at a time when silence was safer.

What I learned from both the negative and positive comments was that for most people my words made an impact on how people thought about American Muslims. I learned that the core of the problem lies in an understanding of who we are. I learned that speaking up is essential.

Never has the responsibility to educate been so important for American Muslims. And never has the responsibility to be active learners in an ever-diversifying world been so great for all Americans.

The size of the world is rapidly shrinking; we are becoming closer and closer to new and different kinds of people. Unfortunately, we as Americans do not always feel as connected to the kinds of people we do not understand or those we mistrust.

Education sets the foundation of a peaceful, understanding world. But education does not only happen in classrooms and through books; it also happens in the relationships we share with others.

American Muslims cannot expect silence to protect them for long. America itself cannot expect our silence to be healthy.

Source: Faisal Mohyuddin, "Many Muslim Americans Have Adopted Silence as Self-Protection," *Chicago Daily Herald* (Special Section), September 11, 2002, p. 18.

Statistics on world population cannot indicate how intensely people hold their religious beliefs or how significant religion is in their everyday lives. But such statistics do reveal that people adhere to a wide array of religions and that massive numbers of people around the world share common religious beliefs. Based on 1994 data on the world's then-estimated population of 5.7 billion people, fewer than 1 billion profess to be nonreligious. Of the remaining 4.7 billion people who do adhere to a religion, almost 4 billion belong to the largest religious groups. For example, there are 1.9 billion Christians (including over 1 billion Catholics and more than 391 million Protestants). The other large religious groups are Muslims (1 billion), Hindus (764 million), and Buddhists (339 million). Smaller groups, but still with significant numbers, are adherents of Chinese folk religion, tribal religionists, Sikhs, Jews, Shamanists, Confucians, Baha'is, Jains, Shintoists, and followers of new religions of various kinds (www.geohive.com/global/religion_top.php).

How can one account for the persistence, and in some cases the revival or resurgence, of religion in the face of secularization? Sociologists have been struggling with this question in recent years. One idea that has been suggested is that religion may in some cases actually be *stimulated* by secularization processes. This is the position taken by sociologists Rodney Stark and William Sims Bainbridge (1985). Let us briefly look at their analysis.

Stark and Bainbridge begin with the premise that religion assures people of highly desired rewards that cannot be achieved through any other means. Religion offers the possibility of an afterlife, thus helping people to endure tragedy by promising an end to their suffering. Indeed, *only* religion can offer people the possibility of an afterlife, which means they will not simply become extinct. The existence of an afterlife is something science can neither prove nor disconfirm. Stark and Bainbridge state: "We see no reason to suppose that the diffusion of science will make humans in the future less motivated to escape death, less affected by tragedy, less inclined to ask 'What does it all mean?'" (1985:431). They thus posit that religion assumes important psychological functions for people that other institutions cannot replicate.

In modern times, religion has found itself in tension with the growing influence of other institutions. Forced to compete for people's attention and allegiance with such institutions as education, science, and the state, religion has *itself* in many instances become secularized. That is, many religions have progressively shed their traditional character. They have made changes in their practices and rituals and modified their belief systems in an attempt to reduce the tensions between themselves and other institutions and to broaden their appeal for membership. But in seeking to become more modern and relevant, such religious groups may make fewer claims about the powers of the supernatural. Indeed, they may place less emphasis on the supernatural altogether. In Stark and Bainbridge's view, the secularization of religion diminishes its effectiveness in assuring people that it can deliver the much-desired rewards of the afterlife. This being the case, why should people involve themselves in secularized religious groups?

Stark and Bainbridge suggest that typically the secularization process is uneven among religions. Thus people in a religious group that is becoming secularized may simply shift to more traditional religious groups that relieve their existential anxieties and reassure them of a rewarding afterlife. But the secularization process may also produce two other reactions: revival and innovation (Stark and Bainbridge, 1985). In the case of **revival,** efforts are made to renew and revitalize the traditional orientations of secularizing religions, as in the case of the Catholic charismatic movement and Protestant evangelicism in the United States. An alternative reaction, **innovation,** involves establishing entirely new religious traditions or new religions, such as the Mormons and the Unification Church. The appearance of sects and cults, discussed earlier, is a form of innovation, as is the emergence of feminist spirituality and other forms of nonofficial religion.

Stark and Bainbridge's ideas also shed light on why societies dominated by nonreligious belief systems, such as the political ideology championed by the Communist Party in the former Soviet Union, are unsuccessful in stamping out religion. In their view, the secular character of these societies' belief systems fails to address the highly desired rewards that only religion can promise. Only religion can address certain of people's unmet psychological needs. Thus some form of traditional religion continues within such societies, even if it is in an underground capacity.

Other sociologists have been struggling to come up with a more global understanding of the relationship between secularization and religion. This approach reflects sociologists' view that individual societies must be analyzed as part of a larger, increasingly globalized, world-system environment that influences what goes on within them. Sociologists Anson Shupe and Jeffrey Hadden (1988) draw attention to the possible usefulness of the world-system perspective in this regard. In this view, individual societies are progressively becoming more globally integrated with one another. The development and growth of the world-system involves

> processes by which the world becomes a single place, both in respect to recognition of a very high degree of interdependence between spheres and locales of social activity across the entire globe and to the growth of consciousness pertaining to the globe as such. (Roland Robertson, quoted in Shupe and Hadden, 1988:x–xi)

However, Shupe and Hadden point out that the processes involved in the continued evolution and development of the world-system create "opposing trends." As governments pursue various political and economic arrangements associated with global integration, they make decisions that often pose challenges to religion-related cultural values within their societies. Earlier we saw that the Sanctuary Movement arose in the 1980s in response to U.S. cooperation with repressive governments in Guatemala and El Salvador and to U.S. policies on deportation of refugees from those countries. Efforts by Arab and Israeli leaders to forge peaceful ties between their nations have frequently outraged some segments of the Jewish and Arab communities, in some instances leading to additional violence.

Other governmental decisions may pose unwanted changes in traditional ways of life of societal members. The Shah of Iran's efforts to modernize the institutions of Iranian society in the 1960s and 1970s are thought to have helped promote the rise of Islamic fundamentalism, which fueled the 1979 Iranian revolution and led to his overthrow. In periods of social change and uncertainty, when all that is familiar seems subject to transformation, traditional religion can provide people with moorings to hold on to. The Shah was replaced by a religious leader, the Ayatollah Khomeini, who created a state governed by Islamic clergy.

Thus some groups or populations may view secularization processes as inappropriately crossing over into domains of thinking and behavior traditionally occupied by religion:

> As a result, any secularization that accompanies globalization, insofar as it involves culture conflict and challenges to the truth claims of various traditional religions, is self-limiting. In other words, secularization turns in on itself and creates the very conditions for a resurgence of religious influence . . . At some point, globalization sets in motion the dynamic for a search for ultimate meaning, values, and resacralization [a return to the sacred]. (Shupe and Hadden, 1988:xi)

Yet another opposing trend to secularization, according to Shupe and Hadden, is the globalization of electronic mass communications. People in even the most underdeveloped nations increasingly have instantaneous access to news of events all around the world. Yet the biases in coverage and superficiality in analysis associated with the mass media may well help fan misunderstandings and conflicts between religious groups and between religious groups and the state. Shupe and Hadden argue that the shortcomings of the mass media may also stimulate religious hostility between nations and even between entire geographic regions (1988).

Thus the demise of religion in the face of secularization, long considered a truism, has come under active reexamination. Sociologists are now pursuing the challenge of understanding the conditions under which secularization energizes or reduces the social significance of religion. On a rapidly changing planet, where the emergence of new discoveries and new issues seems to constantly challenge our taken-for-granted lives, the solace and inspiration provided by religion may be humanly indispensable. If this is the case, we can only conclude that religion—in all its variety of forms—is here to stay.

CHAPTER SUMMARY

1. The continuing significance of religion in societies worldwide cannot be ignored. While scientific and technical knowledge has expanded exponentially, people everywhere continue to harbor traditional religious beliefs or develop new ones that guide their thinking and behavior.

2. Religion can be characterized as a group phenomenon; concerned with the sacred; commonly concerned with the supernatural; possessing a set of beliefs, norms, and practices; and providing group members with moral prescriptions.

3. Official forms of religion include churches, sects, denominations, and cults. Nonofficial forms of religion, sometimes called folk or popular religion, are not authorized by or under the control of organized religious groups.

4. Religion is thought to perform a variety of functions, including psychological and social functions for its participants. Within sociology a functionalist approach to religion stresses ways in which religion promotes social stability within society. In contrast, a Marxist approach stresses the role religion can play in justifying and rationalizing societal inequalities.

5. In some cases religious beliefs buttress the existing order, legitimizing even the most extreme differences in wealth, power, and prestige. However, in other cases religious beliefs inspire oppressed people to challenge the status quo, providing a powerful rationale for social movements aimed at transforming society.

6. The United States has been characterized as a denominational society, one in which there is no dominant church and in which religious pluralism prevails. Religion plays a role in many people's lives in U.S. society, based on evidence of religious group affiliation, attendance at services, exercise of religious beliefs, and prayer behavior.

7. Religion, like other social institutions, often reflects society's systems of class, racial, and gender inequality. In the United States, racial group membership and class position may influence one's religious-group affiliation and religious prac-

tices. The secondary role women play in many religious denominations reflects the pervasiveness of patriarchy and male dominance in U.S. society as a whole.

8. The secularization thesis posits a decline of the significance of religion in people's lives as science and technology become ever more important. However, the hold that religion has over people does not appear to be dwindling, either in the United States or worldwide.

THINKING CRITICALLY

1. Consider your own religion or that of a friend or relative. What were its origins? Is it closest today to the category of church, sect, denomination, or cult? Why?

2. Many people, even those who are members of organized religious groups, hold to beliefs or engage in practices that might be called nonofficial religion. What are some examples from your own life or from the lives of others you know?

3. In recent years there has been a great deal of controversy in the United States over such issues as women's legal right to abortion and proposals to allow gay males and lesbians to enter into civil unions, even to marry. Discuss the different positions taken on these topics by various religious groups with which you are familiar.

4. Sociologists have detected among people a wave of interest in new religions and various forms of nonofficial religion in recent years. How would you explain this, based on your reading of this chapter?

5. Feminist spirituality is said to reflect the feeling of women that they have been demeaned or treated unequally by conventional organized religious groups. Why is there at times so much resistance, as in the case of the Roman Catholic Church, to making changes in this regard?

KEY TERMS

agnostic, *(512)*
animism, *(507)*
atheist, *(512)*
church, *(508)*
civil religion, *(524)*
class consciousness, *(515)*
cult, *(508)*
denomination, *(508)*

denominational society, *(523)*
false consciousness, *(515)*
feminist spirituality, *(531)*
innovation, *(535)*
liberation theology, *(520)*
monotheism, *(507)*
nonofficial religion, *(510)*

official religion, *(510)*
polytheism, *(507)*
profane, *(507)*
religion, *(507)*
revival, *(535)*
sacred, *(507)*
sect, *(508)*
secularization, *(531)*

Chapter Seventeen

Emerging Issues

A key feature of twenty-first century existence is **globalization,** a process whereby the world-system becomes increasingly dominant, linking and integrating ever-larger numbers of societies into a worldwide network of economic and political relationships. This process is neither inevitable nor equitable. It did not just happen by itself, and not everyone in the world benefits equally from it. Rather, globalization is the creation of dominant forces that have asserted their interests worldwide, regardless of the consequences for others. Globalization has been marked increasingly by sharp inequalities both between nations and within nations, between rich and poor, men and women, whites and people of color, young and old (Schaefer, 2003). Nations find their cultures and very life chances are influenced more by transnational forces and less by local interests. International trade agreements, for example, may influence internal labor relations, social expenditures, environmental conditions, and the overall economic health of individual societies. And individuals may find their statuses and life chances dramatically affected by the consequences of these transnational forces.

Many of the issues likely to confront individuals in the new century are linked by this process of globalization. Throughout this text we have periodically discussed globalization and its effects on individuals' daily lives. For example, the global division of labor has produced a widening gap between the wealth of core nations and the poverty of peripheral pp. 47–52; 298–307 ▷ nations (see Chapters 3 and 10). That gap is likely to widen if large, multinational corporations continue to exploit the politically and economically disadvantaged work forces of poverty-stricken peripheral nations. In the United States, continued globalization of the division of labor means more lost manufacturing jobs and pressure toward wage stagnation and decline for many U.S. workers. This change in the labor force is contributing to a widening of the gap between the nation's rich and poor.

On the other hand, the economic pressures and dislocations resulting from globalization have also helped to energize resistance. They have, for example, reignited the labor movement and awakened an international coalition of student groups, unions, and faith communities to challenge organizations like the World Trade Organization.

What other effects is globalization likely to have in the future? In this chapter we explore four emerging issues: population age dynamics; environmental racism; the digital divide; and global militarism.

In the United States, on average people are living longer, and more of them are entering their later years than ever before.

- What does this mean for society and for the quality of life that individuals can expect to have during old age?

(continued)

- Will everyone face the same issues and challenges as they age, or are there differing patterns based on gender, race, and class?

The baby-boom generation promises to be the largest cohort of elderly people in the United States, and it is crucial to address the implications of an aging population. But as individuals assess their own life chances in the United States, people elsewhere face shorter life spans. Peripheral nations often have much younger populations.

- How does globalization affect population age dynamics?
- Why is there a "graying of the core" at the same time as a "youth boom" in the periphery?
- What are the implications for a society in which very young people greatly outnumber the older population?
- How do these differ from the implications of a population dominated by elders?

The second issue we explore is environmental racism. Production and consumption patterns throughout the world, but especially in the core nations, have had a negative impact on the environment globally. Pollution produced by the burning of fossil fuels and the release of a variety of chemicals into the atmosphere have contributed to erosion of the ozone layer that helps protect Earth from cancer-causing radiation. Such polluting activities are also a major culprit in global warming. Environmental issues, then, are global issues—what producers and consumers do in the core is polluting the environment for everyone. Moreover, consumption and production processes in the core raise the problem of what to do with enormous amounts of waste products.

- What is the role of racism in toxic waste siting?
- Why does this matter to everyone?
- What is the role of globalization in processes affecting racism in waste management?

Few analyses of the environment examine the roles of race and racism in decisions about where to put toxic waste. Yet there is evidence that selection of polluting and toxic waste sites may at times be racism-driven. That such practices exist, and why, is important for each of us, because they affect such fundamental matters as health and life span. They also reflect the unequal distribution of political power and access to decision making.

The third issue we examine is the impact of the tremendous growth of the Internet on society and on the world-system. While its supporters cite the great benefits derived from this technology, a critical analysis of globalization leads to several questions:

- What is the Internet, and what can it do?
- Who controls the Internet?
- What are the social possibilities of the information superhighway, and what are the problems it may pose?
- Who has access to the Internet and who does not?
- How does the global spread of the Internet affect world-system relations?

Finally, we explore the globalization of militarism and the rising threat of global terrorism. The Cold War ended in the early 1990s with the breakup of the Soviet Union. In the aftermath of the Cold War, industries devoted to defense contracting have had to find new markets for their goods and services. One strategy the U.S. defense industry has chosen with the apparent support of the state is to increase export of arms to other countries.

- What are the implications—for each of us, for society, and for the world—of the choices these weapons producers make?
- How might the threat of terrorism be related to the globalization of militarism?

The sociological imagination you have developed in this course invites you to examine the social context in which these issues continue to evolve. The structural arrangements, institutional processes, and social relationships that help define these matters as emerging public issues raise critical questions. Armed with sociological concepts and a sociological imagination, you can begin to explore how your biography and others' may be affected by these issues now and in the future.

Global Population: The Graying of the Core and the Youth Explosion of the Periphery

A good place to begin to examine this issue is by comparing a core country like the United States with a peripheral country like Sierra Leone. Figure 17.1 clearly shows that the U.S. population has more people in the older age groups than in the younger age groups. In Sierra Leone, far more people are in the youngest age groups than in the older groups. What might explain these differences?

One way to understand the different population distributions is to look at basic demographic indicators, such as birth rate, death rate, infant mortality rate and life expectancy at birth (see Table 17.1). **Birth** and **death rates** measure the number of births and deaths each year per 1,000 people in the population. The difference between these two rates provides a rough measure of the growth of population overall. The birth rate in 2001 in Sierra Leone was almost three times greater than that in the United States, as was its death rate. This suggests that the overall population in Sierra Leone was growing at a faster rate. It also helps explain why the younger groups in Sierra Leone's population are larger than those in the United States.

To better understand the factors affecting the population distributions in the two nations, look at infant mortality rates and life expectancies at birth. **Infant mortality rates** indicate the number of children who die before their first birthday per 1,000 live births in a given year. In Sierra Leone, the infant mortality rate in 2001 was 26 times greater than the rate in the United States. High infant mortality rates can reduce the impact of high birth rates. However, if the birth rate is high enough, even a high infant mortality rate will not necessarily alter the relative proportions of the age groups in a country's population. This will especially be the case if life expectancy at birth is low for that country. **Life expectancy at birth,** or the number of years someone born in a given year may be expected to live if the existing patterns of mortality that year remain the same throughout that person's life, also affects the size of the age groups. Longer life expectancies mean people will survive to join

Sierra Leone

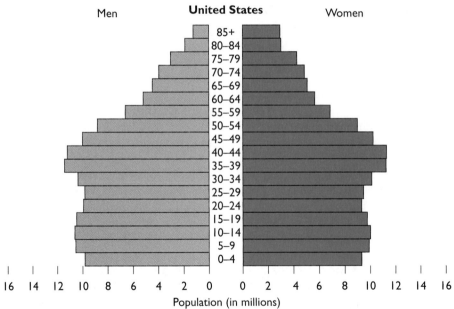

FIGURE 17.1 Comparing U.S. and Sierra Leone Population Distributions: **2000** The sharp contrasts between nations in the core and in the periphery are often starkly illustrated in the comparisons of population distributions. How do differences in the distribution of men and women of different ages affect life in these two countries? (Source: www.census.gov.)

TABLE 17.1 Comparing Population Dynamics in the United States and Sierra Leone

Indicator	United States	Sierra Leone
Birth rate, 2001	15	44
Death rate, 2001	9	25
Adult mortality rate, men, 2000–2001	141	587
Adult mortality rate, women, 2000–2001	82	531
Infant mortality rate, 2001	7	182
Life expectancy at birth, men, 2001 (years)[1]	75	36
Life expectancy at birth, women, 2001 (years)[1]	81	39
Age dependency ratio, 2001[2]	0.5	1.0
Total fertility rate, 2001	2.1	5.7
Adolescent fertility rate, 2002 (per 1,000 women aged 15–19)	48	182
Child immunization rate for DPT vaccine, 2001 (%)	94	44
Child immunization rate for measles vaccine, 2001 (%)	91	37
Population with access to "improved water source," 2001 (%)	100	57
Population with access to "improved sanitation facilities," 2001 (%)	100	66
Children (aged 10–14) in labor force (not including child slavery or military), 2001 (%)	0	14

[1] Source: www.odci.gov/cia.
[2] The ratio of people under 15 and older than 65 to the number of people aged 15–64 years.

SOURCE: World Bank, *World Development Indicators* (Washington, DC: World Bank, 2003).

the older age groups in the population, making these older groups larger than those where life expectancies are low. In 2001, Sierra Leone's life expectancy was about 40 years shorter than that of the United States (World Bank, 2003). Taken together, these data suggest a shorter average life in Sierra Leone than in the United States, so that the older age groups in the United States are much larger than those in Sierra Leone. Coupled with the higher birth rate in Sierra Leone producing larger younger age groups, Sierra Leone's population distribution looks like an inverted version of that of the United States. What factors help to explain these stark differences?

pp. 47–49 Consider, first, our discussion in Chapter 3 of the global division of labor in the world-system. Peripheral countries are among the poorest as a result of centuries of economic exploitation and dominance by the core. As a result, famine, war, natural disaster, chronic malnutrition, and poor health are key factors that limit life chances. For example, in Sierra Leone a civil war has raged since 1991, resulting in the displacement or deaths of more than one-third of the population (www.odci.gov/cia). Much of the fighting is over control of the production and sale of diamonds, a valuable resource in the global economy (www.amnestyusa.org). The displacement of large segments of the Sierra Leone population has resulted in high rates of hunger and malnutrition and a shortage of vital resources such as health care.

The poverty-stricken people of peripheral countries typically have limited access to clean water and sanitation systems, making intestinal bacteria and diarrhea a common and deadly occurrence. In Sierra Leone, 57 percent of the population have access to drinkable water (called "improved water sources" by the World Bank), compared to 100 percent of the population in the United States; 66 percent of the Sierra Leone population have access to "improved sanitation facilities," compared to 100 percent in the United States (World Bank, 2003).

Global inequality between the core and the periphery also means unequal access to medical care and drug treatment for critical diseases. In Sierra Leone, only 37 percent of the children under 12 years old have access to vaccination against measles, and 44 percent have access to immunization against diphtheria, pertussis, and whooping cough (DPT); compare that to the United States, where 91 percent of the children under 12 have access to measles vaccinations, and 94 percent to DPT immunizations (World Bank, 2003). Children in Sierra Leone are thus far more vulnerable to childhood diseases, since their immune systems are likely to be compromised by chronic malnutrition. As a result, any health challenges, from simple diarrhea to more serious illnesses, can frequently kill. Moreover, access to medical care in peripheral nations is scarce. In Sierra Leone, there are so few physicians per 1,000 people in the population that the World Bank does not record it. This compares to 2.5 physicians per 1,000 people in the United States. Even when people become ill with treatable diseases, in Sierra Leone they are less likely to have access to a doctor to prevent the disease from causing death.

The spread of the human immunodeficiency virus (HIV) and the number of cases of autoimmune deficiency syndrome (AIDS) have slowed considerably in core nations like the United States, but they are increasing in peripheral nations like Sierra Leone. This is in part because access to preventive education is more readily available in the core. Moreover, the very expensive drugs currently used to control AIDS symptoms are generally unavailable or unaffordable to most in the periphery. The World Bank noted that Subsaharan Africa has the fastest growing increase in the rate of new adult HIV infections in the world; by 2002 the region held 70 percent of all AIDS cases worldwide (www.allafrica.com). In Sierra Leone, at least 7 percent of the population over 15 was HIV-positive in 2001 (World Bank, 2003). And although infants are vulnerable to maternally transmitted HIV infection, the rate of AIDS cases among those under 4 years old in 1999 was relatively low, 1.9 percent, in Sierra Leone (World Health Organization, 2000).

In contrast, demographers have long noted that the population of the United States is aging. The average life span has been steadily increasing since the 1950s, largely as a result of advances in nutrition, exercise, and medicine. Thus, the baby-boom generation (persons born between 1946 and 1964) is thriving. And although the birth rate since the 1980s has been increasing somewhat in an "echo boom" of the earlier baby boom, it is not as large an increase as that following World War II. This means that the number of people age 65 and over is larger than it has ever been.

Estimates of how large this older group may grow to be vary, but consensus that the increase will be dramatic is widespread. In 2001, some 4.4 million people in the United States were 85 years old or older (www.census.gov/statab: Table 11). Meanwhile, the growth of the younger segments of the population is slowing down. In 1960, for example, 16.5 million children were five years old or younger; by 2001, the number had grown only slightly, to 19.4 million. The growth in the 65-and-older age group was far more pronounced. In 1960 this group numbered 16.7 million people, roughly the same as the youngest age group; but by 2001, the number of elders had more than doubled, to 35.3 million (www.census.gov/statab: Table 11). Moreover, children born in 2001 can expect to live an average of 75 years (World Bank, 2003). Thus observers agree that this elder age group will continue to increase rapidly.

In large measure, then, the core nations' greater access to life-enhancing resources based on their privileged position in the world-system is producing an increasingly aging population, in stark contrast to the experience of peripheral nations, where limited access to vital resources stemming from their exploited and dominated position in the world-system is producing a population that is clearly younger. The globalization process is exacerbating the gaps between the core and periphery. What are the social implications of these population age dynamics?

The Youth Boom of the Periphery

When a population is dominated by younger age groups, it is likely to stimulate population growth, since a younger population is likely to be more fertile than an aging one. Indeed, in 2001 Sierra Leone's **fertility rate** (the number of children that would be born to a woman were she to live through her childbearing years and reproduce consistently at her age group's fertility rate) was almost three times the rate in the United States. More telling is the relative **adolescent fertility rate** (the number of births to women aged 15–19 years per 1,000 women in the same age group) (see Table 17.1): Sierra Leone's adolescent fertility rate was almost four times greater than that of the United States. This means strong pressures toward a continuing increase in population growth rates in a country that suffers limited access to vital resources supporting life chances as a result of its peripheral position in the global political economy.

In a population that has proportionately fewer adults in the age groups usually responsible for production and labor, children become an important asset. High infant mortality rates that threaten the survival of children make high fertility rates a strategy that increases the chances that at least some will survive to contribute labor and income to the family. Large cohorts of very young children coupled with smaller cohorts of working-age adults (15–64 years) means that working-age people are placed under greater pressure to provide for a very large number of dependents. Sierra Leone's **age dependency ratio** (the ratio of people younger than 15 and older than 65 to the number of people aged 15–64) is twice that of the United States. Although this dependency ratio includes those who are 65 or older, in peripheral nations like Sierra Leone people seldom live that long. Thus Sierra Leone's greater age dependency ratio indicates a deficit of working-age people to support a young, dependent population or to provide a labor force sufficient to meet current societal needs. And this dependency ratio is further complicated by the startling number of orphaned children resulting from the high rate of HIV among adults. Since the beginning of Sierra Leone's AIDS epidemic, more than 56,000 children have lost their mother or both parents to AIDS; 36,000 children were orphaned by the disease there by the latest count (World Health Organization, 2000).

Because of the higher dependency ratio in Sierra Leone resources available are insufficient to support the sheer number of people who must be provided for. With so few adults to produce or obtain what is needed, and so many children available, children become a source of labor. Thus children are likely to be found in the formal and informal labor force, and many are abducted or sold into slavery (Bales, 1999).

The youth boom in peripheral countries often means that children are exploited and perform jobs more commonly reserved for adults elsewhere, including mining, manufacturing, slave labor, and military service. Here, a young boy in Sierra Leone wears the face of an innocent child but carries the weapons of an adult combat soldier.

Children are commonly active as slave labor in the informal labor markets of peripheral nations, engaging in street vending and bartering, and even prostitution. In addition, sweatshops and mines frequently use young children as slaves because they are an easily exploitable, readily available labor force. Whereas the extent of child slavery is difficult to count, nations often report the number of children officially employed. In Sierra Leone, 14 percent of children aged 10–14 participated in the formal low-wage labor force in 2001, compared with 0 percent in the United States (see Table 17.1). This figure does not include the number of children who have been forced or sold into slavery.

Children are also more likely to be used as soldiers in countries dominated by younger age groups. There are simply not enough adults to fight the increasing incidence of civil wars and international wars often fueled by tensions arising from the unequal distribution of vital resources. The United Nations issued a report in 2001 noting the rise of child soldiers, particularly in the periphery. It estimated that more than 300,000 children under the age of 18—and some as young as 7 or 8—were involved as soldiers in conflicts in over 30 countries (www.un.org). Amnesty International cited Sierra Leone in particular, where an estimated 10,000 children under the age of 18 (and some as young as 5) are believed to have been used as combatants by both government and opposition forces (www.amnestyusa.org). Participation as both a worker and a soldier means that the notion of childhood that dominates in the core, where children are seen as innocent and carefree and where they are protected from exploitation as laborers or as soldiers, is unlikely to prevail in the periphery. This occurs not because peripheral cultures do not value children or human life as do those in the core; rather the effects of centuries of unequal relations in the global division of labor on population age dynamics have vastly differ-ent implications for the periphery and the core. And a large, poverty-stricken popu-lation with an enormous abundance of very young people becomes more vulnerable to exploitation and slavery of children (Bales, 1999).

The Graying of the Core

Let's look at the United States as an example of a core nation to explore the con-trasting implications posed by an aging population. In this case, the growing popu-lation of elders is occurring in a nation that has benefited from the globalization process, so that more people live longer and more resources are available to assist them. Nonetheless, elders face problems and challenges.

Within the next few decades, the age distribution in the United States will have shifted so dramatically toward the elderly that society is likely to look quite differ-ent than it does today. Imagine the impact an aging population will have on institu-tions such as the family, the economy, and the government. Many social institutions will have to change in order to accommodate the pressures imposed by a large el-derly cohort.

An aging population in general increases pressures on the institution of the state, particularly on programs designed to address the issues and needs of the elderly. pp. 462–463 As was discussed in Chapter 14, people become more vulnerable to chronic illnesses as they age and thus require more medical care. Of course, aging does not necessarily entail becoming frail, feeble, or senile, but the older people get the more susceptible they become to chronic or long-term illnesses such as arthritis, heart disease, Alzheimer's disease, and various types of cancer. Some chronic conditions are exacerbated by extended exposure to environmental pollution and toxins or by other factors such as smoking, alcohol abuse, lack of exercise, or high-fat diets. The longer people live, the more these factors affect them. Chronic ill-nesses are typically among the most expensive to treat; thus the more elderly there are in the population, the greater the expense of health care for the nation.

At present, only the extremely poor are eligible to receive Medicaid assistance to pay for nursing-home and other long-term care (e.g., visiting nurses and caretakers). Relatively few elderly have private long-term-care insurance. Many older persons and their families thus face the terrifying prospect of being bankrupted by the costs of nursing-home care. The average annual cost of such care per person in 2000 was more than $52,000, and some states averaged as much as $80,000 per year (The American Association of Homes and Services for the Aging, www.aahsa.org; Fed-eral Long Term Care Insurance Program, www.ltcfeds.com). The elderly and their families pay more than 56 percent of that cost, with the remainder currently paid by Medicaid. In 2001, when the total national bill for nursing-home care was $99 billion, Medicaid and other governmental health care programs paid $55.9 billion of that amount (www.census.govstatab: Tables 112, 116). Adding the cost of care paid by the elderly and their families to the government bill would significantly increase the tax burden on the younger working population.

The institution of the family is greatly affected by these pressures on the U.S. p. 472 health care system. In Chapter 15 we noted that the high cost of nursing-home care was causing more families to care for their frail or disabled elderly members themselves. Indeed, many of the elderly with disabilities are cared for by their own families, either in the elders' own homes in the same community or in their children's homes. More than one-third of the elderly with disabilities are cared for by their children, compared with only 5 percent in nursing-home care (Cancian and Oliker, 2000). The remainder struggle to care for themselves or are cared for by other aging relatives and friends. The impact this has on families is important. Children of elderly parents with disabilities are often ill-equipped to care for them, since many of the children either are working couples or are unemployed or underemployed. In this way class influences the impact of aging on families.

Gender figures prominently in the effects of elder care. Studies indicate that women are caregivers far more often than men (Merrill, 1997). One study found that 72 percent of elder caregivers were women (Cancian and Oliker, 2000). Such women spend an average of 6 to 10 hours per week on elder care, and many spend much more, depending on the severity of the dependence (Lechner and Neal, 1999).

An aging population also places pressures on the Social Security system. Originally designed as a social contract with U.S. workers, the Social Security system relies on payments from current workers to pay benefits to current retirees; the assumption is that when these current workers retire and begin to collect their entitlements, enough workers will fill their vacated places in the labor market to support them throughout retirement. This assumption may be in jeopardy in the coming decades. If more elderly people in the United States are living longer after they retire, and fewer younger and middle-aged people are in the labor force to pay their entitlements, pressures on the Social Security system could mount to crisis proportions. Indeed, over the past decade many people have debated whether the system is on the verge of bankruptcy or in danger of becoming so. (This debate, of course, conspicuously ignores the option of reducing spending in other areas such as defense or raising taxes on wealthy corporations and individuals, to better meet Social Security needs.)

Such budgetary fears raise the question of the social construction of retirement. Currently, most workers retire between 62 and 65 years of age. Most retire willingly, but for many retirement is involuntary (Neubeck and Neubeck, 1997). Because of improvements in health care and health awareness, most people in the United States are still quite healthy physically and mentally when they retire, and many can expect to live 20 or more additional years. For some, this creates a role strain, for a person may want to fulfill the obligations of a productive citizen but may not have the opportunity to do so. What does retirement mean, then, when a retiree is still able and willing to be productive? And how is an aging person to live for 20 or more years on an income that is just a fraction of that on which he or she may have been relying?

Some retirees seek employment after retirement. Fast-food firms such as McDonald's have made a point of hiring retirees as counter workers. Retirees who do not necessarily need the income of a paying job but want to continue making positive contributions to their communities often perform important volunteer services. Many donate time and skills as daycare workers, hospital aides, soup-kitchen aides, cancer care volunteers, and so forth. All these pursuits suggest that the social con-

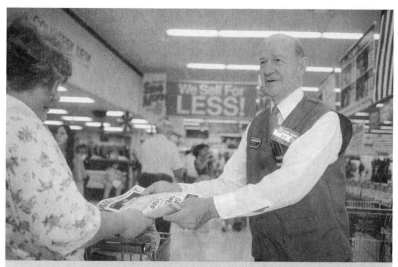

Retirement often means a seriously reduced income. For many retirees it also means being forced out of the labor market at a time when they are still capable of being productive. While some retirees engage in volunteer work to continue making important contributions to society, others find they can be productive and earn much-needed income by working in places like the retail store shown here.

struction of retirement in the United States is driven by antiquated stereotypes of elderly fragility, senility, and declining productivity. Yet a shrinking labor market encourages continuation of these stereotypes, as younger workers pressure older workers to retire to make room for them, and corporations add to the pressure in their search for cheaper (younger) workers.

In addition to its effects on the economy, the state, and the family, the aging of America also affects the political process. As the baby-boom generation ages and lives longer, it has a greater impact on voting and the legislative process, in part because it represents one of the largest age cohorts in the voting population. Studies show that political participation rates tend to increase with age (www.census.gov/ pp. 335; 345–347 statab: Table 477). As we saw in Chapter 11, politicians are paying increasing attention to the issues and needs of older people because of their significant and growing number—and because they vote.

Of course, political clout among elders is dependent on the development of **age consciousness,** the awareness of common interests based on age. Older people can have a tremendous political impact by organizing and mobilizing their collective effort for change. Opportunities for increasing age consciousness are growing as a result of such trends as segregated housing for the elderly in retirement communities and programs that stimulate interaction among the elderly, such as senior centers.

Their potential for organized political clout has not been lost on aging persons in the United States. They have been organizing into powerful political groups ever since the Gray Panthers was founded in the 1970s. With a current membership of more than 70,000 in over 50 networked chapters, the Gray Panthers have frequently challenged ageist stereotypes and age discrimination in the workplace and elsewhere. They also seek to increase awareness among legislators of the need for policies to assist and protect the elderly (see http://www.graypanthers.org/). Much larger groups, such as the 35 million-member AARP (formerly the American Association of Retired Persons), have a greater impact on the political process. As the elderly population increases, and as elders find their voice through influential organizations, the political process will pay more and more attention to issues and interests affecting them.

The shift in the population pyramid has an interesting effect on a culture that has focused primarily on youth since the 1960s, when baby boomers became relatively affluent and the largest and most vocal segment of the population. Films, television, and advertising have strongly celebrated youth. Over the past several years, however, more commercials have been appearing for products pitched to an aging population, such as adult disposable diapers for incontinence, vitamins designed for older people, electric light switches that operate at the clap of a hand, voice-activated emergency alert systems, and life insurance programs available regardless of age. Where once only young models could be seen in advertisements and fashion magazines, now increasingly older, gray-haired models peer out from the pages and the screen. Television programs such as *Judging Amy* and *The West Wing* and reruns of *Golden Girls* feature older actors, who are depicted as vibrant, sexually active, and productive.

Still, the dominant culture's emphasis on the desirability of youth has hardly disappeared. As the population ages, advertisements offer antibaldness products and hair dyes to cover the gray, facial creams to smooth out wrinkles, and senior citizen exercise videotapes promising to make their users look and feel young. While people may be living longer, advertisers emphasize that they need not look "old." The population shift to older cohorts, then, also increasingly affects the culture, whose themes simultaneously celebrate and resist the aging process.

Why is this population shift of concern to you now? First, you may have parents or other relatives who are currently elderly, and thus you are learning firsthand what the population shift already means to their existence (and to that of their primary caretakers). Second, if current trends continue, everyone may eventually become part of those increasingly larger older age groups. Who will underwrite the retirement income and health care programs on which older people will have to rely? How will decisions made today concerning the federal budget and spending affect the reliability of programs such as Medicare, Social Security, and elder care when people are eligible for them? How will current decisions regarding a national health care policy affect the quality of life in retirement? How can people improve their economic well-being while they are in the labor force so as to protect their life chances when they retire? It is important not to frame questions and analyses in terms of a pitched battle between the young and the elderly; rather, these should be framed in the context of people's life-cycle relationships to such macro-level social structures as the economy, the state, and the intersection of race, class, gender, and age within institutions, all of which are affected by the relationship between the United States and others in the globalization process that is currently under way.

Environment: Toxic Imperialism and Environmental Racism

No one lives in environmental isolation. What happens to the environment in one part of the world ultimately affects the environment in other parts of the world. Never was this more clear than in 1986, when an overheated nuclear power reactor in Chernobyl in the former Soviet Union's Ukraine released the most radioactivity into the atmosphere in world history, "equivalent to the fallout from several dozen Hiroshima bombs" (Hohenemser and Renn, 1988:5). Notably, the fallout did not remain over or near Ukraine alone, although the largest impact was clearly in the former Soviet Union and western Europe; it traveled to cover the entire Northern Hemisphere. That event was certainly notable in its enormity, yet it was not simply an isolated freak accident. It raises questions about the relationship between environmental danger and inequality within and between societies, inequality that is in many instances increasing with globalization.

National and worldwide attention has focused on environmental concerns since the first Earth Day celebration in 1970. Increasing awareness of the effects individuals' daily actions have on the health and stability of the environment has caused many to modify their lifestyles and patterns of consumption. Political action has increasingly focused on industrial production and on ways to curb corporate contributions to environmental instability and global warming. However, the sociological imagination leads to several questions: What effect does globalization have on the environment? Does everyone suffer the consequences of environmental pollution equally? How are toxic waste sites selected and pollution cleanups assigned? Are they distributed equitably throughout the world and in this country? How do power relationships and processes affect the selection of sites for toxic waste dumps?

Toxic Imperialism

Scant attention has been paid to exploring the possible intersection of environmental issues and issues of globalization and inequality. Yet evidence suggests that this question warrants close scrutiny (Simon, 2000). For example, international trade agreements appear likely to make the environment worse, as countries seek to minimize or eliminate what they perceive to be barriers to trade and production. The North American Free Trade Agreement (NAFTA), in effect since 1994, has already been implicated in the environmental deterioration of the *maquilladora* factory zones lining the United States–Mexico border as a result of relaxed environmental protection standards in the United States and Mexico, selective enforcement of standards, and the improper disposal of toxic waste byproducts of production—all in the interest of enhancing trade and production (www.globalexchange.org/ftaa/topten.html). This situation is likely to spread, since the United States is currently engaged in a push to expand NAFTA to all of Central and South America.

In addition, corporations and core nations like the United States have been dumping toxic wastes and polluting products in peripheral nations such as Nigeria, Guinea, and Haiti, as well as in black townships in South Africa (Clapp, 2001;

Barrels of toxic waste, as well as polluting industries themselves, are frequently located in communities populated by the poor and people of color, a practice referred to by some as "environmental racism."

Marks and Brown, 1990). U.S. corporations like HoltraChem Manufacturing Company have dumped hundreds of tons of mercury waste products in India (Judd, 2001). And tons of hazardous waste from Australia, Germany, and the United States are routinely dumped in South Pacific nations and islands (www.greenleft.org). The Earth Day/Wall Street Action Group has referred to toxic dumping in semiperipheral and peripheral nations by major multinational corporations and core nations as **toxic imperialism** (Cohen, 1990).

Why are such nations targeted as viable sites for toxic waste dumping? Part of the answer can be understood in the context of world-system relations. Semiperipheral and peripheral nations are far less powerful and much poorer economically than core nations like the United States. Indeed, overwhelming debt has prompted some peripheral nations such as the Philippines and Cambodia to accept toxic waste in exchange for payments as a way of raising money to reduce debt burdens (www.hrw.org).

Loopholes in United States federal laws regulating toxic materials, especially the Federal Insecticide, Fungicide and Rodenticide Act (FIFRA), have encouraged exports of toxic materials, even when use of these substances has been banned in the United States. Legislative efforts since 1978 to close the loopholes have failed. Federal policy initiatives and lax enforcement of regulatory laws have made it profitable for corporations to export products that are deemed a threat to U.S. residents (O'Neill, 2000). Few poor nations have regulatory policies governing toxic substances and pesticides. Governments in those that do often do not adequately enforce them. This gives the large international pesticide producers and toxic waste producers the freedom to export these substances without restriction (www.panna.org/panna/resources).

The governments of many nations do not wish to publicly acknowledge the level of environmental poisoning caused by toxic imports. Press reports of contaminated food, water, and land could severely depress tourism in poor nations. Furthermore, many of their governments are understandably reluctant to admit that their lack of legal controls or inability to enforce them has aided and abetted the endangerment of their own citizens. Finally, any admission that toxic substances are present in the land or water of other nations invites investigation by the U.S. Food and Drug Administration (FDA) of all food imports into this country, thereby potentially damaging poor nations' important source of trade income (Weir and Schapiro, 1981). Taken together, these factors give corporations based in core nations a free hand to dump unsafe substances and toxic wastes in poorer areas of the world.

The corporations that are most likely to pollute the poorer nations may be based in the core, but they are acting like stateless entities: huge multinational corporations doing business all around the world, globally spreading their toxic waste, seemingly beyond control by governments. But multinational corporations do not restrict their practice of dumping of toxic wastes to poorer nations. They also pollute neighborhoods in core nations like the United States (Simon, 2000). What is notable, however, is that they do not spread their wastes randomly. When they dump toxic waste in the United States they tend to select neighborhoods of color and poverty, a practice called environmental racism.

Environmental Racism

The kinds of relationships that exist between global inequality and environmental degradation are reproduced more locally. A growing body of research has begun to focus on the issue of inequality and toxic pollution within the United States (Cassidy, Judge, and Sommers, 2000; Stretskey and Hogan, 1998). In a 1987 study of the relationship between toxic wastes and racial composition of communities, the Commission for Racial Justice (under the auspices of the United Church of Christ) cited "clear patterns which show that communities with greater minority percentages of the population are more likely to be the sites of commercial hazardous waste facilities. The possibility that these patterns resulted by chance is virtually impossible" (Chavis and Lee, 1987:23). Little had changed more than a decade later (Hind and Reese, 1998; Maher, 1998).

Commission for Racial Justice researchers found that poverty-stricken neighborhoods and communities of color continue to bear a disproportionate burden as recipients of the 6 billion tons of toxic waste and environmental pollution produced in the United States annually. As many as 50 percent of African Americans and 60 percent of Latinos/Latinas live in communities in which levels of air pollutants exceed federal regulations (Hatfield, 2003). Indeed, the commission found that communities in which commercial waste sites existed had twice the proportion of people of color as communities that did not have any such sites. And communities that had two or more commercial toxic waste sites had more than three times the proportion of people of color than those that had no such sites. Moreover, racial composition correlated with the location of a commercial toxic waste site more strongly than any other variable, including socioeconomic variables such as average household income and average home values (Been, 1994; Pollack and Vitas, 1995). Researchers came to similar conclusions regarding air pollution (Daniels and Friedman, 1999; Gelobter, 1992), as well as the effects of toxic waste dumping on people who consume fish caught in dumpsite waters (West, et al., 1992).

Some researchers refer to this pattern as a problem of **environmental racism** (Lee, 1992, 1994; Westra and Lawson, 2001), in which an invisible, unearned privilege of whiteness and affluence is the relative freedom from pollution in one's immediate neighborhood. Why have communities of color in the United States become the disproportionate recipients of toxic waste sites? Various studies have begun to unravel this issue. The sociological imagination points to at least four important factors related to inequality.

First, land values in neighborhoods of color and heavily integrated communities are often depressed. This is because properties in white communities are frequently defined by real estate agencies and mortgaging banks as more desirable investments. In fact, banks often **redline** heavily integrated communities and neighborhoods of color, a practice that defines these areas as ineligible for mortgage or repair loans or for small-business loans. One study found that in 2001 African Americans were more than twice as likely to be denied a mortgage as white applicants, regardless of income; Latinos/Latinas were 1.5 times more likely than white applicants to be denied such loans (www.uaw.org). Redlining also frequently hinders small business owners' attempts to obtain insurance, a situation which can escalate the flight of businesses from communities in transition. Land is consequently readily available and cheap, with owners eager for a buyer (Hamilton, J., 1995).

Furthermore, the combination of racial discrimination in housing and poverty often means that both poor and middle-class people of color have far less mobility than middle-class whites. They may not be able to sell their property or afford to move from a community where toxic waste sites are located (Boerner and Lambert, 1995).

People of color also often have fewer political and economic resources and often are not well organized politically. When commercial toxic waste sites are targeted for their communities, they are not able to respond with as strong an organized opposition as that put forth by white middle-class communities (Bullard and Wright, 1987; Chavis and Lee, 1987). And beyond the question of organization is the lack of access to influential governmental and nongovernmental leaders and institutions. People of color and the poor are underrepresented in government and almost entirely absent on policy boards and other key advisory bodies (Pinderhughs, 1996). Therefore, their interests and concerns are far less likely to be heard. As a result, governmental agencies charged with overseeing the environment not only do not recognize the relationship between systems of racial and economic inequality and environmental issues, but they also fail to protect communities of color and poverty. Penalties for violations of environmental laws are often more lax or poorly enforced in these communities compared with those in affluent white communities (Boerner and Lambert, 1995). Mainstream nongovernmental environmental organizations are not any more likely to recognize the role of systems of inequality and to articulate the problem, as most are primarily concerned with the conservation of nature and wildlife preservation rather than with the human health risks of exposure to toxic waste (Austin and Schill, 1994).

Finally, those promoting the toxic waste facilities often promise jobs and other economic benefits for the host communities, thereby mitigating some of the opposition that might develop. Communities of color may have unemployment rates that are two to three times higher than those of white communities. Economically depressed communities are thus vulnerable to promises of much-needed jobs (Hamilton, J., 1995). Nevertheless, people of color have concerns about dump sites in their neighborhoods. Evidence suggests that African Americans are just as concerned about the environment as are whites (Mohai, 1990). Indeed, one recent study found that the poor and people of color are *more* concerned with environmental issues than whites and the affluent (Uyeki and Holland, 2000). Native Americans have organized an environmental action group, Citizens against Ruining Our Environment, which helps residents on tribal lands resist toxic waste dumping in their communities. This task is complicated by the fact that Native lands are not subject to the same state and federal regulations as non-Native lands (Wei, 1991). And the National Association for the Advancement of Colored People increasingly links civil rights issues to the issue of environmental racism (Cole and Foster, 2001; www.naacp.org).

Despite these resistance efforts, toxic waste sitings continue to be overwhelmingly located in communities of color. Resistance is hampered by lack of information. Even when grassroots activists attempt to resist these facilities, they often find it difficult to obtain key information necessary to organize their efforts. Community groups often note that they confronted obstacles when they tried to obtain information, and many cite government agencies as those obstacles (Bullard, 1993). Chavis and Lee (1987) noted that such "institutional resistance" to providing access to information is likely to increase when agencies deal with groups that they believe are not powerful (see also Gould, 1993).

It is crucial for everyone to understand environmental racism and toxic imperialism as a public issue. Why? First, when toxic wastes and other unsafe materials are exported to underdeveloped countries, they can return to the United States in imports of such things as produce, coffee, meat, and fish. Notably, toxic pesticide dumping remains high: between 1997 and 2000 U.S. exports of toxic pesticides increased by 15 percent over the exports between 1992 and 1996 (www.panna.org/panna/resources/panups/panupfi20020111.dv.html). Toxic wastes and carcinogenic materials such as mercury, dioxins, and lead dumped in other countries thus find their way into the food chain, and they may return to the United States and onto people's dinner plates.

The factors uncovered by studies of the relationship between inequality and environmental danger suggest that *all* communities are potentially at risk. That is, any community that is not well organized or does not have access to political and economic resources is vulnerable. Furthermore, in an economy where jobs are continuing to disappear, many communities that are stable now could change and become susceptible to the appeal of jobs and financial compensation in exchange for accepting the risks and hazards of toxic waste facilities. Similarly, a recessionary economy frequently attacks the real estate values of many communities, including previously stable middle-class white neighborhoods. Such depreciated areas become increasingly vulnerable to hazardous waste sitings. Together, these factors suggest that everyone would benefit from an understanding of how the systems of racial and economic inequality relate to toxic waste and pollution.

Finally, individuals may be relieved that such hazards and risks presently occur in someone else's community and not their own, but the fact is that everyone ends up sharing in increased health care costs related to illnesses from dangerous toxic waste siting. Ultimately, tolerating toxic waste sites in anyone's community cedes power to those who produce and dump hazardous and toxic substances. As long as these polluters believe that jobs and cash can appease communities, and as long as governmental agencies feel free to keep information from those who seek to fend off unwanted risks, everyone will be less able to struggle against these forces if or when their own community is targeted.

Technology and Globalization: The Digital Divide

Increasing globalization has stimulated and in turn been encouraged by the development of new technologies. In particular, the Internet, or information superhighway, has dramatically altered the way societies produce and consume goods and services, communicate, and gain access to information and other resources. Multinational corporations that have shifted production overseas to peripheral countries use it to connect management in core headquarters with labor and materials abroad. Likewise, Internet communications enable global military operations to be directed from the United States. With keystrokes, entire communities, nations, and regions around the world are affected by economic, political, and military decision makers.

Those with Internet access can obtain information about jobs all around the country or the world. This greatly expands job search capabilities beyond the local newspaper listings. Increasingly, workers telecommute to work from the comfort of home using personal computers. Such an arrangement can be invaluable to people struggling to balance family responsibilities with the need to earn income, including workers with preschool-age children or family members who require constant care, such as people with disabilities or aging parents. Telecommuting often reduces the need for costly child care or home companion arrangements. And daily errands after work can similarly be made more convenient because in addition to telecommuting to work, shopping online is possible.

The Internet also offers many educational opportunities. Anyone with access can obtain all sorts of reference materials from home, and not be restricted by the limited resources of local library facilities or by geographic isolation of living in remote rural areas. Teachers increasingly place reference materials and reading assignments for courses online, so that commuting students can access them beyond the restricted hours their libraries may be open. Journals, newspapers, and magazines can publish online instead of printing thousands of copies to distribute to libraries and book stores, thus saving trees from wanton destruction. People more and more complete whole courses and degree programs online in distance-learning arrangements, allowing homebound people (such as the frail elderly or people with severe disabilities) and those who live in isolated communities to access educational opportunities they might ordinarily be denied.

The environmental and community benefits of the Internet can be significant. Online shopping and educational opportunities, as well as telecommuting, can benefit the environment as fewer cars (or even mass transit) are needed, thus reducing the pollution caused by burning fossil fuels. The Internet can also offer a virtual community for people who have difficulties connecting to others who live in their immediate geographic communities, providing valuable support networks and information. For example, gay and lesbian adolescents can find refuge in online chatrooms and information sites without risking rejection, punishment, and perhaps violence associated with coming out in their geographic communities (Egan, 2000). The Internet also allows users to "travel" around the world to talk to a diverse range of people about their perspectives and lives in places that are unfamiliar.

On the other hand, the very nature of the Internet's promise poses many new and interesting questions about power and inequality. For example, telecommuting to work using personal computers at home signals a return to a form of cottage industry, as more and more workers become "mobile workers" with PCs, FAX machines, e-mail, and other electronic devices. This may be cheaper for employers and easier for workers, but it also means workers become increasingly isolated from each other and therefore encounter fewer opportunities to develop a sense of community and to organize around common problems. Generally, telecommuters are not unionized, so they are more easily subjected to unfair or abusive work conditions. Emerging evidence, for example, suggests that many telecommuting workers are enduring the same conditions long suffered by workers in sweatshops common in the garment and electronics industries, including low wages, no benefits, long hours, and oppressive supervisory control (Ross, 1999). Furthermore, laws designed to protect the physical environment that workers must endure are difficult to enforce; it is impossible to legislate desk heights, appropriate seating and lighting, fair lunch and coffee breaks, and other occupational health and safety factors in people's homes.

In addition to the problems facing many workers now engaged in telecommuting, increasing reliance on the Internet poses many cultural costs. Online educational opportunities and distance learning certainly offer the potential of linking isolated individuals and schools to the mainstream of society. However, the Internet also has the potential to displace human labor, since fewer faculty will be needed to teach larger numbers of students electronically. And it can mean far less human contact between students and teachers who are online, thereby removing an important piece of the educational process: the give and take of discussion and the mentoring relationship. Who, then, will write recommendation letters for faceless students who complete these courses and then try to find jobs or admission to further educational programs? Placing books, magazines, reference materials, and newspapers online also means a cultural shift in how individuals relate to printed material. It means a substantial change in the social construction of leisure, as it becomes more difficult to enjoy the simple pleasures of reading at the beach, on a subway, under a tree, sitting up in bed late at night, or even while snuggling with a young child in a comfortable chair.

Increasing reliance on Internet publications means that the more affluent will likely have better access to vital information, thereby widening the gap between the haves and the have-nots. For example, access to job ads posted on the Internet is predicated on a working knowledge of how to use the Internet, and, more important, on access to a computer and the ability to pay for an Internet service provider. This is important, since more and more employers are posting job openings on the Internet instead of placing job ads in newspapers. They do this for several reasons. First, it acts as a prescreening device, in that only those with some computer skills will even know about and apply for the job; even if the job does not require these skills, people who have them are likely to have an ability to learn new skills and be able to keep up with technological changes in the workplace. Further, posting jobs on the Internet is less expensive than paying for ads in newspapers, and once the job is filled, its listing can be instantaneously removed from the Internet, unlike newspaper ads that will run for the entire time period that has been paid for, even if the job has already been filled. This means that those with no computer skills or with no regular access to a computer will be left behind in a labor market that is increasingly polarized between a limited number of entry-level jobs with strong potential for upward mobility, good pay, and decent benefits at one pole and millions of dead-end, low-wage jobs with no benefits and little or no prospect for advancement at the other pole.

Because issues of power and inequality rise with Internet use, asking who controls and who uses the Internet becomes sociologically revealing. Although many people think of the Internet as the new frontier where no one controls or censors the content or access, the fact is that several layers of people and organizations control the Internet to some degree (Biegel, 1996). First, the federal government exerts some control over the Internet, which was initially intended to connect the defense and military establishments, universities, and research institutions around the country and the globe. Examples include recent government actions to control the display of pornography, to capture those who would prey on children, and to remove information that might be used by terrorists.

Private corporations are also among those controlling the "information superhighway." Internet service providers (e.g., AOL) affect who has access to the Internet. They determine the service fees to be charged and they can decide to deny services to some users. Communications companies, such as local television cable service providers, are increasingly expanding their services to include high-speed digital and cable connections to the Internet, for a fee. Since they are financing the infrastructure needed to provide this service, they can determine who has access by deciding which communities will receive the infrastructural investment and which will not. In addition to these companies, others develop the computers and the software necessary to connect to the Internet. These firms have a strong ability to influence, if not control, how people use the Internet. Microsoft, for example, has been highly successful in its strategy of preloading most new personal and laptop computers with its Windows file management system, so that almost everyone now uses Windows.

In addition to their role as Internet service providers, corporate actors can shape perceptions by posting or withholding information on the thousands of websites they maintain ("dot-coms"). They are joined by hundreds of government agencies, as well as faculty at colleges and universities who develop new computer programs and post massive amounts of information and data on the Internet. Together, they shape what people see and learn and what they can do on the Internet. Finally, the Internet Society was chartered by the federal government for the express purpose of evaluating Internet policies and acting as federal watchdog over other task forces and committees that address these policies (http://www.isoc.org). Together, these individuals and organizations have the very real capacity to shape, influence, and control the future direction of as well as access to what is increasingly becoming an indispensible resource.

Beyond Internet control, a related issue is who uses the Internet. How diverse is the online community? Does it reflect the diversity of the real world? What are the implications of user patterns? U.S. Census data initially indicated a notable gender gap in computer use and Internet access, with men far more active in cyberspace than women. But that gap quickly evaporated: In 2000, the Census Bureau noted that among adults with online access, 48 percent of users were men and 52 percent were women (www.census.gov/statabs:Table 913). Beyond gender, however, other patterns of inequality noted throughout this textbook are replicated online, a situation referred to as the **digital divide.** Those who are of the dominant statuses relative to class, race, ethnicity, and age enjoy privileged access to the Internet (Luke, 1997).

For example, the Internet is not economically diverse; the poor have very little access. By 1998, it became evident that the poor seriously lagged behind the more affluent in their entrance into the Information Age (see Table 17.2). Worse yet, when the poor do gain access, they do so with technology that is several developmental cycles behind that used by the affluent, thereby being deprived of the latest tools with which to compete effectively for jobs and other opportunities (Goslee, 1998; U.S. Department of Commerce and National Telecommunications and Information Administration, 2000). Notably, the technology gap between economic classes is not the result of personal choices being made by individuals, but rather a function of the inequality of infrastructural development in communities. Telephone, cable, and communications companies have been much quicker to wire affluent communities, particularly in the suburbs, but have ignored poorer neighborhoods.

Why does this matter? The widening technology gap between the poor and the affluent has economic implications for communities and individuals, as well as for the larger society. When poor neighborhoods

TABLE 17.2 Percentage of Households with Computers and Internet Access by Class and Race: 2001

	Have Home Computer	Have Internet Access
Income (per year)		
<$5,000	25.9%	20.5%
$5,000–9,999	19.2	14.4
$10,000–14,999	25.7	19.4
$15,000–19,999	31.8	21.0
$20,000–24,999	40.1	31.8
$25,00–34,999	49.7	42.2
$35,000–49,000	64.3	55.0
$50,000–74,999	77.7	70.6
$75,000 +	89.0	84.8
Race:		
African American	37.1%	30.8%
Latino/Latina	40.0	32.0
American Indian, Eskimo, Aleut	44.7	38.7
Asian American/Pacific Islander	72.7	68.1
White	61.1	55.4

SOURCE: www.census.gov/statab, Table 1135.

lack the infrastructure to help individuals link to the Internet, this poses obstacles to economic development in those communities. Communities with obsolete telecommunications capabilities are unattractive locations for businesses. The result is likely to be a downward cycle of limited economic opportunities and jobs for residents, many of whom already have limited means of mobility to travel to jobs that are increasingly located in communities wired for state-of-the-art technology. The deepening poverty of urban communities, for example, makes them even more unattractive for other investments, thus intensifying the cycle of poverty as jobs evaporate in poor city neighborhoods while they sprout in the suburbs. The result is a highly "fractured" labor market in many urban areas. The only work remaining for the unskilled is increasingly found in the service-sector in jobs where, as seen in Chapter 12, wages are low, and benefits, job security, and opportunity pp. 369–371 for advancement are frequently nonexistent. The U.S. Office of Technology Assessment cited the poor distribution of information access technologies and the supportive infrastructure as increasingly significant factors contributing to inequality in the United States because of "the concentration of poverty and the deconcentration of opportunity" (see also Goslee, 1998:2; Bucy, 2000).

The effect of this digital divide on individuals is not only a loss of possible employment opportunities for those who lack access to the Internet (Sangmoon, 2001). Increasing reliance by the state on the Internet to connect individuals to vital services introduces further obstacles to the poor in gaining access to important resources. Since three-fourths of all interactions between individuals and the state, including the delivery of food stamps, Social Security benefits, and Medicaid information, occur online, people with little or no access to the Internet are at a serious disadvantage (Goslee, 1998).

Ironically, at precisely the time when the state is demanding that the poor be self-sufficient, technological inequality makes it far more difficult for impoverished communities and individuals to help themselves. This is because more and more of the occasions that once nurtured leadership development and citizen participation occur online. With fewer face-to-face meetings and associations that previously were significant in the development of communication, coordination, and encouragement of community action, poor communities find themselves increasingly bereft of the necessary networks to address social problems. This does not mean there are no community organizations actively pursuing strategies to help their neighborhoods address the serious social problems confronting them. But lack of access to the communications technology that can link isolated, small, and poor communities in more powerful networks greatly increases the difficulty of obtaining needed resources. Finding out about funding opportunities, pertinent legislative developments, and strategies used in other neighborhoods becomes harder for such communities.

While lack of access to new technology impairs the ability of poor communities and individuals to help themselves, democratic processes themselves may also be harmed (Hurwitz, 1999; Lockard, 1997). Increasingly, political leaders are communicating with their constituents online, so those with greater access to the Internet will be more likely to have access to those who make policy decisions. As we saw in Chapter 11, access to legislators is a key factor in shaping how p. 351 they define problems and policy solutions to them. Political Action Committees

(PACs) have been an important mechanism enabling the affluent and corporations to gain the attention of legislators and thus to increase their chances of achieving favorable treatment in legislative policies. Technological inequality reinforces PACs' privileged access to legislators, and thus effectively magnifies their political clout.

Patterns of technological access relative to racially defined status echo those relative to class: Racially-dominant groups have a strong advantage. Whites and Asian Americans are more likely to have access than are African Americans, Latinos/Latinas, and Native Americans. Owning a computer is closely associated with household income levels. Our discussions in Chapter 7 indicated a strong intersection of class and race in the United States, such that African Americans and Latinos/Latinas are three times more likely than whites or Asian Americans to be poor, and therefore unlikely to have enough financial resources to support computer ownership or Internet access.

Beyond the ability to purchase computer equipment and Internet access service is the problem of a sort of high-tech "redlining" of African American and Latino/Latina communities. When communications companies install high-speed fiber optical cables to connect users to the Internet, they often focus their efforts on affluent communities and areas serving businesses. The result is that the information superhighway infrastructure put in place often bypasses communities of color. Technology is thus less likely to be available to support Internet access to people of color, even if they have their own home computers.

One alternative to providing individuals access to the Internet at home is to provide it through public institutions such as schools. But funding school budgets through property tax revenues means fewer resources in poor communities, including poor communities of color, to finance either the infrastructure of high-speed fiber optical cables or the computers themselves. Without fundamental changes in how schools are financed, schools in such communities will continue to be shortchanged in their access to computers and the Internet. Public libraries are in a similar bind.

In addition to aggravating patterns of inequality relating to class and race, increasing reliance on the Internet may deepen inequality based on able-bodiedness. People with disabilities, such as illiteracy, dyslexia, and blindness, face barriers to fully participate in the great potential future promised by the Internet (Borchert, 1998). While this is not surprising, the implications are significant: If people are becoming increasingly reliant on the Internet as a critical resource, many individuals with disabilities will likely be left behind. Unless societies develop tools to connect them with the mainstream of the Internet, they will have a difficult time benefiting from all that this resource has to offer, thereby increasing the gap between the able-bodied and those with disabilities.

Age inequalities are also replicated and reinforced in the virtual world of the Internet, mimicking earlier patterns of inequality witnessed in the United States in the first half of the twentieth century. Adult immigrants to the United States during this period often found that their native language and culture limited their ability to interact and participate in the social mainstream. But their children quickly learned English and the new culture through their participation in the public school system. Children often became their elders' teachers, translators, and protectors, producing a role reversal and a generational status inconsistency. Now, the older, less Internet-savvy native-born generation is much like these earlier geographic adult immigrants. Today's older generation is less literate in computer language and culture, but their children, particularly affluent children, are more likely to be computer-literate and well-versed in usage of the Internet because of computer education and access in school. Today's children often become the Internet teachers and computer use translators for their parents, producing the same generational role reversals and status inconsistencies earlier geographic immigration created between young and old.

These patterns of inequality of access to the Internet reverberate globally, thereby intensifying the global inequalities discussed in Chapters 3 and 10. Although inequalities in access between classes certainly appear in every nation, core and periphery alike, members of the core nations generally have privileged access to the Internet while the semiperiphery and the periphery lag woefully behind. Most nations, regardless of their world-system status, have at least some direct Internet connection, since such connections are necessary to support multinational corporations doing business around the world. These connections link managers in the core with production facilities and workers in the semiperiphery and the periphery and with markets everywhere. But some peripheral nations, particularly in Africa, have no Internet connection at all. Others, again primarily in Africa, have only e-mail capabilities (www.isoc.org/images/mapv15.gif). This pattern of unequal access to global connectivity means that the periphery is being left behind in the great information revolution. Why does this matter? If Internet connectivity is an increasingly critical resource for development, the gap between the wealth and power of the core and the poverty and relative powerlessness of the periphery is sure to widen even further, intensifying the differences in people's life chances that already exist in the world system. The lack of connectivity discourages foreign investment, impedes economic development, and reduces the chances of global political participation.

Even in nations with Internet connection capabilities, individuals in the periphery and semiperiphery have far less access than do individuals in the core. This is because connectivity in these countries is more typically over telephone lines rather than through the high-speed fiber optic cables more common in the core. The number of telephones per 1,000 people provides a picture of the difficulty of individual access to the Internet: the fewer phones to be shared by more people, the less likely that one will be able to tie up those lines to be connected to the Internet for very long, if at all. In the core, there are significantly more phones than in the periphery and semiperiphery. In the United States, western Europe, and Australia, for example, there are 400–700 phones for every 1,000 people, but in much of Latin America, Asia, and Africa, this figure drops sharply, to 1–99 phones per 1,000 people (United Nations Development Programme, www.undp.org). People in the core, then, have a much better opportunity than those in the periphery or semiperiphery to gain access to information for empowerment and, perhaps, enhanced life chances.

Ironically, technology itself is beginning to offer an important resource for bypassing these limitations to development in the periphery and semiperiphery. The rapidly declining cost of cellular telephones is making global interconnectivity an increasingly real opportunity for people in countries left behind in the revolution taking place on the Internet. This is because cell phones do not depend on the expensive infrastructure required of conventional telephone lines and are not subject to the whims of private investors, despotic rulers seeking to keep populations ignorant and under control, or the ravages and disruptions of wars. Particularly in Africa, cellular phones are becoming an increasingly common possession. In Botswana, for example, more than 12 percent of the population owns a cellular phone. The result: a "quiet revolution" of potential political and economic empowerment. In Senegal 40 years of one-party rule finally ended in 2000, when voters ousted President Abdou Diouf. Cellular phones enabled poll watchers to immediately report election results to independent broadcasters, making it all but impossible for Diouf to preserve his rule by incorrectly claiming to have won (Ashurst, 2001). The use of cellular phones to provide access to the Internet is likely to increase in such countries, as wireless technology now increasingly available in the core spreads to the periphery and semiperiphery.

Cyberspace and the Promise for Social Change

Many people throughout the world have turned to the Internet as a potent social movement resource, particularly when states have sought to silence them. Women in Chiapas, Mexico, for example, have found the Internet a useful networking tool, sending news of state oppression and human rights violations there outside of the remote isolation of the area, and gaining political and financial support for their cause beyond their immediate location (Glusker, 1998). In Taliban-controlled Afghanistan, women in RAWA (Revolutionary Association of Women in Afghanistan) sought and gained international support through the Internet for

Although a digital divide has accelerated global inequality between the core and the periphery, wireless technology may actually help close that gap. Here, a man in Africa uses a cell phone to communicate from a fairly isolated area.

their struggles against the fundamentalist dictatorship that denied women education, health care, employment, and freedom of movement as well as speech. Their efforts succeeded in the unprecedented inclusion of at least two women in the provisional governing alliance put in place in Afghanistan after the fall of the Taliban government in 2001.

In recent years, a number of citizen groups in the United States have experimented with the use of computer networks as a tool for monitoring government agencies and organizing citizens, thereby creating virtual communities among individuals who are otherwise marginalized from power and participation (Stoecker and Stuber, 1999). Today, using the Internet, information on a wide range of important topics may be obtained and shared among literally millions of persons at a very low cost. Bulletin boards are used for announcing demonstrations and other actions that one can join, posting addresses to write letters, and listing companies currently being boycotted for various reasons. The Internet sites are often interactive, allowing citizens to talk with each other, exchange feedback, offer pointers, and debate facts and strategies. Some provide links so that people can contact their legislators to register their point of view. In 2003, as the United States pushed for a war against Iraq, antiwar activists used the Internet and e-mail to rally hundreds of thousands of protestors in a "virtual demonstration," clogging legislators' e-mails and phone systems with messages imploring them to withdraw their support of President Bush's planned attacks. Empowerment is enhanced when citizens have free or low-cost access to the Internet, databases of government information, and e-mail systems. The Internet can be enormously empowering, if one has such access and knows how to use it.

The key issue of the future in cyberspace, then, is democratizing access. One way to encourage greater access is to install more computers in public schools and libraries, senior centers, daycare centers, welfare and unemployment offices, community centers, and the like. Public Internet cafés where anyone may come and use the Internet, much like a public library's noncirculating reference materials, might also help. Such cafés might also become community gathering places, encouraging greater interaction between neighbors than could otherwise be accomplished when individuals are isolated in their own homes away from other community members. While these would seem to be steps in the direction of improving access to the Internet, there are storm clouds on the horizon of democratizing the Internet.

Globalization, Militarism, Terrorism, and Social Change

The power of globalization is such that even the core must deal with the ramifications of alterations in the structure of the global economy. By the 1990s, the Cold War between the East and the West had come to an end. The Berlin Wall separating East and West Germany had been torn down, and the German Democratic Republic and the Federal Republic of Germany reunited after existing separately since World War II. The Soviet Union ceased to exist following the restructuring of Soviet society, or *perestroika,* and its republics became independent nations. The end of the Cold War escalated the process of increasing globalization as former Eastern bloc nations shifted their economies to mixtures of capitalism and socialism and sought inclusion into international security and trade organizations from which they had previously been excluded. The end of the Cold War opened new markets for core capitalist nations for a wide range of products, from soda and burgers to guns and other weapons.

Furthermore, despite evidence of a rise of neofascist, ultra-right-wing parties and candidates in Russia and other eastern European countries, the military threat posed by the communist bloc largely disappeared for the West. With no identifiable enemy to fill the void, the United States was left with the question of how to deal with its huge industrial apparatus developed in support of the military. One response to this challenge facing the United States military-industrial complex was to increase the sale of arms and weapons systems abroad (Bixby, 1992; www.fas.org). This response may make economic sense to the defense-contracting corporations, but it raises critical questions: What are the consequences of this globalization of arms? How does government justify continuing large-scale military expenditures and weapons production as the communist threat evaporates? In light of the insistence of all of the components of the military-industrial complex that external threats remain, who or what might those threats be? Are military responses likely to be effective against such threats? Who benefits and who is hurt by the military-industrial complex's response to these questions?

The question of what to do with massive sectors of the economy devoted to defense production is not simply a question of United States foreign policy and the future of its military. It is inextricably linked to the structure of the entire military-industrial complex, as well as to the health and future of the U.S. economy as a whole. While the end of the Cold War raised fitting debates about what to do with the anticipated "peace dividend" of money no longer needed for defense that could have resulted from that momentous change in global politics, and some defense spending cuts occurred, the U.S. Department of Defense has nonetheless continued to absorb significant proportions of the federal budget. The total military budget expenditure in 2000 was $291 billion (www.census.gov/statab:Table 566). That same year, United States military spending accounted for 37 percent of total world military expenditures of $798 billion (www.fas.org). U.S. military expenditures have since been growing, particularly with the 2003 war against Iraq.

Prior to the September 11, 2001, terrorist attacks, some observers suggested alternative approaches to the continued high levels of military spending, arguing that winding down the East–West arms race in and of itself would make the world a more secure place. More attention could be focused on severe domestic problems such as hunger and homelessness, unemployment, deteriorating infrastructure, inadequate education facilities, and racial inequality. Further, with reduced military spending, research and development money previously allocated to military projects could be turned to civilian needs. Finally, workers who would be laid off from defense contractors are highly trained and educated; such workers could be redeployed into nondefense skilled jobs where serious labor shortages exist. And some observers point out that civilian expenditures can actually produce more jobs than military spending: Where "$1 billion in military procurement generates 21,500 jobs directly and indirectly[,] the same $1 billion invested in industrial renewal, mass transit, housing, education, and health care will produce on average 33,100 jobs" (Melman, 1997).

Even before September 11, the United States ignored these potential benefits of winding down military production and expenditures with the end of the Cold War, and instead chose a different path. President George W. Bush resurrected Ronald Reagan's hugely expensive and much criticized Strategic Defense Initiative (Star Wars), claiming it to be a desperately needed missile defense system. He did not, however, clearly identify the sources of the alleged missile threats to U.S. security that might necessitate such a multi-billion-dollar program. The September 11, 2001, attacks on the World Trade Center and the Pentagon, and the spread of anthrax through the United States mail, clearly revealed that the greatest threat to security

Increasing political, economic, and cultural globalization has generated increasing levels of international terrorism. Here, the September 11, 2001, attacks that destroyed the World Trade Center towers in New York City became the most infamous symbol of the increase in international terrorist activity.

was not individual nations but international terrorists. Yet the Bush administration increased conventional defense spending to a degree not seen in years. This raises a pressing and undebated question: Do expenditures on conventional military responses and missile defense systems increase U.S. security against terrorist attacks? Meanwhile, defense contractors are busy defending their own economic interests by fueling the international market for arms. What effect does this international market have on United States or world security, and on the rise of international terrorism? Let's look at these emerging global issues.

Export of Arms

In 2001, the United States was by far the leading arms-exporting nation in the world. U.S. arms manufacturers delivered $9.7 billion in weapons to countries the world over, more than twice as much as Great Britain, the second-largest arms exporter. Overall, the United States alone supplied almost half of all the arms exported globally. And, most notably, the United States fueled global conflicts, supplying arms or military technology in more than 92 percent of the conflicts that flared up around the world, often supplying arms as well as military training to both sides at the same time. For example, both India and Pakistan received weapons from the United States, as did both Azerbaijan and Armenia. Many of the nations locked in extended and bitter disputes in the Middle East, notably Israel, Egypt, Oman, Saudi Arabia, Lebanon, and Kuwait, all receive arms from the United States. Conservative estimates are that in 1999 alone, the United States sent about $7 billion in arms to countries where violations of international human rights treaties are rampant, including the use of children as soldiers in combat (www.cdi.org; www.fas.org).

These exports occurred even as the elder Bush administration publicly spoke in 1992 of a "new world order," stimulated by arms restraint, and lectured other countries to join the United States in such restraint. How is it possible to take this position and still sell others arms? One rationale for allowing such exports is the necessity to save U.S. jobs that would otherwise be lost were there to be cuts in government defense spending in the United States. Indeed, in a tight battle for his reelection in 1992, President George H. W. Bush tried the unsuccessful political alchemy of turning jobs into votes by approving several new foreign arms sales, including sales to Saudi Arabia and Taiwan. Such sales have continued unabated into the new century. And although Congress has the constitutional power to veto these sales, the fact is that it has not. Why? Each senator and congressperson has constituents who desperately need jobs, and it would be political suicide to refuse arms sales that give them employment.

Who has benefited and who has been hurt by this strategy of arms export? The main beneficiaries of arming the world have been the weapons-manufacturing corporations. The Center for Defense Information found that such corporations have reaped great profits from international arms sales (Hellman, 2000). In many ways, the first Gulf war against Iraq in 1991 became a live commercial for arms manufacturers such as Raytheon (the manufacturer of the Patriot missile), as potential international buyers saw dramatic videos purporting to show "evidence" (later found to be far less spectacular in reality) of the efficiency and "kill-power" of United States weapons systems.

p. 368 ▶ Not surprisingly, given the changing organization of work and production we discussed in Chapter 12, defense industry workers in many cases have lost jobs. For the arms manufacturers, increased profits from exports in a competitive world market do not offset profit slowdowns when they are unable to obtain enough lucrative contracts from the Department of Defense. For example, United Technologies Corporation, the eighth-largest arms exporter in the United States, decided to downsize in the early 1990s because of government defense spending cutbacks and announced the layoff of 14,000 workers; its Pratt & Whitney division eliminated 7,500 jobs, even as it seemed it would be the likely manufacturer of the engines for the jets sold to Saudi Arabia and Taiwan (Bixby, 1992:A7). By 1996, only about 2.3 million U.S. workers were employed in defense-related industries, a 36 percent decline in such jobs from the height of the Cold War in 1987 (Melman, 1997).

While profits are made by weapons producers, increased arms exports are not making the world any safer. In fact, they are increasing the likelihood of armed conflicts and arms buildups everywhere. Arms have become a key commodity traded in the world system. With nations becoming ever more heavily armed in regions of the world where tensions run high, the probability of future armed conflicts between nations increases immeasurably.

The terrorist attacks in the United States in 2001 raised the question of the role of the international arms market in contributing to the heightened sophistication of and dangers posed by terrorists around the world. The State Department estimates that 28 terrorist organizations operate from 18 nations. Although the United States does not directly sell arms to these terrorist groups, throughout the 1990s it sold weapons and provided military assistance and training to 16 of the 18 governments that host these organizations and tolerate them, such as Saudi Arabia, Algeria, Iraq, Lebanon, and Sri Lanka (www.cdi.org). What may have seemed like a good idea at one time often becomes a highly regrettable one, to say the least. For example, the United States played a significant role in arming and training the Taliban military in Afghanistan in the early 1980s, in support of its military conflict with the former Soviet Union. This was part of the approach the United States has frequently adopted in international affairs, in which "the enemy of my enemy is my friend." Once the Taliban had successfully defended Afghanistan against Soviet forces, the imported weapons and the Afghanis' training expertise remained. These became key in the strengthening of the international al-Qaeda network, which was identified as the terrorist perpetrator of the September 11 suicide attacks against the World Trade Center, the Pentagon, and other targets. These horrific events are forcing people to come to grips with the rise of international terrorism: What is terrorism? Is this a new phenomenon? Will greater investment in conventional military responses provide adequate defense and security against such attacks if they are aimed at the United States?

Terrorism

Global economic and political inequalities—propped up largely by the huge proliferation of military might in the core and elsewhere, U.S. arms exports to other nations, and U.S. military support for "friendly" militaristic regimes throughout the world—have helped fuel international terrorism. But what exactly is terrorism? People use this word to describe a wide range of behaviors, and acts that are described as "terrorism" by some observers may be termed by others as acts of "patriotism." U.S. officials insisted that the September 11 attacks represented acts of war against the United States, requiring a military response. What is the difference between "war" and "terrorism"? It would seem important to sort out these issues, then, in order to understand the new realities of life in an era of globalization.

War is an organized, armed conflict between nations (Palen, 2001:472). Armed conflicts that occur within nations between organized factions are termed "civil wars" to distinguish them from international armed conflicts. Wars can be officially and formally declared or may be unofficially waged (as when the U.S. government referred to its war in Vietnam as a "conflict" rather than declare a formal "war" or when it waged an undeclared war against Iraq in 2003). In either case, war is a fairly constant feature of world history, and certainly of the United States, which has participated in more than a dozen major wars and has sent troops around the world to participate in "peacekeeping missions" and other assorted armed conflicts nearly 200 times (Leckie, 1992).

Terrorism is the use of violence as a strategy to gain political objectives, and it may be used by individuals or groups who usually have relatively little power otherwise. When used in this way, terrorism has been called a "weapon of the weak" (Scott, 1985), and "diplomacy from below" (Kumamoto, 1991). The power of terrorism is its ability to incite tremendous fear and sense of vulnerability in people through acts of unpredictable, random violence, or by leveling violence against society's critical institutions, leaders, and symbols. Terrorism commonly interrupts business and life as usual by altering people's freedom of movement, their comfort in their surroundings, and their confidence that the full force of the state or other social institutions can protect them. Terrorism thus creates a legitimacy crisis for the state and destabilizes or disrupts existing governments. The state often has difficulty confronting terrorism because the enemy is not always apparent, and thus may be unresponsive to conventional social control mechanisms (including police and military repression and counterviolence). Terrorism has tremendous potential to undermine the invisible, unearned privileges that come with living in the core, including the ability to live without the threat of the violence that is so common elsewhere in the world, and to go to work every day, to shop, to travel, to vote, to simply open the daily mail, without fear of loss of life and limb.

While terrorism is frequently a weapon of the weak, it can also be used by governments to coerce their own resistant populations to acquiesce to their will and to eliminate challengers to state power. For example, the military in Argentina and Chile in the 1970s used kidnapping, murder, and torture to purge these countries of leftist critics, thousands of whom remain among the "disappeared." Former president of Yugoslavia Slobodan Milosevic was charged in an international tribunal with sanctioning rape, murder, and kidnapping (among other charges) as terrorist tactics in 1999 in an attempt to "ethnically cleanse" Kosovo of Albanians by scaring them into leaving Kosovo or by killing them.

Terrorism, like war, is not new or unusual, although the incidence of terrorist acts has certainly been on the rise around the world. For example, terrorist bombings occurred in Great Britain, Northern Ireland, the Middle East, and elsewhere fairly regularly throughout the 1980s and 1990s. In the United States, such bombings showed a steady increase from the early 1980s through the 1990s (Eitzen and Zinn, 1997). Terrorism is also not something used only by "others," that is, people outside the United States. The Ku Klux Klan and other white supremacist groups have frequently used terrorist tactics in their disputes with the federal government's policies in support of civil rights, as have antiabortionists and extremists in the antiwar movement in the 1960s, to name a few. When a bomb tore through the Alfred P. Murrah Federal Building in Oklahoma City in 1995, killing 167 people, many people in the United States, including those in the media, immediately assumed that the culprits were probably Middle Eastern terrorists. The perpetrators were quickly identified, however, as United States citizens involved in local militia groups disgruntled with the federal government. In fact, Timothy McVeigh, the man ultimately convicted and executed for the bombing, was a veteran of the U.S. military. This case highlighted the fact that terrorism is a tactic used by "home-grown" groups as a strategy for achieving their political objectives, and not only by groups located elsewhere around the world. The characteristic that terrorists often have in common is the possession of far less power relative to that of the governments they seek to challenge.

What actions should be defined as terrorism is not always agreed on by everyone. Some even view "terrorism" as indistinct from "patriotism." What is the difference? Individuals involved in domestic terrorism in the United States are often part of a loose configuration of groups that refer to themselves the "Patriot" movement. They believe that the federal government increasingly violates the basic premises of the Constitution and consider it their patriotic duty to subvert and challenge that government wherever and however possible (Berlet and Lyons, 1995; Wills, 1995). Similarly, members of the Irish Republican Army (IRA) consider themselves to be patriots defending the right of Northern Ireland to self-determination apart from the control of Great Britain; and members of the radical Islamic jihad movement believe they are being patriotic in attacking governments that violate their interpretation of Islamic law. Indeed, colonists in the American Revolution saw the Boston Tea Party as an act of patriotism. Such examples are not intended to justify the use of property destruction and violence to gain a political objective; but they do raise the critical issue of perspective and relativity—one person's terrorism is another's patriotism. We don't hold that terrorist crimes against humanity are acceptable if they're defined as acts of "patriotism," but considering these issues may help us approach some understanding of why terrorist acts occur.

Despite President George W. Bush's insistence that the world is clearly defined in camps of "evildoers" and "us," reality is much more complex and ambiguous. In an increasingly globalized world, understanding the complexities becomes necessary. For example, consider the relationship between the United States and other core nations on the one hand, and underdeveloped and oppressed populations on the other. Increased expenditures on conventional military responses to terrorism against the core that arise out of that context are unlikely to provide increased security. Viable solutions will likely emerge only when people more fully understand the global context in which terrorism occurs. What social, political, and economic factors are likely to influence the growth of international terrorism? Some research suggests that the experience of intensifying ethnic and religious rifts, accompanied by feelings of alienation, social isolation, and threatened survival, often underscored by a sense of religious imperative, are common features shared by many international terrorist groups (Hoffman, 1995). Other researchers point to the widening global gap between wealth and poverty, the continuing dominating military role of the United States, and the global expansion of the culture-invasive Internet as critical trends to watch (Jensen, 2001).

As the United States struggles to combat terrorism, questions of who will bear the greatest burden of that effort become critical. With an all-volunteer military in the United States, structured racial and class inequality (see Chapter 7) situ- pp. 199–204 ates people of color disproportionately among those called to place themselves in harm's way in conventional military responses against terrorism. For example, African Americans constitute 12.3 percent of the total U.S. population, yet they represent more than 22 percent of the active-duty military. Almost 27 percent of the army, the branch most likely to function as ground troops and therefore to be placed in greatest danger, are African American. They are also far less likely to be among the more elite branches of the military: 14.5 percent of the air force, 16 percent of the marines, and 17.2 percent of the navy are African American (www.census.gov/stabab:Table 577). This means that people of color are at a relatively higher risk than whites to be harmed by the decision to resort to conventional military responses to terrorism.

While it is true that in the military actions in both the Persian Gulf and Afghanistan ground troops played a relatively minor role and suffered few casualties, such troops remain more likely to be injured or killed than jet pilots flying at high speeds above their targets. Those on the ground are closer to the danger (including the potential to become part of the "collateral damage" of erroneous bombing and other forms of "friendly fire"). In the 2003 war with Iraq, ground troops figured prominently as the troops pressed toward Bagdad in a search for both presumed "weapons of mass destruction" and personnel such as Saddam Hussein himself. Tens of thousands were potentially exposed to feared biological and chemical weapons, which fortunately were not used against U.S. troops (and may not have been in the Iraqi arsenal at the time of the U.S. attack).

In addition to the unequal burden of danger faced by people in the military, individual civilians face serious consequences of war and terrorism. In such instances, the consequences are not just individual: everyone stands to lose. As the "Social Forces/People's Lives" reading illustrates, xenophobic fear and anxiety fueled by a combination of international terrorism and the U.S. military-industrial complex's hunger for war produces suspicion of visitors and immigrants from abroad. In the reading, a graduate student from Iran lost his ability to reenter the United States from Canada to continue his studies after leaving briefly to visit his family. This student's considerable talents and potential for making serious contributions may very well be lost, not because he himself has done anything wrong, but because of his national origins. Fears of terrorism have led U.S. government agencies to profile individuals in an attempt to defend the nation against future attacks.

Might there be other, perhaps more effective, responses to international terrorism? How helpful, for example, might the United Nations be in focusing widespread international pressure on states that support terrorists? Might the creation of an international court of justice devoted to handling terrorists be effective in convening fair trials, meting out appropriate sanctions and upholding international norms outlawing terrorist acts? Is it useful for the United States to isolate itself from the concerns of the rest of the world except when it serves its own dominant interests? And, perhaps most important, how do societies address the global problems that feed terrorism, such as poverty, lack of democratic governance, violations of refugees' human rights , and so forth? Would addressing these issues help reduce the fertile grounds spawning terrorism? How these questions are answered will affect everyone in this new century.

Our discussion of emerging issues suggests that using a sociological imagination helps to begin to frame questions about new issues and concerns as they develop. Waiting for someone else to do the research before asking questions is not necessary. A well-developed sociological imagination should provide the tools to analyze aggregate statistics and averages; to figure out who benefits and who is hurt by certain relationships and processes; and to see the implications changes might have for different members of U.S. society and those in other societies around the world. Individuals armed with a toolkit of sociological concepts such as those we introduced in this text and applied in our analysis of emerging issues may be able to anticipate future trends. In short, people can learn to link their personal, individual biographies to the larger institutions in society and their history, and thereby better understand the societal patterns and processes that affect them. This may lead individuals to see how *they* can collectively contribute to change, and thus give them the greater freedom to be actors in their world, not just people who are acted upon.

Social Forces/People's Lives

Stranded: Cut Off from Life in the U.S.

LISA CHEDEKEL

International terrorism has raised anxieties and fears in the United States, prompting sweeping changes in everyday cultural patterns in an attempt to increase security. The need to feel secure has led, unfortunately, to racial and ethnic profiling of individuals, especially those from other countries who work and study in the United States. This reading illustrates in very personal terms how individuals can find themselves caught in a web of fear that defines them as potential threats to security, whether they have engaged in terrorism or not. The promising graduate career of the man in this reading has been put on hold indefinitely as he struggles to negotiate his return to the University of Connecticut from Canada.

TORONTO—In the summer and fall, at least he had the lake.

Ali Ghodsi Senejani could drive his '92 Chevy down to the shore of Lake Ontario, squint across the invisible aquatic border and imagine himself reclaiming the life he lost in a single misstep.

"You can't see the land," he says, "but you can feel, across the water, there is the U.S."

But the winter has changed everything. The shore, with its punishing arctic winds, is deserted and forbidding. The sun's silver glare is blinding. The months in limbo have sapped his spirit.

Now, as he makes his 34th weekly call to the U.S. Consulate in Toronto, Senejani says he is ready to give up.

"I know exactly what they will say: 'Administrative processing of your visa is not yet complete. You may call again next week,'" he mimics. "The words never change."

Still, when a female voice comes on the line to take his name, date of birth and nationality, he feels the familiar swirl of adrenaline. Maybe he will finally be allowed to return to the University of Connecticut to complete his studies. Maybe he will soon be reunited with his young wife, Maryam Kahlili, who left their native Iran in August and has been waiting for him in Storrs.

At any moment, the U.S. government could decide to give Ali Senejani his life back.

"Administrative processing of your visa is not yet complete. You may call again next week," the clerk at the consulate says.

He hangs up. He exhales. He retreats.

Hope, once his salvation, has become his captor.

All kinds of walls have gone up in the 16 months since Sept. 11, but Senejani, 29, finds himself in an unusual prison.

Born and raised near the industrial city of Arak, Iran, he left home eight years ago to attend college in India, then earned a master's degree in science in Germany. It was there that he met a UConn professor, J. Peter Gogarten, who urged him to come to the States to pursue a doctorate in molecular biology.

Senejani completed his master's thesis at UConn in June 2000, then enrolled as a Ph.D. candidate and graduate research assistant. He won a prestigious fellowship in his first year and was chosen to be a teaching assistant by a senior professor in the department of molecular and cell biology. His research on inteins—complex genetic elements—was gaining attention in scientific journals.

Then came the fallout from the terrorist attacks—a host of new immigration rules and the inclusion of Iran on President Bush's "axis of evil."

When school got out last spring, Senejani decided to visit his grandmother and uncles in Toronto, as he had done a few times before, and try to arrange a quick trip home to Iran from there. He has been stuck in Canada ever since.

Once Senejani crossed the border on May 19, he knew he would need a new student visa to re-enter the U.S. Just weeks earlier, the State Department had announced that students from Iraq, Iran, Syria, and four other countries deemed to be state sponsors of terrorism would no longer be able to renew their visas automatically after visits to Canada or Mexico. Senejani had called the U.S. Consulate before he left and was told it could take as long as a month for his re-entry visa to be processed.

That was eight months ago.

Today, Senejani is unable to return to UConn and is reluctant to return to Iran, where he would have to forgo his research. The walls are closing in; his Canadian visitor's visa expires in mid-February and if he does not receive a three-month extension, he may have no choice but to go back to Iran.

Some days, Senejani berates himself for leaving the States. At the time, he was trying to make things right in his family. He and Maryam, 24, had been legally married by a cleric in their hometown in the summer of 2000, but they had not had the traditional marriage celebration that an Iranian woman deserves. His plan was to return to Iran for the wedding party and then re-enter the U.S. with his wife, who had stayed in Iran to finish college.

"I didn't want her or her family to feel like I didn't have the interest," he said.

To obtain a student re-entry visa, Sanejani had to leave the U.S., which does not provide such approvals. There is no U.S. consulate in Iran because the country has no diplomatic relations with America. He thought he best option would be Canada.

"His only real choice was to forfeit his family obligations in Iran and stay here," said Mark Wentzel, UConn's director of International Services. "At the time, no one could have foreseen these consequences."...

In some ways, Senejani is not alone. As many as 5,000 students from 26 mostly Muslim and Arab countries missed the start of classes this year because their visas were delayed by new security checks, according to surveys and other information from U.S. universities. A State Department spokesperson acknowledged "significant delays" for some visa applicants, most of whom remained in their home countries.

In addition, more than 88,500 applicants for student "F-1" visas, the most common type, were denied in the 12 months that ended Sept. 30—a rejection rate of 27 percent, up from 23 percent the year before.

What makes Senejani's predicament unusual is not only the length of the bureaucratic limbo, but that he is still pushing through it. By now, officials at UConn, Yale University and other colleges say, the majority of delayed students have received visa decisions, or have given up and opted for schools in England, Australia or elsewhere. Many were trying to enroll in U.S. schools for the first time.

Senejani, who is more than halfway to his doctorate, cannot seem to cut his losses and go home. There is always the promise of next week, or the week after, or the week after that.

"How can I leave," he asks, "when I would always wonder, what if I had waited another week?"...

Senejani is majoring in genetics. He was examining the evolution of inteins, benign parasites that insert themselves into DNA—a line of research that might someday be of help in fighting disease.

Now his professors worry that his two years of work will be lost. Gogarten has trouble accepting that the driven, talented student he had spotted while lecturing in Germany may have vanished.

"There are many eager and bright people around who can't get an experiment to work. But Ali is very talented at the bench... He has put so much energy into getting where he is, it's really tragic," he said.

Source: Lisa Chedekel, "Stranded: Cut Off from Life in the U.S.," *Hartford CT Courant*, January 26, 2003, pp. A1, A4.

CHAPTER SUMMARY

1. Globalization of economic relationships increasingly dominates social life and has a significant effect on social arrangements and individuals alike. The global division of labor has worsened the gap of wealth and poverty between core and peripheral nations, contributing to stark population patterns. The gap between wealth and poverty among nations is widening, and core nations increasingly act to protect their economic interests in peripheral and semiperipheral nations.

2. While core nations are increasingly dominated by older population cohorts, the periphery struggles to support an ever-younger population. Societies with large older cohorts must find ways to address the medical, economic, and social needs of an aging population. Those with significantly larger populations under the age of 15 face quite different challenges, including the care and feeding of more dependent members of society as well as the problem of production of necessary goods and services and the defense of the nation.

3. Increasing globalization creates a problem of what to do with the toxic waste generated by the production of the world's goods and services. The power imbalances of the world-system and the related economic disparities created by the global division of labor means that core nations have the power to discard their toxic waste in peripheral countries with very little challenge.

4. Unequal power, coupled with systems of inequality around race and class in core nations like the United States, leads to environmental racism. Poor neighborhoods and communities of color are far more likely than affluent and white communities to become the unwilling recipients of much of the toxic and nuclear waste of the nation.

5. Globalization is furthered by the rapid rise of the Internet, which offers tremendous promise for information and communication access for everyone. There is a substantial digital divide, however, in which access to the Internet and all that it promises remains sharply unequal. Poor people, people of color, and peripheral nations have far less access to the Internet and to the new opportunity structures for improved integration and participation in society. Some—including many nations in Africa, people with severe visual disabilities, and the very poor—are left out entirely.

6. Increasing globalization of economic relations, in addition to promoting greater opportunities for trade and wider distribution of goods and services, also promotes increasing political tensions around the world. The end of the Cold War in the 1990s presumably made the world safer from the threat of nuclear war between the East and West; in fact, it worsened the promise of world peace. Core nations, particularly the United States, stepped up their sale of arms worldwide, and hence substantially contributed to a widening destabilization of global relations and violence around the world.

7. International terrorism has spread the threat of violence from its previous concentration in peripheral and semiperipheral areas of the globe to the core as well. Responding to terrorism spawned by networks of groups across many nations is much more difficult than responding to violence from an easily identifiable single nation.

THINKING CRITICALLY

1. Suppose you were in charge of developing strategies to close the digital divide. What approaches would you suggest to accomplish this goal? How would you work toward greater access for the poor? For people of color? For people with disabilities? For the elderly? For peripheral and semiperipheral countries? Who will likely benefit and who will likely be hurt by your proposals, and why? What institutions would need to be changed, and how? What institutions will likely be changed by your proposals, and why?

2. Increasing longevity is causing more people to reconsider the meaning of retirement and "old age." Perhaps some people you know are currently retired. What have they done to redefine their retirements? How do their experiences compare with how their parents defined retirement? What factors may explain the differences, if any, between the people you know and their parents? Which institutions affect the retirement experiences of the people you know and their parents? How? How might these institutions need to change in the future in order to accommodate the presence of a larger elderly cohort?

3. Is an unannounced plant shutdown an act of terrorism? Why or why not? Is rape an act of terrorism? What differentiates these acts from the attack against the World Trade Center in 2001, if anything? How are they similar?

4. Suppose you were asked to offer a plan for toxic waste disposal that addresses the problem of environmental racism. What factors would you consider in the development of your plan? Why? Who is likely to benefit and who is likely to be hurt by your proposal? Are there things that you can do to minimize or eliminate the differential impact of your plan? What institutional changes, if any, would have to take place to accommodate your plan?

5. Select an emerging issue that has not been covered in this chapter (perhaps reproductive technology, privatization of public services like prisons, gays in the military, decriminalization of drugs, or any other that you may find interesting). Using your sociological imagination, explore the institutional arrangements that might contribute to the issue. Examine who benefits and who is hurt by the issue as it currently stands, and try to assess why. What alternative arrangements would you suggest to deal with the issue? Are there race, class, and gender factors to be considered when examining this emerging issue? Be specific.

KEY TERMS

adolescent fertility rate, *(547)*

age consciousness, *(551)*

age dependency ratio, *(547)*

birth rate, *(543)*

death rate, *(543)*

digital divide, *(561)*

environmental racism, *(556)*

fertility rate, *(547)*

globalization, *(541)*

infant mortality rate, *(543)*

life expectancy at birth, *(543)*

perestroika, *(566)*

redline, *(556)*

terrorism, *(570)*

toxic imperialism, *(554)*

war, *(570)*

ableism Prejudice and discrimination against a group of people because of their physical or mental disability. (Chapter 7)

absolute deprivation The state of being unable to purchase the things related to basic survival. (*Compare with* relative deprivation.) (Chapter 10)

achieved status Social status acquired through a person's application of resources, talent, effort, and opportunity. (*See also* status; *Compare with* ascribed status.) (Chapter 4)

activity theory The view that aging does not necessarily require people to withdraw from work and leisure activities in which they have been involved, and that such withdrawal may be harmful to elders. (Chapter 7)

adolescent fertility rate The number of births to women aged 15–19 years old per 1,000 women in the same age group. (Chapter 17)

affirmative action Regulations requiring that employers not discriminate in hiring and that they take positive steps to increase the number of members of racial minority groups and women in their job applicant pools. (Chapter 7)

age consciousness The awareness of common interests based on age. (Chapter 17)

age dependency ratio The ratio of people younger than 15 and older than 65 to the number of people aged 15–64. (Chapter 17)

age inequality A system of inequality in which members of a particular age group are thought of and treated as less worthy than those of another; usually refers to older people. (Chapter 7)

ageism Prejudice and discrimination against a group of people because of their age; usually directed against older people. (Chapter 7)

agnostic A person who denies or disbelieves the possibility that one can know that a god or gods exist. (Chapter 16)

alienation A withdrawing or separation from something; for example, in Marxist theory, workers experience a sense of estrangement from their work. (*Compare with* apathy.) (Chapters 9, 11)

alterative movement A type of social movement that focuses on changing individuals' thinking and behavior in a specific, limited way; for example, Students against Drunk Driving. (*Compare with* redemptive movement, reformative movement, *and* transformative movement.) (Chapter 10)

animism The belief that spirits exist in other people or in the natural environment. (*Compare with* monotheism *and* polytheism.) (Chapter 16)

anticipatory socialization Preparation for future roles in society; for example, parents prepare their children for the world of work they are likely to be a part of when they are adults. (Chapter 6)

antithesis According to Marx and Engels, the contradictions and antagonisms within the structure of society that challenge that structure. (*See also* dialectic, thesis, *and* synthesis.) (Chapter 10)

apathy Indifference or lack of interest or concern. (*Compare with* alienation.) (Chapter 11)

appearance norms Standards of attractiveness, often applied to women. (Chapter 9)

ascribed status Social status over which a person has no control, such as race, sex, and class. (*See also* status; *Compare with* achieved status.) (Chapter 4)

atheist A person who denies or disbelieves the existence of a god or gods. (Chapter 16)

basic needs What a country's population requires for survival, including health, education, food, water, and sanitation. (Chapter 10)

bias Unwanted influences that can produce research results which are invalid or without foundation. (Chapter 2)

birth rate The number of births each year per 1,000 people in the population. (Chapters 3, 17)

blended families Families consisting of two partners and their respective children from previous relationships. When these new marriages produce children as well, they create a family consisting of stepsiblings, half-siblings, stepparents, and parents. (Chapter 15)

bourgeoisie The ownership class or group of capitalists who are the principal private owners of the society's means of production under capitalism. (Chapter 1)

bureaucracy An organization characterized by clear-cut division of labor, hierarchy of authority, adherence to formal rules, impartiality, and rewards based on merit. (*See also* secondary group.) (Chapters 1, 4)

business dominance theory (*also known as* **instrumentalism**) The view that the state is not a neutral arbiter of the common good because capitalists have captured it and use it to further their own interests. (Chapter 11)

capital The means of production. (Chapter 11)

capitalism A political economy characterized by an arrangement of production in which workers cooperate to produce wealth that is then privately owned by whoever hired the workers. (Chapters 1, 7, 11)

capitalist interests Individuals and organizations that benefit from amassing and maintaining private profits. (Chapter 11)

capitalist state structuralist theory Theoretical argument that an economy based on capitalism *forces* the state to shape its policies in ways that are consistent with capital-accumulation interests because the fate of the state rests on the economy's health. (Chapter 11)

capitalists Those who have invested in business and therefore own the means of production. (*Compare with* proletariat.) (Chapter 10)

catastrophic leave policy Allows workers to donate unused paid time off (such as sick leave, vacation time, and personal leave time) to fellow workers facing family crises. (Chapter 15)

church In the generic sense, religion or religious membership. (Chapter 16)

civil religion According to Bellah, a set of widely held beliefs, akin to a national religion, that a nation and its institutions are under the special favor of God, thus promoting national cohesion among heterogeneous groups. (Chapter 16)

class A segment of the population whose members are similar in their possession of and access to economic resources. (Chapter 7)

class consciousness According to Marx, workers' understanding of what capitalism was doing to them and their realization that it would be desirable to join others in a struggle against the capitalist class. (*Compare with* false consciousness.) (Chapters 1, 16)

class dialectic perspective The view that the conflict between the working and capitalist classes results in compromises in state policy that are not necessarily in the best interests of the capitalists. (Chapter 11)

class identity The sense of belonging to a particular economic class, resulting from shared life experiences, as, for example, that experienced by members of an elite. (Chapter 11)

collective embezzlement Situation in which the lack of supervision encouraged a great deal of fraud to occur in the savings and loan industry as standard operating procedure. (Chapter 11)

communism Political economy in which workers must cooperate to produce the goods and services needed, but the means of production are collectively owned by the workers themselves. (Chapter 11)

competitive individualism The belief that individuals are completely responsible for their own economic condition so that economic success (wealth) or failure (poverty) is the result of individual effort. (Chapter 5)

competitive sector A part of the formal labor market in which production is medium to small scale and which relies primarily on human labor rather than machinery for production. (Chapter 12)

compulsory heterosexuality The norm requiring adoption of a heterosexual public persona as a prerequisite for acceptance in mainstream society. (Chapter 6)

conflict perspective The view that social divisions and struggles characterize society; also the belief that social change is a result of conflict. (*See also* cyclical theory, equilibrium theory, *and* evolutionary theory.) (Chapters 1, 3, 6, 10)

conflict perspective on economic inequality A view holding that extreme economic inequality in a society is neither natural nor inevitable but gives rise to conflict within society. (Chapter 7)

containment theory A social-psychological explanation that suggests that deviant behavior is limited in society because of internal (personal) and external (societal) controls that contain the behavior of individuals. (*See also* social-psychological explanations; *compare with* control theory, differential

association theory, *and* social reinforcement theory.) (Chapter 9)

contingency work Employment that is temporary, contracted, leased, part-time, and other 'nonstandard' arrangements. (Chapter 12)

control group In research, a group of subjects that does not receive the special treatment designed for an experimental group. The control group serves as a baseline of comparison for the experimental group. (*Compare with* experimental group.) (Chapter 2)

control theory A social-psychological explanation for deviant behavior that suggests that such behavior results from the absence of social control or constraints. (*See also* social-psychological explanations; *compare with* containment theory, differential association theory, *and* social reinforcement theory.) (Chapter 9)

co-optation The socialization of prospective and new members of the power elite so that they come to share the worldview of that elite. (*See also* power elite.) (Chapter 11)

core concepts Fundamental ideas that are helpful in analyzing features of a society. (Chapter 1)

core nations In a world-system, countries in which production is based on technology that relies more on machinery than on human labor and in which human labor is relatively skilled and highly paid; they are usually relatively wealthy nations. (*See also* world-system; *compare with* peripheral nations *and* semiperipheral nations.) (Chapter 3)

corporate crime Violations of the law by corporations in their policies or operating procedures. (Chapter 9)

corporate culture The relationships and structures created in societies by corporate ideologies that promote and enhance the production of private profit; corporations in the core frequently export these ideologies to peripheral countries. (Chapter 5)

corporate welfare State policies and expenditures that redistribute wealth to corporations and the affluent by directly or indirectly subsidizing, supporting, rescuing, or otherwise socializing the cost and risk of investment and private profit making. (Chapter 11)

corporatization of medicine A trend in health care in which large private firms have entered the health care services field for the purpose of making a profit. (Chapter 14)

cottage industry A business whose labor force consists of family members who work at home using their own equipment. (Chapter 10)

counterculture A subculture whose members embrace values, norms, rituals, and lifestyles that directly challenge those of the dominant culture. (Chapter 5)

crime A form of behavior considered deviant because it is in violation of the law. (Chapter 9)

cult A religious group that generally accepts the legitimacy of other religious groups but has a negative tension with its social environment. (*Compare with* denomination *and* sect.) (Chapter 16)

cultural capital Material and nonmaterial goods that are socially valued, such as education or important social connections. (Chapter 13)

cultural diffusion The sharing and incorporation of a diversity of cultures from one society to another, or of subcultures within the dominant culture. (Chapter 5)

cultural hegemony A situation in which the ideas and values of the dominant members of society are diffused throughout society's institutions and imposed on less powerful members. (Chapter 5)

cultural lag The time it takes from the point at which a new subculture, technology, or idea is introduced to the point at which it is accepted or incorporated into the dominant culture. (Chapter 5)

cultural leveling Situation in which the diverse and distinctive differences between cultures become blurred as they increasingly come to resemble each other because of the common, dominating presence of corporate culture. (Chapter 5)

cultural myth of romanticism Ideology that explains female sexual activity as the result of being "swept off her feet" in the heat of a romantic moment. (Chapter 15)

cultural relativity A perspective that considers other cultures and their points of view as worthy of respect and understanding. (*Compare with* multiculturalism.) (Chapter 5)

cultural synchronization A condition in which people have shared cultural values and traits; according to Irvine, for example, many African Americans have cultural traits not shared by the dominant "Eurocentric" majority, and the two groups therefore lack cultural synchronization. (Chapter 13)

culture The social construction of reality of society's dominant groups, often imposed as a shared way of life among members of a society; it is sometimes shared and frequently challenged by subordinate groups. (Chapter 5)

culture of poverty The belief that poor people are poverty-stricken because of a shared lack of motivation to work hard, earn a living, or gain an education. (Chapter 5)

culture shock A feeling of confusion, uncertainty, surprise, or anxiety experienced when people are exposed to a different culture or behavior that does not conform to the prevailing norms. (Chapter 5)

cyclical theory The view that society is like a natural organism and that each society passes naturally and inevitably through the same life cycle phases as individual biological organisms, so that ultimately social change may be viewed as part of a natural cycle. (*Compare with* conflict theory, equilibrium theory, *and* evolutionary theory.) (Chapter 10)

de facto segregation Segregation as if by law; for example, schools may be segregated because neighborhoods are segregated, and it is "unwritten law" that neighborhoods will remain segregated. (*Compare with* de jure segregation.) (Chapter 13)

de jure segregation Segregation as a matter of law; for example, in the South before the 1964 Civil Rights Act was passed, there were laws to segregate schools. (*Compare with* de facto segregation.) (Chapter 13)

death rate The number of deaths each year per 1,000 people in the population. (Chapters 3, 17)

debt dependency A strategy of development based on reliance on aid and loans from other countries, international aid agencies, and banks. (*Compare with* dependent development *and* trade dependency.) (Chapter 10)

debt-for-nature swaps Arrangements in which debt-ridden governments agree to purchase or set aside land to conserve as state-owned parks and to protect the land's natural resources in exchange for debt cancellation. (Chapter 10)

declining significance of race The belief that because of changes in attitudes, passage and enforcement of civil rights laws, and efforts to promote educational and occupational opportunities, one's race is no longer a key social determinant in the United States. (Chapter 8)

definition of the situation *See* Thomas theorem.

degradation ceremony The process in which socialization agents attack and devalue an individual's existing identity in an effort to break it down and build a new one. (Chapter 6)

deindustrialization A state of decline in a nation's manufacturing activity; for example, goods may be produced in other countries and only assembled domestically. (Chapter 12)

democracy A government, organization, or group ruled and controlled by the people, usually the majority. (Chapter 4)

denomination A religious group that accepts the legitimacy of other religious groups and coexists peacefully with its social environment. (*Compare with* cult *and* sect.) (Chapter 16)

denominational society A society characterized by religious pluralism rather than by one dominant church. (Chapter 16)

dependent development A dual strategy combining import substitution and export processing adopted by peripheral nations in order to combat the drain on their resources and the unequal benefits of trade dependency. (*See also* export processing *and* import substitution; *compare with* debt dependency *and* trade dependency.) (Chapter 10)

dependent variable A variable in which change is caused by an independent variable. (*See also* variable; *compare with* independent variable.) (Chapter 2)

deregulation The process of removing or significantly relaxing government restrictions on an industry. (Chapter 11)

desegregation The elimination of the barriers separating or isolating the members of a racial minority group from the rest of society. (Chapter 13)

deviance Behavior or a condition of being that is in violation of or departs from social norms. (Chapter 9)

dialectic According to Marx and Engels, the ongoing process of social change marked by conflict. (*See also* antithesis, synthesis, *and* thesis.) (Chapter 10)

differential association theory A social-psychological explanation for deviant behavior that suggests that such behavior results from an individual associating with people who are already disposed toward deviant behavior. (*See also* social-psychological explanations; *compare with* containment theory, control theory, *and* social reinforcement theory.) (Chapter 9)

digital divide Pattern of inequality in which those who are of the dominant statuses relative to class, race, age, and nation enjoy privileged access to the Internet. (Chapter 17)

direct democracy A government, organization, or group in which all members participate in decision making. (*See also* democracy; *compare with* representative democracy.) (Chapter 4)

disengagement theory The view that it is natural for all elderly people to withdraw from the social roles they occupied when they were younger because of inevitable biological and psychological decline. (Chapter 7)

division of labor Arrangement of work in which tasks are broken into steps or jobs performed by different individuals or nations. (Chapters 3, 12)

domestic labor Work done to maintain the home and family, usually unpaid. (*Compare with* formal labor market *and* informal labor market.) (Chapter 12)

double day A situation in which women who work full time also perform most or all of the domestic chores at home; *also called* **double shift** or **second shift**. (*Compare with* triple shift.) (Chapters 6, 8, 12, 15)

double shift *See* double day.

economic inequality A system of inequality characterized by a vast difference in wealth and income possessed by families and individuals. (Chapter 7)

economy The institution made up of structures, relationships, and activities whose manifest function is to produce and distribute goods and services throughout society. (Chapters 3, 11)

education The institution whose manifest function is to transmit the knowledge and skills that all young members of society need to become productive members of the economy as adults. (Chapter 3)

ego As described by Freud, the rational self that controls the urges of the individual. (Chapter 6)

elite pluralist theory A perspective in which competing elites coexist and compromise to achieve a balanced government for the common good. (*Compare with* interest-group pluralism.) (Chapter 11)

employee stock option plans (ESOPs) Program in which workers purchase shares of stock in their own companies. By providing workers with a share of the profits their labor helps create, this approach may motivate them to become more productive. (Chapter 12)

environmental racism The dumping of toxic wastes in racial minority communities to a disproportionate degree compared to dumping in other areas. (Chapter 17)

equilibrium theory The view that society is like a biological organism such as the human body; according to this notion all systems in the organism are interdependent, and any disturbance or alteration in one of the systems requires adjustments in the other systems for the organism to maintain its equilibrium. (*Compare with* conflict perspective, cyclical theory, *and* evolutionary theory.) (Chapter 10)

ethnic group People with a shared racial, religious, or national heritage who possess the same cultural traits and sense of community. (Chapters 7, 8)

ethnocentrism The view that one's culture is the standard against which other cultures should be evaluated. (Chapter 5)

evolutionary theory The view that society is like a biological organism that evolves to a higher life form with each change, so that social change is viewed as evolutionary. (*Compare with* conflict perspective, cyclical theory, *and* equilibrium theory.) (Chapter 10)

experimental group In research, a group of subjects that receives special treatment designed by the researcher so that the effects of that treatment may be studied. (*Compare with* control group.) (Chapter 2)

experimental research Research conducted to determine how a particular organism or object is affected by different types of treatment selected by the researcher. (*Compare with* field research *and* historical research.) (Chapter 2)

export processing The strategy adopted by peripheral nations of manufacturing goods for sale abroad in order to combat the drain on their resources and the unequal benefits of trade dependency. (*See also* trade dependency.) (Chapter 10)

extended family A family that includes the nuclear family plus other members of one or both of the parents' families of orientation, such as grandparents or aunts and uncles. (*See also* families of orientation; *Compare with* nuclear family.) (Chapter 15)

false consciousness According to Marx, the failure of workers to understand that capitalism and not themselves is to blame for their alienation and misery. (*Compare with* class consciousness.) (Chapters 1, 16)

false universalism The belief that all persons with a given status experience life in the same ways; for example, that all women have the same life experiences regardless of their race, class, or age. (Chapter 8)

families of choice A family form defined not by biology but by choice, marked by stable relationships based on shared economic and emotional ties in one or more households, such as those found where heterosexual or homosexual couples live together but are not married. (*Compare with* families of orientation *and* families of procreation.) (Chapter 15)

families of orientation Families into which people are born or adopted. (*Compare with* families of procreation *and* families of choice.) (Chapter 15)

families of procreation Families into which people marry and produce offspring. (*Compare with* families of orientation *and* families of choice.) (Chapter 15)

family An organized ongoing network of kin and nonkin who interact daily, sharing economic and household responsibilities and obligations, providing for domestic needs of all members, and ensuring their survival. (Chapters 3, 15)

feminism Belief in the political, economic, and social equality of the sexes which may be held by any person, male or female. (Chapter 7)

feminist spirituality An unofficial religion that supports the beliefs that people need to be ecologically sensitive and that they are part of nature and its cycles. (*See also* non-official religion.) (Chapter 16)

feminization of poverty A situation in which a growing percentage of the poor live in female-headed households; subtly suggests that women choose to be poor and stay on welfare or somehow bring poverty on themselves. (*Compare with* pauperization of motherhood.) (Chapter 15)

fertility rate The number of children that would be born to a woman were she to live through her childbearing years and reproduce consistently at her age group's fertility rate (Chapter 17)

field research Research conducted at the place where the subjects are located so that the researcher may gain information through firsthand observation. (*Compare with* experimental research *and* historical research.) (Chapter 2)

flextime An arrangement of work hours that allows more free time for the worker so long as a full day or week of work is performed; for example, some workers work four-day weeks with 10 hours of work a day so that they can have three days off to take care of their families. (Chapter 15)

folkways The least formal or important norms, usually involving conventional routines such as how many meals a day we eat. (*See also* norms; *compare with* laws *and* mores.) (Chapter 5)

formal labor market Consists of people who are paid for their work, usually performed outside the home. (*Compare with* domestic labor *and* informal labor market.) (Chapter 12)

functional imperatives According to functionalists, the social needs that must be met in order for a society to survive. (Chapter 3)

functionalist perspective The view that societies are adaptive social structures that help human beings adjust to their physical, political, economic, and social environment. (Chapters 1, 3)

functionalist perspective on economic inequality The belief that economic inequality is the result of beneficial forces and that different occupational levels in society should receive markedly different rewards. (Chapter 7)

functionalist theory of deviance The belief that deviant behavior is a necessary and possibly even desirable thing; for example, criminals perform a service to society in that their crimes anger and upset members of society who then come together and become more cohesive as a group. (Chapter 9)

gatekeepers Schools that open different doors of opportunity for different student populations through such policies as tracking, thus depriving students from economically disadvantaged backgrounds of knowledge and school credentials that could facilitate their future upward mobility. (*See also* tracking.) (Chapters 2, 13)

gender The category of masculine or feminine, determined by societal expectations for behavior and ways of relating to others based on sex. (*Compare with* sex.) (Chapter 7)

gender inequality A system in which males and females are perceived and treated as unequals, usually characterized by a belief in male supremacy. (Chapter 7)

generalized other A concept developed by George Herbert Mead to refer to the attitude of the larger community assumed by an individual to be important. (*Compare with* significant other.) (Chapter 6)

genocide The systematic extermination of a group of people by those who consider themselves racially superior. (Chapter 7)

gilded welfare State policies and budgetary expenditures that redistribute wealth from the poor and working class to the middle class and the affluent. These include Social Security, Medicare, federal income tax deductions for home ownership and local property taxes, dependent children tax deductions, and home business tax deductions. (Chapter 11)

glass ceiling A level in a company or bureaucracy above which women or racial minorities rarely are able to rise. (Chapter 12)

global division of labor Situation in which the work required to produce the world's goods and services is broken into separate tasks, each performed largely by different groups of nations or groups within nations. (Chapter 3)

globalization A process whereby the world-system of economic relationships becomes increasingly dominant, linking and integrating ever-larger numbers of societies into a worldwide network of economic and political relationships. (Chapters 12, 17)

government The politicians who occupy the structure of the state. (*See also* state.) (Chapters 3, 11)

greenhouse effect An increase in Earth's temperature that results when carbon dioxide is released and trapped in the atmosphere; occurs, for example, when fossil fuels are burned. (Chapter 3)

group A collection of individuals who have regular interaction. (Chapter 4)

health A term that can carry varying meanings, such as the absence of illness and death, or the ability of people to use their full physical and mental capabilities. (Chapter 14)

health care system A system whose participants include physicians and other medical professionals; clinics and hospitals; universities, research centers, and corporations; government agencies; and insurance firms. (Chapter 14)

heterosexism The belief that homosexuality is unnatural and immoral. (Chapter 7)

historical research A type of research that is concerned with establishing facts about the past. (*Compare with* experimental research *and* field research.) (Chapter 2)

homogenization of news A single perspective and analysis of news stories resulting from a few large conglomerates owning several media outlets. (Chapter 6)

household A common residential unit in which related and nonrelated individuals may live. (Chapter 15)

human agency The ability of humans to react to and change the social conditions surrounding them. (Chapter 1)

hypothesis A carefully formulated proposition that may be either verified or discarded on the basis of the examination of relevant data. (Chapter 2)

id As described by Freud, a primitive, almost feral self that compels individuals to focus on their own personal pleasure. (Chapter 6)

ideological hegemony The dominance of a set of ideas that govern actions and make other options appear not to make sense. (Chapter 7)

ideology A systematic body of ideas (e.g., doctrines or myths) held by members of a class, institution, or group. (Chapters 5, 7)

immigrant minorities Groups who came to the United States voluntarily, such as Asians and Latin Americans. (*Compare with* involuntary minorities.) (Chapter 13)

import substitution The strategy adopted by peripheral nations of substituting locally produced goods for imported goods in order to combat the drain on their resources and the unequal benefits of trade dependency. (*See also* trade dependency.) (Chapter 10)

imposter syndrome The feeling of people from the lower classes who succeed in life that they have fooled others into thinking that they are deserving of recognition, respect, and acceptance. (Chapter 6)

income Money received in the form of hourly wages or annual salaries, or government benefits, or return on investments. (Chapter 7)

independent variable A variable that affects another variable. A change in the independent variable causes the other variable to change. (*See also* variable; *compare with* dependent variable.) (Chapter 2)

inequality based on able-bodiedness A system of inequality in which members with physical or mental disabilities are thought of and treated as less worthy than others. (Chapter 7)

inequality based on sexual orientation A system of inequality in which members with a particular sexual orientation are thought of and treated as less worthy than others. (Chapter 7)

infant mortality rate The number of infants who die within the first year of life per 1,000 live births. (Chapters 3, 14, 17)

informal labor market Consists of people who are not paid for their work; may include both voluntary and involuntary work. (*Compare with* domestic labor *and* formal labor market.) (Chapter 12)

informal organization A social structure that emerges spontaneously as people interact in bureaucratic or formal organizational settings. (Chapter 4)

innovation With respect to religion, the establishment of new religious rituals or entirely new religions as a response to the secularization of a religion. (*See also* secularization; *compare with* revival.) (Chapter 16)

institutional racism Racial prejudice or discrimination embedded in the routine functioning of societal institutions. (*Compare with* personal racism.) (Chapter 7)

institutional sexism Prejudicial or discriminatory practices that foster advantages for males that accompany the routine operations of societal institutions. (Chapter 7)

institutions The social structures societies possess to fulfill fundamental social needs; five institutions are found in all societies—family, religion, economy, education, and the state. (Chapter 3)

instrumentalism See business dominance theory.

interchangeability of elites The mobility of members of the power elite to progress from one institutional sphere of influence to another; for example, someone may be a leader in a corporation and then move to a position of power in the state. (*See also* power elite.) (Chapter 11)

interest-group pluralism A perspective in which a variety of competing interest groups coexist and compromise to produce a balanced government for the common good. (*Compare with* elite pluralist theory.) (Chapter 11)

interlocking board of directors See interlocking corporate directorate.

interlocking corporate directorate A relationship between two corporations formed when one person serves on the board of directors of both corporations. (Chapter 11)

inventions New practices and objects developed out of existing knowledge. (Chapter 10)

involuntary minorities Groups who were incorporated into U.S. society through colonization, conquest, or slavery, for example, Native Americans and African Americans. (*Compare with* immigrant minorities.) (Chapter 13)

iron law of oligarchy The inevitable tendency for organizations to be ruled by a few people, even those organizations that purport to be democratic. (Chapter 4)

label An identifying or descriptive word or phrase, often with a negative connotation when applied to people, for example, a "label of deviance" or "labeled an outcast." (Chapter 9)

labeling theory A theory of deviance that draws attention to how people come to be labeled as deviants and the impact of this label on such individuals and their subsequent behavior. (Chapter 9)

language Patterns of written symbols, audible sounds, and gestures that convey meanings. (Chapter 5)

latent function An unintended and sometimes unrecognized result that is produced as institutions carry out their manifest functions. (*See also* institutions; *compare with* manifest function.) (Chapter 3)

latent social change Social change that is largely unrecognized and unintended; for example, the effects of the baby boom in the United States. (*Compare with* manifest social change.) (Chapter 10)

laws The most formal and important norms, which are considered so vital that they are written as legal formalizations. (*See also* norms; *compare with* folkways *and* mores.) (Chapter 5)

learned helplessness The learned lack of confidence in one's abilities, usually resulting as a response to how one is treated. (Chapter 13)

Liberation Theology Religious teaching that stresses non-acceptance of poverty, challenge of authority if it is oppressive or punitive, civil disobedience, and the legitimacy of nontraditional lifestyles. (Chapters 6, 16)

life chances One's ability to experience life and all its beneficial offerings. (Chapters 1, 3)

life expectancy The average number of years a group of people all born in the same year are expected to live. (Chapters 14, 17)

looking-glass self People's evaluation of themselves based on how they imagine others perceive and react to them. (Chapter 6)

macro-level social structures The large-scale social structures that organize and distribute individuals into social positions, for example, institutions, societies, and the world-system. (*See also* social structure; *compare with* micro-level social structures *and* midlevel social structures.) (Chapter 3)

male chauvinism A form of sexism through which men express the belief that males are superior to females and have a right to insist on the subordination of females. (*See also* sexism.) (Chapter 7)

managed care A system by which insurance companies set forth strict terms and conditions under which they will pay for services for individuals' health problems. (Chapter 14)

managerial revolution The separation of the functions of ownership and control in corporations, with the power of corporate decision making going to managers. (Chapter 12)

manifest function The basic social need an institution is intended to address. (*See also* institutions; *compare with* latent function.) (Chapter 3)

manifest social change Social change resulting from a deliberate organized effort on the part of one group, for example, the American Revolution or the feminist movement. (*Compare with* latent social change.) (Chapter 10)

Marxist theory of deviance A sociological explanation for deviant behavior that suggests that such behavior within the working class results from a sense of alienation, low wages, and unemployment. (*See also* alienation *and* sociological explanations; *compare with* opportunity structure theory.) (Chapter 9)

master status The one status (among several that each individual has) that overrides all others, thus dictating how a person is treated. (*See also* status.) (Chapter 4)

material culture Physical artifacts that define a society, such as a flag, style of dress, or housing. (*Compare with* nonmaterial culture.) (Chapter 5)

maternal mortality The number of women who die as a result of pregnancy and birthing per 100,000 infants born. (Chapter 14)

McDonaldization of society As described by Ritzer, the exportation of U.S. corporate culture around the world and the consequent homogenization of global culture. (Chapter 5)

medical model The perspective that health consists of the absence of illness or disease. (*See also* proactive health care system *and* reactive health care system.) (Chapter 14)

merger The takeover or absorption of one company by another, often accomplished by the purchase of the company that is taken over. (*See also* merger mania.) (Chapter 12)

merger mania A situation in which many mergers or company takeovers occur. (*See also* merger.) (Chapter 12)

meritocracy A system that rewards people based on their merit. (Chapter 13)

micro-level social structures Social structures through which individuals relate to one another, such as an individual's status or role in society. (*See also* social structure; *compare with* macro-level social structures *and* midlevel social structures.) (Chapter 4)

midlevel social structures Medium-sized social structures such as groups and organizations. (*See also* social structure; *compare with* macro-level social structures *and* micro-level social structures.) (Chapter 4)

middle class Loosely defined as a category of people whose income places them above the poverty line but below the wealthiest fifth of the population. It may also be conceptualized by lifestyle, including home ownership and the ability to send one's children to college. (Chapter 12)

military-industrial complex A structure, composed of the uniformed military, the aerospace-defense industry, the civilian national security managers, and the U.S. Congress, each of which works to advance the interests of its members while simultaneously promoting and reinforcing the interests of the others. (Chapter 11)

minority group An inferior status assigned by the dominant group in a society to another group of people regardless of their numbers within the society. (Chapter 7)

modernization theory The view that poor countries can move from traditional to industrial economies by adopting the value systems of industrialized Western nations. (Chapter 10)

monotheism Belief in one god. (*Compare with* animism *and* polytheism.) (Chapter 16)

mores Norms specifying behaviors that must or must not occur, and to which strong feelings may be attached, such as those relating to the selection of a marriage partner. (*See also* norms; *compare with* folkways *and* laws.) (Chapter 5)

motherhood norms A standard of behavior holding that normal women want to have children; in contrast, women who do not have children or who choose not to have children are exhibiting a form of deviant behavior. (Chapter 9)

multiculturalism A perspective that acknowledges the heterogeneity of societies, examines the contributions and the intersection of many different groups at crucial moments in history, and explores the factors that affected the experiences of each group. (*Compare with* cultural relativity.) (Chapter 5)

multinational (*or* **transnational**) **corporations** Companies that operate production and trade facilities in countries other than their own. (Chapter 11)

nations Political entities with clearly defined geographic boundaries usually recognized by neighboring nations and characterized by the viewpoint and interests of their dominant groups or societies. (Chapter 3)

nature-versus-nurture debate Disagreement among social scientists concerning whether genetics (nature) or environment (nurture) exerts a stronger influence on human behavior. (Chapter 6)

negative sanctions Social control in the form of punishment meted out to those who violate the norms of society by exhibiting deviant behavior. (*See also* sanctions; *compare with* positive sanctions.) (Chapter 9)

net worth The value of one's assets (wealth), minus the value of one's outstanding debts. (Chapter 7)

New Federalism A political philosophy that endorses the belief that the federal government should be involved only in taxation and national defense and that all else is the responsibility of state or local governments. (Chapter 11)

no-fault divorce The dissolution of a marriage in which neither party must attribute blame or misconduct to the other in order to be granted the divorce. (Chapter 15)

nonmaterial culture The body of abstractions that defines the way a society's members live; abstractions include knowledge, beliefs, values, customs, rituals, and symbols. (*Compare with* material culture.) (Chapter 5)

nonofficial religion A departure from the beliefs and practices of official religion; also called popular or folk religion. (*Compare with* official religion.) (Chapter 16)

normative indoctrination The teaching of norms to individuals. (*See also* norms.) (Chapter 5)

norms Rules or standards of proper behavior that are formed by interacting individuals. (Chapters 4, 5, 9)

nuclear family A family consisting of two parents and their offspring. (*Compare with* extended family.) (Chapter 15)

official religion A formal, organized religious group. (*Compare with* nonofficial religion.) (Chapter 16)

open-ended research questions In research, exploratory questions that leave the sociologist flexibility in deciding what should be considered relevant data. (Chapter 2)

opportunity structure theory A sociological explanation for deviant behavior that suggests that such behavior results from a society that stresses the importance of material success but does not provide all members with the same means to achieve that success. (*See also* sociological explanations; *compare with* Marxist theory of deviance.) (Chapter 9)

pandemic A disease found throughout the world and affecting a large number of people. (Chapter 14)

participant observation A type of field research in which the researcher plays an active role in the group to the point where he or she becomes an active participant. (*See also* field research *and* passive observation.) (Chapter 2)

passive observation A type of field research in which the researcher observes the group and records the events for later analysis and interpretation. (*See also* field research *and* participant observation.) (Chapter 2)

patriarchy A social system in which male dominance is considered a natural, inalienable right. (Chapters 5, 7)

pauperization of motherhood A situation in which a growing percentage of the poor have female-headed households; subtly suggests that women are impoverished as a result of institutional forces. (*Compare with* feminization of poverty.) (Chapter 15)

perestroika The restructuring of the Soviet Union. (Chapter 17)

peripheral nations In a world-system, countries in which production is based on technology that relies more on inexpensive human labor than on expensive machinery; such countries are usually economically poor. (*See also* world-system; *compare with* core nations *and* semiperipheral nations.) (Chapter 3)

personal racism The racial prejudice or discrimination expressed by individuals or small groups of people. (*Compare with* institutional racism.) (Chapter 7)

personal troubles Matters involving a person's character and his or her relations with others over which the individual has control. (*Compare with* public issues.) (Chapter 1)

physiological explanations Within the context of explaining deviant behavior, explanations that attribute such behavior to a physical peculiarity or malfunction or to heredity. (*Compare with* psychological explanations, social-psychological explanations, *and* sociological explanations.) (Chapter 9)

pluralism The theory that competing interest groups or elites coexist, cooperate, and maintain a balance of power to create government in the common good. (Chapter 11)

political economy The intersection of the institutions of state and economy (Chapter 11)

political socialization The process through which people internalize a political identity that defines who they are and how they should behave in the political and economic institutions of society. (Chapter 6)

polytheism Belief in more than one god. (*Compare with* animism *and* monotheism.) (Chapter 16)

positive sanctions Social control in the form of rewards given to those who conform to the norms and abide by the rules of society. (*See also* sanctions; *compare with* negative sanctions.) (Chapter 9)

power elite People who fill the command positions of strategically important institutions, such as the state, the corporate economy, and the military, and who come from a similar background and share a single worldview. (Chapter 11)

Power Elite Theory Theory of power in which there is a select, or elite, group of individuals in whom power is concentrated, ensuring that their interests will prevail over all others. (Chapter 11)

primary group A collection of individuals who interact frequently and share important connections that bring the members together, for example, family, friends, and coworkers. (*See also* group; *compare with* secondary group.) (Chapter 4)

primary sources Sources of information used in historical research that have not been interpreted, evaluated, or analyzed by others, for example, original records, diaries, official documents, eyewitness accounts, and oral histories. (*Compare with* secondary sources.) (Chapter 2)

proactive health care system A preventive system of health care aimed at enhancing people's overall well-being and potential. (*See also* medical model; *compare with* reactive health care system.) (Chapter 14)

profane Ordinary, everyday, or nonreligious. (*Compare with* sacred.) (Chapter 16)

proletariat The working class; those who do not own the means of production and must therefore sell their labor power in order to live. (*Compare with* capitalists.) (Chapters 1, 10)

psychological explanations Within the context of explaining deviant behavior, explanations that attribute such behavior to emotional problems or unusual personality traits that often result from experiences with family members or other people in a position to influence one's psychological development. (*Compare with* physiological explanations, social-psychological explanations, *and* sociological explanations.) (Chapter 9)

public issues Societal conditions that transcend the individual and lie beyond his or her personal environment and control, such as rising unemployment. (*Compare with* personal troubles.) (Chapter 1)

race A category into which people are assigned based on the social meaning and significance given to certain physical (and sometimes cultural) characteristics of members of a society's population. (Chapter 7)

racial formation According to Omi and Winant, the process in which the dominant groups establish the content and importance of racial categories. (Chapter 7)

racial inequality A system of inequality in which members of one race are thought of and treated as less worthy than members of another, resulting in discrimination and exploitation. (Chapter 7)

random A system of sample selection in which every individual in the total population has an equal chance of being selected. (Chapter 2)

reactive health care system A health care system organized to respond to existing illness or disease rather than prevent it. (*Compare with* proactive health care system.) (Chapter 14)

recidivism A tendency to relapse into a previous mode of behavior; for example, people who have gone to prison more than once are recidivists. (Chapter 9)

redemptive movement A type of social movement directed at totally changing individuals rather than society as a whole; often a religious movement. (*Compare with* alterative movement, reformative movement, *and* transformative movement.) (Chapter 10)

redline A banking practice that defines certain areas, such as those with a large minority population, as ineligible for mortgages and small-business loans. (Chapter 17)

reductionism A process that reduces complex ideas or information to simple terms; for example, people who attribute deviant behavior to physiological or psychological reasons only and do not consider larger societal influences are practicing reductionism. (Chapter 9)

reference group A group to whom people look for approval, guidance, and role models; for example, peer groups. (Chapter 6)

reformative movement A type of social movement that aims to make limited but specific changes in society rather than just in individuals; for example, the civil rights movement. (*Compare with* alterative movement, redemptive movement, *and* transformative movement.) (Chapter 10)

relative deprivation According to Davies, the state in which people's understanding of deprivation is relative to the conditions around them, to conditions they expect, or to conditions that previously existed. (*Compare with* absolute deprivation.) (Chapter 10)

religion A body of beliefs and practices (embraced by a social group) concerned with the supernatural and the sacred that encourages followers to conduct themselves in accordance with moral prescriptions associated with the beliefs. (Chapters 3, 16)

representative democracy A government, organization, or group in which people choose or elect others to make decisions for them. (*See also* democracy; *compare with* direct democracy.) (Chapter 4)

research methods The research tools used by sociologists, such as surveys, that help to generate new knowledge. (Chapter 2)

resocialization The process in which an individual's previous self is replaced with a new, more acceptable social identity. (Chapter 6)

resource mobilization theory The view that social movements and revolutions will not occur regardless of how strong the feelings of the people may be unless human and supportive resources are available and deployed for use. (Chapter 10)

revival With respect to religion, an effort to renew and revitalize the traditional orientations of religions that are becoming secularized. (*See also* secularization; *compare with* innovation.) (Chapter 16)

rituals Regularly practiced formal ceremonies, usually marking important personal or social events. (Chapter 5)

role conflict The distress individuals experience when the demands of two or more roles they play are at odds. (*Compare with* role strain.) (Chapter 4)

role set The multiple roles that a given individual is expected to fulfill and the relationships of these various roles to the roles of others. (Chapter 4)

role strain The distress individuals experience when one of the roles they play contains contradictory demands. (*Compare with* role conflict.) (Chapter 4)

rolelessness The absence of socially sanctioned roles. (Chapter 8)

runaway shops Work facilities that are moved to locations where labor is inexpensive and often nonunionized and taxes and laws favor business interests. (Chapter 12)

sacred Relating to religious objects, beings, and situations that inspire awe, reverence, or fear. (*Compare with* profane.) (Chapter 16)

sample A set of subjects that is representative of the total population of subjects. (Chapter 2)

sanctions Social control in the form of punishment meted out to those who exhibit deviant behavior or rewards given to those who conform to the norms of society. (Chapters 5, 9)

sandwich generation Generation of adults caring for both elders and children. (Chapter 15)

Sapir-Whorf hypothesis Notion that people's understanding of the world around them can be limited by their language; they only know the world by the very words they learn and use. (Chapter 5)

second shift *See* double day.

secondary data analysis The analysis of data that have already been gathered by others, often for totally different purposes. (Chapter 2)

secondary group A collection of individuals who come together for a specific purpose such as accomplishing a task or achieving a goal; primary groups may form as a result of people's participation in secondary groups. (*See also* group; *compare with* primary group.) (Chapter 4)

secondary sources Sources of information used in historical research that have been interpreted, evaluated, or analyzed by others, for example, publica-tions of scholars. (*Compare with* primary sources.) (Chapter 2)

sect A religious group formed by people protesting their social environment, including other religious groups. (*Compare with* cult *and* denomination.) (Chapter 16)

secularization The decline in significance of religion in people's lives. (Chapter 16)

segmented labor market A divided labor market resulting from the fact that men and women, and people in different racial categories, compete in different labor markets for different jobs. (Chapter 12)

self-fulfilling prophecy The phenomenon in which people achieve to the level expected of them rather than to the level of which they may actually be capable. (Chapters 6, 13)

semiperipheral nations In a world-system, countries in which production is based on a mixture of intermediate levels of machinery and human labor and in which human labor is semiskilled and paid intermediate levels of wages. (*See also* world-system; *compare with* core nations and peripheral nations.) (Chapter 3)

sex The category of male or female, determined by fundamental biological characteristics. (*Compare with* gender.) (Chapter 7)

sexism The systematic subordination of people on the basis of their sex. (Chapter 7)

sexual division of labor A division of responsibilities for women and men based on biological differences; for example, because women bear children, it is often the custom that they stay home and be caretakers. (Chapter 7)

significant other An individual who serves as the most important person, and therefore a crucial role model, in another individual's life. (*Compare with* generalized other.) (Chapter 6)

single-payer plan A system of health care in which the government controls fees, streamlines administration, and has all bills submitted to it for payment. (Chapter 14)

social aggregate A collection of individuals with no real interpersonal ties or patterned relationships, such as people who attend a concert or sporting event. (Chapter 4)

social capital A crucial social resource that all people possess to a greater or lesser degree. (Chapter 4)

social change Significant variations or alterations in social structures and cultures over time. (Chapter 10)

social construction The creation of ideas regarding people and their relationships to others by members of a social group; for example, the idea that there are biologically distinct races, some of which are inferior to others. (Chapter 7)

social construction (of deviance) The social process by which people come to define others as deviant, either in their behavior or by their being. (Chapter 9)

social control Means of minimizing socially deviant behavior. (Chapter 9)

social Darwinism An extension of the evolutionary perspective which holds that as societies evolve and change, only the fittest will survive and those that are less fit will die out. (*See also* evolutionary perspective.) (Chapter 10)

social determinism The view that important features of society are determinants of what happens to individuals. (Chapter 1)

social facts Social and cultural features of a society, existing independently of the individuals who make it up, which influence people's behavior. (Chapter 1)

social movements Large-scale, persistent efforts in which individuals working together may alter how institutions and whole societies operate. (Chapters 3, 10)

social networks The complex patterns of social relationships and ties to others in which individuals are caught up. (Chapter 4)

social-psychological explanations Within the context of explaining deviant behavior, explanations that attribute such behavior to conditions in people's immediate social environment that influence their thinking and actions. (*Compare with* physiological explanations, psychological explanations, *and* sociological explanations.) (Chapter 9)

social reform An adjustment in the content of cultural patterns of behavior or normative systems that does not fundamentally alter the social structure. (*Compare with* social revolution.) (Chapter 10)

social reinforcement theory A social-psychological explanation for deviant behavior that suggests that such behavior results from the belief that the rewards of deviant behavior outweigh the punishments. (*See also* social-psychological explanations; *compare with* containment theory, control theory, *and* differential association theory.) (Chapter 9)

social reproduction Maintenance rather than change of existing social systems; for example, by conserving the status quo, schools perpetuate racism and sexism. (Chapter 13)

social revolution A fundamental and radical upheaval of existing social structures. (*Compare with* social reform.) (Chapter 10)

social role The behavior expected of individuals in the various positions or statuses they hold. (Chapter 4)

social stratification Ways in which people occupying different social positions can be ranked from high to low. (Chapters 1, 7)

social structure The way in which recurring patterns of relationships within a social system are organized. (Chapters 3, 4)

social systems The ongoing ways that groups of people organize themselves and relate to one another in order to survive. (Chapter 3)

social welfare State policies and expenditures which redistribute wealth from the affluent to the poor and working class to reduce poverty and economic inequality. (Chapter 11)

socialism Political economy in which production of goods and services involves the social cooperation between workers to create wealth. The means of production are likely to be owned or controlled by the state. (Chapters 1, 11)

socialization The ongoing process of learning the ways of a culture. (Chapter 6)

socialization agents Elements that bring about the process of socialization; the agents can be grouped into seven categories—family; peers; school; religion; work; media; and toys, games, and recreational activities. (Chapter 6)

society An organization of people who share a common territory, govern themselves, and cooperate to secure the survival of the group. (Chapter 3)

sociobiology The study of the biological basis of social behavior. (*See also* nature-versus-nurture debate.) (Chapter 6)

sociological explanations Within the context of explaining deviant behavior, explanations that attribute the behavior to societal factors outside the control of individuals. (*Compare with* physiological explanations, psychological explanations, *and* social-psychological explanations.) (Chapter 9)

sociological imagination A way of thinking that enables individuals to understand how they are affected by broad features of the society and the times in which they live. Chapter 1)

sociology The study of people as participants in and creators of society. (Chapter 1)

state The institution made up of political positions and the structure of political relations whose manifest function is to protect society's members from internal and external threats. (Chapters 3, 11)

status The position a person occupies in a group or organization; for example, in a family a person may have the status of son and brother. (Chapter 4)

status inconsistency A situation in which one indication of a person's standing in society is out of sync with the others; for example, someone with an advanced academic degree working at a blue-collar job. (Chapter 15)

stigma A negative mark that discredits a person's worth. (Chapters 7, 9)

subculture A group whose members participate in the larger society and its institutions but who share values, norms, a heritage, and rituals that differ from those of the dominant culture. (Chapter 5)

superego As described by Freud, the conscience that functions as the restraining force of the id and the ego, reinforcing the limiting rules of social behavior. (Chapter 6)

supply-side economics An economic philosophy that supports the belief that benefits to capitalists will trickle down to benefit labor and ultimately to benefit everyone; also called trickle-down economics. (Chapter 11)

surrogate mother A woman, usually hired by a married couple, who carries a fertilized egg and gives birth to a child but then turns over the baby to the other woman, who will be the child's legal mother. (Chapter 10)

survey A type of research in which the participants fill out a questionnaire or answer questions in person or over the phone. (Chapter 2)

symbolic annihilation "The absence of experience of a group of people in the media" (Lont, 2001:119). When individuals see few people of color, women, gays and lesbians, people with disabilities, or the poor, or hear few of their voices talking about their experiences as valid, it suggests that these people do not exist or are unimportant. (Chapter 6)

symbolic interaction An interpersonal process that uses language and other symbols, and sanctions, to create, maintain, and alter culture and society. (Chapter 6)

symbolic interactionism A sociological perspective that focuses on such topics as the ways in which shared meanings among individuals develop or change through social interaction. (Chapter 1)

synthesis According to Marx and Engels, the result of the conflict between the thesis and the antithesis; a whole new social structure containing elements of both the thesis and the antithesis. (*See also* antithesis, dialectic, *and* thesis.) (Chapter 10)

systems of inequality Sets of social relationships built around an attribute, such as wealth or sexual orientation, to which members of society accord a great deal of meaning and importance in everyday life. (Chapter 7)

terrorism The use of violence as a strategy to gain political objectives, often by individuals or groups who usually have relatively little power otherwise. (Chapter 17)

thesis According to Marx and Engels, the current or temporary state of existence of a society. (*See also* antithesis, dialectic, and synthesis.) (Chapter 10)

Thomas theorem The view that if a situation is defined as real, the consequences of actions based on that definition are quite real, regardless of whether the definition is accurate; for example, if women are defined as inferior to men, they will be treated as inferior regardless of the reality; also called definition of the situation. (Chapter 5)

total institutions Institutions in which individuals are completely isolated from the rest of society for an extended period of time; for example, mental institutions. (Chapter 6)

toxic imperialism Toxic dumping in underdeveloped countries by major corporations and industrialized or core nations. (Chapter 17)

tracking A policy in many schools wherein students are grouped for instruction on the basis of the presumption that their past classroom performance and standardized test scores are valid indicators of their ability and potential; for example, schools may divide students into academic (college-bound) and vocational (employment-bound) tracks. (*See also* gatekeepers.) (Chapters 2, 13)

trade dependency A relationship between nations characterized by limited numbers of core trade partners for peripheral countries. (*Compare with* dependent development *and* debt dependency.) (Chapter 10)

transformative movement A type of social movement that aims to make sweeping, rather than limited, changes in society, for example, revolution. (*Compare with* alterative movement, redemptive movement, *and* reformative movement.) (Chapter 10)

trickle-down economics *See* supply-side economics.

triple shift A situation in which women work in the formal labor market and the informal labor market in addition to working at domestic labor. (*See also* domestic labor, formal labor market, *and* informal labor market; *compare with* double day.) (Chapter 12)

underdeveloped nation A peripheral nation that has experienced historically disadvantageous relationships with more powerful industrialized or core nations and thus has been limited in its development opportunities. (*See also* core nation *and* peripheral nation.) (Chapter 10)

underemployment The situation in which individuals are employed at jobs that do not fully utilize their skills, that pay less than a living wage, or that offer no opportunity for full-time employment. (Chapter 12)

values Assumptions and judgments made about the goods, goals, or states of existence that are deemed important, desirable, and worth striving for. (Chapter 5)

variables Attitudes, behaviors, or conditions that can vary. (Chapter 2)

war An organized, armed conflict between nations. (Chapter 17)

wealth The value of the assets or property that one owns. (Chapter 7)

whistle-blowers People, usually workers, who speak out against unfair, unethical, unsafe, or illegal practices of the institution for which they work. (Chapter 9)

white-collar crime Violations of the law by individuals in the course of their occupations or professions; crimes that benefit them. (Chapter 9)

white-skin privilege Social advantages, usually unearned, provided to members of the white majority. (Chapter 8)

work Any activity that produces something of value for other people. (Chapter 12)

worker cooperative A company that is owned and operated by its workers. (Chapter 12)

world-system An international social system of cultural, normative, economic, political, and military relations organized around the exchange of goods and services; the most complete macro-level social structure, which encompasses all other levels of social structure. (*See also* macro-level social structure *and* social structure.) (Chapter 3)

References

Aaron, Vanetta, Keith D. Parker, Suzanne Ortega, and Thomas Calhoun. 1999. "The extended family as a source of support among African Americans." *Challenge: A Journal of Research on African American Men* 10(2):23–36.

Abbott, Franklin, ed. 1998. *Boyhood, Growing Up Male: A Multicultural Anthology.* Madison: University of Wisconsin Press.

Abdolali, Nasrin and Daniel S. Ward. 1998. "The Senate Armed Services Committee and defense budget making: The role of deference, dollars, and ideology." *Journal of Political and Military Sociology* 26(2):229–52.

Aberle, David. 1966. *The Peyote Religion among the Navaho.* Chicago: Aldine.

Abowd, John M. and David S. Kaplan. 1998. "Executive compensation: Six questions that need answering." BLS Working Papers No. 319. Washington, DC: U.S. Department of Labor, Bureau of Labor Statistics.

Abraham, Laurie K. 1994. *Mama Might Be Better Off Dead: The Failure of Health Care in Urban America.* Chicago: University of Chicago Press.

Abramovitz, Mimi. 1996. *Regulating the Lives of Women: Social Welfare Policy from Colonial Times to the Present.* Boston: South End Press.

———. **2000.** *Under Attack, Fighting Back: Women and Welfare in the United States.* New York: Monthly Review Press.

Acuña, Rodolfo. 2000. *Occupied America: A History of Chicanos.* 4th ed. Boston: Addison-Wesley.

Adam, Barry D. 1987. *The Rise of the Gay and Lesbian Movement.* Boston: Twayne.

Adler, Patricia. 1985. *Wheeling and Dealing.* New York: Columbia University Press.

——— **and Peter Adler, eds. 1994.** *Constructions of Deviance: Social Power, Context, and Interaction.* Belmont, CA: Wadsworth.

Afkhami, Mahnaz. 1997. "Promoting women's rights in the Muslim world." *Journal of Democracy* 8:157–66.

Akers, Ronald L. 1985. Deviant Behavior. 3rd ed. Belmont, CA: Wadsworth.

Albelda, Randy and Chris Tilly. 1997. *Glass Ceilings and Bottomless Pits: Women's Work, Women's Poverty.* Boston: South End Press.

Alexander, Jeffrey C. and Paul Colomy, eds. 1990. *Differentiation Theory and Social Change: Comparative Historical Perspectives.* New York: Columbia University Press.

Allan, Graham and Graham Crow. 2001. *Families, Households, and Society.* New York: Palgrave.

Allen, Mile and Nancy Burrell. 1996. "Comparing the impact of homosexual and heterosexual parents on children: Meta-analysis of existing research." *Journal of Homosexuality* 32:19–35.

Allen, Tammy D., Stacy E. McManus, and Joyce E. A. Russell. 1999. "Newcomer socialization and stress: Formal peer relationships as a source of support." *Journal of Vocational Behavior* 54(3):453–70.

Allen-Meares, Paula. 1990. "Educating black youths: The unfulfilled promise of equality." *Social Work* 35(3):283–86.

Almquist, Elizabeth M. 1989. "The experience of minority women in the United States." p. 414–45 in Jo Freeman, ed., *Women: A Feminist Perspective,* 4th ed. Mountain View, CA: Mayfield.

Alpert, Rebecca T., ed. 2000. *Voices of the Religious Left: A Contemporary Sourcebook.* Philadelphia: Temple University Press.

Alter, Jonathan. 2000. "The death penalty on trial." *Newsweek* (June 12):24–34.

Alwin, Duane F. 1984. "Trends in parental socialization values: Detroit, 1958–1983." *American Journal of Sociology* 90:359–82.

Amato, Paul R. and Frieda Fowler. 2002. "Parenting practices, child adjustment and family diversity." *Journal of Marriage and the Family* 64(3):703–16.

American Association of University Women. 2001. *Hostile Hallways: Bullying, Teasing, and Sexual Harassment in School.* Washington, DC: AAUW.

——— **and the Wellesley College Center for Research on Women. 1992.** *How Schools Shortchange Girls.* Washington, DC: AAUW Educational Foundation.

American Sociological Association. 1997. *Code of Ethics.* Washington, DC: ASA. Available at www.asanet.org.

Amott, Teresa. 1993. *Caught in the Crisis: Women and the U.S. Economy Today.* New York: Monthly Review Press.

——— **and Julie A. Matthaei. 1996.** *Race, Gender, and Work: A Multicultural Economic History of Women in the United States.* Rev. ed. Boston: South End Press.

Ancheta, Angelo N. 1998. *Race, Rights, and the Asian American Experience.* New Brunswick: Rutgers University Press.

Andersen, Margaret L. 1990. "Feminism and the American family ideal." *Journal of Comparative Family Studies* 22:35–46.

——— **and Patricia Hill Collins, eds. 2004.** *Race, Class, and Gender: An Anthology.* 5th edition. Belmont, CA: Wadsworth.

Anderson, Elijah. 1976. *A Place on the Corner.* Chicago: University of Chicago Press.

———. **1999.** *Code of the Street: Decency, Violence, and the Moral Life of the Inner City.* New York: W.W. Norton.

Anderson, Kristin L. 1997. "Gender, status, and domestic violence: An integration of feminist and family violence approaches." *Journal of Marriage and the Family* 59(3): 655–69.

Anderson, Kristin L. 2000. *"Not to People Like Us": Hidden Abuse in Upscale Marriages.* New York: Basic Books

——— **and Debra Umberson. 2001.** "Gendering violence: Masculinity and power in men's accounts of domestic violence." *Gender & Society* 15(3):358–80.

Anderson, Sarah and John Cavanagh, with Thea Lee. 2000. *Field Guide to the Global Economy.* New York: The New Press.

Anderson, Tammy L. 1998. "A cultural identity theory of drug abuse." *Sociology of Crime, Law, and Deviance* 1:233–62.

Andrews, Edmund L. 1996. "Don't go away mad, just go away: AT&T's gentle but firm effort to cut 40,000 jobs." *New York Times,* February 13, pp. D1, D6.

Anti-Defamation League of B'nai B'rith. 1999. *Anti-Semitism and Prejudice in America.* New York: ADL.

Antill, John K., Jacqueline J. Goodow, Russell Graeme, and Sandra Cotton. 1996. "The influence of parents and family context on children's involvement in household tasks." *Sex Roles* 34(3–4): 215–36.

Apple, Michael W. 1992. "Constructing the captive audience: Channel One and the political economy of the text." *International Studies in Sociology of Education* 2(2): 107–31.

Applied Research Center. 2001. *Racial Profiling and Punishment in U.S. Public Schools.* Oakland, CA: ARC. Available at ww.arc.org.

Arnett, Jeffrey Jensen. 1995. "Adolescents' uses of media for self-socialization." *Journal of Youth and Adolescence* 24(5):519–33.

Aronowitz, Stanley. 1998. "The new corporate university: Higher education becomes higher training." *Dollars and Sense* 216(March–April):32–35.

———. **2000.** *The Knowledge Factory: Dismantling the Corporate University and Creating True Higher Learning.* Boston: Beacon Press.

——— **and William DiFazio. 1994.** *The Jobless Future: Sci-Tech and the Dogma of Work.* Minneapolis: University of Minnesota Press.

Ascenzi, Joseph. 2000. "Toxic suit cites PG&E in 4 deaths: Action by 56 plaintiffs says toxic water used to fill swimming pools." *The Business Press,* August 14 (www.fumento.com/buspress.html).

Asch, Adrienne and Michelle Fine. 1988. "Introduction: Beyond pedestals." pp. 1–37 in Michelle Fine and Adrienne Asch, eds., *Women with Disabilities.* Philadelphia: Temple University Press.

Asher, Carol. 1992. *Successful Detracking in Middle and Senior High Schools.* New York: ERIC Clearinghouse on Urban Education, Columbia University.

Ashurst, Mark. 2001. "Now, a 'quiet revolution.'" *Newsweek,* August 27, p. 32.

Associated Press. 2000. "Associated Press Poll." May 17–21.

Auerbach, A. J. and L. J. Kotlikoff. 1987. "Life insurance of the elderly: Its adequacy and determinants." pp. 229–67 in G. Burtless, ed., *Work, Health, and Income among the Elderly.* Washington, DC: Brookings Institute.

Austin, Regina and Michael Schill. 1994. "Black, brown, red, and poisoned." *The Humanist,* July/August, pp. 9–16.

Auvinen, Juha Y. 1996. "IMF intervention and political protest in the Third World: A conventional wisdom refined." *Third World Quarterly* 17(3):377–400.

Awad, Nihad. 2002. "The effect of racial and religious profiling in the American Muslim community since September 11, 2001." Paper presented to the United States House of Representatives House Judiciary Committee (http://www.cairnet.org).

Ayers, William, Jean Ann Hunt, and Therese Quinn, eds. 1998. *Teaching for Social Justice: A Democracy and Education Reader.* New York: The New Press.

Babbie, Earl. 2000. *The Practice of Social Research.* 9th ed. Belmont, CA: Wadsworth.

Bacon, David. 2000. "No justice for janitors." *In These Times,* May 15.

————. **2001.** "Health, safety, and workers' rights in the maquiladoras." *Journal of Public Health Policy* 22(3):338–48.

Baker, Robin. 2000. *Sex in the Future: The Reproductive Revolution and How It Will Change Us.* New York: Arcade.

Bales, Kevin. 1999. *Disposable People: New Slavery in the Global Economy.* Berkeley: University of California Press.

Banfield, Edward. 1974. *The Unheavenly City Revisited.* Boston: Little, Brown.

———— **and James Q. Wilson. 1963.** *City Politics.* New York: Vintage.

Baptist, Willie, Mary Bricker Jenkins, and Monica Dillon. 1999. "Taking the struggle on the road: The new Freedom Bus—Freedom from unemployment, hunger, and homelessness." *Journal of Progressive Human Services* 10(2):7–29.

Baratz, Steven S. and Joan C. Baratz. 1970. "Early childhood intervention: The social science base of institutional racism." *Harvard Educational Review* 40:29–50.

Barker, Martin and Julian Petley, eds. 1997. *Ill Effects: The Media/Violence Debate.* London: Routledge.

Barlett, Donald L. and James B. Steele. 2001. "Corporate Welfare." pp. 87–97 in Amanda Konradi and Martha Schmitt, eds., *Reading between the Lines: Toward an Understanding of Social Problems,* 2nd ed. Mountain View, CA: Mayfield.

Barnett, Bernice McNair. 1993. "Invisible southern black women leaders in the civil rights movement: The triple constraints of gender, race, and class." *Gender & Society* 7(June):162–82.

Barnett, Mark A. 1977. "The role of play and make believe in children's cognitive development: Implications for social class differences and education." *Journal of Education* 159(4):38–48.

Barnhurst, Kevin G. and Ellen Wartella. 1998. "Young citizens, American TV newscasts and the collective memory." *Critical Studies in Mass Communication* 15(3):279–305.

Barringer, Felicity. 1993. "School hallways as gantlets of sexual taunts." *New York Times,* June 2, p. B7.

Barry, David S. 1993. "Growing up violent." *Media and Values* 62(Summer):8–11.

Bartfeld, Judi. 2000. "Child support and the postdivorce economic well-being of mothers, fathers, and children." *Demography* 37(2):203–13.

Basu, Malika. 1996. "Humanization and development: The question of basic needs." *Social Action* 46(3):249–61.

Battles, Kathleen and Wendy Hilton-Morrow. 2002. "Gay characters in conventional spaces: Will and Grace and the situation comedy genre." *Critical Studies in Media Communication* 19(1):87–105.

Beaulieu, Lionel J. 1998. "Welfare reform: An overview of key provisions." *Southern Rural Development Center Information Brief* 1 (January):1–3.

Becker, Howard S. 1963. *Outsiders: Studies in the Sociology of Deviance.* New York: Free Press.

Been, Vicki. 1994. "Locally undesirable land uses in minority neighborhoods: Disproportionate siting or market dynamics?" *Yale Law Journal* 103:1383–1413.

Beeson, Elizabeth and Marty Strange. 2003. *Why Rural Matters 2003.* Washington, DC: Rural School and Community Trust. Summary available at www.ruraledu.org.

Bell, Daniel. 1973. *The Coming of Post-industrial Society.* New York: Basic Books.

Bellah, Robert N. 1967. "Civil religion in America." *Daedalus* 96:1–21.

Benson, Michael L., Greer Litton Fox, Alred De Maris, and Judy Van Wyk. 2000. "Violence in families: The intersection of race, poverty, and community context." *Contemporary Perspectives in Family Research* 2:91–109.

Berger, Peter L. 1999. *The Desecularization of the World: Resurgent Religion and World Politics.* Grand Rapids, MI: William B. Eerdmans.

———— **and Thomas Luckmann. 1966.** *The Social Construction of Reality.* Garden City, NY: Doubleday.

Bergleiter, Henri and Benjamin Kissin, eds. 1995. *The Genetics of Alcoholism.* New York: Oxford University Press.

Berle, Adolph and Gardiner C. Means. 1932. *The Modern Corporation and Private Property.* New York: Harcourt, Brace & World.

Berlet, Chip and Matthew N. Lyons. 1995. "Militia nation." *The Progressive* 59(June): 22–25.

Berman, Daniel M. and John T. O'Connor. 1997. *Who Owns the Sun? Politics and the Struggle for a Solar Economy.* White River Junction, VT: Chelsea Green Publishing.

Best, Joel. 1998. "Too much fun: Toys as social problems and the interpretation of culture." *Symbolic Interaction* 21(2):197–212.

Bianchi, Suzanne M. and Jane Lawler Dye. 2001. "The participation of women and men in the United States labor force: Trends and future prospects." pp. 460–72 in Dana Vannoy, ed., *Gender Mosaics.* Los Angeles: Roxbury.

Biegel, Stuart. 1996. "Does anyone control the Internet?" *UCLA Online Institute for Cyberspace Law and Policy.* (www.gse.ucla.edu/iclp/control.html).

Bienefeld, Manfred. 2000. "Structural adjustment: Debt collection device or development policy." *Review—Fernand Braudel Center* 23(4):533–82.

Billings, Dwight B. and Kathleen M. Blee. 2000. *The Road to Poverty: The Making of Wealth and Hardship in Appalachia.* New York: Cambridge University Press.

Binkley, Bonnie. 2001. "A case study of the impact of deindustrialization in Memphis, Tennessee." Paper presented at the annual meetings of the Southern Sociological Society.

Bixby, Lyn. 1992. "Peace dividend: More markets for arms makers." *Hartford CT Courant,* October 25, pp. A6–A7.

Black, Amy E. and Jamie L. Allen. 2001. "Tracing the legacy of Anita Hill: The Thomas/Hill hearings and media coverage of sexual harassment." *Gender Issues* 19(1):33–52.

Blau, Joel. 1999. *Illusions of Prosperity: America's Working Families in an Age of Economic Insecurity.* New York: Oxford University Press.

Block, Fred, Richard A. Cloward, Barbara Ehrenreich, and Frances Fox Piven. 1987. *The Mean Season: The Attack on the Welfare State.* New York: Pantheon Books.

Blumberg, Rhoda Lois. 1991. *Civil Rights: The 1960s Freedom Struggle.* Rev. ed. Boston: Twayne.

Boerner, Christopher and Thomas Lambert. 1995. "Environmental justice." *Public Interest* 118(Winter):61–81.

Boggiano, A. K. and M. Barrett. 1991. "Strategies to motivate helpless and mastery-oriented children: The effect of gender-based expectancies." *Sex Roles* 25:487–510.

Boggs, Carl. 2000. *The End of Politics: Corporate Power and the Decline of the Public Sphere*. New York: Guilford Press.

Bonilla-Silva, Eduardo. 2001. *White Supremacy and Racism in the Post–Civil Rights Era*. Boulder, CO: Lynne Rienner.

Borchert, Mark. 1998. "The challenge of cyberspace: Internet access and persons with disabilities." Pp. 49–63 in Ebo Bohash, ed., *Cyberghetto or Cyberutopia? Race, Class, and Gender on the Internet*. Westport, CT: Praeger.

Bornschier, Volker and Christopher Chase-Dunn. 1985. *Transnational Corporations and Underdevelopment*. New York: Praeger.

Bose, E. Christine and Rachel Bridges Whaley. 2001. "Sex segregation in the U.S. labor force." Pp. 228–39 in Dana Vannoy, ed., *Gender Mosaics: Social Perspectives*. Los Angeles: Roxbury.

Boserup, Esther. 1970. *Women's Role in Economic Development*. New York: St. Martin's Press.

Bouchard, Thomas J. Jr. and Matthew McGue. 1990. "Genetic and rearing environmental influences on adult personality: An analysis of adopted twins reared apart." *Journal of Personality* 58(1):263–92.

Bourdieu, Pierre, and Jean-Claude Passeron. 1991. *Reproduction in Education, Society, and Culture*. Rev. ed. Newbury Park, CA: Sage.

Bowker, Lee H. 1972. "Red and black in contemporary history texts: A content analysis." Pp. 101–10 in Howard M. Bahr, Bruce A. Chadwick, and Robert C. Day, eds., *Native Americans Today: Sociological Perspectives*. New York: Harper & Row.

Bowles, Samuel, and Herbert Gintis. 1976. *Schooling in Capitalist America: Educational Reform and the Contradictions of Economic Life*. New York: Basic Books.

Bowman, Philip and Cleopatra Howard. 1985. "Race-related socialization, motivation, and academic achievement: A study of black youth in three-generation families." *Journal of the American Academy of Child Psychiatry* 24:134–41.

Boyle, Sarah Patton. 1962. *The Desegregated Heart: A Virginian's Stand in Time of Transition*. New York: William Morrow.

Bradsher, Julia E. 1996. "Disability among racial and ethnic groups." Abstract 10 (July). San Francisco: Disability Statistics Center, University of California.

Brady, David and Michael Wallace. 2001. "Deindustrialization and poverty: Manufacturing decline and AFDC recipiency in Lake County, Indiana 1964–93." *Sociological Forum* 16(2):321–58.

Brady, Susan M. 2001. "Sterilization of girls and women with intellectual disabilities: Past and present justifications." *Violence against Women* 7(4):432–61.

Bramlett, Matthew D. and William D. Mosher. 2001. "First marriage dissolution, divorce, and remarriage: United States." Department of Health and Human Services

Centers for Disease Control. *Advance Data* No. 323 (May 31).

Brand, Peg Zeglin, ed. 2000. *Beauty Matters*. Bloomington: Indiana University Press.

Braude, Ann. 2000. *Women and American Religion*. New York: Oxford University Press.

Brecher, Jeremy, Tim Costello, and Brendan Smith. 2000. *Globalization from Below: The Power of Solidarity*. Cambridge, MA: South End Press.

Brint, Steven. 1998. *Schools and Societies*. Thousand Oaks, CA: Pine Forge Press.

——— and Jerome Karabel. 1989. *The Diverted Dream*. New York: Oxford University Press.

Broman, Clifford L. 1988. "Household work and family life satisfaction of blacks." *Journal of Marriage and the Family* 50:743–48.

Brown, Dee Alexander. 2001. *Bury My Heart at Wounded Knee: An Indian History of the American West*. New York: Henry Holt.

Brown, Tina A. 1993. "Police seek motive in murder-suicide." *Hartford CT Courant*, August 8, p. B1.

Bucy, Erik. 2000. "Social access to the Internet." *Harvard International Journal of Press/Politics* 5(1):50–61.

Budig, Michelle J. and Paula England. 2001. "The wage penalty for motherhood." *American Sociological Review* 66(2):204–25.

Bullard, Robert D. 1993. *Confronting Environmental Racism: Voices from the Grassroots*. Boston: South End Press.

———, ed. 1997. *Unequal Protection: Environmental Justice and Communities of Color*. San Francisco Sierra Club Books.

——— and Beverly Hendrix Wright. 1987. "Environmentalism and the politics of equity: Emergent trends in the black community." *Mid-American Review of Sociology* 12(2): 21–38.

Burkhauser, R. V. and G. J. Duncan. 1989. "Economic risks of gender roles; Income loss and life events over the life course." *Social Science Quarterly* 70:3–23.

Burkhauser, R. V., Holden, Karen C. and D. J. Feaster. 1988. "The timing of falls into poverty after retirement and widowhood." *Demography* 25:405–414.

Burnham, James. 1941. *The Managerial Revolution*. New York: John Day.

Burns, Ailsa and Ross Homel. 1989. "Gender division of tasks by parents and their children." *Psychology of Women Quarterly* 13(1):113–25.

Burris, Val. 1992. "Elite policy-planning networks in the United States." *Research in Politics and Society* 4:111–34.

Business Week. 1980. "Industry's schoolhouse clout." October 13:156–60.

Butsch, Richard. 1995. "Ralph, Fred, Archie, and Homer: Why television keeps recreating the white male working-class buffoon." Pp. 403–12 in Gail Dines and Jean M. Humez, eds., *Gender, Race, and Class in Media*. Thousand Oaks, CA: Sage.

Butterfield, Fox. 2003. "Prison rates among blacks reach a peak, report finds." *New York Times* April 7, p. A11.

Calavita, Kitty and Henry Pontell. 1991. "'Other people's money' revisited: Embezzlement in the savings and loan insurance industries." *Social Problems* 38(1):94–112.

Campbell, Anne. 1991. *The Girls in the Gang: A Report from New York City*. New York: Basil Blackwell.

Campbell, Nancy D. 1999. "Regulating 'maternal instinct': Governing mentalities of late twentieth century U.S. illicit drug policy." *Signs* 24(4):895–923.

Cancian, Francesca M. and Stacey J. Oliker. 2000. *Caring and Gender*. Thousand Oaks, CA: Pine Forge Press.

Cannon, Carl M. 1993. "Honey, I warped the kids." *Mother Jones* 18(July–August):16–17.

Casey, Timothy J. 1998. "Welfare reform and its impact in the nation and in New York." New York: Federation of Protestant Welfare Agencies (www.wnylc.com/frames/menus/. . . law/resource-material/welrefor.htm).

Cassell, Justine and Henry Jenkins, eds. 1998. *From Barbie to Mortal Kombat: Gender and Computer Games*. Cambridge: MIT Press.

Cassidy, Elizabeth, Rebecca P. Judge, and Paul M. Sommers. 2000. "The distribution of environmental justice: A comment." *Social Science Quarterly* 81(3):877–78.

Castellani, Paul J. 1987. *The Political Economy of Developmental Disabilities*. Baltimore: Paul H. Brookes.

Castro-Vasquez, Genaro. 2000. "Masculinity and condom use among Mexican teenagers: The Escuela Nacional Preparatoria No. 1's case." *Gender and Education* 12(4):479–92.

Centers for Disease Control. 1999. "Youth risk behavior survey." *Morbidity and Mortality Weekly Report* 49(SS-5):66.

———. 2002. *Youth Risk Behavior Surveillance—United States, 2001*. Washington, DC: U.S. Department of Health and Human Services.

Cermak, Sharon and Victor Groza. 1998. "Sensory processing problems in post-institutionalized children: Implications for social work." *Child and Adolescent Social Work Journal* 15(1):5–37.

Cerulo, Karen A. 2000. "Packaging violence: Media, story sequencing, and the perception of right and wrong." Pp. 153–76 in Mark Gottdiener, ed., *New Forms of Consumption: Consumers, Culture, and Commodification*. Lanham, MD: Rowman & Littlefield.

Chang, Grace. 2000. *Disposable Domestics: Immigrant Women Workers in the Global Economy*. Boston: South End Press.

Chapple, Constance L. 1998. "Dow Corning and the silicone breast implant debacle: A case of corporate crime against women." Pp. 179–96 in Lee H. Bowker, ed., *Masculinities and Violence*. Thousand Oaks, CA: Sage.

Charlton, James I. 1998. *Nothing about Us without Us: Disability Oppression and Empowerment.* Berkeley: University of California Press.

Chase-Dunn, Christopher. 1997. *Rise and Demise: Comparing World Systems.* Boulder, CO: Westview Press.

———. 1998. *Global Formation: Structures of the World Economy.* Lanham, MD: Rowman & Littlefield.

——— and Thomas D. Hall, 1997. *Rise and Demise: Comparing World-Systems.* Boulder, CO: Westview Press.

Chavis, Benjamin F. Jr. and Charles Lee. 1987. *Toxic Wastes and Race in the United States: A National Report on the Racial and Socio-Economic Characteristics of Communities with Hazardous Waste Sites.* New York: United Church of Christ Commission for Racial Justice.

Cheney, George. 2002. *Values at Work: Employee Participation Meets Market Pressure at Mondragon.* Rev. ed. Ithaca, NY: Cornell University Press.

Chesler, Mark, Joseph Sanders, and Debra S. Kalmus. 1988. *Social Science in Court: Mobilizing Experts in the School Desegregation Cases.* Madison: University of Wisconsin Press.

Chisolm, June F. 1999. "The sandwich generation." *Journal of Social Distress and the Homeless* 8(3):177–91.

Chomsky, Noam. 1997. *Media Control: The Spectacular Achievements of Propaganda.* New York: Seven Stories Press.

———. 1999. "The current bombings: Behind the rhetoric." *Znet* (www.zmag.org/current_bombings.htm)

Chossudovsky, Michel. 1997. "Dismantling former Yugoslavia, recolonizing Bosnia." *Capital and Class* 62(Summer):1–12.

Christ, Carol P. and Judith Plaskow, eds. 1992. *Womenspirit Rising: A Feminist Reader in Religion.* San Francisco: Harper–San Francisco.

CIA. 1999. *World Factbook, 1999.*

Cimons, Marlene. 1990. "GAO cites bias in health research." *Los Angeles Times* (June 19):A20.

Citizens for Tax Justice. 1996. "The hidden entitlements" www.ctj.org/html.publist.htm.

Clapp, Jennifer. 2001. *Toxic Exports: The Transfer of Hazardous Wastes from Rich to Poor Countries.* Ithaca, NY: Cornell University Press.

Clark, Charles S. 1991. "Youth gangs." *Congressional Quarterly Researcher* 1(22):753–76.

Clark, Kenneth B. and Mamie P. Clark. 1947. "Racial identification and preferences in Negro children." Pp. 169–78 in Theodore M. Newcomb and Eugene L. Hartley, eds., *Readings in Social Psychology.* New York: Holt, Rinehart and Winston.

Clarke, Victoria. 2001. "What about the children? Arguments against lesbian and gay parenting." *Women's Studies International Forum* 24(5):555–70.

Clawson, Dan. 1980. *Bureaucracy and the Labor Process: The Transformation of U.S. Industry, 1860–1920.* New York: Monthly Review Press.

———, Alan Neustadtl, and Mark Weller. 1998. *Dollars and Votes: How Business Campaign Contributions Subvert Democracy.* Philadelphia: Temple University Press.

Clawson, Rosalee A. 2002. "Poor people, black faces: The portrayal of poverty in economics textbooks." *Journal of Black Studies* 32(3):352–61.

——— and Elizabeth R. Kegler. 2000. "The 'race-coding' of poverty in American government college textbooks." *Howard Journal of Communications* 11(3):179–88.

Clendinen, Dudley, and Adam Nagourney. 2001. *Out for Good: The Struggle to Build a Gay Rights Movement in America.* New York: Touchstone Books.

Clinard, Marshall B. and Robert F. Meier. 1992. *Sociology of Deviant Behavior.* 8th ed. Fort Worth, TX: Harcourt Brace Jovanovich.

CNN/Time. 1998. "CNN/Time Poll." October 14–15.

Cockburn, Alexander. 1997. "The big win." *The Nation,* September 8/15, p. 8.

Cody, Paul J. and Peter L. Welch. 1997. "Rural gay men in northern New England: Life experiences and coping styles." *Journal of Homosexuality* 33(1):51–67.

Cohen, Mitchell. 1990. "Toxic imperialism: Exposing Pentagonorrhea." *Z Magazine,* October, pp. 78–79.

Cole, David. 1999. *No Equal Justice: Race and Class in the American Criminal Justice System.* New York: The New Press.

Cole, Luke W. and Sheila R. Foster. 2001. *From the Ground Up: Environmental Racism and the Rise of the Environmental Justice Movement.* New York: New York University Press.

Coleman, James S., et al. 1966. *Equality of Educational Opportunity.* Washington, DC: U.S. Government Printing Office.

Coleman, James William. 1989. *The Criminal Elite.* New York: St. Martin's Press.

Collins, Chuck and Felice Yeskel with United for a Fair Economy. 2000. *Economic Apartheid in America: A Primer on Economic Inequality and Insecurity.* New York: The New Press.

Collins, Patricia Hill. 2000. *Black Feminist Thought: Knowledge, Consciousness, and the Politics of Empowerment.* 2d ed. New York: Routledge.

Collins, Randall. 1979. *Credential Society.* New York: Academic Press.

Collins, Susan. 1998. "Economic integration and the American worker: An overview." Pp. 3–45 in Susan Collins, ed., *Imports, Exports, and the American Worker.* Washington, DC: Brookings Institution Press.

Coltrane, Scott and Michele Adams. 2001. "Men, women, and housework." Pp. 145–154 in Dana Vannoy, ed., *Gender Mosaics: Social Perspectives.* Los Angeles: Roxbury.

Compa, Lance. 2001. "NAFTA's labor side agreement and international labor solidarity." *Antipode* 33(3): 451–67.

Comstock, George, and Haejung Paik. 1991. *Television and the American Child.* San Diego, CA: Academic Press.

Comte, Auguste. 1966. *System of Positive Polity.* Vol. 3. New York: Burt Franklin.

Connecticut Department of Education. 1999. *Connecticut Public Schools: Town and School District Profiles.* Hartford: State Department of Education.

Conway, M. Margaret. 2000. *Political Participation in the United States.* Washington, DC: CQ Press.

Cook, Christopher D. 2000. "Temps demand a new deal." *The Nation* March 27:13–19.

Cookson, Peter W. and Caroline Hodges Persell. 1985. *Preparing for Power: America's Elite Boarding Schools.* New York: Basic Books.

Cooley, Charles Horton. 1902. *Human Nature and the Social Order.* New York: Scribner.

———. 1929. *Social Organization.* New York: Scribner.

Cooper, Marc. 1999. "No sweat: Uniting workers and students: A new movement is born." *The Nation,* June 7, p. 11–15.

Cooper, Margaret. 1999. "The Australian disability rights movements lives." *Disability and Society* 14(2):217–26.

Cormier, David and Harry Targ. 2001. "Globalization and the North American worker." *Labor Studies Journal* 26(1): 42–59.

Cose, Ellis. 1995. *The Rage of a Privileged Class.* New York: Perennial.

———. 2002. *The Envy of the World: On Being a Black Man in America.* New York: Washington Square Press.

Costello, Barbara J. and Paul R. Vowell. 1999. "Testing control theory and differential association: A reanalysis of the Richmond Youth Project Data." *Criminology* 37(4): 815–42.

Cowley, Geoffrey. 2002. "The disappearing mind." *Newsweek,* June 19, p. 45.

Crane, Diana. 1999. "Gender and hegemony in fashion magazines: Women's interpretations of fashion photographs." *Sociological Quarterly* 40(4):541–63.

Cress, Daniel M. and David A. Snow. 2000. "The outcomes of homeless mobilization: The influence of organization, disruption, political mediation, and framing." *American Journal of Sociology* 105(4):1063–1104.

Croissant, Jennifer L. 2001. "Can this campus be bought? Commercial influence in unfamiliar places." *Academe,* September-October, pp. 44–48.

Cubbins, Lisa A. 2001. "The legacy of patriarchy in today's Russia." Pp. 174–183 in Dana Vannoy, ed., *Gender Mosaics: Social Perspectives.* Los Angeles: Roxbury.

Cuklanz, Lisa M. 2000. *Rape on Prime Time: Television, Masculinity, and Sexual Violence.* Philadelphia: University of Pennsylvania Press.

Cumming, Elaine and William E. Henry. 1961. *Growing Old: The Process of Disengagement.* New York: Basic Books.

Cummings, Scott and Del Taebel. 1978. "The economic socialization of children." *Social Problems* 26(December):198–210.

Cummins, Robert A. and David Dunt. 1988. "Evaluation of a de-institutionalization program in Australia: The St. Nicholas Project." *International Journal of Rehabilitation Research* 11(4):395–96.

Cunningham, Mick. 2001. "Parental influences on the gendered division of labor." *American Sociological Review* 66(2):184–203.

Curb, Rosemary, and Nancy Manahan, eds. 1985. *Lesbian Nuns: Breaking Silence.* Talahassee, FL: Naiad Press.

Curra, John. 2000. *The Relativity of Deviance.* Thousand Oaks, CA: Sage.

Currie, Dawn H. 1997. "Decoding femininity: Advertisements and their teenage readers." *Gender & Society* 11(4):453–77.

Curtiss, Susan. 1977. *Genie: A Linguistic Study of a Modern Day "Wild Child."* New York: Academic Press.

Cutler, James Elbert. 1969. *Lynch-Law: An Investigation into the History of Lynching in the United States.* Montclair, NJ: Patterson Smith.

Cypher, James M. 2001. "NAFTA's lessons: from economic mythology to current realities." *Labor Studies Journal* 26(1):5–21.

Dandaneau, Steven P. 1996. *A Town Abandoned: Flint, Michigan Confronts Deindustrialization.* Albany: State University of New York Press.

Daniels, Arlene Kaplan. 1988. *Invisible Careers: Women Civic Leaders from the Volunteer World.* Chicago: University of Chicago Press.

Daniels, Glynis and Samantha Friedman. 1999. "Spatial inequality and the distribution of industrial toxic releases: Evidence from the 1990 TRI." *Social Science Quarterly* 80(2):244–62.

Davies, James. 1962. "Toward a theory of revolution." *American Sociological Review* 27(1):5–19.

———. 1969. "The J-curve of rising and declining satisfactions as a cause of some great revolutions and a contained revolution." Pp. 671–709 in H. D. Graham and T. R. Gurr, eds., *Violence in America.* New York: Signet.

———. 1974. "The J-curve and power struggle theories of collective violence." *American Sociological Review* 39:607–10.

Davis, Angela Y. 1983. *Women, Race and Class.* New York: Vintage.

Davis, Kingsley. 1940. "Extreme social isolation of a child." *American Journal of Sociology* 45(January):554–64.

———. 1948. *Human Society.* New York: Macmillan.

——— and Wilbert Moore. 1945. "Some principles of stratification." *American Sociological Review* 10:242–249.

Davis, Nanette J. and Clarice Stasz. 1990. *Social Control of Deviance.* New York: McGraw-Hill.

DeBoeck, Guy. 2000. "Green zones or greenbacks? The debt-nature exchange: Green neocolonialism and environmental exploitation." *Contradictions* 92:99–110.

Debt Crisis Network. 1985. *From Debt to Development: Alternatives to the International Debt Crisis.* Washington, DC: Institute for Policy Studies.

Deegan, Mary Jo. 1998. "Harriet Martineau, patriarchal gatekeeping and sociological theory: Multiple assaults on the historical canon." Paper presented at the International Sociological Association.

Deere, C. and M. Leon deLeal. 1981. "Peasant production, proletarianization, and the sexual division of labor in the Andes." *Signs* 7(2):338–60.

———, J. Humphries, and M. Leon deLeal. 1982. "Class and historical analysis for the study of women and economic change." Pp. 87–116 in R. Anker, M. Buvinic, and N. Youssef, eds., *Women's Roles and Population Trends in the Third World.* London: ILO.

Dei, George, J. Sefa, Josephine Mazzuca, Elizabeth McIsaac, and Jasmin Zine. 1997. *Reconstructing "Drop-Out": A Critical Ethnography of the Dynamics of Black Students' Disengagement from School.* Ontario: University of Toronto Press.

Delacroix, Jacques and Charles C. Ragin. 1981. "Structural blockage: A cross-national study of economic dependency, state efficacy, and underdevelopment." *American Journal of Sociology* 86:1311–47.

Delaney, John T. 1996. "Workplace cooperation: Current problems, news approaches." *Journal of Labor Research* 17(1):45–56.

D'Emilio, John, William B. Turner, and Urvashi Vaid, eds. 2000. *Creating Change: Sexuality, Public Policy, and Civil Rights.* New York: St. Martin's Press.

Demo, David H. and Alan C. Acock. 1993. "Family diversity and the division of domestic labor: How much have things really changed?" *Family Relations* 42(3):323–31.

Dennis, Everette E. and Edward C. Pease, eds. 1996. *The Media in Black and White.* New Brunswick, NJ: Transaction Publishers.

Dennis, Rutledge M. 1981. "Socialization and racism: The white experience." Pages 71–85 in Benjamin P. Bowser and Raymond G. Hunt (eds.), *Impacts of Racism on White Americans.* Beverly Hills, CA: Sage.

DeOliver, Miguel. 1995. "Structural consolidation: The Colorado Delta Region, 1900–10." *Review* 18(4):565–88.

DeParle, Jason. 1990. "War, class divisions, and burden of service." *New York Times,* November 13, p. A14.

DeVaney, Ann, ed. 1994. *Watching Channel One: The Convergence of Students, Technology, and Private Business.* Albany: State University of New York Press.

De Witt, Karen. 1992. "The nation's schools learn a 4th R: Resegregation." *New York Times,* January 19, p. E5.

Dickinson, Torry D. 1997. "Selective globalization: The relocation of industrial production and the shaping of women's work." *Research in the Sociology of Work* 6:109–29.

Diebel, Linda. 1993. "Unions not welcome: That's the message workers get as they try to organize to defend themselves in North Carolina." *Toronto Star,* June 6, p. F1.

Dietz, Tracy L. 1998. "An examination of violence and gender role portrayals in video games: Implications for gender socialization and aggressive behavior." *Sex Roles* 38(5–6):425–42.

Dill, Bonnie Thornton. 1983. "Race, class, and gender: Prospects for an all-inclusive sisterhood." *Feminist Studies* 9(1):131–50.

———. 1988. "'Making your job good itself': Domestic service and the construction of personal dignity." Pp. 33–52 in Ann Bookman and Sandra Morgen, eds., *Women and the Politics of Empowerment.* Philadelphia: Temple University Press.

Dines, Gail. 1992a. "Pornography and the media: Cultural representation of violence against women." *Family Violence and Sexual Assault Bulletin* 8(3):17–20.

Dobash, Emerson R. et al. 2000. *Changing Violent Men.* Thousand Oaks, CA: Sage.

Dolbeare, Kenneth M. 1986. *Democracy at Risk: The Politics of Economic Renewal.* Rev. ed. Chatham, NJ: Chatham House.

Domhoff, G. William. 2002. *Who Rules America? Power and Politics.* 4th ed. New York: McGraw-Hill.

Dougherty, Kevin. 1981. "After the fall: Research on school effects since the Coleman report." *Harvard Educational Review* 51(2):301–8.

Doyle, Bertram Wilbur. 1971. *The Etiquette of Race Relations in the South: A Study in Social Control.* New York: Schocken Books.

Du Bois, W. E. B. 1989/1903. *The Souls of Black Folk.* New York: Penguin.

Dudley, William, ed. 1999. *Media Violence: Opposing Viewpoints.* San Diego, CA: Greenhaven Press.

Duncan, G. J., and S. D. Hoffman. 1985. "Economic consequences of marital instability." Pp. 427–67 in M. David and T. Smeeding, eds., *Horizontal Equity, Uncertainty, and Economic Well-Being.* Chicago: University of Chicago Press.

Duneier, Mitchell. 1992. *Slim's Table: Race, Respectability, and Masculinity.* Chicago: University of Chicago Press.

Dunning, Eric. 1993. "Sport in the civilizing process: Aspects of the development of modern sport." Pp. 39–70 in Eric G. Dunning, Joseph A. Maguire, and Robert E. Pearton, eds., *The Sports Process: A Comparative and Developmental Approach.* Champaign, IL: Human Kinetics Press.

Durkheim, Émile. 1954. *The Elementary Forms of Religious Life.* Trans. Joseph W. Swain. Glencoe, IL: Free Press.

————. 1964. *The Division of Labor in Society.* Trans. George Simpson. New York: Free Press.

Durning, Alan Thein. 1994. "Redesigning the forest economy." Pp. 22–40 in Lester R. Brown, ed., *State of the World, 1994.* New York: Norton.

Dye, Thomas R. 1990. *Who's Running America? The Bush Era.* Englewood Cliffs, NJ: Prentice Hall.

————. 2002. *Who's Running America? The Bush Reconstruction.* Upper Saddle River, NJ: Prentice Hall.

Economist Book of Vital World Statistics, The. **1990.** New York: Times Books/Random House.

Edelman, Marian Wright. 1988. "Growing up black in America." Pp. 143–62 in Jerome H. Skolnick and Elliott Currie, eds., *Crisis in American Institutions,* 7th ed. Glenview, IL: Scott, Foresman.

Eder, Donna and Stephen Parker. 1987. "The cultural production and reproduction of gender: The effect of extracurricular activities on peer-group culture." *Sociology of Education* 60(July):200–213.

Edgerton, Robert B. 1978. *Deviance: A Cross-Cultural Perspective.* Menlo Park, CA: Cummings.

Edin, Kathryn and Laura Lein. 1997. *Making Ends Meet: How Single Mothers Survive Welfare and Low-Wage Work.* New York: Russell Sage Foundation.

Edsall, Thomas B. and Mary D. Edsall. 1992. *Chain Reaction: The Impact of Race, Rights, and Taxes on American Politics.* New York: Norton.

Edwards, Richard. 1979. *Contested Terrain: The Transformation of the Workplace in the Twentieth Century.* New York: Basic Books.

Edut, Ophira, ed. 1998. *Adios, Barbie: Young Women Write about Body Image and Identity.* Seattle: Seal Press.

Egan, Jennifer. 2000. "Lonely gay teen seeking same." *New York Times Magazine* December 10, pp. 110–17, 128–33.

Egan, Timothy. 1998. "The swoon of the swoosh." *New York Times Magazine* September 13, pp. 66–70.

Ehrenreich, Barbara. 1986. "Is the middle class doomed?" *New York Times Magazine* September 7, pp. 44 ff.

————.2001. *Nickel and Dimed.* New York: Owl Books.

———— and Arlie Russell Hochschild, eds. **2003.** *Global Woman: Nannies, Maids, and Sex Workers in the New Economy.* New York: Metropolitan Books.

Eisenstein, Sarah. 1983. *Give Us Bread but Give Us Roses: Working Women's Consciousness in the United States, 1890 to the First World War.* London: Routledge & Kegan Paul.

Eitzen, D. Stanley and Maxine Baca Zinn. 1989a. "The forces reshaping America." Pp. 1–18 in D. Stanley Eitzen and Maxine Baca Zinn, eds., *The Reshaping of America: Social Consequences of the Changing Economy.* Englewood Cliffs, NJ: Prentice Hall.

———— and ————, eds. **1989b.** *The Reshaping of America: Social Consequences of the Changing Economy.* Englewood Cliffs, NJ: Prentice Hall.

———— and ————. **1997.** *Social Problems.* 7th ed. Boston: Allyn and Bacon.

———— and ————. **2000.** "The missing safety net and families: A progressive critique of the new welfare legislation." *Journal of Sociology and Social Welfare* 27(1):53–72.

Elias, Robert. 1986. *The Politics of Victimization: Victims, Victimology, and Human Rights.* New York: Oxford University Press.

England, Paula. 2000. "Marriage, the costs of children, and gender inequality." Pp. 320–42 in Linda J. Waite, Christine Bachrach, Michelle Hindin, Elizabeth Thomson, and Arland Thornton, eds., *The Ties That Bind: Perspectives on Marriage and Cohabitation.* New York: Aldine de Gruyter.

————, **Jennifer Thompson, and Carolyn Aman. 2001.** "The sex gap in pay and comparable worth: An update." Pp. 551–65 in Ivar Berg and Arne L. Karleberg, eds., *Sourcebook of Labor Markets: Evolving Structures and Processes.* New York: Kluwer Academic/Plenum.

Enloe, Cynthia. 1989. *Bananas, Beaches, and Bases: Making Feminist Sense of International Politics.* Berkeley: University of California Press.

Entman, Robert M. and Andrew Rojecki. 2000. *The Black Image in the White Mind: Media and Race in America.* Chicago: University of Chicago Press.

Epstein, Cynthia Fuchs. 1993. *Women in Law.* 2d ed. Urbana: University of Illinois Press.

Erikson, Erik. 1963. *Childhood and Society.* New York: Norton.

Erikson, Kai T. 1966. *Wayward Puritans.* New York: Macmillan.

Estey, Ken and Betsy Bowman. 2000. "What is a co-op?" *GEO (Grassroots Economic Organizing) Newsletter* 43(September–October): 2.

Euben, J. Peter. 1997. *Corrupting Youth: Political Education, Democratic Culture, and Political Theory.* Princeton, NJ: Princeton University Press.

Evanoff, Richard. 2001. "Co-ops for older workers on the rise in Japan." *GEO (Grassroots Economic Organizing) Newsletter* 46 (March-April), geonewsletter.org

Evans, Chris. 1999. "Work and workloads during industrialization: The experience of forgemen in the British iron industry." *International Review of Social History* 44(2):197–215.

Fabig, Heike and Richard Boele. 1999. "The changing nature of NGO activity in a globalising world: Pushing the corporate responsibility agenda." *IDS Bulletin* 30(3):58–67.

Falk, Ursula Adler and Gerhard Falk. 1997. *Ageism, the Aged, and Aging in America: On Being Old in an Alienated Society.* New York: Charles C. Thomas.

Farley, Reynolds and Walter R. Allen. 1987. *The Color Line and the Quality of Life in America.* New York: Russell Sage Foundation.

Farrell, Bill and Larry Koch. 1995. "Criminal justice, sociology, and academia." *American Sociologist* 26(1):52–61.

Fausto-Sterling, Anne. 2000. *Sexing the Body: Gender Politics and the Construction of Sexuality.* New York: Basic Books.

Feagin, Joe R. 2000. *Racist America: Roots, Current Realities, and Future Reparations.* New York: Routledge.

———— **and Clairece Booher Feagin. 1999.** *Racial and Ethnic Relations,* 6th ed. Englewood Cliffs, NJ: Prentice-Hall.

———— **and Melvin P. Sikes. 1994.** *Living with Racism: The Black Middle-Class Experience.* Boston: Beacon Press.

Featherstone, Liza. 2000. "The new student movement." *The Nation,* May 15 pp. 11–18.

Federal News Service. 1993. White House press briefing: Secretary of the Treasury Lloyd Bentsen (March 10).

Fei, John C. H. and Gustav Ranis. 1997. *Growth and Development from an Evolutionary Perspective.* Malden, MA: Blackwell.

Fein, Melvyn L. 1990. *Role Change: A Resocialization Perspective.* New York: Praeger.

Feltey, Kathryn M. 2001. "Gender violence: Rape and sexual assault." Pp. 363–373 in Dana Vannoy, ed., *Gender Mosaics: Social Perspectives.* Los Angeles: Roxbury.

Ferber, Marianne A., Brigid O'Farrell, and La Rue Allen. 1991. *Work and Family: Policies for a Changing Work Force.* Washington, DC: National Academy Press.

Ferree, Myra Marx. 1990. "Beyond separate spheres: Feminism and family research." *Journal of Marriage and the Family* 52 (November):866–84.

———— **and Elaine J. Hall. 1996.** "Gender, race, and class in mainstream textbooks." *American Sociological Review* 61(6): 929–50.

————, **Judith Lorber, and Beth B. Hess, eds. 1999.** *Revisioning Gender.* Thousand Oaks, CA: Sage.

———— **and Mangala Subramaniam. 2000.** "The international women's movement at century's end." Pp. 496–506 in Dana Vannoy, ed., *Gender Mosaics: Social Perspectives.* Los Angeles: Roxbury.

Feyerick, Debby. 1998. "Baby boomers feeling strain of caring for older parents" (www.cnn.com/health/9807/31/elder.care/).

Fields, Jason and Lynne M. Casper. 2001. "America's families and living arrangements." In U.S. Census Bureau, *Current Population Reports.* Washington, DC: Government Printing Office.

Fine, Gary Alan. 1986. "The dirty play of little boys." Pp. 171–79 in Michael S. Kimmel and Michael A. Messner, eds. *Men's Lives.* New York: Macmillan.

————. 1987. *With the Boys: Little League Baseball and Preadolescent Culture.* Chicago: University of Chicago Press.

Fine, Michelle. 1992. "Sexuality, schooling, and adolescent females: The missing discourse of desire." Pp. 31–59 in Michelle Fine, *Disruptive Voices.* Ann Arbor: University of Michigan Press.

———— and Adrienne Asch. 1985. "Disabled women: Sexism without the pedestal." Pp. 6–22 in Mary Jo Deegan and Nancy A. Brooks, eds., *Women and Disability: The Double Handicap*. New Brunswick, NJ: Transaction Books.

Finlay, Andrew. 1996. "Teenage pregnancy, romantic love and social science: An uneasy relationship." Pp. 79–96 in Veronica James and Jonathan Gabe, eds., *Health and the Sociology of Emotions*. Oxford, England: Blackwell.

Finn, Patrick J. 1999. *Literacy with an Attitude: Educating Working-Class Children in Their Own Self-Interest*. Albany: State University of New York Press.

Fischer, Claude S. et al. 1996. *Inequality by Design: Cracking the Bell Curve Myth*. Princeton, NJ: Princeton University Press.

Fischer, David H. 1978. *Growing Old in America*. New York: Oxford University Press.

Fishbein, Diane H. 1990. "Biological perspectives in criminology." *Criminology* (28):27–72.

Fitzgerald, Joan and Peter B. Meyer. 1986. "Recognizing constraints to local economic development." *Journal of the Community Development Society* 17(2):115–26.

Flanagan, Cara. 1999. *Early Socialisation: Sociability and Attachment*. New York: Routledge.

Folbre, Nancy. 1985. "The pauperization of motherhood: Patriarchy and public policy in the U.S." *Review of Radical Political Economics* 16(4):72–88.

————. 1995. *The New Field Guide to the U.S. Economy*. New York: The New Press.

Foner, Phillip S. 1965. *The Case of Joe Hill*. New York: International Publishers.

Ford, D. Y. 1998. "The underrepresentation of minority students in gifted education: Problems and promises in recruitment and retention." *Journal of Special Education* 32 (Spring):4–14.

Ford, Ramona L. 1988. *Work, Organization and Power*. Boston: Allyn and Bacon.

Fordham, Signithia and John U. Ogbu. 1986. "Black students' school success: Coping with the burden of 'acting white.'" *Journal of Urban Review* 18:176–206.

Foster, John. 1999. *The Vulnerable Planet*. New York: Monthly Review Press.

Fox News/Opinion Dynamics. 2000. "Fox News/Opinion Dynamics Poll." January 12–13.

Frahm, Robert A. 2002. "Court backs vouchers: Landmark ruling provides boost to school choice movement." *Hartford (CT) Courant*, June 28, p. A1.

———— and Theresa Sullivan Barger. 1993. "Four of five teens sexually harassed in school, survey says." *Hartford (CT) Courant*, June 2, pp. A1, A6.

Frank, Andre Gunder. 1967. *Capitalism and Underdevelopment in Latin America: Historical Studies of Chile and Brazil*. New York: Monthly Review Press.

Frank, Francine and Frank Anshen. 1983. *Language and the Sexes*. Albany: State University of New York Press.

Frank, Gelya. 2000. *Venus on Wheels: Two Decades of Dialogue on Disability, Biography, and Being Female in America*. Berkeley: University of California Press.

Frankl, Razelle. 1987. *Televangelism: The Marketing of Popular Religion*. Carbondale: Southern Illinois University Press.

Franklin, Barry M. 1986. *Building the American Community: The School Curriculum and the Search for Social Control*. Philadelphia: Falmer Press.

Franklin, Raymond S. 1991. *Shadows of Race and Class*. Minneapolis: University of Minnesota Press.

Franklin, Sarah and Helena Ragone, eds. 1998. *Reproducing Reproduction: Kinship, Power, and Technological Innovation*. Philadelphia: University of Pennsylvania Press.

Fraser, Jill A. 2001. *White Collar Sweatshop: The Deterioration of Work and Its Rewards in Corporate America*. New York: Norton.

Free, Marvin D. 1996. *African Americans and the Criminal Justice System*. New York: Garland.

Freiberg, P. 1991. "Separate classes for black males?" *APA Monitor*, May, pp. 1, 47.

Friedman, Devin. 2002. "Dr. Levine's dilemma." *New York Times Magazine*, May 8, pp. 64–67.

Freud, Sigmund. 1946. *Civilization and Its Discontents*. London: Hogarth Press.

Fromberg, Doris Pronin and Doris Bergen, eds. 1998. *Play from Birth to Twelve and Beyond: Contexts, Perspectives, and Meanings*. New York: Garland Pub.

Gallas, Karen. 1998. *"Sometimes I Can Be Anything": Power, Gender, and Identity in a Primary Classroom*. New York: Teachers College Press.

Gallup Organization. 1999. "Gallup Poll." February 19–21.

Gamoran, Adam, and M. Berends. 1987. "The effects of stratification in secondary schools: Synthesis of survey and ethnographic research." *Review of Educational Research* 57:415–35.

———— and Robert D. Mare. 1989. "Secondary school tracking and educational inequality." *American Journal of Sociology* March, pp. 1146–83.

Gans, Herbert. 1982. *The Urban Villagers*. Rev. ed. New York: Free Press.

Garfinkel, Harold. 1956. "Conditions of successful degradation ceremonies." *American Sociological Review* 61:420–24.

Garfinkel, Irwin, Sara S. McLanahan, Daniel R. Meyer, and Judith A. Selzer. 1998. *Fathers under Fire: The Revolution in Child Support Enforcement*. New York: Russell Sage Foundation.

Garson, Barbara. 1994. *All the Livelong Day: The Meaning and Demeaning of Routine Work*. New York: Penguin.

Gault, Barbara and Annisah Um'rani. 2000. "The outcomes of welfare reform for women." *Poverty and Race* 9(4):1–6.

Gelles, Richard J., and Murray A. Straus. 1988. *Intimate Violence*. New York: Simon & Schuster.

Gelobter, Michel. 1992. "Toward a model of environmental discrimination." Pp. 64–81 in B. Bryant and P. Mohai, eds., *Race and the Incidence of Environmental Hazards: A Time for Discourse*. Boulder, CO: Westview Press.

GEO. 2001. *An Economy of Hope*. Stillwater, PA: Grassroots Economic Organizing.

Gerschick, Thomas J. and Adam Stephen Miller. 2000. "Coming to terms: Masculinity and physical disability." Pages 135–37 in Tracy E. Ore (ed.), *The Social Construction of Difference and Inequality: Race, Class, Gender, and Sexuality*. Mountain View, CA: Mayfield.

Gerson, Kathleen. 1993. *No Man's Land: Men's Changing Commitments to Family and Work*. New York: Basic Books.

Gerstel, Naomi and Dan Clawson. 2001. "Unions' responses to family concerns." *Social Problems* 48(2):277–97.

Gerstle, Gary and John Mollenkopf, eds. 2001. *E Pluribus Unum? Contemporary and Historical Perspectives on Immigrant Political Incorporation*. New York: Russell Sage Foundation.

Gerth, Hans and C. Wright Mills, eds. 1968. *From Max Weber: Essays in Sociology*. New York: Oxford University Press.

Gervasi, Sean. 1996. "Why is NATO in Yugoslavia?" Paper presented at the Conference on the Enlargement of NAT in Eastern Europe and the Mediterranean, January, Prague, Czech Republic.

Gibbs, Jewel Taylor, ed. 1988. *Young, Black and Male in America: An Endangered Species*. Dover, MA: Auburn.

Gifford, A. L. et al. 2002. "Participation in research and access to experimental trials by HIV-infected patients." *New England Journal of Medicine* 346 (May):1373–82.

Gilens, Martin. 1999. *Why Americans Hate Welfare: Race, Media, and the Politics of Antipoverty Policy*. Chicago: University of Chicago Press.

Gill, Gurjeet K. 1998. "Female feticide as a contemporary cultural practice in the Punjab." *Dialectical Anthropology* 23(2):203–13.

Gilligan, Carol, Nona P. Lyons, and Trudy J. Hanmer, eds. 1990. *Making Connection: The Relational Worlds of Adolescent Girls at Emma Willard School*. Cambridge, MA: Harvard University Press.

Gilmore, Sean and Alicia Crissman. 1997. "Video games: Analyzing gender identity and violence in this new virtual reality." *Studies in Symbolic Interaction* 21:181–99.

Gismondi, Michael. 1988. "Conceptualizing religion from below: The Central American experience." *Social Compass* 35(2–3):343–70.

Glasberg, Davita Silfen and Dan Skidmore. 1997. *Corporate Welfare Policy and the Welfare State: Bank Deregulation and the Savings and Loan Bailout*. New York: Aldine de Gruyter.

Glasberg, Davita Silfen and Kathryn B. Ward. 1993. "Foreign debt and economic growth in the world system." *Social Science Quarterly* 74(4):703–20.

Glass, Jennifer L. and Sara Beth Estes. 1997. "The family responsive workplace." *Annual Review of Sociology* 23:289–313.

Glassner, Barry. 1988. *Bodies.* New York: Putnam.

Glazer, Morton Peretz and Penina Migdal Glazer. 1999. "On the trail of courageous behavior." *Sociological Inquiry* 69(2): 276–95.

Glazer, Nona Y. 1987. "Servants to capital: Unpaid domestic labor and paid work." Pp. 236–55 in Naomi Gerstel and Harriet Engel Gross, eds., *Families and Work.* Philadelphia: Temple University Press.

Glazer, Sarah. 1990. "Why schools still have tracking." *Editorial Research Reports,* December 28, pp. 746–59.

Glusker, Susannah. 1998. "Women networking for peace and survival in Chiapas: Militants, celebrities, academics, survivors, and the Stiletto Heel Brigade." 39(7–8):539–57.

Goffman, Erving. 1961. *Asylums: Essays on the Social Situation of Mental Patients and Other Inmates.* Chicago: Aldine.

———. 1963. *Stigma: Notes on the Management of Spoiled Identity.* Englewood Cliffs, NJ: Prentice Hall.

Goode, Erich. 1996. "The ethics of deception in social research: A case study." *Qualitative Sociology* 19(1):11–33.

Goodlad, John I. 1984 *A Place Called School.* New York: McGraw-Hill.

Goodwin, M. H. 1980. "Directive-response sequences in girls' and boys' task activities." Pp. 157–173 in S. McConnell-Ginet, R. Borker, and N. Furman, eds., *Women and Language in Literature and Society.* New York: Praeger.

Gopaul-McNicol, Sharon-Ann. 1988. "Racial identification and racial preference of black preschool children in New York and Trinidad." *Journal of Black Psychology* 14 (February):65–68.

———. 1995. "A cross-cultural examination of racial identity and racial preference of preschool children in the West Indies." *Journal of Cross-Cultural Psychology* 26(2): 141–52.

Gordon, Linda. 1988. *Heroes of Their Own Lives.* New York: Viking Penguin.

Gordon, Mary. 2003. "Wall Street firms to pay 1.4b in SEC deal." *Associated Press Online,* April 29.

Goslee, Susan. 1998. "Losing ground bit by bit: Low-income communities in the information age." Washington, DC: Benton Foundation (www.benton.org/library/low-income/).

Gossett, Thomas F. 1997. *Race: The History of an Idea in America.* Rev. ed. New York: Oxford University Press.

Gould, Kenneth A. 1993. "Pollution and perception: Social visibility and local environmental mobilization." *Qualitative Sociology* 16(2):157–78.

Gould, Stephen J. 1996. *The Mismeasure of Man.* Rev. ed. New York: W. W. Norton.

Gouldner, Alvin W. 1970. *The Coming Crisis of Western Sociology.* New York: Avon.

Gow, Joe. 1996. "Reconsidering gender roles on MTV: Depictions in the most popular music videos of the early 1990s." *Communication Reports* 9(2):151–61.

Grammick, Jeannine, ed. 1989. *Homosexuality in the Priesthood and Religious Life.* New York: Crossroad.

Gramsci, Antonio. 1971. *Selections from the Prison Notebooks.* New York: International Publishers.

Granovetter, Mark S. 1973. "The strength of weak ties." *American Journal of Sociology* 78 (May): 1360–80.

Grant, Carl A. and Christine F. Sleeter. 1988. "Race, class and gender and abandoned dreams." *Teachers College Record* 90(1):19–40.

Greeley, Andrew. 1972. *The Denominational Society.* Glenview, IL: Scott, Foresman.

Green, Charles and Ian Isidore Smart. 1997. "Ebonics as cultural resistance." *Peace Review* 9(4):521–26.

Greenberg, Bradley and Jeffrey E. Brand. 1993. "Television news and advertising in schools: The 'Channel One' controversy." *Journal of Communication* 43(1):143–51.

Greenberg, David F. 1988. *The Construction of Homosexuality.* Chicago: University of Chicago Press.

———, ed. 1993. *Crime and Capitalism: Readings in Marxist Criminology.* Philadelphia: Temple University Press.

Greenhouse, Linda. 2003a. "Justices back affirmative action by 5 to 4." *New York Times,* June 24, p. A1.

———. 2003b. "Justices, 6–3, legalize gay sexual conduct." *New York Times, June 27, p. A1.*

Greenhouse, Steven. 2001. "Child care, the perk of tomorrow?" *New York Times, Week in Review* May 13.

Gregory, Raymond F. 2001. *Age Discrimination in the American Workplace: Old at a Young Age.* New Brunswick, NJ: Rutgers University Press.

Griffin, Keith. 1979. "Underdevelopment in history." Pp. 77–90 in Charles K. Wilber, ed., *The Political Economy of Development and Underdevelopment,* 2d ed. New York: Random House.

Grossman, Dave and Gloria DeGaetano. 1999. *Stop Teaching Our Kids to Kill: A Call to Action Against TV, Movie, and Video Game Violence.* New York: Crown.

Grunseit, Anne, Susan Kippax, Peter Aggleton, Mariella Baldo, and Gary Slutkin. 1997. "Sexuality education and young people's sexual behavior: A review of studies." *Journal of Adolescent Research* 12(4):421–53.

Guberman, Nancy. 1999. "Daughters-in-law as caregivers: How and why do they come to care?" *Journal of Women and Aging* 11(1):85–102.

Gutiérrez, Gustavo. 1973. *A Theology of Liberation.* Maryknoll, NY: Orbis Books.

———. 1983. *The Power of the Poor in History.* Maryknoll, NY: Orbis Books.

Gutman, Herbert G. 1977. *Work, Culture, and Society in Industrializing America.* New York: Vintage.

Guy-Sheftall, Beverly and Johnetta Betsch Cole, eds. 1995. *Words of Fire: An Anthology of African-American Feminist Thought.* New York: The New Press.

Hackett, Robert and Megan Adam. 1999. "Is media democratization a social movement? *Peace Review* 11(1):125–31.

Hadaway, C. Kirk, Penny Long Marler, and Mark Chaves. 1993. "What the polls don't show: A closer look at U.S. church attendance." *American Sociological Review* 58(December):741–52.

Haddad, Yvonne Yasbeck, and John L. Esposito, eds. 2001. *Daughters of Abraham: Feminist Thought in Judaism, Christianity, and Islam.* Gainesville: University of Florida Press.

Hadley, Jack. 2002. *Sicker and Poorer: The Consequences of Being Uninsured.* Washington, DC: Urban Institute.

Hagan, John. 1994. *Crime and Disrepute.* Thousand Oaks, CA: Pine Forge Press.

———. 1997. "Crime and capitalization: Toward a developmental theory of street crime in America." Pp. 287–308 in Terence P. Thornberry, ed., *Developmental Theories of Crime and Delinquency.* New Brunswick, NJ: Transaction.

Hagedorn, John M. 1998. "Gang violence in the postindustrial era." *Crime and Justice* 24:365–419.

Hall, Kira and Mary Bucholtz, eds. 1995. *Gender Articulated: Language and the Socially Constructed Self.* New York: Routledge.

Hall, Stuart and Paul du Gay, eds. 1996. *Questions of Cultural Identity.* Thousand Oaks, CA: Sage.

Hallinan, Maureen T. 1994. "Tracking: from theory to practice." *Sociology of Education* 67 (April):79–91.

———. 2001. "Sociological perspectives on black–white inequalities in American schooling." *Sociology of Education* (Extra Issue): 50–70.

Halprin, Sara. 1995. *Look at My Ugly Face: Myths and Musings on Beauty and Other Perilous Obsessions with Women's Appearance.* New York: Viking.

Hamilton, Cynthia. 1995. "Industrial racism, the environmental crisis, and the denial of social justice." Pp. 189–96. Marcy Darnovsky, Barbara Epstein, and Richard Flacks, eds. *Cultural Politics and Social Movements,* Philadelphia: Temple University Press.

Hamilton, James T. 1995. "Testing for environmental racism: Prejudice, profits, political power?" *Journal of Policy Analysis and Management* 14(1):107–32.

Hamilton, Richard. 1972. *Class and Politics in the United States.* New York: Wiley.

Hamper, Ben. 1991. *Rivethead: Tales from the Assembly Line.* New York: Warner Books.

Hanania, Joseph. 1999. "Playing princesses, punishers and prudes." *New York Times,* March 7, pp. 35, 38.

Hanson, Thomas L., Sara S. McLanahan, and Elizabeth Thomson. 1998. "Windows on divorce: Before and after." *Social Science Research* 27(3):329–49.

Harkness, Sara and Charles M. Super, eds. 1996. *Parents' Cultural Belief Systems: Their Origins, Expressions, and Consequences.* New York: Guilford Press.

Harrigan, John J. 2000. *Empty Dreams, Empty Pockets: Class and Bias in American Politics.* New York: Longman.

Harris, David A. 1999. "Driving while black: Racial profiling on our nation's highways." American Civil Liberties Special Report (www.aclu.org/profiling/report).

Harrison, Lawrence E. 2000. "Promoting progressive cultural change." Pp. 296–307 in Lawrence E., Harrison and Samuel P. Huntington, eds. *Culture Matters: How Values Shape Human Progress.* New York: Basic Books.

Hart and Teeter/NBC/Wall Street Journal, 1999 (www.publicagenda.org/issues).

Harvard Law Review. 1988. "Developments in the law: Race and the criminal process." 101:1472.

Hatfield, Heather. 2003. "Toxic communities: Environmental racism" (www.cbcfhealth.org).

Hautzinger, Sarah. 2003. "Researching men's violence: Personal reflections on ethnographic data." *Men and Masculinities* 6(1):93–106.

Havens, Timothy. 2000. "'The biggest show in the world': Race and the global popularity of The Cosby Show." *Media Culture and Society* 22(4):371–91.

Hawdon, James E. 1999. "Daily routines and crime: Using routine activities as measures of Hirschi's involvement." *Youth and Society* 30(4):395–415.

Hawkesworth, Marian. 2001. "Disabling spatialities and the regulation of a visible secret." *Urban Studies* 38(2):299–318.

Hayashi, Reiko and Masako Okuhira. 2001. "The disability rights movement in Japan: Past, present, and future."*Disability and Society* 16(6):855–69.

Hayes, Thomas C. 1991. "Earnings soar 75% at Exxon." *New York Times,* April 25, pp. D1, D10.

Haynes, Jeff. 1998. *Religion in Global Politics.* New York: Longman.

Healey, Kerry, Christine Smith with Chris O'Sullivan. 1998. "Batterer intervention: Program approaches and criminal justice strategies." U.S. Department of Justice, Office of Justice Programs, National Institute of Justice.

Heintz, James, Nancy Folbre, and the Center for Popular Economics. 2000. *The Ultimate Field Guide to the U.S. Economy: A Compact and Irreverent Guide to Economic Life in America.* New York: The New Press.

Held, David, Anthony McGrew, David Goldblatt, and Jonathan Perraton. 1999. *Global Transformations: Politics, Economics, and Culture.* Palo, Atlo, CA: Stanford University Press.

Hellman, Christopher. 2000. "Top 15 U.S. defense contractors of FY '99." www.cdi.org/issues/usmi/complex/top15fy99.html).

Hemenway, David, Tomoko Shinoda-Tagawa, and Matthew Miller. 2002. "Firearm availability and female homicide victimization rates among 25 populous high-income countries." *Journal of the American Medical Women's Association* 57(2).

Henry, Jules. 1963. *Culture against Man.* New York: Vintage Books.

Herideen, Penelope E. 1998. *Policy, Pedagogy, and Inequality: Community College Student Realities in Post-industrial America.* New York: Bergin & Garvey.

Herman, Edward S. and Noam Chomsky. 1988. *Manufacturing Consent: The Political Economy of the Mass Media.* New York: Pantheon.

Herrnstein, Richard J. and Charles Murray. 1994. *The Bell Curve: Intelligence and Class Structure in American Life.* New York: Free Press.

Hesse-Biber, Sharlene. 1996. *Am I Thin Enough Yet? The Cult of Thinness and the Commercialization of Identity.* New York: Oxford University Press.

Hibbard, David R. and Duane Buhrmester. 1998. "The role of peers in the socialization of gender-related social interaction styles." *Sex Roles* 39(3–4):185– 202.

Hill, Nancy. 1997. "Does parenting differ based on social class? African American women's perceived socialization for achievement." *American Journal of Community Psychology* 25(5):675–97.

Hill, Shirley. 1999. *African American Children: Socialization and Development in Families.* Thousand Oaks, CA: Sage.

Hilts, Philip J. 1993. "Why whistle-blowers can seem a little crazy." *New York Times,* June 13, pp. E6.

Hind, John A. and Michael Reese. 1998. "The distribution of environmental quality: An empirical analysis." *Social Science Quarterly* 79(4):693–716.

Hirschi, Travis. 1969. *Causes of Delinquency.* Berkeley: University of California Press.

Ho, Mae-Wan. 2000. *Genetic Engineering: Dream or Nightmare? Turning the Tide on the Brave New World of Bad Science and Big Business.* New York: Continuum.

Hochschild, Arlie, with Anne Machung. 1997. *The Second Shift: Working Parents and the Revolution at Home.* New York: Avon Books.

Hochschild, Arlie. 1997. *The Time Bind: When Work Becomes Home and Home Becomes Work.* New York: Metropolitan Books.

Hodson, Randy. 1991. "The active worker: Compliance and autonomy at the workplace." *Journal of Contemporary Ethnography* 20 (April):47–78.

———. 1995. "Worker resistance: An undeveloped concept in the sociology of work."

Economic and Industrial Democracy 16 (1):79–110.

———. 2001. *Dignity at Work.* New York: Cambridge University Press.

——— and Teresa A. Sullivan. 1990. *The Social Organization of Work.* Belmont, CA: Wadsworth.

Hoffman, Bruce. 1995. "'Holy terror': The implications of terrorism motivated by a religious imperative." *Studies in Conflict and Terrorism* 18(4):271–84.

Hohenemser, Christopher and Ortwin Renn. 1988. "Chernobyl's other legacy." *Environment* 30(April):5.

Holden, Karen C. 1990. "Social security policy and the income shock of widowhood." Working Paper No. 3, University of Wisconsin, Institute of Public Affairs, Madison.

——— and Pamela J. Smock. 1991. "The economic costs of marital dissolution: Why do women bear a disproportionate cost?" *Annual Review of Sociology* 17:51–78.

Holland, Kelley and Linda Himelstein. 1995. "The Bankers Trust tapes." *Business Week,* October 16, pp. 106–11.

Holmstrom, Lynda Lytle, David A. Karp, and Paul S. Gray. 2002. "Why laundry, not Hegel? Social class, transition to college, and pathways to adulthood." *Symbolic Interaction* 25(4):437–62.

Hondagneu-Sotelo, Pierette. 1997. "Affluent players in the informal economy: Employers of paid domestic workers." *International Journal of Sociology and Social Policy* 17(3/4):131–59.

———. 2001. *Domestica: Immigrant Workers Cleaning and Caring in the Shadows of Affluence.* Berkeley: University of California Press.

hooks, bell. 1981. *Ain't I a Woman: Black Women and Feminism.* Boston: South End Press.

Hooks, Gregory. 1991. *Forging the Military-Industrial Complex: World War II's Battle of the Potomac.* Urbana: University of Illinois Press.

Horowitz, Irving Louis, ed. 1967. *The Rise and Fall of Project Camelot.* Cambridge, MA: MIT Press.

Hoselitz, Berthold Frank. 1960. *Sociological Aspects of Economic Growth.* Glencoe, IL: Free Press.

Hossfeld, Karen. 1988. *Divisions of Labor, Divisions of Lives: Immigrant Women Workers in Silicon Valley.* Unpublished doctoral dissertation, University of California at Santa Cruz.

———. 1989. "The triple shift: Immigrant women workers and the household division of labor in Silicon Valley." Paper presented at the annual meeting of the American Sociological Association, Atlanta.

Houppert, Karen. 1999. "You're not entitled! Welfare 'reform' is leading to government lawlessness." *The Nation,* October 25, pp. 11–18.

Houston, Brant, and Jack Ewing. 1991. "Justice jailed." *Hartford (CT) Courant,* June 16, pp. A1, A10–A11.

——— and ———. 1992. "Racial inequity still evident in setting of bail." *Hartford (CT) Courant,* May 17, A1, A6.

Howard, Judith A. and Jocelyn A. Hollander. 1997. *Gendered Situations, Gendered Selves: A Gender Lens on Social Psychology.* Thousand Oaks, CA: Sage.

Huber, Melissa S. and Ellen Ernst Kosser. 1999. "Community distress predicting welfare exits: The under-examined factor for families in the United States." *Community, Work and Family* 2(2):173–86.

Huff, C. Ronald, ed. 1996. *Gangs in America.* Thousand Oaks, CA: Sage.

Hughes, Bill. 1999. "The constitution of impairment: Modernity and the aesthetic of oppression." *Disability and Society* 14(2):155–72.

Hughes, Diane and Lisa Chen. 1997. "When and what parents tell children about race: An examination of race-related socialization among African American families." *Applied Developmental Science* 1(4):200–14.

Human Rights Watch. 2000. *United States: Stark Race Disparities in Drug Incarceration.* New York: HRW. Available at www.hrw.org.

———. 2001. *Hatred in the Hallways: Violence and Discrimination against Lesbian, Gay, Bisexual, and Transgender Students in U.S. Schools.* New York: HRW.

Humphreys, Laud. 1975. *Tearoom Trade.* Chicago: Aldine.

Hungerford, Thomas L. 2001. "The economic consequences of widowhood on elderly women in the United States and Germany." *Gerontologist* 41(1):103–10.

Hurwitz, Roger. 1999. "Who needs politics? Who needs people? The ironies of democracy in cyberspace." *Contemporary Sociology* 28(6):655–61.

Ichilov, Orit. 2002. "Citizenship perceptions of Soviet immigrants in Israel." *International Review of Sociology* 12(1):5–22.

Imam, Ayesha M. 2001. "The Muslim right ('fundamentalists') and sexuality." Pp. 15–30 in Patricia Beattie Jung et al., eds., *Good Sex: Feminist Perspectives from the World's Religions.* New Brunswick, NJ: Rutgers University Press.

Institute of Medicine. 2002a. *Care without Coverage: Too Little, Too Late.* Washington, DC: National Academy Press.

———. 2002b. *Unequal Treatment: Confronting Racial and Ethnic Disparities in Health Care.* Washington, DC: National Academy Press.

Irvine, Jacqueline Jordan. 1990. *Black Students and School Failure.* New York: Greenwood Press.

Isaac, T. M. Thomas, Richard W. Franke, and Pyaralal Raghavan. 1998. *Democracy at Work in an Indian Industrial Cooperative.* Ithaca, NY: Cornell University Press.

Iyengar, Shanto. 1990. "The accessibility bias in politics: Television news and public opinion." *International Journal of Public Opinion Research* 2(1):1–15.

Jackall, Robert. 1988. *Moral Mazes: The World of Corporate Managers.* New York: Oxford University Press.

Jackson, Janine. 2000. "Anything but racism: Media make excuses for 'whitewashed' TV lineup" (www.fair.org/extra/0001/tv-racism.html).

Jaffee, David. 2002. *Organization Theory: Tension and Change.* New York: McGraw-Hill.

Jans, Lita and Susan Stoddard. 1999. *Chartbook on Women and Disability in the United States.* Washington, DC: U.S. Office of Education.

Jargowsky, Paul A. 1998. *Poverty and Place: Ghettos, Barrios, and the American City.* New York: Russell Sage Foundation.

Jaynes, Gerald David and Robin M. Williams Jr., eds. 1989. *A Common Destiny: Blacks and American Society.* Washington, DC: National Academy Press.

Jencks, Christopher and Meredith Phillips, eds. 1998. *The Black–White Test Score Gap.* Washington, DC: Brookings Institute.

Jenkins, J. Craig and Charles Perrow. 1977. "Insurgency of the powerless: Farm workers movements, 1946–72." *American Sociological Review* 42(2):249–68.

Jensen, Carl J. III. 2001. "Beyond the tea leaves: Futures research and terrorism." *American Behavioral Scientist* 44(6):914–36.

Jessop, Bob. 1990. *State Theory: Putting the Capitalist State in Its Place.* University Park: Pennsylvania State University Press.

Jewell, K. Sue. 1993. *From Mammy to Miss America and Beyond.* New York: Routledge.

John, Daphne, Beth Anne Shelton, and Kristen Luschen. 1995. "Race, ethnicity, gender, and perceptions of fairness." *Journal of Family Issues* 16(3):357–79.

Johnson, Allan G. 1997. *The Forest and the Trees: Sociology as Life, Practice, and Promise.* Philadelphia: Temple University Press.

———. 2001. *Privilege, Power, and Difference.* Mountain View, CA: Mayfield.

Johnson, Bradley. 1989. "California moves to ban Whittle's 'Channel One.'" *Advertising Age* 60(May 29):1, 48.

Johnson, Dirk. 1990. "More prisons using iron hand to control inmates." *New York Times,* November 1, p. A18.

Johnson, James E., James F. Christie, and Thomas D. Yawkey. 1999. *Play and Early Childhood Development.* New York: Longman.

———, Walter C. Farrell Jr., and Jennifer A. Stoloff. 2000. "An empirical assessment of four perspectives on the declining fortunes of the African American male." *Urban Affairs Review* 35 (May):708–9.

Johnstone, Ronald L. 2001. *Religion in Society.* 6th ed. Englewood Cliffs, NJ: Prentice Hall.

Jones, Christopher M. 2001. "Roles, politics and the survival of the V-22 Osprey." *Journal of Political and Military Sociology* 29(1):46–72.

Jones, Jacqueline. 1987. "Black women, work, and the family under slavery." Pp. 84–110 in Naomi Gerstel and Harriet Engel Gross, eds., *Families and Work.* Philadelphia: Temple University Press.

Jones, M. Gail and Jack Wheatley. 1989. "Gender influences in classroom displays and student–teacher behaviors." *Science Education* 73(5):535–45.

Joppke, Christian. 1993. *Mobilizing against Nuclear Energy: A Comparison of Germany and the United States.* Berkeley: University of California Press.

Judd, Neville. 2001. "USA/India: Toxic shipment under fire" (corpwatch.org).

Kagan, Jerome, J. Steven Resnick, and Nancy Snidman. 1988. "Biological bases of childhood shyness." *Science* 240 (April 1): 167–171.

Kallianes, Virginia and Phyllis Rubenfeld. 1997. "Disabled women and reproductive rights." *Disability and Society* 12(2):203–21.

Kane, Connie. 2000. "African American family dynamics as perceived by family members." *Journal of Black Studies* 30(5): 691–702.

Kane, Michael B. 1970. *Minorities in Textbooks: A Study of Their Treatment in Social Science Texts.* Chicago: Quadrangle.

Kanfer, Stefan. 1993. *The Last Empire: De Beers, Diamonds, and the World.* New York: Farrar Straus Giroux.

Kaplan, Howard B., Robert J. Johnson, and Carol A. Bailey. 1987. "Deviant peers and deviant behavior: Further elaborations of a model." *Social Psychology Quarterly* 50(4):227–52.

Katz, Jesse. 2000. "For many felons, voting ban is forever." *Hartford (CT) Courant,* April 26, p. A12.

Keith, Jennie, Christine L. Fry, and Anthony P. Glascock. 1994. *The Aging Experience:Diversity and Commonality across Cultures.* Thousand Oaks, CA: Sage.

Kendall, Diana. 2002. *The Power of Good Deeds: Privileged Women and the Social Reproduction of the Upper Class.* New York: Rowman and Littlefield.

Kennedy, Paul. 1987. *The Rise and Fall of the Great Powers.* New York: Random House.

Kennedy, Randall. 1997. *Race, Crime, and the Law.* New York: Pantheon Books.

Kerbo, Harold R. 2000. *Social Stratification and Inequality: Class Conflict in Historical, Comparative, and Global Perspective.* New York: McGraw-Hill.

———. 2003. *Social Stratification and Inequality: Class Conflict in Historical, Comparative, and Global Perspective.* New York: McGraw-Hill.

Kibria, Nazli. 1998. "Vietnamese families." Pp. 176–88 in Ronald L. Taylor, ed., *Minority Families in the United States: A Multicultural Perspective.* Upper Saddle River, NJ: Prentice Hall.

Kilbride, Howard W., David L. Johnson, and Ann Pytkowicz Streissguth. 1977. "Social class, birth order, and newborn experience." *Child Development* 48(4):1686–88.

Kim, Marlene. 2000. "Women paid low wages: Who they are and where they work." *Monthly Labor Review,* September, pp. 26–30.

Kimmel, Michael S. 2000. *The Gendered Society.* New York: Oxford University Press.

Kindlon, Daniel J., Michael Thompson, with Teresa Barker. 2000. *Raising Cain: Protecting the Emotional Life of Boys.* New York: Ballantine Books.

King, Billie Jean. 2002. "Playing field still not level." *Hartford (CT) Courant,* June 23, p. C5.

Kinsey, Alfred, Wardell Pomeroy, and Clyde Martin. 1948. *Sexual Behavior in the Human Male.* Philadelphia: Saunders.

———, ———, ———, and Paul Gebhard. 1953. *Sexual Behavior in the Human Female.* Philadelphia: Saunders.

Kirschenman, Joleen, and Kathryn M. Neckerman. 1991. "'We'd love to hire them, but': The meaning of race for employers." Pp. 203–32 in Christopher Jencks and Paul E. Peterson, eds., *The Urban Underclass.* Washington, DC: Brookings Institution.

Kisker, E. E. 1985. "Teenagers talk about sex, pregnancy, and contraception." *Family Planning Perspectives* 17(2):83–90.

Klandermans, Bert, Marlene Roefs, and Johan Olivier. 2001. "Grievance formation in a country in transition: South Africa, 1994–1998." *Social Psychology Quarterly* 64(1):41–54.

Kleinke, J. D. 2001. *Oxymorons: The Myth of a U.S. Health Care System.* New York: Jossey-Bass.

Knee, Jonathan A. 2003. "False alarm at the FCC: Ending TV–newspaper cross-ownership rules may have little effect" (www.cjr.org/year/03/3/knee).

Kochman, Thomas. 1981. *Black and White Styles in Conflict.* Chicago: University of Chicago Press.

Kohn, Melvin. 1977. *Social Competence, Symptoms and Underachievement in Childhood: A Longitudinal Perspective.* Washington, DC: Winston.

Kopels, Sandra and David R. Dupper. 1999. "School-based peer sexual harassment." *Child Welfare* 78(July–August):435–60.

Koretz, Gene. 2001. "Why married men earn more." *Business Week,* September 17.

Korgen, Kathleen Odell. 1998. *From Black to Biracial: Transforming Racial Identity among Americans.* Westport, CT: Praeger.

Kowalewski, David. 1990. "The historical structuring of a dissident movement: The sanctuary case." *Research in Social Movements, Conflict and Change* 12:89–110.

Kozol, Jonathan. 1991. *Savage Inequalities.* New York: Crown.

Krecker, Margaret L. and Angela M. O'Rand. 1991. "Contested milieux: Small firms, unionization and the provision of protective structures." *Sociological Forum* 6(1):93–117.

Kubitschek, Warren N. and Maureen T. Hallinan. 1996. "Race, gender, and inequity in track assignments." *Research in Sociology of Education and Socialization* 11:121–46.

Kumamoto, Robert. 1991. "Diplomacy from below: International terrorism and American foreign relations, 1945–1962." *Terrorism* 14(1):31–48.

Kurz, Demie. 2001. "Violence against women by intimate partners." Pp. 205–15 in Dana Vannoy, ed., *Gender Mosaics: Social Perspectives.* Los Angeles: Roxbury.

Lacayo, Richard. 1990. "Why no blue blood will flow: On the front lines, a disproportionate number of troops hail from minorities and the working class." *Time,* November 26, p. 34.

LaDuke, Winona. 1999. *All Our Relations: Native Struggles for Land and Life.* Cambridge, MA: South End Press.

Lamb, Michael E., ed. 1997. *The Role of the Father in Child Development.* New York: Wiley.

LaPlante, Mitchell P. 1996. "Disability and employment." Abstract 11 (January). San Francisco: Disability Statistics Center, University of California.

Lappe, Frances Moore and Joseph Collins. 1986. *World Hunger: Twelve Myths.* New York/San Francisco: Grove Press/Food First Books.

Lareau, Annette. 1989. *Home Advantage: Social Class and Parental Intervention in Elementary Education.* Philadelphia: Falmer Press.

Lasch, Christopher. 1977. *Haven in a Heartless World: The Family Besieged.* New York: Basic Books.

Lawson, Steven F. 1990. *Running for Freedom: Civil Rights and Black Politics in America since 1941.* Philadelphia: Temple University Press.

Lay, Mary M. et al., eds. 2000. *Body Talk: Rhetoric, Technology, Reproduction.* Madison: University of Wisconsin Press.

Lechner, Viola M. and Margaret B. Neal (eds.), 1999. *Work and Caring For the Elderly: International Perspectives.* Philadelphia: Brunner/Mazel.

Leckie, Robert. 1992. *The Wars of America.* New York: Harper Collins.

Lee, Charles. 1992. "Toxic waste and race in the United States." Pp. 10–27 in B. Bryant and P. Mohai, eds., *Race and the Incidence of Environmental Hazards: A Time for Discourse.* Boulder, CO: Westview Press.

———. 1994. "Beyond toxic wastes and race." Pp. 41–52 in Robert D. Bullard, ed., *Confronting Environmental Racism: Voices from the Grassroots.* Boston: South End Press.

Lee, Felicia R. 1994. "Grappling with how to teach young speakers of black dialect." *New York Times,* January 5, p. A1.

Lemert, Edwin M. 1967. *Human Deviance, Social Problems, and Social Control.* Englewood Cliffs, NJ: Prentice Hall.

Lengermann, Patricia Madoo, and Jill Niebrugge. 2000. Pp. 436–86 in George Ritzer, *Sociological Theory,* 4th ed. New York: McGraw-Hill.

Lenski, Gerhard. 1966. *Power and Privilege.* New York: McGraw-Hill.

———, Jean Lenski, and Patrick Nolan. 1991. *Human Societies: An Introduction to Macrosociology.* New York: McGraw-Hill.

Lev, Michael A. 2000. "China's One-Child Rule: The Next Generation." *Hartford (CT) Courant,* May 1, B7.

Levin, Jack and William C. Levin. 1980. *Ageism: Prejudice and Discrimination against the Elderly.* Belmont, CA: Wadsworth.

Levine, Suzanne Braun. 2000. *Father Courage: What Happens When Men Put Family First.* New York: Harcourt.

Levine, Rhonda. 1988. *Class Struggle and the New Deal: Industrial Labor, Industrial Capital and the State.* Lawrence: University Press of Kansas.

Lewis, Neil A. 1994. "Prize in an unusual lottery: A scarce experimental drug." *New York Times,* January 7, p. A1.

Lewis, Oscar. 1959. *Five Families: Mexican Case Studies in the Culture of Poverty.* New York: Basic Books.

Lichter, S. Robert and Daniel R. Amundson. 1997. "Distorted reality: Hispanic characters in TV entertainment." Pp. 57–72 in Clara Rodriguez, ed., *Latin Looks.* Boulder, CO: Westview Press.

Liebow, Elliot. 1967. *Tally's Corner: A Study of Negro Streetcorner Men.* Boston: Little, Brown.

"Life sentence in dragging death." 1999. *Washington Post,* November 19, p. A32.

Light, Donald W. 1989. "Corporate medicine for profit." Pp. 294–308 in Phil Brown, ed., *Perspectives in Medical Sociology.* Belmont, CA: Wadsworth.

Ligos, Melinda. 2000. "The fear of taking paternity leave." *New York Times.* May 31, p. G1.

Lincoln, C. Eric and Lawrence H. Mamiya. 1990. *The Black Church in the African American Experience.* Durham, NC: Duke University Press.

Lindsey, Linda L. and Sandra Christy. 1996. *Gender Roles: A Sociological Perspective.* 3rd ed. Saddle River, NJ: Prentice Hall.

Ling, Nan. 2000. "Inequality in social capital." *Contemporary Sociology* 29 (November): 785–95.

Link, Bruce G. et al. 1987. "The social rejection of former mental patients: Understanding why labels matter." *American Journal of Sociology* 92(May): 1461–1500.

———, Elmer L. Struening, Michael Rahav, Jo C. Phelan, and Larry Nuttbrock. 1997. "On stigma and its consequences: Evidence from a longitudinal study of men with dual diagnoses of mental illness and substance abuse." *Journal of Health and Social Behavior* 38(2):177–90.

Linton, Simi. 1998. *Claiming Disability: Knowledge and Identity.* New York: New York University Press

Lipset, Seymour Martin. 1960. *Political Man: The Social Bases of Politics.* Garden City, NY: Doubleday.

———. 1990. *Continental Divide: The Values and Institutions of the United States and Canada.* New York, London: Routledge.

Lipsitz, George. 1998. *The Possessive Investment in Whiteness: How White People Profit* from *Identity Politics*. Philadelphia: Temple University Press.

Liska, Allen E. and Steven F. Messner. 1998. *Perspectives on Crime and Deviance*. Upper Saddle River, NJ: Prentice Hall.

Litwak, Eugene. 1965. "Extended kin relations in an industrial democratic society." Pp. 290–323 in Ethel Shanas and Gordon T. Strieb, eds., *Social Structure and the Family: Generational Relations*. Englewood Cliffs, NJ: Prentice Hall.

Lockard, J. 1997. "Progressive politics, electronic individualism, and the myth of virtual community." Pp. 219–32 in D. Porter, ed., *Internet Culture*. New York: Routledge.

Locker, Mike and Bob Stone. 2000. "Intercooperation is alive and well in the Bay Area!" *GEO (Grassroots Economic Organizing) Newsletter* 43(September–October): 4–5.

Loewen, James W. 1995. *Lies My Teacher Told Me: Everything Your American History Textbook Got Wrong*. New York: The New Press.

Lofstrom, Jan. 1998. "Introduction: Sketching the framework for a history and sociology of homosexualities in the Nordic countries." *Journal of Homosexuality* 35(3–4):1–13.

Logue, John. 1998. "Rustbelt buyouts: Why Ohio leads in worker ownership." *Dollars and Sense*, September–October, pp. 34–38.

Long, Patrick Du Phuoc and Laura Ricard. 1996. *The Dream Shattered: Vietnamese Gangs in America*. Boston: Northeastern University Press.

Lonsdale, Susan. 1990. *Women and Disability*. New York: St. Martin's Press.

Lont, Cynthia M. 2001. "The influence of the media on gender images." Pp. 114–22 in Dana Vannoy, ed., *Gender Mosaics: Social Perspectives*. Los Angeles: Roxbury.

Lopreato, Joseph and Timothy Crippen. 1999. *Crisis in Sociology: The Need for Darwin*. New Brunswick, NJ: Transaction Publishers.

Los Angeles Times. **2000.** "Los Angeles Times poll." June 8–13.

Los Angeles Times. **2001.** "Los Angeles Times poll." November 10–13.

Loveless, Tom. 1999. *The Tracking Wars*. Washington, DC: Brookings Institution.

Lowe, Marcia D. 1994. "Reinventing transport." Pp. 81–98 in Lester R. Brown, ed., *State of the World, 1994*. New York: Norton.

Lucas, Samuel R. 1999. *Tracking Inequality: Stratification and Mobility in American High Schools*. New York: Columbia University Teachers College Press.

Lugar, Richard and Joseph R. Biden Jr. 1998. "Swapping Debt for Nature" (www.csmonitor.com).

Luke, Timothy W. 1997. "The politics of digital inequality: Access, capability, and distribution in cyberspace." *New Political Science* 41–42(Fall):121–44.

Lundberg, George D. 2002. *Severed Trust: Why American Medicine Hasn't Been Fixed and What We Can Do about It*. New York: Basic Books.

MacArthur, John R. 1992. *Second Front: Censorship and Propaganda in the Gulf War*. Berkeley: University of California Press.

Macleod, Greg. 1997. *From Mondragon to America: Experiments in Community Development*. Sydney, NS, Canada: University College of Cape Breton Press.

MacNichol, Sally Noland and Mary Elizabeth Walsh. 1993. "Feminist theology and spirituality: An annotated bibliography." *Women's Studies Quarterly* 21(Spring–Summer):177–96.

Madrid, Arturo. 1992. "Missing people and others." Pp. 6–11 in Margaret L. Andersen and Patricia Hill Collins, eds., *Race, Class, and Gender*. Belmont, CA: Wadsworth.

Magnussen, Paul with Nicole Harris, Linda Himmelstein, Biull Vlasic, and Wendy Zellner. 1997. "A wake-up call for business." *Business Week*, September 1, pp. 28–9.

Maher, Timothy. 1998. "Environmental oppression: Who is targeted for toxic exposure?" *Journal of Black Studies* 28(3):357–67.

Mahler, Jonathan. 2003. "Commute to nowhere: In a new kind of recession, out-of-work executives are being forced to rethink their professional identities, their personal relationships—and their most fundamental sense of who they are." *New York Times Magazine* April 13, pp. 44–49.

Maio, Kathi. 1990. "Hooked on hate? Unfunny comedians, MTV, tabloid television, fright films, and other media invasions." *Ms.* 1(2):42–44.

Majoribanks, Kevin. 1987. "Gender/social class, family environments and adolescents' aspirations." *Australian Journal of Education* 31(1):43–54.

Maltz, D. N. and R. A. Borker. 1983. "A cultural approach to male–female miscommunication." Pp. 195–216 in J. J. Gumperz, ed., *Language and Social Identity*. New York: Cambridge University Press.

Mann, Coramae Richey and Marjorie S. Zatz, eds. 2002. *Images of Color, Images of Crime*. Los Angeles: Roxbury.

Manning, Robert D. 2000. *Credit Card Nation: The Consequences of America's Addiction to Credit*. New York: Basic Books.

Manning, Steven. 1999. "Students for sale: How corporations are buying their way into America's classrooms." *The Nation*, September 27, pp. 11–18.

Marcus, Eric. 1999. *Is It a Choice? Answers to 300 of the Most Frequently Asked Questions about Gay and Lesbian People*. Rev. ed. San Francisco: Harper San Francisco.

Marks, Donovan and Nicole Brown. 1990. "The next link in the dumping chain." Pp. 32–33 in Dana Alston, ed., *We Speak for Ourselves: Social Justice, Race and Environment*. Washington, DC: Panos Institute.

Martin, Judith G. 1993. "Why women need a feminist spirituality." *Women's Studies Quarterly* 21(Spring–Summer):106–20.

Marx, Karl. 1844/1964. *Economic and Philosophic Manuscripts of 1844*. Trans. Martin Milligan. New York: International Publishers.

———. **1964.** *Selected Writings in Sociology and Social Philosophy*. Ed. T. B. Bottomore and Maximillian Rubel. Baltimore: Penguin.

——— **and Friederich Engels. 1848/1967.** *The Communist Manifesto*. Baltimore: Penguin.

——— and ———. **1970.** *The German Ideology*. New York: International Publishers.

Massey, Douglas S. 2002. *Beyond Smoke and Mirrors: Mexican Immigration in an Era of Economic Integration*. New York: Russell Sage Foundation.

——— **and Nancy A. Denton. 1993.** *American Apartheid: Segregation and the Making of the Underclass*. Cambridge, MA: Harvard University Press.

Mater, Gene P. 1989. "Monday memo." *Broadcasting* 117(July 10):23.

Mauer, Marc. 1999. *Race to Incarcerate*. New York: New Press.

Maume, David J., Jr. 1999. "Glass ceilings and glass escalators: Occupational segregation and race and sex differences in managerial promotions." *Work and Occupations* 26(4):483–509.

———. **2001.** "Work–family conflict: Effects for job segregation and career perceptions." Pp. 240–48 in Dana Vannoy, ed., *Gender Mosaics: Social Perspectives*. Los Angeles: Roxbury.

Mayer, Colin. 2001. "Financial institutions and the institutional foundations of a market economy" (www.dse.de/ef/omstm/mayer.htm).

McAdam, Doug. 1982. *Political Process and the Development of Black Insurgency, 1930–1970*. Chicago: University of Chicago Press.

———. **1988.** *Freedom Summer*. New York: Oxford University Press.

———. **1999.** *Political Process and the Development of Black Insurgency, 1930–1970*. Chicago: University of Chicago Press.

McAllister, Matthew P. 1996. *The Commercialization of American Culture: New Advertising, Control, and Democracy*. Thousand Oaks, CA: Sage.

McCarthy, John D. and Mark Wolfson. 1996. "Resource mobilization by local social movement organizations: Agency, strategy, and organization in the movement against drinking and driving." *American Sociological Review* 61(6):1070–88.

McChesney, Robert. 1999. *Rich Media, Poor Democracy: Communication Politics in Dubious Times*. Urbana: University of Illinois Press.

———. **1997.** "The global media giants: The nine firms that dominate the world" (www.fair.org).

McClellan, Jeffrey A. and Mary Jo V. Pugh, eds. 1999. *The Role of Peer Groups in Adolescent Social Identity: Exploring the Importance of Stability and Change*. San Francisco: Jossey-Bass.

McFadden, Robert D. 1991. "Degrees and stacks of résumés yield few jobs for class of '91." *New York Times,* April 22, pp. A1, B6.

McGuire, Meredith B. 1992. *Religion: The Social Context.* 3rd ed. Belmont, CA: Wadsworth.

McGuire, Patrick and Donald McQuarie, eds. 1994. *From the Left Bank to the Mainstream: Historical Debates and Contemporary Research in Marxist Sociology.* Chicago: Nelson Hall.

McIntosh, Peggy. 1992. "White privilege and male privilege." Pp. 70–81 in Margaret L. Andersen and Patricia Hill Collins, eds., *Race, Class, and Gender.* Belmont, CA: Wadsworth.

McKean, Benjamin L. 2001. "Harvard's shame." *The Nation,* May 21.

McKinlay, John B. and Sonja M. McKinlay. 1990. "Medical measures and the decline of mortality." Pp. 10–23 in Peter Conrad and Rochelle Kern, eds., *The Sociology of Health and Illness.* 3rd ed. New York: St. Martin's Press.

McManus, Patricia A. and Thomas A. DiPrete. 2001. "Losers and winners: The financial consequences of separation and divorce for men." *American Sociological Review* 66(2):246–68.

McQuiston, John T. 1990. "Dozens are injured in further outbreak of Rikers Island unrest." *New York Times,* August 22, p. A1.

Mead, George Herbert. 1934. *Mind, Self, and Society.* Chicago: University of Chicago Press.

Mead, Lawrence M. 1992. *The New Politics of Poverty.* New York: Basic Books.

Meadows, Lynn M. 1996. "Discovering women's work: A study of post-retirement aged women." *Marriage and Family Review* 24(1–2):165–91.

Mehlman, Maxwell J. and Jeffrey R. Botkin. 1998. *Access to the Genome: The Challenge to Equality.* Washington, DC: Georgetown University Press.

Meier, Kenneth J., et al. 1989. *Race, Class, and Education: The Politics of Second-Generation Discrimination.* Madison: University of Wisconsin Press.

Melman, Seymour. 1997. "From private to state capitalism" (www.webcom.com/ncecd).

———. **2001.** *After Capitalism: From Managerialism to Workplace Democracy.* New York: Knopf.

Melton, J. Gordon, ed. 1989. *The Encyclopedia of American Religions.* 3rd ed. Detroit: Gale Research.

Merchant, Jennifer. 1996. "Biogenetics, artificial procreation, and public policy in the United States and France." *Technology in Society* 18(1):1–15.

Merrill, Deborah M. 1997. *Caring for Elderly Parents: Juggling Work, Family, and Caregiving in Middle and Working Class Families.* Westport, CT: Auburn House.

Merry, Sally Engle. 2002. "Governmentality and gender violence in Hawai'i in historical perspective." *Social and Legal Studies* 11(1): 81–111.

Merton, Robert K. 1957. *Social Theory and Social Structure.* New York: Free Press.

———. **1968.** *Social Theory and Social Structure.* Enl. ed. New York: Free Press.

Messner, Michael A. 2001. "When bodies are weapons: Masculinity and violence in sport." Pp. 94–105 in Dana Vannoy, ed., *Gender Mosaics: Social Perspectives.* Los Angeles: Roxbury.

Meyer, David S. 1993. "Institutionalizing dissent: The United States structure of political opportunity and the end of the nuclear freeze movement." *Sociological Forum* 8(2):157–80.

——— **and Suzanne Staggenborg. 1996.** "Movements, countermovements, and the structure of political opportunity." *American Journal of Sociology* 101(6):1628–60.

Meyer, Madonna Harrington. 1996. "Making claims as workers or wives: The distribution of Social Security benefits." *American Sociological Review* 61(3):449–65.

Michels, Robert. 1962. *Political Parties: A Sociological Study of Oligarchical Tendencies of Modern Democracy.* New York: Free Press.

Miethe, Terance D. 1999. *Whistleblowing at Work: Tough Choices in Exposing Fraud, Waste, and Abuse on the Job.* Boulder, CO: Westview Press.

Milgram, Stanley. 1967. "The small-world problem." *Psychology Today* 1(1):60–67.

Miliband, Ralph. 1969. *The State in Capitalist Society.* New York: Basic Books.

Miller, Carol Diana. 1997. *Effects of Economic Development, Trade Dependency, and Debt on Women's Share of the Labor Force: A Cross-National Study.* Ph.D. dissertation, University of Arizona, Tucson. Ann Arbor, MI: Dissertation Abstracts.

Miller, Casey and Kate Swift. 1991. *Words and Women Updated: New Language in New Times.* New York: Harper Collins.

Miller, Jerome G. 1996. *Search and Destroy: African American Males in the Criminal Justice System.* New York: Cambridge University Press.

Mills, C. Wright. 1957. *The Power Elite.* New York: Oxford University Press.

———. **1959.** *The Sociological Imagination.* New York: Oxford University Press.

Min, Pyong Gap. 1996. *Caught in the Middle: Korean Merchants in America's Multiethnic Cities.* Berkeley: University of California Press.

Mink, Gwendolyn. 2002. *Welfare's End.* Ithaca, NY: Cornell University Press.

Mintz, Beth, and Michael Schwartz. 1985. *The Power Structure of American Business.* Chicago: University of Chicago Press.

Mishel, Lawrence, Jared Bernstein, and John Schmitt. 1997. *The State of Working America, 1996–97.* Armonk, NY: M.E. Sharpe.

———, ———, and ———. **2001.** *The State of Working America, 2000–2001.* Ithaca, NY: ILR Press.

——— **and Jacqueline Simon. 1988.** *The State of Working America.* Washington, DC: Economic Policy Institute.

Mittal, Anuradha and Peter Rosset, eds. 1999. *America Needs Human Rights.* Oakland, CA: Food First Books.

Moghadam, Valentine M. 1999. "Gender and the global economy." Pp. 128–60 in Myra Marx Ferree, Judith Lorber, and Beth B. Hess, eds., *Revisioning Gender.* Thousand Oaks, CA: Sage.

Mohai, Paul. 1990. "Black environmentalism." *Social Science Quarterly* 71(4):744–65.

Molina, Olga. 2000. "African American women's unique divorce experiences." *Journal of Divorce and Remarriage* 32(3–4):93–99.

Monaghan, Peter. 1993. "Facing jail, a sociologist raises questions about a scholar's right to protect sources." *Chronicle of Higher Education,* April 7, p. A10.

Montgomery, James D. 1992. "Job search and network competition: Implications of the strength-of-weak-ties hypothesis." *American Sociological Review* 57 (October):586–96.

Monti, Daniel J. 1994. *Wannabe: Gangs in Suburbs and Schools.* Cambridge: Blackwell.

Moore, Joan and John M. Hagedorn. 1996. "What happens to girls in the gang?" Pp. 205–18 in Ronald C. Huff, *Gangs in America,* 2nd ed. Thousand Oaks, CA: Sage.

Moore, Molly. 1990. "Crossing the culture gulf: For female soldiers, different rules." *Washington Post,* August 23, pp. D1–D2.

Morgan, Leslie A. 1991. *After Marriage Ends: Economic Consequences for Midlife Women.* Newbury Park, CA: Sage.

Morris, Aldon D. 1984. *The Origins of the Civil Rights Movement: Black Communities Organizing for Change.* New York: Free Press.

———. **1999.** "A retrospective on the civil rights movement: Political and intellectual lankmarks." *Annual Review of Sociology* 25:517–39.

Morris, Joan and Michale D. Grimes. 1996. "Contradictions in the childhood socialization of sociologists from the working class." *Race, Gender and Class* 4(1):63–82.

Morrison, Toni, ed. 1992. *Race-ing Justice, En-gendering Power: Essays on Anita Hill, Clarence Thomas, and the Social Construction of Reality.* New York: Pantheon.

Mortimer, Jeylan T. and Roberta G. Simmons. 1978. "Adult socialization." Pp. 421–54 in Ralph H. Turner, James Coleman, and Renee C. Fox, eds., *Annual Review of Sociology,* vol. 4. Palo Alto, CA: Annual Reviews.

Morton, Emma, Carol W. Runyan, Kathryn E. Moracco, and John Butts. 1998. "Partner homicide–suicide involving female homicide victims: A population-based study in North Carolina, 1988–1992." *Violence and Victims* 13(2):91–106.

Mueller, L. 1977. "Women and men, power and powerlessness in Lesotho." *Signs* 3(1):154–166.

Muller, Ronald. 1979. "The multinational corporation and the underdevelopment of the third world." Pp. 151–78 in Charles Wilber, ed., *The Political Economy of Development and Underdevelopment.* New York: Random House.

Munch, Allison, J. Miller McPherson, and Lynn Smith-Lovin. 1997. "Gender, children and social contact: The effects of childrearing for men and women." *American Sociological Review* 62: 509–20.

Murdock, George. 1949. *Social Structure.* New York: Macmillan.

Murnen, S. K., and L. Smolak. 2000. "The experience of sexual harassment among grade-school students: Early socialization of female subordination?" *Sex Roles* 43 (July):1–17.

Murnen, Sarah K. 2000. "Gender and the use of sexually degrading language." *Psychology of Women Quarterly* 24(4):319–27.

Murray, Stephen O. 2000. *Homosexualities.* Chicago: University of Chicago Press.

Nakano Glenn, Evelyn and Stacey G.H. Yap. 1998. "Chinese American families." Pp. 128–58 in Ronald L. Taylor, ed., *Minority Families in the United States: A Multicul-tural Perspective.* Upper Saddle River, NJ: Prentice Hall.

Nanda, Serena. 1999. *Gender Diversity: Cross Cultural Variations.* New York: Waveland Press.

National Center for Education Statistics. 1992. *Digest of Education Statistics, 1992.* Washington, DC: U.S. Government Printing Office.

———. 2001. *Digest of Education Statistics, 2001.* Washington, DC: U.S. Government Printing Office.

———. 2002a. *The Condition of Education, 2002.* Washington, DC: U.S. Government Printing Office.

———. 2002b. *Digest of Education Statistics, 2001.* Washington, DC: U.S. Government Printing Office.

National Center for Employee Ownership, www.nceo.org.

National Center for Health Statistics. 1998. *Health, United States, 1998: Socioeconomic Status and Health Chart Book.* Washington, DC: U.S. Government Printing Office.

———. 2001. *Health, U.S.A.: 2001.* Hyattsville, MD: NCHS.

———. 2002. "Summary Health Statistics for U.S. Adults: National Health Interview Survey, 1997." *Vital Health Statistics* 10:205.

National Center for Public Policy and Higher Education. 2002. *Losing Ground: A National Status Report on the Affordability of Higher Education.* Available at www. highereducation.org.

National Coalition of Anti-Violence Programs. 2002. "Anti-lesbian, gay, transgender and bisexual biolence in 2000" (www.aup.org/ncavp).

National Commission on Excellence in Education. 1983. *A Nation at Risk.* Washington, DC: U.S. Government Printing Office.

National Institute on Drug Abuse. 1999. *Monitoring the Future.* Washington, DC: U.S. Government Printing Office.

National Issues Forum. 1992. *The Health Care Crisis: Containing Costs, Expanding Coverage.* New York: McGraw-Hill.

National Journal. 1989. "AFL-CIO calls for legislation to control mergers, ease impact on workers, communities." 21(February 18):395.

National Opinion Research Center. 2000. *General Social Survey.* February 1–June 25.

National Organization on Disability/Harris Organization. 2000. "National Organization on Disability/Harris Poll." May 25–June 11.

Navarro, Vincente. 1990. "Race or class versus race and class: Mortality differentials in the United States." *Lancet* 336(November 17):1238–40.

———. 1991a. "The class gap." *The Nation,* April 8, pp. 436–37.

NBC News/Wall Street Journal Poll. 1999. June 16–19.

Neath, Jeanne and Kay Schriner. 1998. "Power to people with disabilities: Empowerment issues in employment programming." *Disability and Society* 13(2):217–28.

Neergaard, Lauren. 2000. "Cesarian sections on the increase." *Hartford (CT) Courant,* August 21, pp. A1, A9.

Neilson, Joyce McCarl, Glenda Walden, and Charlotte A. Kunkel. 2000. "Gendered heteronormativity: Empirical illustrations in everyday life." *Sociological Quarterly* 41(2): 283–96.

Nelson, Fiona. 1999. "Lesbian families: Achieving motherhood." *Journal of Gay and Lesbian Social Services* 10(1):27–46.

Nelson, Margaret K. 1999. "Between paid and unpaid work: Gender patterns in supplemental economic activities among white, rural families." *Gender & Society* 13(4): 518–39.

Nelson, Todd D., ed. 2002. *Ageism: Stereotyping and Prejudice against Older Persons.* Cambridge, MA: MIT Press.

Neubeck, Kenneth J. and Noel A. Cazenave. 2001. *Welfare Racism: Playing the Race Card against America's Poor.* New York: Routledge.

——— and Mary Alice Neubeck. 1997. *Social Problems: A Critical Approach.* 4th ed. New York: McGraw-Hill.

Neuman, W. Lawrence. 2003. *Social Research Methods: Qualitative and Quantitative Approaches.* 5th ed. Boston: Allyn and Bacon.

"New era of segregation, a." 1993. *Newsweek,* December 27, p. 44.

Newman, Katherine S. 1999. *Falling from Grace: Downward Mobility in the Age of Affluence.* Berkeley: University of California Press.

Newton, Barbara J. and Elizabeth B. Buck. 1985. "Television as significant other: Its relationship to self-descriptors in five countries." *Journal of Cross-Cultural Psychology* 16(3):289–312.

Nichols, John. 2000. "Now what? Seattle is just a start." *The Progressive,* January, p. 16–19.

Niemonen, Jack. 2002. *Race, Class, and the State in Contemporary Sociology: The William Julius Wilson Debates.* Boulder, CO: L. Rienne.

Noble, David. 2001. *Digital Diploma Mills.* New York: Monthly Review.

Norberg, Katarina. 2001. "The constitutive values of Swedish schooling: A challenge to the inner life of schools." *Pedagogy, Culture, and Society* 9(3):371–86.

North, Liisa. 1988. "The women poor of Peru." *ISIS: International Women's Journal* 17(March):12–14.

Nosek, Margaret A. and Carol A. Howland. 1998. "Abuse and women with disabilities." Violence against Women Online Resources (www.vaw.umn.edu), February.

Oakes, Guy. 1990. *The Soul of the Salesman: The Moral Ethos of Personal Sales.* Atlantic Highlands, NJ: Humanities Press International.

Oakes, Jeannie. 1985. *Keeping Track: How Schools Structure Inequality.* New Haven: Yale University Press.

———. 1990. *Multiplying Inequalities: The Effects of Race, Social Class, and Tracking on Opportunities to Learn Mathematics and Science.* Santa Monica, CA: Rand Corporation.

———. 1995. "Two cities' tracking and within-school segregation." *Teachers College Record* 96(4):681–90.

———, and G. Guiton. 1995. "Matchmaking: The dynamics of high school tracking decisions." *American Educational Research Journal* 32 (Spring): 3–33.

——— et al. 2002. *Becoming Good American Schools: The Struggle for Civic Virtue in Education Reform.* San Francisco: Jossey-Bass.

O'Barr, William M. 2001. "Language and patriarchy." Pp. 106–13 in Dana Vannoy, ed., *Gender Mosaics: Social Perspectives.* Los Angeles: Roxbury.

O'Connor, James. 1987. *The Meaning of Crisis: A Theoretical Introduction.* New York: Basil Blackwell.

———. 1996. "World economy in the 1990s." *Capitalism, Nature, Socialism* 7(1):113–24.

O'Connor, Lisa A., Jeanne Brooks-Gunn, and Julia Graber. 2000. "Black and white girls' racial preferences in media and peer choices and the role of socialization for black girls." *Journal of Family Psychology* 14(3):510–21.

Ogbu, John U. 1991. "Immigrant and involuntary minorities in comparative perspective." Pp. 3–33 in Margaret A. Gibson and John U. Ogbu, eds., *Minority Status and Schooling.* New York: Garland.

Ogburn, William F. 1964. *On Culture and Social Change: Selected Papers.* Ed. Otis Dudley Duncan. Chicago: University of Chicago Press.

——— and Clark Tibbits. 1934. "The family and its functions." Pp. 661–708 in Research Committee on Social Trends, *Recent Social Trends in the United States.* New York: McGraw-Hill.

Okie, Susan. 2001. "Sharp drop in AIDS toll may be over." *New York Times,* August 14, p. A1.

Oliver, Melvin L. and Thomas M. Shapiro. 1995. *Black Wealth/White Wealth: New Perspective on Racial Inequality.* New York: Routledge.

Omi, Michael and Howard A. Winant. 1986. *Racial Formation in the United States from the 1960s to the 1980s.* New York: Routledge, Chapman & Hall.

———— and ————. 1994. *Racial Formation in the United States: from the 1960s to the 1990s.* New York: Routledge.

O'Neill, Kate. 2000. *Waste Trading among Rich Nations: Building a New Theory of Environmental Regulation.* Cambridge, MA: MIT Press.

Orcutt, James D. 1983. *Analyzing Deviance.* Chicago: Dorsey Press.

Orfield, Gary, Susan E. Eaton, and Elaine R. Jones. 1997. *Dismantling Segregation: The Quiet Reversal of Brown v. Board of Education.* New York: The New Press.

————, and Mindy Kornhaber, eds. 2001. *Raising Standards or Raising Barriers? Inequality and High Stakes Testing in Education.* Washington, DC: Century Foundation Press.

————, and Holly J. Lebowitz, eds. 1999. *Religion, Race, and Social Justice in a Changing America.* New York: Century Foundation Press.

Ortiz, Victor M. 1999. "Only time can tell if geography is still destiny: Time, space, and NAFTA in a U.S.–Mexican border city." *Human Organization* 58(2):173–81.

Ostling, Richard N. 1991. "What does God really think about sex?" *Time,* June 24, pp. 48–50.

Ostrander, Susan A. 1984. *Women of the Upper Class.* Philadelphia: Temple University Press.

"Our bodies, their selves." 1990. *Newsweek,* December 17, p. 60.

Page, Reba Neukom. 1991. *Lower Track Classrooms.* New York: Teachers College Press.

Palen, J. John. 2001. *Social Problems For the Twenty-First Century.* New York: McGraw-Hill.

Papanek, H. 1979. "Development planning for women: The implications of women's work." Pp. 170–201 in R. Jahan and H. Papanek, eds., *Women and Development.* Dacca: Bangladesh Institute of Law and International Affairs.

Parenti, Michael. 1993. *Inventing Reality: The Politics of the Mass Media.* New York: St. Martin's Press.

————. 1998. *America Besieged.* San Francisco: City Lights Books.

Pareto, Vilfredo. 1963. *Treatise on General Sociology.* New York: Dover.

Parker, David. 2001. "Good companions: Decorative, informative, or interrogative? The role of social theory textbooks." *Sociology* 35(1):213–18.

Parkin, Frank. 1971. *Class Inequality and Political Order: Social Stratification in Capitalist and Communist Societies.* New York: Praeger.

Parrenas, Rhacel Salazar, ed. 2001. *Servants of Globalization: Women, Migration, and Domestic Work.* Stanford, CA: Stanford University Press.

Parsons, Jacquelynne Eccles et al. 1982. "Sex differences in attributions and learned helplessness." *Sex Roles* 8(4):421–32.

Parsons, Talcott. 1951. *The Social System.* New York: Free Press.

Pastor, Manuel Jr. 2001. "Economics and ethnicity: Poverty, race, and immigration in Los Angeles County." Pp. 102–38 in Marta Lopez-Garza and David R. Diaz, eds., *Asian and Latino Immigrants in Restructuring Economy: The Metamorphosis of Southern California.* Stanford, CA: Stanford University Press.

Pattillo-McCoy, Mary. 1999. *Black Picket Fences: Privilege and Peril among the Black Middle Class.* Chicago: University of Chicago Press.

Pear, Robert. 2003. "Big increase seen in people lacking health insurance." *New York Times,* September 30, p. A1.

Pellegrini, Frank. 2002. "Person of the Week: 'Enron Whistleblower' Sherron Watkins. Time online edition (Jan. 18). Available at www.time.com.

Peltz, William H. 1990. "Can girls + science – stereotypes = success?" *Science Teacher,* December, pp. 44–49.

Pencavel, John. 2002. *Worker Participation: Lessons from the Worker Co-ops of the Pacific Northwest.* New York: Russell Sage Foundation.

Perez, Lisandro. 1998. "Cuban American families." Pp. 108–24 in Ronald J. Taylor, ed., *Minority Families in the United States: A Multicultural Perspective.* Upper Saddle River, NJ: Prentice Hall.

Peterson, Gary W. and Boyd C. Rollins. 1987. "Parent–child socialization." In Marvin B. Sussman and Suzanne K. Steinmetz, eds., *Handbook of Marriage and the Family.* New York: Plenum.

Peterson, Richard R. 1996. "A reevaluation of the economic consequences of divorce." *American Sociological Review* 61:528–36.

Pew Research Center for the People and the Press. 2000. "Poll: Market shapes news." *Hartford (CT) Courant,* May 1, p. A7.

Phelan, Jo, Bruce G. Link, Robert E. Moore, and Ann Stueve. 1997. "The stigma of homelessness: The impact of the label 'homeless' on attitudes toward poor persons." *Social Psychology Quarterly* 60(4):323–37.

Phillips, Kevin. 1990. *The Politics of Rich and Poor: Wealth and the American Electorate in the Reagan Aftermath.* New York: Random House.

————. 1993. *Boiling Point: Republicans, Democrats, and the Decline of Middle Class Prosperity.* New York: Random House.

————. 2002. *Wealth and Democracy: A Political History of the American Rich.* New York: Broadway Books.

Phua, Voon Chin, Gayle Kaufman, and Suk Keong Park. 2001. "Strategic adjustments of elderly Asian Americans: Living arrangements and headship." *Journal of Comparative Family Studies* 32(2):263–81.

Pilisuk, Marc and Thomas Hayden. 1965. "Is there a military-industrial complex which prevents peace? Consensus and countervailing power in pluralistic society." *Journal of Social Issues* 21(July):67–117.

Pincus, Fred L. 2000. "Reverse discrimination vs. white privilege: An empirical study of alleged victims of affirmative action." *Race and Society* 3(1):1–22.

Pinderhughes, Dianne M. 1987. *Race and Ethnicity in Chicago Politics: A Reexamination of Pluralist Theory.* Urbana: University of Illinois Press.

Pinderhughs, Raquel. 1996. "The impact of race on environmental quality: An empirical and theoretical discussion." *Sociological Perspectives* 39(2):231–48.

Pinkey, Andrea Davis. 2000. *Let It Shine: Stories of Black Women Freedom Fighters.* San Diego: Gulliver Books/Harcourt.

Pirog-Good, Maureen A. 1993. "Child support guidelines and the economic well-being of children in the United States." *Family Relations* 42(4):453–62.

Piven, Francis Fox and Richard Cloward. 1977. *Poor People's Movements: Why They Succeed, How They Fail.* New York: Vintage.

———— and ————. 1982. *The New Class War: Reagan's Attack on the Welfare State and Its Consequences.* New York: Pantheon.

———— and ————.2000. *Why Americans Still Don't Vote: And Why Politicians Want It That Way.* Boston: Beacon Press.

Plaskow, Judith and Carol P. Christ, eds. 1989. *Weaving the Vision: New Patterns in Feminist Spirituality.* San Francisco: Harper & Row.

Polit, Denise F., and Janet R. Kahn. 1987. "Teenage pregnancy and the role of schools." *Urban Education* 28(July):131–53.

Pollack, Philip H. and M. Elliot Vitas. 1995. "Who bears the burden of environmental pollution? Race, ethnicity, and environmental equity in Florida." *Social Science Quarterly* 76(2):294–310.

Ponniah, Gowrie and Geraldine Reardon. 1999. "Women's labour in Bangladesh and Sri Lanka: The trade-off with technology." *Gender, Technology, and Development* 3(1):85–102.

Pooley, Julie Ann, Lisbeth T. Pike, Neil M. Drew, and Lauren Breen. 2002. "Inferring Australian children's sense of community: A critical exploration." *Community, Work, and Family* 5(1):5–22.

Poulantzas, Nicos. 1973. *Political Power and Social Classes.* London: New Left Books and Sheed and Ward.

Poulton, Terry. 1997. *No Fat Chicks: How Big Business Profits by Making Women Hate Their Bodies—And How to Fight Back.* Secaucus, NJ: Carol Pub. Group.

Pozner, Jennifer L. 2001. "Power shortage for media women: Studies document absence from influential roles" (www.fair.org/extra/0108/women-in-news.html).

Press, Eyal and Jennifer Washburn. 2000. "The kept university." *Atlantic Monthly,* March, 39–54.

Presser, Harriet B. 2000. "Nonstandard work schedules and marital instability." *Journal of Marriage and the Family* 62(1):93–110.

Princeton Survey Research Associates. 2000. "Newsweek poll." *Newsweek,* April 13–14.

Project Censored. 2001–2002. "Censored 2003: The Top 25 censored media stories of 2001–2002" (www.projectcensored.org/ yearbook.htm).

Public Law 101–335, an Act to Establish a Clear and Comprehensive Prohibition of Discrimination on the Basis of Disability. 1990. Washington, DC: U.S. Government Printing Office.

Public Perspective. **2001.** "Economy: Bottoming out?" 12(4):45.

Quadagno, Jill S. and M. H. Meyer. 1989. "Organized labor, state structures and social policy development: A case study of old age assistance in Ohio, 1916–1940." *Social Problems* 36(2):181–96.

Quindlen, Anna. 1991. "Women warriors." *New York Times,* February 3, p. E19.

Quinn, Peggy. 1994. "America's disability policy: Another double standard?" *Affilia* 9(Spring):45–59.

Quinney, Richard. 1979. *Criminology: Analysis and Critique.* 2d ed. Boston: Little, Brown.

"Race: Can we talk?" 1991. *Ms.,* July–August, pp. 34–39.

Raffalli, Mary. 1994. "Why so few women physicists?" *New York Times, Education Life,* January 9, pp. 26 ff.

Ramasubbu, K., H. Gurm, and D. Litaker. 2001. "Gender bias in clinical trials: Do double standards still apply?" *Journal of Women's Health and Gender-Based Medicine* 10(October):757–64.

Ramirez, Miguel. 2003. "NAFTA hasn't lived up to its billing in Mexico." *Hartford (CT) Courant,* September 22, p. A7.

Ratcliff, Katherine Strother, ed. 2002. *Women and Health: Power, Technology, and Inequality in a Gendered World.* Boston: Allyn and Bacon.

Raymond, Diane. 1992. "'In the best interests of the child': Thoughts on homophobia and parenting." Pp. 114–30 in Warren J. Blumenfeld, ed., *Homophobia: How We All Pay the Price.* Boston: Beacon Press.

Reckless, Walter C. 1961. *The Crime Problem.* New York: Appleton-Century-Crofts.

Reece, Ray. 1980. "The solar blackout: What happens when Exxon and DOE go sunbathing together?" *Mother Jones,* September–October, pp. 28–37.

Reese, Ellen R. and Carnette Newcombe. 1999. "Welfare rights organizations then and now: The divergent goals and strategies of the NWRO and ACORN." Paper presented at the annual meeting of the Society for the Study of Social Problems, August, Chicago.

Reid, Penny and Gillian Finchilescu. 1995. "The disempowering effects of media violence against women on college women." *Psychology of Women Quarterly* 19(3): 397–411.

Reiman, Jeffrey H. 1996. *—and the Poor Get Prison: Economic Bias in American Criminal Justice.* Boston: Allyn and Bacon.

———. 2000. *The Rich Get Richer and the Poor Get Prison: Ideology, Class, and Criminal Justice.* 6th ed. Boston: Allyn and Bacon.

Reingold, Jennifer. 1997. "Executive pay: Tying pay to performance is a great idea. But stock-option deals have compensation out of control." *Business Week,* April 21, pp. 58–66.

Renard, Marie-Christine. 1999. "The interstices of globalization: The example of fair coffee." *Sociologia Ruralis* 39(4):484–500.

Rendall, Steve and Will Creeley. 2002. "White noise: Voices of color scarce on urban public radio" (www.fair.org/extra/0209/ white-noise.html).

Renold, Emma. 2000. "'Coming out': Gender, (hetero)sexuality and the primary school." *Gender and Education* 12(3):309–26.

Renzetti, Claire M., and Daniel J. Curran. 1992. *Women, Men, and Society.* 2d ed. Boston: Allyn and Bacon.

Reskin, Barbara F. 1998. *Realities of Affirmative Action in Employment.* Washington, DC: American Sociological Association.

Rhem, James. 1999. "Pygmalion in the classroom." *National Teaching and Learning Forum.* February 8(2) (www.ntlf.com/html /pi/9902/pygm 1.html).

Rhym, Darren. 1998. "An analysis of George Jefferson and Heathcliff Huxtable." *Journal of African American Men* 3(3):57–67.

Rifkin, Jeremy. 1995. *The End of Work: The Decline of the Global Labor Force and the Dawn of the Post-Market Era.* G.P. Putnam and Sons.

——— and Randy Barber. 1978. *The North Will Rise Again: Pensions, Politics, and Power in the 1980s.* Boston: Beacon Press.

Riggle, Ellen D. B., Alan L. Ellis, and Anne M. Crawford. 1996. "The impact of 'media contact' on attitudes toward gay men." *Journal of Homosexuality* 31(3):55–69.

Rist, Ray C. 1970. "Student social class and teacher expectations." *Harvard Educational Review* 40(August):411–51.

———. 1973. *The Urban School: A Factory for Failure.* Cambridge, MA: MIT Press.

Ritzer, George. 2000. *The McDonaldization of Society (New Century Edition).* Thousand Oaks, CA: Pine Forge Press.

———. 2002. *McDonaldization: The Reader.* Thousand Oaks, CA: Pine Forge Press.

Ritzer, George and Douglas J. Goodman. 2004. *Sociological Theory.* 6th ed. New York: McGraw-Hill.

Roberts, Dorothy. 1997. *Killing the Black Body: Race, Reproduction, and the Meaning of Liberty.* New York: Pantheon Books.

———. 2001. *Shattered Bonds: The Color of Child Welfare.* New York: BasicCivitas Books.

Robertson, James C. 1999. *The Corporate Practice of Medicine.* Berkeley: University of California Press.

Robinson, Daniel N. 1996. *Wild Beasts and Idle Humours: The Insanity Defense from Antiquity to the Present.* Cambridge, MA: Harvard University Press.

Rodden, John. 2001. "Reeducating reunified Germany?" *Society* 38(5):66–74.

Rodriguez, Clara E., ed. 1997. *Latin Looks: Images of Latinas and Latinos in the U.S. Media.* Boulder, CO: Westview Press.

Roethlisberger, Frederick J. and William J. Dickson. 1939. *Management and the Worker.* Cambridge, MA: Harvard University Press.

Rogers, Mary F. 2001. "Contemporary feminist theory." Pp. 285–96 in George Ritzer and Barry Smart, eds., *Handbook of Social Theory.* London: Sage.

Rollins, Judith. 1985. *Between Women: Domestics and Their Employers.* Philadelphia: Temple University Press.

Rome, Dennis M. 2002. "Murderers, rapists, and drug addicts." Pp. 71–81 in Coramae Richey Mann and Marjorie S. Zatz, eds., *Images of Color, Images of Crime.* 2nd ed. Los Angeles: Roxbury.

Romero, Mary. 1992. *Maid in America.* New York: Routledge.

———. 1999. "Immigration, the servant problem, and the legacy of the domestic labor debate." *University of Miami Law Review* 53(July):1045–64.

Roof, Wade Clark and William McKinney. 1987. *American Mainline Religion.* New Brunswick, NJ: Rutgers University Press.

Root, Maria P. P., ed. 1996. *The Multiracial Experience: Racial Borders as the New Frontier.* Thousand Oaks, CA: Sage.

Roschelle, Anne R. 1999. "Gender, family structure, and social structure: Racial ethnic families in the United States." Pp. 311–40 in Myra Marx Ferree, Judith Lorber, and Beth B. Hess, eds., *Revisioning Gender.* Thousand Oaks, CA: Sage.

Rose, Mike. 1989. *Lives on the Boundary.* New York: Penguin.

Rosen, Corey. 1998. "ESOPs." *Dollars and Sense,* July–August, p. 48.

Rosenfeld, Rachel A. 1980. "Race and sex differences in career dynamics." *American Sociological Review* 45:583–609.

Rosenthal, Robert and Lenore Jacobson. 1968a. *Pygmalion in the Classroom.* New York: Holt, Rinehart and Winston.

——— and ———. 1968b. "Teacher expectations for the disadvantaged." *Scientific American* 218(April):19–23.

——— and ———. 1992. *Pygmalion in the Classroom.* Expanded ed. New York: Holt, Rinehart and Winston.

Ross, Andrew. 1999. "Sweated labor in cyberspace." *New Labor Forum* 4 (Spring–Summer): 47–56.

Ross, Catherine E. 1987. "The division of labor at home." *Social Forces* 65:816–33.

Rostow, W. W. 1960. *The States of Economic Growth: A Non-Communist Manifesto.* London: Cambridge University Press.

Rothschild, Joyce, and J. Allen Whitt. 1986. *The Cooperative Workplace: Potentials and Dilemmas of Organizational Democracy and Participation.* New York: Cambridge University Press.

Rousso, Harilyn and Michael L. Wehmeyer, eds. 2001. *Double Jeopardy: Addressing*

Gender Equity in Special Education. Albany: State University of New York Press.

Rowland, Robyn. 1992. *Living Laboratories: Women and Reproductive Technologies.* Bloomington: Indiana University Press.

Rubin, Beth A. 1996. *Shifts in the Social Contract: Understanding Change in American Society.* Thousand Oaks, CA: Pine Forge Press.

Rubington, Earl and Martin S. Weinberg, eds. 1999. *Deviance: The Interactional Perspective.* Boston: Allyn and Bacon.

Rude, George F. E. 1964. *The Crowd in History: A Study of Popular Disturbances in France and England, 1730–1848.* New York: Wiley.

———. 1985. *History from Below: Studies in Popular Protest and Popular Ideology in Honour of George Rude.* Ed. Frederick Krantz. Montreal: Concordia University.

Rushton, J. Phillippe. 1997. *Race, Evolution, and Behavior.* New Brunswick, NJ: Transaction Publishers.

Russell, George. 1987. "Rebuilding to survive." *Time,* February 16, pp. 44–45.

Russell, Katheryn K. 1998. *The Color of Crime: Racial Hoaxes, White Fear, Black Protectionism, Police Harassment, and Other Macroaggressions.* New York: New York University Press.

Russell, Marta. 1998. *Beyond Ramps: Disability at the End of the Social Contract.* New York: Common Courage Press.

Ryan, Jake and Charles Sackrey. 1984. *Strangers in Paradise: Academics from the Working Class.* Boston: South End Press.

Sadker, David and Myra Sadker. 1994. *Failing at Fairness: How America's Schools Cheat Girls.* New York: Scribner.

Sanders, Douglas. 1996. "Getting lesbian and gay issues on the international human rights agenda." *Human Rights Quarterly* 18(1): 67–106.

Sangmoon, Kim. 2001. "The impact of differential access to the Internet on earnings: A cross-sectional analysis." Paper presented at the Southern Sociological Society annual meetings.

Sapir, Edward. 1949. *Selected Writings of Edward Sapir in Language, Culture, and Personality.* Ed. David G. Mandelbaum. Berkeley: University of California Press.

Savage, David G. 2003. "Study: Poor in minority in college." *Hartford (CT) Courant,* April 7, p. B5.

Save the Children. 2002. *America's Forgotten Children: Child Poverty in Rural America.* Westport, CT: Save the Children. Available at www.savethechildren.org.

Scarr, Sandra. 1982. "Development is internally guided, not determined." *Contemporary Psychology* 27:852–53.

Schaefer, Richard T. 2004. *Racial and Ethnic Groups.* 9th ed. Upper Saddle River, NJ: Peason/Prentice Hall.

Schaefer, Robert K. 2003. *Understanding Globalization: The Social Consequences of Political, Economic, and Environmental Change.* 2nd ed. Lanham, MD: Rowman and Littlefield.

Schemo, Diana Jean. 2001. "U.S. schools turn more segregated, a study finds." *New York Times,* July 20, p. A14.

———. 2002. "Study finds parochial schools segregated along racial lines." *New York Times,* June 27, p. A18.

Scherer-Warren, Ilse. 1990. "'Recovering our dignity'—An appraisal of the utopia of liberation in Latin America." *International Sociology* 5(March):11–25.

Schoendorf, Kenneth C. et al. 1992. "Mortality among infants of black as compared with white college-educated parents." *New England Journal of Medicine* 326 (June): 1522–26.

Schofield, J. W. 1981. "Complementary and conflicting identities: Images and interaction in an interracial school." Pp. 53–90 in S. R. Asher and J. M. Gottman, eds., *The Development of Children's Friendships.* New York: Cambridge University Press.

Schram, Sanford F. and Samuel H. Beer, eds. 1999. *Welfare Reform: A Race to the Bottom?* Baltimore: Johns Hopkins University Press.

Schulman, Karen. 2000. "The high cost of child care puts quality care out of reach for many families." Children's Defense Fund. Available at www.childrensdefense.org.

Schur, Edwin M. 1984. *Labeling Women Deviant: Gender, Stigma, and Social Control.* New York: Random House.

Schutt, Russell K. 2001. *Investigating the Social World: The Process and Practice of Research.* 3rd ed. Thousand Oaks, CA: Pine Forge Press.

Schwartz, John and Todd Barrett. 1992. "Can you top this? The war between the states—for new business—rages on." *Newsweek,* February 17, pp. 40–41.

Schwartz-Nobel, Loretta. 2002. *Growing Up Empty: The Hunger Epidemic in America.* New York: HarperCollins.

Scott, James C. 1985. *Weapons of the Weak: Everyday Forms of Peasant Resistance.* New Haven: Yale University Press.

Scott, V. Catherine. 1995. *Gender and Development: Rethinking Modernization and Dependency Theory.* Boulder, CO: L. Rienner.

Seccombe, Karen. 1999. *"So You Think I Drive a Cadillac?" Welfare Recipients' Perspectives on the System and its Reform.* Boston: Allyn and Bacon.

Seeman, Melvin. 1959. "On the meaning of alienation." *American Sociological Review* 24:783–91.

Seers, Dudley. 1969. *The Meaning of Development.* Paper presented at the Eleventh World Conference of the Society for International Development, New Delhi.

Segal, Mady W., David R. Segal, Jerald G. Bachman, and Peter Freedman-Doan. 1998. "Gender and the propensity to enlist in the U.S. military." *Gender Issues* 16(3):65–87.

Seidman, Gay. 1993. *Manufacturing Militance: Workers' Movements in Brazil and South Africa, 1970–1985.* Berkeley: University of California Press.

Seltzer, J. A. 1989. *Relationships between Fathers and Children Who Live Apart.* NSFH Working Paper No. 4, University of Wisconsin–Madison, Center for Demographic Ecology.

Sen, Amartya. 2000. *Development as Freedom.* New York: Anchor Books.

Sexton, Patricia Cayo. 1991. *The War on Labor and the Left: Understanding America's Unique Conservatism.* Boulder, CO: Westview Press.

Seybold, Peter. 1987. "Beyond the veil of neutrality." Pp. 175–93 in Rhonda F. Levine and Jerry Lembcke, eds., *Recapturing Marxism.* New York: Praeger.

Shanklin, Eugenia. 2000. "Representations of race and racism in American anthropology." *Current Anthropology* 41(1):99–103.

Shapiro, Joseph P. 1993. *No Pity: People with Disabilities Forging a New Civil Rights Movement.* New York: Times Books/Random House.

Shapiro, Thomas M. 1985. *Population Control Politics.* Philadelphia: Temple University Press.

Sharma, Sohan and Surinder Kumar. 2002. "Debt relief: Indentured servitude for the Third World." *Race and Class* 43(4):45–56.

Sharp, Deanna L., Joan M. Hermsen, and Jodi Billings. 2002. "Factors associated with having flextime: A focus on married workers." *Journal of Family and Economic Issues* 23(1):51–72.

Shaul, Susan, Pamela J. Dowling, and Bernice F. Laden. 1985. "Like other women: Perspectives of mothers with physical disabilities." Pp. 133–42 in Mary Jo Deegan and Nancy A. Brooks, eds., *Women and Disability: The Double Handicap.* New Brunswick, NJ: Transaction Books.

Shaw-Taylor, Yoku and Nijole V. Benokraitis. 1995. "The presentation of minorities in marriage and family textbooks." *Teaching Sociology* 23(2):122–35.

Sheldon, Randall G., Sharon K. Tracy, and William B. Brown. 1997. *Youth Gangs in American Society.* Belmont, CA: Wadsworth.

Sheler, Jeffrey L. 1990. "Homosexuality doctrines." *U.S. News & World Report,* July 16, p. 55.

Shelton, Beth Anne and Daphne John. 1999. "Who does what and how much do they do? Gender and total work time." *Sociological Focus* 32:285–300.

——— and Rebecca E. Dean. 2001. "Divorce trends and effects for women and men." Pp. 216–26 in Dana Vannoy, ed., *Gender Mosaics: Social Perspectives.* Los Angeles: Roxbury.

Shen, Ce and John B. Williamson. 2001. "Accounting for cross-national differences in infant mortality decline (1965–1991) among less developed countries: Effects of women's status, economic dependency, and state strength." *Social Indicators Research* 53(3): 257–88.

Shepard, Benjamin and Ronald Hayduk, eds. 2002. *From ACT UP to the WTO: Urban Protest and Community Building in the Era of Globalization.* New York: Verso.

Shire, Karen A. 1999. "Socialization and work in Japan: The meaning of adulthood of men and women in a business context." *International Journal of Japanese Sociology* 8(Nov.):77–92.

Shupe, Anson. 1990. "The stubborn persistence of religion in the global arena." Pp. 17–26 in Emile Sahliyeh, ed., *Religious Resurgence and Politics in the Contemporary World.* Albany: State University of New York Press.

———— **and Jeffrey K. Hadden. 1988.** *The Politics of Religion and Social Change.* New York: Paragon House.

Sidel, Ruth. 2000. "The enemy within: The demonization of poor women." *Journal of Sociology and Social Welfare* 27(1):73–84.

Sidel, Victor W. 2000. "Working together for health and human rights." *Medicine, Conflict, and Survival* 16(4):355–69.

Siegel, Jessica. 1991. "What army ads don't say." *New York Times,* January 18, p. A31.

Silverman, Lewis A. 2000. "Vermont civil unions, full faith and credit, and marital status." *Kentucky Law Journal* 89(4):1075–1107.

Simon, Barbara Levy. 1988. "Never-married old women and disability." Pp. 215–25 in Michelle Fine and Adrienne Asch, eds., *Women with Disabilities.* Philadelphia: Temple University Press.

Simon, David R. 2000. "Corporate environmental crimes and social inequality: New directions for environmental justice research." *American Behavioral Scientist* 43(4):633–45.

Simon, David R. and D. Stanley Eitzen. 1990. *Elite Deviance.* 3rd ed. Boston: Allyn and Bacon.

Singleton, Judy. 2000. "Women caring for elderly family members: Shaping nontraditional work and family initiatives." *Journal of Comparative Family Studies* 31(3):367–75.

Sinke, Suzanne M. 1999. "Gender in language and life: A Dutch American example." *Gender Issues* 17(1):26–51.

Sklar, Holly, Laryssa Mykyta, and Susan Wefald. 2002. *Raise the Floor: Wages and Policies That Will Work for Us All.* Boston: South End Press.

Slavin, Robert E. 1990. "Achievement effects of ability grouping in secondary schools: A best-evidence synthesis." *Review of Educational Research* 60 (Fall):471–499.

Sloan, Allan. 1996. "The hit men." *Newsweek* February 26:44–48.

Sloan, Allan. 2002. "Who killed Enron?" *Newsweek,* January 21, pp. 18–22.

Sloan, Lacey M. and Nora S. Gustavson, eds. 2000. *Violence and Social Injustice against Lesbian, Gay, and Bisexual People.* Binghamton, NY: Harrington Park Press.

Smedley, Audrey. 1999. *Race in North America: Origins and Evolution of a World View.* 2d ed. Boulder, CO: Westview Press.

Smith, Christian, ed. 1996. *Disruptive Religion: The Force of Faith in Social Movement Activism.* New York: Routledge.

Smith, Greg B. 2002. "Bad execs do little time." *New York Daily News,* July 14, p. 7.

Smith, Ralph R. and Russell R. Windes. 2000. *Progay/Antigay: The Rhetorical War over Sexuality.* Thousand Oaks, CA: Sage.

Smith, Robert C. 1995. *Racism in the Post-Civil Rights Era: Now You See It, Now You Don't.* Albany: State University of New York Press.

Smitherman, Geneva and Sylvia Cunningham. 1997. "Moving beyond resistance: Ebonics and African American youth." *Journal of Black Psychology* 23(3):227–32.

Sorokin, Pitirim A. 1957. *Social and Cultural Dynamics.* Rev. abr. ed. Boston: Porter Sargent.

Sorrels, Bobbye D. 1983. *The Nonsexist Communicator: Solving the Problems of Gender and Awkwardness in Modern English.* Englewood Cliffs, NJ: Prentice Hall.

Soyer, Daniel. 1999. "Garment sweatshops, then and now." *New Labor Forum* 4(Spring–Summer):35–46.

Spade, Joan Z. 2001. "Gender and education in the United States." Pp. 85–93 in Dana Vannoy, ed., *Gender Mosaics: Social Perspectives.* Los Angeles: Roxbury.

————, **I. Columba and B. E. Vanfossen. 1997.** "Tracking in mathematics and science: Courses and course-selection procedures." *Sociology of Education* 70(April): 108–27.

Spelman, Elizabeth. 1988. *Inessential Women.* Boston: Beacon Press.

Spengler, Oswald. 1926. *The Decline of the West.* New York: Knopf.

Spickard, Paul R. 1997. "What must I be? Asian Americans and the question of multiethnic identity." *Amerasia Journal* 23(1): 43–60.

Sprouse, Martin, ed. 1992. *Sabotage in the American Workplace: Anecdotes of Dissatisfaction, Mischief, and Revenge.* San Francisco: Pressure Drop Press.

Spyrou, Spyros. 2000. "Education, ideology, and the national self: The social practice of identity construction in the classroom." *Cyprus Review* 12(1):61–81.

Stack, Carol D. 1974. *All Our Kin: Strategies for Survival in a Black Community.* New York: Harper & Row.

Stanley, Julia P. 1977. "Paradigmatic woman: The prostitute." Pp. 303–21 in David L. Shores, ed., *Papers in Language Variation.* Birmingham: University of Alabama Press.

Staples, Robert. 1995. "Black deprivation–white privilege: The assault on affirmative action." *Black Scholar* 25(3):2–6.

Stark, Rodney and William Sims Bainbridge. 1985. *The Future of Religion: Secularization, Revival and Cult Formation.* Berkeley: University of California Press.

Starr, Paul. 1982. *The Social Transformation of American Medicine.* New York: Basic Books.

Stauber, John C. and Sheldon Rampton. 1995. *Toxic Sludge Is Good for You: Lies, Damn Lies, and the Public Relations Industry.* Monroe, ME: Common Courage Press.

Stearney, Lynn M. 1996. "Sex control technology and reproductive 'choice': The conflation of technical and political argument in the new science of human reproduction." *Communication Theory* 6(4):388–405.

Steelman, Lala Carr and Brian Powell. 1985. "The social and academic consequences of birth order: Real, artifactual, or both?" *Journal of Marriage and the Family* 47(1):117–24.

Stein, Nan. 1995. "Sexual harassment in school: The public performance of gendered violence." *Harvard Educational Review* 62 (Summer):145–62.

Steinberg, Ronnie J. 2001. "How sex gets into your paycheck and how to get it out: The gender gap in pay and comparable worth." Pp. 258–68 in Dana Vannoy, ed., *Gender Mosaics: Social Perspectives.* Los Angeles: Roxbury.

Steinberg, Stephen. 2001. *The Ethnic Myth: Race, Ethnicity, and Class in America.* 3rd ed. New York: Atheneum.

Stern, Sol. 1998. "The vanishing teacher and other UFT fictions" (www.city-journal.org/ html/10_2_the_vanishing_teacher.html).

Stevenson, Howard C., Jr. 1995. "Relationship of adolescent perceptions of racial socialization to racial identity." *Journal of Black Psychology* 21(1):49–70.

Stiers, Gretchen A. 2000. *From This Day Forward: Commitment, Marriage, and Family in Lesbian and Gay Relationships.* New York: St. Martin's Press.

Stoecker, Randy and Angela C. S. Stuber. 1999. "Building an information superhighway of one's own: A comparison on two approaches." *Research in Politics and Society* 7:291–309.

Stohs, Joanne Hoven. 2000. "Multicultural women's experience of household labor, conflicts, and equity." *Sex Roles* 42(5–6):339–61.

Stolen Lives Project. 1999. *Stolen Lives: Killed by Law Enforcement.* 2nd ed. New York: October 22nd Coalition to Stop Police Brutality, Repression, and Criminalization of a Generation.

Stone, Leroy O. and Andrew S. Harvey. 2001. "Gender differences in transitions to total-work retirement." Pp. 258–69 in Victor W. Marshall, Walter R. Heinz, Helga Kruger, and Anil Verma, eds., *Restructuring Work and the Life Course.* Ontario: University of Toronto Press.

Strauss, Murray. 2000. *Beating the Devil Out of Them: Corporal Punishment in American Families and Its Effects on Children.* 2nd ed. New Brunswick, NJ: Transaction.

Streeten, Paul with Shahid Javed Burki, Mahbub ul Haq, Norman Hicks, and Frances Stewart. 1981. *First Things First: Meeting Basic Human Needs in Developing Countries.* New York: Oxford University Press.

Stretsky, Paul and Michael Hogan. 1998. "Environmental justice: An analysis of superfund sites in Florida." *Social Problems* 45(2):268–87.

Stroman, Duane F. 1982. *The Awakening Minorities: The Physically Handicapped.* Washington, DC: University Press of America.

Stroup, Atlee L. and Gene E. Pollock. 1999. "Economic consequences of marital dissolution for Hispanics." *Journal of Divorce and Remarriage* 30(1–2):149–66.

Sundaram, I. Satya. 1996. "Basic needs approach to development." *Social Action* 46(3): 225–39.

Sullivan, Harry Stack. 1953. *The Interpersonal Theory of Modern Psychiatry.* New York: Norton.

"Survey assesses public role of religion." 2000. *Princeton Weekly Bulletin* 89 (May 8).

Sutherland, Edwin H. and Donald R. Cressey. 1974. *Criminology.* 9th ed. Philadelphia: Lippincott.

Sutton, Terri. 1992. "Bustin' loose: Why big breasts are back." *Utne Reader,* May–June, pp. 60–61.

Swan, Edward T. 1995. "Equitable access to funding." *Contemporary Education* 66(4):202–4.

Szalai, Georg. 2003. "Company sees $45 billion loss, $45 billion write-down in fourth quarter." *Hollywood Reporter,* January 30, p. 1.

"Talking to God." 1992. *Newsweek,* January 6, pp. 39–44.

Taylor, Ian. 1999. *Crime in Context: A Critical Criminology of Market Societies.* Boulder, CO: Westview Press.

———, Paul Walton, and Jock Young. 1973. *The New Criminology.* New York: Harper & Row.

———, ———, and ———. 1975. *Critical Criminology.* London: Routledge & Kegan Paul.

Taylor, Ronald L. 1998. "Black American families." Pp. 19–45 in Ronald L. Taylor, ed., *Minority Families in the United States: A Multicultural Perspective.* Upper Saddle River, NJ: Prentice Hall.

Taylor, Shawn. 2003. "Time to give: Workers donating paid hours off to colleagues in need." *Hartford (CT) Courant,* March 10, p. E1

Thom, Mary. 2001. *Balancing the Equation: Where Are Women and Girls in Science, Engineering and Technology?* New York: National Council for Research on Women.

Thomas, Charles B., Jr. 1997. "Segregation and social inequality in a deindustrializing community: The case of Flint." *Michigan Sociological Review* 11:64–96.

Thomas, Evan. 2003. "Fear at the front." *Newsweek,* February 3, pp. 34–40.

Thomas, W. I. 1928. *The Child in America.* New York: Knopf.

Thompson, E. P. 1966. *The Making of the English Working Class.* New York: Vintage.

Thorne, Barrie. 1989. "Girls and boys together . . . but mostly apart: Gender arrangements in elementary schools." Pp. 138–53 in Michael S. Kimmel and Michael A. Messner, eds., *Men's Lives.* New York: Macmillan.

———. 1993. *Gender Play: Girls and Boys in School.* New Brunswick, NJ: Rutgers University Press.

Thornton, Michael et al. 1990. "Sociodemographic and environmental influences on racial socialization by black parents." *Child Development* 61:401–9.

Thornton, Michael C. 1998. "Indigenous resources and strategies of resistance: Informal caregiving and racial socialization in black communities." Pp. 49–66 in Hamilton I. McCubbin, Elizabeth A. Thompson, Ann. I. Thompson, and Jo A. Futrell, eds., *Resiliency in African-American Families.* Thousand Oaks, CA : Sage.

Tilly, Charles. 1998. "Social movements and (all sorts of) other political interactions: Local, national, and international, including identities." *Theory and Society* 27(4):453–80.

Time. 1982a. "Countdown on the ERA: As the deadline nears, supporters mount last-gasp drives." June 14, p. 25.

———. 1982b. "ERA dies: But its backers will try again." July 5, p. 29.

Time/Cable News Network. 2001. "Harris interactive poll." December 19–20. (www.geohive.com/global/religion_top.php).

Tjaden, Patricia and Nancy Thoennes. 2000. "Extent, nature, and consequences of intimate partner violence: Findings from the National Violence a gainst Women survey." U.S. Department of Justice, Office of Justice Programs, National Institutes of Justice.

Todaro, Michael P. 1989. *Economic Development in the Third World* (4th ed). New York: Longman.

Tonry, Michael. 1995. *Malign Neglect: Race, Crime, and Punishment in America.* New York: Oxford University Press.

Tower, Cynthia Crosson. 1996. *Understanding Child Abuse and Neglect.* 3rd ed. Boston: Allyn and Bacon.

Truman, David B. 1951. *The Governmental Process.* New York: Random House.

Tuchman, Gaye, Arlene Kaplan Daniels, and James Benet, eds. 1978. *Hearth and Home: Images of Women in the Mass Media.* New York: Oxford University Press.

Tumin, Melvin. 1953. "Some principles of stratification: A critical analysis." *American Sociological Review* 18:387–94).

———. 1966. "Some principles of stratification: A critical view." Pp. 53–58 in Rheinhard Bendix and Seymour Martin Lipset, eds., *Class, Status and Power,* 2d ed. New York: Free Press.

Turner, Terisa E. and Benjamin S. Craig. 1995. "Not in our nature: The male deal and corporate solutions to the debt-nature crisis." *Review* 18(2):209–58.

Twaddle, Andrew C. 1999. *Health Care Reform in Sweden, 1980–1994.* New York: Auburn House.

Uchitelle, Louis. 1999. "The American middle, just getting by." *New York Times,* August 1, Section 3, pp. 1, 13.

———. 2000. "Working families strain to live middle-class life." *New York Times,* September 10, pp. 1, 28.

United Nations, Department of Economic and Social Affairs. 2001. *1999 Demographic Yearbook.* New York: United Nations.

United Nations Human Development Programme. 1998. *Human Development Report, 1998.* New York: Oxford University Press.

U.S. Bureau of the Census. 1992. *Statistical Abstract of the United States, 1992.* Washington, DC: U.S. Government Printing Office.

———. 1994. *Income, Poverty, and Valuation of Noncash Benefits: 1993.* Current Population Reports, Series P60, No. 188, Washington, DC: U.S. Government Printing Office.

———. 2002a. *Money Income in the United States: 2001.* Washington, DC: U.S. Government Printing Office.

———. 2002b. *Poverty in the United States: 2001.* Washington, DC: U.S. Government Printing Office.

———. 2003. *Statistical Abstract of the United States, 2002.* Washington, DC: U.S. Government Printing Office.

U.S. Bureau of Labor Statistics. 2001. Annual statistics available at www.bls.gov.

———. 2003. "Employment status of the civilian population by sex and age" (www.bls.gov).

U.S. Census Bureau. 1999. *Current Population Surveys.* Washington, DC: Government Printing Office.

———. 2001. *Current Population Surveys.* Washington, DC: Government Printing Office.

U.S. Central Intelligence Agency. 1999. *The World Fact Handbook,* 1999. Washington, DC: CIA.

———. 2001. *The World Fact Handbook, 2001.* Washington, DC: CIA.

U.S. Congress: Senate. 1989. *Americans with Disabilities Act of 1989.* Hearings before the Committee on Labor and Human Resources and the Subcommittee on the Handicapped, 101st Congress, 1st Session. Washington, DC: U.S. Government Printing Office.

———. 1991. *Channel One: Educational Television and Technology.* Hearings before the Subcommittee on Education, Arts, and the Humanities of the Committee on Labor and Human Resources. 102nd Congress, 1st Session. Washington, DC: U.S. Government Printing Office.

U.S. Department of Commerce, Bureau of the Census. 1993. *Statistical Abstract of the United States, 1993.* Washington, DC: U.S. Government Printing Office.

———. 1999. *Statistical Abstract of the United States, 1999.* Washington, DC: U.S. Government Printing Office.

U.S. Department of Commerce and National Telecommunications and Information Administration. 2000. *Falling through the Net: Toward Digital Inclusion.* Washington, DC: U.S. Government Printing Office.

U.S. Department of Defense. 1999. *Selected Manpower Statistics.* Washington, DC: U.S. Government Printing Office.

U.S. Department of Health, Education, and Welfare. 1973. *Work in America.* Report of a Special Task Force to the Secretary of Health, Education, and Welfare. Washington, DC: U.S. Government Printing Office.

U.S. Department of Health and Human Services. 1985. *Social Security Programs throughout the World.* Washington, DC: U.S. Government Printing Office.

———. 1992. *Health, United States, 1991.* Washington, DC: U.S. Government Printing Office.

———. 1998a. *Facts about Heart Disease and Women.* Bethesda, MD: National Institutes of Health.

———. 1998b. *Women of Color Health Data Book.* Washington, DC: National Institutes of Health.

———. 1999. "A descriptive analysis of patterns of informal and formal caregiving among privately insured and non-privately insured disabled elders living in the community" (http://aspe.hhs.gov/daltpc/home/htm).

U.S. Department of Justice, Bureau of Justice Statistics. 1999. *Highlights of the 1998 National Youth Gang Survey.* Washington, DC: U.S. Government Printing Office.

U.S. Department of Labor. 1985. *Displaced Workers, 1979–83.* Washington, DC: U.S. Government Printing Office.

———. 1991. *A Report on the Glass Ceiling Initiative.* Washington, DC: U.S. Government Printing Office.

U.S. Department of Labor, Bureau of Labor Statistics. 2000. www.stats.bls.gov.

Upchurch, Dawn M., Lee A. Lillard, and Constantijn W. Panis. 2002. "Nonmarital childbearing: Influences of education, marriage, and fertility." *Demography* 39 (May): 311–29.

Useem, Michael. 1984. *The Inner Circle: Large Corporations and the Rise of Business Political Activity in the U.S. and U.K.* New York: Oxford University Press.

Uyecki, Eugene S. and Lani J. Holland. 2000. "Diffusion of pro-environment attitudes?" *American Behavioral Scientist* 43(4):646–62.

Van Dyke, Nella. 1998. "Hotbeds of activism: Locations of student protest." *Social Problems* 45(2):205–20.

Varano, Charles S. 1999. *Forced Choices: Class, Community, and Worker Ownership.* Albany: State University of New York Press.

Velkoff, Victoria A. and Valerie A. Lawson. 1998. *International Brief: Gender and Aging: Caregiving.* Washington, DC: U.S. Department of Commerce Economics and Statistics Administration.

Vigil, James Diego. 1997. *Learning from Gangs: The Mexican American Experience.* Charleston, WV: Clearinghouse on Rural Education and Small Schools, Appalachia Educational Laboratory.

Villa-Vicencio, Charles. 1978. "The theology of apartheid." *Christianity and Crisis,* March 13, pp. 45–49.

Vischer, Robert K. 2001. "Racial segregation in American churches and its implications for school vouchers." *Florida Law Review* 53(2):193–237.

Wagner, Edwin M. 1989. "Air Force first-term reenlistment: The effect of held values." *Journal of Political and Military Sociology* 17(2):223–39.

Wallace, Anthony F. C. 1966. *Religion: An Anthropological View.* New York: Random House.

Wallach, Lori and Michelle Sforza. 1999. "NAFTA at 5." *The Nation,* January 25, p. 7.

Wallerstein, Immanuel. 1974. *The Modern World System: Capitalist Agriculture and the Origins of the European World-Economy in the Sixteenth Century.* New York: Academic Press.

———. 1980. *The Modern World System II: Mercantilism and the Consolidation of the European World Economy, 1600–1750.* New York: Academic Press.

———. 1997. "Long waves of capitalist development: A Marxist interpretation." *Science and Society* 61(2):264–66.

Walsh, Mark. 1990. "N.C. board sues to block the use of 'Channel One.'" *Education Week* 9 (February 28):1, 21.

Walters, Pamela Barnhouse. 2001. "Educational access and the state: Historical continuities and discontinuities in racial inequality in American education." *Sociology of Education* (Extra Issue):35–49.

Walters, Ronald. 1996. "The criticality of racism." *Black Scholar* 26(1):2–8.

Walton, John. 2001. "Debt, protest, and the state in Latin America." Pp. 299–328 in Susan Eckstein, ed., *Power and Popular Protest: Latin American Social Movements.* Berkeley: University of California Press.

——— and Charles Ragin. 1990. "The debt crisis and political protest in the Third World." *American Sociological Review* 55(6):876–90.

Ward, Kathryn. 1984. *Women in the World System.* New York: Praeger.

———. 1990. "Introduction and overview." Pp. 1–24 in Kathryn B. Ward, ed., *Women Workers and Global Restructuring.* Ithaca, NY: ILR Press.

Warner, Rebecca L. and Brent S. Steel. 1999. "Child rearing as a mechanism for social change: The relationship of child gender to parents' commitment to gender equality." *Gender & Society* 13:503–17.

***Washington Times.* 2002.** "The AOL Time Warner debacle." August 8 (editorial).

Watson, Bill. 1971. "Counter-planning on the shop floor." *Radical America* 5(May–June).

Wattenberg, Martin P. 2002. *Where Have All the Voters Gone?* Cambridge, MA: Harvard University Press.

Weber, Max. 1947. *The Theory of Social and Economic Organization.* Trans. A. M. Henderson and Talcott Parsons. New York: Free Press.

Weeks, John. 2000. "Latin America and the 'high performing Asian economies': Growth and debt." *Journal of International Development* 12(5):625–54.

Wei, Ann. 1991. "Dumping on Native Americans." *Multinational Monitor,* October, p. 7.

Weinstein, James. 1968. *The Corporate Ideal in the Liberal State, 1900–1918.* Boston: Beacon Press.

Weir, David, and Mark Schapiro. 1981. *Circle of Poison: Pesticides and People in a Hungry World.* San Francisco: Institute for Food and Development Policy.

Weitzman, Lenore J. and Mavis Maclean (eds.). 1992. *Economic Consequences of Divorce: The International Perspective.* Oxford, England: Clarendon Press; New York: Oxford University Press.

Wellesley College Center for Research on Women. 1992. *How Schools Shortchange Girls.* Washington, DC: American Association of University Women Educational Foundation.

Welner, Kevin G. and Jeannie Oakes. 1996. "(Li)ability grouping: The new susceptibility of school tracking systems to legal challenges." *Harvard Educational Review* 66(3):451–70.

West, Patrick C., J. Mark Fly, Francis Larkin, and Roberts Marans. 1992. "Minority anglers and toxic fish consumption: Evidence from a state-wide survey of Michigan." In B. Bryant and P. Mohai, eds., *Race and the Incidence of Environmental Hazards: A Time for Discourse.* Boulder, CO: Westview Press.

Westra, Laura and Bill E. Lawson, eds. 2001. *Faces of Environmental Racism: Confronting Issues of Global Justice.* Lanham, MD: Rowman and Littlefield.

"Whistle-blowing nuclear worker gains." 1993. *New York Times,* June 10, p. A18.

Whorf, Bejamin Lee. 1956. "The relation of habitual thought and behavior to language." Pp. 134–59 in *Language, Thought, and Reality."* Cambridge, MA: Technology Press of M.I.T.

Wilkinson, Richard G. 1996. *Unhealthy Societies: The Afflictions of Inequality.* New York: Routledge.

Williams, Brett. 1999. "The great family fraud of postwar America." Pp. 65–89 in Adolph Reed Jr., ed., *Without Justice for All: The New Liberalism and Our Retreat from Racial Equality.* Boulder, CO: Westview.

Williams, David R., and Chiquita Collins. 1995. "U.S. socioeconomic and racial difference in health: Patterns and explanations." *Annual Review of Sociology* 21:349–86.

Williams, Gregory Howard. 1996. *Life on the Color Line: The True Story of a White Boy Who Discovered He Was Black.* New York: Plume.

Williams, Heather L. 1999b. "Mobile capital and transborder labor rights mobilization." *Politics and Society* 27(1):139–66.

Williams, Juan. 1987. *Eyes on the Prize.* New York: Penguin.

Williams, Norma. 1990. *The Mexican American Family: Tradition and Change.* Dix Hills, NY: General Hall.

Williams, Robin M., Jr. 1965. *American Society: A Sociological Interpretation.* 2d ed. New York: Knopf.

Willie, Charles V. 1989. *Caste and Class Controversy on Race and Poverty.* 2d ed. New York: General Hall.

Wills, Garry. 1995. "The new revolutionaries." *New York Review of Books,* August 10, pp. 50–55.

Wills, John S. 1994. "Popular culture, curriculum, and historical representation: The situation of Native Americans in American history and the perpetuation of stereotypes." *Journal of Narrative and Life History* 4(4):277–94.

Wilson, Edward O. 2000. *Sociobiology: The New Synthesis.* Cambridge, MA: Belknap Press of Harvard University Press.

Wilson, John. 1992. "Cleaning up the game: Perspectives on the evolution of professional sports." Pp. 65–95 in Eric Dunning and Chris Rojek, eds., *Sport and Leisure in the Civilizing Process: Critique and Counter Critique.* Toronto: University of Toronto Press.

Wilson, William Julius. 1980. *The Declining Significance of Race: Blacks and Changing American Institutions.* 2d ed. Chicago: University of Chicago Press.

———. 1987. *The Truly Disadvantaged.* Chicago: University of Chicago Press.

———. 1996. *When Work Disappears: The World of the New Urban Poor.* New York: Knopf.

Wolff, Edward N. and Richard C. Leone. 2002. *Top Heavy: The Increasing Inequality of Wealth in America and What Can Be Done about It.* 2d ed. New York: Free Press.

Women's International League for Peace and Freedom. 1991. "Victory or defeat for people of color?" *Questions and Answers about the Gulf War* 3(April):1–4.

Wood, Robert E. 1986. *From Marshall Plan to Debt Crisis: Foreign Aid and Development Choices in the World Economy.* Berkeley: University of California Press.

Wooden, Wayne S. 1995. *Renegade Kids, Suburban Outlaws: from Youth Culture to Delinquency.* Belmont, CA: Wadsworth.

Woodford, Maize, California School Board, James Baldwin, Patricia J. Williams, John H. McWhorter, Herb Boyd, Jaquelyne Johnson Jackson, Mumia Abu-Jamal, Geneva Smitherman, and Earl Ofari Hutchinson. 1997. "The Black Scholar Reader's Forum: Ebonics." *Black Scholar* 27(1):2–37.

World Bank. 2000. *World Development Indicators.* Washington, DC: International bank for Reconstruction and Development.

———. 2003. *World Development Indicators.* Washington, DC: World Bank.

World Health Organization. 2000. *Epidemiological Fact Sheets on HIV/AIDS and Sexually Transmitted Infections: Sierra Leone.* New York: United Nations.

Worley, Jennifer Campbell and Dana Vannoy. 2001. "The challenge of integrating work and family life." Pp. 165–73 in Dana Vannoy, ed., *Gender Mosaics: Social Perspectives.* Los Angeles: Roxbury.

Wysong, Earl. 1993. "Conflicting agendas, interests, and actors in disease prevention policy-making: Business, labor, and the High Risk Act." *International Journal of Health Services* 23(2):301–22.

Wrong, Dennis H. 1959. "The functional theory of stratification: Some neglected considerations." *American Sociological Review* 24 (December):772–82.

Xiao, Hong. 2000. "Class, gender, and parental values in the 1990s." *Gender & Society* 14(6):785–803.

Yellowbird, Michael and C. Matthew Snipp. 1998. "American Indian families." Pp. 226–48 in Ronald L. Taylor, ed., *Minority Families in the United States: A Multicultural Perspective.* Upper Saddle River, NJ: Prentice Hall.

Zajda, Joseph. 2000. "The politics of the rewriting of history in Russia: School textbooks and curriculum material." *Education and Society* 18(3):99–123.

Zavella, Patricia. 1987. *Women's Work and Chicano Families.* Ithaca, NY: Cornell University Press.

Zeitlin, Irving M. 2000. *Ideology and the Development of Sociological Theory.* 7th ed. Englewood Cliffs, NJ: Prentice Hall.

Zelnick, Melvin and J. Kim Young. 1982. "Sex education and its association with teenage sexual activity, pregnancy, and contraceptive use." *Family Planning Perspectives* 14(May–June):117–26.

Zey, Mary. 1993. *Banking on Fraud: Drexel, Junk Bonds, and Buyouts.* Hawthorne, NY: Aldine de Gruyter.

———. 1998. "Embeddedness of interorganizational corporate crime in the 1980s: Securities fraud of banks and investment banks." *Research in the Sociology of Organizations* 15:111–59.

Zhu, Xiao Di, Yi Yang, and Xiaodong Liu. 2002. "Young American adults living in parental homes." Joint Center for Housing Studies. Cambridge, MA: Harvard University.

Zick, C. D. and K. R. Smith. 1986. "Immediate and delayed effects of widowhood on poverty: Patterns from the 1970s." *Gerontologist* 26:669–75.

Zinn, Howard. 1980. *A People's History of the United States.* New York: Harper Colophon.

Zinn, Maxine Baca and Bonnie Thornton Dill, eds. 1993. *Women of Color in United States Society.* Philadelphia: Temple University Press.

Zweig, Michael. 2000. *The Working Class Majority: America's Best Kept Secret.* Ithaca, NY: ILR Press.

Zweigenhaft, Richard L. and G. William Domhoff. 1991. *Blacks in the White Establishment? A Study of Race and Class in America.* New Haven: Yale University Press.

——— and ———. 1998. *Diversity in the Power Elite: Have Women and Minorities Reached the Top?* New Haven: Yale University Press.

Photo Credits

Page 2: © Sofronski Michael/Gamma; page 6: © Tony Freeman/Photo Edit; page 12: © Gianni Dagli Orti/CORBIS; page 18: © Isaac Hernandez; page 22: © Spencer Grant\Photo Edit; page 30: © Strauss/Curtis/CORBIS; page 34: © Ted Spiegel/CORBIS; page 36: © Bettmann/CORBIS; page 44: © Bob Daemmrich; page 53: © Steven Rubin/The Image Works; page 58: © Wesley Bocxe/The Image Works; 17p362: © Wesley Bocxe/The Image Works; page 65: © Bettmann/CORBIS; page 69: © Michael J. Doolittle/The Image Works; page 76: © Marilyn Humphries / The Image Works; page 80: © Digital Vision/Getty; page 83: © AFP/CORBIS; page 88: © Mike Brinson/Getty; page 90: © Image Source/The Image State; page 98: © Photo Researchers, Inc.; page 103: © Michael S. Yamashita/CORBIS; page 110: © Laura Dwight; page 115: © Peter M. Fisher/CORBIS; page 125: © Ed Kashi/CORBIS; page 130: © Saxpix/AGE Fotostock; page 133: © Ethno Images; page 137: © Jérome Sessini/In Visu/Corbis; page 142: © Jim Pickerell/The Image Works ; page 147: © LWA-Dann Tardif/CORBIS; page 150: © Eastcott-Momatiuk/The Image Works; page 155: © Laura Dwight; page 159: © Extra Image Production/The Image State; page 165: © Picture Partners/AGE Fotostock; page 176: © Bob Krist/Corbis; page 184: © AFP/CORBIS; page 187: © Bettmann/CORBIS; page 196: © Viviane Moos/CORBIS; page 203: © Johnathan Hourok/Photo Edit; page 207: © Jeff Greenberg / The Image Works; page 211: © David Hurn/Magnum Photos; page 216: © David Lucas/Getty Images; page 225: © Steven Rubin / The Image Works; page 229: © Larry Williams/CORBIS; page 231: © Myrleen F. Cate/Photo Edit; page 239: © Eli Reed/Magnum Photos; page 247: © Jeff Greenberg/Peter Arnold, Inc. ; page 254: © A. Ramey/Photo Edit; page 260: © Elizabeth Crews / The Image Works; page 262: © Laura Dwight; page 268: © Bill Aron/Photo Edit; page 272: © Reuters NewMedia Inc./CORBIS; page 279: © Cathy Melloan Resources/Photo Edit; page 288: © Tom Sobolik/Black Star; page 292: © Sygma Collection/Corbis; page 300: © AFP/CORBIS; page 304: © AFP/CORBIS; page 307: © AFP/CORBIS; page 310: © First Light/The Image State; page 321: © Reuters NewMedia Inc./CORBIS; page 330: © Amet Jean Pierre/CORBIS; page 334: © Baitel Esaias/Gamma; page 337: © Najlah Feanny/CORBIS SABA; page 344: © James McGoon / CORBIS Sygma; page 350: © Jim Rassol/ CORBIS Sygma; page 358: © David Butow/CORBIS SABA; page 364: © Charles Gupton Photography/CORBIS; page 367: © Claudia Kunin/Getty; page 370L: © Bill Stormont/CORBIS; page 370R: © Pedro Coll/AGE Fotostock; page 373: © Groshong Daniel J./Gamma; page 383: © Jim Bourg/Liaison/Getty; page 394: © Tim Boyle/Newsmakers/Getty; page 398: © Gabe Palmer/Mug Shots/CORBIS; page 401: © Seth Resnick/Stock Boston; page 416: © Bob Daemmrich/The Image Works; page 417: © Bob Daemmrich; page 423: © Laura Dwight; page 427: © Keith Dannemiller/CORBIS SABA; page 434: © Terry Gilliam/AP Photo; page 439: © C. Butler/Raw Talent; page 445: © Doug Menuez/PhotoDisc/Getty; page 449: © Richard Falco/Black Star; page 459: © Joao Silva/CORBIS Sygma; page 463: © Owen Franken/CORBIS; page 468: © Ryan McVay/PhotoDisc/Getty; page 473TL: © Bart Geerligs/Taxi/Getty; page 473B: © Laura Dwight; page 473TR: © George Shelley/CORBIS; page 487: © Mimi Forsyth/AGE Fotostock; page 494: © Ariel Skelley/CORBIS; page 496: © Gan Engberg/The Image Works; page 504: © Zen Icknow/CORBIS; page 514: © Mario Tama/Getty Images; page 517: © The Art Archive/National Palace Mexico City / Dagli Orti, © (2003) Banco de México Diego Rivera & Frida Kahlo Museums Trust; page 519: © AFP/CORBIS; page 528: © Peter Yates/CORBIS; page 538: © AFP/CORBIS; page 544: © Robert Patrick/CORBIS Sygma; page 547: © Jack Kurtz/The Image Works; page 550: © Scott Thode/The Image State; page 561: © Strauss/Curtis/CORBIS; page 564: © Lee Snider/The Image Works

Name Index

Subject Index